S.S. CERAMIC
The Untold Story

by Clare Hardy

with the assistance of
Eric Munday
and
Frank McCormick

With grateful thanks to the other contributors to this book,
whose lives were touched by this ship.

"... on November 23, 1942 (the Ceramic) left the Mersey for Australia, independently routed, with 378 passengers. Her subsequent complete disappearance was at first little publicised at home, due to the general censorship of shipping information, and the Admiralty assumed that she had been sunk without survivors from the 500 or so persons on board. It was learned a long time later that she had been torpedoed and sunk on December 6 in latitude 40 deg. 30 min. N., longitude 40 deg, 20 min. W, and that one survivor, a sapper of the Royal Engineers, had been picked up by the U-boat and taken to a German prison camp. **The full story, as far as I know, has never been published.**"

Sea Breezes, November 1963
STEAMERS OF THE PAST
White Star Liner "Ceramic" of 1913
by J. H. Isherwood

This book is dedicated to my grandfather
TREVOR ERNEST WINSER
and to the 654 men, women and children
who perished with him
on the night of 6/7 December 1942.

Also in memory of
ERIC A. MUNDAY
1921-2011
Without whom the story would never have been told.

The diaries, memoirs, letters and other documents in this book are transcribed as they were written for authenticity and to represent the writer's character. Diaries and memoirs remain the copyright of the authors.

First printed 2006.
Second edition 2012.

ISBN-13: 978-1479369713
ISBN-10: 1479369713

s.s.ccramic@btconnect.com
www.ssceramic.co.uk

CONTENTS

Introduction: Whatever happened to Trevor Winser?   5

PART ONE: 1912-1939

1.	From the cradle	14
2.	A triumph of engineering	20
3.	Making the news	41
4.	The outbreak of war	64
5.	The Ceramican	83
6.	The Inter-War Years	123

PART TWO: 1939-1942

7.	War breaks out again	158
8.	Trooping begins	180
9.	Final voyage	285

PART THREE: The truth is finally told

10.	The survivor's story	348
11.	Back home	404
12.	The account of the U-boat crew	461
13.	The Fate of Werner Henke	482

Casualty List   *499*

Mystery of liner sinking cleared after 3 years
—BY THE ONE SURVIVOR
Express Staff Reporter

SAPPER ERIC ALFRED MUNDAY, aged 24, is back in his home at Foulsham-road, Thornton Heath, Surrey —and he has brought with him the first full story of a three-year-old war mystery—the sinking of the British liner Ceramic in the Atlantic.

The 18,000-ton Ceramic, former luxury ship on the Australian run, set out for Capetown from Britain on November 26, 1942, with 656 men, women and children on board.

She went down off the Azores. For ten months relatives of the passengers heard nothing. Then the loss of the ship was admitted in Capetown.

In the House of Commons, the First Lord of the Admiralty said she was not in convoy, but was a "fast, independent ship." That was all.

Sapper Munday was the only survivor of the Ceramic. Yesterday he told me the story of her last voyage.

Captain H. C. Elford had taken the ship through the Atlantic before. He knew what the dangers were, in that winter of 1942. And he protested to the authorities against taking women and children on board. But 155, including 50 British nurses, were in the ship when she left Britain.

SAPPER MUNDAY

On the night of December 6, three torpedoes hit her. She remained afloat for three hours. Everyone on board was got into boats or rafts.

At dawn a storm broke. The boats were scattered. Many sank. Munday's boat, with 40 in it, capsized. He and six other soldiers clung to it. The rest were swept away.

Four hours later the U-boat surfaced near them. A rope was thrown to them, but the boat was swept by a heavy sea. Only Munday was able to grab it, and he was hauled aboard.

"I pleaded with the U-boat commander, Captain Henke, to save the other six men who were still clinging to the overturned lifeboat," said Munday. "He refused."

The U-boat submerged. Munday saw no more survivors of the Ceramic. The next two and a half years he spent in a prison camp.

Since he came back Sapper Munday has made contact with scores of relatives of those who sailed in the Ceramic, and who have waited three years to know exactly what happened.

Trevor Winser, grandfather of the author.

Below: with wife Joyce on their honeymoon, Margate 1938.

4

Introduction
Whatever happened to Trevor Winser?

I was in the Sergeants' Mess one lunch time, and I was reading the paper, and the headline said *'The Only Survivor On Troopship, Torpedoed December 6/7 1942'*. And it had got his name and address, and I cut it out and I went home on the bus to Mum and said to her, "Look, I'm sure this is to do with Trevor I'm sure it is." I said, "Why don't you just write to this fellow and ask for the details?"

(Trevor's brother, Tony Winser, interviewed August 1999)

6 Armitage Place, Hawkhurst, Kent
Oct 17 1945
Dear Mr Munday,

I hope you will excuse me writing to you, but my youngest son who is in the Air Force sent me your account which he saw in the Daily Express & we are very interested as my eldest son was going abroad & we know he left here in Nov 1942 & that his ship was torpedoed Dec, 6th 1942. We were notified the following Sept. that his ship was torpedoed and sunk & as nothing more had been heard of him he must be presumed drowned at sea. This of course has been a very great blow to us & have tried every means we know to try & find out just what happened. Everything you say seems to tally with what we do know that I felt I must write to you & ask you if you could give us any more details. We should be so grateful if you could or better still if you are this way should be so pleased if you could call on us. He was married & had a little girl. She was 14 months old when he left England. His name was Trevor if you should have known anyone by that name. He was a Corporal in the R.A.S.C. Once more please excuse me but if you could give us any more information we should be most grateful to you.
Thanking you. Yours faithfully
(Mrs) L. Winser

Dear Mr Munday,

I feel I would like to write you a few lines to thank you for your letter also for the trouble you are taking in writing to the shipping agents. We should be so glad of any news to relieve our mind. But if only our dear son could come back to us it would be the best news of all. As I told you in my last letter his name was Trevor,

but his wife tells me he was mostly called Tim in the army. I wonder if you might have heard anyone called by that name... You yourself must have had a terrible experience but hope you are quite recovered by now. Thanking you for all the trouble you are taking. Yours very sincerely,
L. Winser

****

Thursday
(October 1942)

My darling Joyce,

Thank you darling for letter of Tuesday. Please excuse short letter this time darling, but we are on field exercises at the moment and time is rather limited. I hope to be down between 2 and 3 on Sat. As far as I know everything is alright and I shall get away at mid-day until 11 o' clock Sunday night. I am looking forward so much to seeing you both. Hope Janet has lost her cold by now. We'll have a lovely week-end darling as we are supposed to be off during next week. So until Sat au revoir my darling. Lots of love and kisses for both Janet and yourself.

Always your very own loving Tim
xxxxxxxxxxxxxxxxxx

Busters for Janet
xxxxxxxxxxxxxxxxxx

Sunday

My darling Joyce

Was so pleased to hear your voice this afternoon darling; guess you thought I was going to say I was off didn't you? I wish to heaven I could say I was darling. Not that I want to go overseas but this place is simply bloody awful. It's just like a concentration camp. The food is elusive and those of us on draft are hardly allowed out of sight. I had to break away to ring you this afternoon. Still I suppose we mustn't grumble too much as this war seems to have taken a definite turn at last doesn't it darling? I do miss darling little Janet and all her sweet little ways. Give her a great big hug for me. This time last Sunday night we were up at the Oak. We had a lovely leave didn't we sweetheart? I keep re-living every moment of it. The house I'm in at present is a large country mansion about 3 miles up a lane. It was so dark when I went to supper the other evening I lost myself. I had to go out the next day and pay out 4/- for a torch. Well my sweetheart I can't think of much more news for the moment but will write again in a day or two. So for the present au revoir my darling. Lots of love and kisses for both Janet and yourself.

Always your very own loving Tim
xxxxxxxxxxxxxxxxxxxxxxx

Busters for Janet
xxxxxxxxxxxxxxxxxxxxxxx

Thursday

My darling Joyce

Thank you so much darling for letter of yesterday, also one of today. They somehow got reversed the Sunday one not arriving until today. Was sorry to hear Janet was off colour. Hope she is back to her darling little self again by now. With a stroke of luck I may be able to get a 48 hour before we leave; will let you know later how it goes. I try not to grumble too much darling but you can imagine how I feel... Yes darling I thought of you out for your walk with Janet last Sunday afternoon. It made me feel so home-sick... Do wish this blasted war would end so that I could get back and have some home life. You bet I'd like to see your hair darling; don't start getting off will you! I played hockey at Byfleet yesterday afternoon, had quite a good game. Well my sweetheart am afraid I haven't much more news at the moment. Please write nice and often won't you darling. So for the present au revoir darling. Lots of love and kisses for both Janet and yourself.

Always your very own loving Tim
xxxxxxxxxxxxxxxxxxxxxxx

Busters for Janet
xxxxxxxxxxxxxxxxxxxxxxx

Sunday

My darling Joyce

Here we are with another Sunday darling. The one day in the week I miss you both more than ever. I am writing this quite early in the morn as I haven't anything else to do and the days seem so long. I am hoping to go to the flicks tonight with two other fellows. I haven't heard from you for several days so hope to get a nice long letter tomorrow. Do hope darling little Janet is back to her old self again by now. I will do all I possibly can to get down some time next weekend but am afraid I shan't be able to let you know anything definite. I think perhaps our draft may have got held up a little with this North African stunt. I am in the same room as a fellow who happens to be a photographer. He has coloured one of Janet's photos for me. She does look sweet. I am suffering rather badly from rheumatism at the moment. I got wet through over on duties last week and my clothes dried on me. It's damned painful and annoying. The doctor has given me some liniment. I am just slightly more confident now that we may not go after all now, but it's rather difficult to look too far ahead. Still we must keep hoping darling. Well my darling am afraid I haven't much more news at the present. So au revoir my darling. Lots of love and kisses for both Janet and yourself.

Always your very own loving Tim
xxxxxxxxxxxxxxxxxxxxxxx

Busters for Janet
xxxxxxxxxxxxxxxxxxxxxxx

Thursday
"B" Company
1 Holding (Bu?)

My darling Joyce

Just a few lines darling to let you know I arrived back safely last night. Guess you are feeling as lonely as I am today. I am still here at the moment but drew all my tropical kit today so expect to be moving shortly. I should write few letters to this address at the moment as they tell us any letters sent to that new address I shan't get until we get there. Hope Janet is keeping free of this cold. I do miss you both so much. Have got my parcel and am drawing my cash tomorrow. Well my sweet must rush, will write again soon. Lots of love and kisses for you both.

Always your very own loving Tim
xxxxxxxxxxxxxxxxxxxxxxx

Busters for Janet
xxxxxxxxxxxxxxxxxxxxxxx

****

Introduction: Whatever happened to Trevor Winser?

(Trevor's brother, Tony Winser, interviewed August 1999):

I always remember the last time I saw Trevor. I was working. I hadn't joined the Air Force then you see. In 1942, I was only 17, and I was at Butchers in Hawkhurst. Well, I went there, see, because they wanted a van driver, and I was so keen on driving, and at that time you didn't have to pass a test or anything, during the war you had a provisional driving licence. And Chris was working there, and she said, "We want a van driver'" and they'll pay you more than I was getting, so I said, "Maybe I'll come up there," and they said, "Yes, you can start." So I had the old Bedford van and when Trevor and Joyce came down to stay, your Mum was only a little toddler, she was only I suppose what, ten months old? Something like that. And of course, Trevor said to me, "Do you think you could get the van, and come and pick us up, and we can put the pram in the back of the van?" So I said, "Yes, of course I can." So he said, "I've got to catch a train at one." And I said, "Don't worry about that, Trevor, I'll come round and give you a hand. So poor old Trevor says, "I love driving, Tony. Can I drive the old van up to the station?" I said, "Yes, of course you can!" So he was so pleased at driving this van, and of course, it was like anything else, it was a job for him to get the gears in! And he was making such a hash of it, old Trevor was, and he was laughing away, and I said, "Oh, you're making a hash of it, Trevor." I said, "I thought you were an experienced driver!" So he said, "Well I can't get used to this!" Well, it only had about three gears on it, I think, that van did. Anyway, eventually he was all right; we got up to Hawkhurst station. The train came in, and it was a slow old train to Paddock Wood, because that's the way he had to go, Paddock Wood, and then change at Tonbridge. And I just said, "Cheerio," to him on the station, and Joyce, he said "Cheerio," to her; kissed Janet in the pram, and he was waving away out the window as he went off, and that's the last time I saw him.

Clare: I've got a clipping here. He was present at church the Sunday before he went overseas.

Tony: *Yes, I was with him. He had a special request for a hymn, and that was, 'Jesu, Lover of my Soul.' And I sat next to him; it was only him and I went; the Parson prayed for him to have a safe return, he was on embarkation leave Trevor, to have a safe return, and he never came back. And Mum was so upset about it she just lost faith. She said, "I can't believe that poor old Trevor, who was a Sunday School teacher at the chapel, he was baptised in the chapel..."*
I remember it quite well when he was baptised, poor old Trevor. At that time they used to have a raincoat on at the church, and they were baptised in this. And I can see it now, a blue, navy blue raincoat, and we dressed him up at home to see how it would look, and he kept worrying because he said, "I know what's going to happen. When I go under, my raincoat's going to come up, and I'll

expose everything!" And he kept worrying about it, so Mum says, "Well, perhaps we can do something about that." So what she done is she got iron things that she sewed in the bottom of the lining and so she said, "That'll be all right. That'll keep it down, Trevor. Don't worry about it." And old Goldie Smith was the Bishop there at that time. So Trevor came down the step, and I was sitting up in the gallery, and old Goldie Smith was saying, "...the Father and Son and Holy Ghost..." and then he put him backwards into the water to bring him up again. And for some reason or other, Trevor happened to slip when he pushed him down, his feet slipped, and he went right down under, and Goldie Smith let go of him. And I was up in the gallery, and I said, "Oh my goodness, Trevor, he's drowned!" And I ran out the church. I ran home, I was so upset. Because I thought he'd drowned. I wasn't very old. And that's what happened. And of course, he came home, and fortunately it was all right; everything was all right.

****

(Ceramic, November 1942)

My darling Joyce

Just a few lines to let you know I am happy and well. Expect you are feeling rather anxious sweetheart but don't worry. I am fine. It's rather difficult to write a letter like this as there are so many things that I dare not mention. Still I know you understand. It was a bit of a blow going so suddenly wasn't it darling? But we knew it had to come sooner or later. Have just had a marvellous dinner of celery soup, roast lamb and mint sauce, baked potatoes, cabbage and Viennese Pudding and custard. At the moment I am in the lounge writing this. Jim Deer and I have a lovely bunk, with sheets and pillows, arm chairs, h&c water, in fact we are in luxury. Hope Janet has lost her cold by now. Give the little darling some big hugs from daddy and tell her to look after mummy for him. Keep smiling my darling. I shall be patiently waiting for the time when we are all together again. Keep writing darling as I shall get your letters eventually. Please forward enclosed letter to Mum. So for the present au revoir my darling. Lots of love and kisses for both Janet and yourself.

Always your very own loving Tim
xxxxxxxxxxxxxxxxxxxxxxx
Busters for Janet
xxxxxxxxxxxxxxxxxxxxxx

****

Introduction: Whatever happened to Trevor Winser?

And after that we had this letter back from him and he said he'd checked with the War Office and that Trevor was definitely on that ship. You see, the War Office never told us that. All they said, we had a telegram, and it just said 'Missing at Sea, December 6/7 1942.' And that was all. 'Presumed Dead", that's right - 'Presumed Dead'.

(Interview with Tony Winser, August 1999)

"Hope Janet has lost her cold by now. Give the little darling some big hugs from daddy and tell her to look after mummy for him. Keep smiling my darling. I shall be patiently waiting for the time when we are all together again."

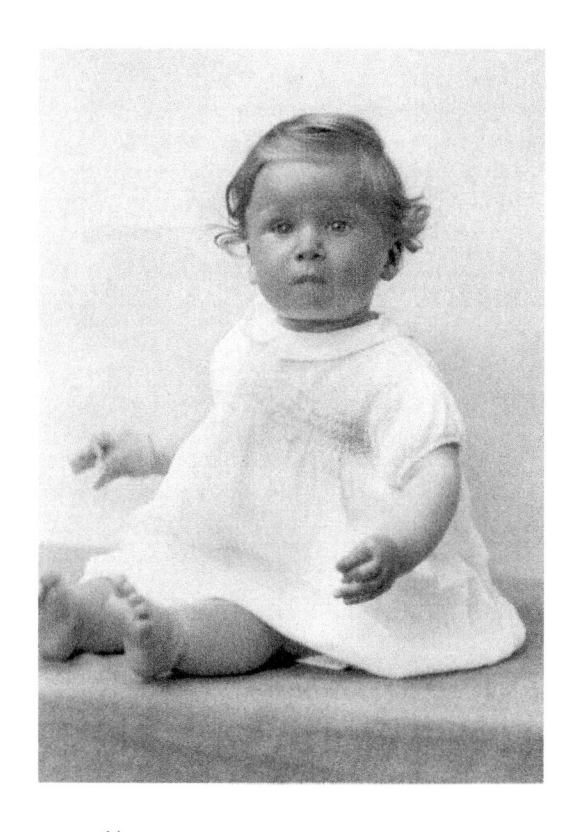

Copyright: John H. Marsh Maritime Collection, SA Maritime Museum.

Part One

1912-1939

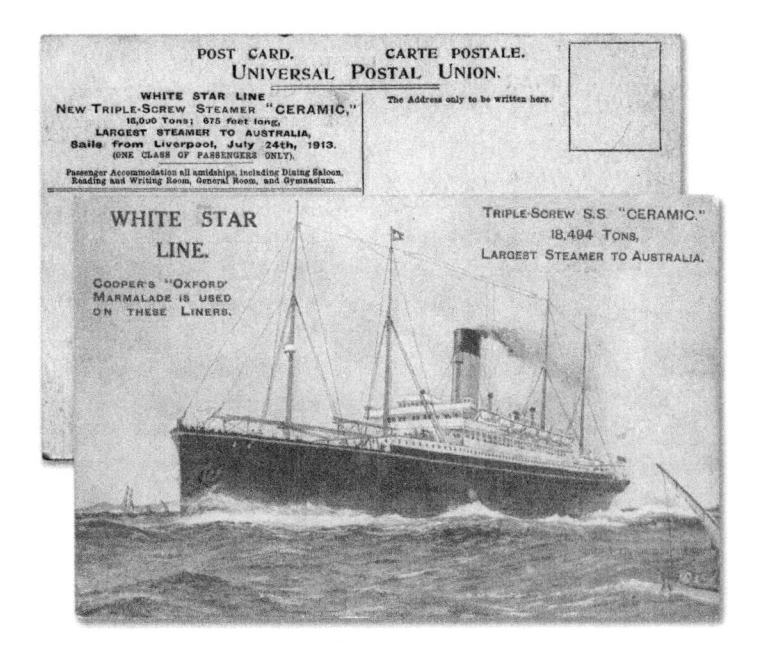

Chapter 1
From the cradle

Somewhere near the top of the list of the twentieth century preoccupations, must be the quest for speed. Throughout the early part of the century, records were being broken by land, sea and air, and new technology was opening up the arena for man to indulge his spirit of competition. Out with the horse and cart, and in with the train and the motor car. A whole new vista of opportunities beckoned for families and individuals to broaden their horizons and discover the country they lived in, to take holidays, to visit relatives, and sometimes to relocate in the search for employment. Journey times by land and sea were being slashed as rival companies in the transport industry vied for the competitive edge. Speed also meant prestige, and sometimes tragedy in the pursuit of it. The allure of the Blue Riband for the fastest crossing of the Atlantic, and the dream of air travel: surely there was nothing man could not achieve. Even the moon was within his grasp as the century unfolded.

The Belfast shipyard, Harland and Wolff, shipbuilders to the legendary White Star Line, were at their zenith at the turn of the twentieth century, as they responded to the nation's appetite for speed, and to the opportunities presented by a shrinking world. No longer just the pink bits on the map, England's colonies were now much closer. Anyone might travel to them, finances permitting. Others might seek an assisted passage for a better life in these lands of opportunity. The passenger liner industry was flourishing and becoming increasingly competitive, the three main British companies of the time being the Aberdeen Line, Lund's Blue Anchor Line and the White Star Line, owners of the "unsinkable" 46,000 ton *Titanic*, whose loss on her maiden voyage in 1912, with its catastrophic human cost, would burst the bubble of the transatlantic superliner programme.

As Britain and America were reeling from this setback, shipbuilding had not ground to a halt in Belfast. At this time, taking shape in the iron-and-redbrick Harland and Wolff shipyard was a superliner of a different kind. Built along the same traditional lines as her sister ships on the 'Colonial' service to Australia via the Cape, which White Star had launched in 1899, the 18,000 ton *Ceramic* would be the company's new trump card, her ratio of 9.5:1 making her the last of the British 'long ships', and the largest in her class.

With work starting in 1912 at the Belfast shipyard, the *Ceramic* would be the next ship launched by White Star after the *Titanic*. Her role was entirely different from her predecessor. She was not destined for the prestigious transatlantic service, but

Chapter 1: From the cradle

The Harland & Wolff Shipyard, Belfast, during the early part of the 20th century.
Valentines postcard.

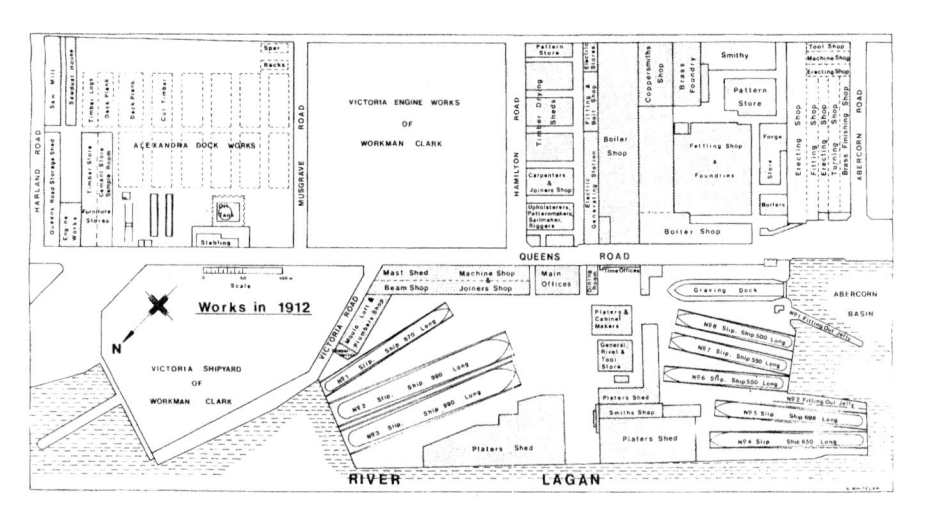

The Harland and Wolff Shipbuilding Works during construction of the Ceramic.
Source: Shipbuilders to the World; 125 Years of Harland and Wolff, Belfast 1861-1986 Michael Moss and John R. Hume;
The Black Staff Press 1986.

Afric   *Medic*   *Persic*

Runic

Suevic

The *Ceramic* featured on the back cover of the White Star Line passenger list which was used for all the Jubilee Class ships to Australia.

The *Ceramic* was celebrated for possessing the tallest masts to pass under Sydney Harbour Bridge.

for the burgeoning Australian route, via South Africa. Her vast cargo holds and single-class passenger accommodation would fulfill a dual purpose; the *Ceramic* would be both a passenger liner and a capacious merchant vessel, a triumph of utility and design, practicality and beauty. Her size set her apart from the other ships on her route, and her lines were classically elegant, the rake of her masts a throwback to the traditional clipper ships, in contrast to the testosterone-fuelled funnels of the transatlantic liners. The *Ceramic* was launched on 11th December 1912, making her first public appearance at the Merseyside Pageant of July 1913, where, decked out in bunting and banners, she joined a ten-mile line of shipping to welcome King George V and Queen Mary. The exuberance with which this Royal Visit is reported in the press, must reflect not only the delight the King experienced to be presented with such a sight, as a former Mariner himself, but also the joy that it brought to the area of Merseyside that would become the *Ceramic*'s adopted home. She later became nicknamed "The Relief of Bootle", or "The Breadbasket of Bootle", because she employed so many of the town's seafarers, keeping them from the dole queue in the precarious inter-war period.

The ships on the Australian run via the Cape were known as the Jubilee Class ships, and all were of a similar appearance, with four masts and one funnel ("four sticks and one stack"). *Afric*, *Medic* and *Persic*, each of 12,000 gross tons and fitted out with generous emigrant accommodation, were first to enter service, soon joined by the larger *Runic* and *Suevic*. These five ships were renowned for being the most spacious and comfortable of any British emigrant ships serving the route. When she joined them in 1913, at a total build cost of £436,000, the *Ceramic*'s physical size heralded a new era in passenger shipping to the southern hemisphere. At 655 feet in length and 18,481 gross tons, she immediately became the largest ship on the Cape and Australian run. Designed to economise power, her length stretched the entirety of Tilbury lock with just one foot to spare. This length made navigation of the bends in the Brisbane River almost impossible, so most voyages ended in Sydney. Douglas Taylor remembers, *"I recall seeing her in Woolwich Dry Dock in Sydney, which was an old style long & narrow graving dock. I seem to remember she took up the length of the dock."* (Letter to the author, March 2000). Until the launch of the post-war P&O liners, the *Ceramic* possessed the tallest masts to pass under Sydney Harbour Bridge. She soon became known as the "Queen of the Southern Seas".

Unlike the *Titanic*, which offered a range of accommodation from first to third class, the *Ceramic* was a single class vessel. She was accordingly fitted out for comfort and practicality rather than luxuriously appointed, though the gymnasium was one indication to her passengers that their journey would be made as pleasurable as possible on a route that might take three months, even on board this super-fast vessel, with a service speed of 15 knots. The *Ceramic*'s accommodation could comfortably hold 600 third-class passengers, with a further

220 if required. The middle and upper decks housed the majority of the two and four-berth rooms. The public rooms could be found on the 395 ft bridge deck, and the main dining saloon was situated on the middle deck over the reserve bunker space, *"a most extraordinary arrangement which must have caused the catering staff a severe headache when coaling was under way."* (Isherwood 1963). Whereas traditionally, the navigating bridge on Harland & Wolff ships would stand alone, on the *Ceramic* it was positioned at the fore end of the 210 ft. boat deck above the bridge deck. Below, were four overall decks and an orlop deck at the ends outside the machinery spaces. Her extensive proportions housed up to 19,000 tons of cargo in seven main holds, and a large bunker hold, totalling 836,000 cubic feet in all, much of which was insulated, and including 321,300 cubic feet of refrigerated space. David Nesbitt recalls, *"I remember the* Ceramic *coming into Newcastle Harbour, New South Wales, Australia and 'tying up' or berthing at a wharf in what was known as 'The Basin' in the late 1920s and early 1930s, when I was a small boy. She could easily be seen from a top floor window in our house, which looked out onto The Basin. To my knowledge, she was the largest ship to come into Newcastle Harbour in those days. She was a source of wonderment to a bunch of small boys of which I was one, during the depression. My father would often call me early in the morning and say, 'Look, the* Ceramic's *in'. She usually came in at night or very early morning."* The homecoming of the *Ceramic* would also bring great excitement as her stores of fresh foods were unloaded, and she was renowned for bringing big Christmas cargoes back to London. One unusual feature for a merchant vessel were the two 4.7 inch quick-firing deck-guns salvaged from an 1887 Japanese cruiser. These were fitted right aft and were carried even in peace time. Though practice they frequently jammed and were rather ineffective, they seemed to signify that the *Ceramic* would not be destined for a quiet life carrying emigrants and fruit to and from the New World.

Marine Engineer, Douglas Taylor, recalls, *"She had triple screws, a reciprocating engine on each outer shaft, and an exhaust turbine on the centre shaft, similar to* Titanic *and* Olympic *of White Star Line, but on a smaller scale. She was coal fired. I don't recall how many Scotch boilers but I did hear that in the centre pass connecting the stokeholds they had coloured signal lamps which were operated so that boiler firing operations were staggered in each stokehold, i.e. firing (with shovels), slicing and raking back of fires."* (Letter to the author, March 2000). The two boiler rooms with their cross bunkers at each end and side bunkers, housed six double-ended boilers, with 36 furnaces and working at 220 lb per square inch. Although she was never converted to burn oil, the *Ceramic*, on account of her great size, maintained a reliable schedule and consistently high average speed that lesser ships on the route could not match. As the last of the great coal burners, she would enjoy a colourful career that embraced the great changes of the first half of the twentieth century.

Chapter 1: From the cradle

Facts and Figures

CERAMIC

Builder	Harland & Wolff Ltd., Belfast	*IHP*	7,750 IHP
Owner	White Star Line and Shaw, Savill & Albion Line (1934)	*Boilers*	6 D.E.
		Furnaces	36
		Fuel	Coal
		Fuel Capacity	3,300 tons
Service	Liverpool to Australia via the Cape	*Screws*	Triple
		Service Speed	15 knots Later 16 knots
Registry	British	*Decks*	Three plus two partial decks
Registered	Southampton		
Home Port	Liverpool	*Crew*	260
Launched	11 December 1912	*Passengers*	Initially 600 third class (plus 220 if necessary) *1936:* Refitted to 480 cabin class *1938:* Refitted to 340 cabin class
Delivered	5 July 1913		
Inaugural Voyage	24 July 1913 (Liverpool - Sydney)		
Gross Tonnage	Initially 18,481 Later 18,713		
Dimensions	655.1 ft long 69.4 ft beam 43.8 ft depth	*Cargo Capacity*	836,000 cubic feet 321,200 cubic feet of refrigerated space
Displacement	34,520 tons		
Features	1 funnel; 4 masts	*Livery*	Black hull; White superstructure; Buff and black funnel; Red boot-topping
Machinery	2 x 4-cylinder triple expansion (wing shafts) 1 x low-pressure steam turbine (centre shaft)		
		Modernised	1936 (Re-entered service August 23)
Cylinders	26.5 in, 42 in, 42 in and 47.5 in diameter	*Call sign*	JCNK
		Official reg.	135474
Stroke	51 in	*Sunk*	7 December 1942

Chapter 2
A triumph of engineering

The Shipbuilder
October 1913

The White Star Australian Liner "Ceramic"

The triple-screw steamer Ceramic, which has been designed and built by Messrs. Harland & Wolff, Ltd., Belfast, for the Australian service of the White Star Line, far surpasses in size any vessel hitherto placed in the Australian trade, and embodies all the latest improvements which the builders' unrivalled experience in the construction of large passenger steamers has enabled them to introduce in regard to both the ship and her propelling machinery. The leading particulars of the Ceramic are:—

Length overall	674 ft. 9 in.
Length B.P	655 ft.
Breadth extreme	69 ft. 5 in.
Depth to upper deck	48 ft.
Indicated horse-power	about 9,000.
Gross tonnage	about 18,500.

The general arrangement of the ship is shown on Plates VI. and VII., from which it will be seen that there are in all seven steel decks, named the lower orlop, orlop, lower, middle, upper bridge, and boat decks respectively. Of these the lower orlop deck occurs only at the forward end; the orlop, lower, middle, and upper decks extend for the full length of the ship; the bridge deck extends for 400 ft. amidships, and the boat deck above the bridge extends for 215 ft. amidships. The main scantlings have been determined by the builders' long experience with large vessels, and are such that the hull structure is very strong. In conformity with the more scientific distribution of structural material which has been evolved during recent years, largely due to Messrs. Harland & Wolff's initiative, advantage is taken of the presence of the bridge to increase the depth of the structural girder by thickening the bridge deck plating and sides to form an efficient top member, instead of providing the required strength in the form of a greater amount of material at the upper deck level.

The keel is formed by a single flat plate more than one inch thick, to the underside of which is attached a horizontal slab 18 in. wide by 2 in. thick.

Chapter 2: A triumph of engineering

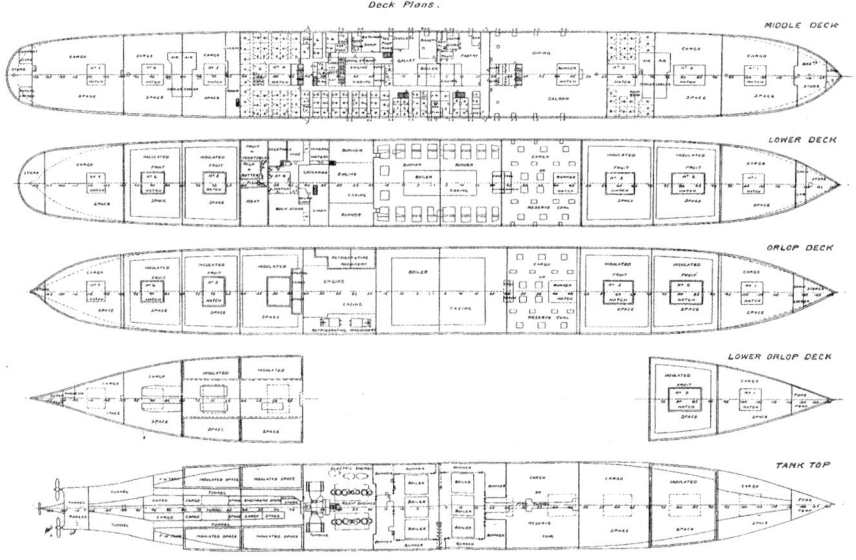

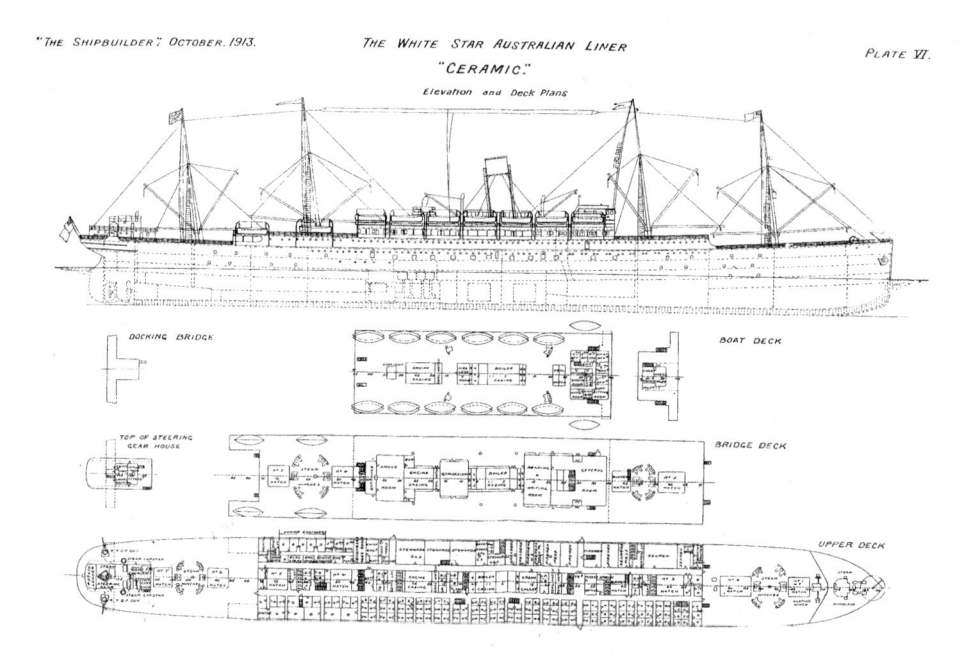

Above the keel plate is the centre girder of the double bottom, which has a normal depth of 4 ft. 6 in., but is increased to 4 ft. 10 in. deep in way of the engine room. The cellular double bottom extends right out to the ship's sides except in the forward and after holds, where the usual form of tank margin is adopted.

Floors are fitted on every frame throughout. In addition to the centre girder, there are on each side amidships four intercostal girders, while additional girders are fitted beneath the engine rooms. The sub-division of the double bottom into separate tanks is so arranged as to provide ample facilities for trimming the ship, and for correcting any list due to unequal disposition of coal or cargo. The fore and after peaks are also arranged to carry water ballast.

For the outer shell, in order to reduce the number of butts, plates of large size have been adopted. The majority of the shell plates are about 30 ft. long by 6 ft. wide, and weigh three tons each. To ensure the best workmanship, hydraulic riveting has been largely employed among the parts thus riveted being the keel plates and strakes adjoining adjoining, and the topside shell plating, stringer plates, and doublings. The seams of the bottom plating are double-riveted, and of the topside plating treble and double-riveted. The butts of the bottom and side plating are overlapped and quadruple-riveted. The largest rivets used are $1^1/8$ in. in diameter.

The frames are spaced $30^1/2$ in. apart for the major portion of the length, but are closer at the extreme ends, the spacing being reduced to 25 in. aft and 24 in. forward. Amidships the frames are of channel section 11" x 50" x 4" x 4" x .60", and extend from the tank top to the bridge deck. At the ends the frames are of the built type and consist of a 7" x 4" x .46" frame angle and a $6^1/2$" x $4^1/2$" x .46" reverse angle forming a 10 in. girder. Web frames extending to the middle deck are fitted at about every third frame in the engine rooms, and every fifth frame in the bunkers. Those in the engine rooms are 30 in. deep, and in the bunkers 34 in. deep. Great transverse strength is also ensured by the transverse watertight bulkheads.

The beams of the main structure are also of channel section 9 in. deep amidships, and are connected to the frames by bracket knees 30in. deep. The beams of the bridge and are supported by three longitudinal girders, which are in turn carried by solid round pillars spaced 5 ft. 1 in. apart. Below the middle deck the pillars are of built section, about 18 ft. apart, the girders being increased in depth to suit the larger span.

To minimize rolling in a seaway, bilge keels 15 in. deep are fitted on each side for about 300 ft. of the vessel's length amidships.

Chapter 2: A triumph of engineering

In addition to the double bottom, watertight sub-division of the ship is effected by twelve transverse watertight bulkheads, which extend to the upper deck. These bulkheads are carried much higher than has been the usual practice in times past, and thus provide exceptional flotation capacity in case of danger. The watertight doors in the engine and boiler-room bulkheads are arranged on the latest system. These doors are of massive construction, to the builders' special design, and are protected with oil cataracts governing the closing speed. Each door is held in position by a suitable friction clutch, which can be instantly released by means of a powerful electro-magnet controlled from the navigating bridge, so that in the event of accident the officer on watch can, by simply moving an electric switch, instantly close all the doors and make the vessel practically unsinkable. Each door can also be closed from below by operating a lever fitted in connection with the friction clutch. As a further precaution floats are provided beneath the level of the stokehold or engine-room floor, which, in the event of water accidentally entering any of the compartments, lift automatically, and thereby close the doors opening into the compartment if they have not already been closed by those in charge of the ship. An escape ladder is provided to each watertight compartment, in order that the closing of the door shall not imprison the men working inside, but the risk of this happening is lessened by electric bells placed in the vicinity of the doors, which ring prior to the closing down and give warning to those below.

The stem and stern castings of the Ceramic are of Siemens-Martin mild cast steel. The rudder frame and stock are of forged iron. The vessel having triple screws, the stern frame is provided with a boss and aperture for the centre or turbine propeller, while the wing or reciprocating propeller shafts are carried by boss arm castings, round which the shell plating is carried to form "bossing" of the builders' improved type. The stern frame is of dished section 14 in. by $9^{1}/_{2}$ in. where attached to the shell plating, and of solid section 17 in. by $9^{1}/_{2}$ in. in way of the aperture. The total height is about 42 ft., and length 21 ft. The boss arms for the wing shafts are in two pieces, which are connected at the centre line by strong deep flanges to form a continuous web right across the ship, and this is again reinforced by a steel bulkhead extending across the vessel at this part. The rudder is of the built type, the diameter of the head being $15^{3}/_{4}$ in. The stem bar is of the usual rolled section, and is connected by a steel casting to the centre keelson and foremost keel plate. The weights of the castings and forgings are as follows:—

Stern frame	21 ton.s.
Brackets (2 pieces)	$20^{1}/_{2}$ tons.
Rudder	25 tons.
Stem bar	4 tons.

Returning to the general arrangement of the ship, it will be seen from Plates VI. and VII. that all available space beneath the middle deck outside the engine and boiler rooms and coal bunkers is devoted to the carriage of cargo, with the exception of that utilized for the ship's provision stores. In addition, a large portion of the 'tween decks between the middle and upper decks is devoted to the same purpose. Special attention has been devoted to the carriage of perishable cargoes, there being thirteen large insulated compartments, comprising three holds and ten 'tween decks with a total capacity of more than 310,000 cubic feet, devoted to this purpose. Indeed, the Ceramic has one of the largest installations for the carriage of meat, fruit, and dairy produce in the Australian trade. The 'tween decks, in addition to being provided with the usual arrangement of brine grids, are fitted with air return and delivery trunks for the circulation of cold air at about 34° when carrying fruit. These trunks are collapsible and can be hinged up overhead when not in use. The refrigerating installation also comprises the cold storage spaces for the ship's provisions, which include separate chambers for meat, fish, milk and butter, and fruit and vegetables, which can thus be kept at the temperature most suitable for preservation in each case. In addition, there are a number of cold larders in the bars and pantries, as well as arrangements for making ice and cooling the drinking water.

The refrigerating engines and accessories are situated on the orlop deck at the sides of the engine casing. On the starboard side there are two horizontal duplex CO_2 machines of Messrs. J. & E. Hall's make, each of which contains two complete units capable of independent working, so that actually four refrigerating units are provided. The cooler grids and the other accessories are placed on the port side.

The brine circulation is arranged on the open brine system with a separate flow and return on each circuit. All brine pipes are externally galvanized. The various circuits are of moderate length, and are interlaced in the chambers to ensure even distribution of the cooling effect, even in the remote contingency of one section being thrown out of action. Separate air coolers, four in number, are fitted in steel houses above the spaces arranged for the carriage of fruit, in which the air from these compartments is circulated over a nest of brine grids by electrically-driven "Sirocco" fans.

No. 1 hold is fitted and lined throughout specially for the carriage of copra. Large hatchways are provided to all the cargo spaces, and the loading and discharging appliances are of a very ample nature. For working each hatch three tubular steel derricks are provided. In addition, there are four derricks on the boat deck for coaling purposes; so that the total number of derricks is twenty-eight. Of the cargo derricks six are carried by each of the vessel's four pole masts. The coaling derricks are carried by posts. The number of steam winches installed is twenty-nine, one for each derrick and one for warping purposes forward. It will thus be seen that the Ceramic places at the disposal of shippers not only enormous

Chapter 2: A triumph of engineering

Fig. 1. Dining Saloon of the "Ceramic." H1891 The Harland & Wolff Collection at Ulster Folk & Transport Museum.

capacity, but the most carefully devised arrangements for the transport of cargo.

In regard to the passenger accommodation, the most interesting feature is that only one class of passengers is provided for, an arrangement which has already proved to be exceedingly popular in the White Star Australian service. The accommodation is arranged on the middle, upper, and bridge decks amidships, communication between the decks being effected by two main stairways, which have large entrance halls at each deck. The stairways have oak-panelled dados, the remaining parts being finished in white. Accommodation has, in the first place been provided for about 600 passengers, but arrangements have been made so that additional staterooms for 220 more people can be readily installed should the demand for berths warrant the extension. The staterooms are situated on the upper and middle decks, and are arranged mostly for two and four people. These rooms are finished in white and are large, airy, and comfortable. The public rooms are large, attractive apartments, and include a dining saloon, reading and writing room, general room, smoking room, and gymnasium. A novel feature is the provision of two swimming baths, one for ladies and one for gentlemen, on the upper deck.

The dining saloon (Fig. 1) is situated on the middle deck just forward of the funnel casing, and extends the full width of the ship for a length of 94 feet. Seating accommodation is provided for nearly 500 people. This room is panelled and framed in pine, finished in enamel white, and contains sideboards and a piano. Large sidelights are arranged in pairs along the sides. The remaining public rooms are arranged in three large deck houses on the bridge deck. The foremost of these deckhouses which is 68 ft. long by 39 ft. wide, contains the general room (Fig. 2), 45 ft. long by 39 ft. wide, and the reading and writing room (Fig. 3), 23 ft. long by 39 ft. wide. The former is panelled and framed in oak and has large brass-framed opening windows arranged in pairs along the sides. The furniture is of wicker-work, and includes card tables, chairs, writing tables and settees. A vestibule is arranged at each side at the entrance doors.

The middle deckhouse contains the gymnasium (Fig. 4), which is 23 ft. long by 27 ft. wide. Here all the latest appliances are provided for recreation and health-giving exercise. The smoking room (Fig. 5) occupies the after deckhouse, which is 31 ft. long by 37 ft. wide. The actual dimensions of the smoking room are 22 ft. by 37 ft., the remaining part of the house being devoted to a bar on the port side and a lavatory on the starboard side. The smoking room is panelled and framed in oak, and also has large brass-framed opening windows arranged in pairs as in the other rooms. A large teak skylight surmounts the centre. The furniture includes writing tables, card tables, and chairs, a number of the small tables being arranged in comfortable bays round the walls.

Chapter 2: A triumph of engineering

Fig. 2. General Room. **H1878** The Harland & Wolff Collection at Ulster Folk & Transport Museum

Fig. 3. Reading and Writing Room. **H1879** The Harland & Wolff Collection at Ulster Folk & Transport Museum

Fig. 4. The Gymnasium. H1888 The Harland & Wolff Collection at Ulster Folk & Transport Museum

Fig. 5. Smoking Room. H1880 The Harland & Wolff Collection at Ulster Folk & Transport Museum

The floors of the main entrance and most of the public rooms are laid with linoleum tiles. The lavatory and sanitary arrangements are on the most up-to-date lines. Hospital accommodation is provided on the port side at the after end of the bridge adjoining the surgery and doctor's room, and there is also an infectious hospital right aft on top of the steering-gear house. The kitchen and culinary department is arranged conveniently just abaft the dining saloon, and the efficiency of the catering will be in keeping with the well-known practice of the White Star Line. Special attention has been given to the important subject of ventilation. Indeed, the utmost advantage throughout has been taken of the size of the ship to ensure the highest degree of comfort to the passengers, officers, and crew.

The captain and officers' quarters are arranged in a steel house 31 ft. long by 39 ft. wide, situated on the forward end of the boat deck. Surmounting this house is the navigating bridge, upon which is placed a steel house containing the steering station, chart room, and pilot's quarters. The engineers' and crew's accommodation occupies the whole of the port side of the bridge adjoining the working passage.

There are two warping capstans aft and a powerful steam windlass forward. The steam steering gear, which is of the builders' well-known design and manufacture, is situated in a steel house on the upper deck aft. The Ceramic is one of the first vessels to come into Mr. Winston Churchill's scheme for arming merchantmen to protect British commerce. For this purpose two 4.7 in. Q.F. guns are installed on the upper deck aft, and will enable the vessel, should the occasion arise, to protect the food supplies she carries.

Electricity, as in all large modern steamers, plays a most important part on board the Ceramic. The main generating sets are located in the main engine-room on the port side, and consist of three main engines and dynamos supplied by Messrs. W. H. Allen, Son & Co., Ltd., of Bedford. Each set has a capacity of 74 kilowatts at 100 volts. The engines are of the vertical two-crank compound enclosed type with forced lubrication, and have cylinders 10 and 15 in. in diameter with a stroke of 7 in., taking steam at 120 lb. per sq. in. Each engine provides 110 B.H.P. at 450 revs. per minute. The dynamos, which are directly coupled to their respective engines, are of the compound-wound continuous-current type. The main switchboard (Fig. 6), placed near the generating sets is provided with switches and circuit breakers for the three generators and with the ammeters and voltmeters necessary for registering and controlling the current generated. It has 24 feeder circuits ranging from 300 to 100 amperes. The power supply is entirely independent of the lighting supply, there being separate power and light busbars on the switchboard which can be paralleled or kept separate as required. Distribution of the current is effected on the single-wire system. The cables,

Fig. 6. Electric Generators and Main Switchboard.
H1894 The Harland & Wolff Collection at Ulster Folk & Transport Museum

Fig. 7. 40 inch "Sirocco" Fans for Engine Room Ventilation.
H1885 The Harland & Wolff Collection at Ulster Folk & Transport Museum

Chapter 2: A triumph of engineering

except those to the machinery spaces, are carried from the switchboard up the port side of the engine-room casing to the upper deck level in insulating clips, from whence they run along the main passages of the different decks and feed in turn distribution, switch and fuse boxes. From the latter current is taken by wiring to the various groups of lights and motors. The main cables and branch wires are of tinned copper, covered with rubber, and heavily braided, except in the machinery spaces, where they are lead sheathed, armoured, and externally braided.

The incandescent lights range from 16 to 100 c.p. and number about 1,500. Lamps of the Osram type have been adopted, except in the cargo spaces and for the portable fittings, for which it was considered preferable to use carbon filament lamps.

For ventilation seventeen powerful electrically-driven "Sirocco" fans have been installed comprising:—

No. 1 Fan.	Exhaust from pantry on middle deck, and crew's galley on upper deck.
No. 2 Fan.	Delivery to forward boiler room, port.
No. 3 Fan.	Delivery to after boiler room, port.
No. 4 Fan.	Delivery to forward boiler room, starboard.
No. 5 Fan.	Delivery to after boiler room, starboard.
No. 6 Fan.	Exhaust from gentlemen's lavatories and baths on upper deck, and baths on middle deck.
No. 7 Fan.	Exhaust from galley on middle deck.
No. 8 Fan.	Ladies' lavatories and baths on upper deck, and chief engineer's bath on middle deck.
No. 9 & 10	Delivery to engine room.
No. 11 Fan.	Delivery to engine room after end.
No. 12 Fan.	Exhaust from ladies' and gentlemen's lavatories and baths, and seamen's lavatories and w.c.'s.
No. 13 Fan.	Exhaust from gentlemen's lavatories and baths, engineers' lavatories and baths hospital bath, and electric store.
No. 14-17	Delivery to cargo spaces.

Photographs of two of the electrically-driven fans are given in Figs. 7 and 8.

In addition to the main generating sets an emergency dynamo, driven by a four-cylinder Diesel oil engine, is provided in the steel house on the upper deck aft well above the water-line. This generating set has a capacity of 75 kilowatts and provides an independent source of supply in the event of the main dynamos being put out of action. Connected to the emergency circuit are about 200 incandescent

Fig. 8. Ventilating Fan on Boat Deck.
H1893 The Harland & Wolff Collection at Ulster Folk & Transport Museum

lamps, placed at suitable positions to enable anyone to find their way from one part of the ship to another. The emergency dynamo can also be connected by change-over switches to the wireless-telegraphy apparatus, electrically-operated watertight doors, signal lights, whistle control, and two electrically-driven bilge pumps, one placed forward and one aft, each having connections which would enable water to be pumped out of any hold, even though the steam pumps and main electric plant were disabled.

The wireless telegraphy apparatus consists of a Marconi $1^{1}/_{2}$ kilowatt standard ship's set, the house for the instruments being situated on the boat deck at the after end of the funnel casing. Two parallel aerial wires, attached to light booms, are extended between the main and mizzen masts. From the aerials connecting wires are led to the instruments. There are two complete sets of apparatus, one for transmitting and one for receiving messages, the latter being placed in a sound-proof chamber in one corner of the house. There is also a battery and coil, which provide a third source of supply for working the apparatus, independent of the main and emergency dynamos. The vessel is provided with marine-signalling apparatus of the usual type, by which signals from submerged bells are received by microphones placed in small tanks on the port and starboard sides of the ship below the water level, these signals being communicated by connecting wires to a receiver in the chart room. An installation of Graham's loud-speaking telephones of Navy pattern is fitted for communication between the following stations:—

Captain	to chief engineer's room.
Chief engineer	to engine room starting platform.
Bridge	to engine room starting platform.
....	to wireless room.
....	to forecastle.
....	to after docking bridge, with extension to after wheel house.

These telephones are operated from the ship's lighting circuit, but an automatic switch is provided so that the supply may be taken from a battery in case of emergency. Other electrical appliances include the whistle (which can be either switched on by hand or set to blow automatically at given intervals during fog), boiler room telegraphs, stoking indicators, rudder indicator, thermostats, and a large number of small motors for various purposes, including the motors for driving the dough mixer, potato peeler, ice rocker, sounding machine, and other appliances.

The propelling machinery of the Ceramic is arranged on the combination system, and consists of two sets of reciprocating engines driving the wing propellers and one low-pressure turbine driving the centre propeller. The arrangement of the machinery is shown on the elevation, plan and sections through the engine room

SS CERAMIC The Untold Story

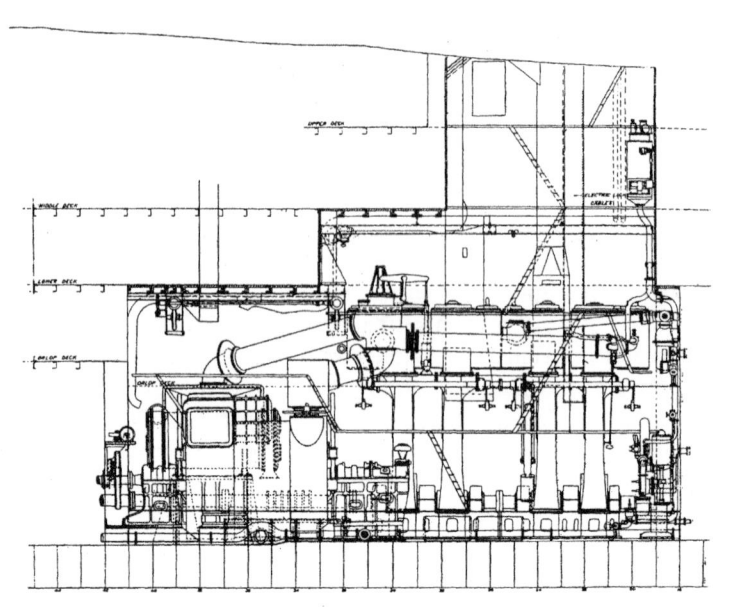

Fig. 9.—Elevation of Engine Room.

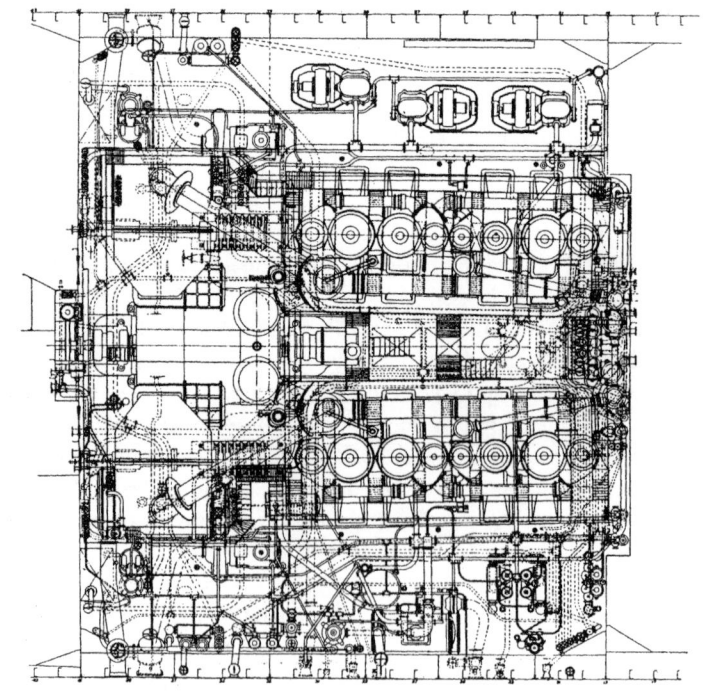

Fig. 10.—Plan of Engine Room.

given in Figs. 9 to 12. The design generally is that adopted in the Olympic and other vessels built by Messrs. Harland & Wolff having combination engines. The power transmitted by each of the three shafts is approximately equal under normal conditions of running.

The reciprocating engines are of the fourcrank triple-expansion type, balanced on the Yarrow, Schlick and Tweedy system. Each set has four inverted direct-acting cylinders $26^1/_2$, 42, $47^1/_2$ and $47^1/_2$ in. in diameter, with a stroke of 51 in. The cylinders of the reciprocating engines are formed by independent castings of strong hard cast iron, liners being fitted to all. The bottoms of the cylinders are double and strongly ribbed. All piston rods and valve spindles are fitted with Beldam's packing. The cylinder and casing covers are of box section, the material used being cast iron. The columns supporting the cylinders are of strong and substantial box section, also in cast iron, and are firmly bolted to the sole plates and cylinders, the tops being securely connected together by tie bars. The sole plates are made of cast iron, and have a box-shaped section provided with semi-circular recesses for the shaft bushes. Six bearings are arranged for each crankshaft.

The h.p. pistons are of cast iron and the i.p. and l.p. pistons of cast steel, their shape being conical. The piston rods are of forged ingot steel. The piston packing throughout is of Lockwood & Carlisle's type. The piston and slide valves are of cast iron, and are arranged for steam to enter between the valves in the case of the h.p. and i.p cylinders, the top piston being larger in diameter than the lower one in order to balance the weight of the valves and gear.

The reversing and hand gear is of Brown's steam and hydraulic type, a hand pump being provided for reversing by hand if required. A worm and wheel turning gear, capable of being worked by steam or hand, is installed for each set of engines. The governors are of Aspinall's type and are driven by levers from the main engine crossheads. Means are also provided for disconnecting the governors and working the throttle valves by hand levers.

The low-pressure turbine is of the Parsons type and is arranged to operate in the ahead direction only when utilizing the exhaust steam from the reciprocating engines and to pass the same to the condensers under a vacuum of 28 in. and a temperature of injection water of 60°F. A thrust block is provided at the forward end of the turbine, having rings in halves fitted into steel carrying blocks.
The steam thrust is arranged to approximately balance the thrust of the propeller. The rotor drum is hollow and made of forged steel. The rotor wheels are of cast steel and the shaft of forged steel. The turbine casing, bearing blocks, and bushes are of cast iron, the latter being lined with white metal. The blading is of brass. The turbine bearings and thrust block are provided with forced lubrication.

Turbine lifting gear, operated by an electric motor, is installed for lifting the rotor and top half of the turbine casing.

Two cast-iron change-over valves are fitted in the steam pipes to the turbine, so that when manoeuvring the steam may be passed directly from the reciprocating engines to the condensers. These valves are of the piston type fitted with Ramsbottom packing rings and are operated from the starting platform by direct-acting engines of the steam and hydraulic type. An emergency governor is arranged to operate the change-over valve engines, and thus shut off the steam supply to the turbine should the speed of the latter become excessive.

All main steam pipes are of lap-welded wrought iron with cast steel bends and junction pieces, and gunmetal sleeves in the stuffing boxes.

The crankshafts of the reciprocating engines are made of Siemens-Martin ingot steel. Each is built in two pieces and has a diameter of $15^3/_4$ in. The crank angles are arranged to suit the balancing of the engines. The thrust shafts are also $15^3/_4$ in. in diameter. Each shaft bears on seven cast iron shoes lined with white metal on both sides, and is supported at the ends on bearings lined with white metal. The intermediate shafting for the reciprocating engines is 14 in. in diameter. The wing propeller shafts are of Siemens-Martin ingot steel and have a diameter of 16 in. The line shafting for the centre propeller is $10^3/_8$ in. in diameter and propeller shaft $11^1/_2$ in. in diameter. The stern tubes are of cast iron and have gunmetal liners extending for their full length. Forced lubrication is provided for all the tunnel bearings.

Each wing propeller has a cast-iron boss and three built manganese bronze blades. Each blade is secured by steel studs and gunmetal capped nuts. The diameter of the wing propeller is 18 ft. Cast iron cones are fitted over the propeller shaft nuts. The centre or turbine propeller is made of solid manganese bronze. The wing propellers are outward turning, while the centre propeller turns in the right-hand direction.

The two condensers are placed one on each side of the turbine, as shown in Figs. 9, 10 and 12. They are pear-shaped in cross section, and have a combined cooling surface of about 9,900 square feet. The circulating pumps are of the centrifugal type and have inlet and outlet pipes of 20 in. bore. Each pump is driven by an open-type engine having a cylinder 14 in. in diameter with a stroke of 12 in. The air pumps are of Weir's independent "Dual" type, having cylinders 24 in. in diameter by 18 in. stroke.

The auxiliary machinery throughout is of the latest type and of ample capacity. The main feed pumps, of which there are two, have cylinders 17 in. in diameter,

Chapter 2: A triumph of engineering

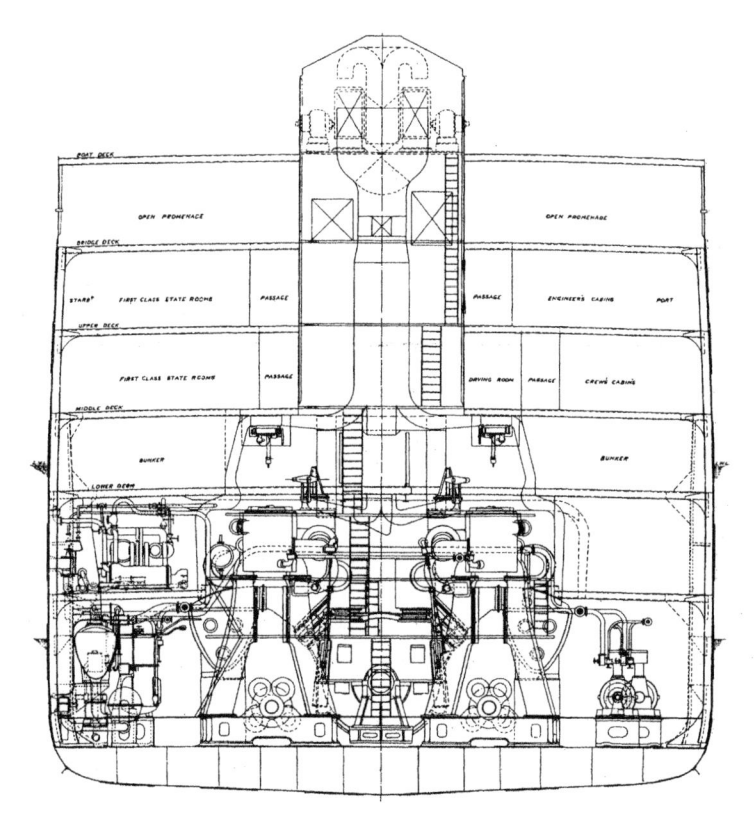

Fig. 11.—Section through Engine Room at Frame 25, looking Aft.

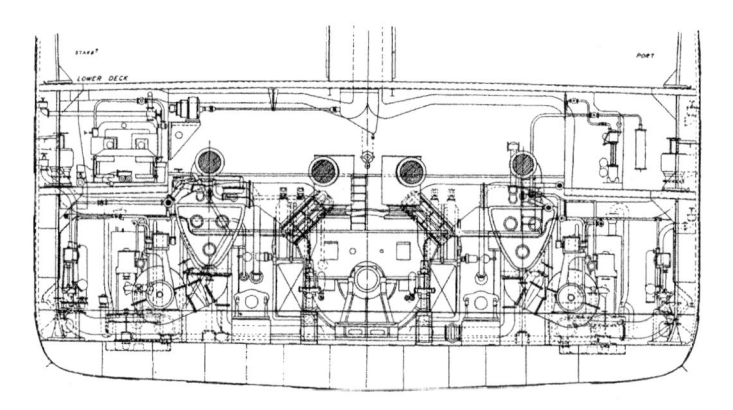

Fig. 12.—Section at Frame 35 showing Turbine and Condensers, looking Aft.

SS CERAMIC The Untold Story

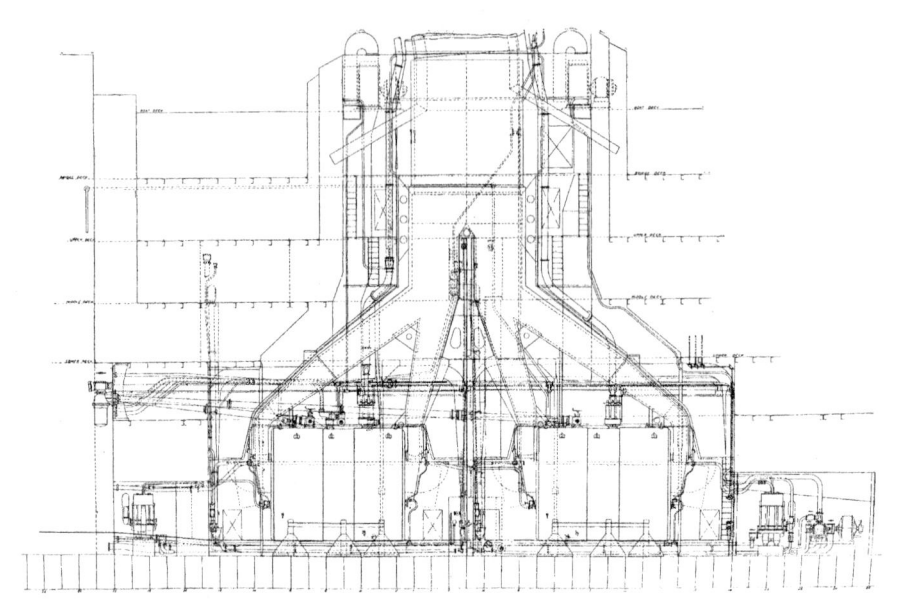

Fig. 13.—Elevation of Boiler Room.

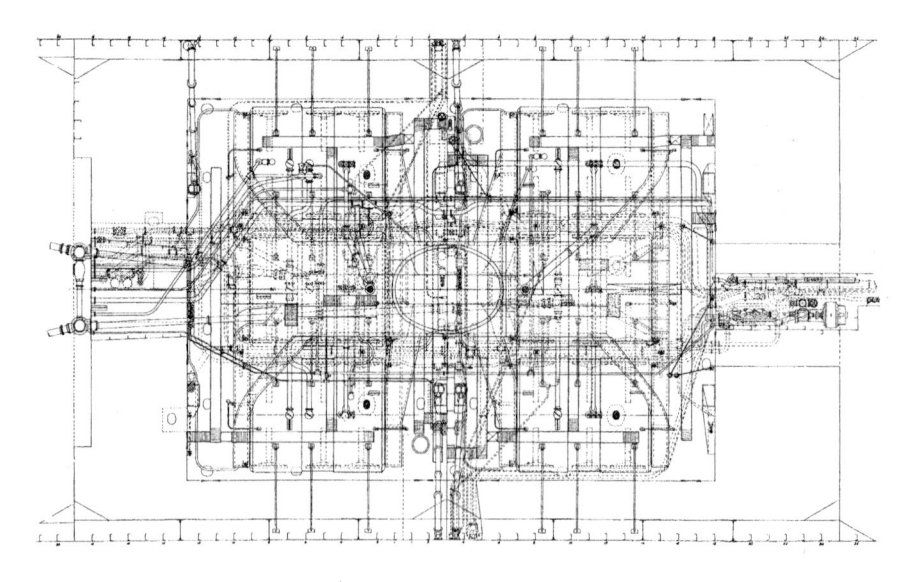

Fig. 14.—Plan of Boiler Room.

pump ends $12^1/_2$ in. in diameter, and a stroke of 26 in. The pumps are interchangeable, and each is capable of dealing with the whole of the feed water. The hot-well pump is of the single-cylinder type, and is also capable of dealing with the whole of the feed water at a low speed. There are two sanitary, three bilge, and one ballast pump of the builders' own make, the latter being capable of discharging 250 tons per hour. In addition the above, there are the two emergency bilge pumps, one placed forward of the boiler rooms and one placed in the forward end of the tunnel, to which reference has already been made. Both these pumps are of the electrically-driven rotary type, and are connected to the ballast system.

The arrangement of the steam-generating plant is shown in Figs. 13, 14 and 15. Altogether there are six double-ended cylindrical boilers $15^1/_2$ ft. in diameter by 19 ft. long, designed for a working pressure of 215 lb. per sq. in. Each boiler has six furnaces of the Morison suspension type, having an inside diameter of 3 ft. 8 in. Opposite furnaces are led into a common combustion chamber. The boiler shell plates are connected in the longitudinal direction by double straps treble riveted, while the circumferential seams are treble riveted at the centre of the boilers and double riveted at the ends. The tubes are of wrought iron and have an external diameter of $2^3/_4$ in. The uptakes are arranged for natural draught and are led to a single funnel, which has been provided with an outer casing throughout. One set of White Star whistles and one Harland & Wolff's 6 in. organ whistle are provided, the former being fitted with Willett Bruce's automatic control gear.

The engine room is well ventilated by two 40 in. and one 35 in. electrically-driven fans, from which trunks are led down to the starting platform and engine room wings. The boiler rooms are ventilated by four 40 in. fans, from which trunks extend to within about 7 ft. of the stokehold floor.

The Ceramic left Belfast on the 5th July, and, after an extended trip which passed off in every way satisfactorily, arrived at Liverpool on the 7th July. During her official tests the vessel attained a speed of 16.5 knots. She occupied a leading position in the naval pageant which took place in the Mersey in the presence of the King and Queen on the 11th July, and sailed on her maiden voyage to Australia on 24th July. A photograph of the ship at is reproduced in Fig. 16.

During construction the Ceramic has been under the supervision of Mr. E. Lionel Fletcher, manager, Captain Bartlett, marine superintendent, and Mr. W. J. Willett Bruce, superintendent engineer of the White Star Line.

We are indebted to Messrs. Harland & Wolff for placing the plans and particulars of this interesting vessel at our disposal.

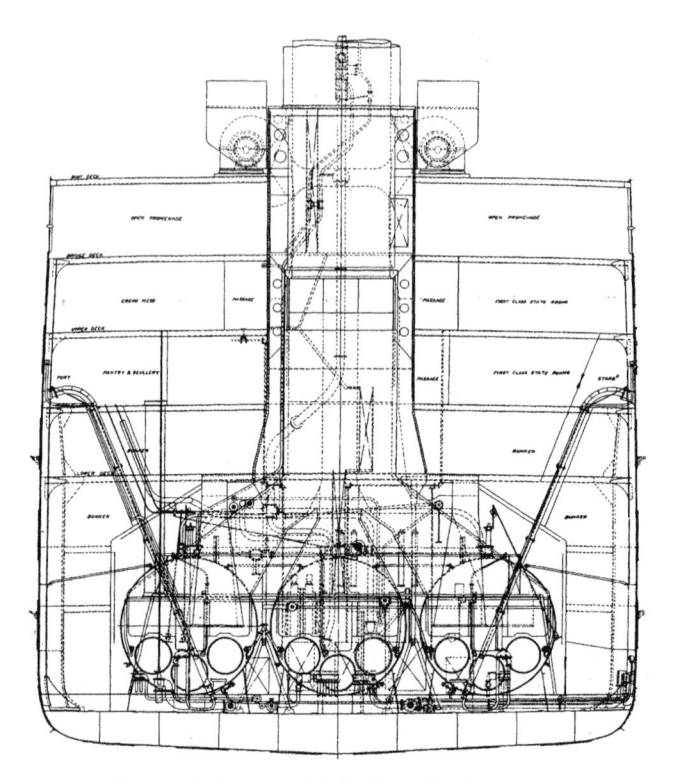

Fig. 15.—Section through Boiler Room, looking Forward.

Fig. 16. Ceramic at Sea. H1865 The Harland & Wolff Collection at Ulster Folk & Transport Museum

Chapter 3
Making the news

The Times - Finance, Commerce and Shipping supplement.
Thursday December 12th 1912.

LAUNCH OF THE WHITE STAR LINER CERAMIC.
LARGEST VESSEL IN THE AUSTRALIAN SERVICE.

Messrs. Harland and Wolff, Belfast, yesterday launched from their North yard the new liner Ceramic, of about 18,000 tons, for the White Star Line. The Ceramic is the biggest vessel built in Belfast this year, and is unique in that she will be the largest ship trading to Australia, and will be the finest triple-screw White Star liner on that berth.

The connexion of the White Star Line with the Australian trade began somewhere back in the sixties. It has within recent years been developed by vessels of the largest type in the trade. Within the last decade the development has been phenomenal through the introduction of such magnificent vessels as the Afric, Medic, and Persic (12,000 tons), Runic, and Suevic (12,600 tons), and now the Ceramic far surpasses in size anything hitherto placed on the Australian berth, and is a vessel representing the highest excellence in marine architecture and engineering and combining those qualities so indispensable to modern requirements — viz., large cargo capacity and extensive passenger accommodation.

The Ceramic, which is a triple-screw steamer, is 676 ft. long by 69 ft. 3 in. beam, and will have a gross tonnage of about 18,600 tons, and will have accommodation for 600 passengers, ordinarily, with arrangements for possible extension for a further 220, or a total complement of 820 if required. It is anticipated, in view of the remarkable development in Australian immigration from the Mother Country and the popularity of White Star vessels, that even this extensive accommodation will be taxed to its utmost capacity.

EFFICIENT LIFEBOAT ACCOMMODATION.

The Ceramic is of very strong construction, built under survey of the Board of Trade for passenger certificate and having 12 watertight bulkheads dividing the vessel into 13 watertight compartments. Eleven of the bulkheads are carried to the

SS CERAMIC The Untold Story

*Port Stern on Ways,
No1 Yard, prior to launch,
10 December 1912.*

H1791 The Harland & Wolff Collection at Ulster Folk & Transport Museum

*Starboard Bow on Ways,
No1 Yard, prior to launch,
10 December 1912.*

H1790 The Harland & Wolff Collection at Ulster Folk & Transport Museum

42

Chapter 3: Making the news

Launch, stern entering water. 11 December 1912.
H1793 The Harland & Wolff Collection at Ulster Folk & Transport Museum

Port Bow view, at quay, 11 December 1912.
H1794 The Harland & Wolff Collection at Ulster Folk & Transport Museum

upper deck, and the aftermost bulkhead to the middle deck. There are eight steel decks, and all the facilities for working the ship and cargo embody the latest improvements. The vessel will be lighted throughout by electricity and will have a complete installation of wireless telegraphy and sufficient lifeboats to accommodate every soul on board, the boats being manipulated by patent davits. The passenger accommodation would leave nothing to be desired.

Full advantage has been taken of the vessel's size in designating the public rooms, and the state-rooms as usual in White Star ships, are large, comfortable and well ventilated. The dining saloon on the middle deck will seat about 1540 persons; it will be finished enamel white with large side-lights arranged in pairs. On the bridge deck, in oak, with suitable furniture and Harland and Wolffs large brass framed opening windows, arranged in pairs, with be another fine apartment, as also the general room on the same deck just forward of the reading and writing room and the smoke-room amidships. These two latter rooms are also panelled and framed in oak with large side lights in pairs and suitable furniture. A feature in the vessel will be the well-equipped gymnasium on the bridge deck just forward of the smoke-room. The state-rooms are arranged mostly as two or four berth rooms. The Ceramic will take up her sailings about the end of next spring.

****

Liverpool Courier
8th July 1913

THE CERAMIC
WHITE STAR LINE'S AUSTRALIAN SERVICE

AN ARMED MERCHANTMAN

Another striking example of the enterprise of the famous White Star Steamship Co. is seen this week anchored in the Mersey, and is certain to afford a great deal of interest to the thousands of visitors who will sojourn in Liverpool during the visit of their Majesties the King and Queen, and also be a source of great pride to citizens who are keenly alive to the maintenance of the mercantile supremacy of the Mersey port. This is the new triple-screw steamer Ceramic, which arrived in Liverpool yesterday morning from Belfast, where she was built by Messrs Harland and Wolff, and which will be one of the most attractive features of the great maritime display to be witnessed on the Mersey on Friday. The Ceramic is a vessel of 18,500 tons register, and is the latest addition to the Australian fleet of the White Star Line. She will be the largest vessel in that service, and has been specially fitted out to meet the increasing trade with the colonies of Australia and South Africa. The necessity has long been felt for accommodation at Australian ports for steamers with great cargo capacity if that colony was to successfully compete with the River Plate area in the chilled meat and kindred provision trades, and that is now being provided. The Ceramic is specially equipped for the carriage of meat, fruit, and dairy produce in the Australian trade, and the refrigerating installation embodies all the latest improvements. She will carry only one class of passengers, for whose comfort the most perfect accommodation is arranged. The vessel is not fitted out with that decorative elaboration which is a characteristic of the great Atlantic liners, but for the particular trade in which she will be engaged she is absolutely everything that could be desired, and the guests who were privileged to travel with her on the trial trip from Belfast to Liverpool were delighted with her passenger equipment, and also with the excellent sea-going qualities of the steamer. The Ceramic is the first armed merchantman from which practice has been made with big guns, and the public will be interested to learn that on Friday she will fire a Royal salute during the visit of their Majesties to the city.

Amongst those on board for the trial trip were Mr. Harold A. Sanderson (chairman of the White Star Line and president of the International Mercantile Marine), Mr. H. Concanon and Mr. E. Lionel Fletcher (managers of the White Star Line), Rear-Admiral H. H. Campbell, C.V.O., Rear-Admiral H. S. Savory, M.V.O. (director of Transports), Commander C. A. Bartlett, R.D., R.N.R. (marine superintendent White Star Line), Commander Buckle, R.N., Mr W. J. Willett Bruce, R.N.R. (superintendent engineer of the White Star Line), Mr. W. W. Bradfield (London manager of the Marconi Company), Captain J. D. Dick, R.N., Mr. T. H. Drummond (Australian passenger manager, White Star Line), Mr. Percy Hunter (Australian Immigration Commissioner), Mr F. W. May (assistant manager, Atlantic Transport Line), Lieut. R. J. Noal, R.N.R. (marine superintendent, Shaw, Savill and Co.), Mr Thomas Rowley (principal engineer surveyor, Board of Trade, Liverpool), Mr. John Dykes (principal engineer surveyor, Lloyd's Register, Liverpool), Commander C. M. Forbes, R.N., Capt. T. F. Gambell, Mr. W. H. Savill, Mr. R. J. A. Shelley (publicity department manager, White Star Line), Mr. L. C. Shapley (victualling superintendent, White Star Line), Mr. E. A. Beazley, Mr. James Parton, Mr. J. A. Potter, and a representative party of British and Colonial journalists.

DESCRIPTION OF THE VESSEL

The Ceramic far surpasses in size anything hitherto placed on the Australian berth, and is in keeping with the White Star Line's record of continued progress and development. Her length over all is 674 ft. 9 in., extreme breadth 69 ft. 5 in., depth 48 ft., and indicated horse-power 9,000. She has been built on the latest and most approved principles, with a double bottom extending right fore and aft, and with twelve transverse water-tight bulkheads carried to the upper deck. There are seven steel decks. The cargo arrangements in such a vessel are, of course, of the utmost importance, and shippers will find in the Ceramic not only enormous capacity, but also the best facilities for working both ship and cargo. The vessel has the largest capacity for the carriage of meat, fruit and dairy produce in the Australian trade, and the refrigerating installation embodies all the latest improvements. The insulated compartments have a total capacity of over 310,000 cubic feet. In addition to the refrigerating space, one of the holds is also fitted and lined throughout for the carriage of copra*. The passenger accommodation is in keeping with the general character of the ship. There is accommodation for about 600 passengers ordinarily, with a further 220, or a total of 820, all in staterooms. These rooms, which are situated on the upper and middle decks, are arranged mostly in two and four berth rooms. The public rooms consist of dining saloon, reading and writing room, general room, and smokeroom, and there is a gymnasium on the bridge deck. There are two swimming baths on the upper deck, one for ladies and one for gentlemen. The staterooms and public rooms are large comfortable apartments. The utmost advantage has been taken of the size of the vessel in their arrangement and disposition, and special attention has been given to the important subject of ventilation. The dining saloon on the middle deck will seat nearly 500 people. The Ceramic has lifeboats of sufficient capacity to accommodate all on board, and every provision is made for the safety of both passengers and crew.

THE TRIAL CRUISE

The Ceramic left Belfast at 9 a.m. on Saturday and went down Belfast Lough to adjust compasses, which operation was completed at noon. The vessel then proceeded towards Mew Island, and carried out steaming trials between that point and Skulmartin Rock light vessel, averaging 16.5 knots per hour. Turning again to the northward the course was run over at a similar speed, the trials throughout being entirely satisfactory. In Belfast Lough a number of builders' representatives left the steamer, which then proceeded to a position off the shore, when the firing tests of the ship's two 4.7 guns were carried out. About seven o'clock the Ceramic proceeded on her extended trial cruise towards Rathlin Island. Turning to the southward again at 11.22 p.m. she steamed towards a position off Rockabill Light, where the turning and manoeuvring trials were carried out during the morning. At midnight the White Star liner Megantic, outward bound for Montreal, was met

---

* COPRA is derived from coconuts. If the nut remains on the tree it continues to ripen, the outside becomes harder and the meaty inner lining thickens and hardens while the milk turns to water. The shells are then split and the meat is left to dry in the sun, becoming "copra" from which coconut oil is extracted.

and the Morse light signalling apparatus found most efficient; the wireless operators were also in constant communication. After carrying out the turning evolutions the steamer proceeded towards South Stack, Holyhead, and from there to a position off Douglas, Isle of Man, to carry out further manoeuvres. In the evening she steamed towards Liverpool via Point Lynas, and completed a most successful cruise of 564 miles early yesterday morning. The Ceramic proved of the high standard always required in vessels of the White Star line.

GUN TRIALS

The Ceramic is one of the self-defensive merchant steamers under Mr. Winston Churchill's scheme for the protection of British commerce. Some four or five ships have already been similarly armed, but the Ceramic is the first ship in which firing practice has actually been carried out. Her armament consists of two 4.7 in. quick-firing guns. They throw a shot of 45 lbs. weight to a range of six miles. The guns are placed astern for several reasons. The first and one of the most important is that they are intended more for defence than for attack and to be used in case of pursuit. Then regard must be had to the general arrangement and convenience of the ship and its working. During firing tests each gun fired ten rounds. Commander Forbes, R.N., of H.M.S. Excellent, with a squad of special men from that ship, was in charge, the whole proceedings being supervised by Rear-Admiral H. H. Campbell, C.V.O. Captain J. R. Dick, R.N., Assistant Director of Naval Ordnance, was also present. The ranges varied from 1,300 yards to 5,500 yards (about three and a quarter miles). At the latter range the target was practically out of sight, and had to be picked up by telescope. It was stated that the aim as to direction was very good, but accuracy of elevation varied. The guns were also tried for extreme elevation and extreme depression, with a view of bringing them to bear the utmost possible strain on the structure of the steamer. The guns were mounted by Messrs. Harland and Wolff on specially constructed platforms, which most successfully resisted the shock of all the explosions, no damage whatever resulting either to the ship herself or to any materials, however fragile, on board. The firing of several of the rounds was entrusted to members of the Ceramic's crew, who are attached to the Royal Naval Reserve, under the charge of Lieut. Davey, R.N.R. The drill of the men was creditably carried out, and the firing proved very good, the aim of the target being wonderfully accurate. The Ceramic carried both officers and men of the Royal Naval Reserve, and will therefore be able to provide gun crews from her own complement. The experiments amply demonstrated that arming merchant vessels in this way will provide very effective defensive power, and thereby add to the security of Britain's mercantile marine. Of course, in a vessel thus armed the safety of passengers and crew is an essential consideration. To secure this it is arranged that the ammunition does not carry its own means of ignition, and does not become active until actually placed in the guns. It is therefore not an explosive in the ordinarily accepted meaning of the word.

The Ceramic is under the command of Captain J. Stivey, retired lieutenant R.N.R., four others of her officers being also members of the R.N.R. and her chief engineer holding the rank of chief engineer in the Royal Naval Reserve. It is the intention of the White Star Line to mount all their ships in the regular Australian trade with guns similar to those on the Ceramic.

The Ceramic leaves Liverpool on her maiden voyage to Australia, via Capetown, on the 24th inst.

****

Liverpool Weekly Mercury
Saturday July 12, 1913

THE CERAMIC
White Star Steamer's Trial Cruise

GUN PRACTICE AT SEA

After a successful two days' trial cruise in the Irish Sea of close upon 600 miles, the White Star Company's newest steamer, the Ceramic, which will be the largest vessel in the Australian trade, arrived in the Mersey this week. An important feature of the trial run was the testing of the two 4.7 quick-firing guns with which the vessel has been equipped for the purpose of self-defence under the scheme recently introduced by the Admiralty for the protection of British commerce. These gunnery trials, which took place at sea, were accounted thoroughly satisfactory by the representatives of the Admiralty who were on board, and were all the more interesting because of the fact that, although several other British merchant steamers have already been similarly armed, the Ceramic has the distinction of having been the first to put the armaments to a practical test.

The Ceramic has been built by Messrs. Harland and Wolff, of Belfast, and in the general principles of her construction follows pretty closely the lines of other fine vessels which form the White Star Company's excellent fleet of "all-one-class" passenger steamers on the Australian service, although she surpasses them all both in size and elegance and comfort. Her gross tonnage is 18,500, her indicated horse-power about 9,000, and her principle dimensions are:– Length over all 674 ft. 9 in.; extreme breadth, 69 ft. 5 in. She has been built with a double bottom extending right fore and aft, and has seven steel decks. The steamer has accommodation, in the ordinary way, for 600 passengers, but when necessary this can be extended for a further 220; and her capacity for the carriage of meat, fruit, and dairy produce is the largest in the Australian trade. She is driven by a triple-screw, and following the principle initiated with such highly satisfactory results on the Laurentic, for the Canadian service, combines the advantages of reciprocating engines with a low-pressure turbine, the former driving the wing propellers, while the turbine drives the centre propeller. She is scheduled to leave Liverpool on July 24 for her maiden voyage to the Antipodes, via Cape Town, under the command of Lieutenant John Stivey, R.N.R.

THE CRUISE

When she left Belfast at nine o'clock on Saturday morning for her trials she had aboard a company of about a hundred guests. Her passenger list included Mr. Harold A. Sanderson (the chairman of the White Star Line), Messrs. H. Concanon and E. Lionel Fletcher (manager), Commander C. A. Bartlett (marine superintendent of the line), Mr. W. J. Willett Bruce (superintendent engineer R.N.R.), Rear-Admiral H. H. Campbell, C.V.O., Rear-Admiral H. S. Savory, M.V.O., Captain J. R. Dick, R.N. (Assistant-Director of Naval Ordnance), Commanders C. M. Forbes and Buckle (R.N.), Messrs. W. H. Saville (of Shaw, Saville, and Co.), W. W. Bradfield (London manager of the Marconi Company), Thomas Rowley (principal engineer-surveyor of the Board of Trade at Liverpool), John Dykes (principal engineer-surveyor of Lloyd's Register), Percy Hunter (Immigration Commissioner for the Australian Commonwealth), R. J. A. Shelley, and a large number of representatives of the English and Australian Press. After completing the adjustment of compasses in Belfast Lough about noon, the Ceramic made for Mew Island, and carried on steaming trials between that point and Skulmartin Rock light vessel, maintaining an average of 16.5 knots, which is well in excess of what will be required of her on the Australian service. This average speed was also well maintained on a northward course, and the trials throughout gave complete satisfaction to the owners and builders. The gun-firing tests took place on Saturday evening, and on their completion the cruise was continued in the direction of Rathlin Island. Shortly before midnight she turned southward again, and when off Rockabill Light went through a number of turning and manoeuvring evolutions during the morning. Then followed a visit to the points off Holyhead and Douglas, I.O.M., the latter being reached on Sunday evening, and an easy passage from thence to Liverpool, by way of Point Lynas, brought the extremely pleasant cruise to an end. The company's guests were very agreeably entertained during the trip, and appreciated their cruise as much as they admired the vessel. The gymnasium, equipped with all the most modern apparatus, and the open air swimming tank were very popular, and the various deck games were played with much enjoyment. Of these games the most notable was a cricket match between a Royal Navy team (so representative as to include a rear admiral along with several gunners), and a side composed of civilians.

SELF-DEFENSIVE GUNS

The gun-firing practice, however, eclipsed everything else in the interest of the passengers. The Ceramic's two quick-firing guns are capable of shooting a projectile of 45 lbs. weight within a range of six miles. As they are intended for defensive purposes rather than for attack, and so that they may be brought effectively into action in case of pursuit, they are mounted on the after-deck, an arrangement which has also the advantage of being most conformable to the general convenience of the ship and its working. Commander Forbes, of H.M.S. Excellent, with a special squad of gunners from Portsmouth, was in charge, and the practice was supervised by Rear-Admiral Campbell. Each gun fired ten rounds, at ranges varying from three-quarters of a mile to three and a quarter miles. At the longer range the targets had to be located by telescope. It was reported that, as to direction, the firing was accurate, but in the matter of elevation the accuracy varied. In order to test to the utmost the strain upon the structure of the ship, the guns were also tried for extreme elevation and extreme depression, but the shock was so effectively resisted by the special platforms on which the guns were mounted that not the slightest damage resulted either to the vessel or to the most fragile material on board.

Several members of the Ceramic's crew, who belong to the Royal Naval Reserve, took part in the firing under charge of Lieutenant Davey, R.N.R. and acquitted themselves with great credit. It was thus made abundantly clear that the Ceramic will be able to furnish efficient guns' crews from her own complement. In an official statement issued by the White Star Company it was claimed that the practice demonstrated that arming merchant vessels in this fashion will provide an effective defensive power, and thereby add to the security of Britain's merchant marine, and as evidence of their firm conviction of this fact the company announced their intention to mount all their ships on the regular Australian trade with guns similar to those on the Ceramic.

Gun mounted on port side of stern.

H1898 The Harland & Wolff Collection at Ulster Folk & Transport Museum

Chapter 3: Making the news

View of Starboard Stern showing gun mounted on deck.
H1897 The Harland & Wolff Collection at Ulster Folk & Transport Museum

Liverpool Echo   *(Ceramic's first outing)*
July 10 1913

THE ROYAL VISIT TO LIVERPOOL
CITY READY
A LAVISH SCHEME OF STREET ADORNMENT

RIVER PAGEANT

Liverpool is donning its carnival dress, not with hasty carelessness, but with the premeditated precision that seeks a good effect. It wants to assure the King and Queen, so far as bunting and banners can do it, of the loyalty of one of the greatest cities in their dominions, and so, all along the line of tomorrow's route, buildings, public and private, are being more an more smothered with the decorator's stock.

Here and there the effect may be garish, but displays such as this have to be judged as a whole, and there appears to be every prospect that the city adornment will be ample for the occasion.

The spirit of holiday is already asserting itself. At noon to-day the elementary schools "broke up" for the summer vacation, and parents had no rest until they did one of two things – took their youngsters to the fun fairs in the parks, so that the little ones might watch the building up of those ponderous mechanical contrivances which produce such varying human sensations, or brought them into the centre of the city for a look at the decorations.

The main streets have been crowded since noon, in spite of a threatening sky, and, given fine weather, their Majesties are sure, to-morrow, of a hearty welcome from a city thoroughly at play. Shop window spaces on the line of the route are being eagerly bought up, and every detail of information is being closely studied by those who, trusting to such chances as the streets afford, are selecting the spot most likely to yield them a satisfactory view of the Royal procession from Knowsley.

From a spectacular point of view Liverpool's function will surpass in picturesqueness anything seen in the other parts of the county through which their Majesties have passed this week. Our river is a valuable asset in more ways than one. To-morrow it will put on one side, for a few hours, its purely utilitarian aspect, and lend itself to a scene likely to make a lasting impression on the memory of those privileged to witness it.

In opening the Gladstone Dock the King fits the very stone, so to speak, to a work

Chapter 3: Making the news

undertaken in the best interests of the port, and when the Galatea steams down the river between lines of merchant ships, representative of the best fleets in the Empire, Liverpolitans may well be forgiven if they indulge in a little boasting.

The arrangements for this striking marine display are complete. The arrival in the Mersey of the warships Liverpool and Lancaster whetted public interest in this branch of the city's rejoicings. It is an item in the programme which has touched the public imagination by its appropriateness as well as the colossal scale on which it is to be carried out.

****

Liverpool Echo
11 July 1913

THE KING AND QUEEN IN THE CITY
SCENES
AN ENTHUSIASTIC WELCOME
THE ROUTE
MANY THOUSANDS WITNESS ROYAL PROGRESS
ADDRESS
HIS MAJESTY'S TWO SPEECHES

To-day takes its place among the great days in the history of Liverpool.

The city has had its share of Royal visits, for no monarch of these realms who wants to know what his people are doing can afford to ignore the Mersey side; but there is nothing hazardous in saying that no occupant of the British throne ever received more enthusiastic acclamation than that which is being given to King George and his gracious Consort.

The streets for miles upon miles echoed the homage of a populace delighted to have the opportunity of seeing their Majesties, and of testifying their feelings of affectionate loyalty.

On their part, the King and Queen were equally delighted to come into such intimate contact with a city whose ships go to every sea, whose commerce is an epitome of the world's activities, and whose people are second to none in the support they consistently give to all those agencies which make for the greatness of the King's dominions and the happiness of his subjects.

"What will the weather be like?" This was the question which leaped to the lips of thousands upon thousands of Liverpool people this morning.

Early rising was the rule. There was no workshop or office to go to, for the hum of industry had been hushed, but there was the Royal procession to see somewhere and somehow, and in the hurry to get to some portion of the line of route breakfast was but a hurried meal.

At first the skies were somewhat threatening, but by nine o'clock the eagerly looked-for sun made his appearance. Ominous clouds sped elsewhere, and the holiday spirit got that impetus which a fine summer day always gives it.

Every tramcar bound citywards was crowded, taxicabs were speeding from point to point, and there was a stream of pedestrians – some seeking positions at the barricades, some taking leisurely the booked window seats or temporary standing places, others lining the roadway on those outskirts of the route taken by the Royal equipages from Knowsley.

No one minded the long wait, for the warmth of the day was comforting, and the stream of life went surging past.

"Let us be glad for a few hours. To-morrow will come, bringing with it the anxieties of our common life. We will await its arrival, and in the meantime enjoy the good things the gods have sent us – surcease from toil, the opportunity of giving vocal expression to the loyalty we feel rather than talk about."

These were the felt, if unlisped, thoughts of the crowded streets, and as the King and Queen passed from point to point they were continuously occupied in acknowledging the full-throated plaudits of a delighted people.

"Doesn't she look nice?" That is how the ladies commented on the smiling Queen, who, bowing right and left, left onlookers in no doubt as to the pleasure she was deriving from this renewal of her acquaintance with Liverpool and its people.

"He looks pleased with himself," remarked a typical Dicky Sam as the King passed own Edge-lane. The phrase exactly described the impression his Majesty conveyed. Blended with kingly dignity were those characteristic British qualities which endear him to his people.

But the remark was capable of a universal application. Everybody looked pleased and was pleased, for Royalty's part in the procession and the functions of the day, especially that on the river, was rightly interpreted as the King's encouraging approval of Liverpool's place in the scheme of things and of her determination to keep what she has won.

The King has conferred the honour of knighthood on the Lord Mayor of Liverpool (Mr J. Harmood Banner M.P.). ...

MERSEY PANORAMA

On the river the panorama was far-extending and impressive. There was a far-away light in the atmosphere which enabled the spectator to take in the whole scheme of the mercantile marine and naval display. The cruisers lying off the Gladstone Dock could easily be seen by ferry passengers, while the eye could reach on the southern so far as the single line of vessels stretched. The view thus took in some miles of brightly decorated shipping, each vessel being spanned from stem to stern with streamers, the whole combining to form a picture which is rarely seen except at Spithead. The Mauretania, which was anchored opposite the Landing-stage, looked magnificent as the eye swept the decks and noted its handsome outlines.

Up and down stream the exhibition of loyal feeling found expression in emphatic manner. Probably such a fluttering mass from ships' decks was never before witnessed in the Mersey.

IN THE CITY

The city itself began quickly to fill up with visitors from other towns. As the hours went by the railway stations deposited their loads of trippers in almost countless numbers. This influx was swollen by the suburban traffic, which was very heavy, the tramway system being fully requisitioned by eager travellers. There was animation in every direction along the whole Royal line, and never was a more grandiose or artistic welcome given to any Sovereign of the realms.

The popularity of the King and Queen has been increased, if that were possible, by the intense interest displayed in the occupations and homes of the working classes. There was at some points almost a plethora of bunting, but it was held in check by good taste, and its demonstrativeness was nowhere open to cavil...

A MASS OF HUMANITY

Gradually the aggregation of people swelled to numbers of which no account could be taken. It was a solid sea of heads, and the mass of humanity as seen from there along the plateau and the south end of Lime-street baffled description. Every person filling up his quotas in the crowd was decked out in holiday attire, and they were not silent when occasion offered to show their loyalty.

Troops of police, mounted and on foot, hurried into position, and the happy panorama, as it increased in volume, also became more intense in the expression of its joyousness in a variety of forms.

Peals of bells from the municipal tower and St Nicholas's Church commenced to ring out merrily over the still, clear atmosphere, about nine o'clock and the flowing music was caught by the ear at a considerable distance, the usual roar of city trams being hushed for the day.

The weather grew brighter as time went on. In the early hours of the morning there was a sharp downpour of rain. At 4.0 a.m. the sky was as black as a lake of ink, and for hours onward it was doubtful if there would not be another downpour.

By 9.0 a.m. the sky had cleared, and at half-past the blue vault of heaven was seen, only flecked by fleecy, gossamer clouds. This intensified the joy of countless spectators who settled down quietly and happily to wait and welcome their King and Queen.

The intense interest shown by the people in the visit of the King and Queen was more strikingly displayed at the various points where the civic functions in which they were to take part occurred, beginning at the Exhibition Grounds in Edge-lane.

To control the traffic, and to supervise the safety of spectators in Liverpool to-day, the services of over 1,700 police officers were required.

ON THE RIVER
A TEN-MILE LINE OF SHIPPING

The Mersey presented an appearance which was as festive as it was impressive. A line of vessels ten miles in length had quietly and with great skill been formed in accordance with the prescribed arrangements, with the result that by eight o'clock a marine display of a unique character was witnessed in the river.

The number of vessels taking part in the display, including his Majesty's ships Liverpool and Lancaster, yachts, tugs and miscellaneous vessels is 109, of a gross tonnage of over 225,000 tons.

It was not possible, as in the case of a naval review, to collect vessels specially for the purpose from all over the world, and the line of vessels consists only of those which are in the Mersey in the ordinary course of their trade, but the spectacle represented to the full the commercial greatness of the port.

The dressing of the liners and other craft was quickly completed this morning. It consisted in the main of flags arranged rainbow fashion, from stem to stern, showing the flag of the country traded to at the fore, the house flag at the main, and the blue and red ensign at the mizzen or staff. Such a sight has not before

Chapter 3: Making the news

been seen in the Mersey.

The river was alive at an early hour. Fussy tugs darted about with visitors to different vessels, some of them conveying bands, who added gaiety to the occasion by playing happy tunes en route. Sedate ferry-boats carried their heavy human freight to and fro, anxious, it appeared, to do all the work they could before their compulsory stoppage in the afternoon.

A scene on the Mersey during the Royal Visit, 11 July 1913.
Liverpool City Libraries Local Records Office.

The Landing-stage was packed by sightseers, a great proportion of whom were visitors, to whom the sight will be a memorable one.

Royal Visit

PLAN SHOWING PROPOSED POSITION OF VESSELS TAKING PART IN THE MARINE DISPLAY ON THE RIVER.
11TH JULY 1913.

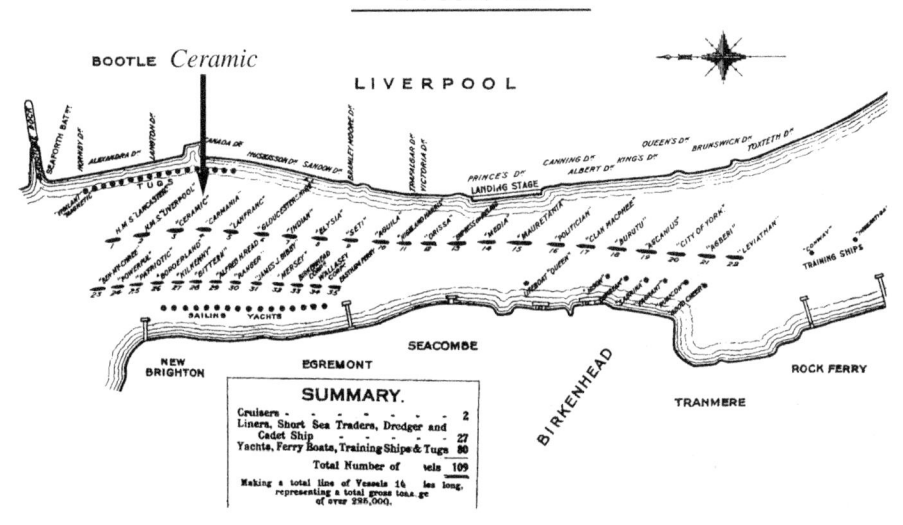

57

Liverpool Echo
July 12 1913

WALLASEY

The loyal inhabitants of Wallasey were early astir, and during the first half of the day continuous streams of people crossed over to Liverpool, doubtless attracted by the more elaborate arrangements of the city. Large crowds, however, remained to witness the marine procession from the Cheshire side of the Mersey, and long before two o'clock the river front, from Seacombe to New Brighton and beyond, presented an unusually animated appearance. There was a plentiful display of bunting from the public institutions and churches of the borough, and not a few diminutive Union Jacks were much in evidence in whatever direction one turned.

During the period of waiting the picturesque display up and down the river was the subject of much favourable comment. On the approach of the Galatea, with the Royal visitors on board, the National Anthem was sung with great unanimity, followed by ringing cheers. At half-past four, when the traffic on the river recommenced, the Daffodil proceeded to and entered the Gladstone Dock, the journey to and fro being undertaken amidst tokens of great enthusiasm on the part of those on board the numerous craft, large and small, which lined the river…

The grand pyrotechnic display on the river front in the evening brought together a dense mass of spectators along the whole length of the promenade…

ON THE GALATEA
CORDIAL SEND-OFF ON RIVER REVIEW

Few parts of yesterday's processional course were so densely crowded as that between the Town Hall and Prince's Parade. When the Royal visitors re-entered their coach the progress was continued down Water-street into St Nicholas-place, and passed under the Overhead Railway just by the Pierhead Station. The Dock Board marked the entrance to their estate by a banner of welcome, and, with its series of streamers, the covered carriage-way, from which spectators had been rigorously excluded, looked exceedingly pretty.

No. 6 Bridge, embellished with palms and flowers, and laid with a crimson carpet, was the halting-place, and here their Majesties were received by Mr. Helenus Robertson and Mr. Robert Gladstone. Chatting with these two Dock Board leaders, and preceded by a couple of giant policemen, they walked down to the Prince's Stage. The National Anthem once more resounded, and from a pole erected on one side of the gangway, and as a companion to a Union Jack which flew from a second pole on the other side, there was unfurled a monster Royal Standard. Its career was brief. Little time was wasted on the platform, and as soon

as their Majesties passed on to the tender this flag was hauled down, while
another Royal ensign made its appearance on the rear mast of the Galatea.

UNFURLING THE STANDARD

The Queen led the way to the boat, followed by the King and the Prince, and the three were received on board with low bows by Commander Mace and Mr. Alfred Chandler. Each of them exchanged a word or two with Mr. Mace resplendent in his full blue and gold naval dress, and then moved to the far side of the boat, where it would appear that they spoke with many of the privileged passengers, who had preceded them from the Town Hall, about the outlook on the Mersey. The Galatea was spic and span in appearance, and was manned by an exceptionally large crew, all the members of which wore their distinctive nautical costumes. She was promptly released from her moorings, and at half-past two precisely the engines were set in motion, and the vessel at the outset steamed seaward. The King and Queen, for whom easy chairs had been placed in the forefront, just below the bridge, came to the land side and acknowledged the cheers of those on the Stage. Her Majesty, less formal than is often her characteristic, engaged at this point in a particularly hearty laugh, and seemed more than ordinarily interested in the plaudits of the spectators, who included the lusty-lunged Sea Scouts and ninety cadets from the Conway.

"Many rejoicings have been held here lately as you see by the papers. This P.C. is the King on his way to inspect the Mauretania & open the Gladstone Dk. There was an awful crowd in L'pool that day. I saw the King pass from an office window." Allan Russell 29/7/13.

Fortunately the conditions for the review could not have been more ideal.
Not only was the atmosphere perfectly clear, but the sun, tempered with a gentle breeze, shone with a summer-like brilliance and warmth, and reflected playfully on the rippling waves. Every craft, however small, could be seen in the river for miles along. When the Galatea commenced her journey a salute of twenty-one guns was thundered forth by the warships Lancaster and Liverpool, stationed off the Gladstone Dock. They were not distinctly heard at the Pierhead...

MARINE DISPLAY

If not the most important function of their Majesties' visit to Lancashire, their inspection of the shipping in the Mersey may be described as the most pleasant and picturesque event of their long and varied programme. Favoured by glorious weather, and regulated by perfect arrangements, the marine display in the Mersey was unique in the annals even of so great a port as Liverpool. It certainly exceeded anything ever before attempted here or in any other seaport. The number of vessels which took part in the display, including his Majesty's ships Liverpool and Lancaster, liners, short-sea traders, dredger, cadet ships, yachts, ferryboats, tugs, and training ships, was 109, of a gross tonnage of over 225,000 tons. The total line of vessels measured ten miles in length. It was not possible on such an occasion, as in the case of a naval review, to collect ships specially for the purpose from all over the world, but yesterday's fleet, consisting of vessels which are in the Mersey in the ordinary course of their trade, was representative of the commerce of Liverpool. All the vessels were dressed with flags, rainbow fashion, from stem to stern, showing the flag of the country traded to at the fore, the house flag at the main, and the blue and red ensign at the mizzen or staff.

From an early hour yesterday morning the river was alive with craft. Speedy little tugs steamed to and fro with passengers anxious to view the various liners, and some of them conveyed bands which played catchy airs and added gaiety to the proceedings. The Landing stage was thronged with a brightly-clad crowd as the King and Queen left the Town Hall and embarked on the Galatea at 2.30 p.m. Enthusiastic cheers greeted their arrival, a Royal salute being fired while the band played the National Anthem.

HRH King George V and Queen Mary on the Galatea.
Liverpool City Libraries Local Records Office.

In brilliant sunshine the Galatea steamed forth on her tour of inspection followed by the Claughton, on board which there was a representative gathering of members of the City Council and prominent citizens. Viewed from the Claughton the scene on both sides of the river was magnificent. The Stage was a kaleidoscope of colour. The ladies' costumes, in endless variety of shade, and the

Chapter 3: Making the news

scarlet uniforms dotted here and there with a background of decorations, made a gay and attractive picture. On the Cheshire side, from Seacombe to New Brighton, the promenade, the banks, and the beach were thronged with a multitude of loyal people, the sight of whom must have considerably impressed the Royal visitors.

At the Galatea moved off further cheers were raised. The Claughton, on the top rack of which luncheon had been served, followed, and both vessels steamed along the line of ships at anchor to the southward of the Mauretania, which was an imposing spectacle in mid-river opposite the Stage. On some of the vessels it was noticed that a part of the crew were Asiatics. In one case they were picturesquely dressed in immaculately white costumes with red belts and fezzes, and their "Huzzas" were not less enthusiastic than anyone else's. From the Burutu came clear across the water, through the megaphone, "Bravo, Liverpool! Long live the King!" And on passing the Clan Macphee the equally appreciate welcome was heard from the band, who played "Rule, Britannia."

The Mauretania was reached shortly after three, and as the Claughton was stopped within a short distance of the Galatea, those on board had an excellent view of the Royal party as they made their way on to the giant liner. As the King and Queen stepped on deck the band of the Indefatigable played the National Anthem. It was observed that the Conway cadets were drawn up close to the entrance gangway, and the King proceeded to inspect them.

HRH King George V and Queen Mary leaving the Mauretania.
Liverpool City Libraries Local Records Office.

At the close of the visit to the Mauretania the Royal party again went on board the Galatea, which steamed along the northern section of vessels, so that the King and Queen had a fine view of the marine display. The Claughton took up a position near the entrance to the Gladstone Dock, and as the Galatea cut the purple ribbon the Lord Mayor's guests witnessed at close quarters the salute from the warships.

The Maiden Voyage of the Ceramic
24th July 1913

Liverpool Daily Post & Mercury
25 July 1913

The White Star Line dispatched two ocean steamers yesterday. In the early afternoon, the new triple-screw steamer Ceramic, 18,481 tons, the largest vessel in the Australian trade (Lieutenant John Stivey R.N.R), left for Australian ports via Capetown, with over 400 (one class only) passengers. The Ceramic, with her two 4.7 guns mounted aft, attracted much attention while lying at the Stage*, and was given a hearty send-off on her 12,000 mile voyage.

Later in the day the twin-screw steamer Baltic sailed from the Mersey for New York with a goodly list of passengers in all classes.

Liverpool Courier
Friday July 25th 1913

*Prince's Landing Stage at the Pier Head where all the big liners picked up their passengers - the docks themselves then being used for on and off-loading of main cargoes.

ARMED LINERS

In the House of Commons yesterday Mr. Douglas Hall asked the First Lord of the Admiralty if he would state the estimated cost of arming the White Star liner Ceramic, whether any sum of money, and if so, what sum, is to be paid to the owners of the ship for permitting her to be armed; if in view of the fact that the White Star liner is controlled by a foreign corporation, any terms have been introduced into the agreement between the White Star Line and the Admiralty which are not contained in the agreements made in respect of ships which are British-owned and controlled; and if so, would he state what those terms were.

Mr. Lambert – I have no information as to the cost to the owners for arming the Ceramic. No sum of money will be paid to them, and no special agreement, additional to that of 1903, has been entered into.

Mr. Hall – How is it intended to enforce an agreement with a company that is controlled by a foreign Power which might possibly be a belligerent Power?

Mr. Lambert – I think the hon. member had better examine the special agreement of 1903, in which he will find an answer to his question.

Chapter 3: Making the news

Arrival in Melbourne.
Author's collection.

Ceramic picnic, Clifton Gardens, 19 September 1913.
Located on the northern side of Sydney Harbour, just around from Bradleys Head, Clifton Gardens was an old time picnic ground.
Author's collection.

Chapter 4
The outbreak of war

No sooner had White Star's pride of the Australian run entered service, than war broke out, and on her fourth visit to the continent, the newly finished liner was taken over by the Australian Government on October 20th 1914, for the transport of troops to the battlefields of Europe.

Known as Troopship A40 (Australian Troopship A40 HMAT Ceramic), her wartime operations began on 14th December 1914. For thousands of young Australians and New Zealanders, the last glance of their mother country would be from the deck of the Ceramic as she sailed towards an unknown horizon.

****

My Dear Mother, At last I am on the boat; and am feeling quite well; But I am anxious for you all. As I cannot hear how you all are after the terrible experiences of the past hours, I desire only to commend you to the All Wise God. Do not worry about me, but look after one another Pray and trust without ceasing. The parting for the moment causes grief but if it is His Will, all will be well. My fondest love Mother & Father & Ethel & Hilda. Be brave. Sidney.

****

Dear Linda, Just another line to let you know I am still alive and another day from (censored). We were told they would put the mail off at (censored) although our first stop they tell us will be (censored) and probably not till (censored). We ran into a storm this morning and the sea is fairly rough now, we have all the port holes screwed up, and the water is running off the decks. I am glad she is (censored) thousand tons instead of 6 or 8 as we have a few cases of sea sickness aboard but us chaps are all O.K. As for myself I have gained an awful appetite instead so don't expect to get sick now, quite disappointed I don't think... the sea tonight just looks like snow. Wish you were here to see it.
Ray Sharp, 2nd reinforcements, 1st Pioneer Battalion.

****

Dear Fred. Just a line to tell you that I am leaving Alexandria today for England. Have managed to get a bullet wound in my left thigh. Am getting along tip top now & will soon be about as usual. Write soon. Kind regards to all. From Jack B.

Chapter 4: The outbreak of war

Images kindly donated by the Australian War Memorial

King George's Sound, WA. 1914-12-31. Arrival of the Second Detachment of the Australian and New Zealand Imperial Expeditionary Forces.
Australian transports: *A29 Suevic; A30 Borda; A32 Themistocles; A33 Ayrshire; A34 Persic; A35 Berrima, A36 Boonah; A37 Barombah; A38 Ulysses; A39 Port Macquarie; A40 Ceramic; A42 Boonara; A43 Barunga; A44 Vestalia.*
New Zealand Transports: *HMNZT Knight of the Garter; HMNZT Willochra; HMNZT Verdala.*
Submarine AE2.
(Original print housed in the AWN4 Archive Store) (Donor D. Roche)
Photographer: A.G. Sands
Negative Number: P02085.004

Melbourne, Vic. Troops line up at Station Pier prior to leaving Port Melbourne on troopship A40 *HMT Ceramic*. Troops on the right are lined up waiting to embark, while those on the left are waiting with their kit bags before they are called.
(Neg given by Herald Ltd)
Negative Number: J00340

65

Records of Capt. P.R. Paull, 16th Battalion AIF, Conflict: 1914-18
AWM file: 419/63/28 PR88/137
Daily entry of events from departure in Melbourne aboard A40 "CERAMIC", training in Egypt with the Signal Unit, landing at Gallipoli, activity on the Peninsula and eventual evacuation to Lemnos due to dysentery.

At Albany until 31/01. Left at eight in morning 31/12/14. Had four letters from Dad but couldn't get ashore. 17 ships started & heading for *(Colombo)*. Had a good New Year's Day lovely & calm.

January 3 Sunday
First all Signallers got *(illegible)* then church parade at 11 o' clock then I had *(torn)* to go in charge of a Watch on the Bridge at 12 till 4. Very interesting reading Penant Signalling. Now at Dinner in mess. Very calm.

January 4 Monday
On watch *(torn)* & 4 till 6 at night. Instructing 9.30 until 12.30. Dinner *(torn)*. Had a read and a sleep. Went on Bridge. Very interesting have flag code nearly *(?)*. Changed my sleeping place. Slept in Life Boat. Very good. Nice & breezy. Very hot all day.

January 5 Tuesday
On Bridge today. Received a message from flag ship. Had good breakfast. *(Torn)* 9.30 till 12.30. Getting hotter every day & sea lovely & calm. On Bridge & at NCO class in good health although the Hospital is full. A lot of sickness…

January 6 Wednesday
Identification issued today. No 344.
(Torn) sleeping on Life Boat as usual & about 4 in morning it rained & I had to shift. It is getting hotter every day. We are now about 4 days off the *(Line)*. She is travelling about 3 degrees a day so we will be at the present rate on Colombo in a week. Routine today as usual now getting lecture.

January 7 Thursday
… sea calm. Feeling very tired & went to bed early on Deck. Raining lightly.

January 8 Friday
Instructing 9.30 to 12… All Boats stopped. Mail closed *(blot)* for Australian boat left side of ships 4pm & went to flagships & brought back mails. One from Lily & Dad. I wrote to them both half an hour before. Sea just like glass. Fine sight of fleet.

January 9 Saturday
Weather a little rough. Not so hot. About 8% south of equator. Too wet to have

Chapter 4: The outbreak of war

class on deck. gave a lecture on Heleograph in Mess. Not many slept on deck on account rain so chose below for me.

January 10 Sunday
(Largely illegible)
All signallers had inspection of vaccination marks mine just taken nicely. Church Parade 10am. Sent for at church & had to go to orderly *(illegible)* & make out pay slip. Getting paid *(?)* tonight 1/- a day £1-0-0. Nice weather not rough just nice sea.

January 11 Monday
Ordinary classes filling up pay roll in *(blot)* room. Sea lovely a bit rougher. Not so hot. Crossed line this morning about 2 o' clock.

January 12 Tuesday
Branched off. North of Equator now. Ships Suevic & Persic & us Ceramic all White Star liners going direct to Aden. All others going in to Colombo left us about 7 *(?)* in the morning. Soon out of sight. We going faster now.

January 13 Wednesday
Usual routine of work in morning. Sea a little rougher. In afternoon passed troopship empty going from Egypt to India quite close could see everything on board. Went bed late. Playing cards troop deck.

January 14 Thursday
Fine lighthouse. First land since Albany. Sea lovely & calm. Passed sea weed & a branch of tree then saw whales quite close to ship. About 11 o'clock islands on North East coast of India. Boat went half way round island. Boats of Indians came out a good way. Island very thickly *(fold)* coconut & palms.

January 15 Friday
MINNIKOI ISLANDS.
Sort of *(illegible)* very black. They are a group of islands & some fish in bands others work inland growing stuff. They exchange off one another. Women wear white *(shawls?)* over shoulders...
Usual class. Have a headache. Platoon organisation coming into force.

January 17 Saturday
Sea moderate. Usual training in signalling & rifle exercises. Concert at night. Went bed early. Had shift early & then came to rain. Got a letter. We passing Islands tomorrow.

January 17 Sunday
SOCOTRA ISLAND.

Raining sea a little rough. Church Parade 11 o'clock. Too interested in book & missed church. Lazy day reading books all day. Socotra Island about 15 miles off. Very large. Seem to go into the clouds.

January 18 Monday
Ordinary Instructors innoculated 4pm. A slight dose of fever. Sighted a native Barge & went full steam ahead today to overtake it, left the other ships behind. It cut behind Socotra Island & we had to give up. Supposed to be smuggling rifles to India. Went bed about 8pm my arm very sore & feeling dead.

January 19 Tuesday
Had a good sleep. My arm very sore. Going to write letters home today. Letters sent to be cencered *(sic)*. Usual training. Lovely sea. Land in sight, tremendous hub going into the clouds. We are in quarantine a/c fever & measles.

January 20 Wednesday
Sea lovely. Arrived Aden about 2pm... Aden a high rocky island & place all forts. A grand sight. Searchlight going all night. As soon as stopped about 30 boats started selling goods by throwing up ropes with baskets attached. They got money first.

January 21 Thursday
Mail boat arrived West Australia to England. Coaling 1000 tons all Arab labour. Finished coaling today. Arabs cheaper today by half. Auxiliary Adviser in Port. Funeral today a fellow from G Company 6th pneumonia last night. Company & Mess mates gone to funeral.

January 22 Friday
(Badly torn)
... to await fleet. Niggers followed us right out & still selling goods...
Usual instruction today sea a little rough...

January 23 Saturday
January 24 Sunday
(Illegible)

January 25 Monday
Still in Red Sea. It is hot now in winter, let alone in summer. A lot of sickness in hospital. 7 deaths up to date in fleet. Submarine still our only convoy although Paramatta on ahead of us. In land nearly all way.

January 26 Tuesday
Have a headache studying wireless too much. Passed some very interesting islands. Also ships bound for Aden. Usual class signalling, washing clothes & inspecting men.

Chapter 4: The outbreak of war

January 27 Wednesday
Passing islands & mainland of Afracus *(?)*. Now in one long line Ulysses first going into canal now. We have to wait till last. Seeing Doctor getting sleeping draughts at 8pm.

January 28 Thursday
Arrive at Port *(?)*. Anchored all fleet. Fighting going on in Suez Canal (illegible). Today going up in boat. Suez a nice place built on water selling goods on boats. Off signalling three days.

January 29 Friday
Never slept again so got a glass of brandy & slept fine. Started up Suez 9 o'clock. Canal all entrenched. Gurkers & Sieks & New Zealanders, Tommys etc. Anchored in first lake. Fighting on ahead today. 20 Gurkers killed. Aireplanes *(sic)*.

January 30 Saturday
Started again today. Arrived Port Said at 5pm. Very busy shipping. Fine sight Hydroplane coming & going all time scouting. Another man died buried *(illegible)* in Port Said... passing girls enjoying myself.

January 31 Sunday
Left Port Said & anchored out in Mediterranean Sea two miles. Other boats gone to Alexandria. Church Parade. Left again about 6pm. Sea lovely & calm. Packing kits & getting ready disembark.

February 1 Monday
Arrived Alexandria about 7am. Five Port Egyptians all around boat selling *(illegible)* & fruit. One of oldest city in world known (332 BC) in early days a population of 1,000,000. Reduced to ruins in 1700 AD population 6000, present population 300,000. Noted for lighthouse.

February 2 Tuesday
Still aboard. Alexandria expect disembark today. Put in. Day looking at Alexandria through telescope. Went into wharf about 2pm. Great crowd of Egyptians dancing & doing tricks to get the boys to throw down coins.

February 3 Wednesday
15th Batt. disembarked this morning. DAP & DSC going on to England for "Ceramic" is going to Cairo. At Mess when orders came to disembark within 20 minutes. Signallers first to go with left Half Batt. Entrained at 7pm & left Alexandria about 8.30 for we do not know. Very cold in train can't sleep although carriage very comfortable the troops are poorly off. Arrived Cairo about 1pm.

****

The 16th Battalion AIF at Anzac, Gallipoli
25 April – 18 May 1915

On 22 December 1914, the 16th Battalion embarked 32 officers and 979 other ranks on the transport *A40 Ceramic* at Port Melbourne. The men had left Broadmeadows *(training camp)* after two days of continuous rain, and they and their equipment were saturated and muddy.

The ship reached Albany, Western Australia, on 27 December, and Aden in the Persian Gulf on 20 January 1915. The unit diary noted that Private Robinson in 'F' Company had died from pleurisy and measles. On 21 January, a band and 'F' Company went ashore for his funeral. Private Harold Robinson, the battalion's first casualty of the war, age 18, was buried in the Maala Cemetery, Yemen.

On 3 February 1915, the battalion disembarked at Alexandria, Egypt. They travelled by train to camp at Heliopolis and remained there, undergoing training, until early April. On 11 April they boarded the troopship *Hyda Pasha* and on the afternoon of 25 April off the Gallipoli peninsula the battalion assembled in the ship's hold: *There, for the last time in this world, many of us stood shoulder to shoulder. As I looked down the ranks of my comrades, I wondered much which of us were marked for the Land Beyond. We were transferred from the transport to the destroyer, which took us close into the shore, and then we were transferred into the ship's boats and rowed to the shore, amidst a hail of shells.*

[Ellis Silas, drawing, 'The Last Assembly', Gallipoli, April 251915, Crusading at Anzac, AD 1915, London, 1916]

At nightfall on 2 May, the 16th went into attack again up a hill called the Bloody Angle towards Quinn's Post, and throughout the night they continued to fight and dig trenches. The battalion's exposure to continual firing made it very dangerous to carry ammunition to them: *Again and again volunteers were shot as they scrambled up with heavy cases; others took their places only to fall dead across the boxes they were dragging, or to roll down the steep side of the hill.*

[Captain C Longmore, The Old Sixteenth: being a record of the 16th Battalion, AIF, during the Great War 1914-1918, Perth, 1929, p 47]

Near dawn on 3 May, the 16th rose out of their trenches to attack the Turkish position about 100 metres away but were seen and met with heavy fire. Their attempt failed and when dawn came their dead 'lay thickly on the slopes'.

At the landing on 25 April, the 16th had been about 1000 strong.
Overnight on 2 May, they had lost 8 officers and 330 men.
At roll call on 3 May, only nine officers and 290 men answered their names.

http://www.anzacsite.gov.au/1landing/s_sixteenth.html#

Chapter 4: The outbreak of war

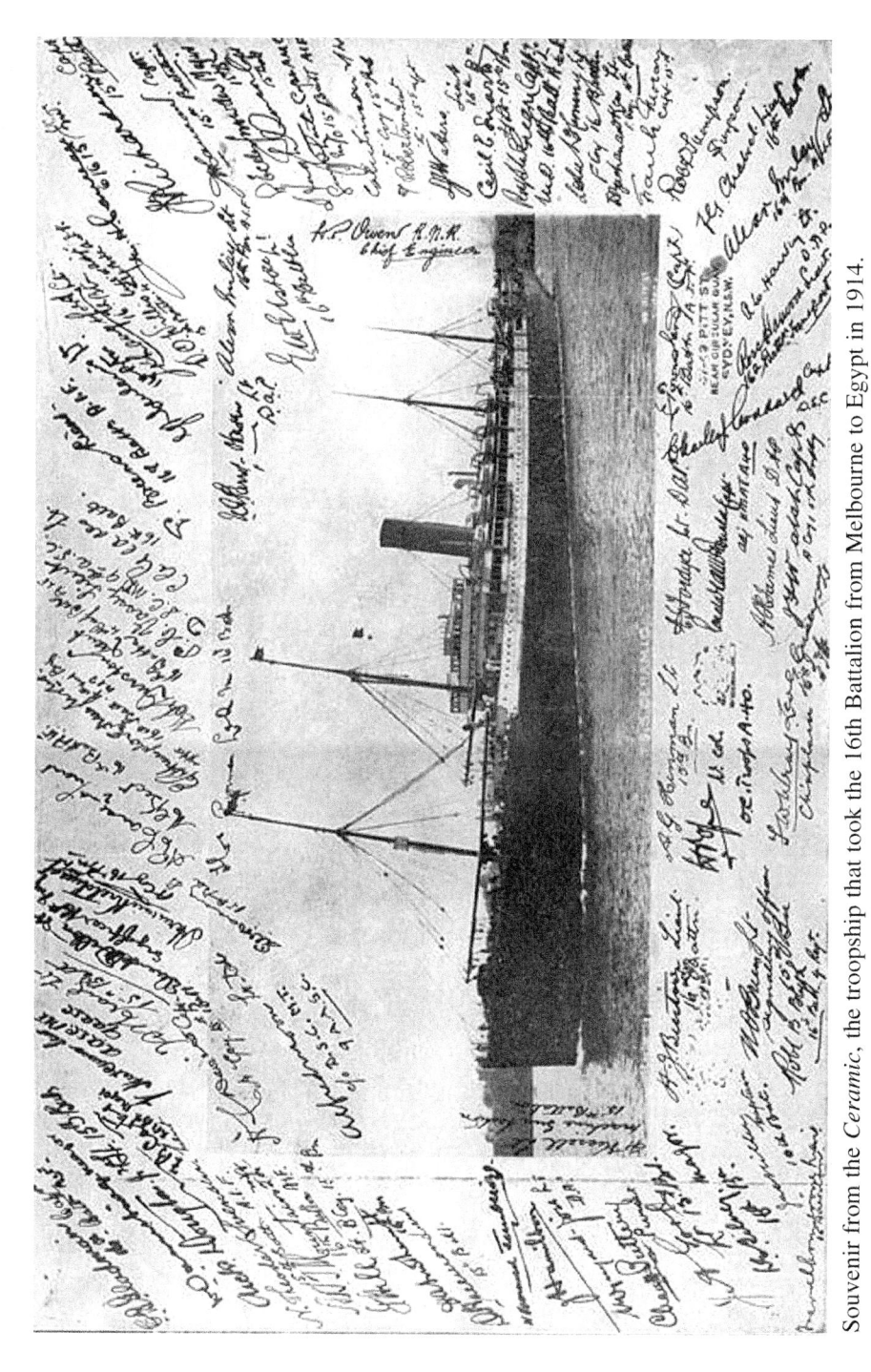

Souvenir from the *Ceramic*, the troopship that took the 16th Battalion from Melbourne to Egypt in 1914.
Captain C Longmore, The Old Sixteenth, Perth, 1929.

Above

At sea. 30 November 1915. On board the *SS Ceramic* requisitioned as troop transport A40 during World War 1. Men of the 5th Battalion, Australian Imperial Force (AIF), relaxing on deck during their voyage to Egypt.

Negative Number: P0851.010

(Donor K McLaughlan)

Left

Men of the 5th Battalion, 12th Reinforcements, Australian Imperial Force (AIF), form the audience watching two men in a boxing contest to relieve the boredom of the voyage.

Negative Number: P0851.007

(Donor K McLaughlan)

Chapter 4: The outbreak of war

Above: Port Said, Egypt. 1915-12. Reinforcement troops of 5th Battalion, Australian Imperial Force (AIF), disembarking from the *SS Ceramic*. The men are crowded aboard three barges being towed by a tug. Other tenders are around the barges. A group of officers are standing at the top of the boarding ladder, The officer at left is Lieutenant Grenado Walter Foreman. Lt Foreman transferred to the Australian Flying Corps., (AFC) on 22 October 1916. He was killed in action in France on 14 July 1917.

Negative Number: P0851.008
(Donor K McLaughlan)

Left: Port Said. 1915-12-18. Elevated view from an upper deck of small boats and tenders ferrying troops of 5th Battalion, Australian Imperial Force (AIF), to shore from the *SS Ceramic*.

Negative Number: P0851.016
(Donor K McLaughlan)

On 25th June 1915, Sydney docks thronged with the infantrymen of the 18th Battalion, as they waited to embark on Troopship A40, the requisitioned Ceramic. Already, the Battalion's first and second reinforcements were on their way, the first having departed on the Themistocles on 12th May, and the second, six days before the Ceramic, on the Kanowra. Of this huge mass of men, bringing with them their hopes and aspirations, leaving behind them their sweethearts and families, only a minority would return, though the parent Battalion on the Ceramic, which stopped over in Egypt for a short while before arriving at ANZAC in August, would be spared the battle for Lone Pine, Hill 60, which was destined to fail, with the loss of 11 Officers and 385 Men of the first and second reinforcements. The survivors would then join the parent Battalion for fierce engagement in the Suvla Bay area, where again casualties were heavy, especially among officers and senior N.C.O.s. Once in France, the 18th Battalion would earn their battle honours in the Somme and the breaching of the Hindenburg Line, and in the battles around Ypres. In 1915, the men who were leaving on the Ceramic knew that they were facing danger, but could they have foreseen the horrors of what they were to face, who knows how it could have turned their thoughts from the immediate pain of parting, tinged with the excitement of adventure, to a more sombre mood of fear. So many men did not return, but for this war at least, the Ceramic would survive to see the peacetime earned at such a cost.

****

George Samuel Willis was born in 1881, the youngest of 11 children, and the only one to be born in Australia. The family had come on an assisted passage in 1878, during which one infant died, as did another soon after their arrival. Before enlisting in 1916, at the age of 35, George was a member of the St. George's English Rifle Regiment. On 7th October 1916, he embarked on Troopship A40, bound for Plymouth. The journey took six weeks. Posted to Etaples, in Northern France, George was hospitalised with "trench feet", and on returning to the battlefield, sustained a bullet wound in his left thigh. On rejoining his unit once again, he was killed in action during the storming of the Bearevoir Line (part of the defence system known as the Hindenberg Line). This action was part of the last major battle of the war; five weeks later the war ended, and on Armistice Day, 11th November 1918, having already lost her husband, son and three other members of her family, George's mother also died.

****

Chapter 4: The outbreak of war

18th Battalion, Australian Infantry, A.I.F.
Photographs courtesy of Lorraine Smith.

Captain Horace Charles McLean Morris, 18th Battalion, Australian Imperial Forces. Taken en route from Sydney to the Middle East, 1915. Captain Morris served in Gallipoli, France and Belgium. The photograph has been annotated on the back by Captain Morris: "Taken on board the *Ceramic* while watching a machine gun being fired at a kite."

Photograph courtesy of Mick Morris.

75

Departures of Australian Troopship A40 HMAT Ceramic
Source: www.unsw.adfa.edu.au/~rmallett/

Australian Army Infantry unit departures – SS Ceramic.
Infantry = Inf. Battalion = Batt.
Division = Div. Brigade = Brig.
Reinforcements = Reinf. Sydney = Syd.
Melbourne = Mel.

1st Inf Batt (NSW) 1st Inf. Brig (1st Div)	5th Reinf	dep Syd 25 Jun 1915
	17th Reinf	dep Syd 14 Apr 1916
	21st Reinf	dep Syd 7 Oct 1916
2nd Inf Batt (NSW) 1st Inf. Brig (1st Div)	17th Reinf	dep Syd 14 Apr 1916
	21st Reinf	dep Syd 7 Oct 1916
3rd Inf Batt (NSW) 1st Inf Brig (1st Div)	17th Reinf	dep Syd 14 Apr 1916
	21st Reinf	dep Syd 7 Oct 1916
4th Inf Batt (NSW) 1st Inf Brig (1st Div)	17th Reinf	dep Syd 14 Apr 1916
5th Inf Batt (Vic) 2nd Inf Brig (2nd Div)	6th Reinf	dep Mel 16 Jul 1915
	12th Reinf	dep Mel 23 Nov 1915
6th Inf Batt (Vic) 2nd Inf Brig (2nd Div)	12th Reinf	dep Mel 23 Nov 1915
7th Inf Batt (Vic) 2nd Inf Brig (2nd Div)	12th Reinf	dep Mel 23 Nov 1915
8th Inf Batt (Vic) 2nd Inf Brig (2nd Div)	12th Reinf	dep Mel 23 Nov 1915
13th Inf Batt (NSW) 4th Inf Brig (4th Div)	21st Reinf	dep Syd 7 Oct 1916
14th Inf Batt (Vic) 4th Inf Brig (4th Div)	12th Reinf	dep Mel 23 Nov 1915
15th Inf Batt (Qld & Tas) 4th Inf Brig (4th Div)		dep Mel 22 Dec 1914
16th Inf Batt (WA & SA) 4th Inf Brig (4th Div)		dep Mel 22 Dec 1914
	1st Reinf	dep Mel 22 Dec 1914
17th Inf Batt (NSW) 5th Inf Brig (2nd Div)	12th Reinf	dep Syd 14 Apr 1916
	16th Reinf	dep Syd 7 Oct 1916
18th Inf Batt (NSW 5th Inf Brig (2nd Div)		dep Syd 25 Jun 1915
	12th Reinf	dep Syd 14 Apr 1916
	16th Reinf	dep Syd 7 Oct 1916
19th Inf Batt (NSW) 5th Inf Brig (2nd Div)		dep Syd 25 Jun 1915
	12th Reinf	dep Syd 14 Apr 1916
	16th Reinf	dep Syd 7 Oct 1916
20th Inf Batt (NSW) 5th Inf Brig (2nd Div)	12th Reinf	dep Syd 14 Apr 1916
	16th Reinf	dep Syd 7 Oct 1916
24th Inf Batt (Vic) 6th Inf Brig (2nd Div)	1st Reinf	dep Syd 26 Jun 1915
30th Inf Batt (NSW) 8th Inf Brig (5th Div)	9th Reinf	dep Syd 7 Oct 1916
31st Inf Batt (Qld &Vic) 8th Inf Brig (5th Div)	6th Reinf	dep Syd 14 Apr 1916
45th Inf Batt (NSW) 12th Inf Brig (4th Div)	2nd Reinf	dep Syd 14 Apr 1916
	6th Reinf	dep Syd 7 Oct 1916
49th Inf Batt (Qld) 13th Inf Brig (4th Div)	6th Reinf	dep Syd 7 Oct 1916

Chapter 4: The outbreak of war

53rd Inf Batt (NSW) 14th Inf Brig (5th Div)	2nd Reinf	dep Syd 14 Apr 1916
	6th Reinf	dep Syd 7 Oct 1916
54th Inf Batt (NSW) 14th Inf Brig (5th Div)	2nd Reinf	dep Syd 14 Apr 1916
	6th Reinf	dep Syd 7 Oct 1916
55th Inf Batt (NSW) 14th Inf Brig (5th Div)	2nd Reinf	dep Syd 14 Apr 1916
	6th Reinf	dep Syd 7 Oct 1916
56th Inf Batt (NSW) 14th Inf Brig (5th Div)	2nd Reinf	dep Syd 14 Apr 1916
	6th Reinf	dep Syd 7 Oct 1916

Summary of *Ceramic*'s departure dates:

22 Dec 1914	Sydney
25 or 26 Jun 1915	Sydney
16 Jul 1915	Melbourne
23 Nov 1915	Melbourne
14 Apr 1916	Sydney
7 Oct 1916	Sydney

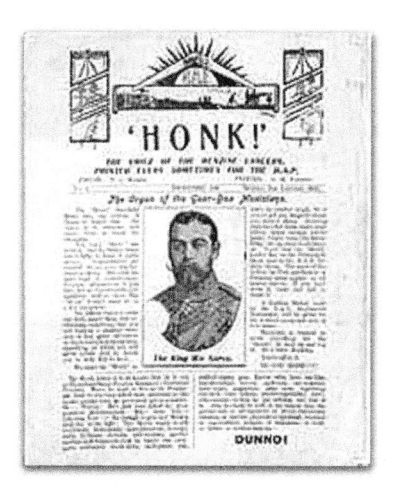

These postcards, and those overleaf, were produced on board the Ceramic by the Australian Imperial Force 1st Australian Divisional Ammunition Park (Motor Transport). The reverse bears the inscription, "Printed on Board Troopship A40 by D.A.P. Press... Mediterranean Sea, Feb 1915".

Honk: The Voice of the Benzine Lancers ([At sea]: Troopship A40, 1915–[1916]). "Honk" was the forerunner to the most famous troop publication "Aussie". Both were produced by Phillip Harris, on his own small portable printing press. "Honk" was first produced on the Ceramic in 1915, and later in the field.

77

The Ceramic also transported British servicemen during the First World War. This period was not without incident. On 9th June 1917, she was attacked by an enemy submarine at the entrance to the English Channel, but the torpedo missed its target. Six weeks later, on 21st July 1917, she was chased by a submarine in the Bristol Channel.

****

Sept 10th 1915
On Active Service

Dear Alice, I am in the best of health. I am now on board this ship, but I do not know quite were (sic) it is taking me but I think it is somewhere nere (sic) Egypt. Hoping you a getting better. Yours, Bert.

****

On Active Service, Am posting this at Bombay

Dear Parents, Just to let you know I'm alright. I have been pretty bad these last few days after being inoculated but am feeling better. Hope all at home are well. Best love Leonard.
P.S. Please write as am longing to hear from home.
Sunday 13th February 1916

Chapter 4: The outbreak of war

No. 1116 7 Platoon B Comp, 2/6 RSR C/o G.P.O. London
This address will find me so don't forget to write.

D.M. (Dear Mother), I am sending you a few lines with the photo of the vessel we are going out on. We arrived here early this morning, had our Breakfast on Board also our dinner on it today (Thursday). Don't know when we are sailing but don't expect it will be long. Now do not worry as that is no good. Kind regards to all at Home and will write to Nance so as you can have it afterwards. I will try and write a bit each day so as you can have something to read when you do get a letter. I remain your Son.

****

Cyd H J Little (1672) No6 Platoon "B" Coy, 1/9 Hants India
My Dear Dot, Just a card this is a Photo of the boat we came over on she is a very fine boat she does about 20 miles an hour on an average. I could not get anymore Photos of the boat or I should have sent one to all at home a letter is on the way. Harry.

****

Feb 3rd 1916
Dear Ede. Just a line to let you know we leave Devenport tonight Wednesday. I suppose you know this boat it is the one we are going on White Star Line I will send address when I get the other side. With Love Your Loving Brother
xxx Will. xx

****

Thursday evening 5.30pm 3/2/1916
My Dear Mater, Just a card to let you know what's what. We arrived down here, Devenport at 1.15pm this afternoon and are now on this boat believe we are sailing to night or tomorrow morning it is a fine boat as you will see and we are very comfortable & nice well will write again shortly. With best love from your son Ralph. (When I say will write again shortly that means first port we stop at).

****

1651 Cyc G.J.W. Yats. 12 Platoon, "C" Coy, 1/9th hants Battn. G.P.O. London.
Feb 3rd 3.30pm Devonport

My Dear Mary. Just a card to let you see we are off at last. We arrived here at 12.45 from Chisledom & are expecting to sail in about an hours time on the "Ceramic". We are supposed to be going to India now, tho' I don't think we shall be there long. Will write you a letter before long. Very Best Love to you and all at home. Your Sincere Cousin xxxxxx Ted.

79

Above: S.S. Ceramic leaving West Chamber of Pedro Miguel locks on the Panama Canal, and entering Gaillard Cut, December 1917. Gaillard Cut is the most narrow portion of the Panama Canal. In 1915, the Culebra Cut was renamed the Gaillard Cut by President Woodrow Wilson, in memory of the engineer who had been in charge of the Cut but who had died just before the canal was completed. A phenomenal feat of engineering, the Gaillard Cut is one of the wonders of the Panama Canal. It is 8.5 miles long, and was carved through the rock and shale of Panama's highland region for most of the distance of the canal, from Gatun Lake in the west to the Pedro Miguel locks in the south

Record Group 185-G; image no. 33-X57 from the Operation of the Panama Canal collection. US National Archives and Records Administration (NARA).

"My dad was the Dock Master at Cristobal and Balboa docks and actually had work gangs doing refitting aboard her as he did in most transit ships. Work was done as the transit progressed. I had heard him speak of her loss by name as a child. My grandfather was a Master rigger (of ships) and also repaired cargo crane riggings aboard her."

Dale C. Clarke Email to author 8th February 2004

Chapter 4: The outbreak of war

Extracts of a World War One Soldiers' Diary
Corporal Ludvig Kristian Johansen GJENVICK
87th Division, 346th Infantry, Company "C"

Ludvig Kristian was born in Trondhjem (now called Trondheim), Norway, 11 January 1892, the youngest of five children of a tradesman family. He was orphaned at the age of nine and was sent to live with elderly relatives who were tenant farmers in the country north and west of Trondhjem. After his confirmation at age fourteen, he worked on farms and eventually gained employment as a shoemaker at A/S Trondhjems Skofabrik in Trondhjem.

In 1913 Ludvig emigrated to the United States, living first in the Davenport, Iowa, and Rock Island, Illinois areas, moving later to Madison, Minnesota, where he worked as a farm laborer in nearby Garfield. It was there that he met his future wife, Clara Seefert.

When the United States entered World War I, Ludvig was drafted into the Army and received his citizenship while stationed at Camp Pike, Arkansas. He was promoted to the rank of Corporal and served in France. He deeply loved his adopted land and was proud of his military service.

Source: http://www.rootsweb.com/~wgnorway/Gjonvik-Ludvig.htm

…we were loaded onto the steamship "Ceramic". Then we sailed from America on the morning of August 24th [1918], accompanied by 11 other ships, and anchored in Liverpool's harbor on September 4, 1918 at 10:30 following a safe journey. Then we disembarked from the ship on the morning of September 5th, [1918] at 6 o'clock, and marched through the streets of Liverpool to the train station, where we were treated to coffee and cookies by the Red Cross…

On the "Ceramic", we had 8 millions worth of (?) with us over the ocean. On the night of August 31, 1918 we were on the Atlantic Ocean, and in thick fog so that no one could see. 5 blasts of the ship's horn were given, and with great alarm all men went on deck, but fortunately they were (only a message?)…

… We got on the old Ceramic, the biggest single stacker afloat, and fed on English grub and fell out for the three whistles every once in awhile. In spite of the fact that a good many will claim that they weren't a bit scared, they will never forget the five blasts of the big ship whistle. Such a thing as a table was a small hindrance and a weasel couldn't have wiggled through the crowd in the stairway. One brought his hard-tack and canteen along. He wouldn't miss his eats anyhow. We landed in Liverpool, got on the train to Winchester and hiked to camp and ate some more English stew and had Tommies telling us "You cahn't do this" and "Out of bounds". This was called a rest camp.

Source: http://www.gjenvick.com/wwi/soldiers_diary/soldiers_diary.html

Returning Sergeants, and contributors to *"The Ceramican"*, 1920.
Private collection. Reproduced by kind permission of Peter Treacy.

"The Ceramican"

"Eric and Daddy" on the promenade deck of the *Ceramic*, 1920.
Photo courtesy of the Treacy family.

Chapter 5
The Ceramican

For the fortunate ones, the cessation of hostilities would lead to an eventual homecoming, though not necessarily immediately. After the horrors of war, a three-month sea journey home, and the expectations of what lay ahead, would have buoyed the spirits of the men on board, and the atmosphere on these journeys back to Australia would have stood in marked contrast to the sombre apprehension of the outward trip. For a total appreciation of life on board, we are indebted to the enterprise of those who returned to their homeland from Tilbury docks at 4.30 pm on 12th March 1920. This voyage would produce, under the leadership of Major P. Dunningham, Officer Commanding Troops, a comprehensive magazine, "The Ceramican" produced on board as a record of the trip, as a spin-off from the daily news sheets and weekly papers circulated to keep the isolated men informed. One of these fragile volumes still exists in the possession of the Treacy family, Sergeant Treacy having participated as part of the Editorial Committee. His son Peter explains, "This voyage was in 1920, so the Diggers were definitely old soldiers homeward bound. Though labelled 'HMT' it was not strictly a trooper mission, but also had wives & children aboard."

****

THE CERAMICAN

Foreword.

It may be of interest to many of the readers of this little souvenir of the voyage to know something of its origin. When first appointed to command the troops returning to Australia in the "Ceramic" I realized that we would be cut off from the outside world as far as news was concerned, and thought it necessary and in the interests of all on board to print a daily news-sheet embracing items received by Marconi; also to print notices of all items of interest from day to day. The idea caught on and a small committee was formed for the purpose of conducting the venture, and from the outset very valuable assistance and support was given by those on board. At the first meeting held it was decided to publish a weekly paper as well at a cost of 2d. per copy and the whole proceeds to be devoted to the cost of production, as well as prizes for Limericks, Competitions, etc. Then came the idea for this souvenir magazine and the support given has more than exceeded my wildest dreams.

My sincere thanks are tendered to the artists for their many illustrations; photographers for their unceasing endeavours to take photographs of everybody and everything of interest, and the many literary contributors for their bright, breezy and humorous articles, and last but by no means least, the working committee, printing and publishing staff, who have been associated with me in the venture and who have devoted almost the whole of their leisure hours in their efforts to make the "Aussiegram," "Ceramican," and the "Souvenir Magazine" the success set out to attain.

I cannot let this opportunity pass without mentioning the names of the Committee and a few others whose efforts have undoubtedly contributed largely to the successful issue of the souvenir "Ceramican." They are as follows: Mrs. Arthur (Miss Bennett Burleigh), Capt. Dinning, Sergt. Treacy, Corpl. Ling (Sub-Editor), Sergt. Ivers (Official Artist), Sergt. McLeod (Official Photographer), Flight-Sergt. Richardson, Corpl. H. F. Shaw, Corpl. Love, W. O. N. White, Hon. Lieut. Beavis, and Sergt. Handcock (Editor). The latter has really been the mainstay of this press venture since I first discussed the proposal with him early in March in Horseferry Road.

In conclusion, I would ask you to remember that all the matter contained herein has been written and compiled At Sea, so, therefore, "Judge not harshly lest ye be judged" and my best wishes go with you all to the many quarters of the globe wherein you will be domiciled. There to reflect on the many happy hours spent on the "Ceramic," and "May those hours be the unhappiest in your lives."

P. DUNNINGHAM, Major, Officer Commanding Troops.
H.M.T. Ceramic

A Few Remarks from the Editor.

We had decided to say a lot of particularly nice things in the following remarks. Indeed, nicer things than we had ever said before. As a matter of fact we had intended to thank a whole lot of people, but this duty as well as pleasure has been kindly done for us.

The Editor, however, sincerely hopes that in time to come those who peruse this little journal will recall happy memories of times spent on board the "Ceramic" in March and April, 1920.

It is not possible that all of us returning to Australia will meet again for we will spread over the great island continent. All of us will be taking up either our old vocation or entering into new. None of us need have any fear for the future if we carry into civil life the earnestness and determination displayed during our military career. Added to this we must equip ourselves with business initiative and enthusiasm of a peaceful environment, for after all: "Peace hath her victories no less renowned than War."

We take with us the appreciation of those whom we have left behind in Great Britain. Appreciation which is so ably expressed by the Dr. Robert Bridges, Poet Laureate, in his eulogistic tribute to Australians:—

"Never shall prouder tale be told
Than how ye fought, as knights of old;
But above all triumphs that else ye have won,
This is the goodliest deed ye have done,
To have sealed with blood, in a desperate day,
The love-bond that binds us for ever and aye."

In conclusion we wish one and all a very prosperous and happy future.

H. M. T. "Ceramic."

The "Ceramic" is owned by the White Star Line of Liverpool, headed by Hon. Captain H. Sanderson, R.N.R., who is chairman of the Company. This Company was the pioneer one in the British steam transport across the Atlantic, and for a long time has been competitor with the famous Cunard liners.

One of the White Star steamers, the R.M.S. "Teutonic" was the first steamer to be subsidized by the British Admiralty as a cruiser. Although at the beginning of the war that vessel was nearly thirty years old, she was immediately purchased by the British Government and was one of the first to get to work on the Hun.

The White Star Company decided to also start an Australian service, carrying one class of passengers only. Their special fleet consisted of the "Medic," "Persic," "Suevic," "Afric," "Runic," and in 1913 the "Ceramic," the largest of the Australian fleet, was launched at Belfast.

All of these vessels have been specially fitted for the Australian trade, for carrying frozen products and for carrying apples from Tasmania, South Australia, and Western Australia.

The dimensions of the "Ceramic" are: length 675 feet, beam 69 feet; tonnage 18,481 gross, 11,729 nett. Her engines are three in number one being a turbine, and capable of driving a ship 16 knots per hour, on a comparatively low consumption of fuel. The "Ceramic" is not only the largest ship trading to Australia but is also the largest which has passed through the Suez Canal and visited Bombay.

She left Liverpool on her first visit to Australia on 24th July, 1913. She was taken over by the Australian Government as a transport in Melbourne on October 20th, 1914, this being her fourth trip to Australia. She was fitted out at Williamstown Dockyard, Melbourne, and very valuable assistance was rendered by the officers of the ship in advising the Australian Transport authorities on the fitting up of not only this ship but of other transports.

She left Melbourne on December 22nd, 1914, with 3,061 officials and troops, and also 24 horses. Troops were commanded by Lieut. Col. Pope. Since that time she has made 14 trips to Australia and New Zealand as a transport, besides which several trips were made across the Atlantic.

During the war she has carried over 30,000 white troops, of which 12,000 were Australian and 18,000 Americans.

She also made a special trip to Halifax and took 2,000 Chinese to France.

Her crew number 290.

The Skipper.

Commander G. R. Metcalfe, R.N.R., who is now Commander of H.M.T. "Ceramic," to which he was appointed in January, 1919, was during the early stages of the war a Staff Captain on T.S.S. "Olympic," on which ship he performed very creditable work.

Commander Metcalfe is of a very quiet disposition and derives great benefit from literature of which he is very fond.

His recreation on land is a good game of golf, and he may often be seen with the glasses watching the barrier go up to a good start.

The O.C. Troops.

Major P. Dunningham, D.S.O., O.C. Troops on the "Ceramic," has always had a leaning towards military. In order to fill in spare time he joined the Citizens Forces in 1904; jogged his way up the ranks till some stars struck his shoulders in 1910.

Chapter 5: The Ceramican

Shortly after war broke out he had a bit of bad luck, in that he suffered from that fashionable complaint, appendicitis. The medicos duly chopped him about and left various identification scars which appeared on his attestation paper early in 1915.

As soon as the medicos could certify that their work had been entirely successful he left for Egypt with the Light Horse and the A.A.S.C.

Things about this time were pretty busy, and he got his baptismal fire in the Senussi campaign in the Libyian Desert. He next gave Sinai a turn and was with Allenby's forces through Palestine and Syria and was D.A.Q.M.G. of the Imperial Mounted Division and afterwards the Australian Mounted Division.

He did special duty in the Gaza-Beersheba-Jerusalem operations in 1917; being on the Desert Mounted Corps Staff and also commanded both the Anzac and Australian Divisional Trains.

Later he was O.C., A.S.C., of Chaytor's Force operating in the Jordan Valley where, for services rendered, he was awarded the D.S.O. He assisted in the final round-up of Turks in 1918 and has been mentioned in despatches three times.

He is an all-round sport, wields a tennis racquet with some skill, is quite at home with boxing gloves or without. Has been known on occasion to say more than his prayers; detests "wowsers." His remarks regarding Pussyfoot are rude; he can when occasion demands be a very candid critic.

He is not entirely adverse to the company of the fair sex, and has a good repertoire of songs and smoke-room yarns.

Takes life pretty easily, is on the unattached list of this ship, does not worry too much, but when aroused one is likely to say: "Oh! What a nice man."

Good-bye England.
(Being a farewell on embarking for Australia and home).

The curtain mist is falling fast,
Another phase of Life is past.
The phase wherein we lived awhile
With English lords and rank and file.
We take back pleasant thoughts of you
Of Sympathy and Kindness true;
As we go South.

When first we reached your English clime,
Our varied natures did not rhyme;
We thought of you as coldish folk,
But soon we saw beneath your cloak
A Heart of real Sincerity.
We take its warmth across the sea,
As we go South.

We say "So-long" to you to-day,
And packed our kits for homeland way
With souvenirs both great and small;
But the grandest souvenir of all:
A mind full of Sweet Memories,
We call to you heartfelt "Coo-ees,"
As we go South.

SUB.

Ye Olde Chronicles of the Ark.

It came to pass that they that had command of the Soldiers of the King who came from the land which is "down under." Not the "down under" which the Padre speaketh of. They even who had fought for their King in the lands of Egypt, and of Palestine, and of France, and of Flanders.

And of they who had kept the front on the plains of the Ancient Britains, and had guarded the Ferry which the Horses passeth over said within themselves: "Is not this the month of the God of War, even Mars?"

It is meet and well that they should return to their own country, so they ordereth that on the twelfth day, even the 3rd day before the Ides of March, they should go down to the sea, to a ship, and pass over the deep waters. So the tablets of the writing were issued and the proclamation went forth.

When the Heralds of the King calleth in highways and byeways of the city, and there was deep wailing in the Street Victoria, and the gentlemen of Israel in the road of Horseferry clothed in sackcloth and ashes. And they who walketh in the perfect way even as they do in the Square Leicester and the Circus Piccadilly, and the places of pleasure, even the Strand, wept with bitter weeping and much gnashing of teeth, and cried: "Now are we undone. Verily we will secure for us the raiment of darkness."

Chapter 5: The Ceramican

But the men of Macready, they who were robed in raiments of blue stood at the crossings of the city and were filled with a great joy.

And said of a truth: "A great peace will now be upon the multitude."

So the day cometh and the soldiers gathered together and then travelled by the road of Iron and the machine of many horses unto the Ark, even that of the Star which is White known as the "Keramos," which being interpreted meaneth potters' earth.

And the place of the leaving was filled with a great crowd, with women and children, with wives, and with some that were not wives – some being even soldiers' allotments.

And the cries went up unto Heaven like as the passing of the Gypo funeral.

And after the passing of the time they came unto the Ark, lying in the waters of the Thames, which she, Lizzie the Virgin, kneweth the foretime even Tillbury.

For did she not there visit he Raleigh, Walter by name, and going unto his ship seeth all things on the ship, but she only saw the cabin of Raleigh and all that it contained.

And as she passeth out again unto her following one murmured so that she heard it not "Honi soit qui mal y pense," which being interpreted meaneth "Look ye not above the garter lest thou be struck with a great blindness."

Then the soldiers of the King entereth the ship two by two even as they went up into the Ark of old. But the soldiers goeth up by the one way and the women and children goeth up by another.

And he who had the care of the ordering of the soldiers was one Dunningham, a soldier of much knowledge and experience.

And the marking on his raiment was that of a crown and his legs were encased in the skin of the hog.

Had he not travelled over many lands and seen many things? Even in the land of the Pharoahs, and had he not been told "Get thee unto Jericho," and he goeth.

Likewise unto the city of the Jews, but being not of that tribe he goeth up with riches, and returneth without a lace for his sandals.

He was a good man and loveth the fruits of the earth, even the vine and the juice thereof. Yet as he standeth one cometh unto him and handeth him a parchment and the reading of the hieroglyphics was thus: "Be it known unto thee that as thou goeth and they that go with thee it seemeth unto me that it is not meet and good that thou shouldst drink of the fruits of the vine and look upon the wine when it is red. Or the amber fluid of Bass, or even the cervesa negra of Guinness, neither shalt thou traffic with the spirits of he, Walker, Johnnie by name. Nor with the spirit rumbullion. Neither is it meet that thou shouldst come in contact with the spirits of he Conan, of the tribe Doyle."

Then the chief of the soldiers was seized with a great sadness, and smote his breast; then, lifting his eyes unto Heaven, and his hands likewise, he cried: "Woe is me. I am worse even than he, Job. Woe likewise unto they Davidson and Whiteside, the makers of the ointments, and the compounders of the number nine. And he Handcock the scribe, peradventure the countenance of these will become pale." And he laughed within himself, saying, "If I suffer, all will suffer likewise," and he murmured, "Wall, oh! Wall, thy day is come."

And with him also was he Blake, the majoribus, not he of the tribe Sexton, the terror of evil-doers, but the servant of the King of the thirty-fifth company of the Guards. Of a truth, he was a man of much austerity, who, saying, "Come," thou camest, or "Go," and thou goeth, and he saw to the ordering of thy going. Some sayeth this man he smileth not with frequency in the gathering of the people. Yet even when he smiled, he smiled with a great smiling, and laughed with a great laughter. For of a truth the sadness of his sadness when he was sad, was only equalled by the gladness of his gladness when he was glad.

And with him also were Chief Macdonald and Dolman, men of much wisdom in the knowledge of the curing of the sick, and the pricking of the arms with a cunning instrument, so that disease came not unto them; Lintott, the centurian, had he not the band of red upon his headgear, and had he not come from the land of Sin, Sand and Sorrow?

And there was Dinning, a man of much learning, who delveth in the inky way,– had he not written many tablets, and had he not a son John by name, who ruleth him with a rod of iron, and with a wife of his bosom, who ruleth them both ?

And there were others, even he Wall, a man of much rotundity, so that the time of passing of the seeing of his knees was great – he seeing them only in the mirror.

So the great ship, even the Ark, goeth forth on the deep waters and heaved with a great heaving, and they therein heaved likewise. So that they eating of the victuals kept them but for a short time, and the fishes rejoiceth much.

Then after the period the sea ceaseth its troubling and the weary rested, so that the

Chapter 5: The Ceramican

decks were filled with a great congregation, with soldiers and the women and the children and the wives and they that were travelling that they may become wives. Which showeth that they who waited for them were men of great confidence and trustfulness, and whose song was, "Oh, come, all ye faithful."

And after the sun was low they gathered no longer together in companies, but in twos by twos.

Some came hither, some thither, mostly thither, and they told tales of a great telling, and the Diggers dug themselves in with a great digging, and Cupid's arrow flew over them all.

And the story of Venus and Adonis repeateth itself with much repeating. Now, of the things which happened, the chronicler knoweth much, but it is hidden within his bosom. For being a man old in years, yet reliable in all matters appertaining to the Goddess, he telleth not these things, peradventure a Why Emma shouldst read of it.

Then if, as Solon tells us, the place of the Gods is filled with Love, of a truth the "Keramos" is a seventh heaven.

Now, the rest of the acts of they that travel in the ship, even of Nightingale that singeth not, and Treacy the counter of talents of silver, and of Richardson who knoweth all things, but no book is yet the size that holdeth all he knoweth not. And of Quartermaine, and he, Ling, the scribe who writeth tales of the light clothing of the ladies of the ballet, and of he, Love, who likes not bacon, because the swine flesh was foreign unto him. And of Stevey, the maker of the tablets, and of the players of the sackbut and the harp and the instruments of brass, who played with a great playing, yet were heard but little.

And then there was Ivers, the painter in many colours, and of much cunning workmanship, so that many said, "He is like unto even Tadema or Leighton or Cox or Lambert."

Are they not written in Ye Book of the Chronicles, even what they doeth, evil or good? Aye, verily so.

The Canal We Knew.

It was like revisiting an old friend to stop at Port Said and pass down the canal again, and to look beyond Kantara out into Sinai. It must have galled those of us who were first comers to the East not to be able to leave the ship; but to those who had known her well, it was just enough to pass swiftly by and say farewell with a wave of the hand. Egypt was our first-love in the world-at-large. She gave us our first taste of foreignness. She will always be dear to us. So it was easier to part with her this way than by renewing the intimacy of going ashore. But to those who had merely read of the East all their lives, it was hard to pass so near without being able to land. It was much to look down on the Canal towns and to gaze over the Sahara for a whole day. This was better than nothing; but to know what the East is, you must go about the streets of the East.

Reminiscence burned up at the first sight of Port Said. The blazing lights of the Casino started it. We re-lived the life of that town as we knew it in 1916. But we came nearer our old home when the "Ceramic" passed down the Canal. The lovely Ismailia was where we left her, sleeping on the edge of Timsah. Rantara, the improvised canvas city, was far from vanishing though we had almost expected her to be gone by now; but she had become the city of debris rather than of canvas. The wastage of war had been salved and piled on this final dump for the Palestine field. This is the sort of finalising sight which puts the wind up those Officers who have had a better time during the war than ever before, and are sorry it's over. Kantara, which is now the exit from the Syrian Field, we knew best as the gateway to it. It was the point we arrived at after leaving Cairo to begin the journey over Sinai to Jerusalem and the Jordan Valley. It is on the desert about Kantara that the Light Horse War Memorial should be reared; and this should be the form of it:—

TROOPER, with full kit up, mounted on waler, beside mounted camelo all very big, in rugged stone, facing out into Sinai, from the Canal bank. Every passing ship would see it for ever. This is the best alternative to the accepted puny project of a highly-finished mounted trooper in some Port Said Garden.

We passed down to Serapeum, above the Bitter Lakes. Serapeum we knew as the place we drilled and languished in for three months after the evacuation of Gallipoli, waiting to go to France. We first learned there the inner meaning of real monotony – a monotony broken only by the daily dip in the Canal. I censored some letters at Serapeum. They showed an inspired power of biting description: "Dear Bill. This place is a fair. Nothing but niggers and sand, sand and flies, niggers and lice, lice and niggers –." "Dear Father. You ask me what the desert is like. Well, it's just miles and miles, and miles and – miles of – all – ."

The Khamseem was blowing mildly as the "Ceramic" passed down to Suez. I say mildly, though the passengers found it uncomfortable. The Khamseem at its height is the desert-storm that approaches you with a solid wall of wind-raised sand, and in which camels die of suffocation. We spent three days at Serapeum in a Dinkum Khamseem. All canvas went down early in the game and lay there till the storm was spent. For three days we saw not more than three yards before us. We were blinded and deafened. When hunger forced us to eat, we ate more sand than beef. The light

Chapter 5: The Ceramican

railway had to run from Scrapeum to the desert railhead, because troops were out there depending on it for rations; but Gyppos were killed by it as it ran, because they could neither hear nor see it coming – and they hadn't the sense to keep off the track. It was like relief from pain when the Khamseem passed.

Suez we knew less well. It had been the nearest halting-place entering the Canal. Yet Suez, though we were going home, was hard to leave, because it stood for the last of Egypt. Egypt, despite its stinks, its filth, its crude lasciviousness, its desert sand and flies, its heat and fiery, dusty blasts, had charmed and amazed and compensated in a thousand ways. If the war leaves Australia with many poor devils who can't settle down, it's to Egypt they will return.

H. W. D.

"Feeding the Diggers."

I often used to wonder when at the Front during the war if any Digger other than those of the A.S.C. ever realised or even thought of the amount of hard work entailed in the preparation, collection, accounting for and distribution of rations for an Army in the field.

The same applies to the ship we are now sailing in to the dear Homeland. Preparations for victualling the "Ceramic" commenced many weeks prior to our embarkation. and were only completed a few hours before the actual sailing time of the ship. We are, indeed, extremely fortunate in being on board a liner so admirably suited to travelling in the tropics from the point of view of a "Trooper."

She has very extensive cooling chambers, storerooms and refrigerators, besides ample storage space for almost every class of comestible carried.

In addition to these rooms, there are on board very finely equipped Bakery (where all bread for daily use is baked), Butcher shop, Vegetable and Potato store, Butter room, Dry Grocery store, Ice Machine, and other rooms too numerous to mention.

The following list of edibles will give the reader some idea of the enormous amount of work entailed by the Victualling Department for a voyage such as we are enjoying at the present time. The stock on board when the ship left Tilbury, and required for the voyage to Australia, are as follows (the figures represent pounds where not otherwise stipulated) :—Fresh Beef 77,763, Mutton 35,806, Pork 9,783, Pickled Pork 10,120, Ox Tails 213 tails, Rabbits 150 cases each containing 50, Salt Beef 700, Brawn 2,528, Corned Beef 16,427, Bacon 9,859, Ham 2,667, 1,590 Sheep's Tongues, Kosher Beef 636, Kosher Mutton 630, Fresh Fish 20,000,

Herrings 2,115, Bloaters 500, Kippers 600, Soles 1,060, Ling Fish 718, Suet 1,113, Australian Butter 14,445, Jam 10,270, Marmalade 418, Prunes 2,800, Lard 538, Cod 5,550, Eggs 44,804, Flour 97,200, Coffee 1,372, Tea 3,400, Pickles 350 gallons, Raisins 560, Dried Apples 880, Apricots 585, Currants 1,511, Peaches 600, Pears 550, Sultanas 1,092, Cases of Apples 207, Oatmeal 6,447, Rolled Oats 780, Macaroni 603, Tapioca 987, Potatoes 224,000, Onions 9,980, Cabbages 10,990, Carrots 9,960, Turnips 9,960, Green Peas 546 pecks, Haricot Beans 3,975, Split Peas 4,141, Dried Peas 9,379, Rice 3,555, Quaker Oats 572, Yeast 680, Fresh Milk 430 gallons, Condensed Milk 1,885 gallons, Tinned Milk 6,111 tins, Cheese 7,633, Sugar 22,919, Pepper 250, Mustard 253, besides a large quantity of Jellies, Condiments and Sauces, etc., etc.

The above is what is supplied by the ship, and, in addition to this, there are large stocks of Red Cross stores, medical comforts, and gifts from the Australian Comforts Fund.

In the whole of my experience, both on the Front and on troopships, I have never seen a better menu than the one at present being supplied to the troops on board. The only genuine "grouse" I've heard is the shortage of the necessary cooling amber ale to wash the above victuals down to the storage compartment of man.

PIP DON.

Tragedy.

Upon the waves lie miles of laughter light,
    The mammoth mechanism of man's brain,
Plough through the fields of wavelets bright,
    Untroubled by the sun, the wind, the rain.
Twelve Beings sit upon the deck enthralled,
    By Voice of Monotone Morbidity – a grouse;
At last the fated number "eight" is called,
    'Tis then the atmosphere is pierced by cries of "HOUSE."

– SUB.

Chapter 5: The Ceramican

"Spurlosversunken:"

(In Glorious Memory of the Officers and Men of H.M.S. "Bergamot," lost without trace, 1917.)

Out from the Northern mists
    Into the gray North Sea;
Seek not to know her mission –
    Orders from Admiralty.

Orders sealed in dead secret,
    Go ye to sea forthwith;
Cast ye about for this raider,
    Be she a fact or a myth.

Small was she with her 4.7 guns,
    Slow was her speed compared with her foes;
But dauntless the spirit of those brave men,
    Who sailed in that ship and passed down below.

Days became weeks, but still came no news;
    Loud spoke the wireless from numberless ships:
Where are you, "Bergamot"? Give you her dues,
    But never an answer from those silent lips.

Did the dread mine, equipped for destruction,
    Smash her in fragments from stem to her stern?
Did the U pirate, with murderous stealth,
    Blow her sky-high? We have yet to learn.

Or in the flames of a glorious action,
    'Midst the shrieking of shells and the crash of guns,
Pass to her rest with the flag of Old England
    Flying in shreds, "Defiance to Huns."

Not till the sea shall yield its dead,
    Nor the God of Battles his tale unfold,
Shall ye learn of the fate of this gallant crew,
    Who died as their fathers died of old.

No stirring reports to herald their end;
    No popular clamour did newspapers send;
Only a line with a short preface –
    His Majesty's sloop, "Sunk without trace!"

– NAVY.

Evening in Bombay.

I looked on pencilled brows o'er eyes of blue,
Red lips that mutely said, I dare you to!
Uptilted nose, two dainty little feet;
"My dear," I said, "a glass of wine with you!"

Morning in Bombay.

Wake! For the sun, who scattered into flight
The gilt before him from the joys of night,
Shines down upon thy aching brow, and strikes
Six empty bottles with a shaft of light.

Last night, ere yet the bottles had run dry,
How many voices cried the old, old cry –
"Haste with the liquor, Comrade! Haste thee here!
One more we'll have, the last, and then good-bye."

And as the cock crowed still ye clamour "More!"
Those of ye not yet tumbled to the floor.
Short is our sojourn here. This is the last!
Till ye were flung feet foremost through the door.

Now with the new day dead to all desires,
Thine aching brow to solitude retires;
And the cool voice of Conscience clamours "Fool!"
And resolution 'mongst the dead suspires.

Glamour indeed is flown, leaving plain prose;
The voyage's wages, too, where – no man knows;
But still one bottle there a fresh'ner yields,
And still a jet from out the syphon flows.

What! For the hazy joys last night ye knew,
When swift ran wine, and fast the rupees flew;
Count now the cost in cash and doleful aches.
"Ah, me!" you moan; "this speed will never do."

Come fill your glass with Scotland's wine, and water from the spring,
And in its cool depths last night's cobwebs fling.
The fires of Youth burn brightly while they last,

And have no hour to waste in suffering.

Come with Old Don't-Care Adam, and leave the lot
Of prating, blue-souled pedants, well forgot;
Let Grundy lay about her as she will,
And Stiggines cry to prayers. Oh, heed them not!

The thin of blood go moaning o'er the earth,
In dolefulness and sighs, and shunning mirth;
Cry "Woe" on joy and pleasure. Then lie down,
Moaning at Death as they have moaned at birth.

– NAUTICUS.

In order to explain his feelings, a sergeant sends in this quotation from Sappho:–

"Hapless and lifeless and deep in love am I, pierced through the bones by the will of the gods, with grievous pains. For such passion for love hath slipped into my heart, and hath shed deep gloom over my tender heart from my breast."

"Australia." – "And there is no kind of dainty wanting there, but all the fruits which the black earth brings forth as food for men are present in abundance." – Solon.

If man would know the present, look into the mirror of the past, and study it. – Confucius.

The man who is best able to manage his country's business is he who can manage his own. – Demosthenes.

"Moisten the lungs with drink." – Alkaios.

Silent grey hairs are more the glory of old age to mortals. – Erinna.

He who serves his country well has no need of ancestors. – Voltaire.

Beware of a talkative woman when she is silent.

When ye sit by the fire yourself to warm,
Take care that your tongue does your neighbors no harm.

– Arabian Proverb.

The Trip
(By W.H. DINNING)

The "Ceramic" left Tilbury at half-past 4 on the afternoon of the 12th March. All the partings had been made in London. There was no heart-shaking at the ship's site, no harrowing fluttering of handkerchiefs as we drew off. It was a happy shipload that dropped down the Canal Basin into the broad and gentle Thames.

The ship carries 1467. This is a goodly number. Only 439 of them are soldiers, and of those, 409 are Australian soldiers. There are 50 "Naval Ratings," as they are curiously called – great thick chested, lion-hearted, cheerful English petty officers for the Australian Navy. The other passengers are women and children. For the "Ceramic" is one of the many phenomena incidentally peculiar to this war. We have had poison-gas and liquid fire, and the aerial bombing of women and children; but ever against these we have the Family Ship. It is true, there has been trooping of wives and families before – if only the mixed trooping to and from the Army of Occupation in India that Kipling has celebrated. But the women and children took their chance in such transporting. It was a poor chance. You should hear Colonel J–, travelling on the "Ceramic" for Mesopotamia, speak of what his mother passed through when she travelled in the seventies to India with her captain-husband and her five children. It is curious that the Colonel should be alive to tell the tale. Such matters are to be judged only by the standards of comparison. The mothers cooped in the squalor of the trooper of the seventies had not known the "Ceramic." They probably thought themselves well off by comparison with the trooping women of the forties. It may be that in the next war soldiers' wives at sea will visualise the "Ceramic" as a poor thing. But we don't.

You must know that the family ship on this run, if less comfortable for the bachelor than a pure trooper, is highly organized for the mother and her child. The bachelor may – and does – curse the crying of babies at table and in cabins adjacent to him in the night watches, though he is glad enough to divert himself by playing with the nippers on deck in the afternoon. The mother disregards the bachelor, and shows her gratitude for the motherly fashion in which the Australian Government provides for her family. She gets a free railway warrant from London to Tilbury.

An attentive fatigue handles her paraphernalia from train to ship. She finds in her cabin a hanging cot affixed to her own bunk. The Government provides her with babies' food – nay, more, it causes the food to be prepared by a staff of nurses, and doled out hot in the bottle. And afterwards her babies' utensils will be sterilised for her. She may summon the doctor to her child at any hour of the day or night on the slenderest provocation. He is glad to come – and he gets no fee. She is provided with a babies' wash-house, babies' drying room, and babies' ironing room. Ship's orders prohibit women from putting through that laundry any garment of a man!

Chapter 5: The Ceramican

None the less you may see, most days, the children's things going unwashed and sodden, because childless ladies are laundering their husbands' shirts, or because girls travelling out to be married are "doing the things" of gentlemen friends with whom they have "picked up" – on the ship. But in theory only the garments of the child may be washed there. In theory, also, there is a period before dinner when all the ship's bathrooms are sacred to the use of the baby. In short, the ship's military fittings have been biassed and modified by the prospect of the baby-passenger, and the ship's daily life is concentric about the mother and her child. And the children, conscious of their rights, rule the ship. Nothing can stand before them. There has been no such competition for a "look in" at any function on this voyage as on the Baby Show that we had before Bombay. Everyone makes way on the deck for the strolling infant. No baby cares who hears it cry. Any afternoon you may see the O.C. himself carrying favor with all the babies on the deck in turn. He knows that if he has "made it right" with the babies he is "on a good wicket" with his ship as a whole. And the babies have ordered the weather, and have seen that it was good. At the first tossing in the Bay of Biscay they took the matter up, and said plainly: "There must be no repetition of such things!" So the sea has been as smooth as a pond, and the tropical sun incredibly gentle.

In fact, so delectable is this family ship that two babies have risen from the foam and joined it – unable to keep away. They came amongst us as a complete surprise – especially to the ladies they adopted as mothers, for each embarked with a written declaration from a doctor in England that she could not possibly achieve child-birth on this voyage. The babies came together, on St. Patrick's Day. One is called Patricia Ceramic, and the other (with fine discrimination) Patrick Daniel Ceramic. Doubtless they will both adopt the sea as a profession. For the day of woman-captains will come. These infants are bound to seek in later life the element which gave them birth.

We reached Port Said at eight on Sunday evening, the 21st March. The blazing lights of the Casino stirred memories of the Port Said we knew before going to France. As we moved in beside the Mole we could just descry in the dusk the gigantic figure of De Lesseps, scroll in hand, pointing proudly the way down his Canal to all east-bound ships. Men and women journeying abroad for the first time got a faint notion of the Orient from the daylight passage through the Canal, and by passing slowly at sundown beside the roofs of Port Tewfik. They could almost decipher the expression on the faces of the Gypos who stood upon the quay.

But the first real taste of the East was enjoyed by the stranger to it at Bombay, which we reached on March 31st. There had been no leave at Port Said or Suez. At first they would give us no leave at Bombay, but because of our importunity, we got it – five days of it. It was a great chance. This Queen of the western ports of India had much to offer those who had been denizens of England all their lives. I remember

Chapter 5: The Ceramican

my first taste of Egypt – my first taste of the world outside Australia. And I can conceive the high exultation of those who were having their first experience of Foreignness in Bombay. The utter strangeness of it must have dazzled them. The magnificence of it dazzled those of us who are blase and hardened travellers. There is a great atmosphere of richness in this City-port; and prices in bazaar and hotel contribute to this atmosphere. The rate of exchange (which reduced the purchasing power of the pound to about eleven shillings) made it hard for us to live up to this. Nonetheless, most passengers squandered their substance on riotous brass and silk and cheroots, dinners and gharries – and drinks. This is a dry ship – very literally so. This is no great hardship to the moderate drinker. But to the man, who, in London, has accustomed himself to the daily, and generous use of spirituous liquors it is a dangerous experiment to be cut off in a single day from every drop. Not only is this a hazardous excursion into the unaccustomed, for beside the deprivation of his drink he is now suffering the pangs of ennui on a long sea voyage and the unwonted heat of the Tropics. He has just emerged from an English winter, and a city of theatres and the like distractions. Ship's concert parties and sports programmes do their best – as does the dispenser of cooling drinks. But the one cannot make up the rich and varied diversions of London, nor the other transform the blazing Tropics into an English winter. So even the super-moderate drinker aches for the prohibited "pint" which would dull the edge of monotony.

So those addicted to drink retrieved in Bombay the enforced abstinence of the voyage. The food on the ship is good. But, of course, everyone insisted on remaining ashore for dinner, partly to acquaint themselves with Bombay in the cool evening, partly to get the flavour of true Indian curry, partly for the pleasure of missing the official ferry steamer in the early evening and putting out at midnight under the moon in a sail-driven felluca.

And, of course, they stayed ashore the later because the ship was coaling. Coaling day and night, she was. If you have never inhabited a ship coaling in the East you know nothing of the vileness of it. Hundreds of coolies are shovelling in the breeze from barge to basket, and the basket-bearers, in a constant queue, are tipping their loads (in the same breeze) into the ship's side. As you approach the ship from shore you will see her enveloped in a fine haze. This filmy thing looks beautiful in the moonlight, and in the light of the coal-barge flares. But aboard the nocturnal beauty of it all is dissipated, and by day there isn't any beauty. The vile black dust not only fills ears and eyes, nose and hair, but penetrates into the remotest recess of your cabin, of which the door and porthole are closed. It will blacken the clothes in the trunk of which the lid is down, but not locked. The khaki you wear is smudged. Every inch of the ship on which you want to lean or sit bears the filthy veneer. Your deck-chair is covered; and as often as you dust it, it will be covered again incontinently. Coal is in your face and on your table-linen. There is no escape or respite, except by going ashore. This is a potent reason for going ashore all day, and for staying there late at night.

We lost some good friends at Bombay. They went to the Indian Army and to the Army of Occupation in Mesopotamia. Great is the intrepidity of him who elects to remain in the Army when the war is over. But these men had done so; and they are in their senses – very much so. But they have wife and family with them – those going to India. This will help to eke out their life in the Army. But the Mesopotamians have not. They are brave men.

On the 9th April we crossed the Line with great ceremony. Neptune came aboard, with spouse complete, and retinue. His satellites included the Imperial Dippers and the Royal High Barber, the Chaplain Archbishop, two policemen, divers whippers-in, and the Marine Band. In theory only those were to be ducked who were crossing for the first time. But once Neptune and his gang had tasted the blood of the official victims the thing became promiscuous, and everyone within coo-ee was ducked. Those out of coo-ee were chiefly people who, for discretionary reasons, had sought the stronghold of their cabins. When Neptune's police had sated themselves, the proletariat took the thing over – and the duckers were ducked. When this act of justice was complete, the ship's hoses were seized, and a clean sweep was made of the decks. After all was over the place was a shambles. But most people enjoyed themselves.

Many bargains had been driven in the native quarter of Bombay. But at least one man left the city with more than he had bargained for. On the (space) of April he was isolated for smallpox. The Marconi operator crackled out the S.O.S. to Fremantle, the retort to which was: "Vaccinate the lot !" So we formed up in the lymph queue with bared arms. One or two ladies who had the presence of mind to cherish their ballroom appearance in the face of death took the M.O. to their cabins later, and were scratched where the wound won't show.

At seven in the evening of April we moved into the lights of Fremantle. We had been gazing on the Southern Cross for many nights. This suggested Home to us very strongly. But the domestic lights of the West, dancing in the dusk, were more than symbolic of our home-coming. Many of us had not seen our country or our people for nearly six years. Many a young wife was coming out from England whose daily habits would be revolutionised in Australia, and whose senses of values would be reversed. Some of us were about to land with a wife and family with whom we did not leave our country. Moving into Fremantle filled us with high and moving expectations.

Next morning we were boarded by the Quarantine authorities, and our sentence was pronounced: "Eighteen days!" There was more in this than you imagine – you readers who are not exiles long overdue to re-enter your Country. It meant that we should

Chapter 5: The Ceramican

crawl lugubriously round the coast to Sydney, stopping at all intermediate ports, but stopping only to drop unhappy wretches into quarantine. No one else could land. These victims would sit in the station, in very sight of their homes, until the uncleanness of one man was expiated. Then the remnant of us would sit in the cage at Sydney, in sight of OUR homes for a week. And so our high home-coming would peter out into a miserable emergence from imprisonment. There were fiancees aboard, whose marriage had been fixed for the day which was their first in quarantine. Their lovers either saw them not at all, or saw them and waved like any mere acquaintance from the launch which scouted round the ship, keeping its prudent distance.

So we left Fremantle on a Sabbath evening, and moped round to Adelaide, where we stayed a day debarking another batch.

Adelaide we left on the 23rd. We cast anchor at Portsea before dawn on Anzac Day. Every potential denizen of quarantine was cheered by the aspect of the Portsea Station, to which we lay quite near. It was like a fine English Hydro to look on. And when the O.C. troops returned after spying it out, he said it was as good within as it looked from the sea. Another thing that cheered us was the statement by the Quarantine Boarding Officer that if the disembarked could show a vaccination "take," or reasonably good scars from the reasonably recent past, they would be discharged in a couple of days. All this augured the best for Sydney.

Here, within march of the Commonwealth Military Headquarters, the narrative should end. So it shall. We slaughtered no albatross to merit this ill-luck, by smallpox at the tail end of the voyage. But for that we could look back on it with unblemished pleasure. But it's good for our souls – this discipline. And it's a good introduction to the rigors of working for a living, now the war is over. But it's only for the moment we feel the sting and indignity of quarantine. Three months hence only the bright spots of this voyage will show in our experience – the unfolding pageant of the East, the games we played, the concerts, the dances, the poker schools, the ices of the Tropics, the dinners we gorged, the livers we cured, the lovely sunsets of the South, the gambolling porpoises, the sport of the flying fish, the sweeps we didn't win, the hot salt baths, the drinks we missed, the personalia of the "Aussiegram," the duty we caught, the scandal we talked, the lymphatic arms we nursed, the meals we missed off Cape Finisterre, the flirtations we had, the night yarns on deck, the wires we got at Fremantle, and the friends we made.

When your friend looks at the wall when you are telling him your troubles or asking him a favor, it's time to grab your hat and get out, for you are wasting your time.

Let our lives be a guidance to a better world of our own making on the basis of love and trust.

Geography of the World.

Geography as taught to-day is all wrong. For instance, we will take Africa – that is, if they will let us. Africa extends from Johannesburg to Park Lane. Its principal exports are diamonds and malaria fever. Its principal imports are Jews and whisky. To the north we have Central Africa, not yet discovered. Livingstone had a try, and then they had to discover him.

Then we have Egypt, the land of Pyramids and other billiard table games. No one is allowed to climb the Pyramids for fear they get snookered. The chief exports are cigarettes and mummies. Mummies a thousand years old are manufactured every day. Famous for its "Wazzer" and Sister Street.

Leaving the land of Sin, Sand, and Sorrow, we go to America. Discovered by C.C. (no, not Charlie Chaplin). America is divided into States. Each State is in a worse state than the other. Sahara Desert was the driest country in the world. America now holds the record. Exports whisky, ragtime, vaudeville artists, and patent corkscrews.

Then we have France. Its principal port is Calais, twenty miles from Dover on a fine day – 150 miles if it is rough. The chief health resort is the Riviera, noted for its champagne and mixed bathing, both of which are intoxicating. The capital is Paris, the gay city. All the streets commence with "Rue de," with the emphasis on the Rude. Famous for "Mademoiselle from Armentieres" and "Vin blanc."

We next take England, a small country north-west of Europe, inhabited by Germans. It consists of mountains, towns, and football clubs, and is governed by the "Daily Mail." Its capital is London, a suburb of Whitechapel. London is noted for its large buildings, including the Houses of Parliament and the "Bull and Bush." The principal river is the Thames, noted for barques down the river and its larks up the river. Its population is a floating one. England is the land of the open door; that's why everybody feels the draught.

To the north we have Scotland, surrounded by four-fifths water, the other fifth being whisky. Scotland is divided into two parts – the Highlands and the Lowlands. The Lowlands are the highest. Scotch people are very religious, and will not allow it to thunder on a Sunday, for fear of breaking the Sabbath. They are very fond of pork, and eat it every New Year's Day, and call it "hogmanay." It is the land of the "O.O." sign. The principal export of Scotland is Scotchmen.

Then we have Ireland. Ireland is an island by permission of the British Government. It is separated from England by the St. George's Channel and the Gulf of Misunderstanding, and is surrounded by Red Tape. Its capital is Dublin, has been Dublin for years, and is now nearly trebling. Dublin is on the Irish Sea, and is the only sea the Irish ever see. The most beautiful spot is Killarney, named after that well-known song. Its principal export is M.P.s.

The next country we take is Japan. A warlike nation on a pacific ocean. It is governed by a Mikado, for which Gilbert and Sullivan are responsible. It is called the Land of the Rising Sun, but it must be understood that this is not the only public-house in the district. It is close to China, which accounts for the many breakages in the past.

In the Southern Hemisphere we find a large piece of land, which is known to cognoscenti as the Land of the Diggers, but to the students of geography it is known as Australia. It is divided into States. Each State is separated from the other by a different railway gauge. Its leading buildings are picture shows, stadiums, and two-up schools. The principal river is the Yarra, owing, it is said, to its strong sense of smell. In the summer-time, when the bands are playing on the boats, you can hear the Yarra humming to the tune. When the soldiers left for the European "stouch" it was found that supports had to be put up to keep lamp-posts, verandah posts, and telegraph posts from falling. The male members are noted for their bigamistic tendencies.

—H.G.M.

Dawn by the Canal.

Still palm-fronds in the wreathing mist;

Still cattle in the lush liersiem;

Still Sweet-Canal* by morning kiss'd;

And still the patient, waiting team, Save the swift East, painting the glowing dawn,

All still, as is the red mid-desert morn.

H.W.D.

*The Sweet-water Canal which ran beside us to Ismailia.

"Dubius Teasar."

Scene: The House of Victuals.

Cassius: What are the mystic contents of this brimful cup.
This murky fluid thou would'st plead of me to sup?
I do not ask of thee some complex question hard.
If thou would'st name it I will straightway drink it up.

Mark Antony: O, Digger swain, of mannerisms gruff,
If thou wilest lend an ear, I will not bluff.
This was a mixture of some Chinese tea.
The trouble is the cook has drowned the stuff.

—SETB.

The Male Flapper.

One does not have to go to school
To learn to designate a fool,
To recognise an arrant ass.
And place him in his proper class.

All any mortal has to do
Is but to watch the fellow who,
Regardless of repeated knocks,
Plays lackey to a thing in frocks.

—PETE.

"A Society Matahorn."

She lived in a mansion in Grosvenor Square, and would be seen daily riding in her elegant Rolls-Royce limousine. Her servants were numerous. Her furniture was of Louis XIV. and Sheraton. The tables were laden with antique silver. She had a box at the opera, and was a patron of the Arts. Her dresses were Parisienne. Linen she abhorred; she wore only the finest silk. Her hats were a dream, and her diamonds were the envy of Duchesses and other members whose names shone large in the 1920 "Who's Who." None knew the origin of her riches. She denied that she was the wife of the Cardiff millionaire. All wondered. It was then that the Census took a call. "Name please, Madame?" "Maria Dorothea de Smithson." "Husband's name?" "John de Smithson." "His occupation?" "Regimental Q.M.S. in India."

Maria Dorothea de Smithson is no longer a mystery in the vicinity of Grosvenor Square.

The Tragedy of a Deck Chair.

They were seated on the saloon promenade deck. They had had a good dinner, one such as maketh the heart of woman and man glad. The moon had just begun to shed her silvery rays o'er the rippling ocean. There was not a movement in the ship. Chairs being scarce, one was doing duty for two. Their hands were clasped as they gazed into each other's eyes, with such looks of tenderness which only the deepest love could arouse. His mind, however, doubtless travelled back to thoughts of dusky ladies of Egypt and Jerusalem, or again, maybe, he remembered without regret Mademoiselle from some village estaminet in France. She, too, had her romance, for memories came to her of a certain Flying Corps Sergeant, an A.M.C. dispenser, and the brightly polished spurs and the mirror-like polish of an Anzac Provost Corps Corporal's leggings, and last – perhaps the one who touched her most – was the little journalistic corporal of Artillery.

A deep silence had fallen upon them for some minutes, but this was compensated by the pressure which he gave her little hand, and which she returned.

Meanwhile she gazed on the diamond and pearl engagement ring presented some nights previously, after his return from urgent business in Port Said. Methinks she wondered what French factory the brilliants [came from], and the size of the pearls seemed to denote a Ciro Bond Street establishment.

He was just about to pour his tale of love into her ear, when she said: "Let go my hand!" "Why, love?" he asked. Her answer came louder than before: "Let go my hand, Sir!" "Why this?" he said. "What have I done? Have I offended you? You know there is no other girl—!" "Hang the other girl! Let go my hand at once!" She stamped her foot. Her brow darkened. Blushes of anger showed through an ample supply of rice powder. Once more she cried in tragic tones worthy of a Sarah Bernhardt:

"Let go my hand, please! You are no gentleman. You are a disgrace to that noble Light Horse Regiment! No longer will I allow your feathered plumes to lightly touch my cheek. Let go! Let go!" He still held on, and on bended knees implored her. She could stand it no longer, and cried, "Fiend! Let go my hand at once! I want to blow my nose !"

—E.H.

Untitled sketch of officer from 'The Ceramican'.

Chapter 5: The Ceramican

"Coincidence."

It was one of those perfect mornings, when the dew-kissed red tiles of the housetops scintillated in the bright morning sunshine, and when the foliage which environed those houses looked greener and richer than ever, that the H.M.A.T. "Ramecci" steamed through the Heads, and plied her way past the anchored ships which rode on the deep blue waves of "Our 'Arbor."

Jack Morrissey, dressed in a well-cut suit, felt excited as the big boat drew into No. 8 Wharf, Woolloomooloo, and looked hurriedly through the Digger passengers aboard.

Suddenly he rushed forward.

"Bill!" he yelled. "How the hell are yer? Haven't seen yer for years!"

Bill Lester thrust out his hand, and gave Morrissey one of those death-grip handshakes, and straightway poured forth all that had happened since Jack had evacuated at Ypres.

Then the discharged man poured forth all that had happened since he had evacuated. How he had met HER! The "wonderfullest" girl in the world.

"Believe me, Bill," he confided, "I've never met anyone like her. The straightest kid on earth, sohelpme!"

"Shake!" interrupted Lester. "I got hitched a fortnight before leavin'!"

"Congrats!" continued Morrissey as he "mitted" with his pal. "I fair did my nut on my girl, but she wasn't perfect. No! She had a very expensive weakness for hats. I had a bit of bad luck. I couldn't get a passage for her at the same time as myself."

"What? She's still in Blighty then?" interrupted Bill.

"Yes – but 'san fairy' I'm expecting her out here any old time now."

"Go on," returned Bill. "I was luckier than you; my wife's with me. Just collecting her odds and ends in the cabin. Hang around for a moment. You must meet her. She is a regular woman. Wouldn't look at another man. Absolutely spoilt me on the trip out!"

A pretty little girl in white, with a big hat-box under each arm, walked daintily down the gangway.

"My wife!" yelled Morrissey, excitedly.

"What?" exclaimed Lester.

"My wife!" repeated Morrissey, excitedly.

"She's mine!" yelled Lester.

And they were both lost in the dust and baggage on the wharf as a Flying Corps officer rushed across and kissed her pretty lips.

—SUB.

"Hats—and Underneath."

Judging from the motionless appearance and obsessed conversation of most of our companions as we crossed the Bay of Biscay, seasickness might be invigorating but for a morbid curiosity regarding the stomach. This fatal weakness reduces its victims to a pitiable state of nervous apprehension, and, moreover, changes their native sweet reasonableness to the murderous thoughts which consume them at the sight of the insolent good spirits of those who are well.

For this state of mind there is nothing but dry biscuits and the last resort of a sick sinner – philosophy.

It remained, for the cause of all the trouble – the gale and rocking decks – to bring the needed distraction on a slippery part of the port promenade deck, by revealing the disquieting psychology underlying one's hat.

Human forms of all ages and sizes, carrying deck impedimenta, appeared unannounced, and slid protesting to the scuppers in admirably varied attitudes. To those whose wits withstood the experience, the obvious first and agonising thought was "Have I still got my hat?" and raising their bruised bodies they gazed around in concentrated anxiety. Oh, woe! There was their beloved fleeing along the deck. Then farewell hope, and welcome speedy death!

They would have spat out loosened teeth without the slightest embarrassment, and maintained unruffled poise with half their clothing hanging from its frame. Why, then, this unreasonable concern for that which at best only serves to give them bald pates?

Chapter 5: The Ceramican

The explanation, of course, lies in man's deep-rooted dignity – a fragment of the serious nonsense he has painfully acquired, exuded through his head, and consolidated into a hat.

But this idea of the dignity growing the hat has gradually been reversed without anyone noticing it, until now we imagine the hat confers the dignity.

And so we have the solemn crowning of kings; women submitting to the unmentionable vagaries of fashion, regardless of suitability or cost; and some of us, not content with our own degradation, have gone so far as to recommend the wearing of hats to little black boys who are content with their virgin wool. Only a race pathetically in earnest could refrain from shrieks of laughter at a full-dress civic function, or fail to weep at the indignities fitted upon the heads of the child-victims of our ostentatious charity "homes." The Church, too, has caught the common madness, displaying funereal symptoms suggestive of melancholia; and even the Law succumbs, and mops its sweaty brow under an insanitary wig. It has been suggested by some who would deprecate their kind that the private soldier only touches his headgear in deference to the superior "brass hat", and that the courtly habit of gentlemen in baring their heads originated in a base desire to accentuate their own dignity.

For us, unfortunately, there is no hope, but the rising generation has found a saviour. The mouths of babies vociferously proclaim him. Charlie Chaplin has invested the hat with a new meaning. By divorcing dignity from hats, he has shown the children a way to emancipate themselves, and to make the hat a thing of joy and airy fancy. It may be that they, in imitation of their forbears, will leave their saviour with his teaching on his hands, and seek the easier way of evolving for themselves merely a new type of the old hat.

They will, of course, in either case despise us, unless our infirmities gain their toleration; but to the unborn, demanding a reasonable cause for everything, how can we escape being a scorn and a hissing?

—H. F. SHAW.

"Northern Lights."
An Australian Incident of the North Russian Campaign.

"Halt! Who goes there?"

We were bivouacked for the night in a collection of rough wooden houses known as the "Tar Kiln" – simply a clearing in the heart of the Russian forest, and five versts from the village of Jitna. A three days' march through primitive bush land had brought us to this desolate place, where we were to remain till the following morning. Being in a position some ten versts behind the enemy's lines, this same post was none too safe, but the British plan of action, if it succeeded, would result not only in the capture of five villages, besides prisoners and booty, but in the annihilation of the Bolshevik army on this front.

At the present moment my pal, Sullivan, and I were doing sentry-go beside a gun-post, and our platoon commander had just come up with news that we were to be relieved. This message was pleasant, as the manoeuvres of the previous few days had exhausted us, and we willingly retired to one of the wooden huts in the clearing. Just as the midnight sun dipped slightly over the forest of pine to announce that the long Arctic day was gone we passed our inner post, and reported "All correct!"

. . . . . .

The next twenty-four hours remain in my memory only like a bad dream. How the 45th Royal Fusiliers (Australian Detachment) "hopped over" at midday and took Jitna; how they swarmed down the Dvina bank and caused three gunboats to surrender; how, after fierce "scrapping," they continued their victorious advance, and took three more villages and a host of prisoners; and how they finally gained their objective line outside Lipovets all this is as a haze in my memory. The fact remains, however, that this unparalleled feat of one battalion in successfully attacking the enemy in the rear should go down to history as a miracle of military skill.

. . . .

Once more it was evening. We were on the homeward trek, having cut into the forest again from the main road, because constant shell-fire ahead signalled the fact that Sieltson, the last strong-post of the "Reds," was not yet ours. The column, led by machine-gunners and our wounded, continued in single file along the narrow forest track. My platoon acted as rearguard to the battalion. Mile after mile we marched, through dense pine and fir, broken at intervals by clearings, bathed in the radiant reflections cast by the Northern Lights, which from time to time swept across the clear Polar sky. All at once we heard firing ahead, and got the order to form a line. With bullets whistling in all directions, we rushed forward, and found ourselves on the bank of a wide marsh. Here I got my bearings, for this was the Shieka River. The Bolshevist army of Seltson, routed and driven out of their village, had taken a short cut through the forest to ambush us here. How we crossed that river is still a mystery to me. We did it, anyway, in the face of intense rifle and machine-gun fire. Thrice I fell in, but recovered myself, and eventually reached the safe side unharmed. Here we found a line, and finally beat off the surprise attack.

Chapter 5: The Ceramican

. . . .

We lost many brave men in that Sheika crossing, and two Australians found heroes' graves beneath its treacherous whirlpools. I met Sullivan later on, and he had little to say of the encounter, or of his own gallant conduct, which I only heard of afterwards. That is why he wears the ribbon of the Victoria Cross.

. . . .

Just as the setting sun turned the distant spires of Yako Church to gold, we filed in again through the opening in our wire at Noal Mill, and later on proceeded to billets in the village.

This ends a sketch of the type of guerilla warfare waged by Britain against the "Reds" during the summer of 1919 – a brief campaign in which "Aussies" played no unimportant part.

'Neath the sapphirine tint of the midnight sun's gleam,
Where the bright Pole-star flashes o'er Dvina's broad stream

—WARRIGAL.

Be sure you put your feet in the right place, then stand firm.—Lincoln.

Things We'd Like to Know.

Is it a fact that whilst in the Bay of Biscay a Digger was found washing another man's face in mistake for his own?

Whether Tassy has transferred his affections, and is no longer seen parading "mit in mit" with the dark "cliner."

Is it a fact that a certain two-striper wished to obtain his discharge in Bombay?

Who is the wag that ran so fast in France that his shadow had to take a short cut to catch him?

Who is Fluffy, and why do the girls adore him?

Who is the joker with the check cap who has the habit of cutting out the other fellow?

Whether the Staff Canteen man loves the kiddies?

Is it a fact that there are a large number of "embryo bottle-ohs" travelling en route to Australia.

Why does the dispenser wear a worried look?

Who was the sergeant in civies who won all the ladies' hearts at Saturday's dance, and why did he sing Kipling's "Pay! Pay! Pay!"

Who is the man who will persist in borrowing tooth brushes?

Is it a fact that the NIGHTINGALE'S song grows fainter and fainter as he goes south?

Is it a fact that the Education Sergeant one-time played Shylock, and is now writing a book called "Bobs, And How to Count 'Em?"

Is it a fact that "Johnno," of the Y.M.C.A., got wounded whilst keeping a lady out of the danger zone when the Naval Brigade were on a submarine expedition?

Whether a certain sergeant, of the Peel instincts, has been studying Jerome K. Jerome's "Three Men in a Boat?"

Replies to Literary Attempts and Contempts.

"W.H." — Poor replica. We have read O. Henry also. "Feebler."—Feeble in name, and feeble in nature. "H.W.F." — Thanks, but "Man Overboard" is frayed with much usage. "Q.F." — Unfortunately, the M.O. would not lend us his microscope to see the joke. "Adam." — After reading "Minced Muchness," we got 'em. "R.J.S."—Before writing a story, you must have a plot. Remember this next time you write. "O.G."— Why didn't you write "To Her" in her autograph book before leaving Blighty. "Geoff" — You say "Her lips, her eyes—they mesmerise," etc. Don't be silly. You'll get over it. "X.Y.Z." — ". . . And he rolled over dead. "We nearly did, too, after reading your tragic spasm. "Light Horse." — We feel convinced that you were told those yarns by the Sphinx. "Brahma." — "Ahmed of Mecca." What a wonderful title, but what a hell of a yarn. "Pomme de Terre." — Try and be funny without being vulgar. "A Brother." — We received "The Curse of Drink." We must say that there is not much spirit in it. Try it on the Y.M.C.A. "Wing." — You say that you have written many things. You are certainly not improving.

Chapter 5: The Ceramican

A.I.F. Education Services.
H.M.A.T. "Ceramic."

The A.I.F. Education Services began work on this ship on the 14th March, 1920. A beginning was slightly delayed owing to the boisterous weather experienced during the early days of the trip.

The Education Staff have been faced with the fact that whilst their work is part of the organisation, and must be attended to, the attendance of students is purely voluntary; but the untiring efforts of the Education Officer and his two assistants will surely be appreciated for their zeal in the furtherance of a scheme whose object is to reduce the ennui of a six weeks' voyage through the Tropics.

The personnel of the Staff is as under:—

Captain H. W. Dinning, Education Officer.
Sergeant R. H. Treacy, Librarian.
Staff-Sergeant L. J. Nightingale, Assistant Librarian.

Arrangements were made for calling classes, and instructors were invited to take these classes. Notification of the procedure to be adopted was promulgated in Ship's Routine Orders, and met with response from a large number of the troops. The first class was opened on the 15th March, 1920, and others were quickly organised. The following classes are now in existence, and the work of both instructors and students is marked by energy and keenness.

Daily Classes

10.45: French — Lance-Corporal W. C. Mortimer, Instructor.
14.00: Bookkeeping — Lieut. R. J. Presswell, Instructor.
14.15: Shorthand — W.O. N. M. White, Instructor.
15.00: Algebra and Geometry — S.-Sergt. W. L. Larkin, Instructor.

In addition, at 10.30 on Monday, Wednesday, and Friday, Staff-Sergeant K. McLeod (an Official Photographer) conducts classes in Photography.

Furthermore, classes have been organised for the purpose of giving the children on board some instruction to prevent them from losing a grip of the knowledge already obtained in their home schools, and to give them some knowledge of their journey. This, too, gives mothers an opportunity of securing some leisure moments during the voyage, and has been largely availed of by grateful parents. This section was organised by W.O. N. White, and he is supported by the following staff of lady and gentlemen teachers, to whom is expressed the appreciation of the Education Service for their assistance: Mrs. L. M. Prentice, Mrs. M. Allen, Mrs C. Wilcox, Mrs. E. Stanley, Mrs. A. Beaman, Mrs. M. Duffy, Mrs. W. Anderson, Captain L. M. Morris, Royal Fusiliers (N.R.R.F.), and Mr. S. H. Mott.

Included amongst the other activities of this Service is a course of highly instructive lectures on "Repatriation," which are being delivered to ex-A.I.F. men by Corporal E. L. Handcock, 28th Battalion.

There are applications for the formation of other classes, which it has not yet been possible to begin. For instance, some men want instruction in Telegraphy, but the apparatus for such tuition cannot be secured. There are some men who want instruction in Wireless Operating, but it is impossible to arrange access for them to the Wireless Room.

It is unfortunate that at this stage of repatriation the ship is necessarily furnished with the tail-end of the educational equipment. This means that the library is meagre; that no sets of tools for Artificers' classes are available; that there is a shortage of such things as blackboards, drawing material, and even paper. It is doubtless the case that the classes already formed are only the nucleus of larger attendances and of a greater variety of classes. There is a proportion of girls and women amongst the students. The most effective means of enrolment is found to be by personal propaganda on troop decks and at meals. This work is being proceeded with.

So far text books to the value of £3 10s. have been sold from the library, and about 35 volumes taken out on loan.

Our Orchestra.

During the voyage an orchestra was formed, under the conductorship of Band-Sergeant F. J. Nott, Mus. Bac., A.R.C.O., the well-known Melbourne organist, who, during his stay in England, gave a series of recitals at the leading London churches.

The orchestra served to greatly assist in the amusement and entertainment of all on board, not only contributing to the concert programme, but also playing for the nightly dances.

Concerts, etc.

Two concert parties were inaugurated, namely, the "Dinkum Diggers" and the Ceramic Vaudeville Troupe. The former consisted of Diggers and their wives; the latter was formed by the members of the boat staff, under the direction of Mr. Cheetham.

Both parties gave a number of talented entertainments of a high-class order, and which were greatly appreciated by the crowded audiences.

Y.M.C.A. Aboard.

The Y.M.C.A., under the control of Hon. Lieut. H. J. Beavis, conducted a lending library, which was well stocked with books by leading authors and authoresses.

Unfortunately, a number of people misinterpreted the word "lending" for "giving," and, being good judges, retained some of the best of the books, which was, to say the least, selfish.

A large number of games and amusements, including cards for whist drives, were distributed freely. With the aid of a good electric lantern plant, kindly lent by Corporal A. Johnson, and a varied assortment of slides, a number of illustrated lectures on places of interest were also given.

In addition to running the lantern, Corporal Johnson worked the electrical effects for the concerts and dances, and, indeed, under the circumstances, did admirable work.

Personnel on Board.

The personnel included Naval Ratings, consisting of petty officers of the Imperial Navy, who were going out to join the Australian Navy; Imperial officers for India and Mesopotamia; noncommissioned officers, their wives and families, bound for India; and also a large number of wives and dependents of soldiers already serving in India; besides returning Diggers, their wives and children, fiancees for Australia, and ex-A.I.F. and Imperial men and their wives.

These totalled 1467, being made up as follows.—Naval Ratings, 1 officer, 49 O.R.; Australian officers, 25; Imperial officers, 15; Australian soldiers, 72 W.O's. and sergeants, 313 O.R's.; Imperial soldiers, 14; ex-A.I.F. men, 3 officers, 191 O.R. Women for India, 150; children for India, 176. Women for Australia, 235; children for Australia, 154; ex-Imperial troops for Australia, 5 officers and 53 other ranks; 4 nurses, A.A.N.S., and 6 special nurses for the voyage only.

If you want to disobey God, seek a place where He cannot see you.

SS CERAMIC The Untold Story

'The Ceramican': vignettes from on board ship.

Chapter 5: The Ceramican

Church Services.

Chaplain-Captain J. A. Jeffries conducted religious services on Sundays for all Protestant denominations.

There being no Catholic Chaplain on board, Captain R. O'Brien filled the breach.

Answers to Correspondents.

"Anxious Mother." – If in need of a nurse, see Tassy, of "D" deck. He can put a baby to sleep quicker than anybody we know.

"Cleanliness." – British commissioned officers and W.O's. are usually particularly cleanly, and would wash before breakfast, and most certainly shave. We doubt muchly from what you say if your deck-mate has told you everything.

"Manchester Bride." – The custom of selling wives after five years' trial is an old custom amongst the natives of Port Augusta district, in South Australia, and may be still honored by the employees of the Broken Hill Proprietary Co.

"Bound for Adelaide." – The "cervus negra," or common ordinary market-garden crow is much appreciated in South Australia, and takes the place of the lark in puddings in the chief hotels of the State.

"Q.C." – Life is too brief. Type is too short. We cannot give you a full description of the average sausage. They are bags of mystery, and, therefore, indulgers of this delicacy need—Faith— faith—FAITH.

"Pussyfoot." – We cannot answer your question re spirits. We have not had a chance of sampling it lately. The only medium we have on board has tried over and over again to get in touch with it, and to-day he informed us that it was like wireless out of range.

"Naval Ratings." – The places which will interest you in Melbourne are Little Bourke Street, Young and Jackson's, and the salubrious suburb of Footscray. You need not worry about the lights not being lighted on Princes Bridge, for the Yarra will lead you home.

"Fiancee in Distress." – We quote you the Latin proverb: "Aut amat aut odit mulier nihil est tertium." (A woman either loves or she hates; there is no third course for her.)

"Poisoned." – Get Professor Whiteside to administer an alexipharmacon.

"First Saloon." – Shirt-tails are not things of beauty or joys for ever, even at a fancy dress ball. We saw the gent. you mentioned, and he looked like a disintegrated Chinese laundry.

"Eighteen Stone." – You are certainly weighty. The Glaxo Company, we understand, state that persons put on weight who inhale the fumes arising from their products.

"The Higgins." – Your ancestors were of the Royal race of Ireland. One Phineas was King of Ballyhooley, and was the inventor of "pothean"; also said to be the first man to run a chip spud cart in County Clare.

"Londonite." – No; you are strictly forbidden to drop sponges or other absorbents into Sydney Harbor, as this harbor will be needed after the arrival of the "Ceramic" as a bath for the Brontosaurus.

"Botanist." – We don't know much about botany. Have made careful inquiries, but cannot find out what is the species of the berry you named. Kew Gardens advise us that it is a new variety, which they have named the "Yhemmar."

Strength of character consists of two things – power of will and power of self-restraint.—F. W. Robertson.

Sound, sound the clarion! Fill the fife!
To all the sensual world proclaim;
One crowded hour of glorious life
Is worth an age without a name.

—Sir W. Scott.

Sports.

A trophy cup of the period, minus its handles, recovered from the sea bed.

A Sports Committee was formed immediately the boat left Tilbury, for the purpose of organising and carrying on the general sports of the ship. The first committee meeting was held on the 15th March, 1920, when it was decided that, owing to the roughness of the weather, the active sports would be delayed for a few days.

On Friday, the 19th, a full sports programme was arranged. and, considering the mixed passengers on board, consisting of troops, ex-troops, wives and children, and fiancees, it was decided to run sports open for all passengers on the boat.

Chapter 5: The Ceramican

In order that prizes be obtained for the different events, a subscription list was opened amongst the saloon passengers, and the sum of £35 7s. was subscribed.

The first heats were run off on the 23rd March, immediately after leaving Port Suez. The events were:—

Potato and Spoon Race – Men.
Potato and Spoon Race – Ladies.
Three-legged Race, Sack Race, and Whistling Race – Men.

A great deal of interest and amusement was caused in the Whistling Race, the ladies sometimes having great difficulty in distinguishing what their men partners were whistling.

On Wednesday, the 24th March, 1920, the heats of the following events were run:—

Potato and Basket Race – Men.
Potato and Basket Race—Ladies.
Cock-fighting, Scratch Pulling, Wheelbarrow and Pick-a-Back.

In the afternoon the preliminaries of the boxing contest commenced. The fights took place on the for'ard well deck. The different events were: Bantam, light, feather, and welter.

Thursday, the 25th, was put down as the Children's Day, when heats were run off for various events. At first it was decided to have open children's races, but owing to the number of children on board, and their variety of ages, it was found fairer to make two classes in each sex, namely: Girls 8 and under, and girls over 8. The same divisions were made for the boys. Great enthusiasm was shown by all the children, and a very busy and enjoyable day was spent. In the early evening the semi-final of the welterweights, took place; also the finals of the Bantam and Lightweight.

Friday, the 26th, proved another day choked full with events of interest. The heats of the Relay Race, Tug-of-war, and Pillow Fighting were finished off during the afternoon.

The Pillow Fighting was well attended, and numerous entries were taken. The event was well contested, and quite a lot of amusement was given. The finals of the welter-weights and feather-weights took place in the evening. This concluded the boxing programme. Throughout some excellent boxing was witnessed, and the many contests were carried out in a clean and sportsmanlike manner. Each day's contests were witnessed by a large proportion of the ship's passengers, including quite a number of the fair sex.

Saturday, the 27th March, 1920. – The finals of all sports events except children were run off. A very busy afternoon ensued, and, thanks to the loyal co-operation of the contestants, all the events were finalised without trouble. In the evening a ship's Baby Show was held. There were four classes open: Under six months; six months to twelve months; boys up to two years; girls up to two years; special prize for ship's champion baby. One of the saloon passengers, the matron, the S.M.O., took upon themselves the most difficult task of judging. In all there were fifty-five entries.

On Monday, 29th, the finals of the children's events took place. This finished the first part of the ship's sports programme.

Tuesday, 30th. – Prizes were distributed by the O.C. Troops.

Wednesday, 31st. – Arrival at Bombay. It was decided to postpone all future events until the weather cooled off.

Sunday, 10th April, 1920. – A further sports programme was arranged, and it was decided to run three sets of sports. The troops were to be given two days' sports to themselves, and one day general and children's sports.

Tuesday, the 13th, "C" deck had a day's sport, commencing at 11.30 a.m., and ran Relay Race, Potato and Spoon, Potato and Basket, Three-legged, Wheelbarrow, and Pick-a-back. The entries were very good, and an excellent day's sport and exercise was the result.

Wednesday, 14th April, 1920 – "D" deck sports. Same events as the previous day. Very good day spent.

Thursday, the 15th. – Children's and women's events and double events.

Keen interest was again shown in the ladies' and children's events, disregarding the fact that we had lost about 150 women and children at Bombay.

Friday, 16th April, 1920. – Boxing contest in the afternoon; exhibition and preliminaries. Chief attraction was a ten-round light-heavy contest. It resulted in a good, clean fight, going over the full ten rounds.

Saturday, 27th April, 1920. – Distribution of prizes by the C.O. Arrived at Fremantle at 8 p.m.

This finished the remaining portion of the sports programme. It was gratifying to notice throughout the keenness and interest that was taken by all contestants in the different sports events.

Chapter 6
The inter-war years

Letter on White Star Line notepaper, addressed to Mr Emmett Kilpatrick, Uniontown, Alabama, United States of America. Dr. Emmett Kilpatrick was an eminent scholar, author, and interpreter for President Woodrow Wilson after World War I. In 1920, he was with a Y.M.C.A. unit connected with the White Army in South Russia; captured by the Bolsheviks and held for a year. Sentenced to death as a spy, he slipped a message out in the clothing of a prisoner being released, and the U.S. government demanded and obtained his release.

10/1/21 Nearing Capetown S.A. S.S. Ceramic

Dear Kil –

Undoubtedly you will have arrived home before this letter reaches you and I sincerely hope that it will find you in better health than when I left you in Paris three weeks ago. I have wondered many times since I came on this boat, how you have made out in Switzerland – where, I am sure you have enjoyed your visit.

I am having a fairly pleasant trip. Good weather and the accommodations are not too bad. There are no interesting people on board, but I have met a woman (English) who has been in Russia with the Quakers – after talking with her for a few minutes, I found that she had absorbed Bolshevik ideas and is quite in accord with them and I told her that I was sorry we were not going into American territory instead of British as I should certainly denounce her to the authorities. She doesn't come near me now – I am glad of it. She made me so damned mad that I wanted to murder her.

We are to remain in Cape Town 36 hours and then continue this long voyage to Albany, Adelaide and then to Melbourne where I shall take leave of the ship.

We should arrive in Melbourne at Nov 1st with good luck.

I forgot to give you an address before leaving Paris, but care of the U.S. Consul, Melbourne, Victoria, Australia is sure to reach me. I will keep you posted on my movements.

Hoping that you are in better health and that I shall hear from you soon after you receive this, believe me,

Yours (illegible)

Don't forget to send me the first copy of the Book.

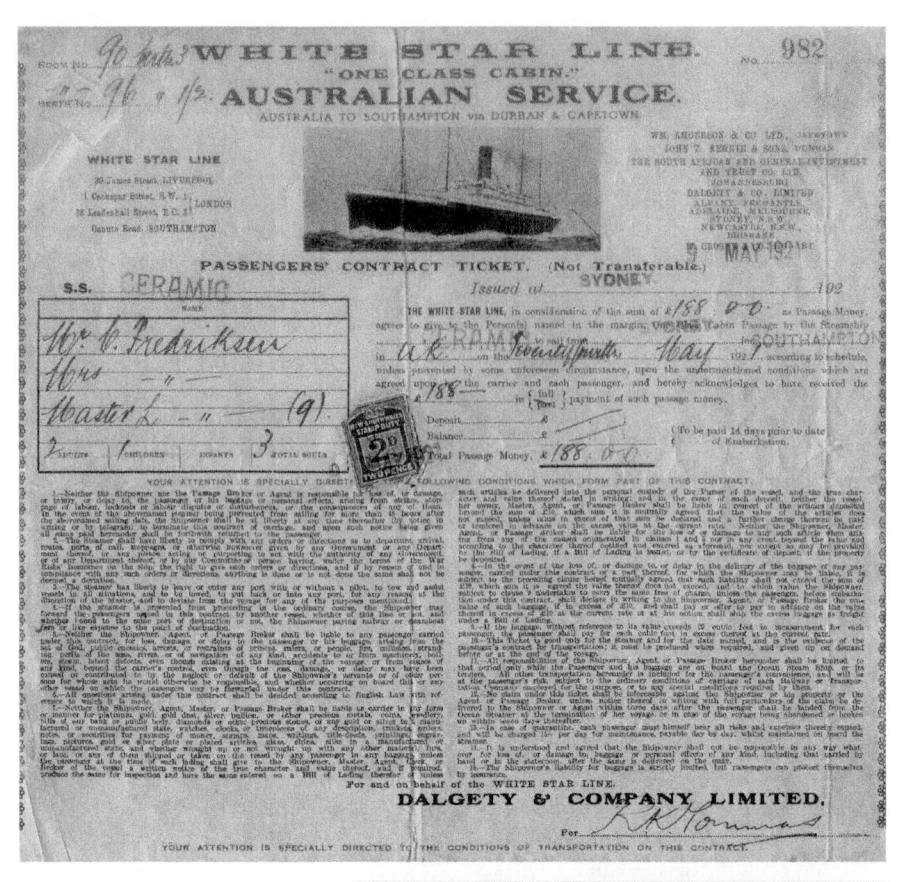

Above: Ticket issued to Mr C. Fredriksen for passage from Sydney to Southampton on the Ceramic, 1921.

Right: Lord Forster, Governor-General of the Commonwealth of Australia, and Captain A. H. Summers at the Ceramic Ball, Sydney, 1923.

White Star Line Magazine in author's collection.

14-11-22.

Dear G. Just to let you know that we are quite alright. We have had a fair voyage so far, last few days rather a rough sea, but neither Colin or I have been sick. We arrive at Cape Town this afternoon, will be nice to be on land for a while. Hope you are better, & rest of family well. Love from Maude.

***

White Star Magazine, August 1924.

REFRIGERATION EXPERTS VISIT CERAMIC
THE WHITE STAR LINE AS PIONEERS

It was on "The Heath," "Before a Hovel" that Edgar, of Shakespeare's "King Lear" kept ejaculating "Tom's a-cold." If he had been one of a group which boarded the Ceramic in Liverpool on June 28th he might have had grounds for his assertion, for not only was the party immediately conducted to the refrigerating chambers of the White Star liner, but the very composition of the party was sufficient to cause a drop in the temperature seeing that they were delegates of the Fourth International Congress of Refrigeration. It is hardly necessary to add that, though associated with various phases of an industry which aims at securing chilliness, the representatives of refrigeration were socially warm-hearted and in no way frosty in demeanour!

Arriving on board the Ceramic, white gloves were dealt round: this ceremony had none of the significance which attaches to it at the assizes, the object being merely to keep hands clean as the descent was made into the refrigerated chambers of the ship. Mr. Willett Bruce and his assistants conducted the explorations, led us round the cooling machine, evaporator and brine return tank room, etc., let loose with surprising ease such phrases as "carbonic anhydride compression system," "granulated cork slabs," "bitumastic cement," and displayed some of the 14 compartments capable of holding over 100,000 carcases of mutton all the way from Sydney to England.

Emerging from the cool depths, the visitors proceeded to the Megantic, where luncheon was served in the cabin dining saloon; Colonel Concanon, Joint Manager of the Line, presided, and in due course gave the toast of "Our Guests." After regretting the absence of Mr. Harold Sanderson and Mr. A. B. Cauty (prevented from being present on account of important business engagements), Colonel Concanon referred to the keen interest with which he and his colleagues had followed the proceedings of the International Congress of Refrigeration. That the White Star Line were pioneers in the field of refrigeration he was well aware; when he and Mr. Willett Bruce (Chief Superintendent Engineer) joined the Line, the question of fitting the steamers which linked Australia and England had not been considered, though there were on the Atlantic service vessels fitted with rather crude arrangements for dealing with refrigeration.

Forty or fifty years ago it was the custom for the large meat-shippers in America to hire the space they wanted on a passenger-carrying steamer; this space they insulated and piped, installing a steam-driven circulating pump. Block ice in bulk and salt in bags provided a mild brine by means of which a suitable temperature around the meat chambers became feasible. A change was made by the White Star Line, which made contracts with the shippers and provided the insulated and piped compartments, as well as the machinery, which consisted of chemical machines of the CO_2, and NH_3 systems; these were arranged for brine or cold air.

To-day, the speaker continued, inasmuch as the White Star Line steamships sailed to Australia and New Zealand as well as across the Western Ocean, the produce which they carried was very varied; hence varied temperatures had to be contrived. For American chilled meat the vital temperature was about 29 or 30 degrees; for Australasian frozen meat a temperature of between 12 and 15 degrees was requisite; dairy produce involved more than one temperature for butter had to be kept at 12 degrees and cheese at 42 degrees; fruit required 88 degrees.

Lieut.-Col. Lord Dudley Gordon, D.S.O. (Chairman of Messrs. J. & E. Hall Ltd., Dartford) in response referred to the excellent work of the White Star Line in putting into practice the results of experiments of investigators. Mr. Hal Williams of London supported Lord Dudley Gordon.

Speaking to the toast "The White Star Line," Mr. Arnold Rushton, Lord Mayor of Liverpool, paid high tribute to the Line and felicitated its representatives upon the fact that in Colonel Concanon they had one who was identified with everything that was being done for the best interests of Liverpool. Mr. W. S. Crichton supported the Lord Mayor and expressed the hope that Liverpool might receive some of the New Zealand trade which at present went elsewhere. Engineer-Captain Willett Bruce, O.B.E., Chief Superintendent Engineer, in responding, referred to the genuine pride felt by himself and his colleagues in being associated with a shipping company of such notable traditions.

His own association with the Line began in the early 'eighties, and it had always been a matter of real delight to him to find that wherever the flag of the White Star Line was found, the public recognised that it stood for efficiency, regularity, confidence, and comfort.

In conclusion it may be added that the delegates present at the luncheon represented 24 nations and that one of the delegates was a Siamese prince.

Chapter 6: The inter-war years

White Star Magazine, August 1924.

Pictures of the *Ceramic* have been forwarded to me from Capetown by Mr. H. C. Hall. He says :– "The *Ceramic* was the first really large vessel to be berthed at the new No. 7 Quay, Capetown Docks. The Quay was not quite completed at the time, but its construction had been pushed on specially fast to provide a berth for the large ships of the White Star and Associated Lines using the port of Table Bay. The *Ceramic* is the longest regular trader using the port, and when she is being docked there is not much room in the fairway for any other craft.

In addition to No. 7 Quay, the Harbour Administration are constructing a new pier which will be able to take four large liners: this is only an instalment of the full programme of harbour construction.

The White Star service to Africa and Australia has made the red pennant with the White Star one of the most familiar emblems amongst the many house flags seen in South African ports."

Left: The *Ceramic* in Gladstone Graving Dock, Liverpool, 1929.
Photo courtesy of Frank McCormick.

SS CERAMIC The Untold Story

This autograph book belonged to A. Bright, who painted the watercolour of an Australian herder opposite. A number of autographs and illustrations were collected en route, on the *Ceramic*'s 34th voyage, leaving Liverpool on 29 January 1927, under Captain John Roberts.

Chapter 6: The inter-war years

The road be rough the gradient steep
The handrail of life, strong or weak.
The time be short or the time be long
The road we take seems ever wrong!

J.W.Boyce.
15/3/27.
"Ceramic"

"Ceramic" at Sea.
2/3/27

Linger not till tomorrow
The wounded heart to heal
Who knows what added sorrow
Thy waiting may reveal?

M.J. Hartnett.
Sub 3rd Eng?

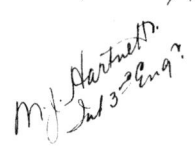

129

SS CERAMIC The Untold Story

The sighing Lover led a "Heart"
The girl for a "Diamond" played
The Father he came down with a "Club"
The Sexton held a "Spade"

Madeleine H. Hill
S. S. Ceramic
11 2/37

P.T.O. I want to get out.

Chapter 6: The inter-war years

"Ceramic" 1-2-27.

All good wishes "Ceramic"

DONALD STUART,
"THE HIGH AND MIGHTY ONE."

Yours, Donald Stuart

The mind of a woman can never be known,
You never can tell it aright,
Shall I tell you the reason? – she knows not her own,
It changes so often ere night,
T'would puzzle Apollo,
Her whimsies to follow,
His oracle would be just a jest,
At first she'll prove kind,
Then quickly you'll find,
She'll change like the wind,
And often abuses,
The man that she chooses,
And what she refuses,
Loves best.

At Sea.
SS Ceramic
(Left Liverpool January 29th 1927 on her 34th voyage.)

With apologies for using two pages of your book.
Sincerely yours,
Sidney H. Paver,
Electrician.

The book was signed by travelling companions, crew and celebrities, all of whom would have become friends over the course of the voyage – the *Ceramic* was a single class ship.

Goza tu del poco, mientras busca mas el loco.
(Enjoy your little while the fool seeks more).

J. Paton. Engr.
S.S. "Ceramic"
2-3-27.

WHS. 2m.
15.3.27

RMS Ceramic.

"Ride a Cock-horse, to the Southern Cross—
To see a Sperm-whale, or an Albatross,
Chalk the Pig's eye — Sit under a hose;
On board the 'Ceramic'—
    wherever she goes."

1st March 1927

J.H. Sharp
Chief Engineer

Chapter 6: The inter-war years

Another passenger, who travelled on the *Ceramic* in 1926 and 1930, collected autographs on a wooden brise fan with a postcard of the *Ceramic* which has been outlined in painted flowers. This is a typical type of souvenir fan that was made between 1900-30 and this type of fan can be found all over the world as a result.

Courtesy of Kathryn Maxwell.

Ceramic football team. 1920s.
Author's collection.

Chapter 6: The inter-war years

Ceramic at Ocean Pier, Hobart. 1920s.
Author's collection.

A little too close for comfort? *Ceramic* almost scraping past the *Arundel Castle* berthed at East Pier, as she is manoeuvred to No. 7 quay. Cape Town 1931.

Copyright: John H. Marsh Maritime Collection, SA Maritime Museum.

Chapter 6: The inter-war years

In the early 1930s, the White Star Line was in desperate financial difficulties due to the decline in the transportation of immigrants, and a failed takeover bid by Lord Kylsant which nearly led to the total collapse of the White Star Line. Between 1930 and 1934, the line was running at a loss. The Great Depression took hold, and shipbuilding ground to a halt. In Clydebank, the hull of the Queen Mary lay incomplete on the slipways. This caused such concern amongst the public that the government agreed to fund the ship's completion on the condition that Cunard and White Star, the two great rivals, must merge as part of the deal, to create a powerful new shipping line.

In the months following the merger in 1934, Cunard White Star Line began a concerted campaign to dispose of as many ex-White Star vessels as it could in the shortest time possible. Many famous liners, such as Vedic, Calgaric, Ionic II, Albertic and Adriatic II were sold for scrap. Ceramic was a little luckier, as she was sold to the Shaw Savill Line. In 1936, the ship had a major refit, but she remained a coal-burner all her life.

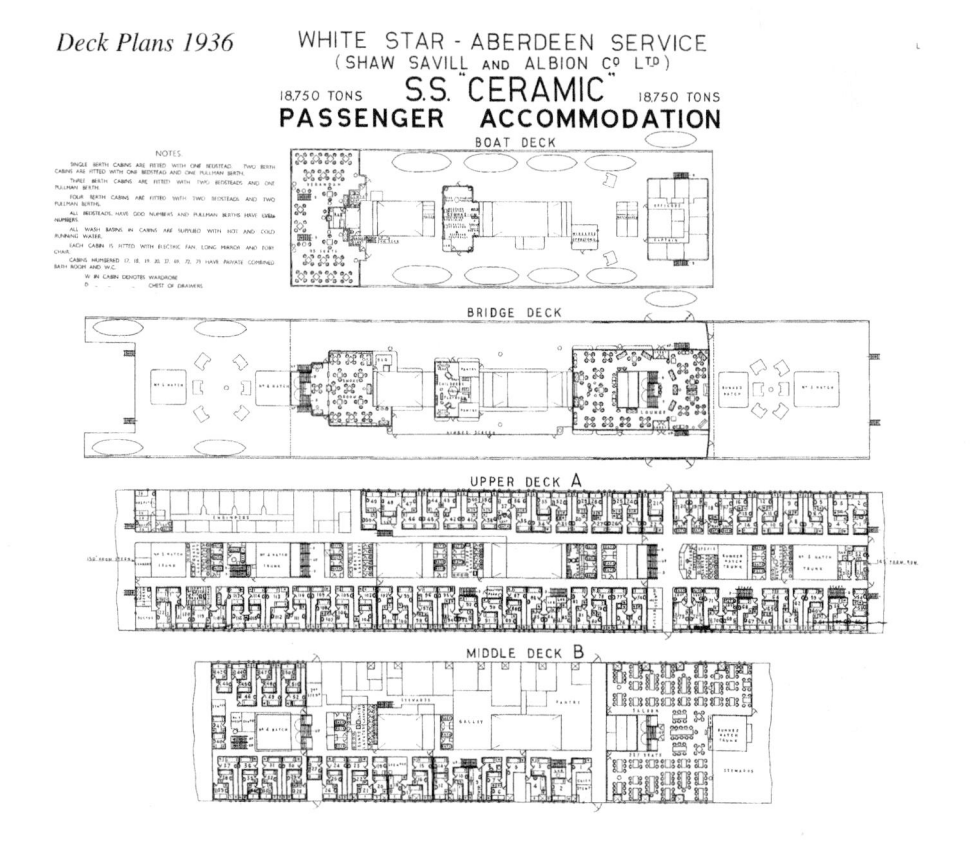

Deck Plans 1936

WHITE STAR - ABERDEEN SERVICE
(SHAW SAVILL AND ALBION Cº LTD)
18,750 TONS   S.S. "CERAMIC"   18,750 TONS
PASSENGER ACCOMMODATION

BOAT DECK

BRIDGE DECK

UPPER DECK A

MIDDLE DECK B

137

Brochure for the Ceramic, 1936

SS CERAMIC
the
CABIN CLASS
SHIP
SUPERB

WHITE STAR-ABERDEEN SERVICE

***

TRIPLE SCREW STEAMER
"CERAMIC"
18,750 TONS

LIVERPOOL TO TENERIFE

CAPE TOWN	DURBAN
FREMANTLE	ADELAIDE
MELBOURNE	SYDNEY

(Through Bookings to Brisbane and Tasmanian and New Zealand Ports.)

VERANDAH CAFE

The Verandah Cafe extends across the Boat Deck for the full width of the Ship. The floor of the Cafe is specially laid so as to be available for dancing when required. The walls are decorated in a soft stone with blue inlays and the ornamental balustrading and wicker furniture give a pleasing effect.

GYMNASIUM

The Gymnasium on the Boat Deck is fitted with all modern equipment for exercise and physical training, including Electric Vibrator and Massage Machines.

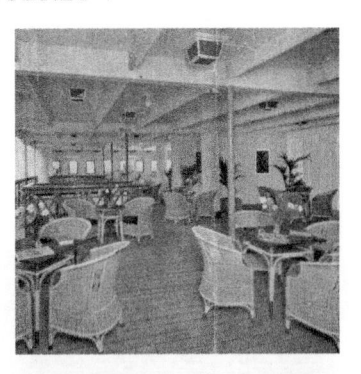

DINING SALOON

A well lighted and ventilated room extending the full width of the steamer. The service and the cuisine of the "Ceramic" are uniformly maintained at a high standard.

SMOKE ROOM

Panelled in various Empire woods with furniture to match, this room, with its recessed window seats, arcaded landing, large skylight and modern electric lighting, has an inviting and distinguished appearance both by day and by night.

LOUNGE

The Lounge is decorated in eighteenth century style in delicate tones of primrose relieved with grey. The walls are embellished by four large oil paintings of picturesque Scottish Lochs and the floor of oak parquetry is partially covered by specially woven hand-made rugs. The artistic lighting, large casement windows, astragel cut mirrors and the luxurious furniture make this a charming room, restful and comfortable.

SINGLE BERTH CABIN

A Special feature of the accommodation is the number of Single Bedstead Cabins, of which there are 53, every one having a Porthole.

The two-, three- and four-berth Cabins are each fitted with one or more Bedsteads with Pullman Berths above.

TWO-BERTH CABIN

All Cabins are luxuriously fitted and contain everything required for the comfort of Passengers – Wardrobe, Chest of Drawers, Chair, Electric Fan, Bedlights, Hot and Cold running water, long Dressing Mirror, etc.

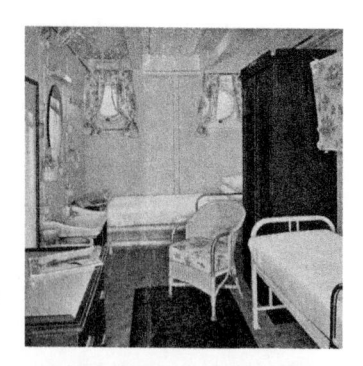

PROMENADE DECK

The "Ceramic" is 674 feet from stem to stern and, as befits a long-distance, fine weather voyage, large deck spaces are provided for games and exercise, as well as ample room for deck chairs.

The deck between the Smoke Room and the Lounge on the Starboard side is fitted with hinged, glazed screens, so that passengers can sit out on deck in all weathers.

The Sun-deck over the Verandah Cafe and the whole of the Boat Deck, in addition to the other Promenade Decks, give a total of over 31,000 square feet of Deck space.

***

T.S.S. "CERAMIC"

This steamer has always been a favourite with the travelling public and now that she has been entirely remodelled and refurnished, it is certain that she will enhance her popularity on the South African and Australian route. Among the principal features of this vessel are :–

All Cabins have either one or two bedsteads and where additional berths are fitted these are of the folding Pullman type. In each room there is a Wardrobe, Combined Chest of Drawers and Writing Table, Chair, Bedside Table, Electric Fan, Reading Light and Bell to each berth. Hot and Cold running water and a long Dressing Mirror in addition to that over the Wash basin.
A number of the Cabins have private bathrooms.

The most modern system of lighting has been adopted in all the Cabins and Public Rooms.

The Public Rooms are large, well-ventilated and tastefully furnished.

A Children's Playroom and Nursery is provided for young children.

The latest type of Sound Film Equipment is installed, and the most recent Sound Films are shown during the voyage. The amplification and illumination are sufficient to enable the films to be shown on Deck under suitable conditions.

A Marconi All-Wave Broadcast Receiver connected to the Panatrope enables Radio programmes and News to be heard whenever the steamer is in touch with a Broadcasting Station.

South African shipping agents, showing a model of the *Ceramic* now in the Iziko Museum.
Photo courtesy of Bart Elford.

Chapter 6: The inter-war years

This page and below left:
Cape Town early 1930s.

Photos by kind permission of the Iziko Museum of South Africa.

Copyright: John H. Marsh Maritime Collection, SA Maritime Museum.

142

Chapter 6: The inter-war years

Joan Willis
Email to Frank McCormick

MARMADUKE PEASGOOD
17 June 1868 - 25 April 1937
Died and buried at sea on board *Ceramic*

My great uncle Marmaduke Peasgood was a journalist by profession; up to his retirement, he worked for the Irish Times. He was born in Bridlington in 1868 to a local farming family, but, when he was a young man, became a journalist, firstly on the local paper, and then eventually went over to Dublin to work in journalism. He also became a representative for a company that sold patent medicines. I understand from the newspaper obituary that I have, that he travelled not only to the Antipodes, but often to America. After retirement, he returned to live in Bridlington, and devoted himself to his favourite occupation of travelling the world.

It was on his return voyage to England on 25 April 1937, that he suffered a cerebral thrombosis and died; he was buried at sea. He was 68 years old. His death certificate states Lat 3.05 S, Long 6.22 E. off the west coast of Africa.

The Bridlington Free Press
Former Journalist Dies at Sea
MAN WHO CROSSED ATLANTIC 28 TIMES

The news reached his friends in Bridlington a few days ago of Mr. Marmaduke Peasgood, a one-time local journalist, who had lived in Bridlington since his retirement a few years ago.

Mr. Peasgood loved the sea and had made twenty-eight round trips to America. In 1934 he went on a Mediterranean trip with Mr. Neal and the late Mr. Hodgson, in 1935 he visited the West Indies, in 1936 he went to Australia with Mr F. Spink and Mr. Cockerill, and it was when on a voyage which embraced Africa, China, Japan, Singapore and Australia that he was taken ill. He was buried at sea on Sunday, April 25th.

A native of the East Riding who spent his boyhood days in Bridlington, Mr. Peasgood as a young man was with the "Bridlington and Quay Gazette" as a reporter and afterwards accepted a similar position in Ireland.

POPULARITY AT SEA

His British views and opinions often found him in difficult positions, and after a time he joined a business firm in Dublin and represented them as their foreign agent for twenty-five years, during which time he made 28 round trips to America. His varied experiences and good nature made him very popular wherever he went, and on many of his foreign trips he was elected chairman of the entertainments during the voyage.

During his 44 years' residence in Ireland he was several times ambushed and the shock of his experiences told their tale on his wife's health and she died some four years ago.

As a boy he was a member of the Priory choir, and on retiring and coming back to Bridlington he renewed many old friendships and made many new ones. On the Conservative Club and Westgate bowling greens he was a popular figure.

It is related of him that three or four years ago he attended a Christmas party. The King's speech had been broadcast and the National Anthem was being played. Mr. Peasgood stood up as if at a public gathering, remarking that he enjoyed the privilege of being able to do so after being denied it so long in Ireland.

****

From Captain Elford's family's collection of news clippings:
The Evening Times, Tuesday January 11, 1938

LINER AGROUND IN THE CLYDE
Early Morning Mishap at Dalmuir

NO PASSENGERS ON BOARD
Lying Clear of the Channel
STATED TO BE IN NO DANGER

AN 18,712-TON LINER, THE S.S. CERAMIC, GROUNDED OFF THE BEARDMORE LIGHT AT DALMUIR EARLY TO-DAY.

The vessel had been loading cargo in Glasgow, and was making for Liverpool when the mishap occurred.

There were no passengers on board, and it is understood that the vessel, which is not obstructing the passage of other ships in the river, is in no immediate danger.

Although the tide was on the ebb the vessel was fortunately so placed that she cleared the channel, and there was no danger of the traffic being held up on the river. In fact, shortly after she went aground a large Blue Funnel liner passed inward bound.

A river boatman informed "The Evening Times" that he did not think there was any likelihood of the vessel being in danger.

It was very unlikely, he said, that she would be swung across the river by the ebb tide.

"It will be necessary to wait for the next high tide early this afternoon to refloat her," he added, "the tide at the present being on the ebb."

Cruise Ship

The Ceramic is of 18,712 tons gross. A few years ago she was taken over from the White Star Line by Shaw, Savile (sic) and Albion, London. Lately she has been sailing between Liverpool and Glasgow, but during the summer months she has been used as a cruise ship.

Firmly Aground

Shortly after 10 o'clock the tide had fallen some 10ft., and it could be seen that the Ceramic was firmly aground about 50 yards from the north bank.

She was lying almost directly opposite the Beardmore Light, where the Queen Mary provided a few anxious moments when she sheered at practically the same point on her trip down the river from John Brown's yard.

An "Evening Times" representative who was on the scene shortly after the Ceramic went aground saw that the liner was lying with a definite list towards the south bank.

With the fall of the tide a large section of her hull below the Plimsoll mark had come into view and the liner appeared to be sitting high up in the water.

The Ceramic was flying "out of control" signals to warn other river shipping to give her a wide berth.

A red flag was placed at bow and stern, while suspended between the masts were two black balls, being the requisite signal to other vessels.

Large quantities of water were being ejected from the liner by her pumps at that time, and from the muddy colour of the water it seemed possible that several of her bottom plates may have been strained in the grounding.

Tug Standing By

The tug Flying Home was standing by, made fast to the liner, but otherwise there was little sign of activity. It was apparent that a period of waiting would ensue until the next high tide when an effort would be made to refloat her.

This probably will be a ticklish task owing to the deep draught of the liner, and also because of the position in which she has settled in the water.

The Ceramic is the longest vessel to ply up and down the river Clyde. She looked gigantic as the tide steadily fell and more of her hull came into view.

Her list was also made more apparent by her four high masts which pointed away at an angle from the north bank.

The point at which the grounding occurred is one of the most desolate on the river. On the north side is the now derelict Beardmore yard while the south bank of the river is low-lying pasture land on which grandstands were erected at the time of the sailing of the Queen Mary.

The grounding of the Ceramic to-day is the fourth mishap which has occurred on the river Clyde during the past eight days.

On Tuesday of last week the Donaldson liner Moveria collided with the Federal steamship Hertford near Dumbarton and late on Thursday night the Blue Star liner Fresno Star, inward bound for Glasgow, grounded near Garvel Point.

While canting prior to going to her loading berth the Harrison Line vessel Merchant hit the pier wall at Prince's Dock and badly damaged her stem as a result of which she had to be drydocked at Govan.

****

Chapter 6: The inter-war years

From Captain Elford's family's collection of news clippings:
(Australian newspaper; no date)

LINER CERAMIC IN DIFFICULTIES

CAUGHT IN SOUTHERLY WHILE BERTHING AT CRANES

Caught in a strong southerly blow while berthing at Nos. 12 and 13 electric cranes, the White Star liner Ceramic (19,000 tons) was in difficulties in the Basin this morning.

The vessel was blown round until it was feared that it might endanger the Mungana and the Kooliga, which were lying at adjacent berths. Fortunately the wind dropped and three tugs were able to bring the vessel alongside the wharf again after an anxious three-quarters of an hour.

Shortly after 10.30 a.m. the Ceramic left No. 1 Lee Wharf *(Newcastle, NSW)*, where she had been loading a cargo of primary produce, for nos. 12 and 13 cranes, accompanied by the tugs Heroine and St. Hilary.

The two bow-lines had been made fast to the wharf when a very strong southerly wind caught the Ceramic and turned it on its bows. The forward anchors were dropped immediately and the tug Heroine endeavoured to pull the vessel round with the St. Hilary pushing the Ceramic on the starboard side.

The vessel continued to swing and had gone within about 100 yards of the Mungana when the wind dropped slightly. The Ceramic then whistled for assistance and was joined shortly afterwards by the tug Aristol, which had been assisting the Mareeba to berth at the Dolphins.

With the Heroine pulling and the St. Hilary and Aristol pushing the vessel round, it eventually began to swing back and was made fast to the wharf about 11.30 a.m.

This is the second occasion in recent weeks on which a vessel has been in difficulties in the harbor. The Nestor was caught in a similar position two or three weeks ago.

The Ceramic will load 3000 tons of bunkers at the cranes and is due to leave for Sydney to-morrow night.

****

From Captain Elford's family's collection of news clippings: (Australian newspaper; no date)

Extensive damage was caused to a ship in Fremantle Harbour yesterday afternoon when the mainmast bent during unloading operations after a stay wire had broken on the port side. The mast fell across the bridge.

FOUR GREAT OVERSEAS LINERS of a total tonnage of 83,529 tons, berthed at Station Pier, Port Melbourne, made this striking picture from the Herald plane today. The ships are the Ceramic (lower left), 18,713 tons, inward bound from South Africa; the Orion (upper left), 23,371 tons, outward bound for London, the Mariposa (lower right), 18,017 tons, from San Francisco; and the Strathmore (upper right), 23,428 tons, inward bound from London.

148

SS CERAMIC The Untold Story

A selection of inter-war souvenirs from the Ceramic.

Betty Hipwell, letter to the author 3 April 2000.

I have had three trips on the Ceramic - the first in 1926 of which I have no recollection as I turned three on the trip home. I possess a serviette ring which I used during the thirties, with the White Star Line badge in it and "RMS Ceramic" written across the top.

In 1938, my mother took my brother and me to England to visit my grandmother and aunt in Hove. (My mother was a war bride from WW1). I have quite a few small black and white photographs taken of activities on deck - quoits, deck tennis, the canvas swimming pool etc, also snaps of Mr Ferries (Engineer), the Purser, J. Paine 1st Officer, G. Stanger 4th Officer and ... Cresswell 2nd Officer. I am taking the rankings from captions under the photos.

I remember the knock out competitions that were held on the deck: Deck Golf, Deck Tennis, Quoits etc. The canvas swimming pool was erected as we got into warmer weather. I was very keen on swimming at that time and not much distance could be swum without having to turn.

I also have 2 faded menus headed "Dinner Au Revoir" dated Tuesday, May 3 1938 and Monday, September 12 1938. They have etchings of the Tower of London on the front.

I celebrated my fifteenth birthday on the way home.

My mother liked the "Ceramic" because it was one class. I remember it had a long deck which was good for walking, I forget how many times around the deck made a mile. I also remember the salt baths with a board across the bath with a basin of fresh water on it to rinse in.

I can still recall the lovely smell of apples which were loaded on the ship at Hobart.

The trip took about six weeks from Sydney to Southampton – 1 week to Perth, 2 weeks to Durban, around to Capetown, 2 weeks Capetown to Tenerife then to England.

I have happy memories of a lovely trip.

Chapter 6: The inter-war years

Life on board the Ceramic, September/October 1938

Reproduced by kind permission of Betty Hipwell; captioned as album.

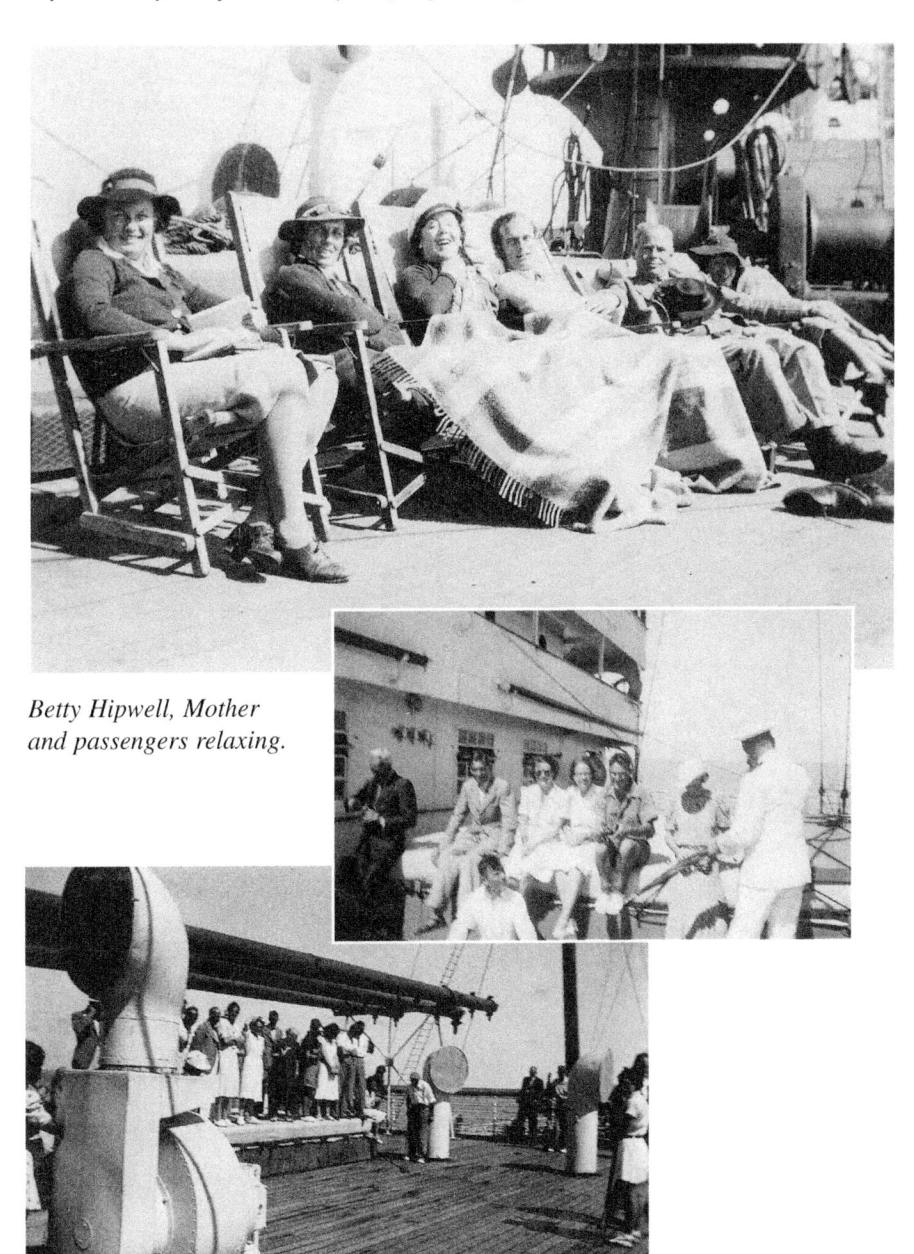

Betty Hipwell, Mother and passengers relaxing.

151

SS CERAMIC The Untold Story

Above: Potato Race.
Below: Deck Tennis Court.

Above: Peg Quoits.
Below: Spectators at the Sports.

The Swimming Pool.

152

Chapter 6: The inter-war years

Fancy Dress

Below:
Gordon Smith
as Don Bradman.

Above: Betty Hipwell (née Smith) as Dairy Maid, with Ceramic Cow.

Lifeboat Practice

153

SS CERAMIC The Untold Story

The Crew

The Purser.

J. Paine 1st Officer
Miss O'Connell
G. Stanger 4th Officer.

2nd Officer Crasswell

Mr Ferries.

Chapter 6: The inter-war years

Around the Ship

*Boat Deck Golf Course
Starboard Side*

The After Deck

The Bridge

DINER AU REVOIR

Grape Fruit, Oporto
Hors d'oeuvre (variés)
Consommé Tosca
Cream of Celery
Fillets of King Klip en Souchet
Asparagus, Hollandaise
Prime Ribs & Sirloin of Beef, York Fritters
Roast Norfolk Turkey Poult, Financière
Baked York Ham & Spinach
French Beans
Tomatoes, Française
Patna Rice
Browned and Boiled New Potatoes
Braised Ptarmigan, Bread Sauce, Game Chips

Cold Buffet

Derby Round of Beef
Corned Ox Tongue
Salade Fermière
Fedora Pudding
Strawberry Flan
Coupe Alexandria
Dessert

T.S.S. "Ceramic" Tuesday, May 3. 1938

DINER AU REVOIR

Caviar sur Croûtes
Hors d'oeuvre (variés)
Clear Green Turtle
Crème d'Asperges
Tay Salmon, Cucumber, Parsley Sauce
Fillets of Sole, Orly
Calf's Sweetbreads, St. Manan
Chicken en Casserole, au Garniture
Scotch Prime Ribs & Sirloin of Beef, Horseradish
French Beans
Corn on the Cob
Patna Rice
Browned and Boiled Potatoes
Roast New Season Grouse, Bread Sauce, Game Chips
Salade Jockey Club
Caramel Pudding
Cherry Flans
Pears, Sabayon
Dessert

T.S.S. "Ceramic" Monday, September 12. 1938

SS CERAMIC The Untold Story

Part Two

1939-1942

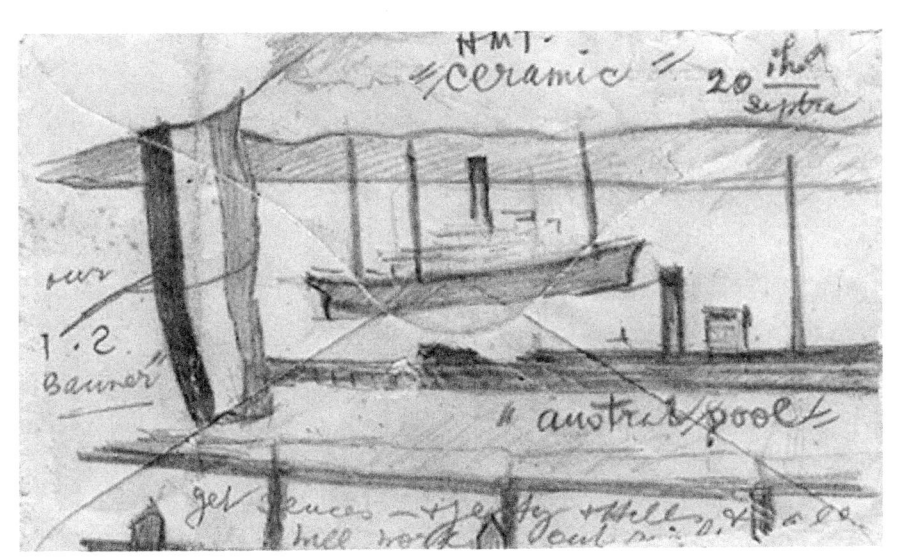

Sketch from the collection of Second Engineer George Churchill Simmons who died at sea in 1940. Courtesy of George Anderson.

Chapter 7
War breaks out again

Michael Towey (father) and Michael Towey (son).

*Children of the Blitz
Robert Westall.*

Courtesy of Mickey Towey.

FATHER AND SON

I left school in 1939. It was late August. The *SS Ceramic* was about to sail from Gladstone Dock. I had to deliver a parcel to my father who was a stoker. I was about to go home when I heard they were looking for a deck-boy. The bosun asked me, and I went there and then, little realising a Great War was looming over us.

Before we reached our first port, Tenerife, we got a message from the Admiralty for all ships to meet at Sierra Leone.

Later, as we left Australia we heard from the wireless that the *Doric Star* had been sunk and we were ordered to pick up survivors.

The *Graf Spee* spotted us, and chased us through the Indian Ocean. But we escaped and joined the convoy at Sierra Leone for the journey home.

We had just reached Africa and on deck I saw these two ladies staring at a wrecked lifeboat. One of the ladies was a stewardess. She said to the other lady, "Let's go and pray in your cabin." I watched them slowly walk away and I never saw them again. I gathered it was somebody she knew.

We were the first convoy of the war at Liverpool, arriving January 1940, about three weeks overdue.

Father kept me at home, saying I was too young for such hazards. I should have sailed on the ship my father lost his life on. He kept going and finally lost his life in December 1942.

Boy, aged fourteen, Liverpool

Doric Star (Blue Star Line) was sunk south of St Helena on 2 Dec 1939 by Graf Spee, which also sank Tairoa (Shaw Savill) next day – both ships Australia to UK.

Chapter 7: War breaks out again

Sea Breezes Vol. 61 No. 502 October 1987.

A VOYAGE TO REMEMBER

When the late Charles Wigglesworth joined the "Ceramic" as second steward in July, 1940, he started a journal, in the form of a letter home, in which he recorded the hopes and fears of a man caught up in events over which he had no control and of which he had little knowledge.

The letter was found recently among the papers of Mr Wigglesworth's stepdaughter, Miss Elsie Arthur, and we are grateful to Miss Arthur for her permission to publish it. Apart from minor editing and the deletion of entirely personal matters it is exactly as Mr Wigglesworth wrote it.

****

Australia and Back, via the West Indies by CHARLES WIGGLESWORTH

I am writing these few lines endeavouring to give a brief outline of our voyage which started on July 20 (1940). I left home on Thursday morning, July 18. It had been my intention to stay at home instead of making the trip but as the voyage would in all probability only take between three and four months I decided to come away in the hope of being back in Liverpool by the beginning of November, when I would settle down for the winter.

I had no idea that we would have to join the ship the morning I left but as soon as we got on board we left the dock and took our place in the river. Everything was kept secret. About 4pm the same day the tender came alongside and we embarked 280 people, mostly women and children for South Africa and Australia. There were all kinds; educated Jews, nurses and some good English types.

In the river besides ourselves were about 56 ships all waiting to go out in convoy. We did not know when we were due to sail but suddenly, on Saturday 20th, there was some excitement as we and the remainder of the ships started to move slowly out of the harbour. We were rather a large convoy to be in the charge of two destroyers.

We began to get settled down, sorting out the children of whom there were about 90. I could see that we were going to have the time of our lives. I have never sailed with so many, but what fine kids they were. The children and nurses were at the first sitting for meals and the adults the second, which kept us very much occupied.

It made a truly wonderful sight to look out over the convoy and see so many ships. Two days out we passed a convoy bound for Liverpool of about the same number, which made for a total of some 112 ships together at one time. Marvellous! The destroyers left us then and we all gradually separated. It was then that our voyage proper really started. For the next seven days we had to be on the lookout as the area we were in was designated as a danger zone.

The passengers had their usual boat drill and wore their lifejackets always. There was complete blackout and very strict rules about parading the deck after dark. We had a mixed crowd, some very well educated, some opera stars and all nationalities but they were all the same financially, only being allowed £10 with which to leave the country. The idea of this was that on arrival at their port of destination they would receive their money in local currency.

When we finally cleared the danger zone things began to brighten up a bit with concerts and children's parties. I was having a great time with the kids and thought often how nice it would be if only you and the children were going to a place of safety.

I forgot to say that when we left the dock for the river and then subsequently cleared Liverpool all communication with the shore ceased, for private messages that is, so it was impossible to get a wire away. We ourselves did not have any trouble during the voyage but ships both ahead and astern of us were being chased and torpedoed.

The time passed very quickly and we were going quite nicely on our way to Cape Town where we were supposed to arrive on Tuesday, August 13. As usual the Saturday before making port we had a concert which was very good indeed and everyone had a good time. When it was over and we had squared things up it was close on midnight. As it was such a nice night but rather dark I went on deck for a breath of fresh air before going to bed. When I went below I had a talk with my mate. He commented on the fact that we were nearly at the end of the first leg of the voyage and were practically safe from surface raiders and submarines.

About 2.30am on Sunday morning, August 11, we were almost thrown out of our bunks by a terrific crash which seemed to come from a little ahead of our room. Dazed for the moment and the light being out I could not make out what had happened. I told my mate that we had probably been hit and we had best get the hell out of it as soon as possible, so we put on our lifejackets and made our way up the main companionway to the lounge where all the passengers were huddled together in all kinds of dress.

I could not make it out as generally when a ship gets hit all the lights go out, but all our lights kept burning. I had a look round and went below again to the

Chapter 7: War breaks out again

purser's office where I assisted a few children with their lifejackets. Considering all things there was no panic.

Shortly afterwards, word came down from the bridge that we had been in collision but it was not thought to be too serious. The captain advised the passengers to get dressed and go to their rooms but to keep handy in case anything else happened. The time then would be about 3.45am but everybody dashed round with cups of tea and took things easy. In the meantime radio messages were sent out for assistance and the weather was very fine, which was in our favour.

Daylight came and we went out on deck to see what kind of a ship had struck us. She was a ship named the Testbank, about 9,000 tons. She had suffered severely and had all her bows stove in but fortunately, like ourselves, there were no casualties. The usual morning's work followed and breakfast was served at the usual time. About 10am the first of the ships appeared on the scene followed shortly by two more which stood by us. We then got word that HMS Cumberland was steaming towards us at full speed and would be with us about two o'clock.

Everybody was calm but serious but we had a large hole forward with water coming through all the time. Right on time HMS Cumberland arrived and after a consultation on board it was decided to transfer the passengers and stewardesses to the cruiser.

They started getting the boats down to the water and about 20 of the cruiser's crew came aboard which helped us considerably. Just as the first boatload was about to start a large P&O liner came towards us. She proved to be the Viceroy of India, outward bound from Liverpool, and being much more suitable for passengers the captain of the cruiser, who had taken command, gave orders to transfer the passengers to the liner.

The last boatload left the ship about 7.30 and the Viceroy of India then continued on her voyage to Cape Town. The baggage was left behind, of course, just allowing the passengers the bare essentials. It was a definite relief to get rid of them as we were way out in the Atlantic where a gale could spring up at any time. The cruiser tried to tow us next morning but it was not a success as we were loaded with heavy, valuable cargo. The forward end of No 1 hatch was where we were hit and the water poured in and the pumps could just about hold their own.

The sea then began to get up so the master and mate decided to jettison some of the cargo in an effort to lighten her. It was heartbreaking to see such good stuff go over the side, big bales of linoleum, crates of best china, lots of useful material.

The ships which had been standing by in case they were needed now left us leaving just the cruiser to escort us. We then started to steam to the nearest port which was Walvis Bay and fortunately the weather moderated and remained calm. After three days the cruiser left us as we were only a few hours away from Walvis Bay, which proved to be a desolate, God-forsaken sort of place. We finally anchored in the bay on August 15. It was a small whaling station but there was little to see but sand.

We eventually got settled down and shortly afterwards a Lloyd's surveyor came aboard and pending his survey we more or less resigned ourselves to our fate. Large lighters next came alongside to take off the baggage which was being sent by train to Cape Town, a journey which took four days longer than it would have taken by sea ...

****

The Times, Wednesday August 14 1940

BRITISH LINER DAMAGED IN COLLISION
NO CASUALTIES

It is officially announced from Capetown (States Reuter) that during the week-end the British liner Ceramic (18,713 tons) and the cargo steamer Testbank (5,083 tons) came into collision in the South Atlantic. Both suffered some damage, but are proceeding to harbour.

Within a few hours of the collision other ships arrived to render assistance if necessary, and as a precautionary measure all passengers in the Ceramic were safely transferred to another liner which was standing by. The weather was calm and there were no casualties in either vessel.

****

The Sydney Morning Herald. Wednesday August 14, 1940.

COLLISION IN ATLANTIC.
Children for Australia at Capetown.
CAPETOWN. Aug.13th (A A P)

Ninety refugee children on their way to Australia have landed in Capetown. They were passengers in the liner Ceramic which collided in dense fog with another vessel in the South Atlantic. There were no casualties and the Ceramic passengers were transferred to the liner which responded to a call. The arrival of the children was unexpected but merchants supplied beds and food, and the Governor's residence at Westbrook was equipped in a few hours to accommodate all the children.

****

Narelle O'Rourke, biography of Nurse Simone Alpen, passenger on the Ceramic.

... Following the family's reunion in England, Mr Alpen, junr., expressed a wish to join the Australian army and the family decided to sail for Australia, where Mr. Alpen had formerly resided – his family lived in Sydney for some years, and he was educated at Riverview and St Joseph's College, Hunter's Hill - but even then they were still adventure bound.

On leaving England in a convoy, which at one stage contained at least 90 boats, the travellers were prepared for U-boat threats and other perils of wartime sea voyages.

Accordingly, they were not unduly perturbed when, after leaving the convoy, they felt something deal their ship a staggering blow during a blackout. It was discovered that the ship had been involved in a mid-ocean collision with a freighter. The latter came off best, as a gaping hole, 20ft by 40ft, had been torn in the liner's side.

To keep the hole above water level, cars and other heavy cargo were pushed into the sea, but it was eventually found necessary to transfer the passengers to another boat.

Both the freighter and the disabled liner, however, later managed to reach a Dominion port.

****

... I was interested about the Viceroy of India rescuing the passengers from the Ceramic as amongst Nurse Simone Alpen's memorabilia is a badge in the shape of a ship's wheel with the ship's flag RMS Viceroy of India engraved on it. It was obviously acquired at this time.

Also a British cruiser, HMS Cumberland came to the passengers' rescue as well as the Viceroy of India, near South Africa.

Narelle O'Rourke

Memoir of Mrs K Stapledon
Imperial War Museum, London
Reproduced by kind permission of Stanley Saunders

... It does not seem possible that only two years have elapsed since Steepy and I were the envy of all our friends in Portsmouth, leaving England and returning to Singapore after eight months leave. I nicknamed by husband Steepy when I first met him, when I was eighteen. Although there is no rhyme or reason for it, simply a mix-up over his surname, the name has stuck, rather to his chagrin. He is a Naval Architect in the Malayan Government Service.

All our goodbyes over, we left Euston Station on July 20th 1940 in a very crowded train for Liverpool, where we had been told to embark. When we reached the ship we found she was the Empress of India and that she was carrying troops to the East. There were several young Army Nurses and Officers travelling with us and it looked promising for a cheery passage.

The journey out was exciting in itself to us, as previously we had always gone East through the Suez Canal and now for the first time we were going round the Cape, which we were greatly looking forward to seeing.

The first two days at sea we were escorted by destroyers, but as out speed was over 18 knots, it was considered safe for us to continue our journey alone. We carried life jackets all the time and at night had warm clothes ready to put on at a moment's notice. At first we were all rather nervous, but after a few days we started to settle down to the usual shipboard life and got deck games organised.

It was rather a shock to hear that our first port of call was to be Gibraltar, to drop some Naval passengers, and these uneasy feelings were fully justified because we arrived there late at night when a heavy raid was in progress and as we lay off the harbour we could see the bombs dropping on the Rock. However, we were not attacked at all and the next morning the passengers got off very early and we put to sea at once.

After leaving we were all very keen to know where we should call next. We were told eventually that it would be St. Vincent, which turned out to be the largest of a group of small islands, off the West Coast of Africa. Viewed from the ship it looked extremely dried up and barren but we were not allowed ashore to see for ourselves. However, the Europeans living there were invited to a dance. This was

Chapter 7: War breaks out again

the first time we were allowed any lights at all on deck, and we all thoroughly enjoyed dancing in the moonlight.

We lay off there for two days in a sticky heat and were overjoyed to get under way again and into the cool sea breezes. The days passed quickly with deck games and tournaments to fill the fine days and chess and bridge to occupy us when it was wet. This peaceful life continued till we reached the South Atlantic, then one Sunday morning after Church, we noticed our ship was turning round and going in the opposite direction, and getting up speed. At first we thought we were being chased by an enemy submarine but the news quickly got round that we were going to the assistance of a large ship in distress.

Great activity was taking place on board, the stewards completely cleared the smoking room of all furniture so that mattresses could be laid for the passengers we expected to pick up. All the married couples had, up till now, single cabins with a connecting door, so the husbands decided to double up with their wives and sleep on a mattress on the floor. This left plenty of empty cabins.

In an amazingly short time the ship was ready to receive the survivors. The Army Nursing Sisters were standing by to give any assistance necessary, when at five thirty in the evening we arrived at the scene of the disaster. We were greatly cheered to find one of our warships standing by the distressed ship, because anything stationary at sea in war time seems to be a sitting target.

We got there in record time doing twenty one knots all the way and found there had been a collision between the British freighter "Testbank" (5083 tons) and the "Ceramic", an 18,713 ton liner carrying 279 passengers and crew. This number included ninety English school children who were being sent to Australia to escape the bombing, only to meet with misfortune at sea. The collision had taken place at two o'clock on the Sunday morning and the "Ceramic" had a hole in her starboard big enough for two buses to pass through. Although the "Testbank" was badly damaged we could see her in the distance making for port.

The "Ceramic" passengers had had an anxious time during the fourteen hours aboard the heavily listing ship, feeling her gradually sinking lower by the head under their very feet. The warship had arrived at five o'clock and the passengers had been ordered to board her as it was thought that our ship would not arrive in time. However, we got there at six and the passengers were then told to board us instead. There was a considerable swell running so oil was poured down on the water and they all got aboard without mishap. The first lifeboat to arrive was full of very green looking women and children who had been in it for about four hours and had been right over to the side of the warship first. They had only been allowed to take small suitcases but even so were better off than all the rest who had to leave the ship quickly to reach us before nightfall and had to leave everything behind. It took three hours to get the passengers and part of the crew on board, and we were told that several of her crew had stayed in the "Ceramic" as it was hoped that she would be towed into port as soon as the weather steadied down.

They were all given hot coffee and we did our best to make them as comfortable as possible. No one had been killed or injured in the collision and apart from fright and the discomfort of an open boat, they were none the worse for their adventure. The children particularly were very brave and behaved splendidly, very few of them were with their mothers, most of them being in the care of friends or relations.

We moved off at nine o'clock and at first the new passengers did not realise that the "Empress of India" (sic) had already over a thousand aboard; they thought she was only half full and started making fantastic demands. One old lady asked if she could choose her cabin and was quite staggered when the steward answered rather drily, "Certainly, madam, stake your claim on the smoke room floor." Fortunately, in the end there were enough bunks for all. There was one bride-to-be who was very agitated because she had lost all her wedding presents and trousseau and at that time there was some doubt as to whether the ship could be towed into port next day. When they realised that we had all put ourselves out, and moved around to make them comfortable, they quickly changed their attitude and were extremely grateful for the assistance they had been given. A letter was posted on the notice board on behalf of them all, thanking the Captain, Staff and passengers for the kindness with which they had been greeted.

When we got to Cape Town two days afterwards over 1000 of the residents waited at the docks for the passengers to disembark. Many of these passengers had no money but most of them had at least warm clothes. The "Ceramic's" Cape Town Agents arranged for them to pass the immigration authorities without passports and accommodated them in hotels where they remained waiting for a ship to take them on.

They were overjoyed to hear later that their ship had made port safely. We only spent one day there ourselves but in that short time enjoyed ourselves enormously, touring the town in a hired car and seeing all the places of interest. It was a great disappointment to us all to find that instead of calling next at Durban, we were going straight on to Mombasa. However, when we got there we found it was a quaint and interesting little place, a curious mixture of the primitive and the very modern. The swimming pool was delightful and there was a fine golf course and a good, comfortable hotel. Most of the Indian business men who had settled there had gone back to India after the outbreak of war. We were only there for about twelve hours and realised that as Bombay was to be our next port of call, it would be some time before we reached Singapore...

Chapter 7: War breaks out again

Collision with the 'Testbank'
Courtesy of G. Landry

Right: The hole in the *Ceramic*'s hull made in collision with the *Testbank*. Water being pumped out.

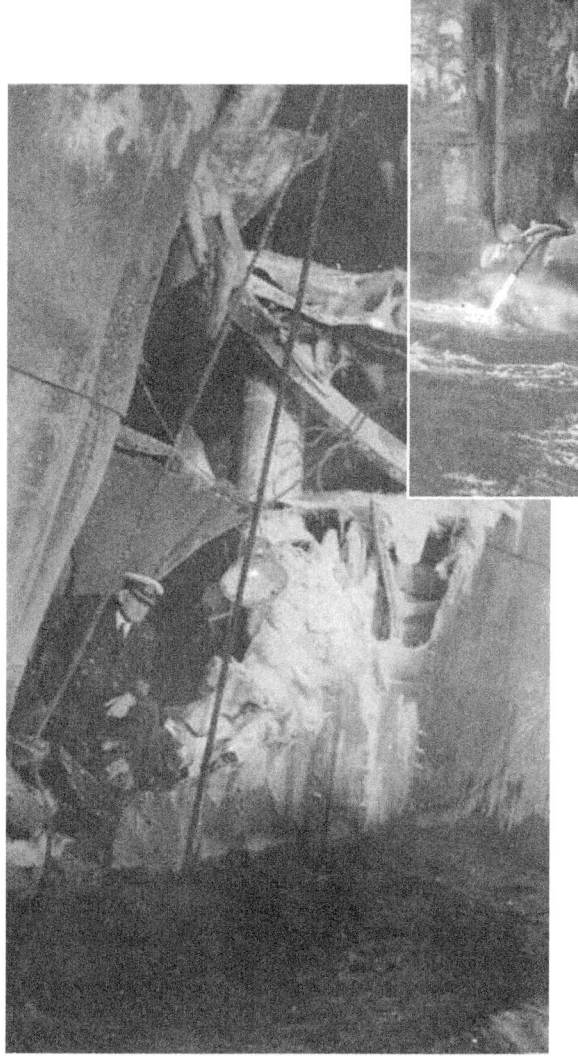

Left: The Captain surveys the damage, inches above the waterline.

Collision with the 'Testbank'
Courtesy of G. Landry

Passengers are transferred from the *Ceramic* to the *Viceroy of India*.

Chapter 7: War breaks out again

Collision with the 'Testbank'
Sunday 11th August 1940

The images in this section are reproduced by kind permission of the Iziko Museum of South Africa. Copyright: John H. Marsh Maritime Collection, SA Maritime Museum.

August 1940 At Walvis Bay. Bow end of the *Ceramic*, showing damage sustained in collision with the *Testbank*.

169

August 15 1940
Testbank arriving at Cape Town with bow squashed flat for about 20 feet after collision at sea with passenger liner *Ceramic*. Tug *John X. Merriman* assisting her.

Copyright: John H. Marsh Maritime Collection, SA Maritime Museum.

Chapter 7: War breaks out again

August 26 1940
After start made on removing crumpled plating from flattened bow and with *Harmonic* (freighter) double-banked alongside her. *Harmonic*'s derricks being used to tranship cargo from *Testbank*.

September 6 1940
With *Harmonic* still alongside and shore cranes helping to empty *Testbank* of cargo. Further progress on stripping twisted metal from *Testbank*'s crushed bow.

Copyright: John H. Marsh Maritime Collection, SA Maritime Museum.

171

SS CERAMIC The Untold Story

October 10 1940 Double-banked alongside *Ceramic*, with which she had collided more than 1000 miles distant 2 months earlier and which had now also reached Cape Town to be repaired. *Testbank*'s bow now fully opened up.

Copyright: John H. Marsh Maritime Collection, SA Maritime Museum.

Chapter 7: War breaks out again

October 10 1940 *Ceramic* at Cape Town being repaired.

Copyright: John H. Marsh Maritime Collection, SA Maritime Museum.

October 10 1940
Testbank being moved to dry-dock with bow still opened up. Tug *J.W. Sauer* assisting her.

November 12 1940
Shows new frames closing up bow end.

October 11 1940
Testbank in dry-dock showing cut away bow section.

February 18 1941
Finishing repairs to bow, freighter *Estrella* alongside her.

Copyright: John H. Marsh Maritime Collection, SA Maritime Museum.

Sea Breezes Vol. 61 No. 502 October 1987.
A VOYAGE TO REMEMBER

Australia and Back, via the West Indies by CHARLES WIGGLESWORTH
(continued)

... Five weeks we lay there and as nobody was allowed ashore it became very monotonous, in fact the only company we had was the crowd of Norwegian fitters who came out each day to patch the ship up sufficient for her to get to Cape Town.

After we had been in Walvis Bay about a month word came through that the Themistocles was going to carry our passengers but as she had left Liverpool with only 12 men aboard we had to send 15 men to Cape Town by rail to prepare the ship. Everything went off all right and on September 24 we gratefully sailed for Cape Town, arriving there on the evening of the 27th. On arrival we had to send an extra 22 stewards and stewardesses to the Themistocles who took two-thirds of our passengers along with all those who had been waiting in Cape Town for a suitable ship to carry them to Australia.

In the meantime I sent a cable to you on August 16 which, according to your letter, you received. It was rather a trying time not being able to get home and not knowing just what was happening to the ship. Quite a few of our sailors and firemen deserted the ship, some I believe on the Empress of Britain, but what became of them I don't know. Some stowed away on the Franconia but were discovered and got six months jail.

There was plenty of excitement while we lay in Cape Town being repaired and the sight of such famous ships made us all feel that we were part of the living world again. There was the Queen Mary, Mauretania, Duchess of Bedford, Dominion Monarch, Aquitania, Andes and the Queen Elizabeth. I got in touch with quite a few of the men who were heartily fed up as they were taking troops to Mombasa which has a terrible climate and is infernally hot.

Without being able to go into a drydock the repairs were rather limited but apparently a drydock was available in Durban so we sailed for there and were told that following this we would be going to Australia. We had lost so many of the crew by now that we had had to send home for replacements and they were due to arrive at Durban on December 20. We got there on the 14th and went immediately into drydock.

As it turned out there was not much to be done and after a few days strengthening us up we left Durban on December 23 for Fremantle. On the 18th I went to the post office and wired you £9 and on the 20th cabled Christmas greetings to you.

As I said, we left Durban on the 23rd carrying a few officials and a Royal Navy captain. It seemed strange to be at sea again, strict watches and the usual blackout until we got away from the South African coast as parts of South Africa are full of fifth columnists and very treacherous to shipping. It was they without a doubt who were responsible for the sinking of the Empress of Britain.

We had Christmas Day at sea two days after leaving the Cape and made the best of things but it was very quiet. I was in my room by nine o'clock thinking about you at home on this day of all days, wondering if you were left in peace to enjoy a quiet day all together.

There was nothing of importance happened on the way across to Fremantle, arriving there on January 5, but we had news that there were ships being shelled and sunk by raiders before we got to Fremantle.

We left there for Adelaide on the 6th with extra watches and a strict lookout being maintained at all times. After 24 hours we had a radio message that a ship was being chased by a raider some 80 or 90 miles astern of us. A further message came through at midnight that she was steaming full speed in our direction. With that we turned round and made for a place named Albany which we had just passed. All hands were up and double watches were kept in the engine-room and we all heaved a sigh of relief when we got into harbour about 2.30am.

At daybreak scouter planes went out and returned at 10am when they gave us the all-clear, which made us a day late getting into Adelaide, arriving Saturday, January 11. We left there the next day, arriving Melbourne on the 14th. Again, a one-day stay and finally arrived Sydney on the 17th.

We were all advised before we arrived in Sydney that we would be there for four days and then a further four days in Newcastle bunkering under the coal tips. After that it would be to Melbourne to pick up a shipload of naval ratings for the UK. That was soon changed, however. We heard that it had been the intention to complete our repairs in drydock at Liverpool but word came from the Admiralty that all repairs had to be carried out in Australia.

I can tell you it was bad news to all hands and everyone was fed up. Still, that couldn't be helped so we left Newcastle and went round to drydock in Sydney. They intended to keep us busy so they drafted on board a large number of armed soldiers guarding the power stations, bridges and the dockyard stores.

During our stay in Sydney all the large ships arrived, the Queen Mary, Queen Elizabeth, Aquitania and others. They had been carrying troops to the Middle East but the last two voyages had been to Singapore, strengthening their defences. We

Chapter 7: War breaks out again

heard while in Sydney that the inquiry regarding our collision had been held in Cape Town, with the verdict going against us. It was a great pity that I did not get the Themistocles as she arrived in England about February 7, safe.

Today is February 27 and we are waiting patiently to leave here. When we do leave we shall be full of sailors, some of De Gaulle's Free French and members of ships' crews that were mined or shelled on the Australian coast. I'm afraid that it looks like being almost the end of May before we'll be arriving home.

We sailed from Sydney on March 20. We had no stewards on board to cope with the crowd we had, so we got 50 men from a ship that had been shelled and sunk by one of the raiders. They were volunteers and could not be signed on as crew because after being taken prisoner they were granted their freedom after signing that they would not take arms against Germany. We have a lot of sailors for England and a lot of young men of the Air Force going into training in Rhodesia and a good many of the crews of different ships sunk by raiders.

We had no difficulty or trouble for the remainder of our stay in Australia and left Fremantle for Durban about April 4. We had a very cold and stormy passage as we had to go on a different course way down in southern latitudes. We all felt better on reaching Durban for the first lap of the long voyage home. We left Durban for Cape Town on April 25, arriving two days later after an uneventful passage.

Finally we cleared Cape Town for home on May 2 going a very long way round, in fact I believe we are going to Halifax to pick up a convoy. Since leaving the Cape we have been on the alert with double watches on the guns. We have a very valuable cargo on board and it would be a tragedy if anything happened.

On May 7 we were met by the armoured cruiser Alcantara who gave us our position and now apparently we are bound for the West Indies. On May 8 we heard that ahead of us the City of Shanghai and the City of Winchester had been torpedoed but another "City" boat got away. Well, that really put the wind up us. The next day we were in touch with a ship who asked us to keep watch for a couple of boats with survivors on board, but though we were on the alert day and night we had no success.

I cannot explain to you just how we all feel, day after day going further into the unknown. I can fully understand what you are all going through at home but honestly I would much prefer to be with you. As I write we are steaming up the Brazilian coast but exactly where to I couldn't say. This is May 15, 10 months since we left Liverpool. Every day will count now.

I am taking things pretty easy now as we have no passengers, only seamen and crews we have picked up from other ships. Listening to the radio we heard about Liverpool being bombed for seven nights in succession and we are all anxious as to just what damage has been done. It is very strange to us, the way we are coming home half way round the world.

We were making for Greenland when we heard of the fate of HMS Hood, what a tragedy. We had to veer away and head for the Hebrides. We have had treble watches on deck but as we have plenty of sailors on board we are able to manage. We have had very heavy and stormy weather. It was a trying time and there would have been little chance for us if anything had happened, but our luck seems to be holding out. We have come all the way from Cape Town on our own, only meeting one ship the whole time until today, Tuesday, the 27th, when we were met by a light cruiser who accompanied us for a while.

As I write now we are making for the bar lightship, expecting to arrive there about four o'clock on Wednesday morning, thus completing our voyage and my longest yet, 10 months and 13 days. It seems like a long, drawn-out nightmare and we are all anxiously waiting for the time to dock and get ashore, to sort of wake up to the reality of living so to speak.

To finish up on a bizarre note, we buried two of our crew a few hours ago. They died this morning within a couple of hours of each other. I don't know if you will ever read this and it doesn't really matter anyway as I shall be seeing you very soon but it may well be of interest to glance through in later years when the war is over and all these things which have so dominated our lives are but memories.

****

Robert Turner
Email to Frank McCormick 19 June 2001

My grandfather, Nathan Redvers Turner ABS, died aboard the Ceramic when casting off in Melbourne Australia in September 1941.

He often told stories of the ship chasing/hunting a U Boat in the Atlantic and sinking it with a shot from the bow gun. Then the ship limped into Rio de Janerio almost out of all supplies.

He also told of a photo that is now lost, but which was in an African newspaper showing a gaping hole in the bow of Ceramic - he was stood in this hole. It was apparently from a collision with the freighter Testbank.

Chapter 7: War breaks out again

Also have the correspondence from SS&A notifying of death. Plus a letter pencil written which arrived about 6 weeks after his death, written as though alive and looking forward to seeing his wife and kids again.

****

Right: Picture and account submitted to the press by Mr Jeffery F. Ibbetson, Engineer on the Ceramic when the collision with the Testbank took place. Mr Ibbetson left the Ceramic just before her final voyage.

The Andrew Weir (Bank Line) vessel Testbank was lost due to enemy action at Bari, Italy on 2nd December, 1943.

Seaman twice cheated death

THIS hitherto unpublished picture shows the gaping bow hole in RMS Ceramic, after she was in collision with the SS Testbank (5,038 tons) off the West African coast on August 14th, 1940.

It belongs to Mr Jeffery F. Ibbotson, a marine engineer, formerly of Liverpool, and now living in Roseville, Sydney.

Jeff was serving with the Ceramic at that time when she was about 600 miles from Capetown, outward bound from the U.K. to Australia.

"She was carrying over 200 passengers including 90 children being evacuated from wartime Britain," he said.

Ceramic managed to make steerage way to Walvis Bay and, after makeshift repairs, she reached Capetown.

But a far worse fate awaited this 18,000-ton Shaw, Saville and Albion liner which sailed regularly from the Mersey.

She was torpedoed on December 6th, 1942, west of the Azores and sunk with the loss of more than 650 lives — all on board, in fact, except for one man, Sapper A. E. Munday of the Royal Engineers.

Mr Munday was picked up by the U.515, the submarine which sank Ceramic, and taken prisoner of war.

Mr Ibbotson bore a charmed life during the war at sea. He left the Ceramic just before this ill-fated voyage and also transferred from the armed merchantman, Jervis Bay, just before she made her brave and historic fight in an attempt to protect her convoy from the German pocket battleship Admiral Scheer.

Jeff retired from the sea in 1944 to become a boiler and pressure-vessel inspector in Australia where he has lived ever since.

He has been in Britain visiting relatives — his brothers Harry (Carlisle), Raymond (Baildon), Oswald (Knaresborough), and sister Kathleen in Dingle, Eire.

179

Chapter 8
Trooping begins

Phil Davenport
Personal Memoirs, extracts from chapter 10
letter to the author 25th April 2000

On Thursday 27 March 1941 we embarked from Melbourne on the "SS Ceramic". Next day the ship remained in Port Phillip Bay to swing the compass before putting to sea in the evening to take departure for Fremantle. The voyage across the Great Australian Bight took six days. The weather was never boisterous but the swells that rolled up from the Southern Ocean were huge. The ship's course was wide across the approaching monsters so that her time on each was more than if they came from directly ahead. Their passing was leisurely. Standing right aft on one side of the main deck, we could sight along its length and gaze, for seconds, down into green depths. Then slowly, to the lift of the next swell, the sea dropped below and we looked up to blue sky above. With the monotonous whirring of the nearby trailing log, the world seemed to be in slow motion. "Ceramic" arrived in Fremantle on Thursday morning. Twenty four hours later we were a long way out in the Indian Ocean.

The great circle track between Fremantle and Durban would have taken us down to the edge of the Roaring Forties. We may have gone even further south to keep us beyond the range of German raiders or U-boats. It was cold and during bad weather we sustained damage to the foredeck. Gangways, railings and a raft were torn adrift and lost overboard. The three services, airforce, navy and merchant navy, in turn, maintained continuous watches, from various stations around the ship. We wore greatcoats and scarves and pulled the flaps of our forage caps down over our ears. The ship's crew kept watch in the crow's nest, high up on the foremast. There, the ship's motion was exaggerated and the victim felt like a missile in a sling shot, and very cold.

In wartime, merchant ships were armed with a four inch gun, mounted at the stern, to deter pursuing submarines or raiders. These guns were maintained and fired by specialist naval gunners assigned to merchant ships. After about eight days at sea "Ceramic" reached its southernmost latitude and started to edge north into less boisterous weather. On a day of moderate conditions, a bright, orange-coloured target was dropped overboard and the gunner was able to fire several practice shells as it receded astern. The result would have been more encouraging to foes than they were comforting to friends.

Chapter 8: Trooping begins

"SS Ceramic" was a graceful passenger liner of the old breed. Built in 1913 — the next ship after the "Titanic" - by Harland and Wolff in Belfast, she was 655 feet long and had a tonnage of 18,495. For many years she was the largest passenger liner on the Australian run. Being slim, she shouldered aside less ocean to reach her service speed of fifteen knots. Her straight stem was plumb but with the subtle raking counter of her funnel and four tall masts, the unbroken line of her main deck and the rounded counter of her stern, she had a harmonious elegance that is missing from the thrusting bows and bulging high-rise of the cruise liners of today.

Twenty months after we disembarked from the "Ceramic" in Durban, she was sunk in the North Atlantic. On the night of 6 - 7 December 1942, she was unescorted on a voyage from Liverpool to Capetown when she was hit by three torpedoes from a German U-boat. She remained afloat for three hours and her complement of 656 persons, including 155 women and children, were all successfully transferred to lifeboats and rafts. In the morning, however, any hope was changed to despair. They were all scattered and sunk or overturned in a fierce winter gale. Only one man survived. He was hauled aboard the U-boat and became a prisoner of war until 1945, when he returned to the UK and told his story. In the meantime the fate of the ship and the people remained a mystery.

Before leaving England on that voyage, the captain of "Ceramic" had protested against taking women and children into the dangers of a North Atlantic winter. It was a period when U-boat wolf packs were operating with utmost savagery; when they came close to isolating and defeating Britain; a period that came to be called "The Battle of the Atlantic". Heading into severe weather and rough seas, "Ceramic" would have been unable to maintain her service speed of fifteen knots, let alone the minimum of seventeen knots necessary for evading U-boats. Nevertheless she was ordered to sea with all of those people on board, and 655 died.

Was the U-boat captain awarded an Iron Cross and did some Whitehall official retire with a knighthood?

During the war I developed a deep respect for the merchant navy. Their task of maintaining supply was crucial. They were in danger from the first shot and then, moment by moment, until the war ended. Whether they were running the gauntlet in a lone vessel or gathered into convoy, they could, in an instant, become a target for bombs, shells or torpedoes. When explosions and raging fires were added to the perils of the sea, the chances of survival were slim.

****

Walter Francis
letter to the author

THE CERAMIC, 1941.

We left Bradfield for an unknown ship in the harbour and as we cast off from the jetty in a lighter we saw an amazing sight. The *Mary* and the *Elizabeth* were both anchored in Sydney harbour. Disappointment was general when we bypassed both liners and pulled alongside a rusty old ship with *Ceramic* painted on the bow. The *Ceramic* was the largest ship ever to visit Sydney during the first world war but on our voyage carried the largest ever cargo of frozen food. As it turned out this was a luxury voyage which accommodated 200 first class passengers in peace time and on our voyage did just that. Each cabin had a typical obsequious English steward to make beds and clean up. The ship maintained a full time entertainment officer. Some of us had single cabins, I shared a three berther, but this was luxury the like of which we never encountered again in our travels. The voyage lasted ten weeks and life for this period was one long party; we were never bored. On the way we stopped on three occasions, Wellington, Panama and Halifax. We left Sydney with 80 Australian airmen, 100 British women and children on their way home for leave. In N. Z. we picked up about 20 of their aircrew just to balance up the sexes.

As it happened we were the first foreign troops to go to Wellington. The Government, Council and the population at large welcomed us in an incredibly warm manner. For the two weeks of our stay, special events were organised for us; a mayoral ball, a special train to take us to New Plymouth and other towns where we were billeted by families who again were very generous. We climbed Mt. Egmont and went to far too many receptions for us to really appreciate the depth of hospitality we were shown. When the party stopped and the we had to leave I experienced one of the most moving events of my life. More than half of the population of this city turned out and with them came massed bands who played The Maoris Farewell without pause for hours. No person either side of the growing water divide had a dry eye.

The trip to Panama was uneventful apart from ongoing entertainment organised by the crew and the passengers. We airmen manned two machine guns night and day and helped man one six inch gun mounted on the stern. Both weapons were virtually useless in the event of a submarine or raider attack but at the time we thought the job was sensible. The Panama crossing was uneventful apart from the fuss caused by the Kiwis in the twin towns of Colon and Christabel. Some of our Kiwi friends declared war on the German Embassy stealing their flag and damaging some property. The outcome resulted only in a change of dress; shore leave thereafter was in civvies for all future troops in transit. We sailed on up

Chapter 8: Trooping begins

through the Bermuda Triangle to Halifax, usually referred to as the a....... of Canada. It was mid winter with black ice covering all roads.

Shore leave for all brave enough, while a large convoy assembled for the Atlantic crossing. Gracie Fields was playing in town but the attraction of young female hostesses happy to support the war effort prevailed and most of us enjoyed the stopover. Eventually we sailed, 65 cargo ships escorted by 16 warships mostly American, although at this time America was not in the war. The weather was cold, grey and miserable; ships hooted often, almost continuously when fogs made collision a possibility. Convoys obviously travel at the speed of the slowest member while at the same time weaving continuously. It was thought that this would make it difficult for lurking U-boats to fire torpedoes accurately. After a week of such slow progress we ran into a storm described by our Captain afterwards, as the worst he had ever experienced in a lifetime of crossing the Atlantic. This happened at night and visibility was so poor and the likelihood of collision so great that all ships were ordered to put all lights on and then to disperse. It would have impossible for a sub to surface or to come to periscope depth, thus we were relatively safe. As had been agreed at the time of dispersal, we steamed back for two days to an agreed reassembly point to find only one other ship there. I never found out what happened to the other ships; the two of us went unescorted to England. Some idea of the storm ferocity can be judged from damage suffered by our ship. All forward rails were torn off or broken and the bow of the ship was dented quite noticeably. We were shadowed by a German F.W. four engine bomber off and on, but, no attacks were made; he was probably directing U-boats in our direction. A few nights before landing, I left my cabin for only a minute when I realised my wallet was left behind. On returning quickly I noticed the cabin steward leaving our cabin. There is no doubt that he took it, we collared him on deck one night, tied him up and then dunked him overboard in the icy Atlantic. He did not confess, I lost three months pay and went ashore broke. In today's currency about AU$ 8000. Liverpool on a cold grey morning looked vastly uninviting, but the prospect of getting safely ashore was appealing.

GREAT BRITAIN

The plan was to leave the ship early before breakfast but things went wrong and we left very late after no breakfast. An air raid interrupted our transportation to the holding camp with an unfortunate outcome, we also missed lunch. Dinner turned out to be welsh rarebit and rice custard. We entrained for London with the minimum of breakfasts, lunch was whatever we were able to buy from Naffi *(sic)* canteens on the railway stations where we stopped en route. On arrival in London my first priority was to send a telegram home asking for food parcels. Our early experience turned out to be a one off and thereafter I never suffered food shortages. The forces, particularly airmen were very well fed, not so the civilian population who were always severely rationed.

Harry Bastian
letter to the author

FROM AUSTRALIA TO ENGLAND
15TH OCTOBER 1941 - 21ST DECEMBER 1941

We must have left the land of our birth about the end of the first week in October 1941. Piled into buses at Bradfield, down the highway and over the bridge to man o'war steps. On the left in Athol Bight were the two Queens, Elizabeth and Mary, and as the ferries headed thataway, we thought you beauty!

Another let down, at the back of the Bight was an old four masted single funnel coal burning troopship of first war vintage, the *Ceramic*. Living in Newcastle all our tender years, she was well known to me in particular. Every trip out, the *Ceramic* had to come to Newcastle to coal and as Dad worked with the Navigation Department, we were always somewhere near. Finished up in a three bunk cabin with Harold Warnock and Jimmy Olliffe.

We must have had the oddest passenger list ever to leave the place. Us R.A.A.F. bods and Navy wallahs on their way to take on high speed tag with 'E' boats, and we had a lot of replacements for the 6th Division A.I.F. Forestry section. With all these, there were hosts of Displaced Persons who, having been held as suspect types in the early days of the war, were now cleared and given tasks according to their abilities, mixed sexes, and a collection of talents not often seen. Quiz shows became quite a feature in our daily routine and the knowledge and abilities of this very motley looking crowd was an education in itself.

We took four days to Wellington New Zealand, where we loaded frozen lamb and other goods. Went to the races in Hutt Valley, a very pretty spot. By invitation some of us went up to Wanganui and we had the pleasure of three days with the White family. At that time, Mr White was Town Clerk.

While in Wellington, there were six of us and our thirst was held in check by a very charming Maori lass in a semi circular bar at the Grand, I think. Walked back in four years later, and Mary said 'Good day Harry' and asked after the others by name, but they were not to join us in the flesh. By some odd twist of fate, there were two Kiwis, whom we had all known through O.T.U. and transit camps thereafter in Africa, so some quiet reflections were in order.

On leaving Wellington, after about two weeks in New Zealand, we took on 20 or so New Zealand airman. The farewell we received from the Wellington people was nothing short of exceptional. Massed bands played for over a couple of hours and a large percentage of the population turned out to bid us farewell.

Chapter 8: Trooping begins

From Wellington, we sailed in a direction which we hoped would hit the Americas about the middle, and the jolly old Pacific really lived up to its name. Forty nine days over this vast ocean, with a strong ripple as a source of interest. Fish and seabird life and activities in daily display, with the albatrosses never failing to show their effortless grace with seldom a movement of the wings.

Away in the distance there was a huge water spout wobbling its way along the surface but we were quite happy to stay away from it. The *S.S. Ceramic* was part of the Shaw Savill and Albion Line, which we had changed to Slow Starvation and Agony, much to poor old Captain Boots' (true) disgust.

We coaled overnight at Panama, and set off through the canal after we had taken on a heap of yankee Marines. They confiscated all cameras pro tem and spent a lot of time trying to assure us that they would soon be in it with us. Chas my younger brother, had written home and told me to make sure to bring every Kangaroo penny I could carry. It was unreal what exchange they commanded and by manipulating the market it was easy to stay in front.

The trip through the canal was really interesting, but we were more interested in all the types of aircraft of which we had only read or seen on gazettes. All the southern side of the canal seemed to be one continuous drome, and everybody flying seemed to be looking for somebody they knew from the little old Boeing P26 to P38 Lightnings, Baltimores and Bostons. We had to remove all insignia from our shirts. We tied up at Cristobal and had all the next day ashore.

We had been given Red Cross chits for a meal at the Hotel Tropico, if my memory serves me right, so took us to a bank to find they would only pay $1 for £5, so I went back to the kangaroo pennies. When we walked into the Hotel Tropico, there were about ten or so of the boys there under the care of a Mr A Cook, who was the leading engineer on the Gatun locks in about the middle of the canal, and whoever came in had a full glass and a seat. God knows what it must have cost him over the day, but he would insist in his generosity.

After lunch we did a bit of shopping and my main interest must have been fruit because my bed was a mass of fruit and cartons of Lucky Strike and Chesterfield cigarettes. We had been joined at some stage by a heap of the Marines, who had come through the Canal as polite guards. Apparently at one stage, one Yank wanted to know as I taught them the intricacies of two-up, why I always took the money whichever way the pennies fell. Saved again by the kangaroo pennies!

Colon and Cristobal were joint cities on the Atlantic end of the Canal, divided by a double railway line. Somewhere in my travels I had acquired an enormous straw hat with a wingspan of about five feet. As we stood being counted a blond driver in a very modern Yank tank with the back window down pulled up just close enough for me to give a yell and dive in, cigarettes, fruit and all. When I came to in my bunk I still had all my illgotten gains and my mates assured me whichever way I went in future they would go the opposite.

We sailed from here in beautiful weather for Halifax, Nova Scotia. Two days before we reached Halifax, we were out on deck each morning with all the clothes we could wear, smashing ice off the rigging with hammers and axes. Fun for a while but even to us colonials with no such bitter winter experience it soon became something to be done only out of sheer necessity.

On advice from Chas, my brother, I did quite a bit of shopping in Halifax, as we had been given addresses of friends, relatives etc. Sugar and butter were the most needed, with an odd pair of stockings for luck. I had a spare kit bag into which these goodies were hoarded under my bunk. By the fates which have hurled me down and helped me up to have another go, we were aghast to come home that night to our nautical mansion to find we only had fluid assets, so to speak. Our cabin was close to the water tank system for the ship and due to some really outstanding finger trouble, some witless twit had allowed the tanks to overflow to such an extent, that ours and several other cabins were awash. Not even an apology was offered, and we were told there was a war on!!!

After trying to clean up the mess most of the night, we were not very happy in the early hours the following day as we left port to form into convoy for our last and most dangerous leg of the trip. There were 48 ships in the convoy and we were what they called the Commodore ship. As escort we had six destroyers borrowed from the Yanks, and made an impressive if slow sight.

Our officer in charge, was a wingless wonder, Wing Co. Kingsbury, a sawn off jerk as it transpired, but more of him shortly.

When we were about ten days out of Halifax, we were hove to in a storm which I have read about in other places, for over 4 days. The *Ceramic* was really a wonderful ship. We lost most of the forward railings, two enormous winches and apart from tons of crockery, Christ knows what else.

Right at the height of all this strife a destroyer came crashing through the waves, they don't bother about going over or around, and he was bashing away with an Aldis Lamp. Some of us had to go up on the bridge to help them read it, and it was all about Pearl Harbour! They would not hear of letting us come home!!

Just prior to all this excitement there had been a furore in the drinking lounge involving officers, but the word was spread that the bar was closed due to bad

Chapter 8: Trooping begins

behaviour - Half a dozen or so of our maligned group interviewed Kingsbury, and he brushed us off by saying 'the necessary steps had been taken' and when I remarked that the wrong people had been blamed, he informed me that I could do one hour on one off on anti submarine watch for the next 48 hours. I hope his Mother and Father do meet officially some day!

After the storm had eased somewhat, we could see one other ship, one more came into view as we plodded steadily on. Later we were joined by a C.A.M. ship, or one with a Hurricane mounted ready for a catapult launch. The ocean had not eased to any great extent, and every ripple was a conning tower to our eyes.
To top it off there was an antiquated machine gun I was to use in emergency.
In the remaining few days of our travel there were about six armourers all trying to make it work. Somebody eventually did the wrong thing and it fired one shot. We nearly bailed out!

****

Diary of Sgt/Pilot Ralph. A. Wilson
405008 RAAF
1922-1942
AWM Ref: PR01043
Reproduced by kind permission of David Wilson.

4/10/41
Saturday morning, it is a bleak morning. I slept until 0715hrs & feel much refreshed.

Went into town at 0800hrs, finally getting to Martin Place at 0900hrs. Cabled Dad to pay return fare at Brisbane office for me, in the Douglas. Left Mascot aerodrome at 1045hrs. The old Doug is certainly very comfortable to fly in. The view was not very good owing to the haze. The airhostess Miss Dalrymple was very nice & took her part well. It was great to go through Brisbane again & meet the people. Spent the afternoon with the family.

Went to Penelope's for tea & had a most enjoyable tea. Met her parents. Mrs Knight is a very decent old stick. Penny was looking great. We went to the Bellevue for a little while after tea. Then went for a run up to Mount Cootha. I think we have clicked. I sincerely hope so anyhow.

5/10/41
Sunday. Dad's birthday. He is 54 now. Said aure-voir to Penny on the phone.

Left old Brisbane at 1415hrs on the Douglas & arrived in Sydney at 1735hrs. Slept most of the way down.

Was glad to get to bed. However I feel much at ease now & very happy. Ready for any number of Nazis.

6/10/41
Still no movement order. There is not much to write about here. It is terribly monotonous. I was in the act of ducking out of a route march this morning, when the W.O. grabbed myself and George Brooks & put us in charge of a couple of flights.

7/10/41
Tuesday. Another day at Bradfield. Told the W/O off this afternoon. The dumb idiot would not give me a chit to go up to I.T.S. for fear that I got an extra little bit of leave. Obtained one from the adjutant. Got to the I.T.S. bank just in time.

8/10/41
Spent morning in camp. In the afternoon, Mac & I went chasing petrol & photographs & ordering photographs. Had tea at Cahills. 3/- for a plate of 1 dozen oysters. 3d per oyster rather expensive.

13/10/41 Mon
Back to camp again. Feel very happy in a way, after seeing Penny. We will certainly make up for it when the show is over. It is a bugger saying goodbye for a couple of years, when there are so many bloody sharks still here.

Friday 17/10/41
At last I have found the time and inclination to enter a few notes in this Diary.

At sea now, on the *Ceramic*. An old coal burner of about 18,000 tons. She was built in 1911 & served as a troop ship in the last war. Used to carry 3,000. Rather different this time. It is all one class. The passengers are composed of a small percentage of civilians. A large amount of Air Force & A.I.F. & few navy members, and a big batch of Refugees. Most of the refugees are of German blood, or German Jew blood.

Much has happened since last Friday at this time. Last Friday night I flew up to Brisbane. We were all certain that it was the last week-end, so I made the best of it. It was a wonderful week-end - I shall never forget it. But the week-end could not last forever, and came to the end all too quickly. I caught the Douglas on Monday morning. Most of the trip was through cloud. When we passed over the harbour, I saw a ship with a ferry boat alongside it. I received rather a shock, for

Chapter 8: Trooping begins

fear that it was ten course leaving. With what missing of heart beats did I hurry to my hut when I got inside the gate. And what relief when I saw the boys' gear still there. And Monday finally passed. On Monday night Mac and myself went to Luna Park. I rather like the Dip railway.

Tuesday was a very easy day, with a closed camp at the end of it. It was great to get a letter from Penelope. Spent most of the day writing letters.

Wednesday was the day. We had all our gear packed & ready. The remainder of ten course are going with a few eleven course chaps. We finally got on the bus at 1400hrs. After being conveyed to one of the Sydney ferries, we were taken to the *Ceramic* with an equal, if not a greater number of A.I.F. & a few naval chaps. What a relief to get away at last.

We have to do this job, therefore the sooner we get away, the sooner we come back, with any luck.

The boat did not waste any time in getting away. At 1730hrs we up anchored & made for sea. I was not sorry to see the last of Sydney. After all one may as well be in England, as well as be in Sydney.

As we left Sydney, the sun was setting A very golden sunset, which enhanced the arched beauty of Sydney's bridge. One of the greatest engineering achievements in the world. In a way it was sad seeing all this slipping away behind points jutting out into the harbour, & finally the harbour disappearing behind the heads, and then the heads and Australia gradually falling below the horizon. The sun had set by now & the Australian coast looked very dark, under a swiftly waning light. And then darkness with the glow of Sydney over the horizon. Dad - oh hell! what's the use of saying what they are doing in Brisbane. I have a pretty good idea.

The ship is a complete blackout at night. It was necessary to show navigation lights near the Harbour because of the amount of shipping. Sleep was most welcome on Wednesday night. I think most of the boys were fairly tired. But one can see that they are all of one mind. Glad to get away & do something definite.

Every one is travelling in passenger berths which are really very comfortable. The rooms are necessarily cramped. But that is a mere detail. We have now been at sea for about 48 hours. It will be 48 hours at 1730hrs tonight. So far the weather has been perfect with a steady breeze from the South East. Typical trade wind. The sea is calm. The *Ceramic* seems to be a comfortable sea boat, with an easy motion. She appears to be very stable with a good bearing. Although she has three screws, she can only do 14 knots at the outside, and seems to cruise along at 10 knots.

There are not very many women passengers which is a good thing. Because if trouble arises they might be a bit of a worry although I should imagine that they would not cause half as much worry as these Refugees. They are a poor looking bunch of specimens.

Wednesday 22/10/41
Quite a lot has happened since the 17th.

We arrived in Pt Nicholson on Monday morning. My first impression of Wellington as I looked from the sundeck of the *Ceramic*, (safely moored at the wharf) towards the north west, was a neat little city. It has a very large hill just behind it, the top of which is covered with very green grass & no trees. There are about 40 wireless masts on the top which belong to a naval wireless station. There was a surprising absence of smoke, indicating that it is not a manufacturing town.

We finally got ashore about 1200hrs. The people are most hospitable. Exceptionally so.

As far as the women are concerned, none I have seen yet can compare with the Brisbane girls. The New Zealand Air Force chaps are as nice as their civilians. On Monday night Vennor, Bill & myself had a most enjoyable evening at the home of Ted Lowe. It was his last night of final leave - I got rather full & arrived back at the ship 5 minutes late. While climbing the gang plank I almost lost my new 15/- pipe. Luckily it fell onto the roof of a railway carriage & not into the water. But alas! It was saved only to be broken. Griff bumped into me in the passage & knocked it out of my mouth. The stem broke off. However I will be able to get two or three made in Wellington.

Tuesday was a busy day from morning till night. I located the Royal Port Nicholson Yacht Club, & met the secretary John Carrol. He will arrange for some of us to go for a sail next Saturday. In the afternoon Mrs Innes took us for a drive in her car. We toured the shores of the harbour & spent a most interesting afternoon. It was a very windy afternoon & some parts of the harbour were whipped white with foam. They get exceptionally strong northerlies here.

As I write now we are moving towards New Plymouth. The government has provided a special train to take the R.A.A.F. to New Plymouth. The trip takes about 10 hours. Much as I dislike train travelling, it is very interesting. The country according to geography books is most typical of English countryside. I think that is the most accurate description. They have just had a very heavy rainfall over the last two months & everything is at its brightest green. The district we are passing through is a dairying & sheep district. The sheep on the round fold hills, covered with smooth rye grass, add the finishing touches to the English

Chapter 8: Trooping begins

scenes one sees in illustrated books.

The people are most disgusted with the government. I am told that the minister for defence, who was a strong advocate for conscription, was in gaol during the last war, because he would not offer his services or do compulsory training.

This route seems to have an ample supply of refreshments. Every 20 minutes or so, the train stops & we have five minutes for refreshments.

Friday 24/10/41
I am in rather a sorry state this morning. When I woke up I thought my head was going to burst. It exploded every time I coughed. However after being violently ill, I felt much better. I do not think that I will mix Beer & whisky in any quantity again.

The boys had a wonderful time in New Plymouth. Yesterday morning we were taken up to Mount Egmont in buses. The top of the mountain was covered with cloud. However we were assured that there is a mountain under the cloud. I saw & touched snow for the first time. There was not very much about, but quite enough to make snow balls. Lunch was provided by three of their leading hotels. In the Criterion Hotel I saw two of the prettiest women that I have seen in New Zealand yet. But unfortunately I did not meet them. Even so they were no prettier than the average Brisbane girl. Rather below average.

The people in New Plymouth were wonderful. They could not do enough for us. We were overwhelmed with hospitality. After lunch, a number of private cars took us up to Pukehura Park. It is a very beautiful park, organised on the same lines as the Botanical Gardens in Brisbane. Afternoon tea was provided at the Kiosk. I met a very nice Western Australian at afternoon tea. She was Mrs Gillingham, the Lady Mayoress. Vennor, Jack, the O.C. & myself sat at the table with her. The O.C. was most lavish & flowery in his praise of New Zealand. He said it was much better than any Australian scenery. I was very pleased when Mrs Gillingham helped me to defend Australia.

Vennor & myself went into town with Mr Gillingham. He showed us the New Plymouth A.N.A. rooms of which he had just reason to be proud.

In the Criterion Hotel I met a very interesting New Zealander. Flying Officer George Braeburn. He is a very decent fellow & we became firm friends almost immediately. He has done 2000 hours & is at present instructing at an airforce station at Christchurch. We did some steady drinking together & then went out to his place for tea. I met Mrs Braeburn and Joan Braeburn who is a very nice kid.

After tea went to the Imperial Hotel, where the boys were having a few pots. I filled up with whisky & beer. It had a disastrous effect this morning. Phew! what a hang over.

Well here we are on the New Plymouth - Wellington express. Most of the chaps are very tired and a number have rather bad hang overs. It is hard to find words that will express ones feelings explicitly. We have met a very nice, generous, warm hearted people. I am beginning to see now, why the British Empire is cemented so firmly together. It is that feeling of cooperation, and that we are all in the right for the same cause. This will hold the Empire together & leave her undaunted. If only that minority does not grow, which does not realise the necessity for immediate action.

(Saw Punga wood from which the Maoris do most of their carving. Also a fire place, once part of a Maori house. The timber is all similar to the English type.)

Sunday 25/10/41. 1300hrs.

Have just had one of the ships dinners. Although we have been in port, they have not put any green food on the table. One would think it worth while putting rabbit's food, & vegetables on the table.

The ship left the wharf about 1900hrs(?) this morning. She is now anchored in the bay. It is the general opinion, or there is a rumour that we will be here for a day or so. I am going mad with the inactivity. However our stay in New Zealand was most enjoyable. The people could not do enough for us.

It was good to get to bed on Friday night & have a sleep. I soon tired of the Air Force ball, and returned to the *Ceramic*. Old Ben is becoming a lad once again. I do not think he has missed taking a lass home one night yet.

Bill Lindley & Max are also making the most of it. We are becoming accustomed, I should say immuned to the beer, now. Max & Ben are able to drink any New Zealander under the table now. So they say. I do not doubt them.

On Saturday morning Bill Francis & myself went into town & tried to buy a case of fruit at the markets. But they had no fruit to spare. The whole market was empty so poor Bill & Ralph had none. We saw an auction sale of fruit. A white man, was auctioning fruit to a crowd of Chinese. As we could not understand the lingo, it all appeared to be most humourous.

Phill Kerr, Bill Francis & myself had lunch at Garlands. We had a big meal of white bait. This appears to be a very small fish. It is battered heavily & served

Chapter 8: Trooping begins

with chips. Rather a nice dish.

We went to the races in the afternoon. Luck was not with us, but the weather was pleasant for once, & it was good to get out in the open. I lost a pound, & Dulhunty lost four.

I sent a couple of cable grams home after tea. They will probably get there about Thursday.

Dulhunty, Jack Lock, & myself went to a theatre after tea. It was the first time I have been for a couple of months. One of the pictures was called Double Date. The name of one of the characters was called Penelope. I found it most interesting.

Monday 26/10/41. 1900 hours.

The Prime Minister of New Zealand came out to the *Ceramic* at seven o'clock this morning. He is the one most responsible for conscription for overseas service in New Zealand. And yet, in the last war, he was in gaol as a conscientious objector. The *Ceramic* weighed anchor at 0800 hours. Old Tom Halsall was right. He seems to be well & truly in the know, as he has been always able to tell us our immediate future so far.

It is good to be on our way again, and moving towards our work. We had to turn back just after lunch as the *Sterling Castle* had a casualty for Wellington on board. However, at 1600 hours we got under way with *Wanganui* as escort. What a relief. I am most impatient to get to good old Angleterre. I wonder if I will be able to get into the fleet air arm.

Life on ship goes on as before.

The boys are fond of a ditty that started as we left Bradfield in the bus. It goes like this.

Someone says
"Who Will drive the coach through Dead Man's Gulch."
"Who are you?"
"I am Tim McKoy.
" Not the McKoy?"
"Yes! the McKoy."
Then chorus. Da da da da da de da, Da da da da da da de da da. To the refrain of the"Stars & Stripes."

Here is a modification.
"Who will play ball with me?"
"I will play ball with you."
"Who are you?"
"I am the Shiny Arse."
"Not the Shiny Arse?"
"Yes the Shiny Arse."
Then chorus

Friday 31/10/41
Five days since I last made an entry, rather a poor show.

The last three days have been very overcast, and mostly fog for the last two. At times it was impossible to see further than the length of the ship. It is excellent weather for getting across the Pacific & avoiding raiders. It would be most annoying if anything should happen to delay us. The confounded ship is terribly slow & the voyage will take long enough as it is. The forces have been allotted duties in the case of hostilities. They are divided up into five parties, stretcher bearers & reserve machine gunners. Some have been allotted babies to take care of. Bill Lindley has Geneva Saunders to take care of. Good man Bill.

We also have to do our turn at watch. The R.A.A.F. have been allotted posts at the gun emplacements on the sun deck, We have to watch from 90° to 150°. Today was the same as the other days. So far the weather has been most agreeable and the sea calm. We have been most fortunate in that respect. There is a fog on the sea & it does not extend much above the level of the masts, although horizontal visibility is absolutely restricted. Ben & myself had to take our turn at the Watch this afternoon, from 1500hrs - 1800hrs. The time passes surprisingly quickly. There is no anxiety in the Pacific however. I should imagine that one will be very alert after Panama.

We had Physical Training again this afternoon. When the period was finished, the boys started a display of strong man stuff. The "Baron" caught Arch Guymer beautifully. The Baron said to Arch, "Here's one that I think you should be able to do Arch." He placed Archie with his feet at right angles, hands clasped with palms downwards, and arms stretched straight down in front. Then he told Archie to look at a spot on the awning above him & stand on his toes. When Archie performed these requirements, looking for all the world like a bathing beauty, Baron gooed in a maidenly voice, "Yoo-hoo!" It looked so ridiculous. And Archie was caught. He eventually decided not to throw the Baron over when his embarrassment finally subsided. Good old Baron, drunkard though he may be. It would be hard to find another wit quite like him. A little of Baron is an excellent tonic for the blues.

Chapter 8: Trooping begins

I am studying Astro Nav from one of the observer's notes. Young Ray Emmelton knows it very well & he is most helpful. I shall be able to get it taped before we reach England. If so it will be an asset worth having.

It is most difficult to find an excuse for writing in the diary. Each day is the same as the previous one, & shipboard life goes on as usual. Tom Halsall seems to think that we will dock in England round about 25th December.

November 1941

Thursday 6/11/41. 2230hrs.
Today was the first fine day since leaving New Zealand We are in latitude 20° South, approximately and almost beneath the sun. The sun came out in earnest about 1230hrs.

After lunch Dulhunty & myself basked on the sun deck. Bill Francis came up later & the O.C. (Shiny Arse). He got very annoyed with the naval chaps who were playing ball disturbing the would be sunbathers. (Shiny Arse) was not in the mood for "playing ball".

The weather so far has been most mild. As for the sea, it has been as calm as it seems possible. There was scarcely a white horse today.

I had to do watch from 2000hrs - 2100hrs this evening. The night is beautiful. The planet Venus, which was visible at our zenith, is very bright tonight. I took the opportunity of learning some practical astro tonight. Learnt the planets Venus, Mars, Jupiter. Also the stars Rigel Kemp, Acrux, Ackenar, Altair, Antares.

The phosphorous was very pretty tonight, being very bright in the small whirl pools travelling alongside the ship, caused by the ship's motion.

After the watch, I went up to the bow to see the bow wave, but it was not very phosphorescent. The moon rose about 2115hrs & made a very pretty picture. As I stood there my thoughts wandered back to Queensland. Back to the time when I used to be burning the midnight oil in the hopes of being a naval architect. The boats I was going to build. And then when the Germans marched on Poland. How times have changed. Oh Hell! What use is it to think of the past, The future is quite enough.

Everyone seems to be delighted with the change of weather. It will be very warm till we get through Panama now. The ladies are actually daring to go without stockings. The R.A.A.F. will wear tropical dress tomorrow, & the navy will probably turn out in white from stem to stern.

SS CERAMIC The Untold Story

Sgt/Pilot Ralph. A. Wilson
Ceramic voyage October-December 1941.
Reproduced by kind permission of David Wilson.

Above: Concert Party.
Below: Deck Tennis.

Ralph and Penny

Outside Halifax.

Above: The Verandah Café.
Left: Sunset.
Right: Sunbathing on deck.

196

Chapter 8: Trooping begins

Monday 10/11/41
What did I do today? Now let me think. Ah yes!

0700hrs	Cup of tea & biscuit.
0800hrs	Had early breakfast.
0900 - 1000hrs	Did watch on the gun bridge at the stem of the ship. Took the opportunity of studying the gun. I am afraid it is rather an ancient specimen. However it may prove useful. Also learnt how the log works.
1000 - 1100hrs	Played deck games & read.
1100hrs	Took class for aircraft identification.
1300hrs	Lunch. (Hebrews 13:8)
1400 - 1630hrs	Slept.
1700hrs	Physical training.
1900hrs	Tea.
1930hrs - 2350hrs	Remained in cabin. Spent most of time looking at what photos I have of Penelope, & reading her letters.

Nothing very much has happened since Thursday. I have not learnt very much more Astro Nav theory. But I have done some practical Astro Nav. There is a Greek on board who is travelling to Panama to take charge of his ship. He has a sextant with him. Therefore I did not lose any time making friends with him. He has taught me how to use the sextant & read it. Although the aircraft sextant is slightly different. When I have learnt more theory I will be able to fix position.

I have also been observing more heavenly bodies. Now please do not mistake me, Diary old son. I mean Planets & Stars. Viz. Planets:- Venus, Mars, Saturn, Jupiter.

Stars - Rigel. Kemp, Mahaut(?) Acenar (Achernar), Peacock(?), Acrux, Canopus, Sirius, Rigel, Bellatrix, Beezlejeeze (Betelgeuse) Antares, & Altar (Altair).

The Southern Cross will be out of sight soon. Seeing the Southern Cross seems to give me the feeling that Home, family, & Penelope are not so far away. But when the Cross drops below the horizon, one realises that they are away down under.

It was a clear night on Friday night, & the moonrise was beautiful. I fell to thinking, while leaning over the rail on the promenade deck, gazing out towards the black and silver lined clouds on the starboard bow. Eventually the moonbeams discovered a break in the clouds, and bathed the ship in semi daylight. I am still amazed about the commissions & have formulated a plan of action for when we arrive in England. We get one week's leave, or perhaps ten days if we are lucky. I shall set to work immediately. If only I can get on to the right man, it should be possible to get posted to a flying boat squadron. It would be great on the water.

Splashing around in water still fascinates me, However I must get the Astro taped, it will be a definite asset in gaining my ends. The fighters are still a terrific temptation & so are the bombers. I like the idea of raiding Germany. However it should be just as important raiding German shipping.

Looking over the moonlight bathed deck, I was impressed with the romance of the scene. It was really very beautiful. I realised that in a few hours this same old moon would be beaming on the folks at home. It would be Saturday night.

Mum may have gone to a show with Bruce, & Pop probably stayed at home with David & the twins. It would do young Bruce a world of good to get away from home for a few months. Penelope. I wonder where she is. Probably some b---- shark is pestering her. I hope Clarence performs his duty. I feel very lonely at times, and long to have you beside me. Pray that your sister will not have any influence for the worse upon you.

Tuesday 11/11/41
Armistice day. At eleven hundred hours we had a parade & observed the two minutes' silence in memory of our deceased heroes of 1914-18. And of the living dead. Men confined to hospital for the rest of their lives. Some kept out of sight because of the horrible disfigurement caused by wounds. One cannot comprehend the awful tragedy of war. Just as men have lost all that is dear to man in the last show, so they are doing now. Men give up ambitions. Their course of life is greatly disrupted. They leave their sweethearts at home. And with so many b---- sharks still at home, it is no joke.

But what a glorious spirit, & what true patriotism. Can there be any doubt that we are wrong? When men volunteer to give up all these things and train to be first class warriors. The nation's best. They are only too glad to gather round the mother country & defend her. What low spineless creatures we should be if we did not make a sacrifice when our country who has provided so much happiness for us, is in dire stress. And what is more, what value would our happy homes, what future would there be for men & sweethearts, if they sat back and watched a brutal organization of gangsters who had overrun their own country, defeat our own dear land. Our homes would become as the dust of ages. Our sweethearts would have a hell on earth, supplying the lust of the gangsters.

Is nothing like a lovely flower
Whose loveliness lasts but an hour?
Sweet tastes the wine preserved an age:
But sweeter still,
In life's new thrill,
Is she whose grace words cannot gauge.

Chapter 8: Trooping begins

Learning to play bridge now. It is a most interesting game. Had an excellent game with Bill Anderson, George Brooks, & Bill Francis this evening. As the sky was rather overcast it was not worth studying any stars.

Thursday 13th November 1941
Not so long to go now, before we reach Panama. What a relief. All cameras have to be handed in today as we are going to pass through neutral territory. The captain states that sentries have shot people trying to take photos of the Canal, as the ship was passing through.

Food is still a grim show. Alas! how I dream of salads. Lettuce, cabbage, carrot, onion, tomato, beetroot, celery, etc. etc.

I slept on deck last night, alongside John Lock. We yarned until the early hours of the morning.

The phosphorescent light in the water was wonderful last night. It is the best I have ever seen. The bow wave was literally aglow. It lit the whole stem. If close enough, I am sure it would have been possible to read a book.

Last night was the best nights rest I have had since leaving Sydney. The deck may have been hard, but it is a pleasant change. The fact that we were breathing fresh air was sufficient.

On parade this morning, I saw flying fish for the first time. I caught a glance of the first one & thought it was a bird, because it flew fully 50 yards without touching the water & then plunged headlong into a wave. Whole schools would leap out, fly for about twenty yards, & then plunge again.

Man has copied the bird, he has copied the fish. I wonder how long it will be before he copies the flying fish. MacNally has a bright idea for the Trans Pacific transport problem. He suggests mixing the flying fish with the whale.

Monday 17th/11/41.
We sighted the first piece of dirt since leaving Wellington on Sunday Morning. As the day progressed more & more land appeared & we finally anchored outside Panama at 1530 hours.

The first welcomer we received from Panama was the Dolphin. They seem to be in abundance about here. Also hundreds of other types of fish.

At last we have completed half the trip. It was great to feel the anchor chain rattling away as the anchor settled on the bottom ten fathoms down. It gives one the sense that something definite has been achieved

Slept on deck on Sunday night, & woke up at 0600hrs this morning with a terrible head.

Dulhunty, Brooks, & myself had a small session last night. I let myself go because I absolutely wanted to forget myself for a while.

As we approached the Locks this morning we passed through a small yacht harbour. There were several very attractive yachts there. Particularly a ketch & a three masted schooner.

There is not much to say about Panama. It is just like any other town. However, the country & vegetation is vastly different. There is genuine jungle coming right down to the edge of the locks. The locks are wonderful. One of the proudest achievements of engineering I should think. The ship is towed from lock to lock by electric mules. The total length of the canal is 47 miles of locks and lakes. We will reach Colon this evening.

The most noticeable feature is the rate at which the locks fill. One can actually feel the ship rise, let alone watch the water rise up the side.

The darky labourers are certainly sunburnt. They are terribly lazy sleepy looking individuals. I think that they just wait for the world to go round. MacNally cracked one of the MacNally standard jokes. He said that they must think that manual labour must be the name of a Spaniard.

I have not seen so many aeroplanes flying about for months. Douglas, Curtiss, PRYs, and others. I believe that there are hidden aerodromes in many parts of the jungle. The canal seems to be well guarded. At times we are so close to the edge of the canal, that it is almost possible to jump on to land. The locks would be easy.

An American lieutenant in charge of the guard, placed on the ship in Panama, informs me that there are crocodiles here. He also confirmed my belief that there are Boa Constrictors & jaguars here. The jungle looks the typical film stuff, à la "King Kong". I would not care to have to travel through it.

At present we are 80 feet above sea level, travelling along a river which has been dammed to cause a big long lake. It seems like travelling the upper Brisbane except for the noticeable difference in the vegetation. Thank goodness the breeze is against us. It would be terribly hot otherwise. We have arrived at Cristobal (1500hrs). After travelling through three large lakes, & about 9 locks. We were 85 feet above sea level on the lakes. The level of the lakes has been raised 30' for the purpose of eliminating the number of locks. This was done by damming all the streams away from the lakes. The canal receives a lot of drainage from the surrounding hills & is therefore always full of fresh water. This water supplies the locks. All feeding is done by gravity. One part of the lakes reminded me very much of Tiplers Channel in Moreton Bay. As the ship approached Colon, we were often well above the surrounding country. It felt more like travelling in a train. At one time between high cliffs, & then another between vast lowlands. The land on the Colon side is very flat & is a strong contrast to the Panama side.

Our American friends certainly drawl. I thought that I would be disappointed. But even the negroes drawl. The negroes are British West Indian Negroes & are intensely loyal to the British, and are very proud of the fact. The living expenses in Panama are very high. Consequently the wages are high. The negro labourer, who seems to do nothing but walk in his sleep, gets 3 dollars 50 cents a day. Equivalent to £1 per day. A white man driving one of the coal cranes gets 16 dollars per day. £5 per day. But the cheapest living expenses are £30 per month.

Tuesday 18/11/41
Army, navy, & airforce were taken by train into Cristobal. Left the wharf at 1000hrs and arrived there at 1010hrs. Jack Lock and myself decided to stick together. Went first of all to the Y.M.C.A. They informed me that the bank was down the next street and so we hurried along. But alas! The rate of exchange is very grim. For some reason or other they do not want Australian money. They say the British Government will not receive any sterling from Panama owing to the German minority there. However the rate of exchange is 1.20 dollars for the pound. This was no good, and so we began to scout around for a good exchange. The money exchange was no better than the bank. Finally we found a Greek in one of the hotels who gave us 2 dollars for £1. This was better than nothing. For a time the prospects looked very poor. Then it was discovered that they wanted Australian silver as souvenirs. By this means we were able to buy dimes for threepence. At times dollars were bought for 4/-. The Panamanians are out to rob any tourist passing through, but I think that if the Australians had been here for a few days, the Panamanians would have been robbed.

After racing around scraping dollars & dimes together, the boys started to look about. What a conglomeration of races there were to be seen. A large number of orientals, alongside, Jamaicans, Mexicans, Spaniards, Costa Ricans, Indians, and then the irish stew tribe. They are a mixture of everything. The American whites, which are in the minority, seem to live mostly in Cristobal. This seems to be the better town. My first ambition was to find some Christmas Cards to send home. Finally selected a couple. One for the family & one for Penelope. They were rather expensive, but it could not be helped. If the rate of exchange had been more favourable it would have been possible to send lots of interesting articles home.

After walking the streets, through every type of humanity it is possible to imagine, from Colon to Cristobal, & back to Colon again, we were ready for the best lunch Jardin Bilgray could give us. The luncheon was no different from our own Australian cafés, except for the fact that it smelt of Colon. Everywhere in Panama there is a smell, which almost suggests evil. The rankness of the tropical jungle is nothing compared with the stench to be encountered in parts of the city. After walking around the block of brothels, in the centre of Colon, I was filled with amazement. Surely this is one of the most evil places in the world. Where the lowest forms of humanity in the world delight in abusing sex, and indulge in the lowest vices. The masses of flesh, that live in the brothels are horrible. They may have been attractive once, but it is hard to imagine. Surely this place is worse than Sodom and Gomorrah of the Bible.

After lunch we had the good fortune to meet a gentleman by the name of Oscar Savage. He is a native of Jamaica, & a very loyal Britisher. The Jamaican natives are intelligent, and seem to do most of the work in Panama Republic. They fill positions of Doctors, car salesmen, & labourers. Oscar was a generous gentleman, & drove us around the town for a couple of hours. His sense of humour, and personal charm made the hours seem like minutes, unfortunately. But alas! Oscar had to attend a business appointment at 3 o'clock, but would not see us go, until we had allowed him to purchase 270 cents worth of fruit, & shout drinks all round. The fruit was most acceptable, as we have had practically no fruit for three weeks. After saying goodbye to Oscar Savage, we went to the Y.M.C.A. and solemnly ate the fruit. It was most enjoyable.

At 1645 hours. All troops, & passengers had to assemble at the train to go back to the *Ceramic*. The sight reminded me of the Brisbane Exhibition. Indeed our troops looked like a crowd of children returning from the Royal Exhibition in Brisbane. But instead of shilling bags, they carried armfulls of various cheap purchases. Several wore tremendous straw hats, and others smoked ridiculous looking pipes. The big bundles of magazines donated by one of the book stalls, added the finishing touches. If the boys had not been so tired there would have been much more hilarity. But even the Balbao beer consumers were too tired to cause any excitement. And so back to the *Ceramic* after seeing one of the strangest places in the world. Where one may meet British consuls, French, & German. And the lowest rats of the waterfront. A really remarkable panorama of many races, is afforded by this Panama Republic. What the night life is like, I do not know, as there was no night leave granted. But one can imagine that it would be rather grotesque. I believe it costs 20 cents for a drink at the Cabaret. But if one escorts a woman, it costs one dollar a drink. The girl simply claps her hands

Chapter 8: Trooping begins

when she wishes to have a drink, & the waiter is on the spot. A fellow is lucky if he gets out of the place spending less than 45 dollars.

But so much for Cristobal & Colon. I cannot imagine any one wanting to live there except espionage agents, & men with demented minds. And yet it is one of the most important places in the world, & has a large influence on the history of the world. Well good luck to the little band of American soldiers, administrators, and natives of Jamaica. These people guard one of democracy's lonely outposts.

On Wednesday, the *Ceramic* remained alongside the wharf until the coaling was finished. This port is one of the biggest coaling centres in the world, & most of the coaling work is done by Jamaicans. The day was hot & humid, making it unbearable below decks. As no shore leave was granted, the passengers sought the shady spots, that were not too dirty with coal, and settled down in deckchairs to read. From my shady spot on the sun deck, I could look over the green jungle vegetation, towards Colon. Naturally enough, the shore held no allure, not after what I had seen yesterday. The coal is everywhere, although it is the fastest the *Ceramic* has been coaled, it is also the dirtiest she has ever been, Tom informs me.

There was coal all over the boat deck & most of the forward promenade deck. By clinging to shoes it found its way to A Deck & the various cabins. Tom & his fellow stewards had a hell of a job cleaning up the floors.

The *Ceramic* left the wharf at half past five in the afternoon, but not until a breeze came in from the north. This was most cooling and refreshing. After a while, what seemed interminable waiting to the more impatient ones, a fussy little tug arrived with the pilot

After the *Ceramic* had given the tug the necessary commands by throaty blasts from her steam whistle, to which the tug would reply with pitiful little squaks like one hears on a Walt Disney cartoon, the tug began to pull & nose at the *Ceramic*, in an effort to get her out into the bay. After much fuss, the *Ceramic* manouvered into the narrow harbour & headed for the gate of the harbour, after very nearly smashing her rudder on one of Colon's wharves, where there is a big dent, marking the spot where the *Ceramic* ceased to go astern. It broke the monotony of the day however, & provided the passengers something to talk about for the rest of the evening. We anchored just inside the gate for a couple of hours, for some reason known to the Captain only. But during that time, latrineograms cabled from stem to stern, and from port to starboard. Rumour had it that one of the propellers was badly bent & the rudder damaged. I suppose I felt the same as the others about it. But the thought that we might be delayed in Colon for a month, worried me intensely. It would be a terrible waste of time, and I did not

SS CERAMIC The Untold Story

join the Air Force for a holiday in the tropics. Indeed the situation looked very grim, so I tried to play bridge with George Brooks, Ben Westerman, & Max McNally. But our fears were allayed, when the engines began to throb, & the ship was blacked out. At 2000hrs the old *Ceramic* once more weighed anchor & wended her way out to sea. What a relief! The game is getting closer now. About three more weeks. It is hard to comprehend that at any time now we may be in practical contact with war. Still there is a chance that we will get across without a scratch. I hope so, it would be terrible to have any delay after all this time.

Thursday 20/11/41
A beautiful day to be at sea. The old *Ceramic* is carving a steady wake across the sunny Caribbean Sea. The weather is wonderful. A fresh North Easter is blowing & it is most exhilarating to stand on the prow of the ship, watching her stem cleave the waves of the jolly old Caribbean Sea into a white mass of curling, thunderous, foam. The flying fish are daringly sportive, and turn on an excellent show, by leaping out of the bow wave, and performing all the hazards of low flying until they are a hundred yards or so away, and then do a slow roll into the deck. Sometimes they just fold their wings and flop, a splash 'Marking the spot. The wings closely resemble those of the 1940-41 Spitfire.

The water must be comparatively shallow here, as there is a large amount of sea weed in the numerous tide rips.

Monday 24/11/41
Five days at sea since leaving Panama Zone. (Colon). Time slips surely & steadily by. Much more surely than the *Ceramic*, who seems to creep towards its next port, like a small schoolboy saunters unwillingly to school. It is almost four months since I have had a fly in an Airforce aircraft. Likewise for the rest of ten course.

Here is the programme for the average day.

0700hrs   Tom (bedroom steward, news reporter, prophet, and wonderful help in general) brings in a cup of tea & two biscuits. This cup of tea is the best to be had on the boat. Tom does his job well. He does not look the steward type, and definitely is not. He stands about five feet seven inches, and has grey hair, mounting pale well defined features of a man about 47 - 50 years of age. Before coming on the *Ceramic* he used to work in one of England's ship building yards, which were blown to smithereens. His information about the raids is most interesting, and most profitable to listen to.

Chapter 8: Trooping begins

0815 hours   Parade. Main object of the parade is to see if anyone has disappeared since last parade and read out Daily Routine Orders. The rest of the morning is free unless there is a lecture.

My morning is usually spent sunbathing while the sun shines. Reading & studying Astro Navigation. Occasionally make a fourth at bridge. But bridge is a waste of time while the sun is shining. Very shortly the sun will be almost a stranger. Deck games provide a great deal of pleasure for some, but deck tennis seems to be the most interesting, & provides the best exercise.

1300 hours   Lunch
Westerman, Lindley. Mackenzie. O'Keefe, MacNally, & myself sit at the same table. Some of the best fun of the trip is to be had at our table. Just to break the monotony we have competitions. For example. The first man to miss a meal is to be fined six bottles. These were provided by Mackenzie. Another one was. Every time we swore, a fine of 1 bottle, 12 being the objective. I was caught for 3. The rest were distributed fairly evenly around the table. The best one was a fine of 1 bottle for every sentence uttered without swearing. Strangely enough MacNally was fined four bottles. A most remarkable event. I was not fined. Almost as remarkable as the MacNally event.

The rest of the afternoon is free until five o'clock. Often in the afternoon, I retire to my bunk and sleep for an hour. Yesterday I was so tired that I slept for three hours. Actually dreamed rather unusual for me. I dreamt that I had returned home to Ardlui. Penelope happened to be staying there, & well - - -.

At five o'clock R.A.A.F. has Physical Training. This is an excellent idea & loosens up the old sinews considerably.

1900 hours.   Tea. Generally very stuffy in the dining saloon owing to the blackout conditions.

Thursday 27th November
Berthed at Halifax wharves at 1630hrs. Just as the sun was setting. We left Colon at 2030hrs on Wednesday 19th November. The trip was most uneventful, the most interesting part being in the vicinity of Cuba, and the Bahama Island,

On Monday night the weather changed most decisively, with the result that we changed into blues on Tuesday, hence it was a more interesting day than usual.

Wednesday was a little colder than Tuesday, but not that much. In the afternoon we had a practice action stations. It happened to rain very heavily while it was on, & a snappy squall hit us. It was nothing for the wind to swing right round through 180° in about four seconds in this storm.

And so Thursday comes. It was very cold this morning, I had to put another blanket on in the early hours of the morning. The temperature was 43° F. The wind was coming off shore with abundant nip. The ship's community donned their woolies in double quick time. It would be a difficult job running a drapers shop here, unless one were any good at weather forecasting. At 0930 land was sighted. But the passengers are getting used to sighting land now, and no one seemed very excited. Nevertheless the foredeck was crowded with bodies craning their necks to get a better view of it. There was a great deal of shipping about, & it so turned out that we arrived at the entrance of the harbour, just as a convoy of about twenty ships was leaving. The weather seemed to be getting colder and more overcast all the time. After the procession of cargo vessels & tankers had passed (some of the tankers may have been wheat carriers), we proceeded up the channel. Snow began to fall very lightly as we entered the channel, but did not fall heavily enough to form a layer on the deck. As we approached the gate, the foghorn was sounded. It is a most cheerless sound, & the *Ceramic*'s is no exception. Although the entrance to the harbour is comparatively narrow, the harbour itself opens out considerably. With Halifax on the western side, & the large suburb of Dartmoor on the opposite side, where the aerodrome & sea plane base is stationed. Further up, the harbour opens up into a large bowl where the convoy is assembled.

As we approached the wharf, the waterfront of Halifax rather resembled the customs house district of Brisbane. The round dome of the post office, closely resembled the customs houses, while the church spires in the rear, resembled those of Ann Street. But that is the only resemblance. There was a great deal of shipping in the harbour, although a convoy has just left. So it looks as if we will not be here too long after all. Finally the old tub berthed at one of Halifaxes wharves just close to the city. The sun was setting as we nosed into the wharf but it did not deprive us of any warmth. I doubt if it could have been colder. The sun set at half past four, & lit the snow clouds up with golden rays, making a very pretty sunset. Although the days are short, the twilight is long and it does not become dark until past five. It was good to get to bed and thaw out, after freezing on deck most of the day.

Next morning it was very cold & I think it was responsible for those who were late on parade. Leave was granted from 1000 hours.

Thursday night, Squadron Leader Gordon, the R.A.A.F. liaison officer, came on

Chapter 8: Trooping begins

board & had a talk with us. He did not waste any time, & sent some officials on board to change money for us. The rate of exchange was $3.50 for £1. Each man was allowed to exchange £2, and more at the bank if necessary. The seven dollars which I received for £2, & the American dollar, made 810 cents. As there is 10% interest on American money. But these cents did not go far after sending air mail letters & cables.

Shortly after ten o'clock, Jack, Heck & myself sallied forth into town. It was a novelty to see all the puddles frozen, & damp mud frozen. The streets had a thin layer of ice on. I believe the automobile accidents are frequent in winter time, & no wonder. It is difficult to walk up a hill, without slipping, let alone drive up & down hills.

We found Kodaks first, where Jack & Heck bought a camera each. The range is very poor, & the price rather high. But we managed to get a fair bargain under the circumstances.

Spent the rest of the morning wandering around the shops, but did not buy anything

In the afternoon I went along to the Royal Nova Scotia Yacht Squadron. It is deserted during the winter, & most of the junior members are away. They have an excellent array of Yachts there, & as they were all up in the yard for winter, it was possible to have a good look at them. The model of the bluenose schooner was very interesting.

Had a tea of greenstuff with John & Hector at the Bon Ton Cafe. The proprietor is Chinese, as in numerous other cafes in Halifax.

While finding my way to the yacht club, I walked through the railway yards & saw some huge locomotives. The town looked very pretty under a light layer of snow which had fallen in the afternoon.

Saturday 29/11/41
Changed 31/- at the bank, and then purchased Christmas cards. Air mail, cables, & Christmas cards have just about left me broke. Went to a shoe store & bought a pair of slippers, as it is getting rather cold.

The prints from the negatives I left at Kodak have turned out very well. I will post some home in the next letter.

The weather was milder than usual. Went along to the Y.M.C.A. in the afternoon & posted some Christmas cards. They will probably arrive a little late in

SS CERAMIC The Untold Story

Australia, but the thought is still there. Went to a theatre with Ted after tea, I forget what the films were about. But theatres are run differently to Australian theatres. To start with, they do not allow smoking. It feels rather strange to sit there with a pipe in the pocket & not be able to have a smoke. There is no interval between pictures, and no interval between sessions. And there are no advertisements. This is the only good point about them. The theatres seem to be packed everywhere in town. Probably because it was Saturday night

We were on our way to the Lantern cafe, when I met Max Wylie & Merv Caddie. They will probably be in the same convoy with us.

On Sunday I spent the day writing letters. I should say most of the day writing one letter which was not able to fit it in a normal sized envelope. Just before breakfast, a ship came into the wharf opposite us. It had a badly damaged stern, where there was a hole large enough drive a car through. After breakfast, Shiny, Mrs Fraser, Mackenzie, & myself strolled over to get a closer look at it. But could learn nothing from the crew. Later I learnt from our own crew that she was travelling from England to Halifax, under blackout conditions. There happened to be a convoy travelling in the same direction under the same conditions. It got in amongst the convoy & hit about six ships, being cannoned from one to the other.

After tea I went into town & posted the letters home. A letter to Penelope & a Christmas card home.

December 1941

Monday 1/12/41
A bitterly cold day. The sky was very clear, & the conditions must have been excellent for radiation. The temperature was 8°F on the average. Even the Halifax people considered it cold. Ice formed on the streets, in the hard crystalline form, making them very slippery. I believe motor car accidents in Halifax are frequent. Not surprising. Went into town in the morning, wrapped up as much as it was thought regimentally fit. By the time we reached the Y.M.C.A, I was wondering if it was possible to knock my ears off.

Had a most enjoyable swim in the Y.M.C.A. indoor pool. The pool is heated to 73°F. The Y.M.C.A. building is very warm and homely. The swim gave me a good appetite & so we went along & had lunch at the Lantern cafe. Had some coffee & toast. Spent the afternoon writing a letter home.

I think I should have been dead twice today. It is strange getting used to the right hand traffic. I habitually look to the right when crossing a road, and walk in front of a street car. The drivers seem to expect this sort of thing, & there have been no

Chapter 8: Trooping begins

Australian casualties up to date. It must be troublesome to street car drivers, & automobile drivers, having to go slowly, & be on the alert to dodge some left handed Australian.

Collected some photographs from Kodaks before coming back to the boat. Kodaks have the nicest pair of girls I have seen since leaving Australia. And they are not even Brisbane average. I cannot help laughing at myself when I think how that White menace brings the average down.

Tuesday 2/12/41
The day was mild thank goodness. The temperature was not as low as usual, being about 34°F. This is warm compared with Monday. Wrote more letters home, & posted the photographs. There was a fall of snow this morning. It is the best so far. There was a layer of about four inches on deck. The same applied to the city. The boys did not waste any time in developing a snow fight. There was much playing of ball, until the snow melted. (Only the draft on the Ceramic will appreciate the playing of ball.) It is a famous expression of the O.C. He was well & truly balled, as he boarded the ship for luncheon.

In the afternoon I wandered into town & spent my last few cents. After selling some of my photographs, I was able to pay the Kodak debt, & had some over to spend.

Saturday 6/12/41
We have been on the Halifax, England hop, for 4 days now. We left the wharf at 1100 hours. I believe that the convoy is rather slow. Hence we will take approximately two weeks to get there. The afternoon was spent doing S turns outside Halifax Harbour, while the convoy got into formation. Just as the sun began to rest on the horizon, the leaders, of which the *Ceramic* was one, headed East. And so on to England. There are about forty one ships in the convoy, in six columns. For an escort we had one destroyer as we left Halifax, with an aeroplane patrol. The forty one ships, of which it is possible to look at about eight at once, make a very impressive sight. It is a great opportunity to study their motion in a sea. If only there was a sea running. I will be disappointed if it does not get a little rough before we reach England.

Thursday was an uneventful day & so I played bridge most of the day. A number of Catalinas & Douglas bombers, intercepted us & escorted us for some distance. They are from Newfoundland. On Friday morning we met three destroyers. And more later on. We now have about five destroyers escorting us. It is consoling to have a few destroyers handy. It would be terrible if anything should happen to delay us now.

Started studying astro nav again, & played a little bridge.

The news bulletin this morning was not very inspiring. Gt Britain has declared war on Finland, Rumania, & Hungary. I hope she can manage it. The idea, probably, is to cut the Germans off from the Black Sea.

On parade this morning the boys had a thrill. A disturbance in the water was sighted astern of the boat alongside us. It resembled an object racing along, under water, spurting the water up. The boys naturally thought submarine. But the submarine was a fog buoy which is towed behind a ship in convoy, so that the ship behind can keep the ship in sight.

Monday 15/12/41
The weather from Saturday the sixth to last Wednesday was mild, and it looked as if we would escape the Atlantic's rough weather. As for myself, I was hoping that it would blow up, being interested in the type of weather. But I did not wish for anything that would break up the convoy & delay our progress. But luck was against us. Some of the ships in the convoy are small, & have a maximum cruising speed of nine knots. Therefore any weather would cause them to heave to & we would have to wait.

On Wednesday evening, a blow developed, in squall fashion, from the South East. The hour seemed more like seven o'clock, than three o'clock. The sun was almost set in the south west, and was immediately obliterated by the sleet squall.

After tea Ian & myself played bridge with Ben & Max. But they finished 1,000 up. The blighters can play, but they also had the cards.

By 2300 hours there was a large swell running, and some of the waves were hitting *Ceramic*'s side with a resounding thud. She creaks like one of Brisbane's worn out trams.

On Thursday morning we were hove to. The sky completely overcast & a very strong breeze blowing. There was a storm on Wednesday night, which caused the convoy to break up. The escorting destroyers spent from seven o'clock in the morning to 12 o'clock noon herding the ships together, and getting the convoy under way again. The sky cleared up for the day, but towards evening, ominous dark clouds came rolling from the north with an ever increasing wind.

When darkness came at four o'clock the convoy had to break up again. The wind was furious by now, and built up a big sea. A number of ships had to heave to, but the *Ceramic* was very steady. We had a close shave, about half past five. The wind was shrieking through the rigging by now, & the ship was showing navigation lights. The *Ceramic* continued on course, in order to get clear of the convoy. Not very far to windward, there was a green light showing, indicating

Chapter 8: Trooping begins

Heavy weather on the deck of the Ceramic.

that there was a ship just to windward of us on the same course. Suddenly out of the fog, there loomed the port light of a ship hove to. She was right across our path, slightly to windward. There was much blowing of fog horns, with the officers running around on the bridge as if the captain was having kittens. The *Ceramic* & our unknown companion to windward, altered course to starboard. The ship to windward stopped & fell behind the *Ceramic*. The ship across our bows, pushed a little harder through the water, & crept up to windward slightly. The *Ceramic* flew past her stern with a few yards to spare. Rather close to be comfortable. By now we were free of the convoy, & proceeded on course for an hour or so, when the old *Ceramic* heaved to, in order to wait for the convoy. I was told later that the wind reached ninety miles per hour on Thursday night.

On Friday morning we were hove to, dipping our nose into a big sea running from the north. The passengers who are not sick, get a thrill of standing behind the shelter of the glass on the promenade deck, watching the waves break over the bow. Occasionally a big green one would bury the nose, much to the delight of the onlookers.

There was evidence of fury of the gale to be seen on the port promenade deck, and the fore deck. On the fore deck, there was a big bend in the rails. On the promenade deck, the seats (garden seat, of the old type) were smashed to pieces. The woodwork around the entrance to the after lounge was practically disintegrated.

The weather cleared a little by nine o'clock & the wind abated slightly. About thirty out of forty one of the convoy were rounded up, and ready to proceed by two o'clock. At two o'clock we set off with a following sea & a westerly wind.

The purser, a big fat individual, has gone mad with the drink, and has to be guarded.

On Saturday morning the *Ceramic* was again hove to in a Westerly gale. Where the rest of the convoy went to seemed to be the main topic of conversation for Saturday morning. All Saturday was spent wallowing about in a Westerly sea, waiting for instructions. The wind was blowing solidly, and steadily building up a big sea. One of the destroyers made contact with us, but did not come close enough to put on a show like Friday. On Friday one passed close by, bucking about like a wild thing. It looked beautiful. And so the *Ceramic* lay hove to all Saturday & Sunday.

Sunday was the roughest day of all. No ships were sighted, & the weather remained thick, & blew solidly. By now the seas were big. It is most interesting to watch the bow plunging into the waves. Occasionally a big one would come along, and cover the bow completely.

It is a pity our cameras were confiscated. Friday was the chance of a life time in observing the behaviour of ships in a sea. They are changed from the huge dead, lumbersome masses they appear to be in port, to a dancing live thing. The tankers are not so lively & spend half their time under water.

Ceramic broke all previous records for rolling yesterday. Unfortunately she chose to do so at lunch time. It amused the boys very much, to see the things slide from one end of the table to the other. But the climax was reached, when the ship gave a record roll half way through lunch. Mrs Brooks (the duchess) who sits at the captain's table, fell over, complete with chair, and slid under the next table. Aubrey Bice, one of our sergeant gunners, collected his plate of soup in his lap. Much to the amusement of the boys. The silly little rat of a waiter at the next table, dropped a tray of cups.

About eleven o'clock last night, just as most of us were dozing off to sleep, an exceptionally big wave broke over the fore deck, and covered the fore promenade deck. It made a terrific row, and gave some of the chaps a fright.

This morning I surveyed the deck above our cabin, but it seemed to be intact. But

Chapter 8: Trooping begins

portion of the starboard rail on the fore deck was missing. There must have been other big ones during the night. The carpenter's shop in the stern house, was smashed in, & timber & tools were floating around in about two feet of water. The ladder to the gun bridge was smashed, & had to be lashed on with rope. The wave that did all the damage to the stern must have severely tested the steering gear.

When the weather cleared today, we headed for the convoy rendezvous but there were only two ships there. The three of us eventually headed east, and are now making good pace with a following wind, & a following sea.

It is good to be going places at last.

STOP PRESS. Todays latrineogram is rather good. It is rumoured that a submarine emerged alongside one of the tankers in the convoy. The commander asked the captain of the tanker to give him some fuel for his cigarette lighter. But the captain of the the tanker demanded that the U-boat commander produce his ration tickets. But when the U-boat commander threatened to sink him, he changed his mind.

But to be quite serious. The troops were informed today that a submarine has been reported in the vicinity, and watches were requested to keep a sharp lookout.

December 24th 1941
Much has happened since the fifteenth.

On Wednesday the seventeenth, an extra watch was appointed. This was for the purpose of aircraft spotting. It consisted of about twelve fellows who knew their aircraft identification. I was one. It was very interesting to be on Monkey Island. This is the nerve centre of the ship. The compass in the lower bridge was smashed at Colon, so they used the one on Monkey Island. But this instrument is rather ancient. I would not be surprised if it was a relic from the days of Christopher Colombus. On Wednesday the skipper was up Monkey Island meddling with the compass. It appears that it works correctly until the gaussing apparatus is turned on. Then it goes haywire. As we had to go through a minefield that night, it appeared to be a grim show.

On Thursday land was sighted on the starboard bow just after breakfast. They are the Shetland Islands. Macnally remarked that they were not the Shetland Islands that he saw on the map. Because the ones on the map were red. We are safe from submarines now, but have to keep a sharp lookout for hostile aircraft. We have been really very fortunate. **The old ship might be terribly slow, but she has amazing luck. The queer part is, the Hun know her whereabouts and are trying to destroy her.** The change of spirit in the ship's crew is most noticeable.

As for myself I am still most impatient.

Just after tea on Thursday night we heard the war news for the first time since leaving Halifax. The expected has happened at last. Japan is taking aggressive action in the Pacific It appears that she will cause quite a lot of trouble before she is through. Although I have expected it for the past six months, it comes as a shock. But I still feel that I am doing the right thing in coming over here to fight the Hun. After all, they are the cause of all this. If I am fortunate to get through this, I will be more than a match for the Jap. I am sure the rest of the fellows feel the same. I feel most concerned about Dad's business. Petrol will be unobtainable in Australia now, and all the cars will be taken off the road. I cannot see how they will continue to function. And yet it gives me assurance to see motor cars for sale in England here. I must visit a lot of motor places & examine their systems.

On Friday we were steaming down the west coast of Scotland, The news on Friday morning was better. The Japs have not landed in New Guinea. But the situation in Malaya, Philippines & Hong Kong is still very grim. America has taken definite action, and has suffered the first losses. But she will strike hard next year. There should not be any need to withdraw troops from overseas now. No doubt our Militia members are rushing for hollow logs out west. Nevertheless it will make some of the loafers in Australia wake up and do something. Nevertheless it is rather worrying to have those little yellow men so close to our loved ones in Australia. But there is no need to worry until they actually land. I rather doubt that they will do that until next year (March), which is rather unlikely.

On Saturday we were not able to go into the Mersey because of a dense fog. A bloody nuisance, what! Saw the Barrage balloons around Liverpool. They certainly present a very demoralising obstacle. We heard the official figures for the gale. The captain gave the official wind velocity as one hundred and twenty miles per hour. It appears that I was a George Washington after all. In the estuary we saw two of the Hurricanes shot off the catapaults on two of the ships that were in the convoy. A hell of a flash is to be seen, then the Hurricane is seen to shoot up about a thousand feet, & then the boom is heard.

On Sunday we proceeded up the channel, weighing anchor at 1100 hrs, & stopping in the Mersey at 1400 hrs. Barrage balloons are tied to buoys along each side of the channel, forming a long lane of them. On either side there are five or six wrecks to be seen. Sinkings from the Hun air raids.

At the mouth of the Mersey the biggest docks in the world are situated. These have been subjected to terrific bombings. Tremendous sheds have been completely gutted. Liverpool is not very impressive. The most noticeable feature

Chapter 8: Trooping begins

is the huge area composed of houses, each are exactly the same as its neighbour.

A tender conveyed us to the wharf. On the way to the wharf I had a yarn with a member of Shaw Savill line. He informed me that they were most surprised to see the old tub arrive. She had been reported sunk & missing about six times.

We were billeted for the night in the Liverpool blind deaf and dumb school. It is a queer experience travelling through a city completely blacked out, and it is necessary to continually ask the way. Liverpool did not seem to be mutilated very much except for some buildings which were completely gutted.

After a snappy breakfast at 0700 hours on Monday morning, we entrained for London. So we left Liverpool without seeing it in the daylight. We travelled in the train all day, & did not have a meal until we were billeted in the Union Jack club at 1800 hrs. The countryside we passed through was just what one would imagine it to be. Castles occasionally, & canals & barges. But the ancient atmosphere was smashed occasionally by the roar of a modern bomber returning from Germany. Only for this, & occasional buildings which are in ruins, one would not know that there is a war on.

Monday night was spent in London. Aubrey Bice & myself went to Leicester Square, where we sought out a post office. I sent two cablegrams to New Farm. Sent the more expensive ones in order that they might get there quickly. After visiting five or six hotels, and a dance hall met some old Australian friends, & went back to the Union Jack Club where we played darts in the air raid shelter until half past two in the morning.

On Tuesday morning we were up early and the draft caught the eight o'clock train at Waterloo station. What legends, the names in London bring back. The atmosphere is one that cannot be described. But I love it. It smells British. To think at here in Whitehall, the Empire's destiny is shaped, and guided. May God guard these men & show them the way. May they meet the Empire's problems with wisdom and God's guidance. There is comparatively little damage. Although we did not get a chance to see it in daylight. We arrived in Bournemouth at No 3 Personnel Receiving Centre, just in time for lunch. In the afternoon we had the usual medical parade. While waiting, I made enquiries about mail. I was overjoyed to receive a letter from New Farm. But I did get any from (?). But it was wonderful to get a letter from Penelope. I was the first one in the draught to get some mail. But when I told the others, the mail was rushed by a mob. Some were lucky, some were not. It sure is great to get a letter. But the photos have not arrived yet.

I went out with Aubrey Bice on Tuesday night. I am afraid I drank a little to much. Went back to the hotel where we are billeted under the impression that I had mislaid my overcoat which had a letter in the pocket. But Jack found it hanging behind the door.

Bournemouth is swarming with troops. Poles, Czechoslovakians, Rhodesians, Africans, U.S.A., Canada, Rnzaf, R.A.A.F all air force members. When I see all these people here to defend Britain it makes me realise that if Britain dies, the whole Empire dies. The Americans can look after Japan until we have finished the Germans. Then Japan will be helpless.

The English people here are most warming to the heart. English people are supposed to be reserved. But they are certainly not unfriendly. I like them very much.

And so we come to Christmas Eve. Today is Christmas Eve. My thoughts dwell upon Australia. After parade this morning, pay problems were attended to, & then we had night vision tests. I only got average. Rather a poor show. However it is not very important.

After the eye test I walked around the town looking at the homes. Comparing it with Halifax I was struck with the absence of children. This is only to be expected. The English girls are very nice on the whole, better than any other ports. They resemble the Brisbane girls very much.

I spent a rather quiet Christmas Eve. After tea I settled down to write some letters. But Jack Lock dragged me into town. We went to the Pavilion & the Rink. I made a few dates with different women. But I cannot see myself keeping them.

Just one other thing. Contrary to the belief in Australia that English Christmas is spent in houses which are almost buried under fathoms of snow. We have very mild Christmas weather. So far it has been wonderful weather. It is only every five or six years that snow is experienced. Thank goodness it is not like Halifax.

END OF THE FIRST NOTE BOOK.
(extracts follow)

Friday 9 January 1942
...This morning I sat around the fire with Jack Lock, Noel Pashen, & a fellow who has been waiting here for seven weeks. Rus Cumberland. Jack and Noel have been posted. We discussed all subjects from Politics to women. From Australia to Australians, and the trip over. The Australians certainly caused a stir on some of the ships in certain convoys. We had some fun with our little draft, but it was

nothing compared to other batches.

On one ship the souveniring was so bad that they needed a kit inspection. The captain was left holding the anchor, & his personal belongings. Considering the numbers packed on some ships, you cannot blame them.

In one case they were so badly fed that they raided the hold, & eventually took charge of the galley. I guess we were lucky after all. That is, comparatively.

Monday 12th January 42
Another bleak cold day. The cold is most penetrating. The only way to keep warm is to stay indoors. It reminds me of Les Wilson's joking remark as we left the *Ceramic*. He said "Why in the name of fortune, do people fight for countries like this?"

7th April 1942
...But in this year of fate, as Nature blooms, so will the horrors of this present war reach a climax. It will be one of the most terrible carnages in history.

From The Portal, 1942 (School Yearbook)

Sergeant-Pilot Ralph A. Wilson was our first Old Boy to join the R.A.A.F. when still at school, volunteering just after his eighteenth birthday in May, 1940, during his final year in the Senior Public class. He spent five years at the College (1936-40), and was a Prefect and one of our outstanding athletes in 1940, securing colours in both rowing and football. He was also an expert amateur sailor, gaining much success in his sailing boats, in open competition on the river. During his training at Tamworth and Amberley, he made rapid progress and showed marked proficiency in "blind" (or instrument) flying and was selected as a bomber pilot. He gained his "wings" in August 1941 and shortly afterwards sailed via Panama, for England, where he underwent advanced training in night flying. In his first flight over Germany he piloted a Hampden bomber and was later transferred to a squadron flying Britain's latest and most up-to-date Lancaster bombers. He was posted missing on July 26th, following a raid over Duisberg, in Germany. No further word has yet been received and any news is sought by his parents, Mr. and Mrs. A.M. Wilson, of New Farm, with whom we join in sympathy in their inevitable anxiety. Ralph early developed a keen sense of responsibility and will be remembered for his enthusiasm and loyalty.

****

Ian Battersby
Letter to the author

Penultimate trip made by the Ceramic
A personal account of the last complete voyage 14th January 1942 to 15th August 1942 by a Sailor Rating.

I completed my second trip on the motor vessel *M.V. Lochkatrine*, five hatch freighter of the Pacific Steam Navigation Company on the l0th December 1941, paying off at Cardiff in the Bristol Channel.

Having been promoted from Ordinary Seaman to a Sailor Rating for the voyage meant that I now performed an A.B.'s job and was paid as such but was not a B.O.T. A.B. My first trip on *Lochkatrine* saw us transport, lashed on the after deck, two enormous replacement gun barrels for a British Battleship – one of the "R" class I think: *"Repulse"*, *"Renown"* etc. 15 inch main armament, to the U.S. Naval Shipyard at Norfolk., Virginia. Also in the dockyard under repair was the Aircraft Carrier *H.M.S.S. Illustrious* which had fought a running battle with Italian and German Airforce warplanes. To memory she accounted for 35 enemy planes but sustained severe damage to herself.

This was the beginning of August 1941 with the U.S. still neutral, so for us engaged in the war at sea, the fact that the U.S.N. would help our cause in this manner was heartening to say the least.

As the convoy broke up into its respective groups in the Western approaches to head for the Clyde, Mersey or Bristol Channel, we joined the latter group to pay off in Cardiff on December 10th.

The news came in as we headed south, of the murderous attack on the U.S. Naval Base at Pearl Harbour in the Hawaiian Islands.

While feeling so sad for our American Naval friends we couldn't help feeling thanks be to providence that our lonely effort must surely be at an end.

Five days leave was spent in the Medway Towns at Kent, The Garden of England in peacetime, the Battlefield of Britain in war time, as I was wont to point out to my North Country shipmates, which seemed to infuriate them, especially as I was born and raised in Lancs and Cheshire. It was what had become a well worn route for me, head up to London on the Southern Railway, cross London on the Underground lugging my sea gear, then the Express north from Euston.

Up until late 1943 I always stayed with Uncle Alf and his very caring lady in the

Chapter 8: Trooping begins

Penultimate trip made by the *Ceramic*
The last complete voyage 14th January 1942 to 15th August 1942 by Ian Battersby.

Alongside at Liver Buildings Landing Stage. Snow on deck.

Inset below:
Target Practice
(Open Ocean).

Passing through Gladstone Dock to lock out. Escort Flotilla signalling. Escorts based here.

Steaming in North Atlantic winter.

219

Liverpool suburb at Fazackerly, which was in the vicinity of Aintree. My mother's sister also lived on the other side of Liverpool, her husband having been taken P.O.W. at Arras in Belgium in May 1940.

After a pleasant Christmas and New Year, there was still some food and drink to be had and the Merchant Seaman Pool people seemingly in no hurry to ship out. Reality finally caught up in the form of a directive to go and front the Mate of some nondescript merchantman. Sighting this rattletrap of an old rustbucket my knees started to knock. Getting the Gen. from a crewman it appeared that the heap was a 43 years old, never went in convoy because it was too slow, a coalburner not much bigger than a large Coaster and to make matters worse, was on the Newfoundland run transporting iron ore.

As I was not then of call-up age, I couldn't see myself committing virtual suicide so told the Mate I couldn't steer. On return to the Pool the official, who would have been a Labour Exchange clerk in peace time, said "So, a smarty are you? well you will take the next one."

The "next one" turned out to be the *Ceramic*; though somewhat big for my liking, nevertheless she would be heading south in convoy to Freetown, Sierra Leone, thence on to Cape Town and a good run alone and Hey Ho for Botany Bay or rather Port Jackson, Sydney, blue skies and warm winds (Merseyside is decidedly uninviting in January). We were as things turned out, in for a disappointment, as I shall explain.

To memory, the deck crowd numbered 14 A.B.s and Sailor Ratings, 6 Ordinary Seamen and 6 Deck Boys. In addition were 3 Quartermasters (who never touched the wheel; the watch-keeping A.B.s did all the steering), 1 Bosun and 1 Bosun's Mate, who was his brother, 1 Lamptrimmer (Deck Stores Keeper), 1 Carpenter and 1 Carpenter's Mate.

After the Deck Crowd had signed on, we were ordered aboard for the following day, and so began the routine of settling in and preparing for sea. The Bosun chose the watches, 12 to 4, 4 to 8, 8 to 12. Three men per watch to do 1st wheel of 2 hours – 1 hour standby – 1 hour look-out, the same again in reverse with the 2 centre hours on look-out and 1st and 4th hours on standby. The Quartermasters pattered about the Bridge and did next to nothing, and the remaining Deck Lads on day work, of which there was plenty once the decks dried.

The living quarters were aft below the main deck, accessed down a skuttle, having the toilets in a line on the after bulkhead facing a line of wash basins. Next came the Mess Room, 4-8 room, companion stair, deck boys, O's, 8-12 room, 12-4 room, QMs and Lampy. The crew's galley was on the upper deck and

Chapter 8: Trooping begins

the Petty Officers lived midships below the passenger accommodation.

As *Ceramic* was such a long ship there was plenty of open deck space aft for the crew and she had laid timber decks throughout. I rather think the timber would have been teak but could have been beech. Nevertheless all this vast area of decking had to be Holeystoned, which involved pulling a block of Sydney Sandstone backwards and forwards with a long handle while sand was spread and sea water hosed; once a week a solution of caustic soda was introduced.

As the Navy had painted over exposed Brass and Timber Decking in the interests of eliminating reflections, some of the dogmatic merchant masters couldn't see why they should comply.

As a Deck Boy in 1940 I was polishing brass thresholds and fittings on the Bridge and Bosun's-Carpenter's quarters regardless that one eventually got 'knocked off' in a Malta convoy in 1942 and no one got off her.

Having chosen the forward and after gangs for stations fore and aft for arrival and departure and the watches chosen and set, we singled up and then let go, and with the help of tugs moved slowly through the dock system into Gladstone dock, past the escorts made fast alongside their Flotilla Club base, and locked out into the River Mersey where tugs manoeuvred us alongside the passenger loading facilities near the Liver Buildings. There was snow on the decks, and we were miserable and cold and thinking of warm winds and blue skies heading down the West African coast.

We had taken on board our passengers, among whom were a Surgeon Rear Admiral and staff, several Imperial Airways Pilots, numerous Australians, New Zealanders and probably South African Service Officers, some with wives and children, various British Army personnel and, as *Ceramic* had been chosen to be the Commodore ship for the convoy, a Naval contingent comprising the Commodore who was a Commander R.N.R. (Merchant Master Mariner in peacetime) a Chief Yeoman of Signals and his assistants and various other naval personnel.

There were other civilian passengers making passage, one of whom I met while following an enquiry for demountable office partitions whilst working as a Company Representative for a Shop and Office Fitting company in Sydney. This gentleman was a Frenchman who made the passage out on the last voyage to Sydney, transferring to Noumea, New Caledonia.

We moved north up the Irish Sea to the now familiar area where the convoys assembled, each ship flying her numeral pennants, one indicating the column, the other her position in the column,

We being the "Commodore Ship", there was much flurry of signal flags appearing on the hoists on the Bridge, as well as lamp signalling.

The convoy formed up without mishap, our invaluable escorts in their respective positions, and we surged forward at our speed of seven knots. As *Ceramic*'s cruising speed was around 15 knots, and the forecast of heavy weather and a North Atlantic mid-winter passage ahead, it looked like a slow crossing. As we headed west the weather worsened and the old rattletraps and rust buckets with their single screws and coal firing had difficulty in making seven knots.

The routine on a Coalburner was that half an hour before the change of the watch, the Fireman being relieved cleaned his fires by breaking up the slabs of clinker and raking it and any other dead junk in his fires out on to the Stokehold deck plates to be barrowed away by his Trimmer. This process caused a loss of steam power and often caused old timers to drop behind the escort screen to become an easy target for a trailing U Boat partially hull down and waiting for nightfall.

The eventual introduction of the escort aircraft carriers put paid to a lot of this caper.

This cleaning of fires followed by restoking caused great columns of black smoke climbing to the sky and did nothing to endear us to our convoy companions, though being the Commodore Ship, everyone else kept their criticism to themselves.

Westward we plodded, day after day of appalling weather, at times barely making headway because some couldn't keep up. One had to feel compassion for the Escort Crews on their relatively small vessels. I watched a corvette close alongside having dialogue with the Commodore go up the side of a mountainous wave until the whole expanse of her port side anti-fouling right down to her keel, literally showing from her knickers to her heels, was visible.

Because of the foul weather, Crows-Nest look outs, 75 feet up in the top nest, were not called for and we kept our look-out periods on the 'Monkey Island' on which was situated the Azimuth bearing Compass. This location is on top of the Wheelhouse and became the domain of the Chief Yeoman of Signals and his very efficient team of Signals Ratings, very pretty to watch as they sent and received by flag hoists to the Flotilla Commander as well as signals to the convoy. In general, Lamp signals were kept to a minimum for obvious reasons.

I felt myself fortunate having scored a place on the 4 to 8 watch. Called at 3-10 am (or 7 bells of the middle watch) we always saw the dawn come up. The dayworkers 'turned to' at 6 am (4 bells of the morning watch) and the man on stand-by was required to join the work which was invariably wash-down fore and aft, so our job was to squeegee the boat deck dry.

Because the 12 to 4 watch got their heads down early in the evening, the 8 to 12 were getting ready to go on watch after, the 4 to 8 watch room became the locale for the usual evening Power game, though a Monopoly board game was usually in progress. And so we finally reached our Trans-Atlantic destination, the Sub-Arctic frozen Eastern Maritimes Canadian port of Halifax, Nova Scotia, a haven for many a torpedoed seamen and the western terminal for the northern convoy route.

As the convoy approached Halifax, it began to part company and disperse, some to head north for Newfoundland to load iron ore, others to head south for a variety of destinations, and others such as ourselves to head into the Port for bunkers or other reasons.

Having been a somewhat frequent caller the previous year on the New Zealand run and what we called the Lend Lease run, I kept a weather eye open for a sighting of their intriguing, to a sailing buff such as myself, Pilot Cutter which was a Newfoundland Grand Banks two masted fishing Schooner, looking exactly like the sailing vessels featured in the film of 1936 and based on the R.L. Stephenson story *Captains Courageous* with John Barrymore and Spencer Tracy. They would meet an incoming vessel, heave-to under sail, and then launch a fishing Dory such as used to be launched when on the fishing grounds, maybe two dozen Dorys single manned and rowed, from which the fisherman would hand-line fish for Cod and, if lucky, Halibut.

Through the Boom Defence and alongside the coaling wharf we went. The Old Girl's thirst for Coal Bunkers usually assured us of at least one night's run ashore.

As there were no Bars or Pubs in the wowserish Eastern Maritimes, certain concerned people had seen fit to establish a well fitted-out Club for Seamen, not to forget a Hospital also.

Something of a Donnybrook got going later in the evening, a score being settled between two of the Stokehold leading-hands, but other crew members managed to throw them out of the club.

Then it was stations 'fore and aft' and we proceeded to sea.

As we cleared the land and set course south, some lines from John Masefield's immortal poem *'The Loch Achray'* came to mind:

In the grey of the coming on of night
She dropped the tug at the Tuskar Light,
'N' the topsails went to the topmast head
To a chorus that fairly awoke the dead.
She trimmed her yards and slanted South
With her royals set and a bone in her mouth.

It wasn't quite like that for us, more of throw some more coal on the furnace fires and keep that Steam Gauge up.

Because of the slowness of the convoy the stokehold gang hadn't had to work at full pressure on the trip over, but now the Bridge called for full cruising speed which meant full effort.

The U Boats had not at this time made their way across to the U.S. Eastern Seaboard after the German Declaration of war on the U.S.A. so the Ship's company settled down to a peaceful run to the Panama Canal, or so we thought. But the news trickled down that we were bound for Rio de Janeiro, queer course to take for Australia thought we. However we would need a good bunkering and Rio is a great place for a Seafarer to have a sojourn in.

Although we could make a top speed of fifteen knots we probably cruised around thirteen. At this speed it would have taken us some thirteen days to reach Rio.

She crossed the Line and all went well,
They ate, they slept, and they struck the bell
And I give you a gospel truth when I state
The crowd didn't find any fault with the Mate.

Mr Marsden to memory, was the Chief Officer or 'Mate' of the *Ceramic*, not big in stature but certainly big in character, with a true humanitarian feeling for his crew. During all our long running campaign to try and improve the diet, Mr. Marsden did what he could – but to no avail – we finished the voyage with the same weekly menu that we started with. By the look of the framed grease and dirt obscured menu pasted on the crews galley bulkhead, it hadn't changed since 1913.

After having his leave, Mr Marsden was posted to S.S. & Albion Lines Commodore Ship *Dominion Monarch* as Chief Officer.

D.M. was something of an experimental vessel being propelled by quadruple diesel engines in a similar configuration to at least one of the German Pocket

Chapter 8: Trooping begins

Battleships, I think the *Graf Spee*, cornered and out of 'Ammo' for her 11 inch guns south of where we were bound. Their crew scuttled this new and wonderfully designed warship rather than be a prize of war to the attacking British and New Zealand Cruisers.

Eventually the Sugarloaf Mountain hove into sight and we steamed into this beautiful harbour.

The off watch firemen and their trimmer mates were on deck with their tongues hanging out, but the word came down that we would be anchoring out in the stream, no going alongside, the coal for bunkers to be transported out to us on barges. The reason for this was that at this time, less than three months after the U.S.A. entered the conflict, Brazil was at the point of declaring which side she would be supporting.

As her neighbours Bolivia, Paraguay and Argentina were pro the Axis side, there was uncertainty as to our reception. Having two R.M. Admirals and their Staffs on board plus a variety of other service Personnel it could be claimed that we were a trooper, consequently steam was kept up and no shore leave.

Brazil subsequently declared for our side and contributed several Battalions of Infantry who served in General Mark Clarke's American 5th Army which fought its way up the West Coast of Italy.

The watch on deck was maintained so that we of the 4-8 came below at eight o' clock that evening and got in a huddle. One of the watch went down on the Coal Barges with some Canadian Dollars and came back with two bottles of Hooch which was some sort of Brandy. A few swigs of this firewater reminded the lads of the fleshpots to be enjoyed ashore, so the idea of lowering away the smaller starboard side after boat took hold and six of us headed to the fray.

As the boat was already swung out with one man on each 'falls' and the others in the boat, we were afloat and cast off in a hurry, the two falls men sliding down the safety lines. As we started to pull away, a Royal Marine, one of the R.M. personnel making a passage to South Africa, who must have been ordered to do sentry duty because of the uncertain situation ashore, called out for us to return or he'd fire. However no shot came and we disappeared into the darkness.

After maybe nearly two hours rowing this cumbersome lifeboat we came to a seawall with a road running parallel to it, on the other side of which were bright lights, bars etc.

Leaving the boat under the watchful eye of a Brazilian who savvied Englisie with the promise of a payola, we hit the nearest bar. In the bar were a group of Canadian Merchant Seamen who became very friendly when two locals who had watched us arrive said we were survivors who'd just rowed in. The Canucks, quite merry by this time of night, bought drinks & souvenired bits of our belts.

Not having much money ourselves to return the hospitality, we couldn't hang around for very long, though time must have slipped by, because the row back took so long that daylight overtook us, and found us within a half mile of *Ceramic* and unable to make any headway against an incoming tide.

Wearily we swallowed our pride and reluctantly accepted a tow from a local motorboat.

The length of the Passenger Prom deck was lined with heads as we came alongside and hooked on the boat falls and were hoisted into position. Several hours later we up-hooked and cleared out for Capetown.

The following day each one of the escapade to the shore-side received a typewritten sheet which was a copy of the entry into the ships log charging us with dire penalties if we blotted our copy books again.

The men charged were as follows:
Charles Freer, Bill Davis, John Wilding, John Roberts, one other
... and Ian Battersby.

Setting course for Cape Town S.A. from Rio de Janeiro involved a long slant south from the Tropic of Capricorn at $22°$S. LAT., Rio being at $22°$ 53 min S., there being 60 n.m. in one degree of LAT meant that we would steam approx, $11°$ (660 n.m.) - further south. Interestingly, the latitude of Adelaide, Australia, is only $1°$ (60 n.m.) further south than Cape Town.

These latitudes are delightful at sea, though just south of the S.E. Trades. Though *Ceramic* had none of the recreational facilities of Cruise Liners such as a Games Deck, Swimming Pool, Ballroom etc., our passengers appeared to have slipped into a Lotus Eating mode. Some became deck dwellers, sleeping out in the open, a favourite location being at the break of the Fore Sun Deck level, out of sight of the Bridge but under the all seeing eyes of the man in the Top Nest.

We of the 4 to 8 always saw the sunrise, the man on lookout being ordered aloft at daybreak to the top Crows Nest, where the only company was an occasional wandering Albatross which used to take up station at the height of the Nest and keep an unblinking eye on the men in it.

Chapter 8: Trooping begins

Right: S.S. *Ceramic*,
4-8 watch, 1942.
Back (L-R):
Albert Armstrong
(Cheshire)
Ian Battersby (Kent)
Charles (Snowy) Freer
(Napier N.Z.)
Front: Bill Davis (Wales)
Johnny Gray (Liverpool)

Port side boats.
Ian Battersby's boat
(Cox) up forward.

Bosun Edward Vaughan, inboard (Chippy's Mate in white).

Twin Marlin Heavy
Machine Gun.
(Replaced with 20mm
Oerlikon Cannons in
New York homeward
bound).

Ceramic's 6" Naval Gun. Maritime Regiment Gunner.

Nothing of much interest happened on this passage. I can recall the Purser, who had a beautiful coal black Persian cat that he used to walk in the night watches as he suffered from insomnia. Also there were three Aircraft Pilots from Imperial Airways making their journey to Sydney. Sunderland Flying Boats, most built by Short Bros. alongside the River Medway up river of the Bridge at Rochester, Kent, being the only Airline connecting Britain & Australia.

Coming on watch at 4 am one morning and having the first hour as standby man, I was told to stand guard outside a particular cabin door and the passenger inside, who was making a bit of a din from time to time, was "one of the airline pilots who was in the grip of the D.T.s" ... just what a lightweight slim seventeen year old was meant to do I never quite figured out.

Every morning the Deck routine involved a washdown fore and aft by day workers, with standby man of the 4 to 8 squeegeeing the boat-deck. The photo of the boat deck shows there was a considerable area to cover for one man.

There were two Rear Admirals of the R.N. and their Staffs making passage to Cape Town, one an Engineer, and the other a Surgeon. To my memory, I think it was the Engineer Admiral, who, every morning positioned himself in a deck chair with a book on the Port side of the Boat Deck outside the officers' quarters in the open area which had to be given the top treatment.

Faced with having to give deference where deference was due, and at the same time placating Gerry Vaughn, the uncompromising Liverpool Bosun, I did my dog trot with the squeegee in a circle, around the Admiral, carefully avoiding his immaculate shoes.

Some mention should be made regarding the job of steering the old girl. As the Wheel House was situated for'ard of midships, the ship was some 760ft long and the steering flat machinery and connections from the rudder to the wheel were thirty years old, plus the fact that she carried approx two full turns of port helm before she would respond. I can assure any reader that after two hours of that caper, the helmsman had had enough.

Further complicating the issue was during a period of zig zag steering. In explanation, the Admiralty had issued at the start up of the convoy system a book of zig zag courses to steer. The wheelhouse clock facing the helm had a steel ring mounted so that the minute hand would just make contact with a point on its underside. When the minute hand made contact a bell would sound. On the steel ring were a number of movable slides which were set at minutes past the hour dictated by the book of courses to steer. The slides were set by the Officer of the Watch and the course to steer at that particular contact point chalked up on a blackboard. Steering this routine in convoy was a sight to see when 50 or 60 ships

Chapter 8: Trooping begins

suddenly at no discernible signal, changed course as much as 10 or 12 degrees.

When steaming alone during a U Boat alert, if zig zagging was reverted to, the two hours on the Wheel seemed to drag as the Helmsman couldn't slip into his usual mental reverie of the girl or whoever or whatever he'd left behind him.

And so we steamed on for Cape Town, that most welcome way station for seafarers over a number of centuries past. Confident of quenching our thirsts built up over weeks, South Africa was a great place for a trot ashore, the currency was on par with Sterling, prices reasonable, the girls more than reasonable, and good ballroom dancers as well.

The British service personnel making passage were due to disembark to go to their different postings, but they were quite sure that they were heading for war zones just as we were, the Imperial Japanese forces having overrun the white areas of influence in the Pacific and South East Asia. Only the Dominions of the British Commonwealth were holding out.

After a routine visit, during which our coal bunkers were replenished and numerous passengers disembarked, the stokehold mob fired up, and what would be today an environmentalist's mobile floating nightmare headed into the Indian Ocean on course for good old Aussie Land.

We were approximately half way across on our way to Adelaide when a telegram received by the ship's radio shack telling me of my elder Brother's loss along with his Aircraft Carrier *H.M.S. Hermes* was passed to me. They had been in action against a Japanese carrier task force of modern carriers equipped with modern planes, off Trincomalee, Ceylon, where they were based. *Hermes* was the first purpose built Aircraft Carrier in the world, of medium size and equipped with ageing, hopeless aircraft. Half the Ship's Company was lost, including Brother Tony who was a Leading Aircraft Electrician aged 20 years.

There are no Roses on a Sailor's grave
No Lilies on an ocean wave,
The only tribute in the Seagulls Sweeps
And the teardrops that a Sweetheart weeps.

The above taken from *'Iron Coffins'* by Kapitanleutnant Herbert A. Werner Kriegsmarine U Boat Officer 1941- 1945.

At last the Australian Mainland hove into view. Though the South-West Pacific was now an intense war zone, it is a vast area, and life seemed perfectly normal under the blue sky and warm sun.

We saw the departure of some passengers and a main gunner or two. The two big guns were manned by Australian Naval ratings, the equivalent of our R.M. D.E.M.S. (Defensively Equipped Merchant Ships). One of them was quite friendly towards myself and was known as Gus, who lived in West Australia and took leave to go home by train which was to take him over the Nullabor Plain, some 700 or more miles, of waterless arid plain. Gus gave me a great description of the journey when he rejoined us in, I think, Melbourne.

Port Adelaide, where we berthed, is some distance from the city, but as the city is not a very attractive place from a thirsty seafarer's viewpoint, it being full of churches, and I think with the stamp of Scottish Presbyterian about it, I don't have many recollections of my two calls there.

I was on the Australian coast in August 1940, having my 16th birthday one day off making Brisbane, outward bound via Auckland New Zealand, as a deck boy making my first trip deep sea aboard the old *Port Hunter* with consumer goods from the U.K. and umpteen drums of special oils and greases from the east coast of the U.S.A. *Port Hunter* blew sky high in the summer of 1942 in convoy trying to make Malta with food and ammo. Nobody got off her, including full Naval 'Dems' gun crews.

While working as a company rep promoting to big builders in the 1960s, I was in the Port Line building in Sydney looking for a firm of Architects who appeared to have moved location. On the 12th floor I came across a Memorial Plaque outside the Company Staff Canteen and stood reading the list of ships lost by the Company with the lists of crew men lost with them. Port Line lost half their fleet of 30 ships and my old wagon was the greatest loss in terms of crew. No one survived.

It was a fleet comprised of old, ageing and very modern fast motor ships, of good crew accommodation and victualling. That highly critical Malta Convoy of summer 1942 comprised mainly of modern fast freighters and the great American tanker *Ohio* with her precious cargo of aviation fuel for the Spitfires and Hurricane fighter planes already flown in off aircraft carriers. Also there were two Port Line vessels, both fast motor ships. The *Port Melbourne* was sunk while the *Port Brisbane* broke away from the fight and made for the North African Coast. At the coming on of night they went hard 'a port and headed for Valletta harbour which she made under cover of darkness. Tragically while discharging her precious cargo she was bombed and sunk alongside.

While working the Australian Coast in the late southern summer we visited the N.W. port of Wyndham, which at that time was truly a frontier place, existing only for support of the meat works. The township comprised of the large abattoir and barrack accommodation for the workers, a substantial pub with cold beer twice the price as down in Fremantle, and a single dusty street of galvanised iron

Chapter 8: Trooping begins

shop shacks occupied by Chinese. The cattle were driven overland from as far as 500 miles away. During the killing season, in the cooler months, any unwanted bits were flumed down into the Wyndham River, there being no local health authority to worry about. This practice attracted giant crocs and equally giant sharks to participate in a feeding frenzy.

The tides on that area of the Australian coast are the same as Darwin, around 18 to 19ft but further down towards Fremantle at the Pearling Port of Broome they record the third highest range in the world at 40ft.

As a Training Ship boy on the *T.S. Vindicatrix* at Sharpness on the River Severn in the spring of 1940, I saw the second highest rise in the world at 43ft. in six hours; quite frightening to watch.

Thinking back to my first trip to Aussie land I was inclined to repeat the lines Rudyard Kipling wrote:

Ship me somewhere east of Suez.
Where the best is like the worst,
Where there ain't no ten commandments
And a man can raise a thirst.

We now departed Adelaide for Melbourne where we entered Port Phillip Bay through the Tide Race there and berthed at one of the long piers.

The reality of the war situation at that time was immediately brought home to us, as the U.S. Army were flooding in, there being nowhere else to go in the S.W. Pacific except New Zealand. There were huge American Transports discharging trucks, staff cars and all the supplies for an Army. They had commandeered the Flying Angel Seamen's Mission, a relatively new extensive premises near the Water Front, for a Port Command headquarters, along with people's private phones and anything else they needed; the Yankees sure meant business.

Our usual routine took place. Having made fast the ship, the stokehold gang drew fires, cleaned up the stokehold and were free to head ashore, which they lost no time in doing. We of the deck crowd had to top derricks, strip hatch covers and prepare to work cargo before we could skedaddle.

Ava Gardner, American film star working on filming the story of the last days of a global nuclear exchange in the northern and western hemispheres and its aftermath and finale in Melbourne, named *'On the Beach'*, observed that "They'd sure chosen the right place to film the end of the world, this place is dead but it won't lay down". Nevertheless we contrived to enjoy our trots ashore, the Mate decreeing that if everybody turned to at 6 am, regardless of sick hangovers or whatever, we could all go shoreside after 2.30 pm, so you can be sure that anyone attempting to lie in was hauled out of his bunk and dragged on deck to the Bosun's muster.

As the very conveniently situated 'Missions' (the Seamen's Mission) had been commandeered by the U.S. Army, we always headed up-town and more often than not drifted out to the Bayside suburb of St. Kilda where there was a dance hall complex called Palm Grove which consisted of three dance floors. There was the main ballroom, an Old Time dance floor and an Hawaiian electric guitar dance band and floor. There were also lots of lovely girls and hordes of American Army personnel. No alcohol of course, a very conservative dance tempo reminiscent of Victor Silvester of Britain and his strict tempo. Jiving and jitterbugging banned on pain of death (almost) but the Yankee boys changed all that. One memorable night the main ballroom was crowded and the resident Australian band put down their instruments and retired backstage for a break. A team of Tank G.I.s must have had things well organised and must also have been an army band because they slipped up on the stage and sat down behind the instrument so one chappie taking up the conductors baton and without musical scores, at the one two three blasted with the opening bars of the current hot jive song in the U.S.A. *"Pardon me Boy, is that the Chattanooga Choo Choo?"*

You would have to have been there to appreciate the reaction that followed. From a staid strictly ballroom tempo the floor simply exploded in a mass of flying legs, twirling bodies and flashing panties, just where these Aussie lasses had picked up the jive I'll never know but some of we seafaring types had become reasonably adept at it. The resident bandsmen came dashing in but let the G.I.s finish their number. The floor discipline was never the same after that performance. Jiving being permitted either side of the band out of the main stream.

Before we cleared out of Port Melbourne an examiner from the Commonwealth of Australia Dept. of Transport visited us to conduct examinations for the Lifeboat Coxswains Certificate for those of the crew who had been interested to study the handbook on the subject. And it was a requisite of the Gravesend Sea School at its wartime evacuation location aboard the *T.S. Vindicatrix* that all Seamen-boys must pass this test before going on home leave prior to shipping out. I had no difficulty with the test which was simple enough I suppose. Nevertheless it wouldn't have mattered if you had a half dozen lifeboat tickets when the time came to lower away and launch into a full gale such as subsequently happened, because no small open boat could survive those conditions.

At last the call came to single up fore and aft, let go the springs and lines and we were away again bound for Port Jackson and Sydney Town. Through the

Chapter 8: Trooping begins

treacherous Bass Strait and up the magnificent coast line of Southern New South Wales past the infamous Botany Bay of legend, now despoiled by an oil refinery at the entrance, a container port at its top end, and two jumbo jet runways built into the bay – developments that have taken the pressure off Sydney Harbour as a working port, much to the satisfaction of recreational boaters and Tourism Operatives.

Sydney is a great port for seamen to be berthed in due to the fact that your ship is virtually in the city itself, instead of being often miles away. We made fast in the area called Walsh Bay close to the bottom of Erskine Street, a walk up which landed you in the C.B.D. Along the street were two hostelries all very convenient, as usual the stokehold mob were way ahead of the deck crew in making for the Shore-side. By the time we reached the first pub, there were all the signs of a 'Donnybrook' brewing, so we passed by and set up headquarters in the second one.

Where Melbourne had become the favoured city for the U.S. Army, Sydney had become the natural base for the U.S. Navy. The R.A.N. Naval Base of Garden Island had all the facilities to cope with the largest of vessels, including the King George V graving dock which was capable of dry docking the two Queens Mary and Lizzie.

The shore side was much the same as down in Victoria, 6 o'clock closing of the hostelries, the usual ballrooms and cinemas, but there were two very good Seamens Missions, one Protestant and the other Catholic, both hosted by friendly girls who did a commendable job of offering a retreat and haven for seafarers. Sunday was a dull day with everything closed – except the Missions.

After a couple of weeks we had discharged the mountain of consumer goods from the U.K. and loaded some small amounts of cargo including butter, cheese, zinc and lead and were ready to depart for Lyttleton, South Island of New Zealand. As we steamed under the Sydney Harbour Bridge into the outer harbour we passed the *U.S.S. Chicago* at anchor, a heavy cruiser that was to bear a charmed life because several days after we departed an attack was made on the harbour by three midget submarines, one getting entangled in the boom net protecting the entrances, and a second was never located and the third one lining up the *Chicago* but its torpedo missed and carried on to sink an old Harbour Ferry being used by the R.A.N. as temporary accommodation, causing the deaths of twenty one personnel. This attack was on the first of June 1942. Four odd months later, the *Chicago* was torpedoed in the bow at the battle of Savo Island in the Solomons, but the collision bulkhead held and the crew were able to get the cruiser back to Sydney where she was repaired at the dockyard on Cockatoo Island, inner harbour.

The time had come to clear Sydney Heads and set course for Lyttleton, South

Island, New Zealand, which lies about 11°S Lat of Sydney. Only a small out port for the town of Christchurch, which is situated on the lovely Avon River which flows through green banks and is reminiscent of Southern England. The distance to cover at that time between the two was approx. 14 miles, the road and railway following the hilly coast for half the distance, but in more recent times a tunnel has been punched through the hills to halve the distance. As the last train back was at 10 pm our gallivantings were somewhat restricted.

Before we departed Sydney, we took on board for the passage back to Britain 360 R.A.A.F. aircrew, mostly pilots destined to join the ever increasing Air War in the Northern Hemisphere, and 160 R.N. survivors of the battleships *H.M.S. Prince of Wales* and *Repulse* as well as several from two destroyers lost in the battle of the Java Sea. These British Naval men had commandeered an old Coal Burning Coaster and had steamed it from the debacle of Singapore to Fremantle emulating Philias Fogg in the story *Around The World in Eighty Days*, by burning everything combustible on board to reach there.

Quite a number of the Australians booked themselves into the White Hart Hotel in Christchurch for the stay in port. With holds frozen down to receive cargo the loading of thousands of tons of telescoped succulent Canterbury Lamb commenced. The Canterbury Plains of South Island N.Z. are extensive and ideal for sheep meat production. To conserve shipping space, the two hind legs of the carcass were sewn off together and inserted into the trunk. With the co-operation of the wharfies, who would slip several loose lambs on top of the net sling after the hatch boss had signalled take the weight, the sling came aboard, momentarily holding up the winch men while we retrieved the carcasses, all for some cigs, and what tea we could scrounge, tea being in short supply ashore. The combined ops that took place in the deck mess room and crews' galley getting this lamb prepared and subsequently roasted was something to see.

As the last train from Christchurch departed at 10 pm there was usually quite a crowd of crewmen on it, and as the only place open for business in Lyttleton appeared to be a café run by a motherly type of lady and her two daughters, lots of the mob headed in for a feed. The family couldn't possibly cope so various lads lent a hand in the kitchen and serving at table. My station was at the stove making omelets and scrambled eggs. Others did veg. peeling and oyster opening 2s-6d per plate of 12 big luscious oysters, a friendly scene.

When the news of the *Ceramic*'s loss reached those good people, I imagine great sadness. Snowy Freer of the 4 to 8 who hailed from Napier on the East Coast of North Island, gained several days leave and headed home on the Inter Island Ferry to Wellington, thence by train, the distance being approx 140 n.m. for the sea section.

Chapter 8: Trooping begins

The 'Mary' clearing out of Table Bay.

Lyttleton, New Zealand.

Sugar Loaf Mountain, Rio de Janeiro, Brazil.

Steaming in Trades.

Coaling Station.

The Old Red Duster. Jigger Mast Gaff.

Steaming in the Tropics.

Foremast. Two nests. Ian Battersby states 'We always used the top one.'

Ian Battersby (right) with Watch Mate Al Armstrong displaying trophy won under Harbour Bridge, Sydney.

235

After two weeks it was all aboard, batten down, get up steam and head for home across the west Pacific to the Panama Canal.

From below 40° S Lat to approx 10° Nth Lat. we steamed placidly along accompanied at times by wandering albatrosses, and for a short time by a giant Hammerhead Shark which I spied from the top nest one forenoon effortlessly keeping pace in the backwash of the starboard bow wave.

Our passengers were now a different kettle of fish, the R.A.A.F. Air Crew doing their fitness routines, while the R.N. Survivors made the most of probably the only free passenger passage they were ever likely to experience.

Finally after approximately fifteen days, the coastline of Panama appeared. As I had by this stage of the war already had transited the Panama Canal three times, I didn't experience the same sense of anticipation that some of our crew did. Nevertheless it was a memorable event, a wonderful example of Surveying and Hydro Engineering.

Once at anchor in Balboa Harbour, the port for Panama City, we became aware of the state of war that the U.S. was now in, with considerable U.S.N. Vessels in harbour.

Eventually it was our turn to start the passage through the great locks and into the system of lakes and rivers to the Caribbean end at Colon. Here we were holed up for ten days to memory, waiting for a convoy to form up before the next leg which was to Guantanamo Bay at the southern end of Cuba, which was a U.S. Naval Base and which, strangely enough still remains so.

This short leg took about four days and we anchored in this placid bay on the line of 20° Lat Nth. the edge of the trade wind zone. While anchored here, the Mate Mr. Marsden, persuaded the R.A.A.F. air crew bods to take part in a lifeboat capacity test, the result of which turned into an hilarious escapade. The ship carried twenty three boats of which there were some three sizes. The largest, which was selected for the test, had a registered capacity of eighty persons. It would have been about twenty feet long.

Snowy Freer the Kiwi was the coxswain, with one A.B. on the for'ard fall in the bow. Once in the water the airmen started climbing down a Jacob's ladder, being counted as they went over the side. By the time there were eighty bods in the boat and attempts were made to get the oars in the rollocks, it became a scene out of an early movie. Strangely enough, some twenty years ago a paperback book was published called *Lifeboat No. 7*, which was the account of a ship's boat from a British Passenger vessel in the South Atlantic sunk by a surface raider. The boat

Chapter 8: Trooping begins

was the same size of our test one, and carried eighty survivors, white officers and Indian crew, most of the way across the Atlantic to the coast of Brazil. The scraps of paper recording the passage written by an R.N. officer in the boat, as well as a tattered diary, are exhibits in the British Maritime Museum in London.

Our next move was to a mined area in the open sea some miles off Key West, Florida. The reason for these short hops was to enable the U.S.N. and supporting bodies to adequately protect the great amount of shipping moving up and down the sea lanes of the Western Atlantic.

For six months since the German declaration of war on the U.S. the U Boat arm had wreaked havoc while the American Authorities organised themselves, eventually with the assistance of the Canadian Navy, the R.N. Escort Groups and units of British Coastal Command. The modern motor vessel *Waiwera,* a unit of the Shaw Savill fleet, had lain alongside at Walsh Bay, Sydney, loading for home. She departed soon after our arrival for Lyttleton N.Z. and remained two weeks ahead of *Ceramic,* departing the Canal independently for New York. Some days out she was torpedoed in balmy weather and the surviving crew spent five days in two boats before being picked up.

To gain entry into this mined area, there being no markers, naturally, very accurate bearings had to be taken, and we could barely see the land. We wondered also if one of those big blows came up, how to clear out without being blown up.

Anyway there we sat in the open ocean, so we soon had a swimming platform rigged up by the port quarter down near the surface of the sea, with a couple of Jacobs Ladders and emergency lines rigged also. Hanging onto the lines and falls and having the swell almost cover you proved very refreshing, while the Leading Seaman Gunner of the R.A.N. patrolled the docking bridge with a loaded .303 rifle taking potshots at small sharks and barracuda on the other side.

We were soon on our way to Norfolk VA. where we were to fill our bunkers with coal for the final leg of our protracted voyage. The coaling facility was at the port of Newport-News which was some distance from Norfolk and involved a longish walk through an open grassed area to reach the Street-Car (tram) for the run in. However, we had a pleasant short stay, and then moved up to Delaware Bay which appeared to be an assembly area before New York and the formation of the Trans Atlantic Convoys.

We were anchored parallel to a large American freighter, which was almost as long as we were. At the turn of the tide, one ship swung opposite the other and brought us quite close. All of a sudden a shower of potatoes came flying over, landing on our deck area amongst the stokehold and deck crew sitting around.

There were shouts of "Have something to eat from Uncle Sam, hungry Limey," from the Yankee crew. They surely paid dearly for their barrage, on the instant several firemen and trimmers dashed down to the stokehold and reappeared with sacks full of throwable coal. A fusilade of coal whistled over and spattered their nice clean decks. Their Bridge Officers must have heaved a great sigh of relief when the two vessels swung out of range.

The assembled convoy began to move out of the bay and proceed down the marked channel. The time was in the last two hours of the morning watch 4-8 and I was on the helm. The master was in heated debate with the American pilot who appeared to refuse to accept that we were of such great draught and wouldn't make it down channel at that state of the tide. While the debate went on, all of a sudden - thump - and the old girl was stuck fast on a mud bank.

First of all an R.C.N. corvette escort took our stern line and went ahead with no result, later a tug hooked on as well but we remained stuck, a sitting target for some ten hours. Then it was up-hook and head to Li'll O'l New York where we berthed on West Side Manhattan up around 50th. St. where all the big Trans-Atlantic liners used to lay.

This was a convenient area to be, as the dock road had bars and grills to cater to the seafaring and dockside workers. Being 12th Ave., it was only four city blocks to 8th. Ave, and Broadway.

Our R.A.A.F. Aircrew rigged themselves out in their summer uniforms of light brown, sporting their flying Brevies and wearing the conspicuous slouch hat, they walked into some dockside bar to the shouts of "Here come the boy scouts". The hecklers very soon learnt that for boy scouts they sure know how to look after themselves.

During our short stay in N.Y.C. all our old World War 1 heavy machine guns were removed and installed in their place were 20mm Oerlikon cannons. We certainly looked well armed when the Armourers had completed their installation.

Then it was the familiar call: Stations Fore and Aft, single up, let go the springs, let go aft, let go for'ard and we were underway for the final leg bound for the port we had left from eight months earlier.

After an uneventful crossing it was up the Mersey Channel, lock in and go alongside in, I think, Gladstone Dock,

We paid-off two days later and went our various ways, myself down to lovely Kent and the Medway Towns.

Chapter 8: Trooping begins

In closing and signing off from AUSSIELAND,

And dirty and careless and old he wore,
As his lamp of Hope grew dim,
He tramped for years till the Swag he Bore,
Seemed part of Himself to Him.
As a Bullock Drags in the sandy ruts,
He followed the outside track,
With never a thought but to reach the Huts,
When the Sun went down, Out Back.

****

Tony Bostock
Letter to the author

I joined the ship in Liverpool as an 18 year old deck cadet in January 1942 and sailed with her for just the one voyage, otherwise, of course, I would not be here today.

We embarked Naval and civilian passengers at Liverpool landing stage and sailed on the 21st January out to anchor off the Bar lightvessel to await a convoy which eventually left the Mersey on the 23rd. We were bound for Cape Town, but like so many orders during the War which were hard to understand, we were routed across the North Atlantic to Halifax, Nova Scotia where we arrived on 7th February. Perhaps there were no convoys going south at the time, and by that stage of the War all the convoys crossing the North Atlantic were not disbanding until they reached the other side because the U boat threat extended right across to American shores. On the other hand judging by what happened later, perhaps it was, to put it politely, a shambles.

After bunkering at Halifax, we joined another convoy headed south which eventually broke up off Bermuda, after which we proceeded independantly. On the 3rd March the *Ceramic* arrived at Rio de Janeiro where we anchored, still a long way from Cape Town though by now we were in the Southern hemisphere, just on the wrong side of the Atlantic. According to our orders we were to load cargo but there was no cargo for us, so we bunkered! You will know that *Ceramic* was one of the last large coal burners, 18,495 tons which was big in those days, triple screwed, and if my memory serves me reasonably well, she burnt several hundred tons of coal a day and carried between two and three thousand tons of bunkers. Consequently, there was a large number of stokers and trimmers in the crew to shovel all that coal. There were some pretty tough customers among them and stays in port could be quite lively!

Off we sailed on the 5th March to cross the South Atlantic. It was during this passage that an incident occurred which caused considerable alarm. Routing by the Admiralty usually ensured that ships were kept well apart and other vessels were hardly ever seen on the open seas. Consequently, when an unidentified ship appeared to close us quite deliberately, there was serious concern that we were about to be attacked by a German raider. However, she sheared away and a collective sigh of relief was heaved. The possibility remained that the unknown vessel might alert a pocket battleship or other enemy ship which were known to be active in the South Atlantic and that during the night we would be approached and attacked under cover of darkness. A particularly sharp lookout was therefore the order of the night. I was on the middle watch, (12-4), it was a moonlit night and at about 2 am while searching the dark area away from the moon's light which was the most likely direction from which an approach would be made, I spotted a vessel on the horizon. Considerable alarm ensued but after a tense hour or so she disappeared and calm was restored. We never found out what these ships were or what they were up to.

On 15th March the ship arrived in Cape Town and many of our passengers disembarked. The next port of call was Durban on the 23rd, then south to Adelaide where we arrived on 13th April to discharge cargo. Melbourne was our next port, then on to Sydney where the ship drydocked, bunkered as usual and commenced loading for home. We left Sydney on 16th May for Lyttleton on the South Island of New Zealand to complete loading, arriving there on 21st May.

On the 2nd June we sailed for Balboa across the Pacific, transitted the Panama Canal on the 24th, bunkered at Colon and then had to wait at anchor in Colon Bay for a convoy which eventually left for Guantanamo Bay, Cuba on 3rd July. After two days at anchor there, another convoy to Key West, Florida, then on to Norfolk, Virginia for bunkers, then to our next stop in the Delaware River. Leaving there we warned the escort that there was insufficient depth of water for the *Ceramic* along the convoy's proposed route but we were nevertheless ordered to proceed and as predicted we went aground. The convoy went on without us and after a salvage tug refloated her, the ship set off for New York arriving there on 24th July. After four days we sailed with a destroyer escort to Halifax. The final stage of this long tortuous journey was in convoy and uneventful, ending where it began at Liverpool on 15th August.

She was a lovely old ship with four masts and graceful lines but I expect you will have photos of her. She was, of course, very old-fashioned having been built in 1913, and although reasonably comfortable, the passenger accommodation which had been modernised in 1936 was cabin class and nothing like that on the later grand ocean liners or the glitzy fun palaces of today, but the food was good especially for a young cadet unused to such 'luxury'. My impression was that the

Chapter 8: Trooping begins

mix of naval and civilian passengers on this voyage had a whale of a time and lived up to the reputation of what people get up to on the high seas away from the constraints of life ashore. Certainly, when we got south of the equator in the nice warm weather of the tropics, it must have been like a cruise holiday for them in the middle of wartime too. Apart from the detours necessitated by the war, the length of time in port in those days which amounted on this trip to seven weeks on the Australian and New Zealand coasts for discharge and loading seems quite incredible when contrasted with the speed of turnround in these days of containerisation.

Cargo was general outward bound, and mostly refrigerated homeward, consisting of frozen lamb, beef, butter, and chilled cheese and apples. Also wool and hides as general cargo. The refrigerated cargo was, of course, vital for the people at home during the war, who would otherwise have starved.

***

Newspaper Report 1942:

CERAMIC FIGHTS U-BOAT

The British merchantman Ceramic (18,713 tons) is being repaired in Rio de Janeiro harbour after a hard voyage from Liverpool lasting 45 days during which she fought a bitter battle with a submarine in the South Atlantic. The ship was damaged, but it is claimed that the submarine was sunk. The Ceramic arrived on March 3. She carried 350 passengers, including women and children. - Associated Press.

Tony Bostock:
There was no gun duel with a sub in the South Atlantic. As I wrote in my account of the voyage to you, we were routed to Rio de Janeiro for cargo but there was none waiting for us when we arrived. In any case, we were only there, at anchor, for 2 days which would not give much time for repairs. I have that in my notes written soon afterwards so where the story of the "battle" came from is a mystery as is the reason for sending the ship there at all. Perhaps we were sent there for bunkers and to route us well south before crossing to Cape Town to keep us away from the Eastern Atlantic because of a greater danger from enemy subs in that area. Our greatest fear in the South Atlantic was of surface raiders, hence the consternation when an unidentified ship took great interest in the Ceramic.
We probably had a firing practice with our 6 inch gun at some stage and this might have been misconstrued by one of the passengers but how it got into "official records" goodness knows. In addition to some civilians, we were carrying a lot of naval personnel including two Rear Admirals, as passengers but I doubt whether the story would have come from that quarter.

Ian Battersby
Regarding your query as to why neither Tony Bostock or myself omitted any description of a recorded running battle with a U Boat is because such an event a never happened, it was just a Newspaper "Beat Up".

There were no enemy submarines operating down into the Tropics on that western side of the Atlantic at that time, and in any case, the U-Boat would have won.

Flat out with the Stokehold crew running and throwing coal like demons, she could only make fifteen knots, the enemy could run at seventeen knots hull down.

***

Diary of Leonard George Peake, F/Lt RAAF, 416453
Reproduced by kind permission of Andrew Peake

14 May 1942
Told today that tonight would be our last leave. Instructed to pack large sea bags in readiness for embarkation. Paid and immediately went into Sydney, made a few last minute purchases. Meet rest of boys at Carlton Hotel, only had about 3 or 4 (port and lemonade), met up with a very amusing American, aircraft hand, a corporal armourer.

Rang up Shirley and made a tea and show appointment. Met Shirley and Mall at the Hotel Grand Central. Mal under the weather, had been drinking with uncle. Shirley and I went and procured seat at the Plaza for *'Dumbo'*, a Walt Disney coloured cartoon. Obtained a ticket for Malcolm Collett. Had tea - porterhouse steak and apple pie. Went along to show. Mal did not show up. Had supper at Carls. Malcolm showed up a bit blithered.

Finished up in Wynyard Park on a three sided affair. Very unsatisfactory? Left at 12 o'clock and came home. In bed by 1 o'clock. Will I ever cease being a sucker - spent 25/- taking a girl out, and left her with somebody else.

Doubtless I can write it off on the education account. Mal came in at 4.30.

15 May 1942
Said to be last day. One cannot be certain until we are well on the way. Paraded at 6.30 with kit. John has just come in to get the Good Guts on last night. Both Mal and I had very little to say. We have done nothing but wait on parades today mustering, medical, pay and embarkation talk. Paid today in sterling 24 pounds, 10 weeks pay in advance also two days pay in Australian. A good watch is being set to stop any one going AWL.

242

Chapter 8: Trooping begins

1900 another Parade. Padre Nesbitt (Presbyterian) from Lindfield, a square man, gave an exceptionally fine address to the boys. I think in their heart of hearts they appreciated it. Sang a couple of hymns. 2100 Roll Call several AWL. Nott cannot be accounted for. Had an exceptionally good shower. I think tonight is about the coldest night we have had in Sydney.

16 May 1942 - 1st day out
Reveille at quarter to 5. Paraded at 5, blankets etc. Very cold morning. Finished packing and paraded with kit. Had breakfast at 6.15. Cleaned out huts then waited around until 8 o'clock. Paraded and left on Double Decker buses at about 8.15. Had a very good trip through Sydney, over the bridge. Every one was just going to work on the trams.

Arrived on the wharf and after a short wait were transferred to a ferry, which when we were all aboard proceeded to Garden Island where we picked up naval officers, petty officer and ratings. We then proceeded to the centre of the harbour where we embarked on the *Ceramic*. Felt a bit shaky going up the gang way which was hanging over side.

Soon had the gear stowed away in cabin, which was a 4 berther, Sgts McWaters, Proctor, Sara and Peake. The bell sounded and we donned great coats and fur felts and life jackets and paraded at boat stations. The Captain gave a short talk on shipboard behaviour, and we were dismissed. Explored her from bow to stern, looked over the guns etc.

Lunch rather sumptuous, very decent mess, meals good, service excellent. Left Sydney about half past 2. Watched the anchor being hauled up and land slip away. Strangely enough I felt no emotion except excitement at the adventure.

Australia slipped away and was soon only a haze on the horizon. Passed the Dutch destroyer, *Van Tromp* doing AA gunnery exercises. Day passed quickly, things at present are interesting. Tea at 7 o'clock. After which I took a turn on the deck. Could see the search lights of Sydney, approximately 60 miles away.

17 May 1942 - 2nd day out Sunday
Had a good sleep for my first night at sea, although cabins tend to be stuffy. Had my first hot salt water bath, and when salt water soap is used they definitely are good. Breakfast at nine, and it was excellent. Porridge, sausages and bacon. Repacked my sea kit bag. Took a turn about the deck and explored the boat deck with Ted Whitehead. An issue of comforts was made. Everyone was given cigarettes, tobacco, razor blades, pull-over, soap, barley sugar, socks etc., and a sheep skin jacket. During the afternoon P/O Quinlan (6), O/C troops held a muster and delivered the GG in regards bounds and meal periods, quarters etc.

SS CERAMIC The Untold Story

Several albatross circling around ship, they all plane rather marvellously. Had a practice alarm boat stations during afternoon, did it in 5 minutes. Sea continues calm, but sky overcast, wind cold. Read until 9.30.

18 May 1942 - 3rd day
A little more order in today's proceedings.

Breakfast at 8 so had to be up a bit more promptly. Table seating clarified and fixed at our table, Sgts Sara, Woods, McWaters, Tinley, Fidg, Gee, Proctor, Collett, Peake.

Cabins inspected, and were paraded, and arranged into flights.

Lot of phosphorescent glowing in water. Had my first beer aboard, made in South Africa, lemonade from Brazil, stout from Sydney. All lollies seem to come from Canada. Quite cosmopolitan. The ship's 'pick-up' playing dance tunes carries me back in an instant to the old peace time dances with Vida, especially those we used to have at the Tusmore Masonic Hall. At the moment I can picture the dancers and hear distinctly the swish swishing of the dancers.

19 May 1942 - 4th day
Parade and PT are about the only things which were different today, than any others. P/O Quinlan took us for PT and we certainly all felt the benefit of it. The skies were dull and overcast with a little rain. Had another boat drill exercise so I spent most of the day in the cabin and lounge.

20 May 1942 - 5th day
Awoke this morning to find that we were in sight of land - New Zealand was on the starboard bow. Later in the day we turned into Cook Strait with land to port and starboard. New Zealanders on board pointed out items of interest. Stevens Island, the island where the Raider Wolfe lurked last war. The scenery was beautiful like a painting. Snow capped peaks could be seen in the distance.

A shore station signaled the boat with Aldis lamp, and a aeroplane was seen in the distance. We hope to dock early tomorrow. Today was bright and sunny, but it was bitterly cold, and we were pleased to wear our overcoats on deck.

The scenery was rugged and the hills came straight down to the sea, a few towns could be seen nestling between hills on the coast.

21 May 1942 - 6th day
Came on deck just before breakfast, the ship was entering harbour. A beautiful sight like a Norwegian fiord, high cliffs coming down to the water edge on either

Chapter 8: Trooping begins

side. The town of Lyttelton was clinging to the side of the hill. It looked as if a push would send it into the sea. Unfortunately I could not wait to see the ship clear the breakwater as I had to go down for breakfast. It was very cold but nearly everyone was on deck to see her berth. Shortly after breakfast we paraded on deck and after a considerable amount of Air Force B we finally got off the ship. Preparations were going forward for the receipt of her freight. More Bull and we were entrained for Christchurch, 3'6" gauge, uncomfortable carriages. But everyone was outside watching the scenery. We went through a long tunnel and came out into level country. The country was cut up into small paddocks, the grass was high and green. We passed through Christchurch and came out to Wigram. We were greeted by Good Old Aussies, struck one as strange.

Detrained, were lined up and marched with out kit to a WAAF pipe band to the Station. All personnel stood to attention as we passed, any who failed were ticked off by the WO. We were shown to our huts and then had dinner (will give my camp impression later). Handed in our money or exchange after CO had given us a chat. Was shown around camp by WO and then came into town. Mal and I spied out the land, and chose a pub to stay at over weekend. Got chatting with some RNZA chaps, very decent fellows (stood us some drinks). Bought some fruit and went up to Union Jack Club. Quite nice. went to the pictures, *"Hold back the dawn"*, not so good, theatre very nice. Home to bed, got lost looking for hut.

22 May 1942 - 7th day
Breakfast at mess very nice although it was a long walk and we had to serve ourselves.

After a long wait we received the NZ money in exchange for our sterling. Mal and I then came into 'C' and booked in at the Excelsior. Walked ourselves tired and bought lunch at the cafeteria. Then we went shopping. I bought a pair of glasses and a pair of slippers. Mal obtained shirt, shoes, sox, gloves. We went into nearly every shop in town, we were well received. Where Mal bought his gloves we received an invitation to tea an Sunday evening (later he rang us up at the hotel and asked us to a party on Saturday night).

Another man where I bought my gloves asked us to meet his wife. He also asked our advice about publishing a song he had written. We were continually stopped and asked to come to a club or a dance. We meet up with John and Spence (groan for Spence).

John, Mal and I managed to lose Spence after tea. John bought a pair of pyjamas and John got all indecisive. I left them and went to the Cosmopolitan Club. They turned up later. Had a pleasant enough evening. New Zealanders were continually asking our opinion of their country.

Bruce Thomas (Wimpy) and Byass (Pitter Patter) arrived at nearly 11 o'clock with whisky and soda. Pitter had the soda siphon in his pocket. He would hold the glass in one hand, and press the lever. Mal took a girl home and woke me up not too late, 1 o'clock. Hotel seems very comfortable, radiator in room, carpeted wall from wall.

23 May 1942 Saturday
Cup of tea early in the morning. Rather loud waitress twitched Mal's nose to wake him. Got up, tried out my new slippers. Had a long soak in the bath. Meandered round town all day in vague sort of way. Visited the gardens in the afternoon and had a look at their Art Gallery which is small, but very good. The building is exceptional and lighting is very effective. Evening Mal and I were invited out and were called for by Mr Thorpe. Had a couple of drinks before we left. Went to a dance in the Returned Soldiers Club, rather crowded, and the dance times were a little strange. After the dance I bought pies and mashed potatoes and beet root. Went to one of the women's home, had prime wine, lemora passion fruit. Quite a good evening though the women were past the first flush of youth. Home at 2 o'clock.

May 24 1942 - 9th day
Rain, rain and more rain, that is approximately the sum of my impressions for today. Went to church, took the wrong tram and had to walk about a mile in the rain. Took the offer of a lift home. Singing in church was rather dull, lacked brightness. Mr Thorpe asked us to get a taxi and call for Miss Kelly at the Zelland hotel. Taxis were scarce so John Talbot, Jimmy Rudd and myself set out. Fortunately a taxi hailed us. Miss Kelly was inside. I explained Jim's presence and we were soon out at the Thorpe's. Spent a very pleasant day in front of the fire, which was of coal, the first domestic coal fire I have seen. It was so cold we had tea in front of the fire. Mrs Thorpe had three daughters, and there was another girl there, Betty. She was very good at the piano and she played very nicely. She played several request numbers. We left at about 9.30 and braved the rain, we came home by bus, and we were properly soaked. I left the radiator on all night and dried my clothes. Malcolm did not return, evidently it was too wet for him to leave.

25 May 1942 - 10th day
Still raining and bitterly cold. Went shopping with John, and on the way back to Hotel called in at Gardon and Gotch. I was well received, and was taken up to the Office, Mr Mortimer being the manager. He discovered that John and he both came from Largs Bay. He took me along to a Business Men's lunch and they had a speaker giving his impressions of USA. He was very good.

Returned to the warehouse and had a look around. Mr Mortimer gave me 3 first editions, very good. Got back to the Hotel at about quarter to 4. Met John and we went and booked for the pictures, 'Big Store' with Marx Bros. It was not too good, and after the show we returned to camp. It was cold in the very extreme. In fact I can hardly write for the cold. Mr Mortimer very kindly offered to have us drive sight seeing should the weather fine up.

26 May 1942 - 11th day
Freezing cold, had to walk a mile through rain to the mess for breakfast. Sat around and froze and dripped rain, just before dinner had a good toast in the Sergeants Mess. Straight after lunch came into town with Stan Allen. Saw Arthur, he invited me out to tea. I read and dozed in the Union Jack Club until 5 o'clock.

Spent the evening at Thorpe's and slept on the couch, had quite a good night. Thorpe's are most informal, eat tea sitting around fire. Mr Thorpe likes some waiting on; the children, are continually dashing for this and that. Arthur is quite a good fellow and is well read, and well informed about a variety of subjects. I promised to obtain in Canada a subscription to Life, he gave me one pound sterling. Rained most of the day, and generally very miserable. The rain is coupled with a driving wind. Even the natives are complaining about the cold.

27 May 1942 - 12th day
Moped about town in miserable weather, although it was showing definite signs of breaking. Went along to see *'Dumbo'* again with John. I enjoyed it more so this time than when I saw it first. Was introduced to Mal's WAAF. I don't think John and I made too good an impression. However she didn't interest us. The fountains and public drinking places have the water continuously running, rather strange to our drought ridden eyes.

28 May 1942 - 13th day
Wandering about as usual, tried unsuccessfully to hire a car. Did some more shopping or at least John and Mal did. In the afternoon went for quite a long walk down the River Avon. Evening went to the Station WAAF dance, had quite an interesting evening. Took a WAAF home, at least I rode with her in the train. Mal did not return all night?? Dropped in at G & G and fixed to be taken motoring tomorrow.

29 May 1942 - 14th day
Visit to Porter Pass. John and I called at G & G at 10 o'clock and met Gregor. He took us up stairs and introduced us to the staff and we partook of morning tea. Went up to Victoria Park, which is on the summit of the hills overlooking CC. An excellent view of the city also the layout of Park was very good. The slope of one valley was entirely given over to rock gardens and trees (some Aust).

In the distance we could see the Southern Alps, and with the sun glinting on them they made a magnificent view. Both John and I expressed our admiration and Mr Mortimer and Jack decided to take us to have a look-see. We returned to the city and Jack warned his wife we would not be home to lunch. Into the city called at G & G. John had a look for Mal. Mr Mortimer picked up his daughter, aged 5, we were to have lunch on the way. Called at one pub, no lunch. Had a couple. Called at another, no lunch, had a couple, ordered lunch at the next town. Arrived at next pub, had a few (I'm not used to this). Had a very excellent lunch, the proprietor and his wife made us most welcome and (Darfield) stood us a few.

Off again, soon snow began to appear on the sides of the road, a little further on it was across the road. Up we went along a narrow unfenced road, the snow was getting deep and skids frequent. Jack stopped the car, and out we hopped into 9" of snow. I stepped into the track made by the car and over I went. Jack and I had a snow fight. It was impossible to turn the car so we had to back her down the road until the snow was clearer.

We took a number of photos and the view was great. Rugged hills, snow, stunted bush, mountain streams, clear blue skies, cold penetrating winds. Back to Darfield, had a few more. Bill M daughter warmed her toes. Mr and Mrs Pavlovitch (prop.) made us very welcome. During the whole day neither Jack nor Bill Mortimer would allow us to stand them one drink. Into the city and Jack took John and I to tea. Tried home cured bacon and eggs, was it great. I finished the day arriving at the pictures at half time with Mr Thorpe and Mother.

30 May 1942, Saturday - 15th day
Reported back at 9 o'clock after a lot of hot cocky in which some chaps were refused leave passes. We were given leave at 12 o'clock, this rather cruelled arrangements. Mal went to find his girl friend. So John and I put in the day shopping and viewing the sport in the Parklands. Finished up at the pictures, saw 'Blood and Sand'. Returned to camp only to find leave had been extended to 12 Sunday night.

31 May 1942, Sunday - 16th day
Lay in bed until late, went without breakfast. Finished some of the letters. After lunch went out to Arthur who was suffering from flu'. Spent a quiet "at home" had tea there and returned to camp about 11 o'clock. Mal and John remained on the camp. Heard that two of our chaps had become engaged to NZ girls. I am sure of one, Sgt Hogan, the announcement was in the local paper.

1 June 1942 - 17th day
Monday, King's Birthday in NZ. Last day in Christchurch. No leave packed all gear, wrote a letter and waited around. Left Wigram at 2.15 and entrained at Stockburn. Made a fairly quick trip to Lyttelton with one stop at Christchurch

where I bought some apples. Detrained on the wharf and after some waiting around we climbed aboard up an incredible steep gangplank. Loading was still in progress and the wharfies are about the slowest I have ever seen. A humour interlude was provided by a drunken sailor who had to be brought aboard in a sling. He was paralytic. Got to bed early. While the light lasted girls were still on the docks talking to the chaps.

2 June 1942 - 18th day
Pulled away from dock about 6 o'clock. Very reluctantly I got up to watch her cleared. Nosed out of docks at about 7.5 at about this time a cable used in towing parted, and tug had to nose us around. We anchored near Heads, some said we were stuck on a mud bank. Anchor was weighed at 7 to 2 and we passed through Heads into open sea at 2 o'clock. A chap was injured in the anchor chains locker by the chains. Extremely cold all day. I found the overalls offered little warmth to my legs. Seemed to be heading south east. Took a turn of deck before turning in, not so dark, but cold, sea running a bit with a swell. Lower deck awash with water.

Most of the conversation today on the promiscuous habits of RAAF personnel ashore. Harry Fidge and others a little worried (VD). Worry unnecessary. Women seemed over easy. KSC. said he had 5 different women in 4 days, Ha! Ha! Ha! P Sara spent a lot of time playing his records purchased in CC.

2 June 1942 - 19th day
Same date as yesterday, crossed International Date Line, called Antipodes Day. Slept badly, bed doesn't suit my back. Very nice day cold but sunny. Had a few brisk walks around the deck. Meeting was called to arrange a programme to keep us occupied, also to give us information re raids and action stations. Read the V Plan given me by G & G. Very dark night. Has been quite a swell, some time water broke over bow. Sara started his "Hit Parade".

3 June 1942 - 20th day
Machinery was set in motion today for organizing the ship from our side at least in case of attack. Volunteers were called for gun crews, and stretcher parties. I have been allotted to No 1 Stretcher Party. Mal is in a gun crew. Only those who had experience previous to RAAF were accepted in gun crews. Today saw also the commencement of the sport, with the first hockey match. Water restrictions also instituted.

4 June 1942 - 21st day
Sea board life is just a little of the same thing everyday. Same scenery to port and starboard. Had an action station at 11.30. Rushed to No 1 Stretcher Post with others of party. Action stations followed by abandon ship.

About 5 chaps have had all their hair cut off during the last few days. It does not improve them and I guess it will not be grown before next port. Tonight we had the complete recording of the *'Pirates of Penzance'*, they awoke happy memories of previous hearings. The traditional scenes were fresh in my mind.

5 June 1942 - 22nd day
Today experienced our first gale. Experienced hands say it is quite a minor-one, well even so it has provided some excitement. Viewed the storm this morning from the sun deck, a magnificent sight, high waves breaking over the ship, with the wind whipping the spray from their crests.

The lounge provided a lot of amusement the chairs and settees were constantly sliding across the floor and not a few finished up on their beam end. While changing a book this afternoon Sgt Saunder collected a wave which broke over the boat deck. It was funny at meals. At lunch time the crockery slid off the table on several occasions, and at dinner they did not fully set the table. They handed out the cutlery with each course.

The seamen move about in sou'westers, oil skins and thigh, boots. The hit parade closed and a large number of entries were received.

The ship steams faster at night than during the day so that smoke will not betray us in daylight. My cabin sprang a leak so I was shifted to temporary quarters.

6 June 1942 - 23rd day
Storm still unabated, old hand say now that it is quite a storm. Very few sea sick. High seas make rather awe inspiring sight as they tower high above the ship. Continues very cold and I was glad to get my sheep skin jacket out of the sea bag. Table of afternoon tea things crashed during a big roll. Many chaps were thrown over in the lounge and many amusing incidents occurred. Winner of Hit of the week was announced.

7 June 1942 - 24th day
High sea continues although wind seems to have lost some of its strength. Anyway the ship has still a lot of rolls, but few have caught us. We are getting used to it. The stewards wet the centres of the table to minimize crockery sliding. Tried to get some sleep in this afternoon. News over wireless told of shelling of Sydney and Newcastle by submarines. Meals are still held under difficulties.

8 June 1942 - 25th day
Little to say about today. The sun came out for a while, although a lot of squalls still hung about. Read most of the day, although I enjoyed the sun while it lasted. Moved back to Room 83, sea having died down. Collection taken up to make up

Chapter 8: Trooping begins

Sgt. Crystal pay which was stolen in Christchurch. I would see money gambled which I had helped contributed. Sgt. Sara remarks during his music hit session get on everyone's goat. But he does a self denial job in working machine.

9 June 1942 - 26th day
Had a parade this morning with BS. No PT but we had an action station at 11.30 followed by an abandon ship. Rather a nice sunny day and I spent quite a time lolling in the sun. Weather should improve, ship is now steering a course of N of E. Sergeant meeting and Mess President and Secretary and representative elected. Some of their complaints seem to be very trivial and unfounded. Meals returned to normal as high seas have dropped.

10 June 1942 - 27th day
Cold wind, spent most of day in lounge. Started letter No. 3 to V. Sea fairly calm. Same as any other day without any high lights. Games of Housie Housie in lounge, no luck. Time is still going forward at 24 minutes per day.

11 June 1942 - 28th day
Heavy fog, ideal sub. weather, very little of interest. Had a game of deck tennis. Wimpy Thomas regaled us with his tales of drunken orgies in the smoke room in the evening (ambiguous what).

12 June 1942 - 29th day
As like yesterday as two peas in a pod. No parade, no PT. Had a lecture by naval surgeon on VD. Nothing else to report.

13 June 1942 - 30th day
Warmer, but moist, spent some time on deck, play Sgt. Proctor deck tennis 6-5 his way. Compulsory parade and talk by P/O Quinlan on general conduct of draft, better feeling resulted. Some deck exercises with Collett, Stan Clarke. Housie Housie in lounge in evening.

14 June 1942, Sunday - 31st day
Quite a nice day. Parade, no PT, wrote some letters for dispatch in Panama. Won hockey match this afternoon. Nothing to note.

15 June 1942 - 32nd day
Good day, warm high wind. Did some photography as cameras have to be handed in for duration of voyage tomorrow. Everyone was making an effort to complete films in camera. Lecture on gun sighting etc.

16 June 1942 - 33rd day
Action stations and abandon ship. Slept in cabin and dozed in sun on deck. Saw

some of Obs. shoot sun with their improvised sextant. Had a tumble with John in lounge this evening. Finished with my good night port.

17 June 1942 - 34th day
Quiet day until 2000. Then had a rough and tumble with Jim Rudd, Mal and John, then went and drunk port and finished on creme de menthe. Wimpy finished telling a good tale. Smoking hot.

18 June 1942 - 35th day
High winds, a lot of spray breaking over deck. Flying fish attracted a lot of attention, only a small variety about the size of a sparrow, they would fly close to water. Practice for concert going on apace. A rope slung from aft starboard ratlines for climbing. I was 2nd up it. Played some deck games. Dressed for first time in tropical dress. Percy Sara wearing his pistol!!

19 June 1942 - 36th day
Rain clouds, sun, wind. Did some sun bathing during the sun period. No PT decks too wet. Heard BBC and America News. British troops pushed back to Egyptian border, Tobruk still holding. Sebastopol defences still holding. Had a merry evening with Mal and John. False alarm about "action stations". Sub said to be operating near at hand. Extra watches set.

20 June 1942 - 37th day
Good sunbathing day. Had two good sets of deck tennis on new forward court. Won a single against Mal. Today continuous watches set on all look out points. Two hours on and 10 off undertaken by gunners. Ship almost heading due north only 9 minutes to put watches on tonight. First ice-cream for tea.
News heard Axis subs spreading mines on eastern seaboard of USA. "Shivers" Sebastopol situation critical. Had no drinks tonight, late news made it impossible to get down to bar.

21 June 1942 - 38th day
Got sun burnt. Hottest day to date. Firing practice by heavy guns aft and machine guns. High elevation gun fired at elevation and at smoke float and scored a direct hit. Heavy gun also scored a hit. Machine gun fire was more noted for stoppages than accuracy. They fired at smoke puff fired by AA gun.

Tobruk fallen and a wedge driven by Germany into Russian defences at Sebastopol. Two heavy kicks in guts.

22 June 1942 - 39th Day
A hot day really tropical, raining in the morning, hot in afternoon. I kept out of the sun.

Paravanes slung out, everyone seemed to be seeing land, drift wood went past. I also saw two butterflies. Sundown still no land. During afternoon had a general health talk by doctor. Lots of chaps sleeping on deck, too much bother for lazy old me, cabin with electric fan OK. Nevertheless it is very sticky. Rumours of subs about.

23 June 1942 - 40th Day (Today 1 year in Air Force)
Up at 5.15 to see a few out lying islands off Panama. Spent all morning watching land come into sight. Islands covered with intensive green verdure, here and there hidden gun emplacements could be seen. Aeroplane patrolling overhead constantly. We followed in a torpedo boat and anchored near reception boat.

Made way slowly up the roadstead passing fortified island, joined by a causeway. Entered the inner harbour through anti sub net, a door was opened by a tug. Tied up to a buoy and am still there. Watched harbour traffic all day. Launches and, tugs moving constantly about. Also a lot of DCs. During evening had a display of searchlights. In the distance we could see a balloon barrage over canal, it was being constantly raised and lowered. Day was hot and steamy and overcast.

All chairs and lounge covered with dust covers and carpets 'taken up. We were told we could have one days leave in Colon.

24 June 1942 - 41st Day
Passed through the canal today. A most interesting experience, the anchor was weighed at about 6 o'clock and by 6.30 when I came on deck we were well in the canal. American marine guards were placed aboard. The passing of the locks was interesting, and the towing mules very ingenious. The locks were protected by barrage balloons and other cunning devices to counter low flying aircraft. The marines were interested in exchanging our badges and money. On either side of the canal was thick tropical jungle. The centre portion of the canal was an uninterrupted water way, the locks being at either end. The passage took about six hours.

We docked at the coaling wharf at Colon. Leave was granted and we went into the town. The roads or at least some of them were ankle deep in mud. On arrival we were immediately in many difficulties and were robbed over the exchange. A Yank soldier took us under his wing and showed us around and treated us to dinner. We had a number of beers. Then we went around the shops, but things were too expensive. We bought some magazines. John bought a watch band.

The women seemed very easy and a number of them it seemed made a good business of it. On the whole I was unimpressed, it being a stinking hole, consisting mainly of drinking places and shops. Returned fairly early to the ship. Saunder had the DTs and went missing which gave rise to an exciting chase.

Everything is continually wet here, it rains a lot and the air is full of moisture. It is strange to see all the Negroes about, they are always trying to clean your shoes. Returned to the ship and had my shirt stolen with my AG badge on it.

25 June 1942 - 42nd Day

Spent a hot uncomfortable night. Leave granted at 2 o'clock. Went into town, Mal and John went to a lot of trouble to change their money. This needed the help of a doughboy. Went to the USO Club. Had a few drinks. Had an interesting talk to an American woman, the first we had met. At last M & J changed their money, they did no better than $2.50 per pound. I got sick and tired of meandering around. Although we saw some sights - squalid houses, filthy tenements, miles of washing, incredible ugly Negroes. Saw a whole street full of school girls marching (shuffling) into school.

I went along to the YMCA and waited for Mal and J. Had an elaborate tea at the Panama Club. Met an American petty officer, had a great yarn with him. Discovered he was a MA, still further talk. He had been in Australia in 1925, a very decent chap. Went to the Atlantic Cabaret, had a few drinks. Saw the much boosted floor show and one of these famous strip tease acts. It is much over rated art. The woman certainly took all her clothes off and paraded in what was supposed to be a seductive manner. She could certainly move independently every posterior muscle. The rest of the show was just so-so. The crowd yelled and howled like maniacs.

Had a few drinks, went out and bought some bananas, a whole stick for $1, took them aboard. Some chaps swapped all their uniform. John had half changed when the MP came along and stopped the arrangement. Took a lot of work to get the fruit aboard.

26 June 1942 - 43rd Day

Still at Colon. Coaling from their elaborate automatic gantries still in progress. Leave granted but I had seen all I wished of this sink, so I remained on board. About mid-day was an extremely heavy storm. I have never heard thunder so loud, the rain fell in torrents for about an hour. This made the remainder of the day unbearably humid. Did a watch at the gang plank for AWL whose leave had been stopped. Think we are leaving today with all the sinking we might be back in a day or so.

27 June 1942 - 44th Day

Left coaling pier early in morning. Drew out into roadstead and dropped. Air was full of rumour of sailing time, and of sub sinking enough to shit oneself.

Had a bad nights sleep, water came in port and I had to jump out. I thought Ferdie

Chapter 8: Trooping begins

had p.... himself. Police came aboard and a parade was held to recover a naval uniform one of our fellows swapped. Several heavy rain storm during the day, water comes down in a deluge often with little warning, everything is consequently moist.

Two new rafts were hauled aboard evidently to compensate for the refugee seamen. Also a number of kegs of beer for free distribution to the men. The gun boat who rescued some of the survivors slipped into the harbour today. Two (said to be) Russian boats drew out of the harbour today. Had an action station and a lecture by Skipper on serious nature of practice.

28 June 1942 - 45th Day
A dull, wet, hot, sticky day - a dreary day. We are still in Colon Harbour waiting for the convoy to assemble. Flooded out of bed again.

29 June 1942 - 46th Day
Another dreary day. Lying in port awaiting the assembling of the convoy. Chap injured at Lyttelton removed to hospital. Preparation being pushed ahead in case of sinking. Captured German sub being tried out in Harbour. Plenty of aircraft about, a number of Catalina on patrol, also Kitty Hawks.

30 June 1942 - 47th Day
Still awaiting convoy. Twelve ships now anchored about us. Now there are about 16. Rumour has it we leave in the morning in convoy. There is one French ship near, supposed to be held since USA entered the war. Had our last practice "abandon ship", if we have another it will be dinkum.

1 July 1942 - 48th Day
Still in Colon Harbour and no hope of moving. Tempers are beginning to show signs of irritation. These are not helped by adverse war news. Germans are within 70 miles of Alexandria. Broke into Mal's drawer as it had jammed with our bananas in it. Had a jolly good feed of them. Days are getting very monotonous. Had a mess meeting with little success, everyone snapped everyone else. Rumour has it the American and British cannot agree on whom the convoy duty will fall.

2 July 1942 - 49th Day
Colon (I am tired of saying still here). We spend most of the time creating rumours as to when we leave here. Sleep and read and get irritable is our daily lot.

3 July 1942 - 50th Day
Left Colon Harbour at fast. Great glee amongst everyone at getting underway. Left in convoy, said to be first to leave Panama, 9 ships with 3 escort vessels. They seem small enough to protect us. It was a very awe inspiring sight to see the

great ships leaving in line, each falling into its appointed position according to number. We were number 6, the speed is very slow, some have difficulty even then in keeping up. The danger is great and we have to carry our life jackets with us all the time. I have prepared a small bag of treasures, e.g. apron, photos, wallets and photo spools in my respirator bag. It is like a furnace in the lounge. News is bad. Sebastopol fallen, serious battle going on in Egypt. Churchill gains vote of confidence. Had a row around ship in practice abandonment.

4 July 1942 - 51st Day
Little to do except walk about carrying life jacket. Convoy still making progress. I counted 5 escort vessels, 2 large and 3 small. Visibility was poor, and there was a fairly heavy wind, a little spray over bow. Did some washing. News from Libya seems better this evening.

5 July 1942 - 52nd Day
Pleasant day, hot and sunny. Had a good bake. Subs said to be about, watches doubled. One of destroyers was closer to convoy. US sub said to be about and ready to appear at 1730, didn't see it however.

6 July 1942 - 53rd Day
Just the same as any other day. Breakfast, cabin inspection, parade etc. Hot, but not unpleasant. Had the concert in the evening in the veranda lounge. Ship's company has erected a stage and curtain of flags. Items were good and entertaining. But it was HOT and sweat just streamed off one and the smell of bodies OH! shades of abos. Still moving north.

7 July 1942 - 54th Day
Dropped another ship during the night making convoy now 7. Air was still full of rumour of our probable destination. Early afternoon land was sighted, convoy went into line ahead, and steamed into a large bay, dropped anchor at 4 o'clock. Said to be near Santiago in Cuba. Seems to be a good harbour, all the shore installations are military barracks. Robbing Hill like Lyttelton, although not so high. Hills seem heavily wooded. Place called Guantanamo.

8 July 1942 - 55th Day
Slightly inebriated, had a session, whisky, lime and soda. Still in port in Cuba. Said to be leaving tomorrow morning early. Nothing today except sun bathe. Few of the fellows went sailing in the life boats.

9 July 1942 - 56th Day
Left port about 6 o'clock and by 8 was well underway. Six ships in convoy, two lines of 3, we lead. Two destroyers, they make a noble sight with the white forelock under their bow. Clouded, dull. Enemy held in Egypt.

Chapter 8: Trooping begins

10 July 1942 - 57th Day
Orderly sergeant today from 0800 to 2359. A lot of Hot Cock getting watches onto the job. I did the job too conscientiously, my legs are dead tired. A lot of shipping passing us by today. We also saw a number of islands and lighthouses. Had some difficulty in waking one of the chaps for watch. He denied his name, either through sleep or laziness. P/O Small soon had him on deck.

11 July 1942 - 58th Day
The day started with raw from lookout who was difficult to get up. Look like he is to receive extra duties. Had a sub scare today. I was lying in bed having a siesta when the whole ship quivered from end to end with the concussion of 2 depth charges. The destroyers scurried around dropping in all about 15 depth charges. They were assisted by the Catalina. It seems likely that the Cat sighted the sub first and dropped depth bombs. I can say it made some excitement, our first taste of the real thing.

12 July 1942 - 59th Day
Steamed into Key West this morning. It is nothing but a huge anchorage, hardly any land visible. Place is full of ships. Later on in afternoon another convoy arrived with a large proportion of tankers. There must be more than 70 ships at anchor here. Lay on deck looking at the stars. The sky is very unfamiliar and strange. We talked of home, and fruit we could eat, and a good dinner.

13 July 1942 - 60th Day
Left Key West early this morning in a large convoy of about 20 ships. Uneventful trip until late in the afternoon when the corvette dropped a number of depth charges. But she was too far off to see any results. The convoy makes an impressive sight, 3 long rows of ships, gray and rust, dipping their prows into the water. During the day we passed several convoys moving in the other direction.

14 July 1942 - 61st Day
Sea like a mill pond. I do not think I have seen it so calm. Two float planes caused some excitement in diving low over the ship several times. Did a lookout 8.30-10.30, a beautiful night, not a ripple in the sea. A few clouds and the other ships like dark ghosts noiseless. Handed in two letters, tipped John and Ern.

15 July 1942 - 62nd Day
On watch again from 8.30 - 10.30. A lovely morning but "look out" makes one very weary. Had several sets of deck tennis. Getting a good tan up. Russian news bad, Egyptian better. Warm and balmy night. The hatch covers are the social centres, a gramophone makes them a cheerio place. Sea like a mill pond, following wind. Convoy going steadily ahead with usually a couple of Catalinas.

16 July 1942 - 63rd Day
Cooler, day of happenings. Depth charges, blimps, and Lockheed Hudson, topped off with Tasmanian apple cider.

Several times throughout day depth charges were dropped. Later in afternoon a US Navy blip circled convoy and a Hudson gave us something to look at by flying low up and down convoy. Apple cider is now the drink, beer has all gone.

17 July 1942 - 64th Day
Spent most of the day steaming into Chesapeake Bay. The convoy was in a long Indian file, we passed a similar convoy going out. In the afternoon we steamed into inner harbour, but did not berth. Several depth charges were dropped at times throughout the day, even as late as lunch time and then we were right in the roadstead. As we came in we passed a huge US battleship, also a tanker with a broken back, said to be mined. It is unusual to see all the harbour installations brilliantly lit up, after the usual black out.

As we were steaming in a passing ship hailed me and asked if I was from down under. Rumour is rife as to whether we get leave or no. We were all inspected by the Harbour Health Authorities, the Doc just looked at everyone.

18 July 1942, Monday - 65th Day
Evidently were wrongly directed, so we upped anchor and came to coaling wharf at Norfolk. There was some difficulty in getting ship in, but they did it. Next we were all lined up and issued with a piece of stamped paper. Then things went to sleep except for rumour. Money and leave was the question but no one had an answer. Leave granted at 4 o'clock.

Went into town, bludged enough money to get into town, then came the usual bother to change money, got some at last at $2.30 to one pound sterling. Wandered around, saw YMCA and then had a big dinner, it only cost me 50c. Had a drink or so. Met some sailors and soldiers and spent the remainder of the evening talking to them. They say the town is a poor one, and we agreed. There are a lot of Negroes living in poor conditions and according to servicemen things are dear here.

Had a most interesting talk to two soldiers from Officers Training School. Returned to ship on a very crowded tram at 12.30. I bought very little and ignored my shopping list. Went into a big store, met several M, also was introduced to Boss. Mal and John rang up Consuls office from there. Bought some mags, which John lost. They also bought some peaches which proved to be green.

Half way home in tram a lot of the crew came on board. They made a big song

Chapter 8: Trooping begins

and dance and made an unholy clatter. Had some difficulty in keeping to the right side of the road. Today was one of hottest day in this part, 104 and it was certainly uncomfortable.

19 July 1942, Sunday - 66th Day
Still at the coaling pier and the coaler have made a hell of a mess, the Skipper says it is the worst he has ever seen. Leave is going to be granted us again, and the Sergeants Mess is trying to arrange exchange. Our officers seem to have no go. Sgt Palmer was brought aboard in a paralytic condition, raving with drink. He had to be carried on a stretcher.

Leave granted and single pound note changed into dollars at 4 to a pound. Mal, John and I came into town per taxi, had a soft drink, and went and had a good look see at a drug store, bought some photo films. Took a taxi out to the beach. Ocean view poor show, poor bathing house, really disgraceful, a poor beach. Returned per tram and checked bathers in YMCA. Had an enormous counter lunch. Went to a movie, saw 'Bahamas Passage'.

Visited drug store and bought some cigarettes for stock and so back to ship. Views. This must be US worst town, hence I will take a unbiased opinion, but it certainly does not come up to the opinion created by American books in my mind of Gods Own Country, perhaps he made this part in the dark. Housing seemed poor, no gardens, no lawns, no public park or gardens.

20 July 1942 - 67th Day
Moved out from coal pier early in the morning. Steamed down harbour passing a large incoming warship. Passed anti sub gates and anchored with other ships. A large number of them, some with aeroplanes and tanks. Slept nearly all afternoon.

21 July 1942 - 68th Day
Still anchored in the roadstead, a slow day. Slept for 2 hours in the afternoon. Four American sailors swam over to the ship, and had to be returned in a life boat.

22 July 1942 - 69th Day
Slipped out of Harbour early in the morning. Had to do two, two hour watches today. A quiet day very much cooler, about 15 ships in convoy, majority British.

23 July 1942 - 70th Day
Slipped out of harbour early, we had anchored for night in Delaware River. We were pulled out of convoy to take a different route as water was too shallow. Just after joining convoy we ran aground. We were aground for about 6 ½ hours. A Royal Navy armed trawler (*HMS St Lornan*) tried to tow us off, we tried running from side to side to rock her off. Finally we had to dump the fresh water and get a

SS CERAMIC The Untold Story

tug. Got off about 4.30. We had a blimp and planes circling us throughout day. Now underway for New York.

24 July 1942 - 71st Day
Early morning found us anchored in New York roadstead. Mist was too thick to see famous skyline. We lay at anchor all day, we watched the shipping of which there was a lot, and also thousands of French letters passing out to sea on the tide.

After tea we up hook and moved up the River. Statue of Liberty loomed out of the mist, and then the skyline. It is most blacked out. It is difficult to conceive looming through the grey mist, it is something like fairy land. Empire State, Chrysler and Woolworth's something like a gigantic mountain range. We pulled into Berth 51 with the assistance of 4 tugs.

Throughout the day the shipping interested us. Ocean greyhounds and an aircraft carrier and literally 100s of tugs and small craft. Washed some clothes in the morning and spent a lot of time watching them. View through day spoiled by fog and in the evening it was too dark.

25 July 1942 - 72nd Day
At Dock 51, we are uncertain if we are to get leave. Workmen came aboard and commenced building new gun turrets. They were putting in 20 mm cannon, 4 on sun deck and 1 near funnel, 2 on bridge, 2 on promenade forward. After endless bother about the money and immigration authorities we were granted leave. They set a watch for saboteurs. I was on at 4.30. Left ship at 2.30, went into town, walked around.

A man invited us to a party at the Carrol Club. Went up Chrysler Building, 2nd highest in world. John and I returned to ship in taxi. Mal went with John. I did two hour watch and then returned to city per subway. After a very long walk I found the place, Mal and John were a bit lit up.

I had a most pleasant evening. The girls were charming and natural, after both I and they overcame their shyness. We had a long chat and dances. Bus and walking got me home. This place is stupendous, it is difficult to take it in. They are so high the mind cannot grasp it.

26 July 1942, Sunday - 73rd Day
Left ship before lunch. Visited Central Park. Had an excellent dinner at a drug store. Rushed through metropolitan Museum, saw Rembrandts and armour. Up town visited Empire State Building, had excellent view. Broadway and the light (now dimmed). Had tea. More walking along Broadway. Went to a Russian picture. Unusual and rugged. Had a good look around town. Dinner was at a kind

Chapter 8: Trooping begins

of theatrical joint, and saw some real painted faces, would turn you over.

27 July 1942 - 74th Day
Leave until 4 o'clock. Came down town, visited Wall Street. Had a good look at the financial section. Returned to end of city, met Mal. Here we were met by 2 women from Australia, Mo's sisters. They stood us dinner, very nice. They want us to write. Looked over Radio City, went on tour of studio of NBC, saw television sets. Caught in heavy rainstorm and had to return to ship by taxi. Pulled out from dock at 8.45. So good bye New York. Much too big.

28 July 1942 - 75th Day
Slipped out of New York harbour early in the morning. Everything obscured by heavy fog which continued all day. Without convoy, but at least 3 escort vessels, destination said to be Halifax. New guns were mounted and magazines loaded. Quiet day everyone was sleeping off effects of leave.

29 July 1942 - 76th Day
Thick fog all around us. It is steadily becoming colder. We are going north flat out. She is swaying with the motion of the motors.

30 July 1942 - 77th Day
Fog lighter. Entered Halifax harbour, very pretty harbour with pine clad slopes. Less shipping in harbour than I expected. Rained during late afternoon. Berthed at pier. I am getting a blasted cold. Money was accepted for exchange.

31 July 1942 - 78th Day
Leave in Halifax after money fuss I am sorry to relate. Town is a typical port, dirty old and tumble down. But it has a sort of thrill. Soldier, sailor and airmen of every kind and description. Posted letters home and had an orgy of shopping, bought a lumber jacket and torch. Visited YM and Anzac Club and had a look around about the main street. Had an excellent dinner and saw a picture show. Visited Anzac Club dance, not enough women. Returned to ship.

1 August 1942 - 79th Day
Leave. Did some shopping. Bought a shower proof lumber jacket. I didn't want yesterdays. Visited Masonic Rooms and was shown over by some old chap. Had a snatch dinner at the Anzac Club. Went to see sports on Navy Recreation ground. Had quite an enjoyable afternoon. Had tea went to pictures, had to stand for 2 out of 3 hours of show. Returned to ship after a visit to the Anzac Club. Town although tumble down near water front is quite nice as you move away from sea front. They have a very nice public garden. John sent home a cable. The girls are quite good looking and to the most part smartly dressed. The trams are poor and you pay 10c. as you leave. Theatres are small and shows continuous.

We were surprised to see the amount of saluting down in the street by Canadian servicemen. Sgt Cusack I hear got into considerable strife in a fight in the town. He was taken in by Naval Shore Patrol.

2 August 1942 - 80th Day
Pulled out from Halifax early this morning. Sailed out of harbour, past British destroyer and corvettes. Target practice with new Oerlikan had a number of stoppages. Dropped naval gun instructor and joined convoy in heavy fog. Speed of convoy very slow, seem almost to be standing still. Deck space is very crowded, now we have 7 invasion barges as deck cargo. There are two sizes of them.

3 August 1942 - 81st Day
Convoy now about 30 ships. Too much fog and mist to see all of escort. The ships are all towing fog buoys, which could easily be mistaken for periscope. Late in the afternoon we had an action stations. Percy Sara is suffering from a cold, a bally nuisance in cabin.

4 August 1942 - 82nd Day
A beautiful day, warm, sunny with a beautiful breeze. The war seems miles away although we are within, bombing range. At 10.30 the convoy had gunnery practice, it relieved the boredom. The convoy makes a pretty sight, the light is not harsh as in tropics.

5 August 1942 - 83rd Day
Fog obscured view all day until about 4 o'clock when it lifted. Little of note, several ships gone from convoy, some lost or maybe gone to St John. Sgt Cheek's heart seems to be turning to butter, he is thinking up ways and means of getting into either a ground job or a discharge.

6 August 1942 - 84th Day
A clear day. Ship, which left convoy for St John, said to have been torpedoed... Ship is being pointed for home.

7 August 1942 - 85th Day
No fog and a clear cold day. Slept and read most of the day.

8 August 1942 - 86th Day
Cold day, no fog. Convoy had a smoke screen try out, it was most effective. Packed my sea kit bag in preparation to landing.

9 August 1942 - 87th Day
Sea running high, very cold. Extra anti aircraft watchers. Mal was subject to practical joke - got up at 2300 hours and dressed. Chap sick with an appendicitis.

Chapter 8: Trooping begins

10 August 1942 - 88th Day
Cold and clear, sea fallen, nothing of interest. Had a couple of ports before bed.

11 August 1942 - 89th Day
Warmer and cloudy. Nothing happening except eat, sleep, read and have afternoon tea.

12 August 1942 - 90th Day
Action station just after breakfast, unidentified aircraft proved to be British. Stood to for about 10 minutes. Several times throughout day depth charges were dropped, some excitement. Said to have passed Hebrides early in the morning.

13 August 1942 - 91st Day
Coast of Ireland was seen first thing after breakfast. Later in afternoon coast of Scotland, Mull of Kintyre and Isle of Roslin. About a third of convoy put into Belfast. At opening of Belfast Harbour there was a large light house, a bit further along coast was a large wireless station. There was a curious feeling of pride at seeing the shores of the land of one's ancestors.

There is sounds of revelry, everyone is slightly drunk. A couple are quarrelling about who is going on watch, they are all drunk. Frank the bar steward is putting chaps to bed. The watch roster has been lost and some chaps are full. The officers are merry. Proctor is drunk. I have packed my kit with most things, have laid in quite a hoard of tobacco, cigarettes, w/pads, soap etc.

14 August 1942 - 92nd Day
Last day. In morning coast of Wales could be seen on starboard side. By afternoon we were in the mouth of the Mersey. The views of the docks and town were quite good and not squalid and dirty. We dock about 2.30 and an Air Commodore came aboard and welcomed us to England. He was a decent sort of chap. Landed our gear which was stowed away on lorries. We marched through Liverpool to the British Council House. A tea dance was put on by a welfare club. We had an enjoyable afternoon.

Had tea, very good. Entrained for Bournemouth. Train rather uncomfortable and sleeping was difficult. English country side was very nice, a beautiful green. The fields are small bordered with hedges and trees. Many streams and canals. The land is gently rolling and beautiful to the eye. The majority of the houses are neat and clean, although some had very small yards and are grimed with smoke. In Liverpool there is some bomb damage, but it is not over extensive.

****

David Man, New York City, April 2004.

THE FALL AND EVACUATION OF SINGAPORE
INTRODUCTION

This description of the fall and evacuation of Singapore in February 1942, followed by the journey from there to England via Australia, New Zealand, the Panama Canal and the US, was written by my father Frank Man (1914 – 1986), on his return to England some nine months after his escape.

Frank Man

My father left England for the Far East in the autumn of 1936 to take up a position at a mercantile house - Edward Boustead. He was originally posted to Singapore but in early 1939 was transferred to Tumpat in Kelantan on the Malay Peninsular, a place he described as 'awful'. He returned to Singapore a year later. He was always keen on the navy and would probably have chosen that as a career but his family placed a greater emphasis on succeeding at commerce and so when war came it was with some enthusiasm that he joined the navy.

***

Frank Man

PART II: RETURN TO ENGLAND

Part I of this record deals with my escape from Singapore on Feb. 14th 1942 and my eventual arrival in Australia on March 9th. Part II deals with the journey from Australia back to England which started on May 12th and ended on August 14th. The interval spent in Australia between March 9th and May 12th has not been recorded as it hardly warrants it, the time there was spent for the most part in buying clothes and generally recuperating. This interval was spent entirely in Melbourne where, apart from trying to start a new wardrobe with the meagre pittance allowed me by the Navy, I tried hard to get transport back to England as soon as this was available. It was not an easy task to get the Naval authorities to take any quick action in the matter nor, to be fair to them, was it very easy for them. I should say at a guess that the number of Naval personnel who escaped from Malaya and Java and arrived in Australia amounted to roughly 100 officers and 800 ratings. All of them arrived in a more or less destitute condition and had to be cared for and eventually given a job; this naturally took time and the task of the Naval authorities was not lightened by the fact that all of them were clamouring to get back to England.

Chapter 8: Trooping begins

It was eventually decided by R.A.N.B. (Royal Australian Naval Board) after about a month of waiting, that all officers and men who had been in the tropics and away from England for a period longer than 3 years should be allowed to return there. The remainder were either shipped straight off to Colombo to carry on their Naval duties there or were incorporated in the Australian Navy. After this decision had been made and those concerned had been informed, the next step was to find accommodation and transport for them. The latter was by no means an easy matter as the question of shipping space was a serious one at that time. Although Australia was importing a vast amount of war material from the U.K. and the U.S.A. she was also exporting an equally large amount of food supplies, so, although there was a large "turnover" of shipping there was still the question of shipping space to be got over.

I had been in Malaya without a break since October 1936 and therefore qualified to return to England for which I was more than thankful. After a seemingly endless wait accommodation was eventually found aboard the S.S. "Ceramic" due to sail from Sydney on May 16th for 10 officers and 150 ratings. I left Melbourne on the afternoon of May 12th 1942 in charge of a draft consisting of 8 officers and 37 ratings. It was an all night journey and the train stopped at very nearly every station, the result being that at every stop I had to clear the station bar and try and get all the draft on board again before the train re-started. This was a difficult and unenviable job, the more so as all the ratings were in exceedingly high spirits at the thought of going home and thus found plenty of excuse to imbibe freely. I eventually gave up the unequal struggle of looking after the draft at every station and resigned myself to the fact that I would very probably arrive at Sydney with only about half the number I had started out with. We arrived at Sydney at 10 a.m. the following morning and roll-call was taken on the platform, much to my surprise the draft now consisted of 39 ratings and 8 officers, so far from losing half the draft on the way as I feared I discovered I had gained two. I was past caring then and sent the whole lot off to the barracks where they could settle the matter amongst themselves.

We had two nights in Sydney which gave us time to have a look at the town. There is a great rivalry between the two cities of Sydney and Melbourne, as an impartial observer I would say that Melbourne is by far the more pleasant of the two. Sydney's only claims to greatness are its harbour and bridge. The latter is without doubt a magnificent and imposing structure and the pride and joy of all Australians. I found it was not diplomatic to mention that it was built by an English firm. I think it is worth mentioning a small incident here which took place in Sydney and had its repercussions in Scotland nearly five months later. One evening I visited the Australia Hotel with a friend, Lieutenant W. B. Bevis, R.N.V.R., we were sitting in the lounge having a few drinks before dinner when an army officer came up to us and asked us whether we would like to join him in a drink. We were pleased to accept his hospitality and after several drinks he suggested that we should all three go out on a party that night and that he would provide the girls. This being our last night in Australia we readily agreed and the party took place and was a great success. The sequel to the party will be told in its chronological place towards the end of this account.

We embarked aboard the S.S. "Ceramic" (above) at midday the following day, Saturday May 16th. Our fellow travelers consisted of a Naval draft of 10 officers and 150 ratings also a draft of about 200 ranks of the R.A.A.F., all of us destined for England. There were no women on board. The "Ceramic" was a single-funnelled cabin-class ship of about 18,000 tons, twinscrew and capable of a maximum speed of about 14 knots. Her main drawback was that she was a coal-burner. She was built on the Clyde in 1912. Until the arrival of the "Queen Mary" at Sydney she had been the largest ship ever to visit Australian waters. She was the flag-ship of the Shaw-Savill and Albion Line. In September 1940 she was rammed by another vessel during a fog off the East coast of Australia, she sustained considerable damage but was repaired and had been doing excellent work ever since. The "Ceramic" eventually met her end under very tragic circumstances in November 1942. It was the trip after she had brought us safely back to England. She was on her way to Cape Town with a full passenger list consisting chiefly of women and children when during a heavy gale off the north-west coast of Africa she was torpedoed by a U-boat and sank within three minutes. There was only one survivor, a gunner in the Royal Artillery, who was picked up by the U-boat after having been in the water for four hours. The official account says that over 500 persons lost their lives. It appears that owing to the heavy seas it was impossible to lower the lifeboats; she was also sailing independently and without escort. The news of this disaster was not released to the public until September 1943.

I shared a cabin on board with two other Naval officers – Lieutenant W. B. Bevis R.N.V.R., whom I have already mentioned, and Lieutenant (E) H. H. Holm R.N.R. It was Bevis who took me out of Singapore in his Minesweeper and we had been together every since that time. I knew him well in Malaya before the War as well as during it; he was married in Penang two days before the War with Japan broke out and had to be recalled from his honeymoon. He had only seen his wife twice since his marriage; fortunately she managed to leave before the collapse and get to Colombo from where she returned to England. He knew she had arrived home safely and therefore was keener than most of us to get home. In peace-time he worked with the Shell Company. Holm was picked up by us off the coast of Sumatra after his ship had been sunk, he was slightly wounded and had literally lost everything he possessed including his clothes. When we picked him up he had been in the water for nearly two days stark naked. He also was a married man and had two children, all his family were safe in England.

Chapter 8: Trooping begins

The Officer-in-Charge of the Naval Draft was Lieutenant Clarke R.N., he had had a shore job at the Naval Base in Singapore and had found his way down to Australia in much the same way as I had although some weeks before. The first Lieutenant of the Draft was Lieutenant Durrant, he had been in Australia for some six years and was returning home for the first time since. Lt. Pirie R.N.V.R. was a kind of secretary to Clarke, he was Anti-Submarine officer on board the destroyer H.M.S. "Jupiter" which was sunk during the battle of the Java Sea. He had had an uncanny experience during the loss of the Jupiter; the ship was torpedoed close in-shore off the north coast of Java and started to sink slowly, as the life-saving equipment was not sufficient for the whole crew to abandon the ship at once the captain ordered it to be done in relays. The shore was only some 2 miles away and although it was dark it was still possible to see the outline of the coast. Lieutenant Pirie was in the first load of survivors and after these had been landed the boats were rowed back to the destroyer to pick up the remainder; on arrival at this position no trace of the destroyer could be found nor were any further survivors seen or heard. What happened to those people left on board is still a mystery as even if the destroyer had sunk there should have been survivors floating in the water near-by[sic], and although the returning boats searched for some hours in the vicinity none were found. There was another amusing tale about the "Jupiter" which is less gruesome than the above. She was based on Batavia shortly before the collapse of Singapore and was sent out one day to investigate a submarine reported off Tanjong Marah[sp?] in Java; unfortunately there are two places of this name, one in Java and the other in Sumatra. The "Jupiter" proceeded to the Tanjong Merah[sp?] in Sumatra, which was incorrect, but surprisingly enough there was[sic] a Japanese submarine there and she sank it with depth charges. Lieutenant Pirie was awarded the D.S.C. for this action.

To return to the officers in the Draft. Surgeon-Lieutenant Seymour R.N.V.R. was the only doctor in the party, and he had plenty of work to do during the voyage. He was a survivor from H.M.S. "Electra", another destroyer sunk during the Java Sea battle. Lieutenant Nixon R.N.R. escaped from Java in the "Angking" (a ship well known on the Singapore-Hong-kong[sic] run), she sailed from Tjilstjap in Java and was torpedoed and sunk about two days out. Lieutenant Nixon and two Malay sailors were the only survivors, they drifted on a raft for three days without food or water under the tropical sun until they were finally picked up and brought safely to Australia. Sub-Lieutenant Barnett-Smith had escaped from Singapore and also found his way down to Australia; I knew him in Malaya when he was Customs Officer in Trengganu one of the wildest of the Malay States. He had had some exciting experiences getting down to Singapore from Trengganu when the Japanese were threatening the town. The only communications Trengganu had with the outer world were by sea, there were no roads out. When the time came to leave Barnet-Smith plus four other European men and three European women had to make their way through the jungle for 120 miles before they were able to find civilized transport. Their exit apparently was so hurried that they had no time to make arrangements for their trek, the women were even wearing high-heeled shoes when they started. The Malays were magnificent to them and guided as well as protected them through the jungle. For food they had to rely on tropical fruits, and at night they lit a fire and slept around it whilst the Malays kept guard. Pay/Sub/Lt. Black R.N.V.R. had originally escaped from Hongkong and then again from Batavia; he was the only paymaster on board and we found him most useful to deal with problems of foreign-exchange and other monetary difficulties at the various ports we visited. S/Lt. Bigley R.N.V.R., like Barnet-Smith, had also been a Customs Officer in Malaya and had only joined the Navy ten days before the fall of Singapore; he escaped in the same way as I had.

The above were the other officers traveling in this draft. The draft was organised into three divisions and provision was made for amusing ourselves during the voyage; each officer had his special duties allotted to him and everything ran extremely smoothly in spite of being idle for three months.

We sailed from Sydney at half past one on the afternoon of Saturday May 16th. It was a glorious day and we stood on the foc'sle[sic] and watched the ship make her way down harbour and out through the Heads, it was a wonderful sight. The cabin I shared with Bevis and Holm was roomy and comfortable, there was also a private bathroom attached so we lived in comparative luxury. Apart from divisions and P.T. in the mornings we had all the day to ourselves and it was not easy to keep everyone amused although the Australian Comforts Fund had been extremely generous to us and supplied all manner of deck games including several medicine balls which were very popular. They had also supplied everybody with a small canvas bag containing warm clothing, razor blades, soap, and two handkerchiefs; in addition to this they provided each man with a sheepskin waistcoat which was a God-send to all of us during the cold weather.

Our destination was unknown to us and it was not until we had been two days out of Sydney that we were informed that our first port of call would be Lyttleton in the South Island of New Zealand. Early on the morning of Wednesday May 20th we sighted land. It was glorious weather and we could see the outline of the coast on both sides of us quite plainly. We were passing through the straits that divide the North and South Islands of New Zealand, the scenery was very grand and quite different from anything I had seen in other parts of the world. Everything appeared to be on such a vast scale, towering cliffs and high mountains in the background impressed me most. We entered Lyttleton harbour early the following morning and we were secured alongside the wharf by about 10 o'clock. The entrance to the harbour is not unlike that of Sydney, narrow, and surrounded by high cliffs, it is only when one has approached within about a mile that one realizes that there is an entrance there at all.

Chapter 8: Trooping begins

We spent altogether ten days in Lyttleton which is part of Christchurch. They are about five miles apart and we lived ashore in Christchurch for the whole period. The new of our arrival had proceeded us so that arrangements had already been made to welcome us. The Secretary of the Navy League took us under his care and was extraordinarily kind to us all through our stay. Parties were arranged for us and we were entertained every day. As the "Ceramic" was coaling as well as loading 3000 tons of cold mutton it was thought advisable for all passengers to leave the ship and find accommodation ashore. On the morning of our arrival both drafts, Navy and R.A.A.F. were accordingly put into a train and taken out to the local race-course where we were to be accommodated in the Grand-Stand[sic]. It was not a long journey but it was sufficient to give us a good idea of the countryside; the country around Christchurch is extremely flat and is known as the Canterbury Plains, it is from these Plains that the famous New Zealand lambs come. Rising sharply from the Plains and about 40 miles distant is a very high range of mountains known locally as the "Alps". They are snow-covered for the majority of the year and in winter they provide excellent facilities for winter sports. The grand-stand at the race-course did not strike any of us as being a comfortable place to live as it meant sleeping on straw on the stone floor of the gentleman's cloakroom. We therefore decided to pay for our own lodgings and returned to Christchurch where we found very comfortable rooms in Warner's Hotel. Here we lived in luxury for ten days and were entertained like lords, the hospitality of the people of Christchurch was overwhelming; they did all they possibly could to make our stay enjoyable and they certainly succeeded. One of our number, Sub-Lieutenant Barnet-Smith even went so far as to get married although it meant leaving his wife behind, and I do not think they have met since. Finally, on June 2nd our stay at Christchurch came to an end and we once more put to sea for the longest leg of our trip. We had enjoyed ourselves so much that many of us were sorely tempted to remain behind and join up with the Royal New Zealand Navy, but the call of home was too much for us and we continued on our way. We left Lyttleton at 9 a.m. and set our course almost due east across the South Pacific Ocean. Our destination was Panama and we estimated the journey would take us 28 days which meant we should arrive on June 28th, we actually arrived on June 23rd. For the first four days out we had good weather, but after that there followed ten days of gale with a strong wind and stern sea. It was difficult at times to remain in one's bunk and meals in the saloon were most difficult although amusing; it was almost impossible to keep any crockery on the table. The temperature dropped considerably and I was thankful for the warm clothing that had been given us in Australia. I quote the following passages out of my diary which I kept throughout the trip and which illustrate very well this part of our journey.

"In the lounge most of the furniture has slid to one side and there have been several amusing incidents of people careering across the floor seated helplessly in an armchair. Barnet-Smith also caused some amusement by being hurled from one side of the ship to the other holding a glass of beer in his hand and finally landing in the lap of an R.A.A.F. officer. The latter was slightly flattened but not a drop of beer was spilt." "I turned in last night wearing a balaclava helmet, sea boot stockings and two sweaters and only just managed to keep warm."

Gradually as the days passed by we journeyed into warmer latitudes until we were in the tropics once more; by June 18th most of us were sleeping on deck at night, it was far too warm down below with all the scuttles closed.

During the trip Bevis and I amused ourselves by taking Star sights and generally polishing up our navigation; this was a golden opportunity to do so. An entry in my diary shows our position at 17.30 on June 17th as roughly 16°S, 96°W. course N.19°E. speed 13.1 knots. In the evenings after dinner I used to play Bridge with Bevis, Black and Holm; I had never played before but became quite a fiend towards the end of the journey. During the day we played deck-games and read books, there was a very good library on board. As we neared the approaches to the Panama Canal we were once more entering the war zone and careful look-out had to be kept for submarines and aircraft especially as we were traveling unescorted. We intercepted several wireless messages from ships who had been torpedoed. On the morning of June 20th we sighted an aircraft but it was too far distant to be identified, we presumed it to be an American aircraft on patrol. On June 23rd at dawn we sighted land, the first for three weeks and at 9 o'clock in the morning we anchored at the entrance to the Panama Canal and picked up our pilot. We remained at anchor the whole of that day and night waiting for a clear passage through the canal, we were not granted any shore-leave which was unfortunate as the landscape looked interesting. At half past six the following morning we weighed anchor and started on our way through the canal. It was one of the most interesting experiences I have had and certainly from an engineering point of view the most impressive. We carried two pilots as well as a platoon of American soldiers who acted as sentries. The latter were there to see that absolutely nothing was thrown over the ship's side, not even an empty cigarette carton; I am not sure whether the reason for this was to prevent sabotage to the locks or to stop rubbish getting into the pipes that operate the rise and fall of water in these locks. The thing that impressed me most was the speed and efficiency with which this great ship was handled, especially the "mules" that actually pull the ship in and out of the locks; the drivers of these "mules" are supposed to be the highest paid officials in the Canal Zone, they certainly have a very responsible job. There are actually three sets of locks through which one has to pass, and they take up most the time of the passage. All groups of locks were heavily protected by barrage balloons and A.A. guns of all types. A very large part of the Panama Canal consists of a fresh-water lake which has been dredged to allow the largest vessels to pass through it. The passage through the Canal took us

Chapter 8: Trooping begins

approximately eight hours and we were tied up alongside the coal wharf at Colon by five o'clock that afternoon.

The weather was now extremely hot, in fact very much hotter than anything I had experienced in Malaya or the East Indies. At times it was almost unbearable especially below decks, even at night time it was very seldom cool. The humidity appeared to be even greater than in Singapore. Colon itself is not a very imposing town, at least I can only judge from the little I saw of it; being a large coaling port it is not easy to keep clean and added to this are of course the old-fashioned ideas of sanitary arrangements still used by the local inhabitants. The latter were a very hybrid lot consisting chiefly of niggers and South American half-castes. I went ashore in the evening with Bevis and Holm, we had dinner at the American Club which seemed to be the only respectable place in town. We drank Pabst beer out of tins and plenty of it. I found it exceptionally good. We then went on a typical tourists' journey of the local night life, visiting about four different night clubs. There were none of them particularly attractive, and their standard of cabaret was definitely low. Most of the cabaret artists were American although the "taxi-girls" were South American. We returned on board at midnight to find the ship practically deserted, a few hours later people began to drift back in various states of intoxication. On the whole none of the draft misbehaved themselves although one member of the R.A.A.F. was stabbed slightly and spent the night in jail. It was impossible to sleep on deck now owing to the ship coaling all night, and there was coal-dust everywhere.

The following morning I went ashore again to try and buy a few things but without very much success. There were no good shops and besides, owing to the rate of exchange ($2 to the £) I did not have very much money. I finally decided to postpone all purchases until we reached New York. I went to the American Club for lunch were I met a very charming American Naval Officer who was serving in a Sloop based on Colon. The U-Boat menace in the Caribbean Sea had just started then and things were looking very unpleasant for the Allies. Convoys had not yet been organised and shipping through the Canal from East to West had almost been brought to a stand-still. The U.S.A. having only recently entered the War, were in no way prepared to meet this menace; the only warships they had available were ancient sloops of the last war and hastily converted fishing boats, all these were working overtime patrolling the coast, and there were no other ships available to do convoy escort duties. I returned on board for tea and did not go ashore that night. In the early hours of the following morning there were the usual scenes of the drunks returning home. The ship was due to leave at 4 a.m. and orders had been issued for all passengers to be on board by 3.30 a.m.; at 3.?5 a.m. the gangway was removed and at 3.55 a.m., a lone reveler was seen walking unsteadily along the wharf towards the ship. He was an R.A.A.F. Sergeant. The problem that faced him now was how to get on board; fortunately for him one of the coal shutes into the bunkers was still in position so he took a running dive and disappeared down the shute. Although he was now on board the next problem was how to get him out of the bunkers; he could be heard singing lustily far down in the bowels of the ship, and seemed to be quite unperturbed. Finally, after some two hours shoveling by his friends he was extricated, looking very dirty, but still very happy.

The ship left the wharf and anchored in the harbour. It was slightly cooler out here and less dirty, but all the same it was still very hot. We remained anchored for seven days and were not allowed to leave the ship. It was a sore test for tempers but we came through it successfully. We weighed anchor at last at 12.20 a.m. on Friday July 3rd. We now had probably the most dangerous part of our journey in front of us. During our week of idling in Colon harbour various stories and rumours had reached us of the dangers that lurked in the seas ahead of us. We even had a practical demonstration of what might happen to us. There were numerous other merchant ships anchored in the harbour with us, all of us were waiting for the first convoy to be formed up before we sailed. One merchant skipper decided he could not wait any longer so, of his own accord and without orders he set sail and left us. We saw him go out, it was about 10 a.m., and at 3 p.m. he and his crew returned in the life-boats, their ship had been torpedoed only a few miles out. This experience certainly did not make us feel any more confident. There is an entry in my diary which illustrated very well our feelings at this period. "They say the passage takes four days – one day out and three days back!"

The convoy consisted of only nine ships and our escort consisted of what looked like three Sloops and two Motor boats. This was the first convoy to sail from Colon, and therefore it was not surprising that a large number of the ships found it difficult to keep their positions, some of the ships were extraordinarily bad at keeping their station. There were the usual rumours of submarines in the vicinity, but the convoy was not attacked nor, I believe, did we even sight a submarine. Our destination was unknown to us, the only thing we did know was that we were heading in a northerly direction. Before leaving Colon we had taken on board some more passengers, all of them Merchant Navy Officers survivors from ships torpedoed in the Pacific Ocean. They had some amusing stories to tell, but in spite of everything they were incredibly cheerful.

At four o'clock in the afternoon on Tuesday July 7th we arrived at Quantanamo [sic] in Cuba. The port is situated in the south east corner of the island and has been lent to the U.S.A. as a Naval Base. It is a perfect harbour but as a town it did not look very impressive from what we were able to see of it from the ship. We remained anchored here for two days and amused ourselves by sailing life boats around the harbour, the wind was quite strong enough to handle them easily, they make a lot of leeway, and usually it meant having to row back to the ship. I wish we had had an opportunity of going ashore as the scenery looked most inviting and it would have been nice to have set foot on Cuba.

Chapter 8: Trooping begins

Early on the morning of Thursday July 9th we set sail again. This time the convoy consisted of six ships escorted by two sloops, the "Ceramic" carried the commodore being the largest ship. Our destination was Key West, the southernmost tip of Florida, which was a general meeting place for the north and southbound convoys. There was some slight excitement on the second day out when a Catalina flying boat reported the presence of two enemy submarines; our escort immediately made an attack and seemed to drop depth charges at random all around the convoy. No "kill" was made, and it seemed very doubtful whether there were any subs present.

At 10 a.m. on July 12th we anchored off Key West with about 30 other ships. Land was only just visible and as there seemed to be no protection of any sort we presumed the anchorage was surrounded by a minefield. At a quarter past six the following morning we weighed anchor and were part of the convoy of 30 ships, most of them tankers. The latter were fully laden and had sailed up from the South American oilfields, most of them were presumably on their way to Europe.

The weather was very hot thanks to the following wind and it became hotter the further north we traveled. Our destination was Newport in Virginia, our reason for calling here was to take on more coal. It had now become a regular feature of the day for the convoy to be attacked by submarines although no ships were lost, we became quite used to the thud of depth charges exploding under water. We also had aerial cover now in the form of Blimps, excellent things for spotting U-Boats but can only be used outside the range of enemy fighters. We were continually passing southbound convoys, usually of about 30 or 40 ships most of them tankers, the average was about two per day; it made one realize the vast amount of shipping still at the disposal of the Allies. It was also surprising to notice that the majority of the escorting ships were flying the White Ensign, chiefly trawlers. On Friday July 17th at 5 o'clock we anchored at the entrance to Newport harbour. The following morning we went alongside the coal wharf, it was not an easy manoeuvre and took $2^{1}/_{3}$ hours to complete owing to wind and tide being against us. Coaling started immediately and the ship was soon covered in a fine layer of coal dust, it was most uncomfortable living on board, being both very hot and very dirty. We went ashore in the evening and had an excellent dinner in town. There did not appear to be very much offered in the way of entertainment, which surprised me in an American city, so we returned on board quite early. The way back to the Docks lay through the negro quarters, we took a tram and were the only white people on board, the remainder being niggers of varying hues. They are an amusing race and full of fun, and as far as I could see were contented with their lot. There was a notice in the tram to the effect that niggers were to give up their seats to white men should they be required. I thought this an unnecessary announcement but perhaps it is needed; it would be unheard of to put such a notice in a tram in Singapore, but perhaps this is no comparison.

It was not until the morning of July 20th that the ship finally finished coaling and we were able to move away from the coal wharf into the comparative coolness of the convoy anchorage. By this time most people were rather irritable and tempers had become frayed due entirely to the heat, dirt, and lack of entertainment ashore. Finally on the morning of July 22nd the convoy set sail, much to everybody's relief. It consisted of 16 merchant vessels and two escort vessels; being so close to land it was possible to have continuous air cover – Blimps and Lockheeds. As usual our destination was unknown; there were rumours of Halifax being the first stop with the hope that something might happen to make us go into New York. The following morning (July 23rd) we entered Delaware Bay, the water here is extremely shallow and we hit bottom several times. Being in convoy it was impossible to alter course into deeper water, although this would appear to have been the natural thing to do if the Commodore of the Convoy knew his job – which apparently he did not. Finally at 10.30 we grounded good and hard, and it was obvious that we would not be able to get off without assistance. One of the escort vessels, a British Trawler, attempted to tow us off but without result. Tugs were wirelessed for from Philadelphia, the nearest port, and whilst we were waiting for these various other attempts were made to try and extricate ourselves. One of these consisted of mustering all hands on the foc'sle where they rushed madly from side to side while the engines went full astern. Even this valiant attempt to "roll" ourselves out of it failed. Eventually three tugs arrived, and with such heaving, bumping and scraping we were hauled off and proceeded on our way northwards escorted by the Trawler. It was obvious that the ship had done itself no good, and on occasions the bumps on the bottom were so marked that it felt as if the ship would break in half. She was too heavily loaded to go into dry dock, but an under-water inspection would have to be made as soon as possible. Early on the morning of July 24th we arrived at New York and anchored between Staten Island and Governor's Island, a hot and misty morning. At 6 o'clock in the evening we weighed anchor and proceeded up stream into the harbour. This short trip up New York harbour in the twilight is the most beautiful trip I have ever done. The silhouette of the tall skyscrapers against the darkening sky with the lights being switched on one by one in most of the buildings was a sight never to be forgotten. The most appropriate adjective to describe this scene is "awe-inspiring", but the description of New York being rather like a wedding cake is also quite apt. We tied up at No. 52 pier at half past eight, no shore leave was granted. The following morning everyone was as keen as mustard to get ashore, but there were endless arrangements to be made over passes, money, and customs; these finally arrived at 1 p.m. so we were able to step ashore before the shops closed. Summer in New York is notorious for its overwhelming heat, and the City maintained its reputation on this occasion. The heat was overpowering and on top of that we had to wear our blue uniforms, not having anything else. Most of the discomfort was walking in the street as in the buildings it was far cooler, and most of them were air-conditioned.

Chapter 8: Trooping begins

I stepped ashore that afternoon with Bevis and Holm, our first object was shopping so we got on the first bus, paid a nickel – for which you can travel anywhere in New York – and proceeded up 8th Avenue to the shopping centre. The local people were always extremely kind and helpful to us, we obviously looked strangers and on top of that, very hot and sticky, when we told them we were English our stock went up 100% and their hospitality was almost embarrassing. I made a few purchases but had to spend a great deal of time watching Bevis and Holm buying "Undies" and "Scanties" for their respective wives, I think they did so more in the way of a peace offering than anything else. Having loaded ourselves with parcels we had to return to the ship to deposit them and then set off again to taste the night life of the City. Our first port of call was the Barbizon-Plaza Hotel which housed the White Ensign Club, this was probably the most palatial and ornate building I have every entered, but in spite of this we got very little out of them, and only two drinks. We then took a bus down 5th Avenue into the heart of the metropolis where we had some bear and club sandwiches at the Bar Parlour, most delicious. We then crossed the street and entered Radio City – the most palatial place of entertainment I have every been to. Here we saw a film called "Mrs. Miniver"- an excellent show, as well as this there was a stage show which consisted of first-class variety turns. Just before the showing of Mrs. Miniver a young lady who was seated next to me, and whom I had never seen before in my life, proceeded to have an epileptic fit much to my embarrassment. She created such a commotion that all the lights were put on and some attendants came and carried her out. All eyes were turned on me and some of them looked most suspicious as if I had made a pass at her. The high light of the stage show was the dancing of the famous Rockettes, chorus girls about 50 of them who danced magnificently and with the most perfect precision. The Show ended soon after 10 p.m. and we then strolled down Broadway looking at the people and at the shops – an amazing experience. There was supposed to be a Black-out in force but there were lights everywhere – it made me realize how little the Americans really knew about war. We had been at a low-down dive, most amusing but rather unhealthy in several respects so we left hurriedly and went to Jack Dempsey's Bar. Here we had several more beers, our financial position not permitting us to have anything more expensive. After this we went to the Night Club called La Conga where we had more beer and sat and watched the dancing and the cabaret. The bands (two) were excellent, and it was an entertainment in itself watching the dancers. It would have taken a great deal of enticement to have persuaded me to perform on the dance floor. We left at 1.30 a.m. and wandered back to the ship. Here there was great activity and they were erecting numerous new gun emplacements, the din of riveters went on all night, but I had consumed a sufficient quantity of beer to sleep soundly. The following day was Sunday, and as conditions on board were rather uncomfortable I went ashore with Bill Bevis to do some sightseeing. We took a bus to the Empire State Building (reputed to be the tallest building in the world) and fortunately we found it open to the public. We took a lift up to the 80th floor, a journey completed in 40 seconds with one's stomach lagging some 10 seconds behind. From here we took another lift to the 102nd floor which was the top. From here we had a really magnificent view. We could see the Normandy lying on her side alongside her berth, with the Queen Mary on the opposite side. A strong wind was blowing which made the whole building sway slightly from side to side, a most uncomfortable feeling which was not helped by a hangover from the night before. To crown it all the Yankee Clipper (flying boat) arrived and proceeded to circle around us, this was too much for both of us, and we returned hurriedly covered in a cold sweat and looking very green. We had an excellent lunch at one of Child's Restaurants, memorable for some really delicious ice-cream. Afterwards we went along to the N.B.C. Building at the Rockefeller Centre – another vast skyscraper. Here we were conducted around the broadcasting studios where we actually saw a play being broadcast, it was most interesting to watch especially the sound effects department which had to produce amongst other things a shipwreck at sea and an aeroplane crashing. There are a total of 157 studios in this building, we did not visit them all; however, we did see a television programme being broadcast. We came out and had tea at an Automat, an incredible experience, you get everything from a slot machine. We then went to the Roxy Cinema, a most palatial building, about the same size as Buckingham Palace. Saw a bad film, but as usual an excellent floor show. Afterwards we had an excellent dinner of fried steak and more ice-cream. We turned in early, feeling very replete. The following day we were still alongside but had no money left, so had to remain on board. Fortunately at about noon we managed to wangle an advance, and I stepped ashore with Bevis and Holm to do some more shopping. We took a bus to 42nd Street which consists of shops interspersed with Cinemas. We made several purchases and were looking for somewhere to lunch when by accident I bumped into a fellow walking along the street. I apologized, and to my amazement, found it was a great friend of mine from Bousteads, Singapore, by the name of Donald Kirk. It was an incredible coincidence especially as he happened to be on two days leave from Canada, and I had to choose that particular time, literally to bump into him. Our meeting was duly celebrated with a most excellent lunch. Unfortunately we had instructions to be back on board by 4 p.m. so we had to break up what looked like being a really first class party – just as well, perhaps. The ship eventually slipped at 9 p.m. and proceeded to anchor down stream. There were only two people missing from all the hundreds on board which was quite good considering the many and manifold temptations of New York; unfortunately they both belonged to my division, and I was saddled with the wearisome task of trying to trace them. They eventually re-joined the ship at Halifax, our next port of call.

We finally sailed from New York at 1200 on Tuesday July 28th. We were alone except for an escort of two destroyers which was very comforting. The weather became much colder as we went northwards and fog accompanied us nearly all

Chapter 8: Trooping begins

the time. On the afternoon of July 30th, we berthed in Halifax, Nova Scotia. There is a considerable difference in the weather after the hot stickiness of New York. We now have mist and cold. As this is our last port of call before reaching England everybody was very keen to get ashore and make some final purchases. Shore leave was granted the following day, July 31st so I went ashore and made numerous purchases chiefly foodstuffs. I had to buy an extra kitbag to carry it all, and I was anxious to know whether I would be able to get it all past the English Customs, if and when we ever reached England. Halifax is not a beautiful city, but I was greatly impressed with the atmosphere of the place, there seemed to be an air of confidence and friendship amongst the inhabitants which was most heartening. Above all I was impressed by the outstanding beauty of the womenfolk, almost without exception they were all very charming. There is not very much entertainment ashore which is not helped by prohibition. The following afternoon Bill Bevis and I attended the official opening of the Navy League Centre which was a Recreation Ground for the Services. It started with a display by the three Services which included a magnificent show of drill and P.T. After that there were several track events helped by several world famous athletes including Charles Dodds, the holder of the World's 1500 metre record. The final entertainment was a baseball match in which Babe Ruth took part; it was an interesting performance more amusing than enlightening, the first ball game I had every seen.

At 1200 on Sunday August 2nd we slipped and put to sea on the last leg of our long voyage. The convoy formed up slowly at slow speed as a thick fog had settled down. There were 30 ships all told. By August 4th the fog had cleared and the weather was fine, the convoy was in good formation and most ships carried out a firing practice. Thick fog came down again the next day, visibility about [?] cable and no other ships could be seen, station was kept on fog buoys streamed astern by all ships. Two ships lost the convoy that afternoon to proceed to St. Johns, Newfoundland, and were torpedoed before they reached their destination, not very heartening news for the rest of us. The fog finally cleared on August 7th and apart from two bad stragglers they were in good position. Various practice manoeuvres were carried out and smoke screens were laid down all very efficiently. The coast of Ireland was finally sighted on the morning of Thursday, August 13th. At 2 p.m. on Friday, August 14th we berthed alongside at Liverpool and after a very quick dispersal we caught the London train, and I was home again once more at 12.30 that night.

http://www.manfamily.org/PDFs/EVACUATION%20OF%20SINGAPORE.pdf

***

FlLt. Jack Liley RAAF
Letter to author

THE VOYAGE TO ENGLAND

We were taken down to Sydney Harbour (near where the Opera House is today) where an old ferry was tied-up. We were embarked on her and taken out to a large ship which we entered up a gangway and through a door open half-way up the side. Once aboard we were allotted cabins, and I found myself sharing a two berth cabin with Bernie Lewis from Brisbane. We had trained together since September 1941 and knew each other very well. The next surprise was finding that we were to have a cabin steward.

The ship turned out to be the *Ceramic* of the Shaw Savill & Albion line, cargo and passenger one class. She had been on the England to Australia via the Cape run for many years. She was 18,000 tons, built in 1914 with a top speed of 14 knots.

It was not long before we found out we were travelling under the same conditions as pre-war passengers. Our accommodation was in two-berth cabins, serviced by a steward who made our beds daily, brought us an early morning cup of tea at 7.30 and generally looked after our everyday wants. Public accommodation dining room, bar, lounge and promenade decks were shared with RN Naval Officers survivors, from the *HMS Prince of Wales* and *Repulse* which had been sunk off Malaya in February, some British. Merchant Marine officers, survivors from sunken merchant ships and our own contingent of RAAF air crew officers and NCOs. On the lower decks were some RN and Merchant seamen but they were not allowed onto our decks.

It was a very comfortable ship. We had no duties and could do as we pleased all day, our time was mostly spent sunbathing and playing games such as deck tennis, deck quoits and walking round the circuit of the deck. Lunch was served in the dining room, dress informal, but at night we were expected to dress for dinner in best blue uniforms. Before dinner we had drinks in the smoke room and dinner was a full menu service. After dinner it was bridge, poker or whatever and the usual routine of a passenger ship except that there were no women.

We were not long on board before we found our first destination was to be Port Lyttleton, on the East coast of the South Island of New Zealand, where we were to load a large quantity of wool and mutton. One of the English Merchant Navy wags said that when the old *Ceramic* was full of wool and mutton she'd be so buoyant as to be almost unsinkable. We hoped that he was right.

Upon arrival at Lyttleton we were offloaded and sent to an RNZAF station near

Chapter 8: Trooping begins

Christchurch to wait until the ship was loaded. It was an elementary flying school and test flight station. We must have been a nuisance because we'd only been there one day when we were told we could have 10 days' leave and go where we liked as long as we came back when due.

After some enquiries four of us, Kevin Howes, Max Patrick, Charlie Harris and I were told the mountains were the place to go and there was a little hotel on the Waimakariri River. We caught the train which took us high up into the mountains to a little whistle stop where the hotel was located, looking across the river valley to the mountains beyond. The scenery was spectacular and bush walking would have been great but unfortunately we were limited by our footwear.

It was a marvellous place, the hotel was very comfortable, we were welcomed and allowed to serve drinks as long as we recorded them on the slate.

When we came back from there we rented an Opel Sedan and toured the Canterbury Plain.

When we returned to the RNZAF Station I was fortunate to meet a pilot who was testing new Hudson Bombers for the RNZAF. He took me for a three hour test flight during which we covered nearly the whole of the South Island with its towering mountains covered in snow. The scenery was magnificent but I nearly passed out because we climbed to 20,000 feet and I had no helmet therefore no oxygen.

Back on board, with the ship fully loaded, the captain called for volunteers from those of us who were trained Air Gunners to man the four anti-aircraft machine guns mounted on each side of the bridge and the after part of the upper deck. Each gun was manned by a No.1 who operated it and a No.2 who was the loader. I was chosen as No.1 on the gun mounted on the starboard side of the bridge from where we could see, hear and talk to the officers and crew on the bridge.

My No.2 was Ted Ebbott who had been my flying partner at 1 AOS Cootamundra and 1 ANS Parkes.

We were a bit surprised when we saw the guns we were expected to operate. They were Hotchkiss .303 which dated back to the 1914-18 war when they were used by the Light Horse. None of us had ever seen one before let alone operated them. They turned out to be quite similar to the Lewis guns which I had learned to operate in the MUR in 1939 so we eventually sorted them out and got them working.

The alarm indicating a submarine or anti-aircraft alert was a bell system which

SS CERAMIC The Untold Story

rang all over the ship. Upon this being heard all hands were to put on their life jackets and tin hats and move to their action stations. Ours was of course at the gun on the starboard bridge. Ted always said that if ever he got to the gun first he would be No.1 and I would have to be No.2, of which more later.

Once we learned how to operate the guns we had practice sessions firing at coloured balloons released by the crew.

After we put to sea and cleared Lyttleton Harbour we noticed that she was steering South East which would take us down to the "roaring fifties" and this in winter promised to be fun. It was obvious to us the purpose of this was to avoid Japanese submarines.

Fortunately the Air Force in Australia had sent along with us some astro navigation books with appropriate calculation tables. They apparently had the idea that we would do some extra study, small hope!

Bernie Lewis and I decided we could put the books and tables to use in calculating our course across the Pacific, so when we were in Christchurch we had bought a large map of the Pacific from a stationer. We reckoned we could make a rough sextant out of cardboard and calibrate it ourselves. Our objective was to take shots of the sun and stars, calculate the result with our tables and then could plot our position within 50 to 100 miles or so. which considering the distances involved would be fair enough.

We continued south-west until we were in the "roaring fifties" and then the storm hit us. It was magnificent and had the old *Ceramic* rolling and pitching like a cork. When she was in a trough between two waves you could see the next wave approaching higher than the top of a 10 storey building, then over she would go and down the other side. It was like the Big Dipper in Luna Park only more magnificent.

The gale was blowing so strongly that the ropes and the rigging stood out horizontally.

Fortunately none of us suffered from sea sickness having been used to some rough flying days. It was just as spectacular in the lounge where heavy lounge chairs and couches careered from one side of the room to another and one had to jump to get out of the way and as for eating that was another adventure especially when soup was on the menu. We then knew what it must have been like in the old sailing ship days going around the Horn because that was where we seemed to be heading, the only difference was that the *Ceramic* was 18,000 tons and the old sailing ships were about 1,000.

Chapter 8: Trooping begins

After some days of this our rough navigation showed us we were now sailing North East and then nearly North up the coast of South America so we realized we were bound for either Panama or the U.S. The ship's officers would not tell us a thing, not surprisingly. Eventually we saw land which turned out to be the islands in the approach to the Panama Canal. We were most excited to find we were to go through the Canal which, even to this day, is one of the man-made wonders of the world.

We knew we were really in the war zone when we entered the Canal. American troops boarded the ship armed with submachineguns and others patrolled along the bank. Barrage balloons flew along both sides of the Canal and there were many anti-aircraft guns. The American Army were clearly nervous of Japanese air attacks and were well prepared to meet it should it come. We were warned not to throw anything however small into the Canal and anyone who did so would risk being shot without warning. The troops had orders to shoot first and ask questions afterwards.

The Canal Zone is in a tropical area so in almost mid summer, as it was by then, there was a severe thunderstorm in the afternoon and almost every day one or more balloons were hit by lightning and came down in flames, most spectacular.

Eventually we passed through the Canal and it was a fascinating experience. At the other end we tied up at a wharf in Colon. We were allowed ashore. Every day was interesting because one part was the U.S. Zone, which was populated with American servicemen and their wives and children, and looked like a typical American town. Over the border, which was over the other side of the street, was a Panamanian town with a largely native population and a much lower standard of living, the like of which we had never seen.

One day when we were in Colon Harbour, Bernie and I were on deck looking at our Pacific map when the Chief Officer came up and said:
"What have you fellows got?"
"A map of the Pacific, sir," we said, "with our estimated course on it."
"Where did you get it from?" the Chief Officer asked.
"We calculated it, sir, with a home-made sextant and a book of astro navigation tables."
"Let me see it," said the Chief Officer. "My word, that is remarkably accurate."
"Well, sir, we are navigators."
"Yes, and if I had known you had it, I would have taken it from you. Don't do it again, will you?"

We stayed at Colon for about a week and it was some time before we were able to find out what the delay was. It turned out there had been a pack of German U

SS CERAMIC The Untold Story

boats hunting in the Caribbean and, as they had sunk many ships, it had been decided no more unescorted ships would travel through it, so we had to wait until enough ships arrived to form a convoy. Also the United States Navy, having only been in the war for only seven months, appeared to be having difficulty in providing enough escorts and trained crews.

Eventually we sailed heavily escorted and after about three days sailed into a landlocked bay which turned out to be the U.S. Navy base at Guantanamo, on the eastern tip of Cuba. We stayed there overnight and next day sailed along the North coast of Cuba to Key West, at the tip of Florida, and from there up the coast of the U.S.

At one time early in our training in Australia a rumour did the rounds that a navigation training school had been set up in Miami Florida, to train Empire Air Training Scheme navigators, and we were going to be sent there. It didn't eventuate so as we passed Miami we thought we should have a wake. We heard the bar was running out of Bass Pale Ale and had only a hundred bottles left so ten of us clubbed together and bought them. We sat around a big round table in the smoke room and drank the lot. It was some time before we recovered the next day.

The U.S. Navy being inexperienced were very nervous and kept trying to shepherd the convoy into the shallow water near the coast, where the submarines could not operate. This was alright for most of the convoy which were much smaller than the *Ceramic*, but we started to bump along the bottom so our captain gave the order to turn out to sea. Next thing we had a USN torpedo boat alongside with a very young officer bellowing at us through a megaphone to obey orders.

Our captain was an old British sea dog and his language was a joy to hear. Eventually it was all sorted out but I got a marvellous view of all the proceedings because I was up on the bridge with my antique machinegun.

We eventually arrived at the USN base at Newport News in Virginia where we were tucked up for the night in a safe harbour. Next day we were off again and eventually after dark arrived off New York. The pantomime that followed was most entertaining. As I have said before the Yanks had only been in the war for seven months and obviously had a lot of untrained or partly trained people in their services.

By this time it was pitch dark and once again I was on duty in the bridge, although what good they thought I could do with my machinegun if we were attacked by a submarine was not clear, but it was a marvellous place to watch an even better pantomime than the first one with the patrol boat off Miami.

Chapter 8: Trooping begins

I haven't mentioned that part of our training was in Morse code by sound and by signalling lamp.

As we came slowly into New York, where the city was partially blacked out, I saw a signalling lamp start up from the shore: "What ship?" then a reply just below me from the bridge "*Ceramic*"; again from the shore: "What ship?", then from us "*Ceramic*" this time more slowly and accompanied by growls from the Chief Officer, who was standing just below me. "Can't those bloody stupid Yanks read plain English," etc, etc. It took a little longer to convince them who we were and that we were friendly, and we eventually berthed in the dock area on Manhattan Island.

We had wondered why we had pulled into New York and the next day we were told that our old Hotchkiss guns were to be removed and replaced by 20mm Oerlikon anti aircraft guns, which would be operated by the present gun crews. I could hardly wait for that to happen but we were told it would take about ten days, during which time we could do what we liked and could choose to stay overnight in the ship.

We were limited by the amount of money we had. Upon embarkation in Sydney we had been given 50 pounds which was about 6 weeks' pay and we had spent most of that in New Zealand, on the ship, and at Panama, so there wasn't a great deal left. People were very kind to us so we managed to see a lot and go to free shows, etc. We even had a day at Coney Island.

Our ten days were soon up and back to the *Ceramic* and first thing I was up on the bridge to see what had been done. I was thrilled to find a large open turret constructed of steel plate and in the middle the Oerlikon cannon with a barrel about 10 feet long and with a strong harness into which the gunner was strapped. The No.2 loader was not so lucky, the ammunition drums were very heavy and although Ted was quite strong he was not very tall and so had some difficulty in lifting the drum up and fitting it onto the gun.

We were soon off again and after clearing New York harbour turned North, destination Halifax in Nova Scotia, Canada, where our transatlantic convoy was being assembled. Halifax was a very dull seaport town where the licensing laws were even more restrictive than the 6 o'clock swill in Australia.

After a few days, a very large convoy of a great variety of ships was assembled to be escorted by Royal Navy corvettes and destroyers. After we put to sea one of my favourite occupations was to watch the ships and their escorts and read the lamp signals from the Navy as they tried to shepherd the ships into their correct stations. Some of the messages were expressed in very choice language as the escort commanders lost patience with the Merchant skippers who seemed to be incapable of doing what they were told.

Being the biggest ship in the convoy the *Ceramic* was placed in the middle to make it hard for the U boats to get at her. This gave us a great view all around.

The Navy was very worried because previous convoys had suffered heavy casualties and this was made worse by the almost perfect calm weather. It was very grey and misty all the way and this may have hindered the U boats in their search for us. It is much harder for U boats to operate effectively when the weather is rough and the waves are high but, in our case we were perfect targets, and it was made much easier by the convoy having to travel at the speed of the slowest ship which was about 10 knots. The *Ceramic* could do 14 knots.

Day by day there was no trouble and on about the fourth day we had passed the halfway mark and I was up early out on the deck watching the convoy when I saw one of the escorting destroyers hoist up a large black ball signal. I asked one of the nearby Merchant officers what it was and he said it was an aircraft alert. I walked quietly down to my cabin, put on my life jacket and tin hat and climbed up to the bridge and into my gun turret, where I strapped myself into the Oërlikon harness.

No sooner had I done this than the alarm bells rang out all over the ship. There was much running and shouting as passengers and crews ran to their actions stations. After a short time I heard great thudding below me as somebody climbed up the ladder of the turret and Ted's face came into view. "Good morning, Ted" I said, "What kept you?" He was furious that I had beaten him to it but he needn't have worried, it was a false alarm.

And so we proceeded on our way until we sailed into Liverpool.

Years later I read in a newspaper article that August 1942 had the highest casualty rate in the whole war. I was glad we hadn't known that at the time; we had crossed the Atlantic without seeing one shot fired in anger.

****

Chapter 9
Final voyage

Harry Hignett
Letter to the author

Early in the last War, I was one of six telegraph messengers based at Bootle, and as part of our district we delivered telegrams to the ships in the local docks. We did enjoy the work and carefully noted the ships arriving and departing. It was interesting but we also hoped to get the first telegram to a ship arriving in the docks. If it was a big passenger ship the crew would always want to send telegrams home to mark a safe arrival. The charge was 1d per word and the average cost would be about 18d. Almost invariably we would receive 3d or 6d tip each time. If it were a very large ship from say another port the number of telegrams sent could be almost 100 and we could collect up to £4. As our wages were 11 shillings per week (55p) with the occasional overtime taking it up to 15 shillings per week (75p) we were sometimes comparatively rich!

We noted the arrival of the *Ceramic* and saw that she was elderly (nearly 30 yrs old) compared to the other large passenger ships docking in those days. But the ship always impressed us as stately and graceful. We saw her cargo discharged in southeast No 2 Branch, Gladstone Dock, and begin loading at the same berth. For almost two weeks she was loading and we noted her deep in the water – she was about to go. It seemed that she could be sitting on the bottom of the dock. Then suddenly she disappeared. One of the boys returned from the docks and informed us that she had gone.

A few days later the *Ceramic* was back in the same berth. We looked on this with amusement. Had she been too deep for the ocean passage? Several weeks later we learned that a tug had damaged one of the dock gates and opened the dock system to tidal flow. The ships had to go out to the Bar and wait until the gate had been repaired.

A few days later I delivered a telegram to the Chief Officer, (then Mr. T. Marsden). As I walked up the gangway I saw several army officers with green tabs of the Intelligence Corps on their lapels. There were also perhaps twenty Army Nurses standing on the deck recognisable with their white full nurses headgear (QANS). I then made for the Chief Officer's room and found him sitting filling out forms. He took the telegram, read it and then looked at me with a querying look. "Do you want to send an answer?" I asked, hoping also for a tip.

He shook his head and looked away. I left the ship.

The next day the *Ceramic* had gone. Several weeks later we heard that the ship had been lost with all hands.

Several years later I joined Shaw Savill & Albion as 5th Officer and then as 4th Officer of the brand new *Ceramic*.

In 1954 I was Chief Officer of the *S.S. Akaroa*. In London when the ship was loading, the Company Loading Superintendent was Capt T. Marsden. "Tommy" was not a tall man, but very pleasant and well-liked. He came aboard for lunch and with ten officers and shore staff sitting around the table he mentioned that he had been the Chief Officer of the *Ceramic*, saying "I received a telegram for me to transfer to another ship. I could have kissed that Telegram Boy when he handed it to me!"

I raised quite a laugh when I replied "You never even gave the beggar a tip!"

****

Dr Bruce Royall
Letter to the author

In November 1942 together with 15 other RAN and ex RN sailors (I had served in *HMS Vanoc* as leading seaman since early in 1941 – Western Approaches – Convoys) I was awaiting passage back to Australia working in the Regulating Office of *HMS Victory*, Portsmouth and annex Scrimshaw. A draft order came through that month assigning all ex RAN sailors (14), except myself for passage home aboard *Ceramic*. I joined *HMS Shropshire*, became HMAS (gift from UK Govt) in Chatham, and returned to Sydney and Pacific duty later in 1943. I lost a number of very close friends when the good ship *Ceramic* was sunk and there is rarely a Naval occasion when I do not think of that sad affair.

I was not aware of the loss of *Ceramic* until the first week of January 1943. However I was not surprised by this sad news. Some weeks before in Scrimshaw Camp, Portsmouth, I had a premonition that a disaster had occurred. In my dream, still realistic after so many years, all my friends were underwater, moving slowly with their hair floating about, air bubbling from nose and mouth – the strangest part of the dream came when I asked tall blond Jack Sorrensen why he had a hole in his forehead – he replied "that's where I was torpedoed."

Chapter 9: Final voyage

John McLean Stewart
b. 7th May 1922
Recollections provided by his daughter, Mrs Anne Tierney
Letter to the author.

My father was a Stoker Fireman. He joined the ship at the Gladstone Dock. It was an eighteen fire coal burner and was loaded with explosive material. My father recalls she was heavily laden - but stressed not over-laden. The expression was "Scupper Deep".

There were young men, women and some children on board.

My father was working with his brother and close friends, it was called "Working By". When she was partly loaded, she went out and took passengers and luggage at Prince's Landing Stage. She was due then to go out mid river to finish loading by barges and cranes. Their job was then done until she sailed. So my father and his brother and some other lads decided to go for a drink, but one of my father's friends said he was staying on board. He was saving up to get married and was going to buy the wedding ring this trip.

"We went home instead of going back to the ship. Next morning when we went to join her, she had sailed prematurely, which was not unusual in those days.

We then reported back to the Pool and were allocated another ship.

It was about two weeks later we heard on the radio the news that the *Ceramic* had been sunk. Lord Haw Haw, alias William Joyce, gave it out. It hit some more than others at the time, because up to seventeen ships a day were being sunk, so unless you were like us, actually booked on or had close friends or relatives, it was just another ship sunk.

We were very involved with one friend - the one who stayed as he was getting married. He was also the son of my mother-in-law's friend, and his sister was my late wife's best friend, so it was always there.

We did not deliberately miss the ship. It was apparently something that did happen. She sailed without us knowing the time of sailing. As I said, it was quite common in those days."

John Stewart married in 1943, and had ten children, 33 grandchildren and currently 6 great grandchildren.

****

SS CERAMIC The Untold Story

LINERS OF LIVERPOOL Part II
Derek M. Whale
ISBN 0 907768 14 8

There must have been many seamen in the last war who lived to thank their lucky stars - because, for one reason or another, they were unable to join ships which were destined to die. And *Ceramic's* story would not be complete without one or two of these "near misses".

Former able seamen Joseph B. Harthen, of Fazakerley, Liverpool, told me how he had been working by *Ceramic* for six weeks. But the night before he was due to sail in her from Liverpool on her last voyage, he "had a few" and, consequently, awoke too late next day to join her.

"I hurried down to the ship, only to see her sailing out of the lock," he said. "All my clothes were on board and I was left on the quay with a fireman, whose name, I think, was Frank Berry."

Joe got another ship, the grand liner *Andes*, and it was not until he returned to Liverpool from New York, with another small army of American troops, that he heard *Ceramic* had been sunk with the loss of many of his old shipmates. "I know that there were a lot of women on board *Ceramic* on that last trip," said Joe who, although in ships torpedoed before and after he signed on for the *Ceramic*, reckons that missing the latter ship "was the luckiest escape of my life."

Just as the *Titanic* had its witnesses to premonitions which stopped them from sailing with her on her ill-fated maiden voyage, *Ceramic* had at least one. Retired able seaman Dan Conroy, of Liverpool, who spent 45 years at sea, told me of that which he believed to be a supernatural occurrence during the last war.

He had arranged to sign on for service with the *Ceramic* one Thursday, two voyages in advance of her final one, and was having breakfast when his landlady asked him what was the matter.

"I must have been feeling a bit fidgety for some reason I couldn't explain," said Dan, who told his landlady that he was going out that morning to sign on for duty with the *Ceramic*. She wished me luck and I went out of the back-kitchen into the yard with the intention of leaving by the back-entry door. This door was unlocked and only on the latch, but I could not budge it. I tried with all my might, but it seemed as if a strong power was barring my exit and I instinctively knew that it was preventing me from leaving for some good reason."

Dan, who experienced all the hell at sea during the Battle of the Atlantic, accepted

Chapter 9: Final voyage

this as a positive sign that he should not present himself at the ship. "I simply went back into the house and did not sign on for the *Ceramic*," he said. "And I was more than ever convinced of that strange warning when I learned that she had been sunk two voyages afterwards."

Mr. Cecil D'Aguiar, of Southampton, who might well have been on board *Ceramic* when she was sunk, told me that he owes his life to a simple incident. For almost a year he had been a catering steward in the liner and then left her because of his annoyance over a leave draw.

The draw, for crew leave, was held in two parts. "My name," he explained, "was drawn with the first lot. But, when the lists were posted, my name was among those on the second list. This was done, I was told, because local men were to go on leave first. I thought, 'I'm not having this', and left the ship, which was sunk two voyages later."

As one of the numerous Merseyside families bereaved when *Ceramic* sank, Mr. Peter Leacy, of Bootle, told me that because the liner employed so many local people, she was also known as a 'family boat'. "We all acknowledged that there were other, greater disasters in terms of life-loss," he said, "but in the context of the time in which *Ceramic* was destroyed, this was probably the biggest single, rivetting incident to reverberate for a long time afterwards in that mile-wide belt between the river and Everton Road."

****

A Lifetime With Ships
The Autobiography of a Coasting Shipowner
Tom Coppack F.I.C.S.
Edited by C.V. Waine and M.E. Waine
1973 T.Stephenson & Sons Ltd. Prescot, Lancs.

"In Loving Memory of my daughter, Elsie"

CHAPTER FORTY-ONE
"Age shall not weary them"

... And now it is May of that fateful (for me) year of 1942. Elsie's marriage to Jack Pickering, at St. John's Church, Chester, had, due to war exigencies, only the immediate family as guests, but a banquet afterwards – the best that Bollands could provide at the time. Then the honeymoon train, and Chester General Station packed with Polish and R.A.F. boys waving and cheering.

289

Later came a card from Conway, showing the smallest house in Wales, and its message – "Happy beyond compare. I saw my old friend, Emlyn Williams. He wishes us well."

They returned to their nice little flat overlooking the Cross at Mold, for Elsie to be near to her job at the bank. Then it was that the Russians told Churchill "You must open a Second Front," and he decided that the Second Front should be through Italy, via North Africa. But how to supply munitions through Italy, a belligerent country? Well, why not a large munition works in South Africa? And each of the big steel works in Britain was instructed to supply its quota of executives – John Summers, Firths, John Brown, Kynochs, and many more – with Major Grindley, of Grindley's Bank, as its managing director.

Summers' quota consisted of their chemist, Jack Pickering, and D. G. Williams (of Sandycroft). That was bad enough for the Coppack ménage, but when they were told it would be, in all probability, for a very long period and that they could take their wives and families with them, that, for us, was the last straw. To argue with Elsie was useless. In her own words, "I am a Coppack, aren't I? Where Jack goes I go. You survived the last war, why shouldn't we this? It won't happen to us."

Jack gave me the transport number – a Shaw Savill liner, under the Alfred Holt management at that time. At least, they were acting as Liverpool agents either for the owners or the Ministry of Shipping, so I 'phoned to them seeking some reassurance.

Holts gave it readily enough. A very important ship is this one. Will be in convoy right through to its destination. I passed this on to my wife and my daughter Marjorie, and indeed we all felt a bit easier - but not much.

(I could see that liner in the previous war torpedoed - all those lassies in the sea- and our own Tarfield, Maurita, under Captain Bob Hutton, and Lady Mostyn, Captain Dan Elliott, all Chester River ships and men.)

Anyhow, 23rd November, 1942, wife Elsie and Marjorie went through to the Adelphi Hotel to meet them against arrival – I saw them off from Shotton Low Level. I ran along the platform, saw the train taking the bend, then sat on a portage truck and wept. Something seemed to tell me, intuitively, that would be the last I would see of that dear lass and her husband.

****

Chapter 9: Final voyage

Grace Marion Alexandra Laing.
Compiled by her son, Dudley Blascheck

Carrycoats Hall (Embossed Address)
Tues. Night Nov. 17th./42

My dear Dudley,

Thank you for your letter which arrived this morning. Yes we heard your broadcast & it was very good. Funnily enough I was wondering earlier in the day if that was the right date. I am afraid we didn't hear any church bells here, except on the Wireless. Yes the War news is very good for a change, but I think we have quite a way to go yet before we get really going, still I daresay next year may see us through. I went to Hexham to day & after lunch at the "Albany" I took Muriel Mail to the pictures & saw a wonderful news reel first of all, of all the excitements in Egypt - the best "news" film I've ever seen. The picture was "Smiling Through" - quite pretty but a bit soft. - Well, you will be interested to hear that the corn has been stacked at last - only yesterday and today - & the thresher is coming tomorrow! The nights have been cold & frosty lately, but the days have been fine & sunny. - When I was in Hogarths' today, I got a lb of Chocolate Biscuits from my "Points" &, as I didn't want them & they won't keep indefinitely, I am sending them to you. They look quite nice. I am going to N/C on Friday & so will post them then. - I am going in by bus & am going to get my hair washed & am having a luncheon party at the "Eldon" consisting of Aunt Constance, Connie Bell, Elsie Clark, Aunt Annie & Aunt Hilda! All Hens! - I am not sure yet whether to leave here on Sunday afternoon or very early Monday morn. The train to Liverpool goes at 9.20 on Monday morning from N/C & in order to catch it, I'd have to leave here about 7 a.m. in the dark, as I would have to pick up Bishop & he would come to N/C with me & luggage & then bring the car back to Corb. - I think I shall probably go in on Sunday afternoon & spend the night at the Station Hotel, as with all my luggage there wouldn't be such a rush on Mon. morning. I get to Liverpool at 3.7. & will spend that night at the "Adelphi" Hotel & go on board early Tuesday. I understand the two little boys & their father will be staying there too & probably everyone else who is going. The father (Mr Harding) will, I suppose hand over "Raymond" & "Vernon" to me Tues. morning! I think I told you they will not be sleeping with me, but will be in the same bunk as a Dr who is going out as "Inspector of Schools". There is also a trained nurse going, so we will be well looked after! I hear from the agents "Shaw, Savill & Albion Ltd" - that I am being given a "room" to myself which they think I will like very much! I don't know the name of anything - it has only a number, but I think it may be more comfortable in a way than the one we came home on. No doubt I will be able to tell you quite a lot about it all in due course. -

The only thing that is rather worrying me is the fact that we may find ourselves landed at C.T. [Cape Town] for Xmas & no train up! However, there again we have rooms booked at the usual hotel so apart from the fact that it will be a waste of time, we should be quite comfy. - I will cable you as soon as we can after arrival, & I will know from the date where you are. I shall also send one to Aunt Constance & she can let Jenny know, but I wonder if you could remember to write to Granny & let her know when you hear from me? Try not to forget. - Everything is alright here, except I think Dobson is very lazy & I had a dust up with him yesterday. Aunt Hilda came for the day Monday. - There was an Airgraph from Daddy yesterday written on Oct. 10th . - He didn't say much, except that he has just received a huge lot of our August, Sept letters & was glad you had had some shooting. Also that the windmill at Nyabira had been mended temporarily and there was water again. - By the way if ever you want to send a cable to me - the best one is by N.L.T. & costs 10/5 (ten shillings & five pence) for 25 words & 5d for each word more. So, as it is rather expensive I shouldn't send one unless it is necessary! If you send one to Daddy - you put on N.L.T. Capt Blascheck, all of which counts as six words, & Light Battery. Salis. S.Rhod. you always have to sign yourself Dudley Blascheck. When you send your report this time, I should address it either to me c/o the Bank address I have given you or to Daddy at the Barracks. - You had better write to me next week to Salisbury & just continue & then I'll get all your news to date in due course. - I am writing this on my knee, so sorry it's a bit scratchy. I am glad you are having an interesting time & that you are getting on well with your Rugger. Uncle Sydney is quite pleased. Well if I write much more, you won't have time to read it! I am enclosing you a..... *(The rest of this letter is missing)*.

The Adelphi Hotel, Liverpool.

Nov. 23rd/42 6.30. p.m. My dear Dudley, Well, so far so good! My train from N/C was an hour late, owing to fog at Manchester. But it is quite nice here. I have never been here before & it's a huge hotel & quite comfy. I walked up the street, but didn't see much except blitzed buildings & there must have been an awful mess. I saw this calendar in a shop & am sending it to you as it reminds me of "Trouble" & anyway you want a calendar to see the date! It was very nice talking to you the other night & what a good connection it was. I am sorry not to have got your letter, but Jenny will send it on & I'll get it in due course, I have no doubt. You seem to be having a busy time anyway & I hope you will write each week so that I know how you are getting on. By the way you can send airgraphs to civilians now in Rhodesia, but they cost 8d instead of 3d! Still it's cheaper than a cable, so if you have any exciting news, you can send one. I left home yesterday afternoon & got all my luggage in the car. Had tea at Shildon, picked up "Bishop" & went into N/C. The first time I've driven that car into town! I went up to Aunt Hilda's for supper & stayed the night at the Station Hotel. It was very frosty at

Chapter 9: Final voyage

home. Oh Dobson came by the midday bus yesterday & so I told him off!! So far I haven't seen my "little boys" but believe the London trains are very late. I have seen a lot of luggage with the same labels on as mine, so quite a number of people must be going. I am going to get washed for dinner now, but will leave this open & post later, in case there is anything to add. I miss you not being here to count my luggage for me! Haven't lost any so far! Later: I am finishing this in bed as it is rather late. I had a good dinner & then saw Mr Harding the two little boys in the hall - they had just arrived from London & the little one was about beat. I had a long talk to them & learnt all about their clothes & various belongings & am now in possession of the keys of their boxes & hope I won't lose them! They are nice little kids - the elder one very excited & the younger one veery tired! Very smart in new grey flannel suits. I have also met the Dr. whose cabin they are going to share & he seems very nice - Dr. Giles - & he originally came from Newcastle & did his training there! He is tall and dark & wears glasses & is about 35 or 40. His sister is here seeing him off & she seems a nice woman. I hear there will be about 12 children all told and we should take about 30 days as we stop at a place I have never been to and always wanted to visit - an island near the other end! Look at the map & I'll tell you later where it is. [St Helena] - The news about Dakar is good tonight isn't it. - I think it will all be quite pleasant & the people whom I have seen who I think are going, all seem decent & not too old. Well I must go to sleep. Goodnight Bunny & be good & work hard & I'll be back before so very long I'm sure & mind you write each week Lots of love & a kiss - from Mummy.

My Dear Dudley,

I find it very difficult to write just now & so you must excuse a short note. Last time I wrote I was looking forward to having Mummy here with us again and instead of a telegram saying she had arrived in Africa - I received the news on New Years Eve, that she had been lost at sea.

It was very difficult for her to decide whether to stay in England with you, or rejoin us here, but having made all arrangements for your well being, she bravely decided to return to us until such a time as we could all be together again.

We have suffered the greatest loss possible - the one we loved most, and we must bear it bravely, as so many have to in these days, and treasure the memory of a very dear woman who died because she wanted to be with those she loved.

I forgot to enclose the cheque for your birthday in my letter - I have sent it off this week.

Love from Daddy

SS CERAMIC The Untold Story

Captain W. Logan Foster from the Bibby Line had been ill with pneumonia and was being sent back to his ship. He had been told that he was to Captain a hospital ship moored offshore. This is his last letter, sent from the Ceramic before departure.

"I had to hang about for a couple of hours, owing to delay through fog. However I eventually did get on board and found that I had a very nice single cabin quite a decent size and comfortable, in fact better than the singles we have [on the Bibby Line]. There is hot and cold water laid on which is a blessing and I think I ought to be comfortable. The lunch here was very good and I enjoyed it for it was 2.0pm before I got down to it with having a light early breakfast I was ravenous. There is a fairly big crowd of people, rather mixed and all looking lost – as I am. It's really a comic position for me, but I'm just going to make the most of it and get as much rest as I can. I don't know where I will get off yet but the office will arrange that and the agents will be fully informed before I get there............Will write from where ever I call at and I hope you will keep well.......I might be home by easter, so I was told, au revoir dear and fondest love, Daddy."

***

Trevor Winser.
(Ceramic, November 1942)

My darling Joyce

Just a few lines to let you know I am happy and well. Expect you are feeling rather anxious sweetheart but don't worry. I am fine. It's rather difficult to write a letter like this as there are so many things that I dare not mention. Still I know you understand. It was a bit of a blow going so suddenly wasn't it darling? But we knew it had to come sooner or later. Have just had a marvellous dinner of celery soup, roast lamb and mint sauce, baked potatoes, cabbage and Viennese Pudding and custard. At the moment I am in the lounge writing this. Jim Deer and I have a lovely bunk, with sheets and pillows, arm chairs, h&c water, in fact we are in luxury. Hope Janet has lost her cold by now. Give the little darling some big hugs from daddy and tell her to look after mummy for him. Keep smiling my darling. I shall be patiently waiting for the time when we are all together again. Keep writing darling as I shall get your letters eventually. Please forward enclosed letter to Mum. So for the present au revoir my darling. Lots of love and kisses for both Janet and yourself.

Always your very own loving Tim
xxxxxxxxxxxxxxxxxxxxxxx
Busters for Janet
xxxxxxxxxxxxxxxxxxxxxxx

Chapter 9: Final voyage

Extract from personal recollections of Charles R J Taylor
The departure of Convoy ON149

LIVERPOOL November 1942. Merseyside was in a thick sea fog off the Irish Sea, which stifled sounds and hid movements as many thousands of troops embarked on many troopships in the port. Merchant ships prominent in pre-war passenger trade, their profiles were obscured by liferafts, scrambling nets, anti aircraft guns mounted on platforms, and other paraphernalia of defensive armament, all blended by grey paint. No crowds to cheer or wave farewell. Just another secret and largely unobserved troop movement, and clandestine ship departures.

I joined *Otranto* at Princes Landing Stage, as contingents of GIs were boarding. From a shared taxi provided by the Merchant Navy Pool office we dropped off two radio operators at a dock gate for *Ceramic*. We knew two of our training shipmates had just joined her. The fog thinned in patches, ropes were cast off, and tugs towed us down river. Through clearer patches as the fog swirled I saw scores merchant ships in the dock basins, painted sombre gray against a drab colourless backdrop of cranes and grimy warehouses, long unpainted because of the war, many gutted and roofless. The scars left by the Blitz on Merseyside.

Flashing lights mounted on buoys warned of wrecks sunk in the fairway during air raids, as their bells responded to water movement round some ships masts sticking up out of the muddy water. We moored to river buoys off Wallasey bank, the fog thickened and closed in early for the long winter night. It persisted next morning in slowly rolling banks. With blasts on her siren, *Ceramic* emerged eerily from one, and slowly edged past us. It was bitterly cold and damp, and only a few crew and some khaki-clad troops were out on deck. I did not see our former trainees among them. Customary catcalls came from them as she slowly disappeared into the next fog bank.

She lay very low in the water, obviously heavily laden. She was not as heavily and defensively armed as other troopships were. Her age showed clearly and many rust scars on her grey painted hull told of her encounters with rough seas. Finer points of ship maintenance were not possible under wartime pressures.

Completed in 1913 for White Star line (a year after their *Titanic* had sunk) she had been designed to cater for sailing ship nostalgia, with four tall raked masts, which in 1942 was an unusual sight. She was managed then by Shaw Savill & Albion Company. One thought of a dignified old lady who had known better times.

Later the fog lifted to a typically dull grey overcast prevalent in those waters in winter. At last we were under way, and sailed along the buoyed channel, over muddy brown shallows. We passed the Bar lightship, (now preserved and moored in dock at the Liverpool Maritime Museum), the water turned to green, and we sailed across to convoy assembly point in Colwyn Bay. *Ceramic* was already anchored there. More ships were arriving as early dusk again fell. Experienced seamen knew the profiles of most, but the identity of others remained anonymous, their names and company livery painted out for the duration.

I had not yet joined a watch, and awoke to the noise of the focsle head winches lifting our anchors. Ships gradually formed five columns, and sailed westward of the Isle of Man, its mountainous profile clearly visible in very bright moonlight shining in a windswept sky and on a calm Irish Sea. The sea was silver to starboard with black silhouettes of ships, and a dark black to port with moonlit grey forms of ships I recall the profile of the fourmaster to starboard.

We left the North Channel astern as a grey overcast dawn broke heading into an ominously leaden grey Atlantic, a heavy swell running capped with white horses. The Irish mountains could be seen to port. An icy wind sent sheets of spray and spume high across every ship. DEMS gunners kept lookout at their respective gun positions, for we were within the possible range of enemy aircraft as well as submarine infested waters.

I recall going on deck as a wintry dusk fell to glimpse the stern view of two ships disappearing into the gloom to starboard, proceeding independently to westward. By her size one could only have been *Ceramic*. She was not part of our transport convoy.

Though southbound for the Mediterranean, we took a course well to westward, possibly a thousand miles from French coast to avoid bomber attacks. We were one of the fast troop convoys for the North Africa campaign, sometimes making 12-14 knots. Later we encountered exceptionally stormy weather that prevailed in the Atlantic throughout the winter of 1942/43. We sailed through this storm for three days or so.

Because of strictly observed zigzag procedures, the westerly deviation, and the delay effect of severe pitching and tossing due to weather conditions it took nine days before we went through the Straits of Gibraltar at night, to make landfall at Mers El Kebir the next evening to disembark our troops.

It is known that *Ceramic* sailed a westerly deviation course, and would have zigzagged as she headed south bound for her first port of call, St Helena Island. It was the practice to allow some ships capable of a reasonable speed to sail independently. There were insufficient naval ships to escort them all. Usually they sailed in an escorted convoy out from British coastal waters, before taking a separate course, just as *Ceramic* did.

Chapter 9: Final voyage

Joe Caffery
Email to Frank McCormick

I am from Liverpool and most of my family still live here, Uncle Jim was a 3rd gen Irish descent, and hailed from the scottie road area. My dad has always sworn, that secrecy surrounded the ship, and far more people than 656 were sailing that day, he had leave from the army and took Jimmy to the docks, he was stopped at the gates and refused entry without a pass (even though he was in uniform). Jimmy got him one a couple of hours later after dad's papers were examined no doubt. He remembers giant red crosses draped over both sides of the ship and the amount of able bodied soldiers that got on the ship not consistent with it being a hospital ship. He asked Jimmy where they were going, he did not know but a whisper had been going round that they were going to South Africa to drop off engineers for a demolition job, but that was only what the crew had heard. Jimmy also told him that there was lots of officers from specialist groups, and a foreign group of officers dressed in civvies along with boffins. Dad never really thought nothing of it and left the ship about 2 hours before sailing.

He left the docks to go to Seaforth to wave it off and noticed a hell of a lot of armed M.P.s and all along the docks were empty army trucks, as if a giant convoy had arrived, there was explosive trucks and personnel trucks. He waved goodbye to the ship which still had the red cross draped over the side and went home.

He told us that it was months after xmas that his Dad got the telegram saying that Jimmy was lost at sea. Dad got the news and was given a weekend pass and went home. He remembers that it was not like a funeral, and a couple of other people who had lost family on board were in the pub together, they knew he had been on board that day and started asking him all sorts of questions which got him thinking... why so many soldiers, why the red cross, why the explosives, he couldnt bear to listen to them and went home.

I always remember him getting letters of the home office and he always wrote back, I wish I had them but they were most probably destroyed after he died.

***

Frank McCormick
Email to the author

... I could well imagine a covert operation being masked by hospital ship insignia whilst in port and until well out to sea, simply to try and confuse informers – there must have been some at every port in the land. But what information or choices were civilians given about travelling?

Harry Hignett
Email to the author

Thank you for your latest. I have no knowledge of that. If a vessel was a hospital ship it would have been painted white with a blue or red band around with the red cross inserted at least three times along the ship's side. To drape a flag or flags like that over the ship's side does not make sense - if it were windy they would blow about and would not easily be seen all over. And who in Liverpool would see them and what would they do with the knowledge? doesn't make sense either. And I'm sure the vessel moved into the river in the dark or late in the day.

***

Charles R J Taylor
Letter to the author

Hospital ships were painted white with red crosses painted on to accord with international convention, illuminated to be seen. Painted tarpaulins wouldn't survive Atlantic weather. Field hospital tents may have been shipped aboard by crane – or army ambulances with red cross markings on quayside or shipped and carried on deck? Such deck cargoes were common then. I can't recall that Ceramic had such (Could it have been a convoy marker, as Ceramic's column in ON149 was headed by the Cross of St George?) That George Cross is an identification pennant (tailed) flown by the escort column leader. Escorts were based down river in Gladstone Dock basin area, near Seaforth, not where Ceramic was berthed. The RN White Ensign flown from stern has St George Cross. But drapes on a ship under way????

... Eric Munday might know more. I wonder if he waved or catcalled to us or stayed below and kept warm.

***

Eric Munday
Letter to the author

I'm afraid it does not trigger any memories. I think that some people feel that because the Ceramic passenger list showed some 50 nursing sisters, that it was a hospital ship. Others may think that because there were 100 or more military personnel, that it was a troop ship. Which category do civilian women and children fall into? It says that the red cross was draped over the side.
I believe that red crosses would be painted on funnels and the superstructure as plain as could be. It would not travel without being fully illuminated. What was a hospital ship doing at Liverpool, when the war zone in December 1942 was in North Africa?

Chapter 9: Final voyage

Prisoner of War repatriation ships sailed under the flag of a neutral country, mainly Switzerland and it is my belief that the Germans would have been informed when such ships were leaving.

At the end of the day I have to believe what I have always said and that the Ceramic was a passenger ship carrying an assortment of small groups of military people. Also that the Ceramic was blacked out during the hours of darkness.

I was once told that a hospital ship was a protected vessel and therefore would not travel within a convoy.

****

Interview with May Bulbrook
24/3/01

The loss of her brother, Basil Bulbrook on the Ceramic

Well, you see, Basil was an Engineer on the Anglo Saxon tankers. He had been torpedoed twice and managed to survive and he was recuperating from the second torpedoing, and my father wanted him to apply for a shore job – he could have because he wasn't really completely fit from the second torpedoing. They were floating on a quarter of a tanker with six Chinese, and Basil managed to save the Captain, he had injured his head you see, but they floated for three days and nights and the German submarine followed them waiting for them to sink, you see. But of course, they were picked up by an American ship which had already picked up some survivors from another ship that was sunk. It seemed that the paths where they were was a sort of harbour for the German submarines. Well I was home, I was in a munitions works in London, and we had been bombed so we were given some leave. And Lord Haw Haw was broadcasting most nights. Basil had gone back, and that photo you've got with him in the garden was taken the last day he was home, and I said to Mum – he used to broadcast about twelve o' clock at night – "Why, turn it up, Mum, I want to hear what he's got to say." And the first words he said was, "What a wonderful feat our commander has done by sinking this big British troopship". But of course, she wasn't a troopship. She carried *some* troops but she also had, I don't know whether it was three hundred or five hundred, but it was in the hundreds, of little children that were being evacuated to Cape Town. And Captain Elford of the *Ceramic*, he pleaded three times with our government not to send these little children on the *Ceramic*, but they wouldn't listen to him. They said she was a big ship - which she was - she had the speed and she should be able to outspeed the German submarines. But Captain Elford said, no, she wouldn't be safe. It wasn't wise to send those children. Anyway, I had been dusting the room – we lived in Devon then – and I opened the window to shake the dust and it blew all the papers off the sideboard, you see. And as I stood to pick them up, I saw the name "*Ceramic*", and I thought "Oh, that's what Basil has gone on." But as I said, Haw Haw said, what a wonderful feat it was to sink this big British troopship – and there were no survivors. Mum said to me, "What's the matter with you? You've gone as white as a sheet," and I said, "Mum, didn't you hear what he said?" She said, "You shouldn't listen to it, and you shouldn't have read your father's papers." I said, "I didn't really read Dad's papers, Mum. They blew all around the room, and I picked them up and saw the name written, "*Ceramic*".

They sailed from Liverpool, and there was a bad air raid that night. I'm not sure that they ***did*** sail, but they were ***due*** to sail. Basil phoned Dad, because we were on the Admiralty – head of the Coastguard you see, so he managed to get through to Brixham to say a last goodbye to Dad, and look after Mum and that. And told him about the *Ceramic*. And as I say, they sailed up, and Mum was very angry with me because she thought I had looked through Dad's papers which I shouldn't have done, you see. And I went back to London, in Woolwich Arsenal, and you know, it was a month before they broke the news in our papers about the sinking of the *Ceramic*. But Haw Haw said this was a wonderful feat, and he was being decorated. He said it was a big troopship on its way to Cape Town where the British had lots of ships, oil tankers and cruise ships waiting for crew to sail them back to Britain, but they couldn't get past this nest where these submarines were. Well, as you know, there was just one survivor of a terrible storm. That young soldier. But of course, we weren't told much. There was nothing much in the papers about it. You know all the rest, but that's about all I can tell you. But I can still hear Lord Haw Haw's voice saying, "No survivors". And anyway, it was a month before the government broke the news and came to tell us that Basil was on the *Ceramic*.

(Was Basil a crew member of the Ceramic?)
Oh, I don't think so. There were other seamen all sailing out to man these ships in Cape Town, you see, there were so many ships that couldn't sail because they had no crew. Especially the tankers, you see, for the petrol and the oil, and of course, food. People didn't really know how much the Merchant Navy did, what with going back from being sunk, but as I say, my father wanted Basil to apply for a shore job, but Basil said, "No Dad", he said, "I won't have anyone say that I showed the white feather, because that was his third sinking you see. He had been up on an enquiry. The government, when they were on a torpedoed ship, if they were saved and came home, they were all at an enquiry in London – of how. Wasn't it awful? And of course Dad tried to help Basil in what to say, and all that you see.

But the strange thing was that Basil, you see, was, they were a Dutch company, I think, the Anglo Saxon tankers, the first one he was on, she came through all the war, but the other three were sunk.

Chapter 9: Final voyage

But as I say, Captain Elford pleaded with the government not to send the evacuated children.

They gave – what do you call it? – a pension. But it wasn't much. About a pound a week I think. And when Dad died, because Basil wasn't married you see, and his money went to his parents, and when Dad died, we were in Fishguard, and the people that used to issue the pension said they would try and get it applied to me, as Basil helped with all my illness. But I said as I wasn't staying down in Pembrokeshire, I wouldn't bother. I didn't want all that trouble. But that broke my mother up, she never got over that, and funnily enough, the Captain from the Anglo Saxon company, that came to tell them that Basil was gone, he died soon after. Not very much I can tell you except I heard it from Haw Haw. He had such a sneering voice, you know. And he knew there were troops on the ship as well as ordinary people, but Captain Elford was very upset to think he had to take all these little children.

But I think the German captain of the submarine - I think he committed suicide. He was upset when he knew there was over six or eight hundred people on board. But I think what he was shocked about was the little children. But they knew all the details about all the ships in Cape Town harbour waiting for their crews to sail them home.

My people tried to keep Basil from the sea. He was a qualified motor engineer as well, you see. And because my other brother - he was a captain of a ship, but Basil **would** go because Dad, my father, was in the Navy from the sailing ship days, so it was in them, you see. He was a very smart young man, and he used to play the guitar. You can see how thin he was. And of course as a young man, mad on motorbikes! He always was very smart, and never seemed to look untidy, you know. And fond of dancing too. All the girls were after him, but he never bothered with them very much. It was motorbikes and the guitar! The other brother was out in Singapore. It was two years before we knew whether he was safe too.

The first time they were torpedoed, they were picked up by an American ship that already had a few that they'd found before. And that small one was taken in America. They were the first lot of British seamen picked up by the Yankees. The American people used to write regularly up until my parents died. But he never went by the name of Basil if he could help it. He didn't like it. He thought it was a bit sissy. So he used to go by his second name of John! No, he thought, apparently when he first went to sea, I suppose some of the people thought Basil was a sissy name, so he used to say his name was John. Because he was Basil John, you see. The same as the other one was Percy Alexander, which he thought was awful!

But as I say, what stuck in me was I heard Haw Haw give it out.

And as I say, Captain Elford, he didn't want to take those children.

I went up when they did that memorial in London. They gave us the invite to go to the dedication of it. I went up to that, and lots of tears were shed. And I remember Mum had a letter from the Queen, you know, but as she said, "A bit of an honour, but what good did it do?"

I don't think people realised what the Merchant Navy did during the war. I mean Basil was only one of hundreds that went back after being bombed. And I think it must have taken a bit of courage to do that.

Anyway, of course, it's a funny thing that I'm the only one left now, and I've always been a creaking gate, with rheumatoid arthritis all my life, but I went out and worked in the bomb factory after Basil went, although Mum and Dad were angry that I did it, and the doctor said I shouldn't, and funnily enough the creaking gate lasts longest, doesn't it? I'll be 95 in a month.

Well, as I say, Basil managed to phone Dad on that night, but he said, "The way I've managed it Dad is because there's a terrible Blitz on Liverpool," so whether she sailed I don't know, but she was supposed to sail, but he said, "Everybody's gone to the shelters and left the phones unmanned". And because Dad was on government premises you see they used to put it through when he said, "Just to say a last goodbye, Dad."

But funnily enough, I've lived alone most of my life, but sometimes in the night it's as if I hear them, hear their voices. Probably because I've got their photos around. But I remember one night, I heard Dad as plain as anything, I even got up, but there was nobody there. Probably because the few bits and pieces I've got are from their homes, you feel that they're there. And we were always as children, we were always loyal to each other. I was the eldest girl, and Mum was a bit on the strict side she used to say, "You wait until your father comes home!" And we wished he would - because her hand was lighter than Dad's. And now, you see, it's just hitting me now that I am old, when I don't feel old - but there you are. But there again, I used to play the piano well, in fact I had a little dance band when I was in my teens. I had to give it up because my fingers have gone. Then the deafness hit me more than anything. I don't hear my own voice, and it's a bit of a strain trying to hold a conversation when you can't hear what you're saying. But there we are. I miss the music more than anything. We were all musical, both the boys played the guitars and mandolins, Dad did. But he was a sailor from the sailing ship days in the Navy, and when he married Mum he transferred to the Admiralty Coastguard. So we moved around the country and lived in quite a few places.

Chapter 9: Final voyage

Public Record Office
CAB 56/1

25 November 1942
17 ships are listed as to leave from Liverpool to begin convoy O.N.149, eventually comprising 50 ships from Milford Haven, Clyde, Belfast, and Aultbea. The Liverpool ships are as follows:

61 *Sarpedon* (Commodore)	Flag B	Speed 14	Height of mast 132	No of guns 6
51 *Taranaki*	Flag B	Speed 13.5	Height of mast 106	No of guns 7
62 *Ceramic*	**Flag B**	**Speed 13.5**	**Height of mast 133**	**No of guns 15**
54 *Meliskerk*	Flag Bu	Speed 12	Height of mast 122	No of guns 5
71 *Moveria*	Flag B	Speed 10	Height of mast 90	No of guns 6
43 *Lechistan*	Flag Pol	Speed 10.5	Height of mast 82	No of guns 7
72 *Beaverhill*	Flag B	Speed 14	Height of mast 104	No of guns 6
31 *Empire Reynolds* (Vice Commodore)	Flag B	Speed 11.5	Height of mast 70	No of guns 10
74 *Henry Stanley*	Flag B	Speed 11	Height of mast 94	No of guns 6
32 *Sinclair Opaline*	Flag Am	Speed 15	Height of mast 90	No of guns 8
81 *British Vigilance*	Flag B	Speed 11.5	Height of mast 77	No of guns 5
14 *Nicania*	Flag B	Speed 11.5	Height of mast 76	No of guns 10
82 *Texas Sun*	Flag Am	Speed 11	Height of mast 105	No of guns 8
91 *Bayano* (Rear Commodore)	Flag B	Speed 12	Height of mast 112	No of guns 12
92 *Stuart Prince*	Flag B	Speed 11	Height of mast 77	No of guns 8
94 *Bothnia*	Flag B	Speed 10	Height of mast 72	No of guns 8
101 *Luculus*	Flag B	Speed 10	Height of mast 90	No of guns 8

Ships are to proceed in single line from the river to the end of the swept channel five cables apart.

When ordered by Commodore Columns:

51	61
54	**62**
43	71
31	72
32	74
14	81
92	82
94	91
	101

All A/A Guns, PAC, Holman Projectors should be loaded and ready for instant action against approaching aircraft, from the time of leaving the Bar. The men should be standing by the guns etc.

Normal Cruising Speed of Convoy 9.5 knots

CRUISING ORDER: MERCANTILE CONVOY

Convoy No. O.N.149
Date 25th November 1942
CONVOY CODE WORD – "RAPTURE"

Commodore A. J. Davies, CB, RNR, & Commodore W. Van Den Donker RNR in S.S. SARPEDON for New York.
Vice Commodore Master of S.S. EMPIRE REYNOLDS for New York
Rear Commodore Master of S.S. BAYANO for Halifax

OCEAN ESCORT
Broadway
Sherwood
Polyanthus
Morden
Pictou
Orillia
Primrose
Local Escort – *Molde (this would be for the Irish Sea leg of the journey)*

RESCUE SHIP
In the event of any ship being damaged while in convoy REAR SHIPS OF COLUMNS will stand by as Rescue ships to save life and then rejoin convoy.

Ceramic is shown in position in the centre of the convoy. Her key codes denote:

CERAMIC
L = Liverpool Ships
CL = Coloured Lights
M/F = DF Guard
P = Passengers
R/T = Radio Telephone
Pendant 62 - 350 passengers
133 Feet

Ships carrying explosives are denoted "X". *Ceramic* **is not amongst them.**

Chapter 9: Final voyage

Ships within RED lines for West & South Africa & South America. Figures in RED denote dispersal pendants, issued to Commodore, Vice Commodore & S.O. Escort only.

Ceramic's dispersal pendant is 87, along with *Meliskerk, Serooskerk, Henry Stanley, Bothnia, Peter Maersk, Cape Breton, Catrine, Tarantia* and *Empire Highway*, which is crossed through. A subsequent document shows latecomer *Fresno Star* as the 10th ship for dispersal for the South Atlantic.

****

Public Record Office
Ref: ADM 199/356
Lieutenant Commander E H Chavasse (Royal Navy)

SECRET

H.M.S. "BROADWAY"
7th December 1942

Sir,

I have the honour to forward the following report of my proceedings while in command of Task Unit 24.1.12 escorting Convoy O.N.149 across the North Atlantic.

2. **27th November**
The escort sailed from Moville as follows during the morning:- *Polyanthus* and *Primrose* to take over from the local escort (*Molde*) at Altacarry.

Morden, escorting the tanker VANJA, to join the convoy at Oversay.

Pictou, to join at Oversay.

Orillia was delayed in Moville with engine trouble, and *Sherwood* stayed behind to assist with repairs. Both sailed at 1430 to overtake near Oversay.

Broadway spent the day calibrating HF D/F and M/F D/F off Lough Foyle and sailed at dusk at 12 knots to overtake.

3. **28th November**
At 0810 I read an S.O.S. from an aircraft in a position some 60 miles fine on my starboard quarter. As my object was the safe and timely arrival of convoy

O.N.149, I considered that the very serious delay in my joining the escort that would be entailed in attempting rescue work did not justify my turning back.

4. MELISKERK was passed, circling with defective steering gear, *Primrose* screening. She shortly afterwards regained station.

5. At 1500 Z I joined the convoy in position 55°46' North, 14°07' West and took over duties of S.O. Escort from *Polyanthus*.

6. At 1726 *Pictou* dropped five charges on a fair contact, which was then lost. (55°44' North, 14°48' West).

7. **29th November**
At 0915 *Broadway* had to go into hand steering. At 0930 I obtained a very good contact, but flexibility of manoeuvre was even less than usual, and the target got inside my turning circle. Port throwers only were fired, and a whale rose slowly to the surface stern first, waved its flukes sadly in the air, commenced to blubber and disappeared. Contact was regained, but the target had by now lost its doppler, and probably much else besides.

8. *Sherwood*'s Asdic transmission failed and she could keep listening watch only. She carried out repairs, which were only completed by dusk. *Pictou*'s R.D.F. was shaky, and she could not transmit on R/T. *Broadway*'s R.D.F. was working only in short scale. Type 67 R/T tests were almost a complete failure, but R/T on 2410 KC/S was apparently alright, except for *Pictou*.

9. At 1204 Z I received orders from C-in-C, W.A., to divert the convoy to the Westward as a U-boat had been sighted close ahead of us (presumably by aircraft). At 1227 Z., in position 54°27' North (illeg.) West, course was altered to 272°. With *Sherwood*'s asdics out of action I exchanged places with her, putting *Broadway*'s on the port bow, i.e., towards the submarine. Shortly after this, *Broadway*'s steering bar was repaired. Net defence ships streamed their gear.

10. Visibility was extreme and the weather flat calm, sunny and warm (November!). I did not put out a distant screen as to do so would unnecessarily widen our front, and might allow an otherwise unsuspecting U-boat to sight the distant screen and infer the convoy's presence beyond.

11. At 1529 Z, I obtained an H/F D/F bearing of a U-boat on the other bow of the convoy, and within one hundred miles. The signal was a weather report. (54°28' North 20°25' West).

12. At 1911 Z I obtained an E-bar nearly right ahead of the convoy, but at a great

distance. (54°30' North, 21°27' West). By my plot this probably referred either to O.N.S. 148 or S.C. 110.

13. I had considered taking advantage of the calm weather by fuelling escorts, but I decided not to on account of the known presence of a submarine and the fact that little fuel could be taken in so near the beginning of the voyage, probably insufficient in some cases to last us out.

14. Pendants 111 (EMPIRE TIDE) reported that she had received R.D.F. transmissions on 54 Megacycles. I understand this is the frequency of Type 286. The only ship in the escort to hold this type was *Sherwood*, who by my orders was not operating it.

15. **30th November**
EMPIRE NUGGET straggled during the night but regained station in the morning.

16. During the morning watch a U-boat transmission was heard fairly close to the southeastward making a weather report. This was probably on account of which we had been diverted to the westward. The convoy altered course to 208° at 0930 Z. (54°54 North, 25°29' West) and later to 203°.

17. The weather continuing fine with a slight swell, I embarked on a fuelling programme. BRITISH GOVERNOR was at my disposal. *Sherwood*, being shortest was sent first, but as she had been unable to obtain the full oiling-at-sea outfit before sailing, she took the whole day over it. I also oiled her first because her water situation was acute and it might be necessary to detach her to the Azores or elsewhere at high speed. In the evening she reported she had only four days water left, and just before dark I sent a round robbin asking if anybody had any water to spare.

18. Admiralty reported a U-boat in our approximate vicinity at 1300 Z, but no transmissions were heard locally.

19. **1st December**

***

CANADIAN JOINT STAFF WASHN 149 INFO COMINCH C&R CTF 24 ADMTY NSHQ FONF COAC CTG 24.7 20, FROM CINWA)

149 NK ALTERING FORTHWITH TO (A) 50-30N 35-00W THENCE (P) OMIT (M) (N) AND (O) STRAGGLER ROUTE CANCEL (U) AND (V) SUBSTITUTE (F) 49 40 34 30 (G) 46 01 43 02 THENCE TO (W)

SOUTH ATLANTIC SHIPS ARE NOT TO BE DETACHED UNTIL FURTHER ORDERS.

***

FROM: COMINCH

U BOAT POSITION BY DF AT 1800/01 WITHIN 100 MILES 52-00 N 29 W X 10510 XCS GROUPS ENIGMA

***

Sherwood's water situation was critical, (evaporators defective), and unless she succeeded in watering from the convoy during the day I decided to detach her at high speed for Fayal. (To water her from a corvette at the same time as *Broadway* was fuelling would have unduly weakened the escort).

20. At 1050 Z however, C-in-C, W.A., drastically amended our route to the westward and at 1110 Z convoy altered course to 257°. (51°33' North, 27°52' West). The new route had the effect of
(a) greatly easing the fuel situation in the escort generally
(b) putting the Azores out of court for the *Sherwood*, as she could never have rejoined the convoy from there.

21. The Tanker was not yet ready, so I postponed the oil fuelling operations, and told *Sherwood* to make an effort at watering from a ship in the convoy. A fair swell was now running and after a prolonged effort, during which much gear was carried away, *Sherwood* reported that she considered watering was not possible. I accordingly detached her at 1615 Z to St. John's at 18 knots (51°22' North, 29°08' West). The tanker reported that the towing pendant was much chafed and she would not be ready to fuel *Broadway* until 1200 Z the next day.

22. Pendants 112 (EMPIRE HEATH) dropped astern with boiler trouble, but later rejoined.

23. **2nd December**

***

SHIPS ESCORTING ON 149, INFO CINCWA, NSHQ, CTG 24.7, AOCINCCC FROM ADMIRALTY

DF BEARING ON 10510 KCS AT 0929Z INDICATES U BOATS MAY BE IN THE VICINITY OF THE CONVOY

Chapter 9: Final voyage

At 0120 Z *Broadway* dropped one depth charge on a doubtful contact on the port bow of the convoy. At 0210 Z flames were seen in the convoy, but the Commodore reported by R/T that all was well. It turned out that one ship had had a flaming funnel. The glare was only seen for a few minutes.

24. Owing to an Admiralty report that a U-boat was apparently in our vicinity, the absence of *Sherwood*, and the recently shortened route, I cancelled fuelling operations.

25. EMPIRE NUGGET again dropped astern, but later overtook. She also straggled during the night. On each occasion *Primrose* escorted her back to station.

26. After dark, HENRY STANLEY's steering gear broke down, and she collided with MAJA which resulted in that section of the convoy resembling a Red Light district. I am informed that damage was only superficial.

27. *Broadway* burst a boiler tube and had to stop for a short time ahead of the convoy.

28. **3rd December**

***

FROM CINCWA

(SECRET CYPHER SHORE, SECRET CODE SEA. SHIPS ESCORTING ON 149. FOR COMMODORE)

ALTER COURSE FORTHWITH FOR
(B) 048 30 NORTH 042 01 WEST THENCE (P)
STRAGGLERS ROUTING FROM (F) TO (B) WHICH IS ON CONVOY ROUTE THENCE (W) OMITTING (G).

***

At 1100 Z *Broadway* went to oil from BRITISH GOVERNOR, and temporarily turned over duties of S.O. Escort to *Polyanthus*. At about the same time the convoy's route was again altered to the westward. The fuelling operation was unsuccessful as a fairly heavy swell was running and the gear provided by the oiler was much too light and parted repeatedly. The length of tow provided (alleged to be 320 feet but I believe to be much less) was far too short for comfort in that sea. When *Broadway*'s oil fuel pump broke down and main steam was temporarily lost which finally parted the tow, I abandoned the attempt after four hours hard trying.

FROM: COMINCH (F-35) (THIS IS AN URGENT U BOAT WARNING)

U BOAT ESTIMATED YOUR VICINITY BY DF 1658Z/03 HAS MADE SIGHTING REPORT OF CONVOY OR IMPORTANT UNIT. 10510 KCS.

***

(COMINCH C&R, INFO CINCWA 391 FROM ADMIRALTY)

ON 148 ON 149 HAS BEEN DIVERTED TO PASS THROUGH 48-30 N 42-00 W TO AVOID U/B IN 4730 N41-30 W

RECOMMEND 148 SHOULD OMIT KING TO AVOID 149

***

29. At 1900 Z I received a message that a U-boat, estimated to be either in our vicinity or that of O.N.S. 148 had made a sighting report. This transmission was not heard by me. It was then dusk, with a wind freshening to gale force, and I kept the escort close round the convoy. O.N.S. 148 had heard the transmission, but did not think it referred to them.

30. Between 1800 Z and 0200 Z/4 the barometer dropped from 1016.5 to 991 millibars, and a strong southeast gale veering later to southwest caused a considerable amount of scattering among the convoy and escort.

***

War Cabinet
Weekly Resumé (No 170) of the Naval, Military and Air situation
from 0700 November 26th to 0700 December 3rd 1942

Anti-Submarine Operations
A U-boat was sunk off Bone on the 28th by H.M. Destroyers Quentin and Quiberon. Fifteen other attacks were reported during the week: 10 by aircraft and 5 by surface craft. Of these, 4 were carried out in the Bay of Biscay, 3 east of Newfoundland and 3 in the Mediterranean. Several of the attacks probably caused damage, notably one by Corvettes south-east of the Azores and one by a Halifax aircraft in the Bay of Biscay...

U-boats
Although there has been remarkably little activity in the Gibraltar area and the Western Mediterranean during the week, there are signs of a renewal of

Chapter 9: Final voyage

operations by 8 or 10 U-boats between Gibraltar and Western Sardinia. **Six or more are estimated to be between Cape St Vincent, Madeira and the Azores.** *The total number operating in the Atlantic is probably about 85.*

***

Public Record Office CAB 56/1
SHIPS FOR SOUTH ATLANTIC ETC

	Distance to go Miles Days		First port of call & destination	ETA
CATRINE	2720	11	FREETOWN, Takoradi, Lagos	16/12
HENRY STANLEY*	2720	11	FREETOWN, Takoradi, Lagos	14/12
BOTHNIA	2400	10	BATHURST, Gambia	13/12
CERAMIC*	**4200**	**13**	**ST. HELENA, Cape Town, Durban**	**17/12**
			*(Changes: Saldanha**)*	
(onwards)	**1700**	**6**	**Sydney**	
SEROOSKERK*	6900	21	DURBAN, Calcutta	31/12
			*(Changes: Saldanha**)*	
TARANTIA	6900	27	DURBAN, Pt. Sudan, Pt. Said, Alex	7/1
			*(Changes: Saldanha**)*	
PETER MAERSK*	10200	36	ADEN, Alex *(Changes: Saldanha**)*	17/1
MELISKERK	3500	13	PERNAMBUCO, Durban, Mombasa	15/12
CAPE ORETON	5900	24	BUENOS AIRES	25/12
FRESNO STAR	5900	23	BUENOS AIRES	25/12

Note: "Distance" to go is based on route anticipated today (3/12/42). No allowance made for zig-zagging.

* Sunk
** *The Port of Saldanha Bay is 60 nautical miles northwest of Cape Town.*

***

31. 4th December
During the middle watch *Broadway*'s steering gear broke down, gyro broke down and lighting circuit for the magnetic compass failed. The R.D.F. however remained loyal, and warned us that we were steaming straight at the convoy instead of away from it. Repairs were effected.

32. At dawn the weather moderated, but the horizon was littered with ships. *Broadway*'s steering gear and tiller flat Sperry repeater again broke down for an hour or so while we were in the middle of a bunch of outlying ships, and entertaining manoeuvres resulted. *Broadway* also had a cracked ship's side plate below the waterline.

33. All escort eventually rejoined, the convoy re-formed, and at 1300 Z the Commodore reported only EMPIRE HEATH was absent. I reported this fact.

***

4 DECEMBER 1942
FROM ADMIRALTY

(TO COMMODORE AND SHIPS NAMES FOR ACTION WHEN DISPERSAL IS ORDERED)

ALL SOUTHBOUND SHIPS OMIT POSITION Z. SOUTH AMERICA SHIPS - MELISKERK, CAPE BRETON MOVE POSITION Y 010 DEGS. A 012 DEGS. B 007 DEGS. OF LONGITUDE WESTWARD. FRESNO STAR MOVE Y 012 DEGS. A 014 DEGS. AND B 010 DEGS. OF LONGITUDE WESTWARD. THENCE THESE SHIPS ARE CLOSE THE COAST AS SAFE NAVIGATION PERMITS CAPE BRETON AND FRESNO STAR TO NEW P 010 SOUTH 034 WEST THENCE D AND AS ROUTED. ALL WEST AFRICA N AND CAPE SHIPS MOVE POSITION Y 005 DEGS. OF LONGITUDE WESTWARD. FROM AMENDED Y AS FOLLOWS. BOTHNIA DIRECT TO DESTINATION. HENRY STANLEY AND CATRINE TO H AND K ON ALTERNATIVE ROUTE AND TO FREETOWN. **CERAMIC TO H NEW M EQUATORIAL 013 30 WEST DIRECT TO ST. HELENA.** TARHORIA TO H NEW M 000 01 NORTH 013 02 WEST, NEW R 016 32 SOUTH 009 59 EAST. SEROOSKERK TO NEW L 018 02 NORTH 021 00 WEST NEW M 000 03 NORTH 012 29 WEST NEW R 015 48 SOUTH 010 15 EAST. PETER MAERSK TO NEW L 017 01 NORTH 022 02 WEST NEW M 000 05 NORTH 014 03 WEST NEW R 017 10 SOUTH 010 05 EAST. LAST 3 SHIPS FROM R AS CLOSE INSHORE AS SAFE NAVIGATION PERMITS TO SALDANHA BAY.

***

NAVAL MESSAGE
From C-in-C, W.A.

Eire ship IRISH PLANE has twice been sighted by convoys mid-Atlantic recently. When an Eire vessel is expected to pass within 50 miles of a convoy in a British strategic area Admiralty will inform escorts in advance with an indication of voyage. Any such vessel sighted without warning should be regarded with suspicion and should be boarded if possible for examination of route. If off her route to an unreasonable extent ship should be directed back on it and warned the incident will be reported. Report should be made to Admiralty on occasion of breaking W/T silence so that Eire Government may be informed and interception or examination at port of arrival considered.

To: O.N. 149 (R) CONNAV BROADWAY
From: ADMIRALTY

Estimate Irish Plane eastbound will pass 40 miles to south of you p.m. tomorrow.

***

5 DECEMBER 1942
FROM COMINCH C&R

ACTION CTU 24.1.12 INFO ADMIRALTY CTF 24 NSHQ OTTAWA FONF NEWFOUNDLAND X

DISPERSE SOUTHBOUND SHIPS AT NIGHTFALL SATURDAY FIFTH X

REF 051045-ON 149 RECOMMEND DISPERSE SOUTHBOUND SHIPS NIGHTFALL TODAY SATURDAY PROVIDED ESCORT HAS NO LOCAL EVIDENCE OF U BOATS PAST 24 HOURS. ROUTES WILL BE PASSED TO COMINCH C AND R ON DISPERSAL.

***

34. **5th December**
During the middle watch, an encounter was made with an Irish merchant vessel who called herself IRISH BEECH HOUND and who acted suspiciously. A separate report of this episode (which was reported by signal to Admiralty at the time) is being forwarded to Captain (D), Newfoundland.

35. As there was every possibility that this vessel had reported the convoy's position and course, I requested the Commodore to make a bold diversion to the southward, which he did at 0645. Course for WESTOMP was set at dusk, and **ten ships for South Atlantic ports were dispersed in position 45°08' North, 46°08' West.**

***

FROM COMINCH 5 DECEMBER 1942

U BOAT POSITION BY DF AT 0343Z/05 WITHIN 100 MILES 47-30 N 42 W. ENIGMA 4798 KCS 69 GROUPS X

***

SS CERAMIC The Untold Story

NARRATIVE

0200 Z *Broadway* 5,000 yards Red 30 from port wing of convoy.
Polyanthus 5,000 yards Green 30 from starboard wing.
Orillia port beam of convoy.
Pictou port quarter.
Morden starboard beam.
Primrose starboard quarter.
Course 231º speed of 8.5 knots.

0215 Z *Broadway* sighted bright light bearing 265º. Steered 270º at 12 knots to investigate.

0220 Z *Polyanthus* sighted and also steered to intercept, course about 180º.

0230 Z *Broadway* fine on ship's starboard bow. Estimated course as 070º, steering straight for convoy. Before challenging, *Broadway* made the signal "STEER SOUTH" repeatedly. There was no reply.

0235 Z Ship altered course to South-east. *Broadway* challenged. No reply.

0240 Z *Broadway* fired lewis gun tracer across her bow. Ship immediately spelt her name IRISH BEECH HOUND. From then on, *Broadway* repeatedly signalled STEER SOUTH which was ignored despite another burst of lewis gun fire much closer to her bridge.

0248 Z *Broadway* altered course to port parallel with merchant ship and on her port quarter; also to avoid *Polyanthus*. *Polyanthus* turned to starboard and regained station,

0300 Z *Irish Beech Hound* signalled "SHALL I PROCEED". *Broadway* replied "STEER SOUTH FOR ONE HOUR".

0310 Z Merchant ship from convoy (out of station), burning bow lights only, seen approaching from port bow.

0313 Z *Broadway* stopped and went astern.

0315 Z *Irish Beech Hound* turned to starboard, and steered parallel to convoy and abeam of it. She made no attempt at disengage. *Broadway* followed her.

0326 Z *Broadway* signalled "PROCEED ON YOUR VOYAGE". There was no reply.

Chapter 9: Final voyage

0340 Z *Broadway* signalled "I WILL REPORT YOU FOR NOT OBEYING ME".

0344 *Irish Beech Hound* replied "I AM TRYING TO KEEP CLEAR OF SHIPS ON PORT SIDE". She then slowed down, and when the other merchant ship had drawn ahead, altered course to the eastward.

NOTE The precise movements of *Orillia* and *Pictou* are uncertain. Both ships left their station and closed the *Irish Beech Hound* at about 0320 Z on her port side, but observing that *Broadway* was dealing with this situation, regained their stations on the screen.

****

To: Admiralty (R) CANNAV C-in-C W.A.
From: BROADWAY

Sighted illuminated EIRE ship at 0220 Z 5th December in position 46°53' North, 45°20' West steering about 070 degrees. Weather unsuitable for boarding. Gave name IRISH BEECH HOUND. She sighted convoy. Consider deliberately slow in answering and obeying signals. Used very bright lantern. When directed clear of convoy nearly fouled straggler and used this as pretext to turn and follow parallel to convoy for some time. Warned she would be reported.

****

From: The Commanding Officer, H.M.S. BROADWAY.
Date: 9th December,1942. No.Y/103 SO.TU.24.1.12/7
To : The Captain (D), NEWFOUNDLAND.

ENCOUNTER WITH EIREANN VESSEL
"IRISH BEECH HOUND"

Submitted:-

While escorting Convoy O.N. 149 on the night of the the 4th-5th December, 1942, an Irish merchant vessel was encountered under suspicious circumstances. I had previously been warned by signal that the ship IRISH PLANE was expected to pass about 40 miles to the southward of me during the night, and a standing order exists that a report was to be made if any such ship were encountered off her route, and that she should be boarded if possible and directed back on to it. (C-in-C W.A's 2149 A/14th November).

2. Circumstances did not admit of boarding. The sea was too heavy for boat work. Also, U-boats had been reported in the vicinity and I did not wish to weaken the escort.

3. A narrative of events and track chart (the latter in original only) are attached. I claim accuracy for neither, since few records were kept at the time. They were made up from memory immediately after the event, and by subsequently comparing notes with the other Commanding Officers concerned.

4. The position of the encounter was 47°02'North, 44°45' West, and not as stated in my 0415 Z/5, which was based on an inaccurate dead reckoning. Heavy adverse weather had delayed the convoy.

5. The Irish ship, whatever her true name, was brilliantly illuminated, and it was difficult in the dazzle of light to make out details of her appearance. She appeared to be about 3,000 tons gross and had one funnel and two masts. Two Eireann flags were painted on her port side, and the word EIRE between them. These marks were floodlit. Many upper deck lights were burning. On the port side of her bridge, the first part of her name - the word - IRISH - was painted in bold white letters. the end of the name was obscured by some object.

6. Visibility was good, and I used a blue light for signalling to her. This light later proved effective at a much greater range when signalling to the Commodore, I am of the opinion that she deliberately failed to answer my signals (until shot up with our sporting gun - a stripped lewis - from the bridge) in the hopes of making me continue signalling and if possible use a brighter light. She herself made accurate Morse. She could, moreover, easily have disengaged to the southward at any time between 0230Z and 0310Z. Her turn to the southwest gave her an excellent opportunity to judge the convoy's course. In brief, it is my opinion that throughout the episode, she deliberately "acted wet".

7. No W/T transmissions which might have come from her were subsequently heard, but I judged it prudent to divert the convoy to the southward (O.N.S.148 was close to the north of us) which I accordingly requested the Commodore to do.

8. As a Cork man myself, I can only express shame at the behaviour of my misguided fellow countrymen, and regret that a breakdown of my loudhailer prevented me from offering them a word of advice in a Cork brogue.

(Sgd.) E.H. Chevasse
LIEUTENANT COMMANDER ROYAL NAVY
in command.

Chapter 9: Final voyage

FROM ADMIRALTY
6 DEC 1942

SOUTHBOUND SHIPS DISPERSED IN 45-08 N 46-08 W AT 1830Z/5.

ON 149. ROUTES AS AMENDED BY 1816Z/3 DECEMBER, NOT TO COMINCH C&R.

CERAMIC	(Y)	38-00	37-24	ST HELENA/CAPETOWN/
	(H)	17-00	21-48	DURBAN/FREEMANTLE/
	(L)	BLANK		ADELAIDE/MELBOURNE/
	(M)	00-00	13-30 W	SYDNEY.
	(R)	BLANK		

CERAMIC FROM ST HELENA TO (D) 17-00 S 11-00 E, THENCE AS CLOSE TO COAST AS SAFE NAVIGATION PERMITS TO (E) 33 S 17-20 E AND TO SALDANHA BAY APPROACH.

CALL SIGN UG OUTCON 320

Above: Believed to be the only photograph in existence of the *Ceramic* on her final voyage, three days before she was sunk, this photograph was taken by a crew member from another ship in the convoy. As photography was not permitted, the camera was concealed in a condom and strung up with fishing line outside one of the ship's portholes.
Photograph courtesy of Tony Denny.

The Impact of German Technology on the Royal Canadian Navy in the Battle of the Atlantic (extract)
by Rob Fisher http://www.uboat.net/articles/?article=44

What happened between August and December 1942 to reduce the RCN's ability to destroy enemy submarines? Or was it just chance or bad luck? Several factors stand out as potential causes of the autumn drought. First of all, the atrocious weather in the North Atlantic in the autumn of 1942. A series of unrelenting gales swept the transatlantic convoy routes almost continuously from October to December. Rough seas played havoc with asdic conditions and made the RCN's outdated radar virtually useless. While the weather was abnormally bad for autumn, the winter months of the period that followed were not much better...

German technological developments were, perhaps, the hidden cause of the autumn drought. In August, as the RCN basked in the glory of its recent successes, U-Boat Command acquired the first prototypes of the Funkmessbeobachtung 1 (FuMB 1) radar detector. The Germans commonly called it Metox, after its French manufacturer. It contained French, German, and even American parts. In addition to the search receiver, it included a wooden aerial in the shape of a cross, known as the "southern cross" or "Biscay cross". The aerial had a horizontal and a vertical antenna and had to be detached and taken below before submerging. FuMB 1 intercepted radar transmissions from both air and surface escorts on wavelengths between 1.25 and 2.5 metres. Thus, Allied radar types which used wavelengths of 1.4 and 1.5 metres – such as the Canadian naval radars SW1C and SW2C, British naval type 286, and the airborne ASV Mark II – were vulnerable to Metox. However, it could not detect the 9.7 centimetre transmissions produced by newer British naval type 271 radar...

Allied authorities realized by November that the Germans had developed a radar detector. Intelligence revealed that FuMB (known as the German Search Receiver or GSR to the Allies) could only detect metric radar transmissions. Western Approaches Command issued a general order to that effect which escort group C3 incorporated into its standing orders. Thus, during the pursuit of SC 109 from 16-19 November, the Senior Officer, Lieutenant-Commander K.L. Dyer, RCN, ordered strict radar silence for three of his six escorts – those without centimetric radar. His move was sound because the shadower, U-43, had FuMB rigged. It made a number of detections against aircraft before the convoy moved out of the range of Newfoundland-based aircraft. Dyer considered the risk of detection by Metox greater than the chances of SW2C or type 286 radar uncovering the U-boat. **Later in the month, HMS Broadway, the Senior Officer of escort group C2 with ON 149, ordered HMS Sherwood not to operate her type 286 radar. In effect, FuMB had neutralized metric radar and escorts equipped with it basically operated without anti-submarine radar by late November.**

Chapter 9: Final voyage

"**The second steamer**": a rare image of the *Peter Maersk*, sunk with the *Ceramic* by U-155 (KK Adolf Piening). All on board were lost: 48 crew, eight gunners and 11 passengers. *Copyright: John H. Marsh Maritime Collection, SA Maritime Museum.*

U-515s log:

6.12.42
CD2572
1838
2 smoke trails in sight, rw 220°, 7000 ton freighter, rw 70° a large 4-Master. Set myself before 4-Master. Ship increases steam at dusk and runs now 17 sm. Get alongside only after a drive lasting for hours. (Breakdown of Bunker 7 and 4). Exhaust gas pipe leaky, burnt gases, minor breakdowns repaired quickly, excellent attitude of the technical staff. Message regarding the second steamer by radiotelegraph. (Later sunk by Piening). Both ships course 110°.

FROM: HENKE TO: COMSUBS
2142

Kapitänleutnant Werner Henke
U-Boat Archive

AT 36 METERS. 2 ZIGZAGGING STEAMERS, NAVAL SQUARE CD 2580 AND 2810, GENERAL COURSE 120 DEGREES, SPEED 15 KNOTS.

2359
Begin attack.
Double shot from pipe I and IV. Depth 5, speed 15.5, bow right hand, position 80 E=12 hm, runtime 30 sec. strike in the centre of the engine room. 2. Shot impact heard, apparently failed. Steamer transmits, it is 'Ceramic' 18800 BRT.

CD2927
7.12.42
0018
Finishing shot pipe V. Depth 3. Strike in the front 20. Steamer gets illuminated and lowers boats, nearby I can see several boats occupied with soldiers.

0038
Finishing shot pipe VI. Depth 4. Strike in the rear 40. Steamer doesn't sink, many rafts and boats get lowered.

0100
Finishing shot pipe II. Depth 6. Strike in the front 20. Steamer breaks apart, sinks in 10 sec. Suddenly strong detonation nearby. Run away, fearing defensive action.

0715-1100
CD 2916
Test dive

***

TO: HENKE ((515))
0730

REPORT AT ONCE WHETHER TROOP TRANSPORT WAS LOADED WITH TROOPS AND WHETHER THERE IS ANY INDICATION OF ITS PORT OF DESTINATION

FROM: HENKE TO: COMSUBS
1110

1. HAVE JUST TURNED AROUND. CD 2927. TROOP TRANSPORT CERAMIC 18713 GR. REG. TONS. 16 KNOTS 110 DEGREES. SECOND STEAMER WAS PIENING'S.
2. 1 PLUS 5 TORPEDOES, 98 CUB. METERS.

FROM: HENKE
1147

CERAMIC FULL OF TROOPS. AM GOING TO THE PLACE OF SINKING IN ORDER TO CAPTURE THE CAPTAIN.

Chapter 9: Final voyage

1200
... heavy swell, overcast C 10, visibility 3-4 sm, rain and hail showers,
Return to site of sinking, to take captain prisoner.

At site of sinking, many corpses from Army and Naval soldiers, about 60 rafts and numerous boats determined, airplane parts.

1600
1 English soldier taken on board despite severe weather. According to statement of survivor, there were 45 officers on board, approximately 1000 men, couldn't find out port of destination. Cargo I assume exclusively war material

1735
Dived because of weather conditions.

***

8 DEC 1942
FROM: ADMIRALTY
(NA LISBON RPTD VA GIBRALTAR 408 CONNAV FROM ADMTY)

GERMAN BROADCAST CLAIMS SINKING OF CERAMIC WEST OF AZORES. THIS IS CONSIDERED PROBABLE AND THERE ARE INDICATIONS THAT SINKING MAY HAVE OCCURRED ON NIGHT OF 6TH/7TH DECEMBER BETWEEN POSITION 41-30 NORTH 41-35 WEST AND 39-20 NORTH 39-00 WEST. SHIP CARRIED 350 PASSENGERS. AS WE HAVE NO SHIPS IN THE VICINITY WE WOULD GREATLY APPRECIATE PORTUGUESE ASSISTANCE IS SEARCHING FOR SURVIVORS.

***

9 DEC 1942
FROM: ADMIRALTY
(HMS ENTERPRISE REPEATED FOC NO AT STAT COMINCH C & R FOCWAF FROM ADMIRALTY)
REF: ADMTY 0805A/9 SECRET

PROCEED TO POSITION 040-30 N 040-20 W TO SEARCH FOR SURVIVORS FROM CERAMIC AND PETER MAERSK TORPEDOED NIGHT OF 6TH/7TH DEC. PORTUGUESE DES. DAO FROM HORTA IS ALSO PROCEEDING

***

The *Ceramic* was sunk at co-ordinates 40.30N/40.20W, in the North Atlantic, west of the Azores. The ocean depth at this point is 4260 metres, or 14,000 ft. (The *Titanic* lies in slightly shallower water at 3800 metres, or 12,600 ft.)

***

Public Record Office CAB 56/1

From Reporting Officer Horta.
Date 9.12.42
Addressed Admiralty for D.N.I., Repeated S.O. (I) Gibraltar.

IMPORTANT

1130 G.M.T. 9th Acting on instructions Portuguese Destroyer DAO left for position 500 miles west Flores to search for survivors from torpedoed ship CERAMIC. Southerly gale here since evening 7th.

***

War Cabinet
Weekly Resumé (No 171) of the Naval, Military and Air situation from 0700 December 3rd to 0700 December 10th 1942

Enemy Attack on Shipping
During the week U-boats are reported to have attacked 5 ships of which 3 are known to have sunk. Two ships in a homeward bound convoy were torpedoed S.E. of Greenland.

The s.s. Peter Maersk (5,476 tons) bound for the Middle East with war stores and the s.s. Ceramic (18,713 tons) outward bound for Australia with Government personnel and war stores, were torpedoed west of the Azores.

***

10th December 1942
From N.A. Lisbon
Addressed Admiralty, repeated V.A. Gibraltar

My 0031 9th Portuguese Ship DAO sailed a.m. 9th but now reports unable to make headway on account of terrible weather and will probably be obliged to return to Horta.

Chapter 9: Final voyage

12th December 1942
From N.C.S.O. Ponta Delgada
Addressed Admiralty, repeated S.O.(I) Gibraltar, N.A. Lisbon.

Portuguese Destroyer DAO sustained heavy weather damage whilst proceeding to search for survivors of S.S. CERAMIC on instructions from local Portuguese naval authorities. She was compelled to return to Fayal.

***

13th December 1942

From: Admiralty
IMMEDIATE to both.

Your 1540/12 regret no further information. Probable that boats endeavoured to make Azores from area indicated in A.M.1934/8 and would in any case be leeward of that area now. Request you will convey the Ministry of Marine, Admiralty's grateful appreciation of action taken and consideration of air reconnaissance and their regret that DAO has suffered damage.

*Damaged in their search for survivors:
Dao (above) and HMS Enterprise (right).*

WAR CABINET 168 (42)
CONCLUSIONS of a Meeting of the War Cabinet held at 10, Downing Street, S.W.1, on Monday, December 14, 1942, at 5.30pm.

Present:
The Right Hon. WINSTON S. CHURCHILL, M.P., Prime Minister (in the Chair)
The Right Hon. C. R. ATTLEE, M.P., Secretary of State for Dominion Affairs.
The Right Hon. OLIVER LYTTLETON, M.P., Minister of Production.
The Right Hon. ANTHONY EDEN, M.P., Secretary of State for Foreign Affairs.
The Right Hon. ERNEST BEVIN, M.P., Minister of Labour and National Service.
The Right Hon. HERBERT MORRISON, M.P., Secretary of State for the Home Department and Minister of Home Security.
The Right Hon. R. G. CASEY, Minister of State.

The following were also present:
The Right Hon. S. M. BRUCE, Representative of the Government of the Commonwealth of Australia.
The Right Hon. Sir KINGSLEY WOOD, M.P., Chancellor of the Exchequer.
The Right Hon. L. S. AMERY, M.P., Secretary of State for India and Secretary of State for Burma.
The Right Hon. A. V. ALEXANDER, M.P., First Lord of the Admiralty.
The Right Hon. Sir ARCHIBALD SINCLAIR Bt., M.P., Secretary of State for Air.
The Right Hon. Lord LEATHERS, Minister of War Transport.
The Right Hon. Sir ALEXANDER CADOGAN, Permanent Under-Secretary of State for Foreign Affairs.
Air Chief Marshal Sir CHARLES F. A. PORTAL, Chief of the Air Staff.
H.H. THE MAHARAJA JAM SAHEB OF NAWANAGAR, Representative of India.
The Right Hon. VISCOUNT CRANBORNE, Lord Privy Seal.
Colonel The Right Hon. OLIVER STANLEY, M.P., Secretary of State for the Colonies.
The Right Hon. Sir STAFFORD CRIPPS, K.C., M.P., Minister of Aircraft Production.
The Right Hon. BRENDAN BRACKEN, M.P., Minister of Information.
Admiral of the Fleet Sir DUDLEY POUND, First Sea Lord and Chief of Naval Staff.
General Sir ALAN BROOKE, Chief of the Imperial General Staff.
Secretariat: Sir EDWARD BRIDGES, Lieut.-General Sir HASTINGS ISMAY, Mr. NORMAN BROOK, Mr. L. F. BURGIS.

... Including belated reports, shipping losses for the previous week amounted to 109,000 tons. Included in this figure was the liner *Ceramic* which had 656 persons on board, including some 244 Government personnel* stated to be from the Colonial Office and other Government Departments.

The War Cabinet –
    Invited the Secretary of State for the Colonies, in consultation with the Minister of War Transport, to submit a short report giving details of the Colonial Service and other Government personnel on board the *Ceramic*.

(*This figure would include the 226 "military" personnel on board.)

Chapter 9: Final voyage

Official composition of passengers on the *Ceramic*

Crew	264
DEMS Gunners	14
Total Crew	**278**

British Army Officers	43
Royal Navy Officers	11
Merchant Navy Officers	9
Nurses	30
Royal Engineers	50
Military/Naval (other ranks)	83
Total Military	**226**

Men	90
Women	50
Children	12
Total Civilian Passengers	**152**

TOTAL	**656**

Cargo
12,362 tons of general and government stores, including aircraft spare parts.

***

From ENTERPRISE
Date: 16. 12. 42.
Time: 1126.

Your 0805A/9. Arrived 090 degrees position of sinkings 250 miles at daylight 11th December. Searched towards position of sinkings at 18 knots zig-zag number 8 until 1255Z/11 when forced to heave to head north. Wind veered from south west force 7 to north force 12 within 15 minutes and in my opinion the resulting heavy confused seas, of typhoon character rendered it virtually impossible for any boat to survive in this area. At 1700Z/11 I decided search must be abandoned and to proceed to Clyde when weather permitted. Northerly gale continued until 0600Z/12. After proceeding a capsized white boat with red bottom colour was passed in position 45 degrees 19 minutes north 33 degrees 33 minutes west at 1600Z/12. Nothing else was seen.

***

To: C-in-C S.A. Governor St. Helena
Date 21.12.42

From: Admiralty
Your 1121/24 CERAMIC was claimed as U-boat casualty on enemy broadcast and has not replied to signals. Another ship will be sent for survivors.

***

Maritime and Coastguard Agency Archives

German Home Service via Allouis 1700 20/2/43

THE SINKING OF THE CERAMIC: ADD
On 6th December 1942 a U-boat under the command of Senior Lieutenant Henke sank the British Transport Ship Ceramic of nearly 19,000 grt. west of the Azores as was reported by the German Special Announcement of 9th December.

1348 Troops Lost
It is now possible to give details of this important success of the German U Boat. Henke's account disproves Churchill's assertion in the House, according to which only 1348 soldiers out of all those transported across the ocean under the protection of the British Navy, had been lost.

Henke to Broadcast Tonight
Henke will speak tonight from the Front. Reports state he had to fire his two torpedoes from a very short distance because of bad weather and high seas. After the torpedo hit, orderly life saving manoevres could not take place on the British Troop Ship. Life belts and rafts which had been lowered onto the sea capsized and sank. By next day when the German U-boat sailed into the scene strewn with wreckage, the storm had dispersed the battered boats and rafts over a great area. Among the wreckage hundreds of dead British soldiers were floating in their life jackets. The U-Boat could save only one survivor. According to his statements two to three thousands British Officers, NCOs and men of British Pioneer Regiments (Royal Engineers), Sailors and Crews were on board.

5 Other Transports Sunk
Similar scenes to those on the Ceramic took place during the sinking of the troop transports President Cleveland, President Pearce, Exeter, Excalibur and Santa Lucia, whose loss the U.S. Navy admitted before the sinking of the Ceramic, all in all the British and American losses in soldiers who were being transported to North Africa or England were more than 75,000 during December alone.

Chapter 9: Final voyage

Transocean (DLG) in English for the Far East 14.58 20.2.43

CERAMIC: DRAMATIC ACCOUNT OF HER LOSS

Berlin: The first dramatic account of the sinking of the British Troop Transport Ceramic which is still not admitted by British Official Quarters, was given Transocean by a reliable source.

Ceramic of 18,713 tons which had British Sappers and Marines in large numbers on board was sunk on 6th December west of the Azores by a German submarine under command of Kapt. Werner Henke aged 34 and owner of Knights Cross of Iron Cross, just when a heavy Atlantic storm was coming up.

It was pitch dark when the German submarine attacked at one minute before midnight. Owing to bad weather two torpedoes were fired simultaneously from close range. The ship was hit near the engine room and slowed down. There was much running to and fro on the upper decks but as more and more men came up from the interior of the ship and the scene was lighted up by torches, the confusion increased. This was due no doubt to bad weather affecting the land soldiers on board and to the tearing of a huge hole in the side of the ship by the torpedo. Despite this desperate situation lifeboats were swung out. But before they could be lowered the oncoming seas had crashed them against the ship's side. The ship's list increased. Rafts were thrown overboard, many of which also broke to pieces, so that most of the men had to rely on their life belts. The ship sank rapidly.

Next morning the submarine returned to rescue what could be rescued in the heavy gale blowing. Among the many bodies of drowned men, Sapper Eric Munday of Thornton, Surrey was rescued. With the rescue of this one man secrecy maintained by Britain (torn) the sinking of the Ceramic can be cleared up. According to (torn) the ship had a crew of 350 and more than 1,000 officers (torn) on board.

***

Supplement to Lloyds List
CERAMIC – London, Feb. 19. – A survivor of the British steamer Ceramic broadcast from Calais on Feb. 17 stating that the vessel was torpedoed and he took to lifeboat with a number of others but during a storm lifeboat capsized and after swimming for four hours was picked up by a German submarine. Note – Ceramic was posted as an "Untraced Vessel" on Jan 27.

Supplement to Lloyds List
CERAMIC – London, Feb. 21. – A broadcast from Germany to-day states that the steamer Ceramic was torpedoed west of the Azores on Dec. 6 in bad weather and sank in six minutes. – Reuter. (See issue of Feb. 20.)

SS CERAMIC The Untold Story

"...We used to get the Echo delivered, but our next door neighbour, another evacuee, named Mrs English, went up to Wallgate Station for hers. I remember one of her children came knocking for my father, and he made the excuse when he came back that there was some night work available, and he was taking the Echo with him. He met the boy on his rounds, in fact Mrs English had shown him the headlines in the Echo "Ceramic Sunk." My father joined all the other relatives outside the shipping offices. They waited there all night, then an official came out and told them it was a German lie. It wasn't until the New Year's Eve that a telegram arrived saying that the vessel was sunk with all hands. I am eighty now, but I have never forgotten that awful day.

***

29th December 1942

Dear xxx/Madam,

We deeply regret to inform you that we have this morning received advice from the Admiralty that the vessel on which both your brothers were serving as Bosuns is gravely overdue and that she must be presumed lost, due to Enemy Action on 6/7th December.

Bosun Edward Vaughan (left) and Ernest Vaughan (right and below).
Courtesy of the late Annie Jennings.

Up to the present we have received no information whatever in regard to the ship's personnel for whom we are gravely concerned. Deeply though we regret it, the probability must now be faced that the vessel has been lost with all hands, and we hasten to assure you of our deepest sympathy.

Under the Government War Pensions Scheme, allowances will be payable to Dependants of those serving in the vessel. In the case of Wives and Children the allowance will be payable under a definite fixed scale, according to the Rank, but in other cases it will be necessary for the Claimant to establish that he or she is in pecuniary need. There is no need for Wives to make any application to the Ministry of Pensions as they will hear from that Ministry direct in the very near future. In other cases the Dependants should get into touch immediately with the Local Regional Officer of the Ministry of Pensions, whose address may be obtained at any Post Office, and this Officer will advise them regarding procedure.

In order to assist you, the Company proposes to continue the payment of allotments up to and including the payment which will fall due on 18th or 19th January.

We are, Yours faithfully, SHAW SAVILL & ALBION CO. LIMITED.

Chapter 9: Final voyage

BRITISH OVERSEAS AIRWAYS CORPORATION

TELEGRAMS: 'FLYING', BRISTOL
TELEPHONE: BRISTOL 35068

WELLINGTON HOUSE
CANYNGE ROAD
CLIFTON, BRISTOL 8.

December 30th. 1942

Dear Sir,

We deeply regret to inform you that we have today received information from the Admiralty that the vessel in which your passengers (see attached list) were travelling is gravely overdue and that she must be presumed lost, due to enemy action on (censored).

Up to the present we have received no information whatever in regard to the ship's personnel or passengers for whom we are gravely concerned. Deeply though we regret it, the probability must now be faced that the vessel has been lost with all those aboard, and we hasten to assure you of our deepest sympathy.

We are,
Yours faithfully,
SHAW SAVILL & ALBION CO. LIMITED.

***

1st January, 1943.

HE.47.884.

Mrs. H.S. Tedford,
550 Ohio Street,
BELFAST, Ulster.

Dear Mrs. Tedford,

I very much regret that we have been informed by the Shipping Company that the boat in which your husband was travelling to Durban is reported missing and up to the present there is no news of passengers and crew. I am enclosing a copy of the letter we have received from the Shipping Company informing us of this.

I shall advise you immediately if any further news is received, and meanwhile on behalf of the Corporation I extend our sincere sympathy to you for the anxiety that this letter must cause.

Yours faithfully

**

Public Record Office

TO BE KEPT UNDER LOCK AND KEY
It is requested that special care may be taken to ensure the secrecy of this document.

THIS DOCUMENT IS THE PROPERTY OF HIS BRITANNIC MAJESTY'S GOVERNMENT

SECRET
WAR CABINET

6th January 1943

Loss of s.s. "CERAMIC"
Summary of Passengers.

Note by Minister of War Transport.

In accordance with the conclusions of the War Cabinet at their meeting on 14th December, I attach herewith a summary analysis of the passengers on board the s.s. "CERAMIC".

	A Returning from leave	B Taking up new appointment	C Ordinary posting to Service
ADMIRALTY CIVILIANS			
C.E.II Branch			
(a) Durban		1 (M)	
(b) Port Elizabeth		1 (M)	
(c) Simonstown		2 (M)	
Director of Armament Supply			
(a) Simonstown		1 (M)	

Chapter 9: Final voyage

	A Returning from leave	B Taking up new appointment	C Ordinary posting to Service

Labour Branch
(a) Simonstown   2 (M)
(b) Durban   3 (M)
(c) Trincomalee   1 (M)

COLONIAL OFFICE
(a) St. Helena   1 (F)   1 M
Plus 1 (F) Wife accompanying husband to St. Helena
(b) South Africa for East African   3 (M)
Colonies
Plus 1 (M) returning to Kenya on completion of education in U.K. to join local Military Forces - age 18 years.

SUDAN GOVERNMENT   3 (M)

(?) for SOUTHERN RHODESIA   2 (M) 1 (F)
Plus 1 (M) mine owner returning to Colony to work mine as Manager had been called up.
4 (F) returning to homes.
2 (Ch) boys of 9 and 6 years respectively. Mother killed in Air Raid in U.K. and boys being sent out to Aunt resident in Colony.

B.O.A.C.   11 (M)

ADMIRALTY Signal Dept.   4 (M)
(Cape Town for Tristan da Cunha)
Plus 4 wives 3 children and 1 wife (joining husband) accompanying ratings (special party for Tristan da Cunha)

MILITARY PERSONNEL
(a) St Helena   49 (M)
(b) South Africa   54 (M) 30 (F)
Plus 1 (M) 1 (F) repatriation of officer and wife to South Africa on completion of officer's military service.
(c) Australia   6 (M)

British Council
1 (M) Regional Officer for a 3 months tour of duty in Egypt

331

	A Returning from leave	B Taking up new appointment	C Ordinary posting to Service
(?) for SOUTH AFRICA Plus 7 (M) 29 (F) 10 (Ch.)	1 (M)	23 (M) 6 (F)	1 (M)
Belgian Government		8 (M)	2 (M)

NAVAL OFFICERS (BRITISH)   7 (M)
for South Africa
Plus 1 (M) repatriation following discharge from Royal Navy.

NAVAL OFFICERS (AUSTRALIAN)   4 (M)
for Australia

NAVAL RATINGS (R.N.) for
(a) South Africa   31 (M)
Plus 1 (M) repatriation following invaliding in U.K.
(b) Australia
1 (M) repatriation following discharge in U.K. on account of age.

NAVAL RATINGS (R.A.N.)   8 (M)
for Australia
Plus 1 (M) repatriation following invaliding in U.K.
NAVAL RATING (R.NED.N.)   1 (M)
for South Africa

MERCANTILE MARINE PERSONNEL
(a) South Africa   11 (M)
(b) Australia   7 officers
    14 (M)
Plus 1 child

Miscellaneous priority passengers   4 (M)
sponsored by Government Departments
Plus 2 (M) members of the Friends Ambulance Unit sponsored by the Foreign Office making a tour of the Units in Abyssinia, Middle East and China.
1 (F) wife of a Naval Officer also on board, she went to the port with her husband with a view to securing a berth if any of the passengers were cancelled. As two people were unable to travel she accordingly embarked.

= **TOTAL 378 passengers.**

PASSENGERS SPONSORED BY THE HIGH COMMISSIONER FOR SOUTH AFRICA IN OTHER THAN "A" "B" AND "C" CATEGORIES

MEN   1   Repatriee discharged from Imperial Forces through ill-health.
              4   Industrialists returning after business visit to UK.
              2   Students returning after completion of education.

WOMEN   2   Wife and adult daughter of industrialist.
              3   Educationalists.
              4   Returning on medical grounds
              5   Rejoining husbands posted to South Africa (husbands in South African Govt. service).
              1   Returning after business visit to U.K.
              9   Wives of husbands in categories "B" and "C"
              1   Fiancée of South African proceeding to marry and then take up work of National importance.
              3   Widows returning home after deaths of husbands.
              1   Proceeding to join daughter in South Africa (this passenger travelled to Port of embarkation on the chance of a berth becoming vacant and made a "pier-head" jump).

TOTAL   29

CHILDREN   4   with "B" passengers
                  6   with "other" passengers

TOTAL   10

****

Translation of a Radio Berlin Broadcast made on the return of U-515 to Lorient, January 1943

For several weeks we have had a report which until today we haven't used. Knight's cross holder **Lieutenant-Commander Henke** describes how he sank the English troop transport *Ceramic*, which had a displacement of 18,713 gross registered tons with a crew of 350 and a complement of several thousand British air force and navy troops. This sinking had been announced then by a special news bulletin from Wehrmacht High Command.

Then we did not use this report for broadcasting as we wanted to wait and see how Churchill would react to that blow. As usual, he did not react at all and until today has shrouded the sinking of the *Ceramic* in silence. Recently he even announced in a speech given to the House of Commons that only about 1,348 soldiers had been killed in troop transport sinkings so far. This would be only a fraction of those which had only been killed aboard the *Ceramic*.

Luckily, one man who survived the *Ceramic* catastrophe is still with us. It is the English Royal Engineer Eric Munday, service number 2148754, from Shearkin in South Surrey, who was rescued by the German U-boat and is now a prisoner of war in Germany. He confirmed to us, as you will hear shortly from himself, that he is most likely the sole survivor of the thousands who couldn't rescue themselves because of severe gales. The lies of the British Prime Minister, Winston Churchill, are clearly countered by the statement of the British soldier, Eric Munday. We now broadcast first the interview of our reporter with Lieutenant-Commander Henke.

Announcer: This steamer, *Ceramic*, which you sank on your last patrol, that was built before the war, wasn't it?

Lt.-Cmdr.: She was a ship of which the British report in Lloyd's register that she had been attacked twice in the war and also in Spring 1918 by U-boats without success. They took great pride in this fact. Scuttlebutt also has it that this ship had the highest masts ever to pass beneath the Sydney harbour bridge.

Announcer: She was a big one, then?

Lt.-Cmdr.: She was a beautiful ship, my first really big hit. We have always wanted that. When I talked with my torpedo officer about work, we always said, yes, if we sank a 20,000 ton steamer, that would suit us nicely. She wasn't exactly 20,000 tons - we estimated her a bit lower than that - but we were quite satisfied nevertheless. We sighted them at dusk. They were two ships, one to port and one to starboard. I found mine fairly quickly. She had four beautiful, high masts, was larger and so I said to myself: "Take her." I did an end-around maneuver and in the approaching darkness then we got her. She got hit beautifully, aimed amidships, but the shot went home in the engine room because of her great speed. They had increased speed at nightfall to get rid of potential pursuers. She also zigzagged. Suddenly her speed was gone. Her great bow wave just vanished, we could see that through our binoculars. Only a little bow wave was still there and also the stern wave had vanished. As she did not show

Chapter 9: Final voyage

	any signs of sinking, I shot two further torpedoes. And now I could see that suddenly the ship's company livened up. The so far totally blackened out vessel lit up all her lights and several lifeboats and floats were lowered into the sea. Because of the torpedoes, naturally some of these always get damaged, it can't be helped. The ship now lay very deep in the water. I decided to shoot another fish to hasten her demise. When the torpedo hit home, I saw the most terrible thing for as long as I have been in submarines. The great, 200 metre long ship appeared to be gripped by a mighty fist from below, was broken in two, the masts fell over and within six seconds she was gone.
Announcer:	She was really gone after only six seconds?
Lt.-Cmdr.:	Yes, it had come about through our previous hits, and the last one finished her off in a coup-de-grace.
Announcer:	But the countless lifeboats and rafts surely had many people on board?
Lt.-Cmdr.:	Certainly they had many people aboard. Through using my searchlight I noted that in most of the boats were soldiers, also on the rafts. On the day after, I could see that they were English, their apparent destination Africa. The crew was especially delighted about this, as we could give our Rommel some relief.
Announcer:	So she was a troop transport?
Lt.-Cmdr.:	Whether she was a dedicated troop transport, I couldn't say. However, she had lots of troops on board. On the following day I returned once more to the site of the sinking and I found a most horrific sight. I noted many corpses. The dead English sailors and soldiers had been thrown off the rafts. The floats themselves had completely disintegrated. Hundreds and hundreds of splintered boards, casks and boats could be seen. It was not a very nice sight. I tried to help several people. However, with the sea being that rough (force nine waves) and gale force winds (force ten to eleven) it was not really possible to carry out rescue missions. I managed to rescue an English soldier, by pulling him aboard. I nearly lost my first officer and a crewman during this maneuver and I finally broke off. In any case, my job is not to rescue people but to wage war on the enemy.
Announcer:	Here we interrupt the interview with Lieutenant-Commander

Henke and would like to give the English soldier, Eric Munday, Royal Engineers, who was rescued by the U-boat, an opportunity to talk. Now you'll hear a small sample of our interpreter's interview with him.

	... *you were probably the only survivor of the Ceramic?*
(Prisoner)	*Yes, I think so, that I am the only survivor of the ship.*
(Interpreter)	*...*
(Prisoner)	*I think I am the only survivor. It was a very bad ...*
(Interpreter)	*And were you expecting to be torpedoed? I mean were there...*
(Prisoner)	*The officer of our ship ... to have our life belts always...*

Eric Munday definitely confirms in these few sentences that he thinks he is the only survivor of the *Ceramic* because of the bad weather, he even says so twice. He also says that the troop transport was on her way to Africa and that the soldiers were reminded by the ship's officers of the possibility of being torpedoed. Therefore, they had to have their life belts with them at all times.

Now let's return to the recorded interview with Lieutenant-Commander Henke.

Announcer: And could you identify other war material?

Lt.-Cmdr.: During my search I discovered several aeroplanes with English markings. Obviously, we were very happy about this.

Announcer: And the other steamer, the one you sighted the evening before?

Lt.-Cmdr.: The other steamer, got shafted at around 2200 hrs by my colleague on my left flank, who is a very experienced U-boat commander. It was a really lucky coincidence, when he reported his success: just sunk etc. - the usual phrase. So the two steamers which together wanted to reach Africa went jointly to the bottom of the sea.

***

Unknown newspaper, undated

Ceramic Sunk?
German Claim In The Atlantic

A special announcement form Hitler's H.Q. to-day claimed that in the North and Central Atlantic German U-boats have sunk 15 more ships, totalling 108,000 tons.

Chapter 9: Final voyage

"Two more ships and an escorting destroyer were torpedoed. In these operations enemy supplies for North Africa were especially hard hit," said the announcement.

Among the ships sunk was the British passenger liner Ceramic, of 18,713 tons, on her way to North Africa as a troop transport. Heavy loss of life must be expected.

"Three more ships laden with war materials and sailing in the same convoy were sunk."

Formerly one of the largest vessels trading between the United Kingdom and Australia, the Ceramic was reported to have had an encounter with a U-boat in the South Atlantic last March, when passengers believed that her guns sank the submarine. She was bound from Liverpool to South Africa at the time. Afterwards she put in at Rio de Janeiro for repairs.

In August 1940, she was in collision with a cargo ship in the South Atlantic whilst taking 90 children to Australia from England. There were no casualties.

***

Unknown newspaper, undated

CERAMIC 'SINKING'

How a U-boat was said to have sunk the British troop transport Ceramic west of the Azores while she was on her way to North Africa on December 6, was described over the German radio last night.

"Owing to the very bad weather, the U-boat had to come very close to the transport before it released two torpedoes simultaneously," it was stated.

"The attack came so suddenly that the troops on board the ship and the crew were unable to reach their boat stations in an orderly fashion. Lifeboats and rafts which had been lowered into the water were smashed by the storm.

"Only one survivor was taken aboard the U-boat.

"According to this survivor, there were 2,000 to 3,000 officers and men of British engineer units, naval personnel and crew on board."

***

Standard
Thursday February 18 1943

"HAVE YOU A SON NAMED ERIC?" ASKED A VOICE ON PHONE

Londoner "Lost at Sea" Turns Up in a U-Boat.

4 WEEKS WITH RAIDERS

Three weeks ago Mr. Ernest Munday, a commercial traveller, of Thornton Heath, heard from the War Office that his son, Sapper Eric Munday, had been lost at sea on his way to North Africa. This morning he and his wife were roused by a telephone call. A woman's voice said, "Have you a son called Eric? because I have just heard his name mentioned on the radio."

To-day when I saw them, Mr. and Mrs. Munday were overjoyed by the news. Said Mrs. Munday who is a shelter marshal, while her husband is an air raid warden: "I can hardly believe it."

This is the story that came over the radio. Sapper Munday said that he was a survivor of the troop transport Ceramic torpedoed on December 6. He said that he was in a lifeboat with 40 or 50 other men, but a storm capsized the boat and the others were lost. He swam four hours. Then he was picked up by a U-boat, in which he spent four weeks before being taken ashore.

Fine Swimmer

To-day at the Munday's home Eric's father told me how he had trained his four sons to be good sportsmen.

"Eric was the best swimmer of them all," he told me. "He always said that he could swim for ever."

Eric must have spent his 21st birthday, on December 12, in the U-boat. He volunteered for service in North Africa and was the only one of his unit who went on the ill-fated ship.

He volunteered for the Royal Engineers two years ago, and before that was a clerk on the Southern Railway, playing football and cricket in the company's team.

***

Chapter 9: Final voyage

Unknown newspaper, undated

"MISSING" MAN BROADCASTS

Kept Four Weeks In German U-Boat

Sapper Eric Alfred Munday, son of Mr. and Mrs. E. A. Munday, of Thornton Heath, who was reported missing at the beginning of this month, is now known to be a prisoner of war, and he broadcast on the German-controlled Calais radio on Wednesday night. He said he was in a ship which was torpedoed on its way to North Africa last December. He scrambled with fifty other men into a lifeboat which eventually capsized. Sapper Munday is a powerful swimmer and after being in the water for four hours he was picked up by a German U-boat. With several other men, he spent four weeks in the U-boat, including Christmas. Subsequently he and his mates were landed at a French port.

***

Unknown newspaper, undated

IN U-BOAT FOR FOUR WEEKS

LONDON PRISONER'S GERMAN BROADCAST

German radio brought to the microphone Sapper Eric Munday (21), of Foulsham Road, Thornton Heath, who was reported "missing at sea" three weeks ago. He broadcast his account of four weeks at sea in a U-boat before being landed on the Continent as a prisoner of war.

He said that he was a survivor of the Ceramic, a troop transport, which the Germans claimed torpedoed and sunk on December 9. He said that when the Ceramic was torpedoed on the way from Britain to North Africa he and 40 or 50 others got into a lifeboat, which capsized in heavy seas.

His Birthday

The other men were lost, but he swam for four hours and was picked up by the U-boat, in which he was kept for four weeks. He spent Christmas and New Year's Day in the U-boat.

Munday's Army number was given by the German radio as 2148743. Before he joined the R.E.s about two years ago he was employed by the Southern Railway as a clerk at Purley.

"He must have celebrated his 21st birthday on December 12 in the U-boat." said his father, Mr. Ernest Munday, to an Evening News representative to-day. "The first news we had of him was about three weeks ago when we were notified by the War Office that he was 'missing at sea.'

"We Had Faith"

"No one knew what had happened to him, and the War Office asked me to let them know if we heard anything from him from any other source. Last night scores of people called and telephoned to tell us about the broadcast. My wife and I had great faith that he was still alive, as he was the most powerful swimmer in the family."

The Ceramic (18,713), a Shaw Savill liner, was said by the enemy to have gone down immediately when hit by a torpedo. Hitler's H.Q. added that "Owing to heavy seas and raging storms heavy loss of life must be expected."

***

Former Shaw Savill Officer, email to the author 2001:
"One thing which everyone (not just the Masters and myself, but it has been an ongoing situation for many many years) agrees is the questionable accuracy of his statements and that he did broadcast from Germany – did he broadcast freely? We hope not."

Eric Munday
Letter to the author 5 September 2001
Regarding the proposed 'Broadcast', firstly, I never did broadcast at any time from Germany. I did however answer questions made to me by a German officer on the day we landed at Lorient, the 6th January 1943. I say we because on that day five English officers (3 Army, 1 RAF and a Ship's Captain) also landed and all agreed that we should give the answers as to our regiment, rank and number. The answers regarding myself were known to the Germans because my Army pass book was taken from me on U-515. In addition I sent my love to my Mother and told her not to worry. I also told her that as far as I knew at that time, that I was the only known survivor.

***

Chapter 9: Final voyage

THE PROPAGANDA WAR

"The Norden Broadcasts"

CDR Robert Lee Norden, USN, was the cover name for LCDR Ralph G. Albrecht, America's answer to Lord Haw-Haw. Albrecht made 309 broadcasts for OP-16-W Special Welfare Branch of ONI as a means of psychological warfare against the German submarine effort. An unashamed lie, the broadcast has often been taken literally, and has been the root cause of much of the misinformation that has been propagated in books and articles since the ship was lost. It is claimed that its effect on Henke, especially after his capture by the Americans, led to his paranoia of falling into British hands, and his subsequent suicide in a futile escape bid in broad daylight from Fort Hunt, the camp in which he was being held. The story of U-515 and Werner Henke may be read in Timothy Mulligan's comprehensive biography, *Lone Wolf*. ISBN 0-275-93677-5.

Norden Broadcast No. 23
25 March 1943
(Broadcast in German)

I make an accusation. I accuse Lieutenant Werner Henke of murder. Lieutenant Henke has murdered 264 helpless survivors of a sinking.

War is war. But there is a tremendous difference between war and murder. We Americans know very well that the majority of the German people did not want this war. But individuals among you who have become guilty of special cruelties, individuals who have untold human lives upon their conscience – they shall not escape full responsibility.

We know these war criminals. We keep a log of their crimes. They can be perfectly sure that not a single one of their crimes will remain concealed.

To make sure that they shall not forget, I will name some of these war criminals at regular intervals and reveal their misdeeds. The documents concerning them increase daily. Nothing will be forgotten. And one day, when there is peace again, we will place these papers at the disposal of a German court. And a German court - not a Nazi court - will condemn these criminals. For these criminals are not men who have committed crimes against just the English or the Americans or the Russians. They have committed crimes against the idea of humanity. They have become criminals against humanity.

Among the men who will face their judges there will also be Lieutenant Werner Henke.

You know the name. You know this name from a radio program of February 20, in which he described how he had sunk the British passenger steamer CERAMIC.

You heard the details. You heard how during the sinking of the CERAMIC, a fearful storm raged. It was such a fierce storm that the lifeboats capsized, the rafts were rendered unseaworthy by the waves; in short, that of the total number of the passengers and crew – 350 men, women, and children – only a single one could be saved.

Fortunately, this terrible news was exaggerated. As a matter of fact, all in all, 86 human lives were saved. One became a prisoner of war, 85 escaped to England.

The 85 have a different story to tell than Lieutenant Werner Henke. They reported that the storm during the sinking of the ship by no means assumed such proportions that a rescue was impossible. On the contrary, all the lifeboats and rafts were able to be let down into the water, the boats were manned – and the majority of the survivors could have been saved. This is, if it had not been for Lieutenant Henke. In the excitement, Lieutenant Henke had apparently forgotten that such things as articles of war existed. He had the waters combed with his searchlights and wherever he found a boat with survivors, or women and children, who, clad in lifesaving jackets, were struggling with the waves – he had his guns trained upon them. Yes, he ordered the survivors slaughtered with machine guns. He drove his crew to supreme efforts in order to murder as many of the helpless people as possible.

Werner Henke knew very well what he had won. For that reason he fished up one of the survivors on board his U-boat and then forced him to tell fairy tales over the German radio about how the Lieutenant had rescued him personally. That was a touching scene over the radio, but this alibi, too, will not help the Lieutenant. Against this one statement made under coercion, there stand 85 statements of those who returned to England.

I accuse Lieutenant Werner Henke of the murder of 264 survivors. No matter how much the German propagandists may celebrate him – this charge will continue to ring in his ears; no triumphal fanfares of the German radio can drown it to the very day on which he will stand before his judges. From the Fuehrer he has received the Knight's Cross – but that, too, will not help him on the day of judgement.

On the day on which he will have to answer for his crime, before himself, before the German people, before humanity.

***

Chapter 9: Final voyage

German News clipping (publication unknown) 1943.

The Fate of the Ceramic

Own report Berlin 6 October.

As we have reported the British admiralty have accepted that the British passenger ship Ceramic 18713 BRT was sunk whilst making a detour to Cape Town.

Reuters commented that this was 'one of the most shocking tragedies of the war' as there are no survivors to report fate of the ship, which was simply lost in the ocean.

The 'traceless sinking' of the Ceramic is not as traceless as Reuters had claimed.

Immediately after the loss of the ship, the British admiralty had the opportunity to share with the nation that in November last year the Ceramic was sunk on its way from England to Cape Town.

3 days after the sinking, namely 9 December 1942 The head (illegible) ... a special announcement about the sinking of the Ceramic, in particular, making the name of the ship known.

While the British, as usual, deny the loss of a large and valuable ship, the Germans release further details given by Captain Lieutenant Henke, which leave no trace of doubt as to the fate of the ship and its occupants.

Furthermore, the testimony of the British Royal Engineer, Eric Munday, Service Number 2148745, from 19 Foulsham Road, Thornton Heath, Surrey, was made public. He was the single survivor to be fished out by the submarine from amongst the wreckage and hundreds of dead bodies hanging in their life jackets.

Despite these facts the British kept silent about the loss of the ship and still talk about the 'traceless sinking' and the 'uncertainty of the fate of the passengers' just to avoid admitting that the message from the German Submarine Commander was right.

They prefer the cruelty of leaving the next of kin in the dark for almost a year than to inform them of fate of the 500 victims.

***

Associated Press
October 1943

British Liner Lost Without Trace; 500 on Board.

CAPETOWN, Oct 2. – News of one of the worst ocean tragedies of the war – the sinking without a trace of the 18,700-ton British liner Ceramic with more than 500 passengers aboard last November – was officially released today by naval authorities.

The Ceramic was sunk, presumably by an enemy submarine, somewhere in the Atlantic while en route to Capetown from England. The official announcement was withheld almost a year because of uncertainty over the fate of passengers and crew.

The exact number of casualties was not known, but it was reported the ship carried more than 500 persons and authorities are still without official news of any survivors.

The Germans announced last December they had sunk the Ceramic with a submarine torpedo in heavy seas and claimed to have picked up one survivor. A person representing himself as the survivor later broadcast over the German radio a version of his rescue by a Nazi U-boat.

According to the German version the Ceramic sank quickly during a gale and lifeboats could not be launched.

The passenger list included many South African and Australian families.

The German announcement had said the ship was carrying troops to North Africa.

The Ceramic, owned by Shaw, Savill & Albion Co., had its home port at Southampton, England. It was built in 1913 at Belfast and was 655 feet long. It normally ran between Australia and England.

The ship battled a submarine in the South Atlantic in 1942, and was said to have probably sunk the submarine. She had left Liverpool carrying 360 passengers to South Africa, but turned in at Rio de Janeiro with fuel and stores exhausted after that U-boat encounter.

***

Chapter 9: Final voyage

Extract from personal recollections of Charles R J Taylor

...Coincidentally, about November 1943 I was crew member of Empire Grace, an intermediate refrigerated ship also managed by Shaw Savill & Albion, engaged O.H.M.S at the time. In 1946 she was renamed Wairangi, and like Ceramic had done for the same ship owners, sailed the Australia run. We carried about eighty five soldiers as passengers for St Helena. We anchored in the lee of the island, near the cliffs on top of which we could see Napoleon's first tomb. Locals came out in their bumboats to market table mats made from marine life crustaceans, and we spoke to a British soldier who was aboard one for a pleasure ride, but anxious to hear news from home. He advised us that they had expected a relief garrison some twelve months beforehand, but that this had failed to arrive. Neither had they received any mail for a very long time. I now know that Ceramic had carried a relief garrison for St Helena Island.

****

Captain Herbert Elford
Photos courtesy of Bart Elford.

Above: Herbert Elford with his wife Elizabeth and son Herbert (Bart).

Above: Shortly before his last voyage.

THE KING GREETS SEA CAPTAINS
The King and Queen in conversation with Captain Elford, when their majesties met the men of the Merchant Navy. Captain J Livingstone and Captain J G Johnstone are also seen.
'The Herald' Thursday, March 6, 1941

Part Three

The truth is finally told.

For various reasons, the loss of the ship without trace, sketchy reports, the necessary secrecy of wartime, protection of interests and the propaganda war, more misinformation than fact has been recorded about the sinking of the *Ceramic*, and what happened to the hundreds who lost their lives.

The families of those who died deserve to know the truth; the historical record needs to be set straight; and we need to know why, as well as how, such a tragedy occurred.

For the first time, the story of the sole survivor is told in full.
Also, for the sake of completeness and to help in our understanding, the remaining survivors of U-515 were invited to share their version of events, at a reunion in Germany in May 2001, attended by the author and Eric Munday.

I can assure you that I will not write about it again in the future. I just did it to do you a favour. I am still very emotional and I hate the damned war.

Willi Klein

Chapter 10
The survivor's story

Interview with Eric Munday 26/9/99

It was quite a luxury ship for those days. Well, the food alone - you didn't know there was a war on. You could order your breakfast, and have it with bacon and eggs, or kippers. With something like a troop ship, there was no comparison. We thought we were lucky at the time.

We had a few officers who were difficult, and they closed several bars to us, to other ranks, and the ship's captain came to us, and he said "Don't worry about that" he said, "I've fixed you up with your own bar, and I suggest you make it out of bounds to military officers." Which we did, but we did attract the 50 Red Cross Nurses, because they were there on board. They used to come into our bar. After a few days though, they threw the whole ship open to us.

(When the torpedo struck, was it sudden?)
Eric: Oh yes, there were three before we got off, and then they told me, another two. You know something's happened - and it was dark. From memory it was about 8 o' clock - we were still up in the bar playing cards. And I remember one of the chaps we were playing with bending over scooping up the money and putting it in his pocket!

Diary kept by Eric Alfred Munday after being torpedoed in the 'Ceramic'

Note: I started writing this diary on the 10th Dec 1942. The reason being that I had nothing whatsoever to do.

1942
6th Dec   8.00 pm. Playing solo with Andy, Harry and Jack in smoke room.
8.15 pm. First torpedo, two more at about five minute intervals. Practically all of R.G.O.X.O. manage to get in the same life boat. Some difficulty in getting away from side owing to ropes being caught, about 45 or 50 in boat, only 2 women. The sea by 12 o'clock was very heavy with frequent downpours of rain, it was all we could do to keep her head on in the wind, and bale the water out. Owing to a number of the lads being ill I had to row right through the night, but where in one way it made me very tired, it kept me warm, and prevented me from laying down and thinking of what lay ahead of us.

Chapter 10: The survivor's story

7th Dec   The night seemed endless, but when at last the light came we found quite a few rafts around us and we were able to exchange a few words with one another. About 8am the wind got up, and the storm started. We now had much difficulty in not hitting the other rafts. The storm now was very high and it was impossible to keep our boat head on in the wind, so we just let it drift and concentrated on baling. We were now shipping water by the gallon, and I seemed to think that we would not last very long, also it was too much to expect to get help that day. I did not relish though another night in this weather, as the rain chilled me to the bone, but on the whole I felt cheerful and confident that we could hold out, that is if things did not get any worse. It is impossible to describe my thoughts, except that I did ask that Mum and Dad would not worry about me, and to thank them for all they had done for me, indeed I thought no one could have had two finer parents, also that Norman could be spared this war, and Ron and Doug would soon be back home. I also thought a lot about Pam and what a pity I had only known her for such a short while. I was sitting forward on the starboard side when the boat capsized and I was the first in the water. The others coming on top of me prevented me from reaching the surface; I really did feel scared, but at last there was a gap and I came up. The lads were clambering over the overturned boat, but there were too many on one side and over it went again. I did not attempt to get on because I never thought it would again be seaworthy. I began searching about for a raft but all I could find were a few pieces of wood, which were very helpful. I was now all on my own and if possible, the storm seemed worse. I could see the boat some way away and so made my way towards it. Jack and Ramsbottom were two that I recognised, so I hung on. The next thing I saw was a big shape in the water about 100 yds away, the waves were so big though that we only saw it for a few seconds. I immediately swam out in that direction and after a couple of minutes I saw it again, but this time could see that it was a submarine. I felt very happy and wanted to shout and laugh, but my hardest job was getting alongside. One time I was so near I could see the faces of the men in the conning tower, the next minute I was swept right away and I thought at first that the submarine had submerged, but after another few minutes I saw it again and made one last effort to reach it. I got alongside and they threw two ropes, but I missed them both. They threw again and this time I managed to hold one. The man who threw the rope caught hold of my hand, and then I was on the boat and a German one. They gave me some food and dry clothing and then fixed me up a hammock. I was feeling quite well but very tired. Our time 12.00 hrs.

8th Dec   I awoke feeling very sore and aching so much that I could hardly move. In a day or so though it wore off. Everything was very strange and besides feeling none too good I felt very depressed. In the evening the Commandant and presumably 1st Officer questioned me as to the movements of the 'Ceramic'.

9th Dec   I cannot shake off feeling of depression, it would make all the difference in the world if there was only some one to talk to. There is a wireless and occasionally I hear some English. Also there are many English and American tunes set to German words. It is very ironic to hear a German U. Boat broadcasting English Jazz.

10th Dec Today they gave me a tooth brush, paste and a comb which were very useful. They let me have my first breath of fresh air and to me it was like a million dollars. I was also allowed to smoke a cigarette.

11th Dec Nothing of importance. No air or smoke.

12th Dec My 21st birthday, but one vastly different to one I had meant to have. It is another thing I must make up for when I reach England. I was allowed some air and time to smoke two cigarettes.

13th Dec It is a week today the 'Ceramic' went down. Life in a U. Boat is no joy ride and I am longing for the day when we reach land. It is just like riding in the underground, but much worse. I heard the B.B.C. for about 10 minutes broadcasting to forces in Africa. I had some air and a smoke.

14th Dec I have now been on board a week. They fished out about 50 cases of New Zealand butter that was floating about in the water*. No air or smoke. Lying in my hammock I heard the 10.30-11 'music while you work' programme, but only for about 10 minutes. It makes home seem very near. Our time about 9.30 pm.

Chapter 10: The survivor's story

The cases of New Zealand butter came from the Hororata, torpedoed by U-103 - Kaptlt. Gustav-Adolf Janssen - on 13th December.

The Fourth Service - Merchantmen at War 1939-45 John Slader 940-545-SLA

13 December 1942 saw her homeward bound from Lyttleton for Liverpool, with a full cargo for war torn Britain. North of the Azores and in gale conditions, the Hororata was torpedoed by U-103. Because of her speed the ship was sailing without convoy or escort. The torpedo struck on her port side. Her Master and crew showed great seamanship in working the slowly sinking ship to an anchorage at Santa Cruz Bay, Flores Island. It was then decided to make for Horta, Fayal Island and the Hororata sailed after dark on 17 December, on the dangerous 150 mile passage. She arrived the following day.

15th Dec   Not so good today, am still getting my old stomach trouble. No air or smoke.

16th Dec   Still not feeling so good. No air or smoke.

17th Dec   Feeling a little better; was allowed some air and a smoke. The sun was shining beautifully, but I was not allowed up for long. I heard a snatch of the American Command performance and also some of Bobby Howes musical comedy hits.

18th Dec   Was allowed no air or smoke, I think it possible we might be near land. I am going to write a letter to Mum and Dad on the off chance that I shall be able to post it when we reach land.

19th Dec   As my hands are now quite better (they were cut slightly when leaving the 'Ceramic') the Commandant has told me that I must help with the general duties of the ship. No air or smoke. I have just had my first shave since being a prisoner. I thought at one time I should have to grow a beard.

20th Dec   Nothing of interest, but was allowed some air and smoked two cigarettes.

21st Dec   Ditto. No air or smoke.

22nd Dec   Ditto. No air or smoke.

351

23rd Dec   They have started to prepare the food for Christmas. As they have plenty of butter they are making piles of cream to pour over the cakes. The men in the U. Boat are considered amongst the best fed men in Germany. I was allowed a smoke which I very much enjoyed.

24th Dec   It seems the custom in Germany is to give and receive your gifts on Christmas Eve. As you know there is not a lot of room in a U. Boat but the men have made it as comfortable as possible. In the evening about six all the lights were turned off and they lit a small Christmas tree; it was very effective. They then sang songs, equivalent to our carols I believe, because one of them was to the tune of our carol 'Silent Night'. We drank hot punch and ate chocolate and biscuits and also a piece of thickly creamed sponge cake. They gave me a present of some chocolate. No air or smoke.

25th Dec   <u>Christmas Day.</u> Awoke feeling none too good, but felt better by dinner time after I had had a shave and cleaned my teeth. This was my second shave in three weeks. For dinner I had some potatoes and tinned chicken and four half peaches (tinned) for afters. I shall be glad when it is all over, and the new year; it brings back too many memories. Also in about a week we might be back on land, and believe me I am very much looking forward to that, especially to be able to talk to some one who is English. I have just finished learning the morse code, which I have been practising for several days. Smoked two cigarettes, but have not seen daylight since the 17th. I smoke on a platform just before reaching the top.

26th Dec   I am feeling better today. There was an alarm at dinner time. When we have these I always get the feeling that I might be saved and land up in England, but the chances are practically nil. I had to wait until 9pm for a smoke.

27th Dec   Norman's birthday. His 14th I think. Last night I heard the National Anthem but it was switched off rather hurriedly. Made 2 handkerchieves from an old piece of material that I found. Smoked two cigarettes.

28th Dec   Am not feeling so good today, but I think it is because the weather is pretty bad. I have now been here three weeks, and on the water five and I have not yet been sea sick. No smoke.

29th Dec   Still not feeling up to much. Since coming on board I have had practically no air or exercise, which has made me very weak at the moment. I would not even be fair match for Norman. If I stay here much longer they will have to take me off in a stretcher. By the way, I have a nickname; the only name they knew was 'John Bull' so I was christened 'Johnny'. They woke me at 22.30 hrs to go and peel potatoes until 00.30 hrs. No smoke.

30th Dec   Nothing of importance. No smoke.

31st Dec   Am hoping that tomorrow will start a better year for everyone. Went to bed about six feeling groggy. Had 2 doughnuts for tea. At 12 o' clock they woke me and wished me a happy new year, with some hot punch. No smoke.

U-515 training patrol in the Baltic Sea. 21/2/42 - 31/8/42.

1943

1st Jan   Feeling a little better. Had a shave. No smoke. Three alarms.

2nd Jan   Feeling about the same. My big trouble now is that I have a boil on my neck about the size of a football. The doctor or whoever it is looking after it says it is the biggest he has ever seen. About 11.30 pm a can of water fell over me while I was asleep. It seems funny when writing about it, but it was no joke at the time. No smoke.

3rd Jan   Had an alarm about 11 am, much excitement, another at midnight. No smoke.

4th Jan   Nothing of importance. No smoke.

5th Jan   Tomorrow we reach land, and I am just as excited as the others, but I am wondering what is just in store for me. Had a shave, but no smoke.

(Up to this point, Eric's diary has been written on 2 loose sheets of paper. It continues in a small pocket book)

6th Jan Arrived in Lorient amidst general excitement, and was pleased to see that there were 4 more prisoners from another U. Boat. They were all officers, 3 army and 1 R.A.F. We were all taken from the harbour and given plenty of warm clothes. They were all on their way to England for a month's leave after being in W. Africa for 2 years. My pleasure though was short lived, because after about 30 minutes I was separated from them. During the afternoon I was interviewed by a German interpreter, who allowed me to make a recording of a message which he said would be broadcast to England. I only hope it was heard, because it will be some time before I shall be able to write. I was allowed a bath, the first for nearly five weeks. At about 6 pm I rejoined the others together with a Ship's Captain. My five comrades are all very decent fellows, but naturally they would be. We spent a pleasant evening playing cribbage, and I had the best night's sleep since leaving the 'Ceramic.'

Photographs courtesy of Wolfgang Altenburger.

Chapter 10: The survivor's story

Admiral Karl Dönitz
Head of U-Boat Command.
U-Boat Archive

Interview with Eric Munday 26/9/99

(Can you tell me more about when you landed in Lorient and Dönitz was there?)
I can only remember that they told me what was happening, the crew, and they told me that we were landing in Lorient, and that Dönitz would probably be there to meet them. And they said, you've got to eat as much as you can now because once you get into Germany you won't get any food like this. Because they did reasonably well; they gave me lots of cigarettes as well. But Mr Dönitz wasn't interested in me! The whole flotilla landed at that time, and they all came in. When we landed in Lorient, the submarine base, they asked me if I would agree to, just on the radio, give my name and number to say that I was a survivor, which I did. There was quite a number of sea captains, and we all agreed to do it. We thought well, we can't do anything wrong, at least they'll know. In fact, the British government knew all along, but they hadn't put the information out. Oh yes, they knew all right, because on the night we were hit a destroyer came out from Portugal to try and pick up survivors, so he didn't come all that way for nothing.

7th Jan	Started at 12.00 hrs on a 36 hr train journey to Wilhelmshaven which up to now has been uneventful. Did not think much of French countryside or the food, except for a bowl of soup at about 17.00 hrs. My five comrades, as I have said, are all very decent fellows. They are Major Kirk, Capt Harrison, both R.A.S.C. and from Bedford and friends before the war. Major Burnett R.E. and Flying Officer Hall. They were from Windsor; all four picked up from the 'Nigerian'. The other is the Ship's Master of the 'Ocean Starling', Capt Monckton, whose home is at Lydney in Glos.
8th Jan	Still on train; at Rosendel bought 6 meringues for 2/-; the chap thought it was a mark. Arrived Oldenburg 21.30 hrs and had to make our 1st change for 33$\frac{1}{2}$ hours. Am writing this whilst waiting for the connection to Wilhelmshaven which leaves about 23.40; all six of us are rather tired of travelling. It is tough luck on Major Kirk as he has malaria pretty "bush". "Bush" is an expression used by Capt Harrison to mean pretty awful. We are waiting in the station buffet, and watching people drink beer. It was as near as we got though to the beer. Important stations passed through were Nantes, Paris, Antwerp, Rotterdam. Arrived Wilhelmshaven 01.30. We were all given beds in separate rooms. Time about 02.30hrs.
9th Jan	Was awakened at 06.45 hrs. Was able whilst washing to have a few words with Capt Monckton. Other than that I have not seen or spoken to the others. I have three times asked for a book, but it has not been forthcoming. Blackouts put up 16.00 hrs. We are given 3 cigarettes a day. Food consists of soup, bread and a little butter and marmalade. Air raid from 19.30 to 20.15 hrs.
10th Jan	Still one man, one room. Food the same as yesterday. Was allowed to walk in the grounds from 9 to 9.30 am. For a couple of hours this afternoon I helped a chap wash up and dish out the food. The break was very welcome and I was able to catch sight of the others in their rooms. It was good to know that Major Kirk's malaria was a little better. I think it must be worse for him than for us, and that's saying something.
11th Jan	MON. Still one man, one room. Food the same except no butter. Did a spot more work this morning and afternoon and had my walk from 9.30 - 10 am. The cigarettes they give us are very coarse and burn your throat, but are very welcome. Have asked if I can write home and was told yes, but not until the next post and goodness knows how long this will be. Things will be much better when I reach the camp but this probably won't be for a week or so. But for me it can't be too soon.

Chapter 10: The survivor's story

12th Jan Still one man, one room. Food the same. Had my walk from 8.30 - 9 am and did a little more work, which certainly breaks the monotony if only for ten minutes. Asked this morning for something to read and some paper and ink so as to catch up with writing this diary, but up to now have not received anything. The weather outside is very cold with plenty of snow and ice, but my room is quite warm.

13th Jan Still one man, one room. Food the same except no marmalade. The bread by the way is not as good as at home; it is much darker, but on the whole quite eatable. I often think of what Dad used to say about "When you are hungry." Had my walk from 9.30 - 10 am. It was very cold but the exercise was welcome. Spoke to the interpreter this evening and he said this would only last for a day or so, but of course this may mean anything.

14th Jan Still one man, one room. Today they have let me write a post card and letter. The post card should arrive in about two weeks and the letter in three or four. Food the same except no butter. No walk. Did some more work, and this afternoon washed some clothes. This evening an officer came to see me and said he would see about getting me a book and also some company. I feel much better though having now written home.

15th Jan Still one man, one room, but this afternoon I thought I was going to join the others, but I merely had to change my room, for one a little smaller, and also better as I don't think there are any rats in this one. Major Burnett and Capt Harrison I know are now together, and I think the other two are also. Had a bath but no exercise or work. Food the same except for some hot fruit juice and cheese, but no marmalade. Had a long interview this morning with a German Captain, but nothing serious transferred. The letters I wrote yesterday have not yet been collected.

Eric Munday, Prisoner of War.

Interview with Eric Munday 26/9/99

When I was picked up they got my pay book, and also there was something in there. Because prior to that was when the Americans had come into the war. We went down to Cardiff Docks to unload and supervise ammunition, and shells. And somehow they knew about this, the Germans did, and that's what they interrogated me about - about Cardiff Docks, and I used to say 'Well, I don't know anything about it.'

***

16th Jan   Still one man, one room. Food the same but no marmalade. Worked for 1/2 hour this morning but no walk. This afternoon had another interview with the Captain and after we had finished we talked about the war. Points of interest were the Jews, the starting of hostilities, incompetence of English Parliament and leaders, and after the war. The talk has set me thinking and I wish I had a companion with which to talk it over. The best news of the day is though I have been given two books and an English newspaper, printed in Germany. The books are "The Life of our Land" by Charles Dickens, and "The Cow Puncher" by Robert J. C. Stead. <u>Note</u> The Captain had a copy of the London Times dated 15th Dec. He also told me that Neville Henderson died last week *[Sir Neville Henderson, Britain's Ambassador to Germany, who on 3 September 1939 delivered the ultimatum stating that if hostilities did not stop at 11.00am, a state of war would exist between Great Britain and Germany]* and that a convoy of 16 tankers from America to W Africa had been destroyed. Capt Harrison is now with Major Kirk and Major Burnett on his own. The Skipper has another seaman as companion. The German Capt said he would try and arrange that the three officers and myself met to play bridge. Two air raid warnings lasting until 22.00 hrs.

17th Jan   Still one man, one room. Food the same except for an additional 15 or 20 cold potatoes. Had my walk from 8.30 to 9 am but other than this have not seen anyone. I think F.O. Hall must have gone as I have not caught sight of him for several days. I am myself hoping to go tomorrow or Tuesday. I have read both of my books and "The Life of our Land" twice; I found it very interesting. The newspaper called "The Camp" gives you football results and film notes. The Palace in this edition lost to Q.P.R. 3 - 0. Air raid from 9.30 - 10.45pm. Major Kirk had to be carried down to the shelter. He did not look any too well.

18th Jan   MON. Still one man, one room. Food the same. Walk from 8.30 - 9 am. Was ticked off for saluting three D.E.M.S. who have been here

Chapter 10: The survivor's story

about a week. Had another interview with the Capt (Osterman?). Conversation more on general lines, such as rationed goods, army and civilian pay, bombing, and a point he's very interested in 'coal'. From a railway and shipping point of view. He is very interesting to listen to, and also very thorough. I only wish I were more learned so as to put up a better opposition. The P.C. and letter written on the 14th were taken away this morning, also my 2 books.

19th Jan   Still one man, one room. Walk from 8.30 to 9 am. Food a little different. No soup, but a meat rissole and potatoes boiled in their jackets. Bread, butter, a little cheese, and lunch sausage. Helped this afternoon to clean out my own and another room. Not feeling too good today but my boil is now better. Given 3 more books.

20th Jan   Still one man, one room. Food the same. Walk from 8.30 to 9 am. Am not feeling so good today, have caught a rotten cold from somewhere. Major Kirk I learn is now feeling much better. Ron's birthday, 23rd, and his 3rd in the army.

21st Jan   Still one man, one room. Food the same, no walk, but had a bath. Did some work for an hour this morning. The other three are all now in separate rooms.

22nd Jan   Still one man, one room. Food a little different; we had same after pudding, consisting of jam sauce and baked custard. Walk from 8.30 to 9 am. Another short interview this afternoon with the Capt, but nothing of importance transferred.

23rd Jan   Still one man, one room. Food the same. Walk from 8.30 to 9 am and it rained hard all the time. Air raid this afternoon lasting a couple of hours. Given another copy of "The Camp", in which there is an article and photographs of U. Boats and U. B. tankers.

24th Jan   Still one man, one room. Food the same. Walk from 8.30 to 9 am. If they would only let us speak to one another for an hour or so a day, it would ease things; but no. I expect this is some form of punishment agreed to under International Law, I only wish though they would tell us how long it will last. I think to myself sometimes that we shall be here to the end of the war, and then emerge with long white beards looking much like Father Time, but then I console myself with the thought that I am lucky to be here at all, with the prospect of ONE DAY going home. Don't think I'm crying. It's just a morbid moment that passes.

***

Prison Without Bars
Eric Munday
25th January 1943
Written whilst a prisoner of war in Wilhelmshaven.

I left England on the 25.11.42 on the passenger ship 'Ceramic' bound for S. Africa and Australia. Everyone on board was in high spirits, especially the few military personnel. I was one of a draft of 14 Engineers bound for somewhere in S. or W. Africa, the actual port of disembarkation I never knew. The sea was smooth and the weather good, and so for that matter was everything else; in fact my friends and I were having the time of our lives. Plenty of beer, whisky, cigarettes, women, entertainments, and above all plenty of real good food. After a few days though we started a submarine and aircraft watch which at first was pretty thick, 4 hours on, and sometimes 6 off, this was reduced later though to 2 on and 6 or 8 off. Everything was going fine until the 6th Dec; we were just getting our sea legs, and looking forward to the warmer weather, we had made many friends among the passengers, and it can be said we were thoroughly looking forward to at least another 3 or four weeks of travelling. Until, as I said before, the 6th Dec. I came off watch at 19.30hrs, washed and changed my clothes and went off to the smoke room to have a drink and play solo, with 3 of my friends. At 20.15 hrs the first torpedo hit us and was followed by two more at about five minute intervals. They were all on the starboard side, the first forward, and the other two as far as I know amidships. (I learnt later that 2 more were fired after an interval of about 3 hours). Emergency stations was sounded but followed almost immediately by boat stations. It was quite dark outside and the sea fairly rough, it was also quite cold. The portside boat stations light was lit which made things a little easier, and the boats were lowered. I saw several boat loads of women get away, and the boat that I eventually got into was in the water, so I had to drop down a rope, cutting my hands pretty badly in doing so, but the pain was easily forgotten in the general excitement, which I thought afterwards was quite accounted for. It is impossible to imagine that a boat of that size with women and children on board could be abandoned with the ease that you see Guardsmen being drilled on a barrack square. If anyone cares to contradict me they are quite at liberty to try, but my opinion will remain the same.

I won't waste my time by describing the following hours of darkness, let it suffice that they were pretty dreadful. At dawn though, the worst was to come: a storm came up and one so terrible, that I was told later by some seamen that the like of it had hardly ever been seen before. At roughly 08.00hrs 7.12.42, the boat I was in capsized and after being in the water 2 or 3 hours I was picked up by the U. Boat. This can only be described as an act of God and nothing else, and I consider myself to be one of the luckiest persons alive today. Anyhow, as I have

Chapter 10: The survivor's story

said I was picked up, but practically more dead than alive. This followed with 4 weeks and 2 days with life on a German U.Boat. This experience is not unique, as many others have had the same experience, but as I was the only one picked up, and only about 2 of the crew could speak English, and only a little at that, things seemed to me none too good. For the first week or ten days I felt pretty ill, what with swallowing too much water and upsetting my stomach to the extent that I could not look food in the face, and my hands, both being bandaged, prevented me from washing, cleaning my teeth or combing my hair. On top of all this I was unable to sleep. After about ten days though things began taking a more active shape and I was allowed to go up into the conning tower for fresh air and a smoke. All the time I was on board though I only saw daylight 3 times and smoked eleven cigarettes. I began eating well, but apart from this and a few odd jobs such as peeling potatoes I had nothing whatsoever else to do. I was, naturally I suppose, all the time in a very morbid state of mind and just longing for the time when I could speak to somebody English. I was on board for my 21st birthday, a thing I had practically forgotten about if it had not been for one of the crew reminding me (he had seen the date in my pay book which had been taken from me). Also Christmas and the New Year. On the whole I was treated very well, in fact exceptionally well, as I was to realise later.

We eventually landed at Lorient in the south of France on Wednesday 6th Jan. I was joined by five Englishmen from other U. Boats, two Majors, a Captain, a Flying Officer and a Ship's Captain. We all spent quite a pleasant evening together, and on the following morning we left for Wilhelmshaven, a journey which took $37^{1}/_{2}$ hours. The first big thing that was brought to my notice on reaching land was the fact that Germany has no supplies of tea, coffee and cocoa, their only drink being Kaffee, called Ersatz I believe, but I personally have a far better name for it, but feeling that discretion is the better part of valour, won't mention what it is. It is black in colour and must, I think, be made from herbs, but I for one, even if the war lasts ten years, will never be able to drink it. Water, from now on is my drink unless I can get a tin of cocoa from home. Well, we arrived at W'haven and this for me was the start of the worst and unhappiest 23 days to date of my life. It was very cold, with snow and ice, whilst in Brittany it had been quite warm. The time was 2.30 am and we were all tired and miserable. We were all put into separate rooms, and awakened at 6.45 am. For the first week I literally did not see a soul, except the guard who was stationed outside the door. If you wanted a match or a wash or wished to go to the toilet, you simply had to knock on the door. The only person who came to see you was the essen mann or in other words the chap who dished out the food, ersatz and your 3 daily cigarettes. Meals consisted of Kaffee at 8 am, soup 11.30 am and again at 3.30 pm, Kaffee again at 4 am with a piece of bread, butter and marmalade sometimes. I admit I never went hungry, but I do admit to feeling very lonely and caged in. In short I had nothing to do and all day in which to do it. My room was on the top *floor in the attic and the rats were so tame that they even showed themselves in the day time. This lasted for 7 days, then I was given a better room, but still no companions, but I was allowed now to have some books. I had several interviews then with a German Captain and at the end of these I was told that we should all be going to the camp in two or three days, but that now is ten days ago and I am beginning to wonder if we shall ever leave here. Every morning at 8.30 until 9 we promenade in the grounds, but if we so much as look at one another a voice quietly tell you it is 'varbaden'. At night if the siren sounds we are marched down separately under an armed guard into the basement. All these precautions for keeping us from talking to one another I could understand perhaps if I was acquainted with the rules of International Law, because I can only put it down as some form of punishment under this agreement. It can't be for what we would talk about because prior to our coming here we had spent three whole days in one another's company.*

On Wednesday 27th Jan at 8 pm (I was in bed) they came and told me that I had got to move into another room, and you can imagine how pleased I was when I was put in with three other lads; 2 Maritime A. A. Gunners and a Merchant Navy Deckhand. I naturally thought on the face of this that I should be going with them to the camp, but no, my pleasure was short lived. On the Friday the other 3 were sent to the camp, and I had to stay behind and go to an army camp, so once again I was sent back to my old room and my lonely night. The 3 army officers whom I accompanied from Lorient also left here on the same day. I now found my own company far worse than before, and must admit that I was feeling none too pleased with what had taken place, it would have been far better, I think, if they had let me stay where I was.

***

25th Jan   MON. Still one man, one room. Food the same. Walk from 8.30 to 9 am. This afternoon washed out some clothes.

26th Jan   Still one man, one room. Food the same. Walk from 8.30 to 9 am. Washed out some clothes for Major B and Capt H.

27th Jan   Still one man, one room. Food the same. Walk from 8.30 to 9 am. Three daylight alarms, and during the first one bombs were dropped very close. To have your own country's bombs fall on you is not very pleasant. At 8.30 pm was moved to another room with 3 companions.

28th Jan   The happiest day since I arrived here. Food the same. No walk but had a bath. My 3 companions are: - 2 Maritime A A lads and a Merchant

Chapter 10: The survivor's story

Navy lad. Their names are Doug Meadows from Bristol, Arthur Hopkins from Manchester, and Ralph Hopkins from South Shields; the first 2 are the Maritime A A lads. They are all 3 survivors of the 'Empire Gilbert' torpedoed on her way to Russia. They are all very decent fellows and we have spent a very enjoyable day. I even got a kick out of sitting down and eating with them.

29th Jan   The three officers went away early this morning. At 11 am an interpreter came to our room and said we were going at 11.30 am, but only the other three, not myself. I said goodbye to them and we promised to write after the war. So I am once again one man, one room. Food the same. Walk from 8.30 to 9 am. It appears that they have gone to the naval camp whilst I have to go to an army one, but when this will be now goodness only knows. It would have been far better if they had never put me with them.

30th Jan   Still one man, one room. Food the same. Walk from 8.30 to 9 am. Did some work for an hour. Four daylight alerts but no gunfire. Night alert from 2.45 am until 4.30 am.

31st Jan   Still one man, one room. Food the same. Walk from 9.30 to 10 am.

1st Feb   MON. Still one man, one room. Food the same. Walk from 8.30 to 9 am. Air raid from 6.15 - 7 pm.

2nd Feb   Still one man, one room. Food the same. Walk from 8.30 to 9 am. Did some work this morning, and also spoke to an interpreter about England. He knew London quite well and also Uckfield. Washed some clothes this afternoon and had a shave. Tomorrow I leave here at 5 am and I feel as pleased as if I were going away on holiday. It is no false alarm either, as I have been issued with rations for the journey including a russet apple.

3rd Feb   Was awakened at 3.30 am. Left Dulag Nord 5 am. Wilhelmshaven Dep 5.30. Changed at Berlin. Dep. 2.15 pm. Before leaving I asked (on the off chance) if there was any chance of getting my daily ration of 3 cigarettes. I nearly had a fit when they gave me a packet of 20. Arrived Lamsdorf 10.30 pm. The camp 11.30. Although very tired could not sleep owing to bitter cold. It was Stalag VIIIB. And of course I naturally thought of Ken.

POW Ken Harrison

363

Stalag VIIIB

4th Feb   Up at 6.30 am and had a cup of ENGLISH TEA. Boy, was it good. Registered officially as P of W, my No. being 27370. Delousing parade at 11am followed by a clothing parade; was given an overcoat, 2 prs socks, pants, vest, cap, 2 shirts. Jerry soup at 12, and ¼ R.C. parcel with 15 Players. In the afternoon moved to arbeit compound. The lads here have been grand to me and I only hope I shall one day be able to repay some of them or at least be able to do the same for some other fellow. My pal (rock and comforter) is an Aussie Clarry Wragg (cousin to Harry Wragg the jockey). I shall never be able to repay him for all that he has done for me. He was captured and wounded in Crete with the 7th Div. If ever a fellow has had a tough time he has.

4th Feb 1943
Dear Mum & Dad. Am now at the camp, and feeling fit and well. Plenty of food and enough clothes, so please don't worry about me. Socks and handkerchieves, shaving gear, chocolate and fags always welcome. Send fags in lots of 100. There are a grand lot of fellows here, and I'm trying to get in touch with Ken. Please let me have his P. of W. No. Write soon, and let me have all the news. Remember me to everyone. Letter No. 1, dated 16 Jan. Writing again soon. Love Eric.

5th Feb   Morning tea at 6.30. Roll call at 7. Issue of ½ RX parcel. The arbeit compound is the one where you go out to work. Clarry is going to try and get me to his job at Steinberg, a woodwork factory. This of course, may not be possible.

6th Feb   Went sick with my stomach. Small concert in the evening. Weather still very cold. VIIIB is about the largest in Germany. 30,000 appx. registered here. Probably half of these aren't working. The camp is divided into compounds, working, convalescent, repatriation, and several others. The gates of these are locked at 9 pm. There are men of all nationalities and men from every battle that has been fought. The Dieppe lads and R.A.F. are in a compound in chains.

7th Feb   Church service 9.30 am. Symphony concert in the evening.

7th Feb 1943
Dear Mum & Dad. Letter No. 2. I am now established in the camp, and am feeling very fit and well, in fact if you were to see me now, you would see no change in me. I have already made many friends, mostly Aussies, in particular one who is cousin to Harry Wragg the jockey. If we keep together when we go out

to work I want you to send me some things for him, as he has been more than decent to me. Would you please send me tooth and shaving brush, 3 hole blades, scarf, photos, Bible, chocolate (a little) and 100 Players every 2 weeks, but you must promise me that you will take it out of my money. By the way, how do I stand with the Southern? Give Doug 10/- every time he gets leave and Norman 1/-6 every week. Tell Doug not to do anything rash, as it's all going to be over by Christmas, and then we'll all have the time of our lives. We must just be patient and not worry. Would you phone the Paynes and Len Funnell and explain everything and then I shall be able to write you more often? I will tell you about Pam as soon as I hear from her, if I ever do. Write me as often as you can, as all scraps of news will be more than welcome. I am still trying to trace Ken; I have met, though, a lad from Gillett Rd. I am hoping to go out to work in a week or two, and then I shall be more settled. This, by the way, is where Ken is, but I doubt if I shall be able to get on the same job, but there is always a chance. All of you look after yourselves and keep smiling. Love Eric.

8th Feb   MON. Interrogation

12th Feb   Left VIIIB at 8 am. Lamsdorf dep 8.30. Changed Neisse dep 11am. Made a brew of tea in the Red X hut. There are 6 of us on this arbeit party to a woodwork factory at Sternberg, a place about 3 km from the Czech border. Am writing this on the train. I did not like leaving Clarry but he hopes to be following on later; in any case I shall see him in Blighty. Changed at Olmütz, arrived at the lager 6 pm. We actually crossed the border a few km into Czechoslovakia. The Sudetanland scenery, mountains, woods and hills, is the best I have seen in Europe.

13th Feb   Awakened at 5.45 am. Started work at 6.30 until 1 pm (half day Sat). It consisted of stacking timber. I found it hard going at first, as it was the first real work I have done since leaving England, anyhow the exercise did me good, and I was able to enjoy my dinner. There are about 60 lads here and we live in 2 rooms; it is quite warm and comfortable, but not extra clean. I am beginning to realise how much of a pal Clarry was during the past week. I miss him a hell of a lot, but content myself with the thought that I may be joining him, Blanche and Kiwi in a week or two. There are many seasoned Gefanganers *[prisoners]* here, most of them captured in France and I must say their outlook and conversation is rather melancholy.

14th Feb   Sunday and a day off; here we are confined to our barrack room. Had bread pudding for afters, also we are on a $^1/_2$ parcel.

14th Feb. 1943
Dear Mum & Dad. Am working in a timber yard at Sternberg with 60 others. Am feeling in the pink of condition and just waiting for the boat, which I don't think will be very long. Have spoken to several fellows who have been with Ken, and he is quite well. Tell Googs and everyone else to write as I am eagerly awaiting news of everyone and everything. Please don't forget fags and a pair of slippers. Will write you every Sunday, so keep smiling, your loving son Eric.

15th Feb   MON. Started work at 6.30; break from 9 - 9.20. Dinner 12 - 1 and finished at 5.40. It's hard graft, and me being soft I feel very tired. Good news of the day is that we are now getting an extra $^1/_2$ parcel on Wednesday and a whole one on Saturday, also a full ration of 50 cigarettes. I have been rather browned off the last day or so, but if I've got to settle here I will, but I'm hoping to be able to join Clarry in about 2 weeks.

16th Feb   Finished work 3.30, feeling fagged out; it consists of stacking and unstacking timber

17th Feb   Finished again at 3.30; actually it should be 5.40, but by getting stuck into it we finished early which quite suits me. Issued with 25 fags and $^1/_2$ R.X Pcl.

18th Feb   Finished 5.40. Am now beginning to settle down and feel better. Find that the work makes the time go quickly. The food that Jerry gives us, that is, extra to our R.X parcel, is soup at 12 o' clock (vegetable) and again at 6 made with horse flesh with a good helping of cabbage or sauerkraut, a ration of about 6 potatoes, $^1/_5$ of a loaf and marg. 3 brews of ersatz.

19th Feb   Had a good jaw with Bill Channings, a New Zealander captured in Greece. He's a market and landscape gardener in civvy street and I'm hoping to get some useful hints from him, but Sat. afternoon and Sundays are the only times we get for really doing anything. During the week, by the time you've cooked your meal it's time for bed.

20th Feb   Half day. 1 R.X. Pcl. 50 Players cigs. Bill received a clothing pcl. from home and presented me with a scarf, balaclava helmet, shaving and tooth brush, chocolate and 3 pkts P.K. Had a discussion with a chap from Highgate, a N. Zealander and an Aussie about the war, communism and N. socialism, also America's position after the war with regards to the colonies.

Chapter 10: The survivor's story

21st Feb   Played football this morning. Bill wrote home one of his cards to assure Mum that I was O.K. Played him crib in the evening.

21st Feb. 1943
Dear Mum & Dad. You should by now have had news of me, so I am eagerly awaiting your reply. My first week's work has made me very tired, but I am feeling very fit. They are a very decent crowd of fellows, and we have some good times; this morning we played football and tonight I have a crib match on. I will describe later exactly how we live but I assure you there is no need to worry. Please look after yourself and don't worry, because that's what I'm doing.
Love Eric.

22nd Feb   MON. Finished 5.40. Did some washing. Went to bed early.

24th Feb   Finished 2.30. Made myself a pair of wooden soled slippers. Had a pint of beer.

25th Feb   Finished 3 pm. Made a coat hanger.

26th Feb   Stomach bad again this afternoon. Moved my bed. Bill gave me a pair of khaki socks. Have now been here 2 weeks and the time has gone very quickly. Am feeling much fitter, but have cultivated an enormous appetite. If it was not for the long working hours everything would suit me fine.

27th Feb   Half day, finished at 12. The job that I am on is called a firearm. Which means that we are given a job and when we are finished we can go. It's pretty hard going at the time, but I would rather have it this way. Issue of <u>Canadian</u> Red X parcel. This consists of 1 lb butter, $1/2$ sugar $1/2$ coffee, tin powdered milk, tin of bully, meat loaf, salmon, sardines, jam, $1/4$ maple leaf cheese, $1/2$ raisins, $1/2$ prunes, 12 thick biscuits, salt, bar of chocolate 80gs, bar of soap. My supper consisted of fried potatoes and a $1/2$ tin of bully and mustard, for afters, 2 biscuits ground to a powder and boiled in milk with raisins, a spoon full of sugar and jam. This gave me a large bowl of something similar to porridge, I found it very tasty and filling. I finished off with coffee, toast, butter and jam. We also received a ration of 30 Players and 20 Capstan. Played 4 handed crib.

28th Feb   Watched a good game of football and spent the remainder of the day very lazily, reading, sleeping and writing.

1st Mar   MON. Finished at 2 pm. Received my first German arbeit money, 9 marks 10. The trouble is there is nothing to spend it on.

2nd Mar   Am now beginning to feel quite fit, and regaining some long lost energy. All I'm wanting now is some mail, which should with a bit of luck arrive some time this month.

3rd Mar   Today finished at 5.40. This means that we were not on our regular job and also that we were not working so hard, this caused one of the "Gaffers" to get rather annoyed, the outcome being that a Scots lad in our party started a fight; before we could intervene two of them were setting about him, and he was rather knocked about before we managed to separate them. I am unable to define or write my thoughts, but I do realise that if we had started anything, a battle would soon have been in progress with perhaps some hot lead thrown in for luck. For the remainder of the day the five of us were watched by the postens like flies. What all the outcome of this will be I don't know.

4th Mar   Finished 2 pm. Have started mucking in with a chap named Ralph Palmer from B'gham. He's a chippy by trade and was in an R.E's field Coy, captured in France.

Interview with Eric Munday 26/9/99

Muckers, as we used to call them, was the chap who you shared your parcel with, or any food, and once you had a mucker, if you bought food from outside, off the locals, you know, eggs and that, you didn't just sit down and eat it on your own, you shared it with your mucker.

5th Mar   Nothing of importance. Time goes very quickly, for which I am very thankful. I have now been here three weeks.

6th Mar   Issue of 1 Red X parcel. Ralph and I had a good assortment between us. Mine was Scottish and his English. Made a bread pudding.

7th Mar   Played football and lost 4-1. Fair game but too much running about and kick and push.

8th Mar   MON. Finished at 5.40. Weather very warm and sunny.

9th Mar   Finished 2.30.

10th Mar Lads selected a sports committee of 7 men. They are all very keen on football and boxing.

Chapter 10: The survivor's story

11th Mar   Although I have been here nearly a month, have only just found out that the Sgt in charge and interpreter comes from Tooting. Was in the same mob as Ken and was captured with him in Crete.

13th Mar   Tomorrow we were to have had a very important football match. A Scotch team v. Londoners, we had even made badges for our jerseys. After dinner four of us went down and marked the pitch out and when we got back to the lager we were told that we were no longer allowed to play on that pitch as the civilians wanted it. The lads were all very disappointed. Had a band concert in the evening and things began to liven up.

14th Mar   We have now made arrangements to send our laundry out for which I am well and truly thankful. 8 of us volunteered to get up at 6 o' clock and take it. It was a grand bright and sunny morning and we had about 3 kms either way to walk. After we had delivered the washing the posten allowed us to walk and inspect an open air swimming pool where we shall be allowed to go in the summer. He also let us go into a gausthaus and have a glass of beer and also a hot drink (like hot lemon cordial). Everyone treated us very decently and whilst we were having our drink we had some Strauss waltzes played on a (penny in the slot machine). It was a thoroughly enjoyable outing and for a couple of hours I forgot I was a gefangener. Have written a card to Ken.

15th Mar   MON. Finished 2.30. Had a nap until dinner time. Heard yesterday that 2 lads from Steinz's escaped and that one had been captured having been shot in the leg.

18th Mar   Went sick with my stomach, but got no satisfaction as time off.

19th Mar   Feeling better. A heap of mail up tonight but none for yours truly.

20th Mar   Had a razor set given me by a Canadian who has just joined this party. Had a good sing song until about 12.30am. Nearly all the tunes though were old ones that I had nearly forgotten.

21st Mar   Took the washing in the lorry and had a very good outing. Started making myself a veneered box. Wrote home, Syd S and Jack McG.

21st March 1943
Dear Mum & Dad. Still without any news of you but am hoping to hear any day now. I am still feeling very fit and if I arrive home in the same condition as I am in now I shall have no complaints. It is heavy outdoor work that I'm doing, and

the only trouble is that I get too big an appetite. I promise you that when I get back I'll eat you out of house and home, especially get a good supply of porridge in. We get a good game of football on a Sunday morning and opportunities for going for walks in the afternoon. The countryside here is very beautiful and amongst the best I have ever seen. But give me the South Downs any time. I wrote to Ken last week. The Sgt. i/c of this party comes from Tooting, was in the same mob as Ken in Crete and knows him very well, also the other lads we went to school with. We have some good news about the Grandison, Locarno, and the Ice Rink etc. I don't know if you ever wrote to Pam, but anyhow she is a girl I was very friendly with at the Spinney. She is 19 and very decent, unspoiled, and a good all round disposition. I think you would like her, and I hope she is going to write me, but if not it's ganz egal with me. Would you please send me a pipe and an ounce or two of St. Bruno. Is your birthday the 7th or 14th July? Please forgive me for forgetting. Give my love to everyone and especially look after yourself. Keep smiling, it won't last forever. Your loving son Eric.

22nd Mar   Finished 3 pm. MONDAY.

23rd Mar   Went to Dentist (civilian) in the town and had one tooth filled. Commando joined this party only P.O.W. for 26 days, captured in Tunis. News he says is good, believes war will be over this year. (I hope he's right).

28th Mar   Sunday. Went with the washing. Picked some water cress.

28th March 1943
Dear Mum & Dad. Still hoping to hear from you any day now. Life continues just the same. I'm still working pretty hard, but feeling very fit especially now the warm weather has set in. Tell Norman and Doug to write and let me know their own bits of news, would you also please send me some books on gardening and copies of the latest dance tunes. Look after yourself Mum, and keep smiling. Kind regards to everyone. Your loving son Eric.

3 April   Recd. first news from home.

4th April 1943
Dear Mum & Dad. No. 5. Received your first letter dated 8th March yesterday. All day I had had a presentiment that I was going to have good news shortly, and believe me I was not disappointed. I feel much better now that I have heard, especially as you all appear to be well. I must say that I had imagined all kinds of things. You seem under the impression that I am actually with Ken, but this is not so, although our address is the same. We are both out at working party camps

Chapter 10: The survivor's story

probably hundreds of miles apart; there is though the possibility that we shall meet before we get back to Blighty. I wrote him a card two weeks ago. Would you please write to Norman Hamer for me and also send a parcel of Players to Gnr. C. Wragg 23681 Stalag VIIIB (Clarry). He was very decent to me when I arrived there from the Naval Camp. You asked if there was anything I was needing, well at present there is not, except for those things I have asked you for in previous letters; some good books though are always welcome, also photographs which can be sent in an ordinary envelope letter. Have you any news of Jim and Tom, who I expect is now back home? Tell Norman that I shall expect some dancing lessons when I get back. I am still keeping very fit (had a good game of football this morning). Look after yourselves. Your loving son Eric.

18th April 1943
Dear Mum & Dad. No. 6. Received 3 letters from you yesterday, dated March 12th, 17th, 26th. One from Aunty D., one from Pam, and one from a person asking for news of her brother who was on my boat; unfortunately though I am unable to help her as I don't know of anyone else who was picked up. I'm sure you won't mind if I write to her next week on the card that I should be sending to you, it may in some little way help her. Was pleased to hear that you are all well and also that some parcels are on the way; I should receive them about June, I am not though in need of any clothing except summer pants and toilet accessories. Everything though is welcome, because if I'm not in need of it, there is always someone who is short. You asked about my 21st, well, it was spent on the bottom of the ocean, and I did not know the date until 8 o' clock in the evening, but unfortunately I was unable to celebrate. I'll make it up, though, when I get back. The photo you asked for is practically impossible to obtain, but I will send one when the opportunity arises. When I asked for a Bible, don't get the idea that the life has turned me religious, for my ideas on the subject are exactly the same, and I go to church whenever it is possible. Remind me to explain this when I get home. What did you mean about receiving a letter from Andy's sister? Well Mum, I'm feeling very fit and sunburnt, and as well as I've ever been. Next Sunday is Easter; we will celebrate it together next year. Look after yourself Mum, and give my love to everyone. Tell Dad to have a couple for me. Your loving son Eric.

2nd May 1943
Dear Mum & Dad. Have received Dad's letter of the 21st and yours of the 31st March and 5th April, there is no need for me to say how pleased I was. Our cards to send home have been rather scarce lately. Last Sunday was Easter and we had Monday off, also yesterday for May Day. We were able to go out on a route march and very much enjoyed ourselves. We also had a whist drive and crib tournament and yours truly won them both. I've been very lucky in this life. Love Eric.

9th May 1943
Dear Mum & Dad. No news from you this week, but one from Auntie D. dated 7th April. Please thank her for me. Am still very fit and sunburned, and hope you are likewise enjoying decent weather. Have you any news of Jim, Bob and Tom? Also Alec. Bill the N.Z. who wrote you has gone back to Stalag with a bad back but he hopes to return in a few weeks. Good luck to you all. Love Eric.

16th May 1943
Dear Mum & Dad. No. 7. Please thank Googs for her letter of the 10th Apl., and thank her for the flowers etc. You all seem far more anxious about Pam than I think I am myself. To be quite truthful, I am unable to define my own feelings; as you know I've never taken things seriously, and I've made too many plans for when I get back; things will just have to take their course. I certainly don't give too much encouragement in my letters, but she writes twice a week. Tell Googs to save all the spirits she is not using and Ken and I will show her how they should be taken. Thanks also for the Bible but don't get the impression that I've suddenly turned religious. Please don't send any spirits or winter underclothes out, but toothpaste, boot polish, brushes, a tin opener and that old pair of brown shoes of mine are things that I would like; also some vaseline for my hair and a few P.K.s. By the way, I have had two teeth filled by a civilian dentist, and he has made a very good job of them. My parcels should start arriving any time now, but I'm not short of fags as my 'Mucker' has received 7,000 in the last five weeks. A mucker means someone with whom you share everything you get, including food and clothes, also you only have to cook alternate days. It will be a change though to be able to share some of my own things. Don't forget the snaps. Best love to you all. Love Eric.

23rd May 1943
Dear Mum & Dad. Received Dad's letter of the 20th Apl. am now getting your letters between 3 and 4 weeks. Why no news of Jim? Will you write to Ken and give him my working party No and ask him to write me as I have not yet heard from him. I hope you are all keeping well and will be able to get away for a holiday this year. Tell Norman to drop a line to his "Jail-bird brother". Give my love to Joan, Googs Etc. and look after yourselves. Best Love Eric.

30th May 1943
Dear Mum & Dad. No mail this week, but everyone here's the same. Had a good game of football this morning, the first for six weeks. Next week we are moving in to a brand new billet, so things will be much better here, especially also as our Red X food parcels are coming through regularly. Tell Norman to write and tell me about all the latest pictures and tunes. Best of luck to you all, keep smiling. Love Eric.

Chapter 10: The survivor's story

6th June 1943
Dear Mum & Dad. *Just received your letter of May 2nd was sorry to hear that you are not receiving my mail, but I assure you I have hardly missed a week for the past 4 months. Your letters to me have been arriving very regularly; I have not heard from Ken or Andy's sister though but I would rather you wrote her as ----. Have just had a 2hrs game of football in the boiling sun and feeling very fit. Love to you all Eric.*

13th June 1943
Dear Mum & Dad. Received your letter dated 23rd Apl. last week and I can't make out why you have not heard from me, as I assure you I have written practically every Sunday. Tomorrow we have a holiday for Whitsun, and that means another lay in until dinner time. No parcels have come through yet, but I am expecting them any post now. By the way, how did Andy's sister get in touch with you, is she old, young or what; has she any news, and for that matter have you, of any of the other lads? I suggest trying the owners. What does Pam have to say? For believe me, all this is beyond me; what does she have to say? Thank Norman for looking after my bike. I expect he's getting a big lad now, but he can't be too big for me to knock hell out of when I get back, as I am honestly feeling in the pink of condition. An inside job with collar and tie won't be much good to me now after comparing it with the state I was in when I joined up. Have you sent any books off yet, as they are always very welcome? I know Googs will give you a hand in selecting a few good ones. Many happy returns on both of your birthdays. I'm sorry I can't send anything, but I do send all my love and best wishes, and hopes for a happier one all together next year. What does Ken have to say? All my love Eric.

20th June 1943
Dear Mum & Dad. No news from you last week, but no matter, it has been coming through very regular. For a long time now I have been going to ask for my old brown shoes (size 9 or 10) also some leather laces and a belt. Have had no reply from Ken, so for the present must rely on news via you and Mrs Harrison. Am still keeping very fit, so I hope you are all looking after yourselves. Kind regards to Saunders' & Griffins. Love Eric.

27th June 1943
Dear Mum & Dad. Had a birthday last Thursday when I received 11 letters: 3 from you, 2 from P., 1 from Andy's sister, 1 from Homer, 2 from lads at the S., 1 from Aunt D. and one from a Mrs Warren of Westbourne, Dartmouth, asking for news of her husband who was on the 'C' (Ceramic). These letters are very difficult to answer as I have very little information to go on myself. I will drop her a post card though today. The one from Andy's sister was very decent and sensible, and at least half a dozen Scotch lads wanted to write to her straight

373

away, but I made up the excuse that she was an old dear about 40, but of course you don't say anything about her, neither does she herself; are photographs out of the question? Please tell her that I will write her the very next time we get an issue of mail. Now for a grouse - please don't fill up half your letters with Pam did this and that. I write to her about once a month merely because I was friendly with her at the Spinney. I will write and tell Aunty D. off later about this, but please thank her for her very nice letter. We had another good game of football this morning against another W.P. (working party). We won 5-1. The lads here are as keen on it as they are of going home. I am very happy and contented to wait for that day, so for goodness sake don't worry about me. Dad always said I was big and ugly enough to look after myself. Thank Norm for his letter. Cheerio and look after yourselves. Your loving son Eric.

11th July 1943
Dear Mum & Dad. Have received three letters from since I last wrote dated May 16th, 20th, 27th. And the best news of all was that Ray was safe. Please tell Mrs Harrison how pleased I was to hear. Do you know if he is getting Red X food parcels and cigarettes? The last news from here is that I have received my first parcel of 500 Churchmans No. 1 from the Southern, this means that I shall be receiving them regularly now; my N. of K. should arrive in about 2 weeks, it's impossible to say how pleased I am about this. Mail from you is also arriving well; 2 letters this week and 1 from Mr Yeo. (Please thank him for me and explain why it is difficult to reply). Now, about this clothing, assuming that you know about boots, slippers, pyjamas, there is nothing else that I am wanting, except in every parcel please put plenty of toilet goods, such as toothpaste, soap, blades (Blue Gillette), brilliantine, blacking, shoe laces, tooth brush, P.K., also a housewife (needles and thread). Thanks for the books and photos, I seem to be causing you a lot of trouble, but perhaps some day I shall be able to repay you, if only a little. Please don't on any account worry about me as I am feeling in the pink of condition. Look after yourselves and thank you again for all that you are doing for me. Your loving son Eric.

18th July 1943
Dear Mum & Dad. Have just received 2 photos and Dad's letter 12th May. They were very nice indeed. Have not yet heard from Ken. Would you please send pyjamas as from Pam, I will write her a letter next Sunday. Had a letter also from Ernie Cook. This weekend we moved into a new billet and it's very clean and comfortable. Am still very fit and sunburned, but no swimming. Plenty of work and football though. Look after yourselves. Love Eric.

25th July 1943
Dear Mum & Dad. The best news of the week is that I have just received my first clothing parcel, and believe me, I could not have asked for a better assortment.

Chapter 10: The survivor's story

Every little thing was something I was wanting so you can tell how pleased I was to get it. I have been waiting for a few days for an excuse to wash my blankets, and the pyjamas was all that I needed. The weather is now boiling hot and the lads went mad when they saw me with a couple of pairs of shorts. Have had no mail from you since receiving the photos, which, by the way, were very good indeed; how about sending one of Ron and Doug in uniform? What does Pam have to say when she writes? I keep promising to write her a letter, but I never seem able to, although I tell her they are in the post (don't let the cat out of the bag). We are quite settled in our new billet and indeed very comfortable and clean, just 40 of us. Have I ever told you that the Sgt. i/c of this party comes from Tooting and was stationed with Ken up until they were captured in Crete. Am still very fit and I hope you are. Keep smiling and for goodness sake don't worry about me. I don't want to see any grey hairs when I come home. Love Eric.

5th August 1943
Dear Mum & Dad. Good news this week, have just received 3 cigarette parcels: from you, the Southern and Miss Andrews, 850 in all. Up to now I have received 11 parcels, so please don't think that I'm not receiving them, and please realise that I'm indeed very grateful for everything. Received also this week your letter of the 22nd July telling me of Barry Pickles. I can't describe how shocked I was, but I hope Mr & Mrs P. are bearing up O.K. I have written Ken but please realise that it is very difficult to get news through, but even if we don't meet this side of the Channel we'll meet the other, and I can wait. You seem to be under the impression Mum, by all of your letters, that life here is one long weary drudge and that laughter and singing are unheard of, but believe me that's all wrong, for we get plenty of work, football and entertainment and good food. Our life is regular: regular sleep, meals, work, and our own time. We don't keep late hours, or go out on the binge, and so you see we must be fit, and believe me that when men are fit they are quite happy enough. Also remember that we all have something good to look forward to; so for goodness sake don't worry about me. The photo I promised last week won't be ready for another 2 weeks but I'll send it as soon as it arrives. Please try for that kit bag I asked for. So cheerio and please remember me to everyone. Look after yourselves and keep smiling. Your loving son Eric.

8th August 1943
Dear Mum & Dad. Have received this week your letter of the 7th June, Aunty D. photos, one from Alec and one from Pat and Aunty M., also another one from Miss Gimpleson, please thank them all for me, especially for the photos, which, by the way, are all framed over the bed. Have also received a parcel of 1lb of tobacco from the S.R. You asked in your letter how we fill our days, well, here goes. Up at 5.45, 10 mins walk to work, start at 6.30, break from 9 - 9.20, dinner 12 - 1, finish 5.45, then a shower and your tea which we cook ourselves; it is then

375

about 7.30. After this we do what we like, either sleep, punt a football about, do some washing, or have an argument (quite friendly), play cards or draughts. Mail and parcels come up pretty regularly once a week. Saturdays we finish at 1 o' clock and get our Red X parcel. In the evening the band usually gets going. Sunday morning we play football, and believe me, there is plenty of interest. In the afternoon I do whatever writing there is to do, and then retire to bed until tea time. Lights go out at 10 pm, and the week starts over again. Well, I hope you are all keeping well, and young Norman is keeping out of mischief. Are you going away at all this year? Give my love to Googs, Joan, etc., and for goodness sake don't worry about me as I am still keeping very fit. Tell Uncle Jack I will keep him to his word about creating a good thirst. Your loving son Eric.

15th August 1943
Dear Mum & Dad. This week I received a clothing parcel and cigarettes from you and one from Swansea, and there's no need for me to tell you how pleased I was. Up to date I've received 2 clothing, 1 tobacco and 3 cigarette pcls. I hope you are all well and that Pam enjoys her stay, please explain why letters to her are scarce. Your mail is arriving very regularly. I only hope mine is as I write practically every week, without fail. Love to you all. Eric.

29th August 1943
Dear Mum & Dad. Am still very fit and well and to prove it will send you a photo next week. Received a parcel of tobacco from the S.R. and one from Carreras this week also two letters from you, the latest dated July 17th, so you see, <u>everything</u> in the garden's lovely. Will you please make up an old kit bag for me for my next parcel, but don't send any pipe tobacco until I say, as I have 3lbs now. Cheerio and look after yourselves. Your loving son Eric.

8th Sept   Italy capitulated.

19th Sept. 1943
Dear Mum & Dad. Hope enclosed photo reaches you O.K. as I know you have been wanting one. The chap in the centre with glasses knows Ken, was in his mob and lives at Tooting. The fellow next but one on the left of him (facing) is my mucker. He comes from just outside Edinburgh, and one of the best lads you could wish to meet; he has a sister that lives at Twickenham. Well, now for the best news of the week, I had a letter from Ron, and he certainly seems to be very fit and well. He gives me plenty of news including his forthcoming marriage either before or after the war. Is there any chance of him getting home before the finish? If so, he'd better save me some cake and a good long drink. I also had two letters from you dated June 26th and July 30th. What is the matter with Bob Heasman? I should be worth quite a bit when I get back, what with another 4/6 increase. The S.R. have certainly been very good, up to the present I've had 1000 cigs, 2lbs

Chapter 10: The survivor's story

tobacco and an extra clothing parcel from them. Since I last wrote you I have received 5 parcels from you, 2 lots of books, including the gardening books, 400 Players and $^1/_2$ lb St Bruno. Thanks for everything and please realise how much I appreciate it all. I am still keeping very fit and well; this Sunday and next we have a big sports coming off, with all the parties in the district taking part. Well cheerio for now, and look after yourselves and don't worry, your loving son Eric.

3rd Oct. 1943
Dear Mum & Dad. Since I last wrote I have received your letter of the 14th July and of the 20th, also 2 letters from Auntie Dorothy and one from Eric Pole. Please thank them for me, but I am very sorry to hear about Alan. What actually happened though? Has Eric heard anything further about the M.N.? I have received since the 19th Sept, 9 parcels; 4 cigs, 1 tobacco from yourself and Dad, 2 from the S.R. and 2 that I don't know who from. I have a good supply now, but no doubt there will be a time soon when they won't be coming through so regularly. If you think it worthwhile you can send me my old football boots, but I myself somehow don't think it is, but whatever you do don't buy new ones. There is nothing else I'm wanting, except the kit bag I asked for several letters back. I wrote last week to Miss Andrews, do you still hear from her? Please thank Googs for her letter which she wrote on her leave, and tell her not to worry about Lyd, as the Charmans have always managed to look after themselves. Have you any message for me yet from Ken as I can't get any news through from him? Well Mum, I'm still keeping very fit and have managed to get plenty of fruit and tomatoes, so don't worry and think that I'm losing weight because if anything I've put quite a lot on. Cheerio for now and look after yourselves. Your loving son Eric.

10th Oct. 1943
Dear Mum & Dad. Received two letters from you, one from Doug and one from Joan this week. Pleased to hear Norm is taking his Oxford; tell him to have a good try and if he gets it or his G.S., I will make him a good present. Mum, don't send the shoes if this arrives in time, as I have since received the boots which I did not know you were sending. Parcels are still coming regularly and I'm still very fit, so don't worry about anything. Love to you all Eric.

24th Oct. 1943
Dear Mum & Dad. Received 2 letters from you, one from Mr Driscoll and one from Eileen, please thank them for me. Well Mum I'm still keeping very well, although the cold weather is just beginning. Last Sunday I played for England against Scotland, it wasn't very exciting though, but we were invited out to a good feed afterwards, and I met a chap from Gillett Road out of the K.R.R.s. Cheerio for now and have a good Christmas, as we certainly intend to. Your loving son Eric.

31st Oct. 1943
Dear Mum & Dad. This week have received the Bible, also Norm's letter and yours of the 11th & 29th Aug. Please thank Aunty for me. Now Mum, about the choc. & P.K. whatever you do you are not to use your own ration cards. One day I will explain why I asked for that, but now you are not to send them. Everything over here is looking very bright, so have patience for a little longer. I'm still keeping very fit, but no word from Ken yet. Your loving son Eric.

7th November 1943
Dear Mum & Dad. This week have received 9 letters and 2 parcels of cigarettes, one from you and one from the Southern. Three letters from you and one from Norman, Mrs Scott, Alec, Peter Letley and two others from some friends in Sully. Please Mum thank them all for me, especially the Southern, when next you write them. Tell Alec I wish him all the very best and will be very honoured to do the necessary when I get back. I was very surprised to hear about Leslie (I suppose he meant to make sure whilst Jim and Bill were out of the way). Don't worry about Doug if he has to go, for I'm sure he wants to, I only wish I had another chance myself. Mum, you seem to be under the impression that you are not doing enough for me, but believe me I receive as much mail and parcels as anyone on this working party, and it's really impossible to write and say how thankful I am. I think one of my muckers wrote you a couple of weeks ago. He comes from just outside Edinburgh but has a sister lives at Twickenham. He's a very decent chap indeed, and you can tell Googs that I will let her see what a mucker is later, as I think she has some wrong ideas on the subject.

Well Mum, all of you have a good Christmas and New Year and don't whatever you do worry about me as I'm feeling very fit and certainly mean to enjoy myself. So look after yourselves and keep smiling. Your loving son Eric.

21st November 1943
Dear Mum & Dad. I do hope you are all still keeping fit, and manage to have a good Christmas, and by now have given over worrying about us over here. I expect though by now you have heard quite a bit about the life, from the 'Repats' who have recently arrived. By the way, there is a chap who got back who was working with me for some time on this party. We have just started making our own plans for the Christmas holiday (4 days last year) and at the moment it consists of a dinner and tea party, with a concert and dance in the evening (no women of course). Boxing day, an international football match in the morning, and a concert in the afternoon. What the food consists of would not be diplomatic to say, but you will certainly be surprised when I do one day tell you. I received a jolly good parcel of books from the S.R. this week, consisting of a dictionary (English - Deutch), a book on Maths, and one on Southern locomotives, which several of us found very interesting! Could you have a look around and see if you could find one or two

Chapter 10: The survivor's story

more, especially ones that give photos and descriptions of famous locomotives and trains. Don't worry though if you are unable to find any as I have several subjects which I can study (when I feel like it). Please thank Joan for her very nice letter received this week dated 15th Sept. I also had one from Jack Heighes written in May. Well cheerio for now, keep smiling. Your loving son Eric.

5th Dec   Returned to Lamsdorf.

5th December 1943
Dear Mum & Dad. First, today is the anniversary of the great event, but tomorrow by date. The year though has gone very quickly, but a hell of a lot of water has flowed under the bridge since then, but if nothing else I am as fit as I could ever wish to be. Secondly, tomorrow my pal Dod and I are going back to the Stalag. I will tell you though all about this later but don't put E338 on your letters any more. Well Mum, this week I received 13 letters: 6 from you, the latest being 1st Nov. (wishing me a Merry Xmas.) two from Pam written from No 19, one from Mrs Harrison, one from Eileen Waller, Auntie D and two re. relatives of people on the 'C' (Ceramic). Well, now to answer some of your enquiries. Thanks a lot for the photo of No 19, photos of any sort are always very welcome. Will be seeing Bill Channings and Clarry Wragg next week so will give you their news later. Now, something that worries me: who is this Mr Uzzell you write about in your letter Oct 10th, as I honestly have never heard of him before, and how does he affect my welfare? Now, what did you think of Pam? Be honest about it, as you all probably know her better than myself. I don't mind what you say, but please tell the truth as I shall write Joan and Aunt D. until I get it. Well cheerio and look after yourselves. (I have written all relatives even Rose Cottage, but have not Uncle Fred's address). Your loving son Eric.

11th December 1943
Dear Mum & Dad. Received 2 of your Oct, letters yesterday also 1 from Pam and Mr Cook. At the moment I am back from the W.P. (working party) but shall be going back shortly. My pal 'Dod' is here with me and believe me he is one of the best of fellows. Have also seen Bill and Clarry and they both thank you for cigs. letters etc. I am still keeping very fit and well, and it's my 22nd tomorrow and I'll be having a far better time than on my 21st. Keep smiling. Love Eric.

19th December 1943
Dear Mum & Dad. Received two letters from you this week both dated the end of November, and it's good to know that you are still in the best of health, but it seems to me that you are still worrying, and I do so wish that you would not, as I am in the best of health, and I now have everything that I require. Dod is still with me and keeping well; he looks after me like a mother. He's only a small chap, but one of the best. He comes from Edinburgh, but has a married sister

SS CERAMIC The Untold Story

living at Twickenham, and he's going to get her to phone you some time. When you write Pam, will you tell her that I'm sorry I haven't written her for some time, but her mail to me is arriving O.K., but I will make it up to her in the new year. By the way Mum, please note that this Stalag has altered its number to 344, whilst Ken's I believe is still 8B, so that now there is little chance of us meeting, but I'm still living in hope. Remember me to all the relations and friends. By the way I did write Meldreth and got a reply from Winnie. Get young Norman something for his birthday, but tell him to get stuck into his Matric. Best of luck to you all. Your loving son Eric.

28th Dec   Entered Revier *(hospital)*. Gastric ward. Had the time of my life.

***

1944

8th Jan 1944
Dear Mum & Dad. Hope the enclosed photo reaches you O.K. It is some of the S.R. Employees in this Stalag. If you don't receive the one sent in Sept. I will get my mucker's mother to send you a copy, as she has received hers. Now Mum, on the 6th Jan. I sent a remittance form to the Regimental Paymaster whereby in appx. 3 months he will send you a cheque for £50. When you receive it will you write to him and ask him how my balance stands? Well Mum, you can do what you like with this, but please don't stint yourself. Last week I received 200 woodbines and several letters: one from Mr Uzzell and Chrissie Munday, both very nice letters indeed, also from Tom, Mrs Scott, Googs, Alec and several from yourself, the latest being 4th Dec. Well, my birthday, Christmas and the New Year are now over, and we had a very pleasant but quiet time. I had a wrist watch given me for my birthday. All of those three holidays though were last year spent under the water, in fact until the 6th Jan. Well this year looks as if it will be brighter, so we must just hope for the best. Keep smiling and keep fit, and remember me to everyone. My weight by the way is now 11st. 10.
All my love Eric.

30th January 1944
Dear Mum & Dad. Since I last wrote I have received quite a number of letters and parcels. Your latest one being 28th Dec; one from Ganville and two from friends in Sully. The parcels were, tobacco from the S.R., cigarettes and tobacco from Uncle Fred, and No. 4 clothing parcel which was very welcome and contained everything that I was wanting. No. 3 parcel I'm afraid is now lost, but never mind, I consider myself lucky to have received 3. Another thing Mum, don't whatever you do use your own chocolate coupons to send me P.K. etc. When I once, foolishly, asked for them I was in a different state to what I'm in now, and I

Chapter 10: The survivor's story

assure you I really can do without them. Well Mum I am now back at E338 and it was good to meet old friends back in Stalag. By the way, I made friends this time with a very decent fellow, this time a South African. He has been a P.O.W. for 2 yrs. and never received a cigarette parcel, so when you send me some would you send him some also. Send him 3 or 4 then wait until you hear that he is receiving them. Craven 'A' are his favourite, and whatever you do you must take the money from my B.B. and if you don't I shall be very annoyed. His name is Cpl. C. W. Chapman No. 35367, Stalag 344. Well cheerio for now. Keep smiling and don't worry (wrote Mr Uzzell 23.1.44). Your loving son Eric

5th Feb   Returned to Knappeks. Unwillingly.

13th February 1944 (dated 1943 in error)
Dear Mum & Dad. Since I last wrote I have received ten letters and one parcel, your latest being 14th Jan. 4 from you, 2 from Pam, 1 Eileen, 1 Mollie, and 2 from friends in Sully. The parcel was six penguin books. Well Mum, you seem to be worrying yourself unduly about my two changes address, so I had better tell you about it. Firstly I went back to the main camp at the beginning of Dec, because of my stomach. (Now, don't get worried. I'm only telling you this to stop you thinking I'm half way in the grave). It was rather bad at the time and I thought I would go and get some treatment. It is a very, very common complaint here, gastritis, but mine was a very mild attack. I was in hospital six weeks on a diet, and came out feeling as fit as a fiddle. The English doctor told me that as long as I keep off fried food, and eat as little meat as possible, I shall never be troubled again. So don't write and ask if my stomach is O.K., because it is. I am now back at the old job and life continues as usual. Stalag VIIIB merely changed its number to 344, has Ken's been altered? Well goodnight Mother dear, keep smiling. Everything in the garden's lovely here. Your loving son Eric.

27th February 1944
Dear Mum & Dad. There is very little news this week, but believe me, I am still feeling very fit; in fact, I've never felt so well since leaving school. Don't, whatever you do, worry about my last letter to you, because the whole thing was an excuse, which I will explain when I get back. The main reason was that I had great hopes of meeting Ken, but there was nothing doing. I have tried five times to get in contact with him, and the next time I hope to be successful, but I am relying on your help. Will you please write him as soon as you receive this, and say I will be back in the Stalag by June. Tell him to try his utmost to be there, and to get in touch with Gnr. C. Wragg who works in the Camp Library. It should be plenty of time to June for you to have had a reply from him and perhaps also to have let me know the result. Have you yet received my second photo and also cheque for £50 sent off beginning of Jan.? Also my request for you to send some cigarettes to the S. African friend of mine. This week I received parcels of cigarettes from Uncle

Jack and Aunty M., also Mrs Stone. Please thank them for me Mum. Well everyone here is very fit, although at the moment we are unable to play football. Remember me to Joan, Googs and the girls etc. and whatever you do look after yourself for just a little while longer. Your loving son Eric.

12th March 1944
Dear Mum and Dad. I received three letters from you this week, the latest being the 18th Feb. I'm afraid that at the moment I'm like you, and that is that I have no news of importance. But I'm keeping very fit and well, and really have no complaints. My stomach has not troubled me since before Christmas, so don't, for goodness sake, write in every letter and ask how it is. We played football last weekend, the first time for a long time, and we were in a state when we finished! This week we had to cancel it again owing to the weather. Last week, by the way, we had a very nice change, when the Stalag dance band came out to give us a show. Nearly every member of the band is a professional, and the leader is Al Burke who used to play for Ambrose. At Christmas also I saw a pantomime 'Treasure Ho' and it was as good a show as I have ever seen. Have you received the photo yet that I sent Jan 4th, also the cheque for £50? Do you still draw the 7/- from my Army pay? Had a very nice letter from Uncle Jack this week; please thank him for me, and also tell him that I think he's just a little bit optimistic. Well Mum, cheerio for now, and remember me to everyone, and above all look after yourselves for just a little longer. Your loving son Eric.

19th March 1944.
Dear Mum & Dad. Received your letter 12th Feb. yesterday. Was glad to hear that you had received the S.R. photo. I also had a games parcel from them this week. They certainly have been good, eh! Now, your first question, about weight; I think if anything I am heavier now than when I left home. I did hear about the 6/- income tax but I'm not worrying about it, there will be time enough for that when I get back. So cheerio for now and all the best. Y.L.S. Eric.

26th March 1944
Dear Mum & Dad. Received four letters this week, from you dated 29th Feb., Mrs Saunders, Miss Grimpleson and Aunty Dorothy. I was relieved to know that you had received the £50, but I wish you had taken more for yourself. As soon as I think I have another 50 in my credit I will send another, as I think it is best that way, don't you? You ask in your letter what I am needing in my clothing parcels, but really as far as clothes are concerned, there is nothing I am wanting. My No. 3 parcel I have now given up as lost, and I think the slippers you sent were in it, so if you could manage another pair I could use them. Here are a few things though that I would like you to put in, if you can get them. Shoe leather, toothpaste etc., blacking, hair oil, boot laces, vaseline and a couple of R.F. cap badges. Well Mum, things are about the same here, although we are still getting

bags of snow. We have, though, started arranging the coming summer's football matches and sports day, and believe me, I am looking forward to some good football. Tell Dad we get the F.A. results each week, also an account of the best match, as for instance, when England beat Scotland 6-2. The return match though on Apl. 22 will have been played when you receive this. We hear also about the raids on London, but I know you will be able to bear up through them, as we did in 39 and 40. So cheerio for now and keep smiling. Your loving son Eric.

2nd April 1944
Dear Mum & Dad. 5 letters this week. 2 from you, 1 from Dad 12th March. Eileen and Mr Uzzell 29th, 2nd. Was very sorry to hear about Mrs Driscoll, please give Pat my heartfelt condolences. Now, what's all this about Norm out at work, it sounds ridiculous to me; he's only a kid. Only a few weeks ago you told me he was swotting hard for Matric, so why this sudden rush. I really did think he was going to try and show us others up, by passing his exam. Well, cheerio for now. Keep smiling. Your loving son Eric.

10th April 1944
Dear Mum & Dad. Please excuse handwriting, as I have just finished playing two strenuous games of football, and am feeling very sleepy. It's Easter Monday; yesterday we played a heat and won, but today in the final we lost 4-2, but boy, was it a good game! I won't say we deserved to win, but we certainly did not lose any laurels in the football itself. This is the first time our party has been beaten, and also we have only 30 men to select a side from, whereas the other parties have over 100. It's impossible to describe the keenness here amongst the lads, and the sportsmanship. It's a real pleasure to play, just for the game itself. Well, that's the football finished with. I received two letters this week, one from you dated 12th March, and one from Pam. By the way, why don't you approve of her joining the W.R.N.S? For myself, I think it is by far a change for the better. Parcels are not quite as regular these days, but don't worry, as everyone else's are the same. The reason is, I think, through the changing over of the number of the camp, but they are bound to come in a rush later on. Don't forget to let me know as soon as you hear from Ken about our meeting in June or July. Remember me to Mrs Harrison and Googs, and also to Syd when you write, and of course poor old Bob: it seems ages since I last saw those two. So cheerio Mum, and keep smiling, everything in the garden's lovely. Your affectionate son Eric.

16th April 1944
Dear Mum & Dad. Hope things are still O.K. with you, as here the hot weather has just started, and sun bathing is in full swing. Even now we are working in shorts and singlet, so you can guess how warm it gets later on. The football team had its photo taken yesterday, so I'll be sending you one in two weeks time. Do you think it's worthwhile sending out an old pair of football boots? Well Mum,

keep smiling, it can't go on for ever. (We hope!) Your loving son Eric.

23rd April 1944
Dear Mum & Dad. Received this week your letter 18th March. Am glad to hear you are all well, but about Norman, I can't make head or tail of what you say, it doesn't seem to make sense; I only hope he is quite fit. Well, the weather still remains good, and the parcels have again started to arrive, so everything in the garden's lovely. Ten new men arrived Friday and I was hoping Ken might be amongst them, but alas, no luck. Don't forget though to let me know as soon as you hear from him. Keep smiling. Your loving son Eric.

1st May 1944
Dear Mum & Dad. Today is Mayday, and we have a holiday, as the celebrations are still kept up in these parts. We have just been given the use of a long strip of garden, and all day today have been amusing myself putting in a few onions and lettuce etc. Even if we are not here to eat them, it passes the time away. Well Mum, I haven't been receiving many cigarette parcels lately, but last Saturday I received three together; two from the S.R. and one from Uncle Fred. A total of 1200 cigarettes; you can guess they were very welcome. I have also received a statement of accounts from the Reg. Paymaster, and everything is quite in order. I am expecting any day now No. 5 clothing parcel, as several of the lads here have already had those sent in January. If the second front hasn't started by the time you get my next one ready, would you put my football boots in, as at present we are playing practically every day, and it knocks hell out of our ordinary boots, and these are an item that we have to go steady on. Tell Doug and Norm to drop me a line some time and give me some of their patter; also try and send me some photos of them. Remember me to Mrs Pole and family, also Griffins and Saunders, whom I hope are all keeping well. By the way, do you ever hear from Pam these days, and what does she have to say? Keep smiling for a little while longer. Your loving son Eric.

7th May 1944
Dear Mum & Dad. Was going to write a letter this week, but am keeping it until next Sunday when I hope to send the football photo. I received this week your letter of March 26th, and was glad to know that you are all well. Don't worry though about Ron looking older, you must remember he's getting on for 26. Although I'm in my 23rd I certainly don't feel any older than when I joined up, in fact I'm a hell of a lot fitter, and I mean to stay like it. Look after yourselves. Your loving son Eric.

14th May 1944
Dear Mum & Dad. Parcels and mail have once again started arriving regularly. This week I received No. 5 clothing parcel, 1lb of tobacco and two cigarette parcels; both Players medium, one from you and the other from Auntie Mary. The clothing parcel was very welcome and contained everything that I was needing. In

Chapter 10: The survivor's story

previous letters I have mentioned a few odds and ends that are always handy; but don't you worry yourself if you have any difficulty in getting them. I will write Mr Uzzell tonight, but please thank Auntie Mary and say that I will drop her a line next week. Well Mum, the much promised football photograph is not forthcoming this week, but we have great hopes for next Saturday. We played football again this morning but unfortunately we lost, nevertheless everybody enjoyed the match. The garden is still in full swing, and the majority of the seeds and plants are coming through very nicely. I received two letters this week, one from you dated 22nd March and one from Pam, the 28th, and I am glad to know that you are all keeping well, as I myself am still feeling very fit. So look after yourselves and keep smiling, remember me to Joan and everybody. Your loving son Eric.

Stalag 8B, E338 football team. Les Bannister (architect of organising photography and much else!) is back left. Eric is back right.

21st May 1944
Dear Mum & Dad. No mail this week, but a record one for parcels. A total of 2100 cigs; 500 from the S.R. 200 from Mrs Stone. The other two are mystery ones; 200 from a Mr W. Ackroyd, and 1,000 from a Mr & Mrs F. W. Dell. Can you enlighten me at all about these? Am still feeling very fit, and have just finished another 90 mins of football; we won 3-1. Our rugby team also won 15-13, so you can guess everyone is very happy. So keep smiling and don't worry. Your loving son Eric.

28th May 1944
Dear Mum and Dad. This week I received a letter from you dated Feb. 20th, and naturally all the news was rather old, as for the last few weeks I have been receiving them dated the end of March. Anyhow, I am glad to know that you are all well and still merry and bright. The hot weather has now set in in earnest, and even at this early stage of the season it is much warmer than it ever is at home. You may be surprised then, why we chose this period to play football. The reason is that the winter months are very severe, and nearly all the time the ground is either deep in snow or covered in ice. Yesterday I played right back for England against Scotland, and we won 5-2. Today is Whit Monday and a holiday, and we are hoping to have another game tonight. Well Mum, I am enclosing this photo, though very much against my will, but the chaps here say it's not so bad as I make out, so as soon as you receive it please do me a favour and lock it up. We only play nine-a-side owing to the size of the pitch. Am writing Eileen and Mrs Stone today, as she might be under the impression that I am not grateful for the cigarettes. Cheerio for now, and look after yourselves. Your loving son Eric.

5th June 1944
Dear Mum & Dad. I received another 200 Players from you this week and 400 State Express from Mrs Stone. Please thank her for me as I only wrote to her last week. Mail at the moment is very irregular but it is probably owing to it now coming by sea. I'm still keeping very fit, and at the moment there is nothing that I am needing, so don't worry about me. Just look after yourselves. Your loving son Eric.

11th June 1944
Dear Mum & Dad. I received this week your letter dated 1st Apl. and it appears that the mail is bad both ways. Anyhow, I had two parcels; one of books from you (which Mum, although it is very nice of you to send them, are really a waste of money, as it appears that the Penguin people sort out all the books they can't sell in Blighty and send it over here. Also about 30 of us here all receive the same books each month! There's no need for me to tell you though what we use the paper for). The other parcel was from Len Funnell: 200 Players. Well Mum, what we have all been eagerly awaiting happened this week (look at the date). I only wish I had Ron & Doug's opportunities of getting into it. But there you are, what is to be, will be. We are playing another important game of football this evening. -

Chapter 10: The survivor's story

Have just returned, 8.30, and alas we lost 3-2, but it was a wonderful game, and I'm feeling very tired. Well Mum, I must scribble these last few lines as the lights will be going off very shortly, and these have to be in first thing in the morning. How are Googs and Joan keeping these days, also 'Pat' and Mr Ward? I dare say everything at the Grange is about normal? Keep smiling just for a short while now, and tell Doug to look after himself. Cheerio for now. Your loving son Eric.

18th June 1944
Dear Mum & Dad. I received a letter from you in the week, and one this morning dated Apl. 10th. Also one from Eric Pole. About my meeting with Ken, the chances are now rather small as he is now at VIIIB, but if I hear from you again that he can get there, I'll be there straight away as there is nothing more I want than a nice long jaw over a cup of tea with him. I wrote to Len Funnell only last week and I am truly grateful for everything that he is doing. Am sorry to hear that Googs is not too well, but don't worry about it Mum, everything will come right in the end. Remember me to Auntie D., Ann Joy, and tell them that I will write them next Sunday. About this Croydon P.O.W. Club: I have not joined, but will have to wait till I get back to explain why. Well Mum, the weather keeps very warm. This morning we played football and this afternoon went for a swim, my first time since I was captured, and I thoroughly enjoyed it. For the majority of the lads, it was their first for over four years. Our garden is now looking a picture and everything is now coming on fine. The latest addition is fifteen strawberry plants. Well, I'll say cheerio for now, so just look after yourselves for a little while longer. Your loving son Eric.

2nd July 1944
Dear Mum & Dad. Well, I hope you are still keeping well, as mail is still generally very bad, but don't you worry about that. Parcels though are still O.K. I received another two from you this week. I'm still keeping very fit myself, and at the moment there is nothing that I'm wanting. So just look after yourselves for a little while longer and keep smiling. Your loving son Eric.

25th June 1944
Dear Mum & Dad. No news of importance this week, as things have been about normal. I did though receive two parcels of Players from you, for which I was very grateful. I hope you are all still keeping O.K. and not having to go up the top too often with Mrs Pole. Remember me to everyone, as I can't seem to settle down to write these days; I am though, still very fit and well, so don't worry.
Your loving son Eric.

23rd July 1944
Dear Mum & Dad. I received two letters from you this week and (for a change) they contained quite a lot of news! They were dated 28th Apl. and 8th May. I also

received a parcel of cigarettes from Mrs Rodder; please thank her for me. Well, Mum, I will now try and answer some of your questions. Firstly, some while back I wrote and said that I had received glasses and letter from the R.P.M. Thanks for news of Norman, but you still don't say what he is working at. 'Dod' and 'Banny' (Les) are still O.K., but I'm afraid Dod and I aren't too friendly these days. Men, I think, are just like women, you have got to live with them to know them. Did Mary (Mrs Banny) ever tell you that she's been married over three years and never had a row with her husband? It's quite true though, but he came abroad a week after being married. It's quite a record I should think. I'm sorry to hear that the vicar is leaving; is he retiring? I was also surprised to hear about Uncle C. I will write Auntie Lyd though this week. Do you ever hear from Pam these days, as we are still keeping up a correspondence, but I honestly could not tell you how serious it is, or will be? Well, I'm still keeping very fit so don't worry about me, just look after yourselves, and remember me to everyone. Keep smiling, your loving son Eric.

30th July 1944
Dear Mum & Dad. Very little news this week so will write a letter next Sunday. I received another 200 Players from you and am expecting No. 6 clothing any day now. I'm still keeping very fit and well, and like yourselves very optimistic about the future. The last letter I received from you was dated 8th May, but there is news of a lot of June mail in the Stalag. Remember me to everyone and excuse me for not writing. Look after yourselves and keep smiling. Your loving son Eric.

6th August 1944
Dear Mum & Dad. I was very pleased to receive your letter of 25th June on Friday to know that you are all still keeping O.K. I have no doubt that Dad is doing a lot of extra work, but I'm sure that he is quite able to cope with it. The picture you referred to was quite correct, but some are more fortunate than others, in as much as they can see both sides. By the way, do you ever hear from 'Al' these days? Do you remember how he always used to come in at one o'clock when it was time for me to go to work? I also had a letter from Pam this week, and although it was rather old, it was very welcome.

Well Mum I'm still keeping very fit and naturally very cheerful, so you have nothing to worry about on my behalf. Also, the same applies to Doug; I guessed that he would have his chance, I only wish I had mine over again. We are still playing football twice every week, and I'm now in unique possession of a pair of football boots. (One of the chaps had a pair sent out, and fortunately for me they happened to be too big for him). Remember me to Mrs Harrison and Heasman, Aunts, Uncles and Cousins etc. also young Norman. Well cheerio for now, and how about looking out for a fatted calf early in the new year? Your loving son Eric.

8th Aug   Sent to Gruby. *(iron ore mine)* E 362.

Chapter 10: The survivor's story

Working Party.
Back 2 rows L-R: Bob Yarrow; Eric Munday; Sam Fotheringham; ?; John Carnie; George Harper; George Frame; Kelman; ?; Charles Doubleday; Les Bannister; ?; ?; Bill Channings; ?; R. Camp; ?; Appleton; Willy Milne; Alf Higgins.
Middle row L-R: Rushworth; John McMahon; Bermondsey Bill; ?; ?; Wright; Alan Graves; John Glendie; Smith.
Front row L-R: R. Palmer; J. Tarpey; Terry Lloyd; ?; Geordie White; Bell; Bird; Gabby McLean; J. Farrell.

8th August 1944
Dear Mum & Dad. I wrote you a letter on the 6th, but since then I have received a letter from Doug, written in April, and also have changed working parties. The news was rather sudden but I have been expecting it for some time, but I will have to tell you about it when I get back. Anyhow, I think it is a change to the good, so don't worry. Remember me to everyone and look after yourselves.
Your loving son Eric.

13th August 1944
Dear Mum & Dad. I've now been a week at the new party, and can't say that I have any regrets for leaving the other one. I'm still keeping very fit and well, and now am just waiting to go out to football. Unfortunately though we only get a game once a fortnight instead of twice a week. Remember me to everyone, and don't worry, as I honestly believe that things are going to sort themselves out very shortly. Your loving son Eric.

22nd August 1944
Dear Mum & Dad. Just a hurried line to let you know that all still goes well. There is nothing of importance to tell you, so will keep a letter that I have for you until such times as there is. I received a letter from you this week dated May 20th, and I'm glad to hear that you are still bearing up. Just keep it up for a little longer, but I quite realise how bad it is at times. So keep smiling.
Your loving son Eric.

29th August 1944
Dear Mum & Dad. Have received no mail this week, but honestly Mum I shan't worry if I don't receive any more, which, with things as they are now seems quite probable, and only to be expected. Anyhow I am still keeping very fit and believe me, I'm going to keep that way. Football is still in full swing, and the weather is warmer than I've ever known it. So look after yourselves and keep smiling.
Your loving son Eric.

19th Sept   German High Command took over R.X. parcels. Gave orders for 2 parcels a week, and stopped all German rations except bread, potatoes and coffee.

26th Sept. 1944
Dear Mum & Dad. I received two letters this week. One from you dated June 11th and the other from Norm. Mail is coming along very well though, considering... I'm still as fit and well as ever and my stomach has been behaving very well ever since last Christmas. The good weather is now finished and tonight we have lit the fire in the room for the first time. The winters here are far more severe than we get at home, but the cold weather doesn't worry me. I also have plenty of

Chapter 10: The survivor's story

warm clothing. If I happen to miss a few weeks in writing you in the near future, do not worry about me as it is only natural to expect at this stage of affairs for everything to be unsettled.

I hope you don't have to go up the top too often these days, and if so, you all look after yourselves. Give my love to all at Ganville, and everyone else. How are the Saunders family keeping these days? I dare say Mary and Jim are quite grown up now! Keep smiling and be good. Your loving son Eric.

1st Oct   Sent away from Mehr Aussee. Owing to the men being moved to a new lager. Was supposed to go to Krackersdorf E 337, but owing to there being no room in that lager for us, we slept at Knappeks and worked at the Wenkestate. This lasted 2 weeks. Then back to the Schact (Adolph) for 6 weeks. After that they were rather tired of us and decided that they would send us back to Lamsdorf. Knappek then decided that we should again work for him. As far as principle goes this looks bad, especially after being once <u>sent</u> away. Anyhow up to now (Xmas) things have turned out OK.

8th Oct. 1944
Dear Mum & Dad. I did not write you last Sunday as I have once again been moving about, but at the moment I am quite settled. Was very pleased to receive your letter of Sept. 3rd as it only took 21 days to reach me. Also one from Aunty D. written June 9th, please thank her and say I will drop her a line next week. It appears from your letter that by the time you receive this, things will be back to normal. Do not worry too much about the parcels being stopped, it's only to be expected, but believe me I have enough kit to see me through. Cigarettes, mind you, are a different question, but it won't trouble me so much now, as it would have done a few months ago, as I have cut my smoking down to a few a day. Well Mum, I'm afraid this is a very uninteresting letter, but honestly there is not anything fresh that I can tell you. The main thing is though that I am still keeping very fit and well and have once again started getting some decent football. Remember me to Ron and Doug and tell Norman to start buying himself some clothes, as we shall probably be needing ours shortly. Look after yourself Mum and keep smiling. Your loving son Eric.

8th October 1944 (Received in Stalag 344)
My dearest son. I know dear, you do understand I cannot send you a card or anything for Xmas, but dear, should you <u>not</u> be with us at 19, do, my dear, remember you will be in my thoughts all day, just hoping & praying it will not be very long before we are all united again. I shall go to Communion as I always have done, dear, & should you, Ron & Doug still be away on the 25th Dec, we shall spend it on our own & celebrate as soon as you all arrive. You

know only too well what my thoughts & wishes will be dear, so here's to you my dear. Good luck, good wishes, health & a speedy return home. God bless you & keep you safe. Your ever loving Mother.

I cannot send a message grand,
But you, my thoughts will understand.
May every day bring fresh good cheer,
And keep our hearts forever near.
The thoughts are not sent in vain;
Tomorrow, sun will shine again,
And mother's love through the days to be,
Will comfort you, & gladden me.

Mum.

Keep this Eric dear for Xmas morn. Xmas greetings:- Dad & brothers Ron, Douglas & Norman.

22nd Oct. 1944
Dear Mum & Dad. I was very happy to hear from you after a lapse in the mail of several weeks, also this week parcels started again and I received the July clothing parcel, containing boots and leather. The April one should be along any time now, also cigarettes so don't worry. No need for me to say that the contents were all very welcome, and each article appreciated. Your letters were dated the 14th and 24th Aug. and I was glad to hear that you had been away for a short holiday; I hope you enjoyed it! Your letters now seem very optimistic about your future, and I can only hope you are right, but please, whatever you do don't fix on any certain time or date as disappointments of that nature are worse than anything. Just have a little patience for a little while longer and I'll be ringing 1885 and you'll be wondering whose voice it is. I'm doing some different work at the moment, but I'm still keeping very fit and well and getting some good football... Well, look after yourselves and keep smiling. Your loving son Eric.

22nd Oct. 1944
Dear Mum & Dad. Don't be too shocked, but I wrote you a letter today and forgot the most important item of news and that is that I have today sent you another remittance of £50. I have sent it home in your name Mum, and I mean you to get yourself something. By the way I never seem to say much about young Norm, so you had better get him something as well. I hope he is now quite well? Keep smiling. Your loving son Eric.

Chapter 10: The survivor's story

29th Oct. 1944
Dear Mum & Dad. I thought I had better look round for a spare letter this week for you as I have received 14; one from Eileen, one from Aunty D and twelve from you including one from Dad and one from Norm. The dates ranged from July 18th to Sept. 29. I also received three cigarette parcels, 200 from yourself, 200 from Len Funnell and 500 from the S.R. They were all Players Medium, and so considering all things, I've had a very good week. On the 22nd Oct. I sent you another remittance of £50 via the Regimental Paymaster, so if you don't hear from him in about 3 months, perhaps you would drop him a line. Remember me to Ron and Doug when you write, but tell Ron that I'm afraid I've lost nearly all interest in dancing, but I would like to get into some good football with him, if he's still interested. It was very decent of you to say that the football photo was O.K. but personally I thought it b____ awful. There's no need to soft soap me too much you know! Well Mum, remember me to everyone, and tell Mary (Mrs Bannister) that Les is still keeping very fit. Look after yourselves and don't worry about me if the mail gets delayed a bit in the near future. Keep smiling. Your loving son Eric.

11th November 1944 (Received in Stalag 344)
My dear Eric. My mind today dear has been with you all day. Do you remember Nov 11th 42, the day we went over to Scotts in that dreadful fog? It is also nearly 2 yrs since I have seen you but I am living, longing & praying that it will not be another 2 months before I see you Eric. Promise me to keep that chin up; I am dear, and really getting ready for our reunion. I quite understand you are not receiving parcels etc. as you were. That naturally worries me, but I understand Red X parcels have started again, so dear, for my sake, be brave as I know you always have been. Your mail to us is also held up - but hoping any post. Dad, Norm & I well; be here for Xmas, we are not going out at all. I feel much better at home until we can all celebrate together. Ron & Doug are both very well last time they wrote. What a day that will be my dear, when you all meet. Norm gets very lonely sometimes without you all; he is writing you tomorrow dear... Eric, my dear, you know I cannot send for Dec 12th, but you know what my birthday wishes to you were just what I pray for daily & hourly. Dad & Norman are both well apart from cold. Keep your promise that you will look after yourself until I can dear, so goodnight, my dearest son, & may God bless you & protect you. Your loving Mother.

12th November 1944
Dear Mum & Dad. Received this week your letter of Sept 15th and 5 parcels. From the S.R. 500 cigs, 1lb tobacco and two lots of books; and 200 cigs from Len Funnell. You can see by this that everything is still O.K. I had a letter from Pam this morning, and she tells me of the good time she is having with you, although from what I hear you had better look after 'young' Norman for me? Be good and look after yourselves. Your loving son Eric.

This letter formed part of undelivered mails which fell into the hands of the Allied forces in Germany. It is undeliverable as addressed, and is therefore returned to you.

15th November 1944
From: E. Uzzell, Welfare Officer, Southern Railway, Waterloo Station, London S.E.1
R.205

Dear Munday,

I hope arrival of this will allay possible anxiety as to whereabouts of our letters. We have been "barred" in preference for n.o.k. to ease the crush under circumstances of the push which has been for the benefit of all.

You will be well primed with all the news, and that preparedness therefore was cause for the hang-up in parcels also.

Last personal parcels were sent you on 13/7, 6/4. Sorry we have not been able to continue with monthly supplies of tobacco and cigarettes since those sent in June. Am optimistic enough to hope to resume soon by a quicker route.

This November is a disappointment to everyone as we all hoped against hope to see "Finis" on the wall. Any rate, we are getting through all right, never fear. Continue this:- "Live one day at a time, and if today is hard for you, remember that tomorrow may bring you a big surprise."

We are not receiving p.o.w. post - a few cards trickle through now and again. Reason appreciated, as I'm sure you are writing.

Now good lad, this must surely be the last Xmas without much in the way of nuts or Peace and Plenty, so here's hoping you will be home in less than a twelve-month. For this festive season - and I'll wager you will make it as gay as possible in your own inventive way - we extend every good wish, and hopes too that next year will really be the best ever.

Remember we all lift our glasses to you at 1.30 Xmas Day - Southern Railway time - so Good Health and Good Luck.

Keep me advised of any changed address.

Last card received from you 6/7. Hope games helped to pass an hour or two pleasantly.

Always yours sincerely,
E. Uzzell

Chapter 10: The survivor's story

19th November 1944
Dear Mum & Dad. I received an old letter from you this morning dated July 1st and also one from Mollie 18th Aug. containing a photograph of herself. She appears to be a very decent sort of girl, but somewhat older than I at first imagined, but of course it's very difficult to tell from a head and shoulders snap. Her people are all very well and she will be writing you. You might Mum, mention this to Pam as she may have forgotten that for the past 2 years she has been going to send one. Just drop a hint will you. I wasn't surprised to hear that Mary is in the Land Army. I should imagine it suits her down to the ground. Remember me to all at 17 as I always forget to mention them in my letters. Also Mr Ward.

I haven't given up all hope of meeting Ken over here but at the present the chances are very small owing to him now being attached to another camp. Well Mum, I am still keeping very fit, and still managing to get a game of football at the weekends although shortly we shall have to stop for a few weeks while the snow is about. Look after yourselves and don't whatever you do worry about me, just keep 'plodding' along, for a little while longer. Remember me to everyone and keep smiling. Your loving son Eric.

26th November 1944
Dear Mum & Dad. This week I received your letter of Oct. 8th containing Xmas Greetings. I'm sure there is no need for me to say that I wish you all the very best and as happy a time as you can get under the circumstances. Don't though worry about me as I shall be quite happy and contented, and although there won't be the usual turkey, we shan't be lacking for good things to eat. Thanks to the Red X. Your loving son Eric.

3rd December 1944
Dear Mum & Dad. I only received a letter from Pam this week, but I trust you are all keeping well, as personally I am feeling very fit and in the best of health. Was Ron one of the lucky ones to get leave? He certainly deserves it in my estimation. Tell Doug to keep his eyes open for me, I don't think I've altered a great deal. Cheerio for now Mum and keep smiling. Your loving son Eric.

10th December 1944
Dear Mum & Dad. I received three letters from you this morning dated 5, 16, 22nd Oct. and one from Pam 2nd Sept. Excuse this letter being a little disjointed, but I'm feeling very tired. We have just finished playing two games of football for a shield. We won the first 6-1, but unfortunately lost the final 5-1. The lads were rather downhearted, as truthfully speaking, we should have won, but as Banny said to me of their lads 'It's easy to smile when you win but a hell of a lot harder when you lose.' Reading the last bit through, it doesn't seem to sound right, but I hope you gather my meaning.

Was glad to hear the good news re. Auntie D. but think it a little premature as yet to send my blessings but think it best to wait until the 'goods are delivered'!! By the way, what have they been doing in Blighty since I left that you are so sure it will be a male? Why the sudden move to Brighton? I should have thought they would have seen the war out, but then, I don't know all the details, and therefore in no position to judge.

Will you please send Norman Bear's P.O.W. No. and then I may be able to contact him. Cheerio for now and look after yourselves, and don't whatever you do worry about me. Your loving son Eric.

17th December 1944
Dear Mum & Dad. By the time you receive this Xmas and the New Year will be over, and so I hope you have all enjoyed yourselves. We are all looking forward to the holidays and I assure you we have plenty of everything with which to satisfy our wants. Remember me to everyone when you see them, and whatever you do look after yourselves. Cheerio for now and keep smiling. Your loving son Eric.

25th December 1944
Dear Mum & Dad. It seems a strange day to be writing letters, but as I have several things to ask you about and because the post goes away in the morning I thought I would break away from the festivities and pen these few words.
I have received six letters from you this week (including one from Dad). The dates ranging from the 7th Aug. to the 6th Nov. Now Mum, to quote a part of your letter for Oct 12th. "Now dear, your B.B. to date is £254.7.0, now at the S.R. I am being stopped 7/- a wk. as the R.E. are now getting that so Dad said if possible you could through your P. Master send along a cheque, he said you would understand." Do you remember writing this? Now to start with, don't think I'm worrying about money, because nothing is further from my thoughts, but from what I can see, I am in debt to the S.R. to the tune of 7/- each week. Therefore I must be drawing something like £3.10.0 to £4 each week. That is, at least 10/- or more per day. This Mum I think is impossible. Also how is the 7/- made up? Perhaps though there is some simple explanation, and I have understood you wrongly.

Well Mum, we are having quite a merry Christmas, and it only lacks the home and female element to make it complete, so I'll just have another one, and wish that we all have it together next year. Keep smiling. Your loving son Eric.

***

1945

This letter has been returned by the Swiss Post Office who were unable to reforward it to Germany because of the interruption of communications.

Chapter 10: The survivor's story

3rd March 1945
My dearest Eric. Still no news of you my dear. But as you know dear, I am hoping any post now, & as long, dear, as I can get news that you are well, I can bear anything. We have naturally wondered & thought all kinds of things, but in our prayers there is just one thing we want to hear, and that, my dear boy, you know only too well without my telling you. Mrs Harrison & I went to our P.O.W. meeting today, & we came back very much happier than we went, as they gave us some comforting news re. 344 & VIIIB, so we are just praying it is so. My prayers are with you day and night, Eric dear. Do please remember this for me, & do try hard to keep that chin up as you have always so nobly done. M. Bannister is phoning me Monday; naturally my dear, like myself, she is very worried, but we do cheer one another up when we can. We do hope that you and Les are together. Pam came down to tea today. She is quite well. Had a letter from B. Channings. He is now M. East & he still seems very well & said he left ____ Jan 15. Mrs H. last card was dated Dec 17th, yours 25 Dec, so you see, dear, how we are all feeling. Aunt M. & Uncle Jack came over last night. Alex is getting married in Sep. all being well. Ron & Doug both are very well, also Sid. G. also has been up today. Norman & Dad both send their love to you, & wish you God speed home, & let the day be very near. God bless you & keep you safe. Goodnight my dear, & God's blessings. Your loving Mother.

Good Friday (postmark 31st March 1945)
Well my dearest, as you will gather from my letter, still no news of you my dear, but Eric, my dear, as I had faith & hope early 43, so I have now that all is well with you & may God hasten the day of our reunion. I am just living & praying for that day, which I feel will not be long now. But you know, dear, if only I could get a few words in your own handwriting, I could rest contented, but I do know you will let me have word as soon as it is possible. Keep an eye open for Doug, as he tells me he is in your country & have scouts out for your no. etc. Ron keeps very well. I shall be going to church after tea to hear the crucifixion, & shall think of you all, not forgetting Ken, Fred, Tom in those happiest days of my life, when you were all in the choir. Dad is busy doing your bedroom out, Norm has gone with Dick & Ken Mott for a hike over to Hedley. Last night I saw Pat Letley & she wished to be remembered to you, & like us all, just waiting to see you. Ann & Jay are getting a little excited now, as their little brother ?? is expected within the next month. Auntie Lely has been very ill, but pleased to say, she is well on the road to recovery. She is still not married. I often wonder if my letters are reaching you. But dear, don't worry about us, just look after yourself. Auntie S. moved last week & the new people are in; very nice indeed, just a young couple with a baby a few months. Well, my dear, let's hope that news from you is on the way. May God help you & look after you. Love from all. Your loving Mother.

SS CERAMIC The Untold Story

From an interview with Eric Munday
26th September 1999

(What was day to day life like as a POW?)
Eric: Not as bad as you might think. We were out on the working party, and we used to work in shifts from about 6 in the morning to about 3 in the afternoon. And then we'd go back and we'd have washing to do, and cooking to do. We used to get Red Cross parcel of clothing, and the Germans supplied bread made out of acorns - not very nice, but that was all they had, it was brown, and beetroot and swede, things like that. But with that coupled with the Red Cross parcels, we were better off than the guards who were looking after us. Because we used to buy stuff off them - eggs for cigarettes. A bar of chocolate would buy you a bag of white flour. A tin of sardines. In the parcels you'd get corned beef, meat loaf... there were two parcels, there was the Canadian red cross parcel, and then there was the British one, and they were different. And they used to mix them up so you got a bit of variety. But you got a bar of chocolate in the English one, and dried milk, tea, corned beef, a packet of biscuits. And what you did, you had a mucker, who you shared your parcels with, so that you got seven meals out of the two parcels. That's what we used to do. So you got a meal every day - of a sort. Oh, and potatoes we used to get from the Germans. *(So they got through to you alright)* Oh, these were from the Red Cross, and the Red Cross used to come and go as they wanted, so there was no problem with the Red Cross. But also, I used to get parcels from home, and cigarettes - that was what we used to barter with - that was our money. The money we used to earn in the factories was what was called 'lagergelt' and didn't buy you anything. Well, cherries, you could buy, in the summer, because all the trees out there were cherry trees lining the roads, so they were quite cheap. Oh and we used to get fruit from the Czechs for cigarettes. You could buy anything for cigarettes! And the Czechs were working in this factory, and they couldn't get cigarettes - well, I think the ration was about three a week. In fact, with our cigarettes we bought a radio, which was hidden, and we used to get all the news! And somebody would write it out and it would be circulated to everybody. We knew the news far better than the Germans did! Because theirs was all censored. They only gave them the good news. The British were like that to some extent, but no, we had all the news we wanted. We knew what was happening. Churchill kept saying that the war would be over by Christmas - but he never said which Christmas! We used to keep quite cheerful really. We used to play football, and they allowed us to do all sorts of things, like concerts. In the big camps, you could take any subject at night school. Any subject you could think of there was somebody there who could teach it. I played in a football team, and I was the only person who wasn't a professional footballer! We used to play other camps. In the end, we even talked them into us taking our washing down to a woman in another village, and she used to do our washing for us, and we used to pay her! *(What, in cigarettes?)* Well, I don't know

Chapter 10: The survivor's story

what we used to pay her - she could take this lagergelt, and she could swap it there for something else. She was happy to do it anyway, I suppose the blokes used to take things down like a bar of chocolate now and again. I remember I was on that party that used to walk down with the washing, because it got you out, and we used to pass by this old village pub, and we talked the guard into letting us in there. We said 'we won't come in there with you, you buy it, and we'll wait outside'. And it became a regular treat for us. And then we found that they'd got a pond at the back, and we asked them is they'd let us swim in it. So you'd gradually build up confidence with the guards especially, they didn't want to upset anybody, because we used to say, you know, if you don't do this we shall report you, and then you'll be sent to the Russian camp. And that was like a death message: they didn't like the Russian camp at all. A lot of the guards were old men. They were too old to be sent to the front. Or they were wounded soldiers, or, if you had six or more children they didn't send you to the front.

(So there was no desire to escape?)
Eric: It wasn't much use to escape. Where I was, there were people there who had never seen the sea, so it was a long way to go. There were lots of blokes who escaped, but just through sheer monotony. They took a chance of being shot. They certainly lost all their possessions that they'd accumulated. Some of those were quite precious: but they still liked a challenge. We moved into a new stalag we used to call it, but it housed about 40 to 50 others, and there were many who escaped from there - they used to go out and come back! Well, you don't worry when you're 21 like you do when you're 51, 71 or whatever you are. I think my mother used to think I was walking around all day with my head down and worried out of my life, we weren't really. Even towards the end, when we knew the war was over - that was the trickiest part of all, because, you know, all the partisans at work in there - the Russian prisoners of war escaped, and they were as mad as a fruit cake. It was an odd time then. And the Germans didn't know where to go. They were saying things to us, hoping that we would take them through to the West.

5th May   Saturday. Left Sternberg 9am. (Russians arr. 4pm). Trouble with D.E. over horses. Arrived Stentzendorf 4pm.

6th May   Dep 6am with horse. Rained all day. Slept in Gasthaus at Hahenstadt. More or less free. 6 men left us inc. Pat, Jim, Mack.

7th May   Bad start. Rain and had to pull our wagon. Steep hills. 5 kms outside H. the whole party split up, including Postens. W. *(Willy, cook)* Banny *(Sergeant)* and self kept together. Met up with Jarrow. Pretty hard march. Gaulich 6 pm. Were told by several officers that we were free. Had a good booze up with a Pole, and stayed the night.

SS CERAMIC The Untold Story

8th May   Away early making for Koniggrestz. Met Swill, Sam, Jim and John. Good weather and everyone in high spirits except Willy whose feet are pretty bad. We decided not to go to Konignetz but to go into the Protectorate. Arrived Garble 11am. Put the cart on a coal wagon of a train that was said to be going to Konignetz. Very slow going and very warm. Left the train at Kysperk. Royal welcome, first Englanders in the town. Bags of food and everything. We were asked to go and stay in Schloss with the Baron and Baroness Van Schnehen and the Countess Van Studenberg. Heard Churchill at 3 pm and the King at 9 pm. Out of Gefangnerchaft into a Palace. We have a wonderful bed, almost too good to get into. We must move on though as we are all itching to get on the move.

Eric Munday 24th October 2005
We arrived in Kysperk on the 9th May 1945, a small town with a railway station on the Sudetanland border. We arrived on a coal tender and decided that the train was too slow for our needs. We still pulled our wooden truck and made for the village centre where we were offered such hospitality it was difficult to believe. A large kitchen in what we thought was the town hall had been fitted out and a very large pot of soup was on the boil. We realised that the soup was for the "locals" but was mainly stolen by the Russians.

We were asked by a very smart gentleman if we would follow him to the Schloss (Castle) where the Baron and Baroness Von Schnehen asked us to stay until we were all in a fit state to travel.

The hospitality was such that it is difficult to compare, living in a POW hut with a castle having a swimming pool and stables for a number of horses. Our group now numbered about 10 from working party E338.

We had an excellent meal and then went to bed. Before going to sleep we were told that Winston Churchill was about to broadcast to officially tell everyone that the war was over.

We all slept well and the following day made ourselves known to the Mayor of the town and to the troops of the Russian Army. They were still fighting as were small pockets of SS troops in Prague. The POWs were however all enjoying ourselves but soon discovered that our money had no use…

9th May   4 am. S.S. troops started firing against partisans in the square. First Russian troops entered Kysperk 10 am. 4 killed. A little fierce fighting. Now 47 in Schloss. Met Olga and Cicilia.

Chapter 10: The survivor's story

Liberated and on the way home, May 1945.
Photos courtesy of Eric Munday.

Eric above left; below second from left.

Eric above second from left.
Below: behind inflatable.

Liberated POWs at the castle of Baron & Baroness von Schnehen.

10th May   Still a little local activity. Czechs very friendly. Burgamaster arranged for ration cards and cigarettes.

11th May   Bought wreath and asked to attend funeral of 4 Russians. At 5 pm the lads decided to leave for Prague but at the last Banny and I decided to stop until things were a little more settled. There are now only 12 left. Another 5 went 17th May.

12-21 May   Best 2 weeks holiday ever. Our hosts have become attached to us and have asked us to see the summer out. We have the freedom of the castle. Plenty of good food and drinks. Swimming, horse riding, dancing, bridge and above all good company and days of laziness just lying in the sun. We all feel sure that no one at home begrudges us this holiday.

Eric Munday 24th October 2005
...Each day we had a shampoo, hair cut and our nails attended to. The swimming pool in the Schloss was in use all day. I went horse riding once, only I had a horse that could not resist eating grass regardless of me on the back. The Russian officers came to the castle several times saying that they required the castle for their headquarters. Leslie Bannister told them that we had commandeered the castle on the orders of our Prime Minister Mr. Winston Churchill.

Our time at Kysperk was running out especially as the trains were now running to Prague. We said our goodbyes and promised that when we arrived home we would tell the authorities how well we had been treated by the Czech people, in particular by the Baron and Baroness and their daughter the Countess Van Studenberg. The Count was a POW in England and although we did not actually see him, we did see the people in London, who showed much interest. Leslie Bannister visited a relation of the Count, Lord Powis.

22nd May   Left Kysperk for Prague 13.30 hrs. Met Luska on train and ended up in her brother's flat for drinks and a bed.

23rd May   Prague wonderful city. Met an American pilot in the Ambassador's Hotel who took us to the authorities, Sankey in charge. Arranged transport for the morning. Met very nice people who gave us a film show and dance band concert.

24th May   Left Prague by lorry 11.30am. Reached Yankee lines 10 km from Pilsen 2pm. Straight to aerodrome to await planes.

25th May   Met Alec C. and several other Steinz chaps. Knappek* shot and Steinz** sweeping streets. 35 planes came.

Chapter 10: The survivor's story

From an interview with Eric Munday 26/9/99
* He was the chappy who owned the factory where we were at Sternberg.
** He was at Sternberg. He owned a similar factory where some of our chaps worked.

26th May   Waited all day on drome. Only 12 planes.

27th May   All day on drome. 12 planes.

Eric Munday 24th October 2005
...We waited in Pilsen aerodrome for many days awaiting a plane to London, but in the meantime the American troops looked after us well.

29th May   Left Pilsen by air. 9.10 am. Arrived Reims 11.50 am. Had tea. white bread, cheese, eggs. Bus lorry to half way house. Yankee kit, delousing bath, medical. Good food.

30th May   Left Reims by car 11.30 am. Arr Dunsfold 1 pm. Deloused and something to eat. Lorry to Worthing. New kit, and medical. Pay and documents.

31st May   More pay. Interrogation.

1st June   Home. 11.30 am.

Finio
24th Nov 1942
1st June 1945

***

From an interview with Eric Munday 26/9/99
When we got back to England just outside Worthing, we were briefed by these RAF chaps and they said 'The first thing we're going to do is you're going to be deloused.' And we said 'Well, we're not,' And he was joking - you know he could have got lynched!

***

Chapter 11
Back home

M.O.D. Debriefing
Official statement given by Eric Munday

REPORT OF AN INTERVIEW WITH SAPPER ERIC MUNDAY, R.E.

We sailed from Liverpool during the forenoon of, I think, the 25th November 1942 in convoy O.N.149, bound for St. Helena, Durban and Sydney. We were detached from the convoy on the 2nd or 3rd December, thence proceeding independently as routed. Nothing of incident occurred until 2000 pm the 6th December, 1942 when (in position 40° 30' N, 40° 20' W)* we were hit by a torpedo forward on the starboard side. The weather was fairly calm at the time, but it was very dark with poor visibility. The vessel took a list but her speed did not lessen as the engines were not damaged.

(This position was not given by Munday, but it is an estimate of the "CERAMIC's" position at the time)

2. Almost immediately "action stations" was sounded, but two or three minutes after the first explosion we were struck simultaneously by two torpedoes amidships, again on the starboard side. The engines stopped immediately and the order was given to abandon ship. All three explosions hit deep as there was no visible damage on deck. I was in the lounge and at once made my way to my boat station on the port side. There was a little panic, probably owing to having women and children on board, but it was nothing serious, and quite understandable as it was so very dark that slight confusion was inevitable.

3. I do not know what happened on the starboard side, but probably the starboard boats were damaged, as there were many more people in my boat than were allocated to it, probably many people came over to the first boat they could find. There were over 50 people in the boat, which was obviously far too many for safety. The boat was lowered successfully, however, and we managed to get away from the ship's side after a struggle.

I think at least 6 or 8 boats were able to get away safely, also numerous rafts. The vessel was not sinking rapidly, and although I did not actually see her sink, I learned later from a midshipman in the U-boat which picked me up that it was 3 hours before she finally disappeared.

Chapter 11: Back home

4. We lay to for the rest of the night, keeping the boat head to sea, as it was too crowded to move about in the darkness, also as there were mostly military personnel in the boat nobody knew much about handling it. By daylight a Northerly* gale had sprung up, with storms of rain and sleet, with high confused seas. Huge waves were breaking over the boat, we bailed furiously, but it was impossible to free the boat of water before another wave crashed over, swamping it so that it capsized and we were all thrown into the water. After a struggle the boat was right, but it was three-quarters full of water; two or three men climbed in and tried to bail it out, but again it was capsized by the huge waves. It was then about 0800 on the 7th, and I decided to swim off. I found some wreckage and clung to that for a little while, but the seas were too strong and it was washed away. I was wearing my life jacket over my battle-dress and did not notice the cold.

5. About four hours after swimming away from the boat, at noon on the 7th December, I was picked up by the submarine. She had surfaced to look for the Captain, but being unsuccessful, and seeing me nearby in the water, I was hauled on board. I do not know the number of the U-boat but I believe the Captain was a Lieutenant Commander named Henke. I did not actually hear his name mentioned whilst I was on board. I was treated well on the whole; several of the crew could speak English fairly well, in particular a young Midshipman, who told me that a number of boats and rafts were seen to leave the ship and that the vessel took about 3 hours to sink. I am of the opinion that the weather was so bad when the storm blew up during the early hours of the 7th December, that no boat could have survived, and this accounts for the great loss of life.

6. The German Midshipman told me about a fortnight before the CERAMIC was sunk, the U-boat had torpedoed a British cruiser. A Destroyer had come to the rescue of her crew, and whilst survivors were being picked up the submarine torpedoed her also. I heard no other reports of any merchant ships being sunk by the submarine on this cruise, which had lasted about a month when the CERAMIC was sunk.

7. We arrived at Lorient on the 6th January, 1943 in company with a Flotilla of U-boats. During the return voyage to that port we were attacked once by Sunderland Flying-boats but no damage was sustained. On arriving at Lorient I met several Army and Air Force officers, also a Merchant Captain, all of whom had been picked up by other U-boats. We were asked if we would like to give our names and addresses, together with the name of our respective ships, so that this information could be broadcast and our relatives thus learn that we were safe. We all agreed to do this; I did not actually broadcast myself, and the German Ministry of Information report to this effect, is not true. I was sent to Stalag 8B in Upper Silesia, remaining there until liberated. The treatment was quite good at this Camp.

From an interview with Eric Munday
26 September 1999

(Looking at transcript of Eric's diary)

Eric: I didn't say much! I did read it and I thought, the day I came home, I just wrote first of June, home, 11.30am! And I didn't say anything.

(Clare: What was it like when you came home?)

Eric: Well, on the day I came home the first thing I couldn't get over was that my father and his friend of his were at the station to meet me. I said 'I hope you haven't been standing there all night!' But it turned out that they had phoned a number in Victoria to find out what time this troop carrier was coming into Victoria. And the friend of my father who came up was only a little chap, but he insisted on carrying my kit bag! And he struggled up the road with it! And I remember my mother making a fuss. And I was expecting, I suppose, to have roast beef and yorkshire pudding and things like that - and it was a piece of boiled fish! And I've never told my mother, but I suppose I was a bit disappointed! And then, I couldn't think what to do next, what to do or where to go, and I was relieved because Les Bannister phoned, and he said 'Come over and rescue me! I'm besieged - they want to have a party in the street for me here!' And that was my excuse to get out of the house and go and see him. I'd only left him about 24 hours.

(Clare: Was it hard to slot back into everyday life?)

Eric: I suppose so but then, hardly a day went by when somebody didn't come home who I knew. In fact, Ken Harrison who I knew and who was also a POW in the Stalag, he was home before me and he used to come round to my mother's, to her home, every day to see if there was any news, you know, when and if, so he was on the doorstep. Of course, he and I had a lot to talk about. I went to school with him, and choirboys with him, and then he was in the Territorials... (Clare: was he the one who was in the same camp, who you tried to meet?) Eric: I never did. In the end, I used to write to my mother and she used to write to him. Because you weren't allowed to use the German post. He never got any of the letters. We did try to meet - I tried to get back to the Stalag at a certain time on some excuse and he would do the same, but in the end we sort of gave up. But I used to get messages from my mother. But he was in Poland - coal mine.

(Clare: I was surprised that you say not a year goes by without hearing from someone who is seeking information about the Ceramic)

After I first came home it was very busy, you know, every day, every post. But gradually it died down, but it's never really stopped. There's at least one a year.

Chapter 11: Back home

Daily Express
15th October 1945

Mystery of liner sinking cleared after 3 years
BY THE ONE SURVIVOR

Sapper Eric Alfred Munday, aged 24, is back in his home in Foulsham Road, Thornton Heath, Surrey – and he has brought with him the first full story of a three-year-old war mystery – the sinking of the British liner Ceramic in the Atlantic.

The 18,000-ton Ceramic, former luxury ship on the Australian run, set out for Capetown from Britain on November 26, 1942, with 656 men, women and children on board.

She went down off the Azores. For ten months relatives of the passengers heard nothing. Then the loss of the ship was admitted in Capetown.

In the House of Commons, the First Lord of the Admiralty said she was not in convoy, but was "a fast, independent ship." That was all.

Sapper Munday was the only survivor of the Ceramic. Yesterday he told me the story of her last voyage.

Captain H. C. Elford had taken the ship through the Atlantic before. He knew what the dangers were in that winter of 1942. And he protested to the authorities against taking women and children on board. But 155, including 50 British nurses, were in the ship when she left Britain.

On the night of December 6, three torpedoes hit her. She remained afloat for three hours. Everyone on board was got into boats or rafts.

At dawn a storm broke. The boats were scattered. Many sank.

Munday's boat, with 40 in it, capsized. He and six other soldiers clung to it. The rest were swept away.

Four hours later the U-boat surfaced near them. A rope was thrown to them but the boat was swept by a heavy sea. Only Munday was able to grab it, and he was hauled aboard.

"I pleaded with the U-boat commander, Captain Henke, to save the other six men who were still clinging to the overturned lifeboat." said Munday. "He refused."

The U-boat submerged. Munday saw no more survivors of the Ceramic. The next two and a half years he spent in a prison camp.

Since he came back, Sapper Munday has made contact with scores of relatives of those who sailed in the Ceramic, and who have waited three years to know exactly what happened.

The following extracts are from letters received either by Eric's parents when news of his rescue reached the press, or by Eric in the immediate aftermath of his return to England. Out of respect, names are omitted. They are included in this book as an illustration of the human cost of the loss of the Ceramic, and the desperation of relatives for news that they could not get from the authorities. Eric has replied to every letter he has received since his rescue. It is intended that this book will now fulfil that role, and that relatives will find the answers they are seeking in its pages.

As you are the only survivor known, who was rescued from the Ceramic, I am writing to know if you can give me any further information, than that received from the Admiralty.

My husband, Cpl. J..., sailed on the Ceramic, & like the hundreds of other relatives of men who were aboard her, I am very anxious for every little bit of news it is possible to get. Perhaps you knew my husband personally, & could tell me if you saw him leave the boat.

If you can give me any information at all, I can assure you that I shall be most grateful.

****

I am writing this letter to enquire of your son Eric Munday who was one of the survivors of the TSS Ceramic which was torpedoed on Dec 6 or 7 1942. My Nephew was Ordinary Seaman on that vessel and if your Son has returned could he tell me if there was any more survivors of that vessel or does he think that any more would be in Japanese hands.

I would be very glad if you could give me any information or where I could apply for the same. Excuse me writing to you but I have just found cutting out of the paper I would be glad of a answer or any information.

****

I almost imagine that you are tired of receiving letters of this nature but I am writing this hoping that you are thinking "One more will not make any difference".

Before me, I have an old newspaper giving the account of your son's escape from death. Believe me when I read it I thanked God that at least his family were rid of

Chapter 11: Back home

all the worry & anxiety which follows such news. You see my husband too was on this boat, so I do know just what suffering it entails.

Since I have not had any more news of my dear husband I am plucking up courage to face a new life without him, & I feel if I really knew the facts of this catastrophe I could settle down & make the best of things.

All this time I have waited, prayed & believed that he was somewhere in Germany, but since all the prisoners have been released I have lost faith…

****

After a very long & disturbed night I sit down to thank you for your very kind letter. It is indeed very good of you to bother about us less fortunate than yourself.

In my mind I have always pictured my loved one struggling in a stormy sea straight away. It is a great comfort to know that it was calm when the awful moment came, I think at least he & the others would not get such a shock at first.

I shall be more than grateful if you would get in touch with me should you hear any more. My heart is full this morning which prevents me from writing any more. But let me on behalf of my family & myself say "Thankyou".

****

My only & much loved daughter was on the "Ceramic" Miss … & I am wondering & hoping if you could give me any information about her & other passengers.

The only information that I have had is from the Admiralty that my daughter is among the missing & that was on 4/1/43. There was a rumour that sailors that had landed at a S. African port had said that many passengers were picked up - & were handed over to the Japanese & then landed on some Pacific Island. Some time back the Red Cross sent me addresses of men in the Navy who were P.O.W. in "OSAKA" camp in Japan & told me to write to them - I did but have had no reply. I will be so very grateful to you if you will let me have all the information you can about the disaster. I have never given up hope that my daughter & other passengers may be safe somewhere & their whereabouts only found after the war. How thankful your family must be at your safe return. Hoping to hear from you soon.

****

...It appears that a report has been circulated in South Africa that a certain number of the passengers were taken prisoner and conveyed to Japan, and naturally it is hoped that ... may be among them. There has never been official confirmation of this report, which on the face of it seems to be rather unlikely; but you can imagine that it would be of great interest to the family if they could get into touch with somebody who could give first hand account of what happened.

****

We were very glad to receive your letter of the 29th August and to learn that you had written direct to ... giving her some of the details of the sinking of the S.S. Ceramic. We also read your account of the sinking as published in the South African press.

Unfortunately, ... seems unable to resign herself to the loss of her daughter and we feel that having heard direct from you may perhaps convince her that there is now little hope of there being other survivors.

****

...My Dear Boy was our all I feel I haven't got nothing to look for now. It has worried me & his father to death so hoping you are both well & thanking you again for your great kindness.

****

I hope you will forgive me writing to you, as I know you must be sick and tired of answering letters about the Ceramic, but I saw your account in the Daily Express and wondered whether you could tell me anything about my son and his wife who were on that ship. They were going to Tristan-Da-Cuna the loneliest island in the world, but were calling at Capetown first. He managed to write me one letter which he wrote on board ship I think as he put his cabin number under the flap of the envelope, which was .... He was in the Navy ... picked for special duty, I believe there were only 5 in his outfit going with their wives and children. My son was 28 and his wife 21 they had only been married 14 months and were thrilled at the prospect of going abroad. He was my only son, the other boy being drowned whilst returning home from school. My son was Champion Athlete at Brecon College so could swim, but his wife could not and hated the water. What I wanted to ask you was, I have seen a letter from a Captain of another ship saying he knew of 7 survivors, and that the 2nd Engineer was on his ship and he was a survivor of Ceramic. Do you yourself think there is any hope at all? My two brothers were killed in the last war, so I really think we have had enough of war to last us a lifetime. What I can't understand is why the news was never released

Chapter 11: Back home

from here, it never has been only from Cape Town. I enclose my son's photo taken with his wife, there might be a faint chance that you may have seen him. I enclose also stamped envelope for return as its the only one I have of them. I do hope you will be able to answer this letter. Why don't the Admiralty tell us the truth about the ship, while the war was on we quite understood it was impossible to release news, but I do think they should do so now. Once again sorry for troubling you, but I felt I had to write.

****

No doubt by now you will be tired of receiving such letters as mine. I am writing to you in the hope that you can give us some news of my brother, ... was lost at sea on the same date that the 'Ceramic' was lost, and although the War Office have given us no definite news, we have reason to believe that he was on the "Ceramic". I am enclosing his photograph, hoping that if you didn't know him by name, you will recognise his face.

Will you please let us have the photograph back, because it is the only one which we have, and, on my mother's behalf, we shall be ever grateful if you can give us some news of him.

****

Thank you very much for your very kind letter. I was hoping I might get a bit more news. I did not have any idea where my husband was bound for, do you think they could have landed in Japanese Hands? The War Office said they did not know the name of the ship he went on but his pal's wife wrote to me saying it was a passenger ship and there were only a few soldiers on it so I wondered if you knew the name by chance.

I wrote to the Red Cross but they could find out nothing. I have been watching the papers for your story as I thought you might have to give an account of what happened.

I am very pleased you are home and hope you are none the worse for your ordeal.

I shall be most grateful if you can pass news of any kind, it is so very hard not to know anything at all, and we keep hoping news will turn up, it is nearly three years since it happened. Thanking you very much.

****

The sinking of the Ceramic was a terrible tragedy for all who had relatives and friends on board. We had a very dear friend on board named ... of the Royal Engineers, he was of medium height and hair almost white. I wonder if your son remembers him & if he could tell us anything about him, whether he was on the same boat as he was that was capsized or not. Any information he could give I should be grateful to have, so that I could pass it on to his brother and sisters.

If your son thinks he remembers him, I could send on a p.c. photograph taken before he sailed, if it would help in identification.

****

I am very grateful to you for giving me what details you could of the sinking of the "Cyramic" (sic) and if by any chance you should hear of any further survivors I should be pleased to hear from you.

By your letter you have certainly helped me draw my own conclusions.

I received your letter yesterday just as we were leaving home to go for our first holiday since 1937, in that year Mother & I spent our holiday at ...'s home, so he is naturally very much in our thoughts at the present time.

I shall send your letter on for his brother to read and ask him to pass it on to other relatives.

****

Despite the fact that I know you are now being kept very very busy writing scores of letters to relatives of those other unfortunate people who sailed on the Ceramic, I venture to ask you if you could give me some news of my uncle who also sailed from England on the same ship.

His name was ... of the Royal Engineers. He was a jovial chappie, rather stockily built, with hair almost snow-white. He was 54 years of age. Perhaps it sounds rather foolish to expect you to bring to mind one man, by my vague description, but the chances are that you may just be able to recollect him by merely having seen him & perhaps not actually knowing, or being sure of his name.

I should be more than grateful to you if you could spare the time to let me know, no matter how briefly, if you have any news at all of my uncle.

****

Chapter 11: Back home

...It was a great consolation to hear from someone who had known & been near to ... during the last few days he was alive. I'm glad too, that you also thought my description of him - "A jovial chappie", was very fitting.

He had lived a very sad & lonely life since soon after the last war, so I know it was no easy task for him to appear so happy & carefree as he always did appear.

Really Mr Munday, I thank you most sincerely in writing to me. I know it wouldn't be easy for you to write of a horror which you want to forget, but you did so in order to help relieve the mind of one who has lost a very dear one. I'm truly grateful.

****

I really am finding it most difficult to adequately convey to you my grateful thanks for writing me, especially as I have no doubt you have many other people to write to, and I know you want to try & forget your terrible experience.

I do so trust that during your captivity the treatment meted out to you was not too harsh & that your health has not suffered.

Please thank your dear mother for her great kindness whenever I have bothered her by phone, but she was so very understanding & consoling in my great grief.

Until your mother told me that the service personnel on board the "Ceramic" were bound for West Africa, I had not the slightest idea of my dear Husband's destination.

****

I was so interested to know a little more about the fate of the "Ceramic" & especially the time & date, as well as its destination. I am sure you will appreciate how anxious I, as well as no doubt all others who lost loved ones, have been to get some first-hand information.

I also was gladdened to hear that during the few days the ship was sailing, all on board had a happy time. It is just a small consolation.

I did try & hope until just after VE Day that my dear husband might have survived, but the small spark of hope has now gone, & I must work as hard as I can to pass my time.

****

...it's true the memory of our loss is painful but through it all we have been hoping for news as we could never understand such a total loss in these days when so many life saving appliances were being carried - so we hoped some might have got to land in some remote spot & eventually bring news of what had happened but I'm afraid those hopes will have to be given up...

I should be grateful to know if you thought there was any chance others to have got away.

****

I expect you must have had hundreds of letters like this and must be very tired of answering them and no doubt want to forget the whole affair. With all those passengers on board, I know it would be a thousand to one chance that you ever came across my friend, but I felt that no harm could be done by writing to you.

His name was ... and he was returning to his home at P... after his training of 5 years in this country. He spent all his holidays with us and it was a very great shock when we heard of his tragic death.

His people are simply heartbroken, as they had looked forward to his homecoming for so long...

I don't suppose there is much you can tell us, apart from what has already appeared in the papers, but I shall be deeply grateful for any information you can give me.

It was a very great tragedy indeed. To think that if the storm had not arisen they might all have been saved.

****

I am most grateful to you for your very prompt reply to my letter. I thought it would be highly improbable that you would have known ..., but I felt that there might just be that chance and so had to write to you. I am forwarding your letter to his mother and I know she will be very grateful to you, as they were told so very little by the Admiralty.

It is very kind indeed of you to offer to get in touch with me if you hear anything further. I'm afraid though that after all this time there is very little hope left, but strange things have happened during this war.

****

Chapter 11: Back home

Later on when you have time could you please fill the envelope I send with his account of the poor "Ceramic". There is no hope we perfectly realise this now for other survivors - but I would like to know the <u>entire</u> truth first hand. This war has hurt so much (our home is still in ... as you know) that nothing will hurt me any more.

****

Thank you so much for your letter. I had very nearly given up all hope of hearing from you, and was afraid maybe as a P.O.W. you were ill or unable to write. Naturally I quite understand the Admiralty wished first to interview you & your letters had to stand over until leave was given you to write. Yes I understand quite well all you write & can picture everything. It was the terrible storm raging when Enterprise & the Portugese destroyer went out to look for survivors that ended the story. Poor poor darlings.

For you & your parents I am so very delighted they have you back. Once again my heart has been torn wide open as our darling son in the Royal Navy was lost only last month in the Pacific Theatre of War after serving on every single front ever since the Wars began... So you see now I know the two devoted brothers are together & did their duty to their last breath in this so called 'Life'. For us there is nothing left... I woke on the Sunday 6th December but it was at night & knew something was very wrong with my son & prayed so hard for you all on that ship. For two months we had no news at all of any disaster, but after Sunday 6th I was not able to walk properly, it was as if I had been blown up by a shell. I was badly concerned.

****

I have received a cutting of the "Daily Express" from my wife today in reference to the sinking of the "Ceramic" which also gives information of you my friend, the man we heard of nearly 3 years ago as being the only survivor, and also one who might give us some definite news of the fate of my brother-in-law ...

I appreciate how impossible it must be for you to know many of the ship's crew but if you have a memory of ... and know something of his final fate I would appreciate your telling me.

I should imagine you must have been piled up with similar queries since back home but am sure you must have been helpful to many, and may you be blessed for all time with the love of God.

****

I must thank you for being so kind as write to me. I must explain it was my niece who wrote to you & she may have made a mistake in the date it was the 19th November my son left home & as far as I imagine it was about the end of Nov he sailed as I had only one letter from him before he sailed & then one off the ship dated on envelope 6th Dec. The news we got was ship torpedoed 6/7 Dec. That was 14th January & then on the 14th August we were notified the ship was torpedoed and sunk & as there was no news from any source about him he must be presumed killed at sea on the 6/7 Dec 1942. We had heard that was the boat he was on, but of course we don't know, but are always trying to look on the bright side. We do hope your son will be spared to come home to you in the best of health. I hope you will not think me too forward in writing to you, but as you are a mother yourself I am sure you will understand my feelings.

****

Having read an article in the eight army news about the loss of Ceramic and that you were the sole survivor I wonder if you could possibly give me any information regarding … whom we think travelled on that boat: Perhaps you could enlighten us as to whether the boat docked any place on the six of Dec as we have a letter from him with that post mark and that's what we can't understand how we received that letter when the ship was attacked on the same day. Have you any idea of your destination, if we could find that out then we would have an idea as to whether he was on that boat or not. I would be most grateful if you could supply me with those particulars and I sincerely hope that you don't think me too forward but I am sure as one soldier to another you will understand our feeling.

****

I am writing to you to ask you If you can tell me anything about my son, who was taking passage on the same ship you was on, the Ceramic, I am his mother who is not the same, through the awful sorrow of his presumed death, he was missing a long time, then was presumed to have lost his life on the Ceramic. I will tell you about him, he was a very bright and happy son always, he was a Sergeant in the Royal Marines in charge of 6 other Royal Marines, he was stationed at the Royal Marine Barracks at Plymouth from being 18 year old, he was married and one baby boy, just over 1 year old when he set sail, his name was …. He was going to Durban Royal Naval College as a P.T.I. to train the troops, he would be about 28 or 29 yr old, his wife has never been the same since the awful news we received, we someway have always felt that he was alive somewhere and have always hoped that we should see him on this earth again his wife would tell you how ideally happy they were, the trouble has altered her a lot she was a lovely young woman, but she has aged of course, I have a letter he wrote to me on the 6th November I read and re read it it is terrible to think that I shall not see him again on this earth

Chapter 11: Back home

it makes one wonder why these things should be, I saw in the paper my younger son had just got, called the War Illustrated, and I cut it out the part saying it could now be told about the Ceramic and how Sapper Munday was the only survivor also your address, as I read it, I thought my son just might have been one of the six clinging to that upturned boat, whom the u boat commander refused to take on board, how dreadful they were to leave people in the water like that. Don't you think if she had been convoyed a lot of people would have been saved...

****

I should be glad of any further information you can give me as to the fate of the people on board. If it was mild at the time of the incident, it would seem possible some would get away on rafts etc. I was to have accompanied my husband, who was going to Capetown to do special work for the Admiralty, but at the last minute my passage was cancelled. I still go on hoping he may be returned to me. He was a first class passenger. I shall be most grateful for your views on this matter. The last report in the paper said 218 had (at least were believed to have lost their lives) and I cannot think it possible that you were the only survivor out of all the lot. My husband could swim, and has travelled all round the world on different ships, and was once shipwrecked off Iceland.

****

I am wondering if you have any further news re the Ceramic. My dear husband was on board, and I am still hoping I may have news. The newspaper reports varied so much from 2 to 3 thousand to 218 believed drowned I never believe only one was saved. My husband was a swimmer and was used to going to sea, and knew exactly how to act in case of emergency. The Shipping Company confirmed to me the ship was in convoy, so in that case the other ships must have rescued some of the passengers.

****

I read an article in the paper today which said you were the only survivor of the liner Ceramic, which was sunk Dec 6-7 1942. My brother ..., was on a ship which was sunk on that date, could you please inform me if you knew anyone of this name on board the ship, or any Corps of Signals troops were aboard the ship at the time of the tragedy.

Thanking you for your trouble will you please reply as soon as possible, it means an awful lot to the whole family.

****

...We have found out from the authorities that my brother was a passenger on the "Ceramic". He was to have been on a ship that went abroad ten weeks before, but as there was some delay in leave, he & some more signalmen had to wait until another boat was sailing to the same destination.

My brother was, as maybe your brothers & sisters may say if you have any, the finest person that ever walked on the face of this earth. He joined the Territorial Army in 1938, and was called up in 1939, on the first day of war, & like you, from that first day he faced many dangers with those Nazi butchers.

He went to France, & was in the battle of Dunkirk, that was a day which in his own words he said he would "never forget", for the majority of his pals were killed on the beaches of Dunkirk.

****

Reference to previous correspondence re loss of Ceramic if your son has now returned Mrs ... would very much like to have a chat with him sometime when quite convenient to him. I think if she can be made to realize the utter futility of hoping any longer for news of our dear one she will be more reconciled to the position.

I myself, who am an old sailor - realized the worse had happened after the German Broadcast.

****

Please forgive me for troubling you with this letter. I know you must have received many more like this, but I feel I must write to ask if it is really true that you were a survivor from the "Ceramic". My husband was the ... of the "Ceramic" and if you could tell me anything about the ship I should be so grateful. Perhaps you would be kind enough to send me a few lines when you can spare the time. Any information at all would be greatly appreciated and I should be very grateful to you for anything you could tell me.

****

You will excuse me writing to you like this, but I happened to see an article in the Daily Express about the Ceramic. As my sister's husband was one of the crew. He was assisting the doctor. His name was ... It is a pretty remote chance, whether you saw him in any of the boats. My sister still maintains that he will come back so perhaps you could let me know whether there is any hope at all.

****

Chapter 11: Back home

I have heard that you were a survivor from the "Ceramic" & that you would be willing to give any information you could about the ship. I had a brother who was a sick bay attendant on the "Ceramic" his name was ... The only information we got was to see in the papers that the German wireless had claimed that they had sunk her on the 6th-7th December & that owing to the heavy seas the loss of life was heavy. Then on New Year's day we got a letter from the shipping company to say that he was missing & then 14 months later another letter to say that he was presumed dead, since then we have heard nothing. If you could give me any information about the ship on that night I would be very grateful.

****

I wrote up to Shaw Savill's some time ago, enquiring for news of 'Ceramic', but they sent me a very nice letter, saying they had been in touch with the Admiralty (had also had an interview with you) but they held out no possible hope of any others being saved. I had always hoped that some news would come from some of the U boat commanders, but apparently this is not to be so. I suppose my Mother told you she was on the Ceramic's previous trip, & only the mercy of God saved her from being on the disasterous (sic) trip. My best wishes to you & many thanks again.

****

Our second boy ... was a ... in the "Ceramic" his first trip to sea & we should be grateful to you if you would kindly give us a call so that we could hear an account of the last few hours of that unlucky ship.

****

I hope you will forgive me for troubling you.but now that I hope your son has been safely returned to this Country I should be grateful if you could tell me if the enclosed report published in the Sunday Express of February 21st 1943 can be considered correct,

My son, who was in the Engineers was a passenger on the 'Ceramic' and the War Office have never been in a position to give me any information beyond the bare statement that he; was "lost at sea"

I have a small estate to settle on behalf of my late son and would feel more resigned and capable of doing so if your son could confirm this report that only one survivor escaped this terrible tragedy.

****

My husband ... was on board the "Ceramic" and I am writing to ask you, if you would be so kind as to let me know whether you have heard any news concerning the last voyage. I do hope that your son has come home with the repatriated prisoners that have arrived in this country recently, and that he is safe and well.

I would be so very grateful if you would ask your son whether he could tell me any news of my husband or any details of the disaster. Also whether he thinks there would be any chance of some survivors being perhaps in Japanese hands.

****

There is just one point that I would like to ask you and that is - were there any other lifeboats full of people and not overturned, within sight of you, when you were picked up by the german submarine?

****

I hope you do not mind me sending you this letter. You see I saw your picture in the paper, and I have been waiting ever since the Ceramic was sunk when I saw your picture then to say you were taken prisoner, and I have looked every night to see if you had arrived home well, and safe to see if you would possibly tell me anything about my husband, ... who was .... I am sending you a small snap of him. It may help you to see if you can remember if you saw him the short while you were both aboard. I would not bother you because it's really not fair after what you have been through. But it would help to soften the blow a bit to know about it from a person who saw it all happen. You see I am left with 2 little girls of 5 and 7 who were both very ill in hospital when the ship sailed, and the younger one was at death's door, and I was sent down to the ship 2 hours before it sailed with a letter from the doctors to get my husband off as they were expecting the child to die any moment. But they would not allow me to go down to the ship, and the last I saw of my husband was when I was waving to him on the top of the ship. Anyhow my child recovered, only to receive the loss of my hubby the day I was bringing young child home as she was fretting for both of us, and a week later my elder child. I myself have never been quite the same since I had all that trouble together. Sorry to tell you all my trouble but it seems to ease a little to tell some one, and I miss him more and more as time goes on, and if he could see (the) children now (they're) a picture after what they have been through. I know you will return my snap and thanking you so much. God bless you for being so kind in answering all these letters.

****

Chapter 11: Back home

I have much to thank you for in your letter of the 8th & though it can throw no light on the tragedy I am indeed thankful that you yourself have survived. While I too echo your final paragraph, I'm afraid there is not any chance of other survivors now. Best wishes to you.

****

I am writing to you wishing you all the Luck in the world after you have got home to see your parents again. I have (been) waiting to see if anyone was saved from the Ceramic because I had a Son in Law aboard of her going to Cape Town. I shall be very much obliged if you can give me any news when being rescued if he were in the same boat or anything about him. His name was ...

****

I have some more news that I thought would interest you. The Captain's sister, Miss Elford rang me the other day stating that the Captain's wife who lives in Finchley wrote and told her about another survivor of the Ceramic. It is a long story.

It appears Mrs Elford went to pay her paper a/c in a shop in Finchley, where she deals. The owner - a lady said she had some news for her. That morning in the Midland bank, she had been talking to a gentleman, who mentioned that his friend's son had been recently repatriated with a lost memory, was from the Ceramic?? Just then the lady was served, & when she looked round to get more particulars, the gentleman in question had got served & left the bank.

Unfortunate, because we do not know if it is from Japan or Germany, this P.O.W. has come from. All he said was - the P.O.W. remembers nothing after the ship sunk - about where he had been, or how he got there.

Up till now Eric has been the only one, although none have lost faith or given up all hope.

It is two yrs & 3 mths now, so where can this other one have been? ...

The 'Ceramic' tragedy broke my heart, I have never been the same. My second son aged 17 yrs went to sea last August. His heart was in it, so I could not be selfish. My only daughter is in the W.R.N.S. & my husband at sea now for 23 yrs, so it is in our family.

****

Have you had any further news of Eric? I thought of you on V.E. Day - like us all you would feel somewhat sad. To us awaiting news - it was not the same. I know what you are enduring & my heart goes out to his Dad & yourself. I cannot understand so many being lost & I hate Doenitz & hope he is brought to trial. I read where he had to be, for giving the order - no survivors to be picked up. We picked their ones up. Germany has at last been brought to her knees & please God we have had our lesson & keep them there.

A few days ago I had a chat with Mrs Elford on the phone - she seems a dear sweet lady, & grieves so much about Captain Elford - to whom she was most devoted. How sad to think he was about to retire for a well earned rest & a little home life, after all those years at sea, & then to be taken like that. Our only hope now I suppose is Japan. I read where both Japs & German Raiders were about at the time of the disaster. Mrs Elford advertised for that repatriate survivor of the Ceramic but no reply.

****

… Thank God you have been spared to return home to your parents safely after your ordeal. At least my prayers in that respect have been answered. We prayed night & day for your safe return, to tell us what really did happen. Your story differs from all the others. I heard you were torpedoed & ship on fire etc. etc. It was a terrible tragedy - the worst of the war - if no others return. The shock nearly killed me - in fact only now am I able to go about as I used to. My Son was only 19 yrs of age - had just got his 2nd Mates Cert. & was a 1st class passenger for Capetown where he had to join a tanker as 3rd Officer for the Shell Oil Co London - same firm as my Husband. Twice before he was a survivor from a tanker torpedoed in the Atlantic & fortunately got away. Before he left home he took a lifeboat cert. etc, so ought to have had all the knowledge required & was a Navigating Officer. However it looks as though the storm beat them all. To me it seems impossible, & I still cling to the slight hope of the Japs having some of them. I don't understand why it has all been so hush-hush, & even yet I feel like telling the Admiralty what I think about it all. I say a disgrace - where was her escort etc?? Women & children should never have been allowed to travel with troops & Naval personnel. Life to them seems nothing, & we are left with our memories. I seem to know you - have talked & written to your parents for a long while now Eric, & only hope you are feeling fit & well now. Please God you will forget your ordeal & enjoy a full happy life. This is my earnest prayer. Thanks once again Eric for the trouble you have taken on my behalf. You must have had hundreds of enquiries. Lots of people in the North lost relatives on the Ceramic. Miss Elford the Captain's sister often rings me up. She was distracted with grief poor soul.

****

Chapter 11: Back home

I was wondering could you give me any information my son ... an Engineer was suppose to be returning home on the Ceramic and I got word telling me he was killed on the sixth of December. I got a cutting from the paper with the notice London Oct 4th only known survivor of about 1500 people aboard the liner Ceramic which disappeared while on a voyage to South Africa is Sapper Eric Munday of Thornton Heath Surrey who is now in a German prison Camp. Part of his story was told in a broadcast from Germany and in letters to his parents. Well I got a cable from my son ... on the 30th of Nov 1942 from P.O.88 Great Britain saying coming home love to all ... Would you tell me the date you left London or when Ceramic left and as I am wondering how I could get cable from him. I also lost my other son on the Mareeba and I went to see his (?) friend and he told me you were in the prison camp in German with him. I was just wondering as I do not think they know them selves as the shipping company seem to be dumb founded my son left here an Engineer on Queen Elizabeth any how I thought I drop you a line and if you ever get this far (?) and call on us and if you could give me any information you would greatly relieve my mind as I think every one is the same. So hoping you are in the best of health and spirits and look after your self and I hope you do not think too hard of me for writing to you.

****

Pardon me troubling you, but I read about you in the Daily Express re your terrible experience on the Ceramic on Dec. 6th 42. I wonder if you had met, or saw anything of ... I knew her very well & she wrote me from Liverpool on Nov 23rd as she sailed on the 26th. She was not very strong, I hate to think of her suffering. If you did not see her on that fateful night, or if you don't know anything about her experience please don't trouble to answer. I apologise once more for troubling you & trust you yourself are well.

****

I have just been reading your experience in the newspaper and hope you will excuse me taking the liberty of writing you but my son ... lost his life at sea on 6th December 1942. He sailed towards the end of November 1942 and I have reason to believe he was on the Ceramic.

The War Office notified me that he lost his life at sea on 6th December 1942 but gave no details and I wonder if by any chance you met him on board and give me any more news.

****

Many thanks for your kindness in letting me know of the happenings of the ill-fated "Ceramic". I know and understand Eric of the Admiralty ways, it would be the same here. I think you have given a wonderful description of the terrible event, which I'm sure must upset you when you look back & think just how lucky you were. It's been a great comfort to me & my poor mother to receive from you yourself, the chosen one as I said in your mother's letter by "God" to be able to tell of the sad event. I read in our papers in Sydney of the bad weather on the Portugal coat at the time in fact I've the cuttings from our own papers.

At that time I had a terrible presentiment that I could not shake off. We had not heard from my poor brother for about 4 weeks, & one of my neighbours came & asked me how I was, I had not been well at that time, & I told her about this presentiment re …, & she said oh don't tell me you are thinking the worst, and for about 10 days I was just helpless & could not shake it off. I knew something was wrong. My neighbour never forgot to this day of my saying. No one would ever credit it was so long long ago as 3 years. Might I ask how you fared as prisoner of war, hope you never met the brutalities like other poor fellows.

****

I hope you will not mind me writing to you, I saw in the Evening News a few weeks ago about your son who was previous "Missing at sea" & is now a Prisoner of War. I experienced the same I was notified by War Office that my eldest son was missing dates they gave 6th or 7th December (at sea) he was in the R.A.M.C. I cannot get any news of him up to now & I have wondered if he was on the same ship as your son. Anyway I felt you might help me if you could. Was the address you had c/o A.P.O. 4230. Draft R.X 0ZY.

My husband has been a prisoner of War in Germany 3 years come May, so you see I've got my lot, like a good many more - 2 sons serving as well. The suspense is terrible, & wishing this terrible war will soon come to an end. I hope & trust your son is keeping well & that you hear from him. I am experiencing the same so can feel for you. Forgive me if I am taking a liberty in writing to you.

****

I hope that your son has got safely home & is fit & well. I am very sorry to trouble him but it would be a great favour to me & to my mother, sister & brother if he would give us some information about the 'Ceramic'. Perhaps you remember that I wrote to you some time ago & told you that my brother, …, was on board & was in charge of 2 little boys. He was going out to S. Rhodesia to take a post as a Medical Officer of Health. We would be glad to know what sort of a journey they had previous to the attack, also on what date the attack took place. A newspaper account some months ago said it was at the end of November but the Shipping Co. told us Dec. 6/7th. I am sure he will know just what to tell us for probably he has had many other requests for the same information, & I am sorry to add to the number. Had I lived nearer I would like to have come & seen him.

****

Knowing what you must have been going through these past few months, I have tried hard not to worry you, but I feel I must ask you if you have heard from your son lately, and to find out whether he has yet arrived in England. When he does arrive in England and has sufficiently recovered his health and strength, perhaps you would be kind enough to let me know anything he can tell you about the sinking of the Ceramic. I am sure you won't mind doing this for me as you understand what it means to us.

****

I hope you won't mind my taking the privilege of writing you, but I feel I know that you will help me. I have wanted to write quite a long time ago but I thought I would wait until the war with Germany was over & that you had got your dear Son safe & well at home again, which I trust is now your happy position. You see we had the dearest son in the world on 'The Ceramic' 21 years of age & it would be a source of great comfort to us to know any details. Was it sunk as the Germans claimed by submarine on the night of Dec 6th or 7th or was there a chance of many survivors. Do please through the medium of your Boy write me Mr Munday giving me what information that you can & I will thank you from the bottom of my heart. I am expecting two of my other Service Boys home within the next fortnight & I would be glad to give them any details. So please Sir at your convenience I will be pleased to hear from you.

****

Many thanks for your very welcome letter. It was a great consolation to us to get the actual details & although remote as the hope seems, it gives us courage to continue hoping. I will write to you at a later date to try & make arrangements to see you. I sincerely hope that you have got over your gruelling experience & are feeling no undue after effects, you have got youth on your side to aid you & that is some consolation to you. It has given my wife & self great comfort to read your letters & I will be for ever grateful to you for your kindness. Wishing you the very best of luck & good fortune in the future.

****

…The news about … is still the same that he will come home again but I must still be patient & content myself with knowing that he is being looked after. A few months ago I got very depressed about him & shed a few tears to myself. The next week Daddy sent a message to me via a medium at Romford church, telling me not to grieve, for all was well with … The medium said he is missing but he hasn't passed on. I always think he is suffering from loss of memory. However there is nothing for it but to patiently wait. I would be much happier about him if Daddy said he is here with me for I think that the ending of the war is only one step in the ladder & that very difficult times lie ahead for us all.

****

I read with much interest your article in the 'Daily Express' regarding the sinking of the British liner "Ceramic" and congratulate you on your miraculous escape.

I had two small nephews on that liner, … and …, 1st class passengers in the care of … and if you can give me any news of them, I shall be forever grateful.

I was very disturbed to read that the liner was not cut in two and "sank like a stone with all on board" as we were given to believe, and I am distressed to read that the poor little darlings may have floundered for hours in the water.

Any news you can give me is anxiously awaited by me and their parent.

****

Many thanks for replying to the letter which my friend wrote to you, re my two nephews It was very kind of you to go to this trouble. Of course you can imagine how anxious I am to receive any information as to what happened to them. I wrote to the Red Cross when the ship was lost & they could give me no news at all & promised to let me know if any information reached them at any time. I have never heard any more.

I thank you very much indeed for promising to let me know should you get any news from the Admiralty.

I did not write myself at first to you, as I didn't want the father of the boys to see the reply in case there was anything in it to upset him too much. He is still very grieved as they were his only two children. They were on their way to … to live with my sister as their mother had died, another sister of mine.

****

Chapter 11: Back home

You will wonder who I am but I happen to pick up this old paper and read about one survivor of a boat sinking in Dec 1942. Well I wish if you were able to ease my mind, my Boy was going out for a second time. He left Nov 20th for North Africa. I got a report missing at sea between 6/7 Dec 1942. After 8 months they presumed him drowned as they said they had received word about the ship from one survivor, who was in Stalag 8B. I thought there was no harm in writing to you, to see if it was the same boat, as it is hard, when you do not know where or when they died. He was ..., was his second time out as he was out in 1939 when war broke out. He was in Egypt. If you can give me any information, if this is the same boat, I will be very much obliged for your kindness.

****

Could you please tell me if my brother ... was on the "Ceramic". He was reported missing at the time of the Ceramic's loss. All we ever got to know was his ship was overdue & must be presumed lost. We never knew the name of his ship. If it will help, he was in the "Maritime Mariners" a gunner I believe. His home is ... His wife & two sons are still there. Sorry to trouble you, because I know you must have had hundreds of letters like this.

****

I am writing to you asking if you could help to give me any information regarding my brother who was on the S.S. Ceramic. I thought maybe your son might be home so I would be very thankful if you could tell me something about the ship. I suppose you must be annoyed with letters with the same question but waiting so long to hear something about the ship if only we knew what really happened to it & how my brother met his death it would relieve me a little. So I hope you will answer this letter as soon as you can.

****

I am writing to you from Australia. I got a letter from Red Cross telling me your Dear Son is the only known survivor of the Ceramic & he is in prison camp in Germany & now the war is over with Germans I thought your Dear Son would be home with you again. My Son, ... was coming home to Australia on the Ceramic. He was in M. Navy. He left Sydney on Queen Elizabeth & was coming home from England on the Ceramic, when she was lost. Would you ask your Dear Son to let me know if there are any more saved. I am nearly mad with worrie (sic). I got a cable from England the day before He sailed to say He was waiting for a boat come home to Australia ...

****

I am quite sure you are heartily sick of receiving letters like this one, & can assure you that I would much rather not write to you. But am doing so on behalf of Mrs ..., of the above address, whose son ... was lost with the Ceramic. Like every other mother she is anxious for any news she can get. If you can give her any news of ... she will be very pleased. He was the only unmarried child she had & was a very good son to her.

****

I take a great pleasure in writing to you, could you give me any information of my youngest son ... who was ... on the Ceramic. Was there any survivors of the ship? If so was he amongst them? I do hope so I've had word that he's gone, but I'm not going to give up hope I can't believe it & won't. If we ever did get any information about him well we'll sure let you no (sic).

****

I presume you are released from Germany & would be very grateful if you could tell me something about the sinking of the Ceramic on which you were sailing. My daughter was a nursing sister on the same vessel & of course has been reported missing presumed killed, but I still feel she may have been taken prisoner although it is a long time ago & I have heard nothing more from the war office.

****

Thank you very much for the nice letter, I still have a hopeful outlook that some good news will come. If you are this way any time I should be very pleased to see you & have a chat, expect you have had very many enquiries from other relatives, & I can say it is comforting to hear from one who knew anything of the disaster.

****

I am sure by now you must have had scores of letters from relatives and friends of passengers in the "Ceramic" but I do hope you will not mind answering one more.

I have already heard from the Red Cross, but should be so grateful if you could let me know if you saw anything of ..., he was on the ship, and his aunt Mrs ... & myself would appreciate any further information you could give.

By the previous account given, we imagined that some of the passengers did not leave the ship, but from what we read in the "Express" the other day I suppose most of the people did get into the boats. I know this must tax your memory very much, but I am sure you appreciate that one wants all the news possible. For ages

Chapter 11: Back home

we just hoped and hoped that if the ship had gone down perhaps there was a chance of some people being picked up, which now is quite impossible I suppose.

...'s description is:- tall (about 6ft) slim, dark hair, hazel eyes, clean shaven.

Thank you in advance for your trouble, and if you cannot write please be assured we shall understand.

****

Please excuse me taking the liberty of writing, but I'm desperately anxious for some news of my husband.

From old newspaper cuttings, I understand your son Eric was the sole survivor of the liner "S.S. Ceramic" and taken prisoner of war. As so many of our boys have been liberated, and I sincerely hope your son is one of them, I should be more than grateful if he could give me any information of my husband ... who was on board the same ship, reported missing and later presumed killed.

****

I find it very difficult to express my appreciation of your extreme kindness in answering my letter regarding my husband. There is very little I can say except to thank you very much. I shall be more than grateful if you will, as you suggest, inform me should you have any further news.

I'm so sorry to have worried you in the first instance, but you see my Husband was my whole life and I'm waiting & praying that by some miracle he will one day come back. Your letter, & newspaper cutting with photograph, are amongst the few items I treasure most. You might have known him.

****

I am writing this letter to find out of my brother ... being lost on the Ceramic, I am quite cut up over it as I miss him very much, and I would be much obliged if you could let me know more about it. He was one of the crew aboard his trade was ..., I am only one of lads myself so hope you can understand my letter as I can't write very much. Well Pal I hope you are O.K. and find a good way in life as I do know you blokes should be helped by the high ups. I am a Liverpool lad myself but I live in Yorks here since being in the R.A.F. Well Pal I hope you write and let me know more about it.

****

I am writing to you against my better judgement, as I realise that it is quite impossible for you to have known personally more than a small percentage of the people who were on the Ceramic, and that in any case, three years is a long time to go on remembering.

Anyway, since I saw the Daily Express on Monday I know I shall not be satisfied until I have written and asked you if you knew my boyfriend, ... who was a cadet on the Ceramic. He was only $17^1/2$, and though I suppose we were a bit young, we had been going out together since we were thirteen. It was only his second ship, and he was really dead keen on the Navy. He wrote to me before he sailed & said he hoped I was not superstitious, as he was in charge of Lifeboat 13! I certainly am superstitious now.

I am afraid you won't be getting much time to yourself on your leave with all these letters to answer, but I am sure it must give a lot of comfort to the relatives to hear from someone who was actually there and really knows what happened. I think the worst part of it was not knowing anything definite, and going on hoping and praying for months, all in vain.

It has helped quite a lot to get that off my chest, and though I don't for a minute expect you to remember ..., I shall be very grateful to you if you have time to answer my letter.

****

After reading in Daily Express yesterday of your experience and capture after the sinking of the Ceramic, I wonder if you can enlighten me any further of what happened that night. I had a nephew on her. He was ... The only word his mother (my sister) received on 31st December 1942, was that the boat was overdue and must be presumed lost with all hands. As he was her only child she collapsed and never recovered. We buried her seven months later. We kept hoping he had been picked up and perhaps taken prisoner, but nothing more was heard. I will be very grateful for any news you may be able to give.

****

In the Daily Express, Monday Oct. 8th, I read your acct. to the papers, of the sinking of the "Ceramic" Nov.-Dec. 1942.

Our eldest son, who was a Civil Engineer, and had an appointment (by the Admiralty) at Simonstown, S.A., was a passenger on this ship.

We learned from the acct. in the papers at that time, that you were the sole

Chapter 11: Back home

survivor, and a P.O.W. in Germany, and I was looking forward to the time when the war would end, and you would return and I might have the chance to see you, and was so thrilled when I saw your acct. in the paper on the 8th. The first acct. said "Sank without trace", but the fact that all were got into the boats puts quite a different light on it. Do you think it possible at all, that some of these might have been picked up later, by some chance? Our other son over a year ago met a seaman in a pub, who said his ship had answered the "Ceramic's" S.O.S., but arrived too late to see anything of it.

Well Mr Munday, I'm sure you are a very busy young man, and will be for some time. Do you mind if I enclose an addressed envelope? I should be very pleased to have just a short note from you, & having the envelope will save you time.

Our son was a young man of 29, tall and fair. He had been issued with a "life jacket" by the Admiralty.

****

I am writing to ask you if you would be very kind and give me some information, however small, about the "Ceramic" from which I am told you were taken P.O.W. in 1942. The reason I ask your help is that my daughter, aged 25, was on the same ship, travelling to join her husband in Cape Town, and nothing has been heard of her since. I do hope you will not mind my writing to you, I know it must be painful for you to remember this terrible tragedy, but I am sure you will understand how very anxious I am to hear something about it. I am asking the Red Cross to forward this to you, as I do not have your address. When you receive this, perhaps you would kindly let me know, also if I could see you to hear about it, it would help to pacify my mind.

****

I hope you will forgive me for writing so soon after your return, but I am wondering if you could spare me a little time. My young daughter aged 24, was a passenger in the Ceramic and, as you realise, I know nothing of what happened. I have been through a very unhappy and anxious time, and I should be so very grateful if you could see me when you feel able, and give me all details that you can.

****

Seeing that many Prisoners of War have returned home I am wondering if your son is home with you again. I most sincerely hope so & also that he is in a good state of health. Since your kind letter to me of January 44 I have heard nothing further except from the War Dept stating that owing to the lapse of time &

absence of news &c my son must be presumed to have lost his life. If your son is home I wonder if he would be kind enough to write the full story for me, from the time of embarkation & also say what was their destination. It is just possible he knew my son whilst on board ship ... Also would you tell me the name of the Shipping Coy. I shall be most grateful for any information as you can imagine.

****

... Not having had a reply from you I am now wondering whether you received my letter, but I think it would have been returned to me if it had not been delivered. Please do not hesitate because it is bad, as I cannot be hurt any more. I dare not tell my wife all that I know as she could not bear it she is thoroughly heartbroken & I am afraid will never be her normal self. Thank God I have another boy or I dare not imagine what would have happened.

****

Thank you very much indeed for your letter of the 28th, I was very pleased to get it, I had not given it a thought that you would have to get permission to reply to enquiries, of which no doubt you have had a large number. I take it from your letter that you have no knowledge of any other survivors, it is terrible really, and if only that storm had not happened it would have been so different, surely that must have been one of the greatest tragedies of the war, and not a word has been given to the public. It is very kind of you to offer to answer further enquiries I may wish to make, but I shall think about that and in the meantime shall leave it to you to let me know if you hear any news.

****

Would it be troubling you to try and find out for me if Mr Alex Munday (sic) could let me know of my son ... who left England in Nov 1944 (sic) for Capetown S. Africa and who was on the "Ceramic". I should be so very grateful to you if you could find anything out for me as to my son's last moments at sea. Mr Alex Munday may perhaps have known my son. I returned to England from Durban in January 30th 1944 after the loss of my husband Captain Jones M.N. & my son Lieut Frederick J. Jones R.N.V.R. within 6 months of each other. Will you kindly explain the reason of my writing to Mr Munday. This morning I had a cutting sent to me from S. Africa from my daughter in law who (was) the young wife of my late son lost in the Ceramic. I should be ever grateful to you if only I could get word from Mr Munday, anything he should know of my son's last moments. They may have been on the same raft together.

****

Chapter 11: Back home

We were very pleased to read in the "Daily Express" that you had arrived home to your parents and hope you are feeling well after your experiences. Your parents will be overjoyed we are sure that you are home again. We wrote to them for information while you was a prisoner in regard to our son who was a passenger on board the "Ceramic", and received a very very comforting letter from them.

I should like to ask you if there is anything further you could tell us beyond the newspaper report as we have been informed of so little. It does seem that there would have been a reasonable chance of some being picked up but for the storm.

****

I am very sorry to intrude on your long looked for peace, but I am writing to you just in case you may have come in contact with any of the crew of that unfortunate ship. My sister's son was a fireman below on the "Ceramic", I have not dared to tell her I am writing to you as I do not want to raise any false hopes, the boy's name was … he was about 22 years old and that was his first trip in her, please did you ever hear his name, I am enclosing his photo, also a cutting from a paper of 2 yrs ago, and the boy lying with his eyes closed at the bottom of the picture seems very like him.

****

I hope you will excuse the liberty I am taking in writing to you, but I am so anxious to know whether your son has been released from the prison camp in Germany. My reason for wanting to know is that my son … a Corporal in the Royal Marines was on the same boat Ceramic as your son when it was torpedoed. You, being a Mother will realise how I feel and I am anxious to know whether your son could give me any particulars. I know it is said there was only one survivor, but I cannot bring myself to believe this, and I can (get) no satisfaction either from the Admiralty or the Red Cross. Could you ask your son whether he thinks there is any hope of there being other survivors, as I still looks long and hope I may hear news of my son. Thanking you in anticipation of a reply.

****

… My son was on that ship, so being a mother, you can imagine my anxiety to hear of any details however small. I should esteem it a great favour if you could give me any information, as the suspense and worry as to whether I shall ever hear from my son again is sometimes more than I can bear.

****

… I am grieved that you do not know what happened to the boat loads of people that you saw leave the ship, but I suppose the storm that came up during the night must have swamped them. It's good of you to give me so many details, and although it doesn't seem possible that there are any more survivors I feel I must still hope and trust that my son may have been saved.

****

Apparently you have not heard of any further survivors or you would have written to me.

I feel now that there cannot be much hopes of my sons survival as the prisoners of war have all been released so the hope that he might have been amongst those has been crushed.

You say you saw the lifeboats pull away did you see any overturned or did you see the Ceramic sink? You must please forgive me for troubling you again but it seems so awful to think that all on board were lost with the one exception.

****

I have been going to write to you many times but I know you have been having a hard time answering the many letters on this subject, and hope you won't mind one more. If you are able to write to me, will you tell me what you can of that night almost three years ago, also if by any strange chance you had come into contact with my husband before the sinking. His name was … usually called …, and he was going to an appointment in …

I was twenty three then and my little girl was seven months old, she is three & a half now, we had our passports and everything ready to go also. I shall be very grateful to you if you can manage to write me any details. If by any chance you should ever come south I would be very glad to see you and have a talk, although I expect you are pretty sick of talking about it by now.

****

I hope you don't mind me writing to you. But I would like to know if your son has arrived home from the prison camp. I lost my husband on the "Ceramic" and read about your son being the only survivor.

I didn't write sooner because I thought I would wait until your son came home then he could tell me if it were true that all on board were drowned. I have been hoping to get good news but it seems hopeless.

Chapter 11: Back home

My Husband was ... he was 25. I hope your son will help me by telling me if it is right what he broadcast from Germany.

Also I hope he is quite fit and well.

Hoping you don't mind me writing to you, I have waited 2 ½ years to write this letter.

****

I must thank you for your very welcome letter. It was nice to hear from you after such a long wait for you coming home from Germany.

I don't think there is anything else to ask you about the ship or any of the men.

It seems hopeless to keep on waiting for good news any longer.

****

I read in today's "Daily Express" your story of the sinking of the "Ceramic" & I am writing to ask if you can give me any information whatsoever of my brother, ... who was also sailing in her.

He was the ... - that point I thought might perhaps help you to recall him - & I enclose a photo as an added help.

I realise you must be receiving daily many such letters as this that it must be a great strain for you to reply to them all & to be thus constantly reminded of the hardships you have been through, both at the actual sinking of the ship & the subsequent years in a prison camp - though I am truly sorry to add to this, I would be more grateful than I can ever express if you can recall my brother in any connection at all & can give me any information whatsoever.

I wrote to you while you were in the prison camp, but perhaps the letter didn't reach you - & of course, as I realised at the time, it would be impossible for you to answer all such enquiries as the letters & cards allowed were so limited.

****

...You know, although such things do not fundamentally make any difference, do not I mean, alter the fact that he has gone, yet just the fact that you actually remember him, & could speak as you did of him, does help terribly.

It was so good to hear you say that he was so well liked, & that he looked after his men so well - yes, you've got the right man alright, that was so typical of him, he was ever popular, & so keen on doing his job to the utmost.

He had just had a leave after two pretty tough years in West Africa - & this time he was on his way to his much loved South Africa, which had been his home for a number of years before the war, & to get back there was his one aim in life.

It was good of you to go into such detail about the actual sinking; & so, if it hadn't been for the storm I suppose there would have been a very fair chance of the majority being saved.

I suppose now there is very little hope that any can have been saved - yet in spite of that, we are loath to give up all hope. We much appreciate your assurance that should you ever hear anything from the Admiralty you will get in touch with us again.

Again, thank you very much for your kindness in writing as you did - we are deeply indebted to you.

****

I do hope that yourself and family are keeping well as all of us here are pretty fair considering all we have been through with anxieties and worries. Please Mrs Munday can I ask you if your boy is home yet as I wrote to you a few weeks ago and maybe I may have put the wrong address or number on your letter as my nerves are very bad at times. However we are both trying to keep up only my girl does know she has lost her husband only 3 months married she is a young widow at the age of 25. I am heartbroken but I am trying to keep up as best I can for the young children sake I have 2 not yet going to school a little boy ... 8 years old and a girl ... she is 12 but what when they leave school I expect they will want to go away somewhere too but I mustn't think of that time yet it's only those who have loved and lost this peace excitement means anything to its just all the same time to me now. I wonder will you spare me a few minutes and let me know if your boy is yet at home and perhaps he may be able to tell some little bit of news no matter how small it may be.

****

I am quite sure you are beseiged with letters & personal enquiries but you will understand the anguish of mind I and other relatives are going through. I am enclosing a photograph of my husband who was an A.B. on the "Ceramic". Do you remember him & can you tell me anything? Please don't think that because

Chapter 11: Back home

the photo is torn that I don't care, there happens to be quite a story about how it got torn but that's beside the point & as you can see I have stuck it carefully together. I won't trouble you with any of my life history but just say that I would be grateful for any bit of information you can give me however small.

****

My son, ... attached to "Movement Control" was on the ill fated ship. We have heard nothing since he left this country, except for the usual curt notification from the War Office, that he is presumed Dead.

I am enclosing his photograph thinking perhaps you might have come in contact with him during the voyage.

Will you please try & help me, his very sorrowing mother. Thank you so much.

****

I am writing on behalf of my mother who has read your story of the sinking of the "Ceramic". You see my brother was on that ship, and my mother also myself was wondering if you could tell us something about him, that is if you did happen to see or know him. I will enclose a photo of him in the uniform he would likely be wearing when he met his death. He had a very good friend with him also. His name was ... If you can tell me anything I would be so very pleased as I have so longed for someone who might be able. May I add that I am very pleased to hear you at least had the good luck to be saved. May God bless you. Please answer my humble letter, and would you please send my photo back as it is all I have left of my poor brother. His name was ... of the Maritime Reg.

****

We had long known of the CERAMIC going down even if no official statement had been issued, and were very much concerned to know if there were any survivors other than yourself.

We had on board a much loved niece, orphaned in the last War we had brought her up as a daughter, she eventually became a Nurse, and was with you as a Nursing Sister in the QUEEN ALEXANDRA'S. We wonder if you ever heard her name mentioned ... but that would be a very remote chance in such a large ship's company.

****

I take the liberty of writing you to enquire if your son has returned to England.

I had a young brother who was a gunner on board the "SS Ceramic" and should like to get in touch with one who might know something.

****

I want to thank you very much for your kind reply to my enquiry. As you say there is not much you can tell me, I suppose it is an ordeal you wish to forget.

For a purely personal reason I should be grateful if you could let me know on what day it happened and at what time.

****

My brother and his wife were sailing on this ship, unfortunately, and I thought you may have made contact with them, or that you would be able to give me some more particulars regarding our sad loss.

My brother ... and his wife, were going to Africa as Missionaries of the Free Church of Scotland, it was to be his first charge, and they were just newly married, he would be about 32 years of age when he sailed, and his wife somewhat younger. ... was of medium height, slim build, and fair complexion, and wore glasses.

If you can find time, (I know you will have many enquiries) to write me a note, I'll be greatly obliged to you.

I write this on behalf of my mother, sisters, and brothers, who will esteem it a favour, if you could throw any more light on our sad loss.

****

... Our son must have been on the same boat though the W.O. do not confirm & cannot tell us the name of the boat! He was in the R.A.S.C. as ... - we quite realise that a boat load of portions of various regiments do not get to know each other personally but naturally one is anxious for any crumbs of news. I have the W.O. permission to advertise & try & get in touch with survivors or relatives - have not yet done so as I guess its a forlorn hope - what do you think? My ... was not 20 when he went in Dec (his 20th birthday came last week!) & he was so full of joy to travel abroad - poor boys - they don't know that war is such a hell - full of fun is youth! My elder son goes into the R.A.F. on 1st May - these two are my all & such dear - truly who'd be a mother - aren't we helpless to do anything to

save them!!! I shall never give up watching for the post & hoping for good news - millions more doing the same thing of course & we have to go on living till <u>our</u> time comes!

****

It is 3 years today that ... went into the R.A.S.C. <u>every</u> anniversary comes like a sickening blow doesn't it when we poor wretched mothers keep on living it over! I have for several weeks past been thinking so much about you & Eric - I know how horrible it must be now that the war is right in Germany & all with sons & husbands held as P.O.W. will naturally be going through hell on their behalf. I expect you have seen in this morning's paper that one has come home from Germany & is making it a sad duty to see the relatives of 127 of his pals left behind - I do hope you are one my dear so that you can get first hand news of what goes on. I have at times wondered if I shall ever see Eric to hear first what happened to the Ceramic on that awful night - I know it is going to be awful indeed for him & you my dear for so many of us will be longing to see him - perhaps it would save him a lot of upset if he could write down all he would say & have it typed off like you so kindly and sensibly did in that first letter. Well time tells everything - we shall all know the whole great plan some day! I wonder if you happen to know of any other relatives of the lost ones who may live fairly near me so I could get in touch - it might help us all to hear each others burdens!!!

****

Thank you so much for your letters yesterday - it must be a great work of sympathy on your part dear Eric to take on all the letter writing it is going to mean replying to all the anxious suffering people who are left in this world as a result of their dear ones being on that ill fated ship... only we who are down in the deep hell of it all can appreciate what you are doing & thank you with all our hearts. I hope the day will come when I can do something for you to prove my gratitude.

As you say, there is little enough to hope for in the news you can give & yet believe it or not I cannot help feeling I shall even yet get some more news of my ... Several times Spain has come into my head & last night Ian & I were talking it all over & he told me for the first time that he too has held that idea! We can only wait & see. For months past I have been getting a 3 - you know I have dabbled in spiritualism a bit since this trouble came & something makes me cling to this 3 - it will soon be 3 years you know & I do feel there is more than we know in it all - time alone will tell.

****

My husband was taking passage on her as he was on his way to Durban to take up a post there in the Barracks, his name was …, nicknamed …, I have been thinking it possible that you may have shared the same quarters as he & am hoping you can give me some definite information of him. I am enclosing a snap which may help, please forgive me for troubling you, I know you must hear from many people & have a busy time answering us, we are all so eager for news, I am sure you will understand & help if possible.

May I add how glad I am that you were spared.

****

I am grateful to you for your letter of the 30th ultimo, it is very kind of you to take so much trouble to answer letters such as mine, for I am sure you must have files of similar letters to answer. Thank you for explaining things so clearly, it seems you were not near land when it happened & I suppose we haven't much hope, yet I don't suppose any of us give up hoping, especially yourself, you have endured so much.

****

I have read your account in the "Daily Express" of your terrible experiences on your voyage out on the Ceramic.

I had a niece on board Miss … & I wondered if you had come in contact with her, she was on her way out to South Africa to be married.

I should be glad to have any information you can give me, I am making these inquiries as she had no parents I was therefore left in charge of her affairs.

****

… Our youngest son - a few weeks short of 19 years of age - was a passenger in the ship and we deeply mourned his loss. He had just taken his Higher School Certificate & we yielded to his persuasion to let him come out to join the E.A. Forces in order to be along with his brothers.

In common with all the other relatives of passengers we have nothing but a complete blank. We wonder if your son can tell us anything about what happened. I don't suppose it will do us any good to know, but naturally we clutch at any opportunity of learning any details. We shall be grateful for any information if your son is able to supply it.

****

Chapter 11: Back home

… I wrote to the Admiralty & Shipping Company & both said as far as they knew "All personnel lost".

I am so glad you hear from your son regularly & trust you may soon meet again. Also that your son in Italy is safe and well. I am sure you are feeling worried about him now. We are living in troubled times & I think the strain is affecting us very much now, especially as the raiders have been over quite frequently.

****

… We have not heard anything from my nephew … who was on the ill fated "Ceramic".

One hopes each day to hear that he is alive & you are sure his wife & mother cling to the last hope & asked me to write to you again.

I wondered if you son did know of any more survivors or any information he could give us. It is now nearly three years since the disaster & almost forgotten except for those who have lost their dear ones.

****

You very kindly told me to write again if there was anything not quite clear. So will you please tell me if to your knowledge <u>you</u> <u>were</u> the <u>only</u> survivor or were there others with you at the time of rescue.

My sister who has been staying at Johannesburg read an a/c in a newspaper there presumably given by you.…

Thanking you so much for answering my letter & if you would just reply to my query I will not worry you again.

****

I trust that you will forgive me for writing to you but presumably you are the only person able to answer some questions that I want to ask.

I have been making enquiries about the loss of the "Ceramic" & when I visited the offices of Shaw Savill & Albion Co Ltd they refused to give me your address but promised to forward a letter from me to you.

My youngest brother … was a passenger on the Ceramic travelling as an employee of British Overseas Airways Corporation. News of what happened has been practically non existent & most of the information I received came from the newspapers long after the tragedy occurred. If it is not troubling you too much I should be very grateful if you will be kind enough to give me whatever information you can. You will no doubt realise that the subject is as painful to myself & my family as it is to you but if you can tell us when how & where he met his death it will be perhaps better than making surmises on such a subject.

I am enclosing a stamped & addressed envelope for your reply & if you consider that any useful purpose can be served if I visit you I will do so at your convenience.

Shaw Savill & Albion gave me to understand that there is no possibility of any further survivors.

****

I feel that I must write a thank you for your letter which reached me today. Although it did much to confirm my fears it is some consolation to know some of the details of what happened & the other members of my family will wish me to convey their thanks to you as well as my own.

In the future I shall continue to make whatever effort I am able to, to obtain information of possible survivors, and, although it is unlikely that I shall be able to learn anything, if I do I will pass whatever news I obtain on to you as no doubt you will have received many letters of a similar nature to mine.

****

I pray you will forgive me taking the liberty of writing to you. I read the news in this morning's Express re. the sinking of the Ceramic. My Boy was ..., Royal Corp Signals; left on the 26th Nov. was reported missing at sea during the night of 6th-7th Dec 1942, almost $9^{1}/_{2}$ months after Killed in Action at Sea. Would it be possible you could have known him? I've written the War Office to try to find out. He was a real Christian boy was $23^{1}/_{2}$ yrs. when reported killed. He was just 5 mths married to a very sweet girl from Darlington whom he met while taking the services in ... Darlington. She has now a beautiful son, the image of his Daddy. If you could ease my mind I would be truly grateful just to know if you had met him.

****

Seeing your story in the newspaper, I would be ever so grateful if you could give me any news about my late husband Signalman ...., he left England about Nov 26, I received a letter from him telling me he was on a civvy liner, so I feel he might

Chapter 11: Back home

of been on the Ceramic, he was about 5ft 3, fair hair & fair complexion, his name was … he had a scotch accent, and the boys called him … Here's hoping you can give me some news as we have heard nothing.

****

… We had an Australian nephew on board also & we have had word from his parents to find out from you if there were any chance of any news of their loved one. His name was… & he was an Australian Engineer Officer. If you have had the good fortune to meet him on board or can give any news about him his parents & ourselves will be very thankful to hear from you & thanks be to God that you have had the good fortune to be saved & may God bless you in the years which be ahead of you.

****

No doubt you will be surprised to get this, as I don't know you & you don't know me, but I do know that you are a mother & will have an idea just how I am feeling being less fortunate than you. I am led to believe that your boy was the sole survivor on the ill fated "Ceramic" our son, our only child was also a passenger on her, he was an Engineer Officer on the "Queen Elizabeth" had signed off in Liverpool & was being repatriated back home. We have heard nothing since we got the notice from the Shipping Coy over two years ago, that the ship was overdue and must be presumed lost, that was all we ever got from them, but I had a paper from home some time ago & it had your boy's photo in it, it also stated that Germany claimed to have many on her hands but that owing to heavy seas we must expect heavy loss of life but I suppose you know all this & have heard it over & over again, but what I did want to ask you, was your boy home yet & if so, he would be the only one who could tell us what really did happen & if there was any hope of other survivors being in Prison camps.

I hope you will not think this presumptuous on my part writing to you, but my Husband & myself are just so very desperate we just don't know what to do, I think if we knew the worst it would be so much easier to bear, than this awful uncertainty. I do pray you have your dear one home with you now, & that he will be able to tell you something our lad also had his 21st Birthday at sea & it was his first trip, hope I have not worried you with my troubles, but if you would be so good, would like to hear from you.

****

Thanks so much for writing to me, I received your letter about a fortnight ago. Yes I know it would not be an easy letter for you to write, it has all been such a mystery, we have hoped & prayed for nearly three years now, that somehow or somewhere our dear boy would be safe. I still cannot imagine how there were not more saved when all were lucky enough to get off the boat & that an S.O.S. was sent out. No matter how rough the seas got surely some effort could of been made to save the men. We have heard such a lot of rumours that they were all picked up & taken prisoners then we heard that the ship was blown to atoms & that there was not even one survivor, but of course we have proved that story wrong, & I made it my business to show the people who were telling the story your kind letter to me which ruled that story out, it would of been much easier for us to bear if we had heard the worst at the beginning but we kept ourselves hoping, with all the stories that were going about that he must be safe somewhere. There is no use in asking you if you got to know our boy. He was an Engineer Officer of the Queen Elizabeth he & several other officers had signed off in Liverpool & were being repatriated home, they had waited about five weeks in Liverpool for a boat, & then had to be put on the ill fated "Ceramic" it was our boy's first trip at sea, as he was only 20 when he left here & had his 21st birthday at sea. He was coming home to get married & everything was ready for him, his poor little fiancee has been very ill since, & like ourselves has been living in hope that we would hear something. ... was our only child so you will understand just how much he meant to us, or perhaps your mother would understand that better, however son, I am glad that you were even spared it did enlighten us a little as to what happened, as they would tell us nothing here, they would not even tell us the name of the boat that the boy was on at first they just told us that the ship our boy was on was overdue & must be presumed lost with all hands, & did not condescend to tell us the name of the ship, we had to write & ask our Minister for External Affairs if he could help us, so he cabled home to Australia House & got a reply to say the ship that ... was on was "Ceramic", that was the first we knew, however Eric, may I call you that, we are coming home as soon as we are allowed to travel, would it be possible for us to meet you & have a talk, it might help us a lot, if you would rather not just say so, & we do sincerely hope that you are getting over your awful ordeal, although we know you will never forget it. You have been very kind in writing to everybody, it is not a nice or yet easy job, I know. Thanks again Eric, & let me know if we can see you when we do come home.

****

... I got a letter from the Australian Red Cross Scty in London dated 31/8/45 which was similar to your own letter. Of course, they were just embodying in their letter any information you gave them at your interviews. Shaw Savill & Albion Co (Shippers) was also similar as you were the only one that survived to give them any news. The Red Cross said the S.O.S. was sent off & was picked up by two ships off the coast of Portugal. Anyone who knows that coast says it could not have been in a worse spot.

Chapter 11: Back home

My cousin (Mrs ...) has been entertaining the boys & girls connected with the British Navy while they have been in Sydney & even when on holiday she had some of them staying with her. Everything to try & keep her mind off the boy (her only child). Her husband & she are trying to get home by April or May of next year. The boy was on his way home to be married. He would have been 24 years old on the 3rd Sept last.

****

I am glad you are back at your home safe & well. Many thanks for your kind letter with details. If only I had been able to have had your letter in June it would have made the Ship's Doctor (who being unwell stood down for that voyage) so much happier - he sort of felt he had let the younger doctors go in his place & being an older man kept saying he ought to have gone in their stead - his heart was very bad & the shock help(ed) his end - but I do thank you for your letter & have passed it on to one of the heads of the (Senior?) Office he will be interested. I am glad you are safe. How happy your home folk must be to have you with them.

****

I expect you are overwhelmed with this type of letter, but I like the other people feel I'd like to write you a few lines.

You see I too had a sister on your boat who was on her way to South Africa, & of course lost. Her name was ... I realise you would not meet all the passengers, but there is a very remote chance that you might have met her during your short time on the Boat, & that is the reason for this letter.

****

I have waited until now to write to you - as I had a cutting out of the B'ham paper about the sinking of the Ceramic & that you were the only survivor on the boat. You will wonder why I am writing but I should like to know if possible what happened as I had my beloved brother on that boat. He was going out to Australia for the War Office. His name was ... He was reported missing believed drowned & I know that he was on that boat.

I am sorry to worry you for I am sure that you have gone through enough without being worried about other people, but it has been such a blow to me & though it is nearly 3 years I cannot get over it.

****

Your son I have been informed is a Prisoner of War in Germany. From details I have received I believe he was travelling on the same ship as my husband - ... I was officially informed that my husband has been missing since Dec 6-7th '42 and have had no further information.

I should be so glad if you could tell me if you have heard from your son, or if he has mentioned any other survivors.

You can appreciate how much I would value any little information which you may be able to let me have.

****

... All the remaining members of my friend's family were on the "Ceramic" and, at the time of the sinking. The Admiralty merely told her that the ship was torpedoed in mid-Atlantic and sank within a few seconds. She was therefore greatly comforted to think that, although she had lost her people, their death must have been practically instantaneous and they couldn't have suffered greatly. Now, however, the accounts in the paper sound so very much worse that she feels her mind will never be at rest until she can hear something more definite about what really happened; yet, on the other hand, if it was very horrible, she would never be able to forget it. I wondered, therefore, if it would be possible for you to see her some time, and tell her something definite but leave out anything that was too awful.

I don't suppose, among all those people you would actually know her relations, but. just in case, the name was ... the fellow was in the Navy, and there were two little children.

****

May I first congratulate you on your fortunate escape from certain death, also your release as a prisoner of war. I have read in the newspaper today your statement regarding the S.S. Ceramic, also your previous account in the early days when you were a prisoner. I now write to ask if you could tell me anything of ... who was on board the ship and nothing has been heard of since. I have not written before as I know it is such a shock to you, but would be glad of anything you could tell me regarding my daughter who left here 3 yrs ago today and was only 25 years of age. She was so keen to do her bit and left her training as a Maternity Nurse at the Aberdeen Hospital. She was trained at Guy's Hospital, London, and only left there in May 1942. I am writing at my office as I do not want my wife to read your letter first.

****

Chapter 11: Back home

I must apologise for the delay in answering your letter, but I have been away on a much needed holiday, as it is the first since 1938 so I think I was entitled to one. Many thanks for your letter with the information you gave me, but I am afraid that it does not help one and you must have had a lot of work answering all the letters. Again I thank you for writing to me.

****

I hope you don't mind my writing to you, and asking permission If I may call on you one of these days in the near future. But as it is a matter which is of interest to both of us, I would be pleased if you could give the matter consideration.
I understand that your son, Eric, now a prisoner of war in Germany, is the sole survivor of the sinking of the Ceramic. I congratulate you on his miraculous escape from what I believe is one of the worst disasters at sea during this War, and I hope that it wont be long before, he comes back to you and makes you still happier. Your faith in his well-being and safety has certainly proved itself, and may it be still further rewarded. My sister, ... was on that ship the night she went down, and my parents in British Columbia were notified by the War Office Casualty Branch last month that "We regret to inform you that ... was killed by enemy action, Dec 5th 1942." Of course they had been notified that she was missing at sea last January, and I made a lot of inquiries at the War Office Casualty Branch in Liverpool last April when I was on my leave up there. The authorities were very kind and showed me all the information possible, including the account of Eric's broadcast over the German radio. I also learned the name of the U-boat commander who sunk the Ceramic. It may or may not be unfortunate for him, should ever we meet.

Of course the news was a terrible shock to my Mother and Father, but I urged them to try and keep up their Faith In ...'s safety, for I felt, and still feel that somehow, somewhere... she is still safe, and I cannot create any other thought to the contrary in my own mind. And that, in spite of the absolute finality of the news regarding the sinking of the ship. I have often gone over the matter and accused myself of "wishful thinking" but the idea persists too much to be just that.

****

I read in the papers that you were making contact with many of the relatives of the missing (crew) passengers, and I know you must have quite a lot of writing to do, but I still wondered and hoped, if you could give me some information of my brother, who is one of the missing.

His name was ... he was a signaller in the R.A. he was a very quiet boy, but still, one must make many friends on board ship, so if you ever came in contact with him, maybe had a few words with him, and I should very much like to know, how things were with him, so if you can help me, I shall be very grateful.

****

I hope you will not mind my writing to you to know if your son Eric has arrived home from being taken prisoner off the ship Ceramic as we read of his account in the paper & I have kept till V. day as we lost a dear friend on the same ship & I have his only child living with me his mother died when he was young & we took his father & the boy into my home as one of our selves till he went to South Africa for his firm on the ill fated ship & no more has been heard about him if only your son is home & can give us some details I would be very much relieved & I hope & pray God has spared your child from this dreadful war I know how you must have felt I have a son in the army myself & is now home on leave which is a real godsend please write me when you can if you have any news at all.

****

Many thanks for your kindness in answering my letter & I wish you the very best of luck & health in the future Well I can only hope & pray that one day our dear friend will turn up with many others for his son's sake who is now in South Africa it was a terrible blow to us all & we could not find anything out at all but Mr ... went to Liverpool to see him off & was told that no soldiers were on board His friend that went with him left a wife & 3 children & she still hopes her husband will return I will not trouble you with our worries but it is nice to know what little you were able to tell us so thanking you once again.

****

Having read in yesterday's edition of the Daily Express of your remarkable escape from the sinking of the Ceramic I wondered if you could give me any information regarding my brother ... who was travelling in the Ceramic as an employee of B.O.A.C. We were duly informed by the Company that he was missing presumed drowned but since then its just been a complete mystery.

****

I saw the article in the Daily Express. I was wondering if you could give me any information about my brother who was on the 'Ceramic'. He was ..., aged 18 yrs. Please let me know. Enclosed you will find a photograph. Can you please return it. It is the only one I have of him. I would be very grateful to you.

****

Chapter 11: Back home

I thank you very much indeed for your most kind letter, although your information will be hard to bear (we had not given up hope) there is one consolation, if she is gone she did not have to suffer like so many others have had to.

****

My brother-in-law ... was a Quarter Master's Sergeant in the Royal Signals and was going out to a garrison on St Helena Island. We received messages to say he was missing, and later presumed killed, and yet even now my sister still thinks there is some hope.

I would be so very grateful if you could help me in any way at your convenience.

****

... First of all she would like to know what you think the chances are of any of them being picked up by Jap raiders. How long (if you have any idea) the storm lasted? And if it was too bad for a lifeboat to remain afloat. I hope you don't mind my writing to you instead of my sister. When it all took place in 1942 I was then only 15 and I don't think I quite realised what the news meant to her. Now I realise only too well and I think it is the least I can do trying to help her in this way.

I've forgotten these two questions - if you don't mind. We would like to know where you all were when the ship was torpedoed (that sounds a crazy question but that's what I've been told to ask!) and if you think any of the lifeboats would have reached land.

I hope you can answer these questions for my sister's sake, I know you will if you possibly can.

****

I have just received a cutting of a newspaper sent by a friend from London with the photo of your boy Sapper Eric Munday a survivor of the S.S. Ceramic. My son ... and his wife ..., he had come from South Africa last May to get married, and was going back in the Ceramic, with special permission. He was six foot in height a well built fellow his wife also was tall. We have never heard a word, only the news we got the 2nd Jan that the Ceramic was sunk by enemy action no survivors but after seeing the photo of your boy we are hoping still that our lad and wife might be picked up. If you hear anything we would be very thankful if you would let us know.

****

I hardly know how to word my letter for I'm sure you have had hundreds of requests similar to mine. The fact is that I would welcome any news you care to give me concerning my auntie and her baby daughter - Mrs ... and ... who were bound for Capetown on the Ceramic on its fateful voyage. I have the newspaper account by me and each time I think of the horrible affair I feel more and more depressed, I'm very pleased, on the other hand, that you have been spared and I hope and pray that the future will be a happy one for you and yours.

We feel our loss greatly, so please tell me what you can and I shall be so thankful.

****

This is another letter of the kind you must have received by the sackfull lately but could you give it your kind attention.

The article in the "Daily Express" says you are the only survivor, but a few months after the "Ceramic" sank my father was approached by a man who claimed he was the only survivor of the ship. This man said he was a quartermaster.

Unfortunately my father only knew the man by sight, and his approach was at a busy time at the local Labour Exchange where my father was working. I mention all this because he, the "only survivor" told us the first definite news about a passenger who was my greatest friend.

I cannot trace this man in any way, so I am hoping you may be able to help remembering a little about my friend. Let me say that whatever details you may be able to supply are not directly for myself, but for this friend's parents in Cape Town. For this purpose I enclose a stamped addressed envelope and also a snapshot of the passenger and her baby taken a few months before the ship sailed.

Here are the details about her that may help you to call her to mind: Her name was Mrs. ... and she was returning to South Africa with her little baby girl, ... Mrs ... was a war widow, her husband having been killed at Malta whilst serving in H.M.S. Maorle in November 1941.

She was a South African by birth, tall, about 5ft 11in, round faced, dark hair and almost grey eyes.

Perhaps after all this time even these details are of not much use but if you can remember any little thing however unimportant it may seem, and would pass it on to this lady's parents via the envelope you would earn their undying gratitude and bring them some comfort in autumn years.

Chapter 11: Back home

During the years of captivity that you endured, we of the Royal Navy were not idle, and I for one gave the Jerry U-Boats a hell of hiding. I was serving in the famous 2nd Escort Group under the late Captain P.J. Walker, and we consisted of five sloops, H.M.S. Starling, Wren, Wildgoose, Magpie and Kite. At one time we bagged six in twenty nine days, and returned to Liverpool with several hundred prisoners. Just after D Day, we got another four, and all told this group was responsible for something like forty five enemy submarines.

The sinking of the "Ceramic" was a score I had to settle, and you can see from what I have said that my account is payed in full!

****

Thank you very much for your kind letter telling me of your terrible experience. I hope you are keeping well after such a wonderful deliverance. I am going to stay in the South later & should like to meet you & hear more. Perhaps you may remember my son - I am missing him dreadfully as he is the last of the family.

****

You will remember me writing you about my Brother in Law some time ago, who I am very sorry to say was lost when the S.S. Ceramic was sunk. He was ...

If your son is at home I shall be so grateful if he could give me any particulars what happened on that night because my wife is so anxious to know if possible what happened or did your son ever see anything of ... on the ship before it was sunk.

A few lines when convenient would greatly oblige.

****

I do hope you will excuse me writing to you, as I have seen in today's paper about you being home. I had some big friends of mine on the Ceramic and wonder if you will be able to give me any information about Their names were Mr ... and his wife ... He was going out to Africa to take up a wireless position, They were inhabitants of ... in Yorkshire, and as I will be going up there shortly, I would be most grateful if you could give me any news to take up to their people.

****

I expect you are tired of receiving and answering letters but after reading your account in the paper I feel I must write and ask you about my husband.

I have been wondering whether to write you ever since May...

I should be very much obliged if you could tell me anything about him as the whole affair was most unsatisfactory. It is disgusting to think it was not convoyed and the War Office do not even tell you the name of the ship.

We were only married 10 months and had only three weeks together.

****

Sorry I have been so long in answering your letter. But first let me thank you for giving me a little idea of what did happen. After so long I don't think I have any chance of having good news.

****

From the Daily papers some months ago we took your name and address as being the only survivor from the ill-fated liner "Ceramic" in the hope that some day you would be in a position to tell us something about the happenings of that terrible night.

We hope that that time may now have arrived and that this letter finds you once more home & free & in as best of health as one can expect under the terrible conditions which you have all had to endure but sincerely hope that you may soon be restored to good health & enjoy the peace which you all so deserve.

As there were hundreds of passengers on the "Ceramic" one cannot possibly expect you to remember any individual person but I write this as my niece, Mrs ... was returning to South Africa on that boat & we of course knew nothing of the loss until some three or four months after.

Her loss seems all the more tragic to us for her husband was a bomber pilot & was killed on air operations over Germany the previous August & it was after the confirmation of his death that she set out for her home in South Africa.

I should, therefore, be most grateful to you if, when you find it convenient to yourself, could give me any particulars of just what happened on the night of Dec 6/7 1942.

****

I feel I must write you a letter in acknowledgement of your very kind letter of the 8th inst.

Chapter 11: Back home

I quite understand the delay in not replying to my previous letter. Your kindness in giving me the particulars is greatly appreciated & I thank you very much indeed for the trouble you have taken.

Knowing what a terrible storm raged on the night of Dec 6-7th we imagined that when the liner was struck there would be little hope of getting the boats & rafts away on such a rough sea. The Shipping Co informed us at the time that no S.O.S. had been picked up & that the first information they had received was over the wireless from some German station, so we rather gathered that the liner must have gone down very quickly or that the wireless room have been hit.

It hardly seems possible that there were no other survivors but yourself, you certainly was a very very lucky fellow.

It seems doubtful that any more news will be forthcoming after this length of time but should you get to know anything I shall be pleased to hear from you.

****

I am writing to you today as I am anxious to know if your son has returned from Germany.

Most of the prisoners around here have arrived home, so I trust your son is home safe & well. I can realise your rejoicings in having him home among you again.

You were very much in my thoughts during V.E. Day, but failed to write as indeed my feelings were mingled with sadness. Our loving child was so near to on it pained us so much. I have beautiful memories of her & a lovely photograph of her which I cherish.

But there is one thing I want to know - the time of the tragedy & what exactly happened after they were torpedoed.

****

I read in the paper the other day that you were the only survivor of the Ceramic and wondered if you could possibly let me know more about her unfortunate end. My mother was one of the passengers and possibly you may have met her. Her name was ... and she was rejoining my father in South Africa - but so much has taken place since then, that I expect that even if you had you would have forgotten her by now.

****

Please forgive me for taking the liberty of writing to you and bringing back an episode in your life which you wish to forget. I had two brothers serving as ... and ... on the Ceramic. Please can you tell me anything about them. I was praying to God they would return to me but after reading your story all my hopes are shattered.

****

... What I want to ask you were there any Royal Marines on the boat that you were on, the reason I am asking you as my son was on that boat, the Navy wrote and told me, he was presumed dead, he was with other Marines, I have not had any news of him since Nov 1942, he was only 18 years old I am enclosing a snap of him I wish you could tell me something. It's a very trying time. It's not like if the War Office told me he was officially dead only presumed. I would be very grateful if you could tell me. I am glad you got home safe to your parents it must have been a great relief to them. My son was one of 12 & we miss him very much...

****

Thank you very much indeed for troubling to write to me yourself. I am so glad to know that you are safe back at home. You must have had a terrible time in Germany at the end, just before the final capitulation. Your parents have been so kind too, letting me know such news as was available about the sinking of the ship.

You have indeed been lucky. It is very fortunate for all of us that you managed to survive to tell the tale, otherwise we would never have known the truth of the matter.

I think we now know all that will ever be known about the happenings that night, and I am sure everything was done that could have been done in the circumstances. It was very bad luck for all of us.

****

I do hope you don't mind me writing this letter, I know that you must be fed up with people writing & asking you about there (sic) relations & friends etc, who were on the "Ceramic". Of course I understand that you can't be expected to have known everyone on the ship or what happened to them. But I expect that everyone thinks there may be just a chance that you may have known that particular person there interested in, the same as I do.

When I read the paper this morning & saw that you are home safe & well I was terribly glad for you. But in a way it made me feel unhappy as you see my Fiancee (sic) was one of the crew, we had just got engaged on that last leave. He was the ... & his name was ... of course everyone called him ... So if you could possibly tell me anything at all I would be very grateful to you. Although it's nearly three years since it happened I still haven't given up hope. He was a very good swimmer but I suppose if there was a bad storm he wouldn't stand a chance, especialy (sic) as it wasnt in a convoy as it should have been by rights. I do hope you are home for good now, & I expect you want to forget it all but if you could let me know anything I would be very glad.

****

I apologise for adding yet another letter of enquiry to the many you must be receiving: my nephew & heir ... was a passenger on board "Ceramic" and is presumed to have lost his life when the vessel was torpedoed. He was proceeding to the Middle East on behalf of the British Consul & I wonder (a) if you knew him by sight or (b) you know anything of his fate. He was very fair, fresh or rather highly coloured complexion, about 5'11" tall & his right shoulder was damaged, the reason why he was not in uniform.

****

I have been trying to get your address ever since the terrible disaster, re the sinking of the Ceramic in December 1942. My dear son was serving as ... on the ill fated ship, and as I cannot get any satisfaction from the local agents here in New Zealand as to what has happened, I am writing to you to know if you could supply me with any news, as I am told that your son Sapper Eric Munday was the only survivor saved. No doubt by this time you have had word from him giving as much news as he possibly can. I am also given to understand that he is a prisoner of war in Germany, also that he had broadcast from the Berlin station just after the sinking however if there is any other new that you could supply me with I would be very much obliged.

I hope and trust that your son is safe and well and the time is not far off when you will all meet again. This has been a terrible blow to my wife as I have been trying to convince her that its almost impossible for all hands to be lost on such a large ship with such up to date equipment for life saving. As its such a long time ago we have very feint hopes of hearing of our dear son again I hope this letter will reach you safe and sincerely trust you will answer it and give me any details if possible. Wishing you all good luck.

****

I shall be very much obliged, if you can tell me about the Ceramic as I have seen in the paper that you are the only one saved. Do you think the other boats might have being picked up by a Raider and taken to Japan. Do you happen to meet ... he was a passenger to Capetown. He is my Nephew, sorry to trouble you but I shall be very grateful to hear from you any news about the above.

****

I'm sure after reading this letter you will forgive me for taking this liberty, I am writing on behalf of my mother who is ill just now, having gone through so much anxiety yourself concerning your son I know you will realise what she is going through.

To come to the point my brother ... was serving on the same ship "Ceramic" as your son. For weeks Mother has kept saying if she could only know of someone else who was on the same ship so you can imagine what we felt when we were sent the cutting out of a London newspaper concerning your son.

I doubt if Sapper Munday came into contact with ... as he belonged to the catering staff and was ... Would it be too much to ask of you if when you communicate with your son you would if possible mention my brother.

I think after reading the paper we realise now the hopelessness of it all as ... couldn't swim at all and under the circumstances it seems that he wouldn't stand much chance.

He was only eighteen years of age and such a popular boy too. But still I'm sure you must have suffered the same so you will understand our feelings.

****

I hope you do not mind my writing to you, a complete stranger, but having read in the Daily Paper about your return from a German prison camp and wondered if the ship on which you sailed from England was the same one on which my dear sister was travelling. ..., her name, was one of the Queen's Alexandra nurses, and all we have heard is that she was reported missing at sea between Dec 6 and 7th, we have been unable to get any more information.

Did you come into contact with any of the nurses, any scrap of news would be so welcome. She was, not too tall, fairly dark and plump.

****

Chapter 11: Back home

I hope you will excuse me writing to you, but my youngest son who is in the Air Force sent me your account which he saw in the Daily Express & we are very interested as my eldest son was going abroad & we know he left here in Nov 1942 & that his ship was torpedoed Dec, 6th 1942. We were notified the following Sept. that his ship was torpedoed and sunk & as nothing more had been heard of him he must be presumed drowned at sea. This of course has been a very great blow to us & have tried every means we know to try & find out just what happened. Everything you say seems to tally with what we do know that I felt I must write to you & ask you if you could give us any more details. We should be so grateful if you could or better still if you are this way should be so pleased if you could call on us. He was married & had a little girl. She was 14 months old when he left England. His name was ... if you should have known anyone by that name. He was a Corporal in R.A.S.C.. Once more please excuse me but if you could give us any more information we should be most grateful to you.

****

I feel I would like to write you a few lines to thank you for your letter also for the trouble you are taking in writing to the shipping agents. We should be so glad of any news to relieve our mind. But if only our dear son could come back to us it would be the best news of all. As I told you in my last letter his name was ..., but his wife tells me he was mostly called ... in the army. I wonder if you might have heard anyone called by that name. Did I tell you he was a Cpl. in the R.A.M.C. (sic). You yourself must have had a terrible experience but hope you are quite recovered by now. Thanking you for all the trouble you are taking.

****

I am writing these few lines in answer to your letter & to say we thank you very much for your kindness in making the enquiries about my son. Had it not been for you we should never have heard any more. Naturally I feel very upset, but as you say it is better to know. Thank you also for your offer of any more help but at the moment I do not know what else to say, but we do still feel we would be so pleased to meet you some time as one can talk better than write.

****

... I daresay you have been worried a lot with people inquiring from you, but please forgive me, my sister is heart-broken, and I have left no stone unturned to get even a glimmer of hope.

****

As you know, I am only one of several thousand no doubt who are wondering if you will be able to tell us anything that happened to our relatives who were on board the Ceramic.

You were kind enough to write me several P.O.W. cards during the period you were a prisoner, but I should be so very grateful if you would let me know what actually happened, & if you think that there is any possibility of there being any other survivors.

****

I hope you will excuse me writing to you, but I am sure you understand how I feel when I tell you my husband was ... on the "Ceramic" and I would be pleased of any information. I had a Daily Sketch cutting handed to me yesterday dated Sept 10th and it mentioned our ship and the (?) as they were trying to trace the crews etc. I still cling to a bit of hope as that has kept me up all this time.

****

I received your letter yesterday & I am deeply grateful to you for writing & giving what information you could give me, my wife also sends her thanks to you. Your details more or less tally's with the U Boats Captain's description of the sinking of which I picked up on the short wave radio, only he said that several life boats were smashed when they were lowered over the side, owing to the severity of the storm.

****

I am writing to thank you for your most kind letter you wrote me, I can't tell you what that letter is to me & my husband & we both will never forget you for the great kindness you have shown to a poor mother. My thoughts are always with my poor boy. He was our only one. We have got no one else.

****

Chapter 11: Back home

19 Foulsham Road
Thornton Heath
Surrey

5/9/45

Dear Mrs ...

Please forgive me for the delay in replying to your letter, but it was only recently that I obtained an interview with the Admiralty and was granted permission to reply to enquiries received. I had also hoped to gain some information regarding the possibility and whereabouts of other survivors but I am sorry to say that they know even less than myself. However, let me give you a few of the details and perhaps you can draw your own conclusions.

It was Sunday 6th Dec. '42 at 8 o'clock in the evening when we were hit and up to that time we had all had a very pleasant and uneventful journey. Of course, we were having lifeboat drill two or three times daily and when the unfortunate moment arrived for us to put this training to use, the operation went off quite successfully. Before I actually left the ship I saw several boat loads of people leave including, as far as I know, all the women and children. At the time the weather was quite mild but during the night a storm broke out preventing rescue ships from reaching us. An S.O.S. signal had been sent out and was picked up by two vessels off the coast of Portugal, but owing to the extremely rough weather they were forced to return in a much damaged condition.

I do not know how the others fared after I was picked up by the U Boat, so as you see, Mrs ... I am afraid I have not been of much help to you. However, if I should receive any further news I will let you know immediately, also if there are any points about which you still have doubt please write and I shall be only too pleased to help you.

Yours very sincerely,

Eric Munday.

Interview with Eric Munday
26 September 1999

They did build another ship that was called the *Ceramic*. I was a bit disappointed as I only found out after it had been launched, because I would like to have gone. It was owned by the Shaw Savill & Albion Shipping Company. There was a letter waiting when I got home. They just wanted my account, and when they realised they couldn't be held responsible, they didn't really show an interest at all. They had a lot of letters that people had written to them and they asked me if I would reply, I had about 100 letters, and I did reply to them, and I wrote to them to ask if they would consider paying the postage, but they didn't reply.

***

The Times
Undated newspaper clipping (January 1947)

THE CERAMIC

Sir, – We are deeply concerned that pain should have been given to anyone by our naming our new passenger-vessel recently launched at Birkenhead after a predecessor which bore the name Ceramic successfully and honourably for so many years in the Australian and Cape trades from this country. As your correspondent recalls, the original Ceramic was torpedoed on December 6, 1942, and after one survivor had been taken aboard the U-boat for purposes of identification the remaining boats with their complement were left by the U-boat commander to their fate in a high sea.

The rule followed by shipping companies, so far as I know, has generally been to avoid repeating the names of any vessels lost from normal marine perils, but this course has not necessarily been followed where vessels have been lost in action in time of war. This differentiation is no doubt due to the feeling that, whereas a marine loss in time of peace spells bad luck for the name of the ship involved, this consideration does not apply to those lost in action with the enemy, whereby the names of many vessels of the Merchant Navy have been crowned with glory. I can assure Mr. Armstrong that in repeating the name Ceramic the Shaw Savill Company had no thought other than to perpetuate an honoured name, and at the same time the company ventured to hope that the existence of a new Ceramic upon the seas might be regarded as a not unworthy memorial by those who were so cruelly bereaved by the inhuman action which followed the sinking of her predecessor.

BASIL SANDERSON,
Chairman, Shaw Savill & Albion Company, Ltd., 88, Leadenhall Street, E.C.3,
Jan 15.

Chapter 12
The account of the U-boat crew

A record of four days in Altenbruch
Clare Hardy

In May 2001, I was to find myself the guest of the surviving crew of U-515 at their annual reunion in Altenbruch, Germany, home of the U-Boat Archive. Eric Munday, with whom I had been collaborating for some eighteen months or more, was also to attend. Almost fifty-nine years after his extraordinary rescue, he would meet, for the first time, the crew of that unlikely saviour that had plucked him from the storm-swept waters. Eric would be accompanied by his wife Joan, and helping us to surmount the language barrier would be my long-suffering sister in law, Helen, whose German degree had proven to be such an asset to me, though perhaps a millstone to herself!

I spent the weeks leading up to this event partly in preparation, both practically and mentally, and partly distracted by my commitment as an Enumerator for the 2001 Census, a job that I had taken on to fund my trip to Germany. As the day drew near, I realised I had overlooked a number of practicalities, including getting a translation of the potentially sensitive questions I hoped to put to the crew of U-515. With one chance only to find out exactly what they had experienced on that night in December 1942, and how it had affected them, I neither wanted to shrink from probing a sensitive subject, nor did I wish to cause offence to men whom I had come to respect, both from Eric's account of the fair treatment he had received as their guest on the boat, and from their openness in welcoming me, the granddaughter of one who had died on the *Ceramic*, as their guest at what could almost be called a family gathering. Here would be a handful of elderly gentlemen, reminiscing about a time in their youth, when they sailed into the jaws of war with little regard for their lives, but only a fundamental belief in the same guiding principles that drove our own side. "Of course both had the same aim," U-515 crewman Carl Möller had written to Eric back in 1958, "to live in peace." What right did I, the fly in the ointment, have to rake up the ugly detritus that might tarnish the memory of that time in their lives?

I had also become aware of the significance of the event, both for myself, and especially for Eric. A regional newspaper and a national radio station had approached me for the story, but I did not feel that publicity would help the cause at this stage. Nevertheless, these approaches had made me conscious of the need to record faithfully the passage of those fleeting few days in the company of men whose memories were still vibrant, and snatched where the march of time might not permit a repeat. Of the options available to me, one stood out as having served well in the course of this history, and that, of course, was the diary. Just as Eric had recorded his memories and emotions while they were still fresh, and as others had done before him in the tradition of the day, and through times when no day was certain to follow the day before, the diary would suit me in the comfort of the longest peacetime in history, the cost of which is so often taken for granted.

Sunday 27th May 2001

For the first time, today I said goodbye to my children and boarded a plane for Germany. If it was hard enough for me to leave them, with the certainty of returning home safely in five days time, I wonder how those who left family behind in November 1942 must have felt, when nothing was certain, least of all arriving at their destination at the height of the Battle of the Atlantic. Helen and I were poor travelling companions: each being less than enthusiastic flyers, and we were not reassured by finding ourselves crossing the tarmac on foot to an apologetic-looking aircraft with propellers, that seemed as if it should be taking off from some grass runway at the back of a disused dairy, rather than waiting in line for take off with the twenty-first century leviathans of the skies, clearly bound for more exotic destinations than downtown Bremen. Eric Munday, and his wife, Joan, had met us at Gatwick, but we were not sitting together. Helen and I were relieved to find ourselves next to the emergency exit.

On landing, uneventfully, at Bremen, the organisers of the reunion, Walter and Waltraud Raksch, who had set themselves the impossible task of fitting a trip to the airport to meet us into their already over-packed schedule, were not to be found. After collecting the keys to our hire car, Eric and I returned to the terminal building for a last look around, but could see no faces resembling those in the photograph we held. In any case, Walter had explained on the phone that they might not make it, so we decided to proceed to Altenbruch - a fairly direct route from Bremen. However, on returning to where Helen and Joan were waiting with our cases, we found Walter and Waltraud with them, and already Helen was in full flow! Though Eric and Joan spoke very little German, and Walter and Waltraud, no English, they decided to travel together, leaving Helen and I to follow with the cases in our hire car - and before you could say, "Is that the windscreen washer or the left indicator?" we were off into the German traffic and onto the rain-lashed autobahn. Whilst tinkering with the controls to work out why a dubious dashboard light kept appearing, we suddenly found the car in front, carrying the Raksch/Munday party, had jammed on the anchors and skidded alarmingly onto (or rather, off of) the hard shoulder, believing we were flashing them to stop! We arrived in Altenbruch with no further rushes of adrenaline, and were greeted by the impossibly sprightly Gunther Altenburger, who would have

Chapter 12: The account of the U-boat crew

us believe he was 86 years old. He had served on U-515, though after the
Ceramic was sunk. In no time at all, we found ourselves in a room reserved for
the U-515 reunion. It was happening all too quickly, and I tried to record as much
as possible with my dictaphone, though regrettably without my camera, as I had
not anticipated that acquaintances would be renewed so soon. Eric was welcomed
as the guest of honour, and it seemed incredible that these remarkably young
looking men could actually have been on U-515 almost 60 years ago. Gunther sat
with us throughout the meal. He was at pains to make clear right from the outset
that he had joined U-515 after the loss of the Ceramic, and therefore was "not
guilty". "No one is guilty," I said through Helen's interpretation. "It was just
war." Gunther replied, "In French, they have the saying, 'C'est la guerre'". We
were speaking the same language.

Into the scene burst an animated Hans Hahn, with a book that recorded the
Christmas of 1942 spent on board U-515 in 1942. "I remember you!" He
exclaimed. "I remember where you were in the Bugraum!" Eric was less sure about
faces - he had many to remember, whereas as the novelty in 1942, it was easier for
the crew to remember him, but certainly memories were already being reawakened,
especially as Hermann Brandt and Herbert Dewald joined the group, and
reminiscences began to flow. With the buzz of conversation, it became harder to use
my dictaphone, but the remaining crew of U-515, of whom I was informed six were
on board when the Ceramic went down, were ready to discuss their experiences
with all the candour I could wish for. With my questions prepared, I suggested we
talk at greater length the next day, and so in the end we retired, for me to phone
home and wish the children a good night's sleep, the miles as nothing in the
communications age. I hoped the metaphor might be reflected in the coming days.

Monday 28th May 2001

As the day has progressed, so has my suspicion that I will be up until the small
hours recording all that has happened. When I came to Germany, the thing that I
feared most was returning home again without achieving my main aim - to talk at
length with the men who were there when the Ceramic was sunk. Although we
had barely met, or I had time to gain their trust, I knew that I could waste no time
in getting down to business, but I was aware that the memories I coveted were not
mine to claim, and I must rely on the generosity of those who had guarded them
for almost sixty years.

After breakfast, we boarded a coach for the river Medem, not far from
Altenbruch. Here we joined a river cruiser, and the weather being inclement, our
party found tables inside. Helen and I sat with Eric and Joan, and we were joined
by Hermann Brandt, who spoke a fair amount of English, which was our main

language of conversation. Eric and Hermann immediately began to discuss the period that Eric was on U-515, reminiscing about the times that Eric was allowed into the conning tower for air. "Never all the way up, only half way," recalled Eric. "We were always practising crash dives, and they used to push me down. I was always in the way."
"Still are," quipped Joan drily.

Hermann told us that Willi Klein, sitting at one of the tables opposite, had been on the bridge when Eric was fished out of the water. "I was very slim then, with more hair," said Hermann, raising his cap to illustrate his point! Eric wondered if Hermann's height had presented a problem on the cramped U-boat, but Hermann explained that he did not move around the boat much, but remained in the engine room, seldom coming up to the top. "You could recognise those who worked below deck," said Hermann. "We were pale and sickly from all the fumes, whereas those on the bridge were fit and suntanned."

Clare Hardy with Hermann Brandt.

The conversation moved on to the sinking of U-515 by the Americans, on the crew's sixth patrol in April 1944. There were approximately sixty men on board, of whom forty survived, and Hermann was one of these. The crew did not want their boat to be captured intact, along with all its log books and vital information, Hermann explained, so they scuttled it by opening the hatches. The first six men to appear on deck were gunned down by the Americans in their determination to obtain the prize, and Hermann Brandt described how he escaped by swimming to the destroyer, and how in the sanatorium, a piece of iron was removed from his leg. With casual arrogance, his American captors requested Hermann's shoes as a souvenir. "What position was I in to refuse?" he said. "In any case, I received new clothes from the Swiss Red Cross. I was transferred to the aircraft carrier Guadalcanal by a rope and bucket from the destroyer. I was not frightened. Henke was by my side, and he said, 'Well, Brandt, we did our best.' We were put into a room full of exhaust fumes, but the officers were allowed a better one. We spent four weeks on board. The Americans were after another submarine, which eventually dived and was bombed." The boat was U-68, from which only one man survived. In the closing chapters of the Battle of the Atlantic, the U-boat crews held only a losing hand, and their fate depended only on luck.

Hermann recalled his time as a Prisoner of War. "I worked in the laundry for 80 cents a day, which might buy a bottle of beer or a packet of cigarettes." But

Chapter 12: The account of the U-boat crew

Hermann admitted to supplementing his allowance by listening out for the clink of metal in the drum, and helping himself to any coins that might have been left in the pockets of his washload. Unfortunately for Hermann, his come-uppance arrived at the end of the war, when he was released in England with a cheque in US dollars. Thinking it prudent to wait for the introduction of the new Deutschmark before cashing his cheque, Hermann was informed at this point that he could only have the old Reisemarks, which by now were virtually worthless.

Eric recounted to Hermann, his experience at the end of the war, when he arrived in Prague just as the S.S. had departed, leaving a legacy of chaos and ruined buildings. He described his next stop in Pilsen - and the delousing parades! Reminiscing about the desperation of the Russians, Eric recalled how, as Prisoners of War, he and his comrades used to send food up to the Russian lager. "Otherwise," he claimed, "they would eat each other."

Hermann recalled U-515's first trip, when they sailed to the warm waters of the Caribbean. In the early days of the war, strict protocol was observed. The U-boat fired at its prey from deck guns before releasing torpedoes, to allow the ship's crew and passengers to evacuate the vessel safely before being sunk. But if the ship returned fire, then they had to shoot back. "It was a simple matter of self defence," Hermann explained. The crew were on this first patrol for three months before returning to Lorient.

On the Medem: Gunther Altenburger, Hermann Kaspers, Willi Klein.

As Hermann had pointed out Willi Klein as an eyewitness to Eric's rescue from the stricken Ceramic, Helen and I took the opportunity of joining him and his friend for the last 66 years, Hermann Kaspers, at their table. "I was on the bridge, and saw everything," recalled Willi. "There were high waves, lots of lifeboats. There were women - a lady with a baby in her arms and her top all torn open." I was a little shocked to hear this fact confirmed, about which I had read but dismissed as sensationalism. I thought it might be distressing to the families of any person who may have fitted this description to picture their relative in such a desperate situation. But of course, there were women and children on the Ceramic, and their fate cannot be imagined. "We shot at the Ceramic by night." Willi continued. "And then during the following day we went back again to find out the ship's destination, but it was not possible. We just had to take the next person. Two men hooked up and made the descent - they were Lamprecht and Hashagen. The waves were terribly high - they were life threatening. It was just by chance that a wave rose up with Eric on it, and washed him on board." I noticed that Willi was shaking as he gave this account, and he explained that even now, he is affected by the trauma of what he saw and experienced. It troubled me that I should oblige him to relive it again, but Willi continued. "Eric was asked where the ship was going, but he said he did not know. I did not speak directly to Eric, as I did not know any English. I found it a bit brutal, because they just fished him out for information. They could have let him come to his senses before interrogating him - that's what I found harsh. There was absolutely no possibility of saving anyone else - it was just the weather. The waves were so high. I had been on U-boats for many years, and I had never seen them that high." What else could Willi recall of the scene? "I could not see very well because of the height of the waves. I could see some lifeboats, but could not make out any details." Willi suddenly fixed his eyes on me, and addressed me directly, rather than through Helen, who was interpreting. "We absolutely did not shoot anyone," he stressed. "We never shot at shipwrecked people." I believed him.

The mood lightened with a switch in the topic of conversation to life in general as a U-boat sailor. "It was small and cramped," Willi explained. "The food was good, though. You could have as much as you wanted. It wasn't portioned - and then they fished out the butter…" (referring to the salvaged crates spilled from the damaged Hororata in December 1942). "Washing was difficult," Willi continued, "and we slept in our leathers because of the possibility of having to get up at a moment's notice. We did not wear pyjamas. We slept in bunks that could be pushed up and pulled down as and when required."

I asked Hermann Kaspers what his role had been. "I was in charge of the torpedo data machine," he explained. I had to enter the distance, size and speed, by typing it into the machine." Willi told us how he had been to Naval School, and four weeks later, found himself on board as a Navigator. He was involved in every attack. When the ship submerged, his position was in the heart of the boat, in charge of the motors. "We mostly attacked at night," continued Willi. "You can travel on the surface at night, and it is faster. You could observe the really big ships without being seen. The position of the U-boat was just above the water. We would follow a ship and try to get in front of it. If it did not zig-zag, and if we were in luck and it travelled past us, then we shot it. The Ceramic took a zig-zag course, and it was very fast. We could see the detail - it was quite close. We first saw its four masts at midday, and followed it all day from some distance. There was no air cover, and we could see the ship, but it could not see us."

Later at lunch, Hans Hahn took up the story. "The Ceramic was a big ship, 18,000 tons - and fast. That is why it did not have any escort. It went on its own. It had guns, war material and troops on board. The Ceramic could do 25 knots, and we

Chapter 12: The account of the U-boat crew

could only manage 16, but there was a storm warning of force 6-8, and large waves, so the ship could not travel quite so fast. We saw the tips of the masts at about 12 o' clock midday, and followed it all afternoon at full speed. The Ceramic did not notice us, although we were travelling on the surface as well. At about midnight, we were one or two miles in front of the Ceramic when the attack began. I was in the tower at the helm. The first torpedo hit the engine room, so the ship could not proceed." Hans explained with his hands on the table how the Ceramic and U-515 had been positioned during the attack. As the Ceramic steamed ahead, the U-boat took up position at right angles to her predicted course, ready to fire when she crossed its path. Once hit, U-515 proceeded to the same position on the opposite side of the now immobile ship to fire a second salvo. It was a simple but deadly tactic. "We sailed around to the other side and sent two more torpedoes into her because she had not sunk - she <u>had</u> to go down! And then the lights came on. It was brightly lit up. The Ceramic had been travelling without lights," explained Hans. "The Portuguese and Spanish ships sailed at that time with their lights on because they were neutral, and we did not attack anything with its lights on. It had its lights off because it was a war ship. The propaganda came about because it should not have had women and children on board. We did not know its name. We shot two torpedoes, of which one hit. It then sent out a distress call to all the ships in the area to say they had been torpedoed by an enemy submarine. The Ceramic had stopped, but it did not sink. That is when we went round to the other side, and the lights came on, and that was when we noticed that they all had their life jackets with a little light on. They swam at night in the water, with their little lights on. We saw people jumping into the water. We did not know there were women and children on board when the ship sank, and so we left the scene." Did all the lifeboats get away successfully? "No, some lifeboats were launched, but they broke away as they were released," Hans continued. "We departed, and then sent a message to Dönitz with the co-ordinates of the site where the Ceramic had been sunk. At 6am, we received a message from Dönitz instructing us to return to the site of the sinking in order to find the Captain, or a survivor. It took six hours to get back to the site, and we arrived there at midday. We saw women and children in the water, but we could not see any boats. No other ships had come to the rescue. They made a grave error allowing women and children on board. The English press wrote that the Germans had shot at the women and children. Two people descended, all hooked up, and dragged Eric Munday on board. His hands were all split open." Eric later explained, "I had helped to load one of the lifeboats,

Hans Hahn and his wife.

when I was ordered to get in it. As it had been lowered, I had to slide down the rope, and that's when I burned my hands."

"Eric was taken on board and given clothing," continued Hans. "He was allowed the occasional smoke, and he was well treated. He experienced depth charges while he was on board and we were submerged. In January we returned to Lorient, and someone came along and took Eric away, and that was it."

Could Hans describe a typical day in a U-boat? "We had three watches. You would be on watch for four hours, and then have eight hours free. There were three different groups of people, and so it would continue, day and night. Each watch comprised five people. The tower formed a circle, and so one person would look after a quarter of it, two looking back and two looking forward. One person sat in the middle at a lower level, and that was me. Four people sat above me on lookout. I could not see anything, I was only steering by means of the compass. In the machine room they operated a different system; six hours on and six hours off. They just sat with the diesel engines and the electric motors. The diesel engines charged the batteries. In our free time we would wash up, peel potatoes, serve food to the officers…" Could Hans describe their sleeping arrangements? "we only used hammocks for overspill. I had a bunk. You could only lie on your side. It was covered with a waxed fabric, and there were only two beds for three people, hence the shift system. It was damp when you got into bed, as someone else had just got out!" Did they wash? The question caused some hilarity. "We had a shower - if it rained, we went outside!" Did they have fresh water? "We had to wash in salt water. Fresh water was only for drinking. We had one glass of fresh water a day, and that was also for cleaning our teeth. We could make fresh water by distilling it from salt water and adding a chemical, but that was needed for the batteries. We had six or seven batteries as big as this table, and they had to be looked after all the time." The batteries seemed to Helen and I to be of greater importance than the men! "There were two toilets for 60 men," Hans continued. "One at the front, and one at the back. But as we left port, the toilet was full of stores for sixteen weeks - bread, potatoes, meat, eggs… You had to ask if you wanted to use the toilet, and if you didn't get permission, you could not go. It was due to the even distribution of weight necessary to balance the boat and the movement of people. But under the engine, there was about three metres of free space to catch the bilge, and we used to piss in that. It was pumped out, so it didn't smell. There were four torpedo tubes in the Bugraum, and people slept there. They ate on top of the torpedo in the middle of the room. There was a heavy hatch in the room, so that if water got in it could be closed off and the room could be pumped out."

Hans continued, "Our longest trip was 22 weeks. Damaged boats returning to base would supply us with diesel and oil so we could stay out longer. But it was problematic connecting a pipe from boat to boat, and watching out all the while that no aircraft were passing overhead. We would look out for places where aircraft didn't fly, but later the Atlantic was completely covered, generally by aircraft taken out to sea by aircraft carriers.

It was hard to believe that these genial men and their cheerful wives, in whose company Helen and I were enjoying lunch at a hostel close to the Medem, could ever have been enemies of our own country. There seemed nothing to differentiate them and their values from those of our own side. "It was war," Hans explained. "We were sunk too, and we are still suffering the effects of the war." Echoing the late Carl Möller's sentiments in a letter to Eric after the war, Hans added, "We were enemies, and now we are friends. This is an example today. Enemies quite often become your best friends."

Hans continued by adding his own experiences of the sinking of U-515 to those I had recorded earlier from Hermann Brandt. "When we were captured, they told us, 'If you do not tell us what trips you are doing, you will be sent to England.' But the Commander did not say anything - it was a threat. We were split up on the aircraft carrier, and we went to Arizona. In April 1944 we were told that Henke had been shot trying to escape, but nobody really believes that. I can't comprehend that a man would try to escape at 3 o' clock in the afternoon over a fence! He couldn't get out, so why would they try to shoot him? They shot him because of the Ceramic, and the propaganda about the shooting of the people in the water. They thought that the English had a price on Henke's head."

How was Hans treated as a Prisoner of War? "I was in Texas in America in 1944, and well cared for. In 1946 I was in San Francisco, and thought I was coming home, but I landed in Liverpool and was loaded into a train. We were dealt with very correctly. I went by train to Edinburgh, and was used by farmers in the fields, not arriving back in Germany until 1948. I was well treated, and what is more, like a normal person. I preferred it in America, because we didn't have to work, and we were well fed, but we weren't treated as people there. In Britain we were treated as people." Why was he detained so long after the end of the war? "I don't know," Hans shrugged. "Other people came home late too. My home was in Czechoslovakia. I was aware that the war was over."

After lunch, we travelled back to the hotel by coach, and Helen and I decided to head for the U-boat archive, a rather optimistic, "five minutes walk up the road," according to Jak Showell! There to meet us was the man himself, and a welcome cup of tea and biscuits. We were shown the files, and had a cursory flick through their contents. I made some copies, but as a trip to the archive is scheduled for tomorrow, we did not spend too long there today. As the predicted small hours now slip by, I feel I will be brief about this evening's interviews, but I have made further tape recordings, and seen collections of photographs in the possession of some of the crew, that I hope I may be allowed to copy tomorrow. Or should that be today? Now if I want to focus on my task, I must get some sleep. Only the eccentric English girl is still awake in this sleepy town, burning the midnight oil to pull her disjointed and rapidly scrawled notes into some kind of order.

Tuesday 29th May 2001

I surfaced today to sunlight - the first I had seen since leaving England. After breakfast, our party had an appointment at the U-boat archive, where we were met at the gate by the legendary Horst Bredow, who is well known for almost single-handedly setting up and running the one and only museum dedicated to the German submarine service in both world wars, and a tribute to the terrible casualties suffered.

U-Boat Archive, Altenbruch.
Horst Bredow and Eric Munday centre.

The emphasis was naturally on the second world war, where the U-boats played such a decisive role. Horst began his tour in the memorial garden, but it soon became clear to Eric, Joan and myself that we were not up to a tour in German. Jak Showell stepped in at this point to provide us with our own guided tour, and so we were fortunate to have the exhibits explained in English by one of Europe's leading authors on U-boats. The museum was truly bursting at the seams, and Jak aired his wish to see some of the overflow housed in England, possibly Bletchley Park, where paradoxically, a greater interest in the subject exists than in Germany. Though charged with the atmosphere generated by a visit of a U-boat crew, the morning proved to be less than ideal for research, as the relevant files were naturally in demand. However, I eventually got my hands on the coveted photograph album, and was able to make use of a handy gadget on which to screw my camera for the purpose of making copies.

From the archive, the Mundays, Helen and myself decided to go into Cuxhaven for lunch, where, by the auspices of the cake gods, we found ourselves parked outside a cafe with all kinds of calorific delicacies on offer. We found Cuxhaven to be an excellent centre for shopping. I fulfilled my duty as Parent In Absence, by purchasing gifts for the children, and Helen was delighted to find a range of children's videos for her German Parent/Toddler group in England. After a bracing visit to the sea front, we were blown back to the car and proceeded to Bremerhaven, where the rest of the party had planned to spend the afternoon.

Chapter 12: The account of the U-boat crew

The weather was bright but windy, and the skies blackened as we made our way past the numerous wind generators flanking the motorway and turning en masse at full speed. We found the U-boat in Bremerhaven harbour with little difficulty, and encountered a few familiar faces in a setting that, for them, was very far from unfamiliar. For me, this was the third submarine I had been inside, but the first German one, and it seemed appropriate to point a camera in Eric's face at every given opportunity. He was a very obliging model, and threw no tantrums at all. The U-boat was considerably less cramped than U-515, being built after the war, and never having entered service. Helen was sure she could find space for the men to take a bath, but as Willi later explained, each man was issued with a bottle of cologne, so really, bathing was quite unnecessary! Of course, we were just playing up to the female stereotype.

Eric gets reacquainted with a U-boat in Bremerhaven.

We returned to the hotel quite hungry, but the evening was testament to the fact that there remained just one insurmountable obstacle to Anglo-German unity, and that was the food! Despite our honourable intentions, and indeed, the Queen must have to face these issues of diplomacy when presented with a plate of chargrilled Stag beetle on her visits to the farther flung reaches of the Commonwealth, we were defeated by a plate of innocuous looking fish fillets, or *'Matjes'*. These were half salted and half soused, the salted offerings presenting the biggest problem to my sensibilities, as they were raw and far too much like living creatures for me. As I surreptitiously tried to remove the skin from my herring, I was confronted by the feisty waitress who insisted it should be consumed in its glorious entirety. Helen, who had the genuine excuse that she is vegetarian, was pushing her portion around the plate in the royal tradition, whilst Eric and Joan did their best, but our lack of enthusiasm did not go unnoticed by the hotel management. By this time, I had lost my appetite, so declined the alternative offer of bread and cheese, but Eric's acceptance became our amusement, as the pile of cheese slices on the plate was found to conceal the blackest rye bread imaginable! I had to take a photograph of Eric's valiant effort to clear his plate, but could barely hold the camera still! When Helen then addressed the cultural slight by ordering the customary post-dinner schnapps, my condition was only exacerbated, as she knocked back a recklessly huge mouthful and then had to decide whether to swallow it, or spit it out! Politeness dictating the former option, she then exclaimed breathlessly, "You could have pulled all my teeth out then, and I wouldn't have noticed!"

As we both needed to sober up - even though I had drunk nothing but mineral water all evening, we decided on a walk to the U-boat archive after dinner, where I made copies of some documents on loan from Hans Hahn. On returning later to the dining room, where

Memories of POW food!

a few were still deep in conversation, we ordered hot chocolate, and Willi Klein beckoned us to his table. "We will talk business in the morning," said Willi, indicating that this was a social invitation. I was pleased to be welcomed by a man who I felt was more conscious of his part in the sinking of the Ceramic than any of his comrades there, and who in many respects was quite guarded. He had been in a senior position, and it concerned me that even after all these years he still felt personally burdened by the human cost of the tragedy. I had not travelled to Germany on a mission of recrimination, but to meet the crew, understand them as men and get at the truth. "You see we are not the monsters we are made out to be," said Willi. I had never seen them as monsters. I had not lived through the war. I felt this was an advantage. Willi would not let us pay for our hot chocolate. His small gesture meant more than the nine mark tab.

We learned how Willi's 'boys' came to him as raw recruits, but how they quickly became such a highly trained crew that with five men on the bridge, they could crash dive to a depth of 15 metres in 28 seconds. It was clear even today how tightly knit they were as a group. I trusted however that we would not be performing any underwater manoevres on our trip to Helgoland tomorrow – a journey Helen and I are anticipating with some trepidation, as it takes two hours each way, and the sea today has been very choppy. Only Hermann Kaspers is staying behind, due to a recent operation on both eyes. When he came, said Willi, his best friend for 66 years, he was very down in spirits, but the camaraderie had given him a boost. Helen and I hoped for a calm sea, and that the trip tomorrow would give us another opportunity to get to know our friends on the last full day of the reunion.

Chapter 12: The account of the U-boat crew

Wednesday 30th May 2001

With our two-hour ferry crossing to Helgoland in prospect today, it was something of a relief to find that the weather was considerably calmer than yesterday, and as the sky cleared and the sun shone through, the day looked full of promise. We boarded the coach for Cuxhaven at 9.30am, most of us sporting our 'fünf-fünfzehn' *[which is how the crew refer to U-515]* baseball caps, courtesy of Gunther and his co-organisers of the reunion. On these occasions, it pays to be in the know, and Hans and Hannelore Schulz were aware of a sun deck where, for ten marks, sun loungers were available for Helen and I to stretch out and quell our constitutions with eyes fixed upon the horizon. It soon seemed worth the price, as others in our party came to join us in our first-class quarters. The outward trip was considerably more bearable than we had anticipated yesterday on Cuxhaven's gale-swept sea front, and Willi attributed the sunshine to the influence of the Angels - with a nod to Helen and myself.

The dot on the horizon that was Helgoland, gradually came into view. It had been the property of the English, until we had swapped it for Zanzibar, a deal that Gunther described as rather like exchanging one's trousers for a button! On drawing near land, it became apparent to the English insouciantes that no harbour existed on the island adequate for a ferry,

Gunther Altenburger nearing Helgoland.

and we would have to transfer to precarious looking motor boats which operated a shuttle service. As we were manhandled onto one of these swaying vessels, Helen and I were concerned for our elderly shipmates, but we underestimated their fitness. This later became even more apparent, when we had the option to scale the cliff, and Helen and I once again found ourselves trailing a posse of 'fünf-fünfzehn' caps on snowy white heads, and having to step up to keep up!

Not wishing to eat too much on account of our meal this evening, we indulged in our favourite German tradition: Kaffee und Küchen! Helen needed no encouragement. Helgoland turned out to be little more than a textbook example of geographic strata, and a sprawling parade of duty-free shops straggling up the cliff. As it does not belong to the EEC, its economy is geared to the duty-free market. Apart from alcohol, tobacco and perfume, there was little else to part us from our deutschmarks that did not appear to be made in China.

Not to be outdone by our octagenarian companions, Helen and I made it to the top, where we enjoyed the view over the azure waters where a succession of white ferries basked in the sun, awaiting their homeward-bound passengers, before we returned via various gift shops, to sea-level.

The route back to the waiting ferry once again involved taking our life in both hands, as we were taken by both arms and squeezed aboard a motorboat that took us to the side of the ship, and, as it rose and dipped with the swell, we jumped aboard with as much dignity as we could muster. Again the sundeck beckoned, and as our friends reclined to enjoy the late afternoon sunshine on their loungers, Willi remarked with the candour of a lifetime's friendship, "Look at your fat tummy sticking up, Hermann!".

As we drew into Cuxhaven, Hermann Brandt chatted to Helen and I, anxious to stress that he had been employed in the Engine Room on U-515, and therefore could not supply any details of the sinking of the Ceramic. "But when I heard about the Ceramic, I didn't shout 'Hooray'," he admitted. "And later, when I learned the full story, it grieved me." Hermann's response echoed that of his comrades, most of whom worked below decks, and were eager to disassociate themselves with an incident that with hindsight they found shameful, though of course, at the time, they were doing their job, which was to sink merchant shipping and troopships heading for North Africa. Blacked out, and in heavy seas, how could they have known of the civilian casualties that, sixty years on, could still cause distress that Helen and I did not feel it appropriate to dwell upon?

"You had better watch out for Hermann," nudged Gunther with a wink. "He's a bit of a Casanova!" Helen and I felt quite safe.

Back in Altenbruch, I borrowed Hermann's photograph album, and made copies quickly before dinner. The evening was not as formal as I had been led to believe, and Eric's speech was the only one, gallantly delivered in German, with a bit of assistance from Helen. I took the opportunity to photograph the six men who were on board U-515 when the Ceramic went down: Hermann Brandt, Herbert Dewald, Hans Hahn, Kurt Hanisch, Hermann Kaspers and Willi Klein. I cannot say that my mind has been changed by this visit, as I did not go with any preconceptions, except that I might find the men behind the sinking of the Ceramic to be ordinary men just like our own, and in this respect, I found what I expected. But as arrangements were made for next year's reunion, with typical German efficiency, and as Eric and Joan signed up in principle, I felt that I didn't want to say goodbye tomorrow, and would welcome the opportunity to meet again. In just a few days, it is possible for friendships to grow. When the past is seen in context, why shouldn't this be the case?

Chapter 12: The account of the U-boat crew

Altenbruch Reunion 2001.
Speech given by Eric Munday at the farewell dinner.

Dear Ladies and Gentlemen,

Thank you for inviting Joan and myself, Clare and Helen to your reunion dinner.

It would have been too much to expect me to recognise any of the survivors of U-515. When I last saw them in January 1943, they were all young and handsome and in their twenties. Now we are in our eighties. After the war Carl Moeller and I wrote to each other and exchanged photographs, likewise to Albrecht Henke, the brother of Werner Henke. This does not mean that any one of us forgets their wartime experiences. After 58 years not one year goes by that I do not hear from a relative of either a crew member or a passenger.

Some of you may not know that Clare's grandfather was lost at sea on the Ceramic and therefore I shall ask her to dedicate her book to his memory.

We will leave you all tomorrow with the hope that we shall meet again next year.

I would like to close with the request to raise your glasses with me to that which connects us: the memory of our common experiences, and the friendship which developed from it.

***

U-515 Crew who were on board when the Ceramic was sunk.

Altenbruch 2001.

L-R Back:
Herbert Dewald
Willi Klein
Hermann Brandt
Hermann Kaspers

L-R Front:
Kurt Hanisch
Eric Munday
Hans Hahn

SS CERAMIC The Untold Story

Recollections of the Ceramic, by Obersteuermann Wilhelm Klein

It was in the afternoon that we were called to the Gefechtsstation. I had to go to the bridge. On the right side of the boat I could see the tips of four masts with my binoculars. We tried to overtake, but the ship zig-zagged. Only when it was dusk could we get a little bit closer. They shouldn't see us at any rate. The sea was rough but visibility was good. It was getting darker, but soon we could see the superstructure of the ship and the bridge - it was a huge ship. To keep up with the ship, we had to follow it at full speed. We were lucky, because if the ship had changed course again, it would have been gone. We had the advantage. We were on the darker side of the sea, whereas the ship was on the brighter side and easy to observe the whole time.

After a few hours of following the ship, we were ready to fire. All torpedoes were ready to shoot. Henke observed the ship with his binoculars, and First Officer Hashagen was standing at the optical sights. (When the boat is well positioned in the optical sights, it is possible to fire).

All went according to plan. The first shot hit the ship. We waited a few minutes and fired a second torpedo. The ship had stopped. Then we heard from the radio room that it was the 18,000 BRT Ceramic (a freight ship). We were happy. But the ship did not sink. In total, there were five torpedoes fired, then the ship collapsed and sank.

Henke moved closer; then we saw the first lifeboats, parts of the wreck, wood and lights, which were on the life jackets of the crew. It was then for the first time that I realised there were people on board - many people. We were taught to sink ships, to destroy freight, but not to kill any people. Damned war.

Henke then moved away. There was the risk of destroyers which would have picked up the Ceramic's radio distress call.

The next day, Henke was ordered to go back to the site where the ship sunk. The sea was very rough. In total, I did 10 trips on a U-boat, but I never saw waves that high. On the bridge, we had all our belts fastened. Pieces of wood indicated to us that we were at the site. Then there were the first life boats. I remember clearly even today, 60 years later. In one boat were women. One had a baby in her arms. Again and again, waves flooded the boat. One time the boat was on top of the waves, then at the bottom, beyond us. It was a storm. I really don't know, and I cannot remember whether I saw more boats.

Then a man drifted towards the U-boat. First Officer Hashagen and Seaman Heinrich Lamprecht were fastened with a rope and went behind the tower on the upper deck. They were drenched again and again, and then - by accident, or by a

Willi Klein

stroke of luck - the man was lifted by a wave to the upper deck and was caught by the two. We lifted him onto the tower. He was absolutely exhausted and his hands were cut to the bone. He was then brought below deck. As far as further developments were concerned, I want to say that it was impossible to rescue anyone from the water, as the upper deck of a U-boat is only 1 metre above water level.

I can assure you that I will not write about it again in the future. I just did it to do you a favour. I am still very emotional and I hate the damned war.

In total, I did 10 trips on a U-boat. In 1940, when I was 20 years old, the boat was hit and I had to exit the boat from 28 metres below water level. Eight comrades died.

***

SS CERAMIC The Untold Story

*Letter from Kurt Hanisch
to the author
15 March 01*

... Around dusk we sighted two ships. The given order 'Battle Stations!' did not tell us anything particular, it was just the command to immediately assume your action stations. On approach, the ships' armament and their zigzag course was noted. To reach a firing position, we had to perform an end around manoeuvre. In the stormy seas, this lasted for several hours and required high engine performance. The second steamer was taken care of by U-155, Lt.-Cmdr. Piening, who was in the vicinity.

Our two diesel engines with their 2,400 horse power required a lot of fuel. Diesel fuel was delivered to them by sea water that forced the fuel from the external tanks inside. In rough seas and through the tossing of the boat, sea water mixed with fuel. The fuel reached a holding tank before entering the engines proper. Viewports on this tank made observation of the fuel possible. As soon as water deposited itself in the lower part of the tank, the engine room artificer had to drain it. My particular task was amongst others to guarantee trouble free operations of the diesel engines.

During the hours-long end around manoeuvre, we did not receive any information about the tactical situation. The engine noise at high speeds was excessive and unbearable in the long run. To protect our ears, we plugged them with cotton wool soaked in wax. Communication was by way of hand signals.

Shortly before midnight, U 515 approached Ceramic to within 1,200 metres. Two torpedoes were fired and reported as hits. After the third hit, Ceramic was fully illuminated, but she did not want to go down. After the fifth torpedo she sank around 0100 hrs. When Ceramic radioed SOS, our side knew what ship she was. U 515 cleared the location of the sinking at high speed. Hours later, we had to go back to retrieve one survivor. This was Eric Munday's rescue.

***

Chapter 12: The account of the U-boat crew

Letter from Carl Möller to Dr Timothy Mulligan, biographer of Werner Henke. November 1987

...Now to your question, what was Henke like from the crew's point of view? During training, hard, often unsympathetic towards others. He kept a very keen eye on discipline and made sure his men were clean. The result was that his crew had to be loyal. On the other hand, he stood up for his men, especially if they received a bad report. As a seaman, he was excellent, and always ready to help. I remember going alongside lifeboats so the wounded could receive treatment from our medical officer, Dr Jensen. According to Heinrich Lamprecht, once he was an American Prisoner of War, he was accused of putting the wounded back in the lifeboats after treatment, which was supposed to be prohibited by the Geneva Convention. Unfortunately, comrade Lamprecht, First Officer on U-515, died shortly after his release from the Prisoner of War camp.

Carl Möller (right) after the salvage of crates of New Zealand butter from the sunk Hororata.
Photo: Eric Munday's collection.

Henke was a "go-getter". His relationship with his superiors was not good, and even we Non-Commissioned Officers had to suffer because of this. He should have been promoted to Kapitanleutnant some time ago, but he remained Oberleutnant for a long time. We prepared for "Front Trials" in the Bay of Biscay: a cruiser and destroyer had to be sunk. His relationship to Leading Engineer Mahnke was not good. The Obermaschinist was accused of sabotage which was a load of rubbish. This was the relationship between the L.E. and Obermaschinist Wilde. Wilde was hauled up in front of a court martial, and we had to take part in this. While refuelling at sea, a hosepipe came undone, and a rubber pipe got blocked up. Wilde was held responsible for it.

We had a dead man on board, which had happened while changing the barrels on the 20mm guns. Henke dealt with this very well. We had an honourable funeral at sea while the engines were stopped. We always tried to take on board the captain or an officer of any sunk ships, and they were all well treated. An officer from the Reedpool even helped with navigation. This meant you could exchange stories. With Henke, you got the impression he wasn't in allegiance with the National Socialists. We had swing music and jazz, and of course, the popular hits of the time sung by Rosita Serano and Rudi Schurike. In spite of this, Henke loathed the English. In 1943 when my family was bombed out, and Lamprecht's parents, wife and children were missing, we requested home leave from Lorient so that we could go to see to our families. Henke refused with these words: "Boys, I need you here on the boat. We'll show the English - I promise you that." He took us both by the arm and said in a low voice, "Bloody war; what's the point?" He was always like that. We were following up some sounds picked up by Funkmaat Heinen, and every few minutes there was a depth charge - it lasted for about nine hours. I was on action stations in the central control room; we were at a depth of about 280 metres. Henke stood like a pillar in the control room. The Leading Engineer was bent double with stomach pains. As the bombs detonated, everyone looked pleadingly at Henke, and he said, "Well, what am I supposed to do about it?" Situations like that you never forget.

The night of the Ceramic also belongs with those unforgettable moments. There were waves tossing about. When the Ceramic was torpedoed, we sped away. Hashagen, the First Watch Officer, and Henke, couldn't agree about the size of the ship. Henke reckoned 10,000 tons, and the First Watch Officer thought it was bigger. The following morning, we sailed back to the site of the sinking. Henke had Lamprecht and I on the bridge. It was a terrible sight - lifeboats, wreckage and people. There were high waves. We were cruising at half-speed, sometimes faster. While this was going on, one man was washed on board, who we immediately brought down into the boat, where I was asked to deal with him, because I spoke English. It was Eric Munday. He later told us about the sinking of the Ceramic. We celebrated Christmas, and experienced some depth charges.

**

Dr Timothy Mulligan is the author of the definitive biography of U-515 Commander Werner Henke.

Lone Wolf: Life and Death of U-boat Ace Werner Henke
Timothy P. Mulligan
Praeger; 1993; ISBN: 0275936775

Chapter 12: The account of the U-boat crew

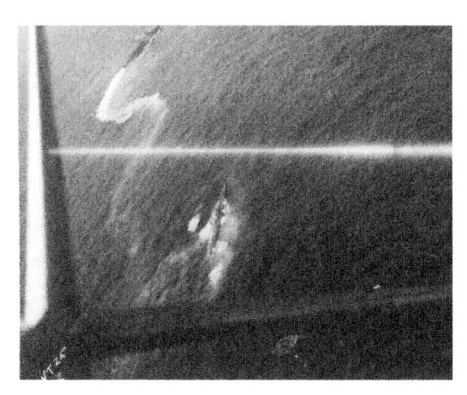

Top left: pursuit of *U-515* by Escort Carrier *USS Guadalcanal*.
Above and left: The capture of Werner Henke and *U-515* survivors by Destroyer Escorts *USS Chatelain* and *USS Pillsbury*.
Photos: USN.

Prisoners of War, *L-R:* ?, Breuer, Herford, ?, Wegemann, Hahn, ?, Hanisch, Oppelt, ?, Kaspers, Zumpf, Goebel, Lüpke. *Photo: Hans Hahn.*

Chapter 13
The fate of Werner Henke

MINISTRY OF DEFENCE
Naval Staff Duties, Empress State Building, London SW6 1TR
Date: 22 January 1986

Dear Mr Heath

Thank you for your letter of 5 December 1985.

U515 was sunk on 9 April 1944 by four US destroyers and three aircraft from USS GUADALCANAL. Forty-four of her ship's company of sixty, including her CO, were taken prisoner.

Yours sincerely,

P R MELTON

Date: 20 February 1986

Dear Mr Heath

In reply to your letter of 28 January 1986 to Mr Melton I can confirm that Kapitänleutnant Werner Henke was the CO of U 515 from her commissioning on 21 February 1942 until her destruction on 9 April 1944. Henke and most of his crew were picked up and landed at Norfolk, Virginia, on 26 April, where they remained for the next three days before being transferred to Camp Fort George G. Meade in Maryland. It was while he was there that Henke was shot dead attempting to escape on 15 June 1944.

The CERAMIC proved a tough nut. In his initial attack Henke fired a salvo of two torpedoes, both of which hit the target but only one of which exploded, in the area of the engine-room. As the CERAMIC was still afloat some 20 minutes later, Henke fired another torpedo to finish her off. It struck the ship forward, following which boats were lowered. A further 20 minutes passed and she was still afloat, so Henke fired yet another torpedo, which on this occasion hit further aft, whereupon more boats and rafts were lowered. The CERAMIC, however, still refused to go down, and it was an hour after the initial attack that Henke fired his fifth and final torpedo. It struck the CERAMIC forward, she broke in two and had disappeared within 10 seconds. Intending to take the Master prisoner Henke closed the position of sinking and discovered about sixty rafts, numerous boats and many bodies of dead Servicemen. He then dived owing to the weather conditions (the wind was SSW force 7 increasing, there was a heavy swell, and additionally rain and hail showers) and withdrew.

Yours sincerely,

R M COPPOCK

***

TWENTY MILLION TONS UNDER THE SEA
Rear Admiral Daniel V. Gallery, USN.
Henry Regnery Company, Chicago 1956.

... This chap that we were after was obviously a tough customer who knew his business. Three times during the morning my tin cans got him on sonar and dropped several full patterns of a dozen depth charges around him. Each time when the ocean quieted down again the destroyer's sonar men could hear telltale noises which indicated a U-boat was fleeing for its life somewhere in the nearby depths. Each time the cans went into our prearranged expanding search pattern and regained sonar contact. After the fourth attack a lot of garbage and oil came up to the surface, but this was an old familiar stunt by this time in the war, and we paid no attention to it. We could still hear the desperate thum ... thum, ... thum of propellors running very deep.

This submarine we were after gambled on staying deep. About 1300, our destroyers were pinging on him again. One took station about half a mile from him and coached another into firing position. Sonar loses contact on a deep submarine when you are nearly over it and the firing ship, if relying on its own sonar, would make the last minute of the approach blind. We had already found out for sure that if you gave this guy half a minute, it was too much.

At 1410 the *Pope* dropped a depth charge pattern and half a minute later the U-boat skipper down at six hundred feet was slammed against the steel walls of his conning tower and knew that the jig was up. Slow all tanks," he ordered. 'Prepare to abandon ship and scuttle."

At 1417 the submarine surfaced within a hundred yards of the *Pope, Flaherty, Pillsbury* and *Chatelain*. I could see him from the bridge of the *Guadalcanal* five miles away. There was no way of knowing that he had surfaced in extremis to abandon ship and scuttle. A deadly rattle snake had just reared his head from the depths-ready to strike, as far as we knew! So we let him have it. All destroyers opened up with everything they had in their lockers, depth charges, torpedoes, four-inch guns, and 20 mm AA guns. All indications were that the U-boat was structurally sound and was quite capable of firing a salvo of six torpedoes from her bow and stern tubes. In such a situation, you don't count the number of men who pop out of the forward and after escape hatches and dive over the side before issuing the order to cease firing. You watch the snake to see if you have broken its neck.

Four minutes after the U-515 surfaced, she slowly reared herself straight up in the air her stem going down. and her bow pointing into the sky with white water pouring out of all the vent holes in the gingerbread around her pressure hull. I suppose a literary man might say she looked like a cobra rearing its head to strike. But on the bridge of the *Guadalcanal,* my seafaring exec, yelled, "Thar she blows ... and sparm at that!"

We fished forty-five survivors from this U-boat out of the water and hauled them aboard the *Guadalcanal.* From some of the first we learned that her number was U-515, which meant nothing whatever to me except another U-boat. I directed the boys to bring the skipper up to the cabin when and if they got him.

Soon my chief master-at-arms and his number one helper escorted a husky, blond, eagle-eyed character, clad in U.S. G.I. dungaree pants and a dry sweat shirt, into the cabin.

"This is the Captain, sir," the CMAA said.

It was hardly necessary for him to say this. The man had a commanding personality and I knew the instant he came in the cabin that he was the skipper. He looked like an All American halfback whose team had just lost a close game and who was beaten but unashamed. I found out later that he was one of Doenitz' aces and though his crew respected his ability as a U-boat skipper, they hated his guts. They said he took unnecessary chances because he wanted an Oak Leaf for his Knight's Cross and they blamed the loss of their boat on his reckless confidence that he would sink the *Guadalcanal* (getting double tonnage credit) before we got him. They were also bitter because for two years he had frozen promotions on his boat to prevent any of his hand-picked crew from being transferred to other boats when they were promoted.

"Your name?" I asked.

"Henke," he said, continuing in English as good as mine, 'Werner Henke, Kapitan Leutnant, Kreigsmarine," and gave his serial number.

Chapter 13: The fate of Werner Henke

"The number of your U-boat?" I asked.

Henke stood mute.

"It was U-515," I said, and the look in his eye admitted it.

"How long were you at sea this cruise?" I asked.

Henke made no answer.

"You sailed from Lorient ten days ago," I said. It didn't take a crystal ball to figure that one out. Lorient was the Nazi main sub base in Biscay; every time we had sighted him he was on a southwest course away from Biscay; and it took eight or nine days to creep out of Biscay now that the RAF and U.S. Navy's Patrol Wing 7 were patrolling over it around the clock.

Henke shrugged his shoulders as if admitting it but said nothing. All this time he had a beaten but defiant look in his eye. Now the look began to harden.

I started to ask another question, "How many ships…" He interrupted, "Captain, I have a protest to make!"

Caught off guard I said, "What is it?"

"You violated International Law and the Geneva Convention," he said.

"How?"

"You killed many of my men while we were trying to surrender."

The answer to that one was easy. I said, "I had no way of knowing whether you were trying to surrender or to torpedo my ships. As soon as we were sure you were harmless we ceased firing and we have rescued forty-five of your men."

"But you killed ten," he said, " in violation of the Geneva Convention."

Henke knew as well as I did that several times wounded U-boats had surfaced to allow the crew to escape and with their dying gasp had torpedoed the ship that had done them in. I've often wondered whether in this situation the survivors from opposite sides should negotiate a truce after their ships go down or should keep on fighting in the water. But there was no point in continuing this argument any further. "Take him below," I said to the MAA.

Some of our skippers in the Battle of the Atlantic treated rescued U-boat captains as guests, and since they themselves lived in the sea cabin near the bridge when in dangerous waters, they turned over their own main cabin to the captured U-boat skipper. I didn't go along with this idea and figured it was better for all concerned to treat U-boat survivors as prisoners of war regardless of rank.

On the *Guadalcanal* we put all officers, including the skipper, in the brig (ship's prison) and separated the enlisted men into groups. We kept all non-rated men in one compartment and all petty officers in another. These three groups could never communicate with each other so they had no chance to give each other pep talks on security, or to hatch any plots to overthrow the government of the United States, or of the U.S.S. *Guadalcanal* especially the *Guadalcanal*.

So Kapitan Leutnant Werner Henke, Kreigsmarine, just awarded the Knight's Cross of the Iron Cross, was incarcerated in the brig. His cell there was bigger than his "cabin" on the U-515, the air was better, and the food that my chief master-at-arms brought him was at least as good as what he had been eating on his own ship.

Next day the master-at-arms brought word up to me on the bridge that Henke would like to see me. "What for?" I asked.

"Something about the Geneva Convention," said the chief.

"Oh, that again," I said, "Okay, bring him up to the cabin after we land the next flight."

When Henke was escorted into the cabin he had lost some of the beaten air of the day before. He registered an official beef against being quartered in the brig and quoted what he claimed was the Geneva Convention to me, saying that under its terms he was entitled to an officer's stateroom and should be allowed to eat in the officers' mess.

This wasn't too hard to answer either. I didn't have my copy of the Geneva Convention handy, but I explained to him that regardless of what the Convention said, we were still in the war zone and had to be practical. I couldn't give him an officer's stateroom without putting one of my own officers out of his bunk, which I didn't propose to do.

"But the Geneva Convention says..." he began.

"Besides," I interrupted, "Many of my officers and sailors are of Jewish or Polish ancestry. They might not be very polite to you if I gave you the freedom of the ship."

486

Chapter 13: The fate of Werner Henke

"According to the Geneva Convention, it is your duty to protect your prisoners."

By this time I was getting a little burned at being lectured on how to run my ship. The next thing I said was just a shot in the dark, on a completely unpremeditated impulse, "Captain, we are going to refuel in Gibraltar about ten days from now. If you don't like the way I'm treating you, I'll be glad to turn you and your crew over to the British. Maybe they will treat you better."

There are several things about this statement of mine which literal-minded people may criticize now. In the first place, we weren't going anywhere near Gibraltar. In the second place, if we had, the whole British Mediterranean Fleet couldn't have taken Henke and those prisoners away from me – I was bringing them home for proof!

My statement had an even greater effect on Henke than I had expected. The beaten look came back into his eyes and he said quickly, "Captain, it isn't that bad. I can put up with this treatment for a few more weeks. I withdraw my protest."

So Henke went back to the brig and requested no more audiences with me.

A few days after this interview, my chief master-at-arms, who had been listening just outside the cabin during this discussion with Henke, came up to me on the bridge with a very interesting story. (Remember that up to this time none of as on the *Guadalcanal* had ever heard of the *Ceramic*.)

It seems that Henke, knowing that the war was over for him, that he would survive it and could look forward to sitting out the rest of it in comparative comfort in the U.S., had done some reminiscing with my MAA. The chief was a sharp operator and had wormed his way into Henke's confidence by assuring Henke that I was a son-of-a-bitch, that all my men would like to shove me overboard, and he personally hated me. This had relaxed Henke so that he did a little talking. The story that the chief brought up to the bridge, given to him by Henke himself, was as follows.

"Just before the U-515 sailed from Lorient, the BBC had beamed a propaganda broadcast at the U-boat bases, saying they had learned that it was the U-515 that sank the *Ceramic*. (Obviously they learned this from Sapper Munday's broadcast.) They went on to say they had also learned that after the sinking the U-515 had surfaced and had machinegunned survivors in the water. Therefore, the broadcast continued, if anyone from the U-515 ever fell into their hands, they would try them for murder and hang them if convicted."

I don't know what prompted Henke to tell this story to my CMAA, except that the chief had established pretty friendly relations with him... and maybe something was preying on Henke's mind. He, of course, denied that there was any truth in the part about machine-gunning survivors, and may have told the story to put the British in a bad light. The British now deny that they ever made such a broadcast, but can offer no explanation as to why Henke, in 1944, should make up such a story. Personally, I take no stock in the part about machine gunning lifeboats, but I do believe the British broadcast such a story.

Anyway, this tale gave me food for thought. I had already found out that Henke did not enthuse when you suggested to him that he might go to England. I began to wonder just how far I could push the idea of sending him there.

After weighing a lot of pros and cons, I decided to try a shenanigan. I had a message to the *Guadalcanal* written up on an official dispatch blank purporting to come from CinC, Atlantic Fleet, saying: "BRITISH ADMIRALTY REQUESTS YOU TURN OVER CREW OF U-515 TO THEM WHEN YOU REFUEL GIBRALTAR. CONSIDERING CROWDED CONDITION YOUR SHIP AUTHORIZE YOU TO USE YOUR DISCRETION."

I also drew up a statement on legal paper with the ship's seal on it ready for signature by Henke:

I, Captain Lieutenant Werner Henke, promise on my honor as a German officer that if I and my crew are imprisoned in the United States instead of in England, I will answer all questions truthfully when I am interrogated by Naval Intelligence Officers.

Signed
Kapt. Lt.

Witness:
D. V. Gallery, Capt, USN
I. S. Johnson, Cdr, USN

Sizing up all the angles on this shenanigan before going into it, the chance of success didn't seem very good. But it was one of those deals where you have nothing to lose and might come out way ahead if it worked. The worst that could happen would be for Henke to spit in my face and tell me to go to hell, which wouldn't affect the outcome of the war one way or the other. If it worked, something pretty good might come of it.

I sent for a large scale anchorage chart of Gibraltar, drew some lines on it as if I were studying the best approach to the anchorage, and left it lying on the table

Chapter 13: The fate of Werner Henke

with parallel rulers and dividers on it where Henke would be bound to see it. I sent for Commander Johnson to come up to the cabin as a witness and explained the pitch to him. Then I had the chief master-at-arms bring Henke up from the brig and handed him the phony dispatch.

His face fell when he read it. A cornered look came back into his eye and he said, "Why do they want me?"

I shrugged and said, "I don't know."

"The Geneva Convention..." he began.

"Wait a minute," I said, "The U.S. and England are allies, you can be legally imprisoned in either place."

After a long pause he looked at me rather pathetically and said, "Well Captain, I suppose there is nothing you can do about it."

"Yes there is," I said. "That dispatch allows me to use my discretion. If you make it worth my while, I'll keep you on board till we arrive in the U.S."

"What do you want me to do?" asked Henke.

"Just sign this," I said, pushing the prepared statement across the table and laying a pen down alongside it.

Henke read the statement carefully twice, thought it over for a while and then said, "Captain, you know I can't sign that."

"It's up to you," I said. "Sign and you go to the United States. If you don't sign, then you and your crew go to England."

Henke was a courageous and tough man, as proved by the decorations he wore. But I had put him in a hell of a spot. Finally he looked at me and I could sense that here was one professional military man baring his soul to another whom he respected even though an enemy. "Well Captain, what would you do if you were in my position?" he asked.

I answered him truthfully and said, "If I were convinced that my country had lost the war and that I could help my crew by signing – I would sign."

Henke and I stood on opposite sides of the table for a few minutes without saying a further word. It was like a scene from a movie. I knew nothing of the real story of the *Ceramic* – at the time, but I'm sure now that all the harrowing details with which he was so familiar ran through his mind again. He knew that no impartial court would punish him for what he had done. He believed a British court-martial would hang him. Finally he picked up the pen, signed the paper, looked at me defiantly, and went back to the brig.

I then circulated a photostat of the agreement which the Captain had signed among the petty officers and non-rated men in the two prisoner compartments, and put a similar proposition to them... Sign and you go to the United States, refuse and you go to England. The proposed agreements for the crew went into much more detail as to what they would say than did Henke's. But they all knew the skipper's signature and there could be no doubt that he had agreed to talk. Every man in the U-515's crew signed, promising to tell all he knew.

Upon arrival in the U.S., Henke reneged on his agreement as I knew he would, saying quite correctly that it had been obtained under duress and false pretenses. But his crew, isolated from him and from each other, never knew this. They figured, "The skipper is talking – why shouldn't we?" When interrogated by our anti-submarine experts they sang like canary birds and our ONI people made quite a haul.

Now that the war is over and we've had time to forget, some bubble-headed people may say that I was guilty of using dishonorable tactics on Henke. However, I fed him well, gave him a comfortable bunk to sleep in, used no rubber hoses or drugs on him, and put him ashore in the United States alive, healthy and mentally undamaged. When I think of Buchenwald and Dachau, and of the brainwashed debris of humanity that the Communists have sent back to us from Korea I roll over and go to sleep with a clear conscience in spite of the finale to this episode which I could not foresee...

***

Classified: NND 750122
Report on the interrogation of P/W Henke, Werner, Kaptleutn.

Subject: **Morale Questionnaire**
14 May 1944
Lt. Tyson, Capt. Brown

I. Outcome of the War
(1) This year will be decisive. He hopes it will be over soon. He does not feel well acquainted with the land war situation, but thinks that it is now 50-50.
(2) Germany never really thought of conquering America; they always wanted to

remain on good terms with the U.S. They would be able to deal with England; to deal with England and America at the same time would be far more difficult. He personally regrets the entry of America into the war; no German is interested in a war with America. If it were not for the U.S., the Germans would now be finished with England.

II. Attitude towards Hitler and Regime
(1a) It may be judged from the parts of the interrogation that P/W does not favour Hitler as the right leader for Germany.
(1b) It is hard to say who would be a good successor. He must be a man who has seen the world and is a good diplomat. It might be von Pappen. P/W regrets that they did not make use of a Navy Ambassador for America. Some elderly admiral would have been a good choice. He would have been better than the persons actually used for these positions.
(2) It may be inferred from (3) below that P/W does not favor the present regime in Germany without qualification.
(3) A system of absolute government is impossible for America. That occurs only through unemployment, hunger, and a lost war, as it was in Germany. Bad treatment at the hands of the Poles contributed. Russia played a part. Following the last war, small countries like Czecho Slovakia could threaten the Germans and uproot the German culture from their lands. The Poles left only unfortunate economic conditions behind them. He knows this because his family comes from Bromberg. His father was an Oberfoerster. His family was there since 1770 and had accumulated their possessions through honest work, not through "speculations". An uncle owned half the village. All this was taken away from his family by the Poles; he states they were paid a very small sum for all the property.

He thinks the Nazis did not conduct their foreign relations very well. He thinks they should have acted differently with reference to the political situation before the war. A "United States of Europe" is a good idea, but how can it be brought about? The many people with their many quarrels make it impossible.

Present day conditions show that Nazism is not the right solution of the German problem. (Before speaking his mind, P/W insisted that his remarks should not be used for propaganda purposes.) Revolution always brings bad people to the front. Think of the French Revolution, and the Russian Revolution, as examples.

He denies that scientists were repressed in Germany.

The Jews always had the best businesses. They came from other parts of Europe and became rich almost immediately. He assumes that there must have been great dishonesty among them. He refers to it as "Geil" and "Schieberei". They were given the chance to work honestly in Germany and to earn their honest money.

P/W adds that he does not wish to be regarded as personally responsible for the treatment of these people. He says that injustice is always punished in the end.

They did not have only two big parties in Germany, but many parties each of which thought it could build up the country. One cannot manage on that basis. Dissatisfaction led to the Nazi movement. This led to the present war.

He expresses his hatred of war, his desire for a peaceful life.

(4) As a Berufsoffizier, he was not a party member.

(5) Question about distinction between people and party not asked. In a rather aristocratic sense, he seems to disclaim knowledge of how the more common people in Germany are affected.

III. Home Front Morale
(1) and (2) Questions about quantity and quality of food not asked. (In this instance it was important to keep up the apparently unmilitary nature of the questions).
(3) Bombardment of German cities with civilian population is unfair. When asked, he does not see much difference between the bombings of English cities and the bombings of German cities. He thinks that bombings raise the people's spirit of resistance. It is a "Scweinerei". "The German who has lost all will fight to the last shot."
(4) Industrial effect of air raids not asked.
(5) Probably has no information by foreign workers.
(6) Was in Hamburg in July 1943; the city was being attacked. Military losses are not greater than those of World War I; but civilian losses are definitely greater.
(7) and (8) not asked.
(9) Lost two brothers-in-law in Russia. No casualties in air raids.

IV. Soldier Morale
People on both sides are tired of the war. He never had to give talks to his men, because their spirit was always good. They trusted him.
(2) The men were not overconfident but their spirit was good. His men were confident of victory because although the entire U-boat war was not going so successfully, his own voyages were always successful.
(3), (4), and (5): Questions did not seem appropriate for a Korvettenkapitaen.

V. Unconditional Surrender
(1) Resistance is definitely increased by the demand.
(1b) Unconditional surrender is not acceptable to the Germans. This is probably because of the post war expectations.

(1c) The German people are encouraged to fight to the finish.
(2) He believes that the Germans would seek an armistice if proper post war aims were explained; it must be assumed that they would be favorable to Germany.
(3) Vergeltung: "I don't know; it is possible."

VI. Post War Expectations
(1) Everyone wants peace; the English do too. But not on the enemy's conditions. They want to make Germany defenseless. Then the Czechs, Poles, and others will uproot the German culture. It is clear that the Germans built up those territories.

The Austrians would have no such (intentions?). The feeling there is just as it is in England; they don't want war any more. P/W's wife is living in the Tyrol right now, and the people there are very pleasant.

The Russians have taken all the border states, such as Lithuania, and gotten rid of the intellectuals. There are families there that don't have men any more.

The Russians would not distinguish between Nazi leaders and the German people.

In Estonia the Russians even stole the hardware from the doors.

(2) Occupation by Western Powers would be preferred.

VII. Attitude toward United Nations
Nothing to add to (VI) above.

VIII. Propaganda
(1) *"I do not know of the effect of Goebbels on the common man"*... *"Personally I always try to develop in my men a positive, national, fighting spirit."*
(2) It might be safely implied that he does not think the people in Germany are well informed, since he himself disclaims a good knowledge of the world situation. It is true his admitted ignorance on this score is due partly to his service at sea.
(3) He sometimes heard radio programs from England. They are pure propaganda. *"Propaganda is necessary in every war."*

He adds that he considers the American broadcasts more effective.
(c) Question about leaflets not asked.
(4) Not asked.

IX. Underground
Not asked.

X. Fighting Qualities
The Russians are not good soldiers. They depend on great masses of men. Neither is their leadership good. The German soldier is superior to them in every way. The Russians are a danger only because of their number.

The English are good seamen. They are not good on land, however. There the Germans are better.

"The Americans are good soldiers."
"No one believes that we will lay down our arms."

XI. American Weapons
American weapons are excellent but not better than those of Germany.

Notes: Conditions were such that Germany could not help entering the war. England should have returned the old colonies.

Attitude: Professional German soldier attitude; sold on German superiority and the justice of Germany's cause. Not an unqualified believer in Nazism. Conceited about his family, background, his military position, and his judgement.

***

TWENTY MILLION TONS UNDER THE SEA
Rear Admiral Daniel V. Gallery, USN.
Henry Regnery Company, Chicago 1956.

When Henke reneged on his agreement which all his people carried out as best they could, our intelligence experts decided to hold him to the terms of the agreement. They told Henke, "Either you talk, or you go to England." When he still refused they made preparations to send him to Canada for further transfer to England. The day before he was due to be shipped to Canada, Henke was pacing the exercise compound of the prisoner's camp. It was broad daylight, there was a high barbed wire fence all around the compound, and even if he got over it there were armed sentries outside the fence. Henke's mind must have gone back to the *Ceramic*. The BBC broadcast about it, which the British now claim is a figment of his imagination, apparently was too much for him.

He waited till a sentry was looking right at him and then started climbing the high wire fence that separated him from this world and eternity. "Halt!" cried the sentry, who didn't know Henke from dozens of others in the camp.

Henke kept on climbing despite two more hails.

Chapter 13: The fate of Werner Henke

The sentry let him have it. When you squeeze the trigger of a submachine gun you can't just put one well aimed bullet in the leg of a fleeing prisoner. You blast a dozen or so slugs in his general direction. Several of the sentry's bullets hit Henke and killed him.

What is the moral, if any, of this grim tale about Henke and the *Ceramic?* A pat answer would be, "He who liveth by the sword shall perish by the sword." That seems to dispose of Kapitän Leutnant Henke quite neatly. But it is much too pat and simple.

Henke's torpedoing of the *Ceramic* and leaving the survivors to drown seems ruthless and brutal, but our own submarine skippers in the Pacific operated in the same way. They had to, just as Henke had to. That's the only way you can wage war with submarines.

I'm sure that if the Allies had lost the war I could have been hung on Henke's accusation that I ruthlessly killed his men when they were trying to surrender. Maybe he could even have convinced a Nazi court-martial that I brainwashed him and violated the Geneva Convention with that shenanigan I worked on him.

If there is any moral at all to this tale, it is one that we refuse to admit in this country – that war is a grim business.

Artists impression from Stern magazine. U-Boat Archive.

SS CERAMIC The Untold Story

Letter to the author

"... I don't know if you may be aware of a book I once read about Commander Henke. It stated that he was captured by the Americans and put in a Canadian prison compound where he tried to escape and was shot. The strange thing was someone had written in pen the words, "This is a tissue of lies as he now lives in luxury in the USA." Unfortunately I cannot remember the name or author of the book with this indelible message. I can only remember obtaining the book from Stanley Road library in Liverpool many years ago. I often wondered if this was ever investigated."

***

Dear Editorial office,

I am a reader of your magazine *Stern*. Unfortunately, I am only in the reader circle, therefore the reports I read are always delayed. I am writing to you with reference to the report *"Verdammter Atlantik"* (Damned Atlantic) by Hans Herlin. It is true, that the lieutenant, Werner Henke, was shot on an escape run in June 1944. I was in the interrogation camp near Washington D.C., i.e. in Fort Hunt near Wellington, a very small camp. Every day we were permitted to walk around in pairs in a small cage for just 1 hour. There, I had the opportunity to talk to Werner Henke. The Americans tormented him badly. He was ready to sing. He was accused of deliberately sinking a Red Cross steamer which was illuminated* and they branded him a war criminal; they wanted to turn him over to the English, and so on. One morning, as he was walking through the left hand side of the cage and I through the right hand side, he took a short run before jumping over the first fence which was 3 metres high. He got over it, then covered the small distance of 2 metres up to the second fence. Exactly at top of the fence he lay still. During the shooting I took cover by laying down on on the ground. The siren howled, and approximately 10 minutes later an ambulance came running and drove quite close to the fence. Four men from the M.P. lifted him down from the fence. I suppose that he was killed instantly. I continued to lay down for protection until I was led back by the sentry. I have made a small drawing for you to get a rough picture. Now, I expect you want to know who I am. You will be astonished, my name is Fritz Kürt** and I was a sailor on the *'Doggerbank'* which was sunk on the 3rd of March 1943 by *U-43* Lieutenant, Schwandke, in the northern Atlantic Ocean. I was the only one to be rescued. Haven't you already written about this?

Yours respectfully,
Fritz Kürt.

Chapter 13: The fate of Werner Henke

*The evidence shows that while she carried medical personnel as passengers, the Ceramic was not a Red Cross ship, neither was she illuminated.

**In the spring of 1943, the tonnage war in the Atlantic reached a climax, when German U-boats managed to butcher convoy after convoy. In addition, boats were sent to more remote areas to sink independent ships. U-43 under Oberleutnant Schwandtke was part of the Tümmler-wolfpack, deployed near the Canaries. In the evening of March 3, 1943, Schwandtke torpedoed a ship which he identified as a Dunedin Star-type ship. He could not suspect he had sunk the Doggerbank, close to completing her journey through the Indian Ocean and Atlantic. Doggerbank had left Yokohama on December 17 1942, and she was steaming about 1000 miles west of the Canaries, when she was hit by three torpedoes. Only fifteen of the crew made it to a small boat, without water or food. On March 29, the Spanish tanker Campoamor found the boat after 26 days with only one remaining survivor, Fritz Kürt. He was taken aboard and brought to Aruba, where he told about the tragic fate of Doggerbank and her crew. According to Kürt, the fifteen men on the raft were quickly reduced to only six after the boat had capsized, including Schneidewind. The captain committed suicide after shooting four of his crew at their explicit request. The number of casualties totalled 364 ... The German high command was apparently very upset about this case of mistaken identity. The pages concerning this sinking were removed from U-43's log.

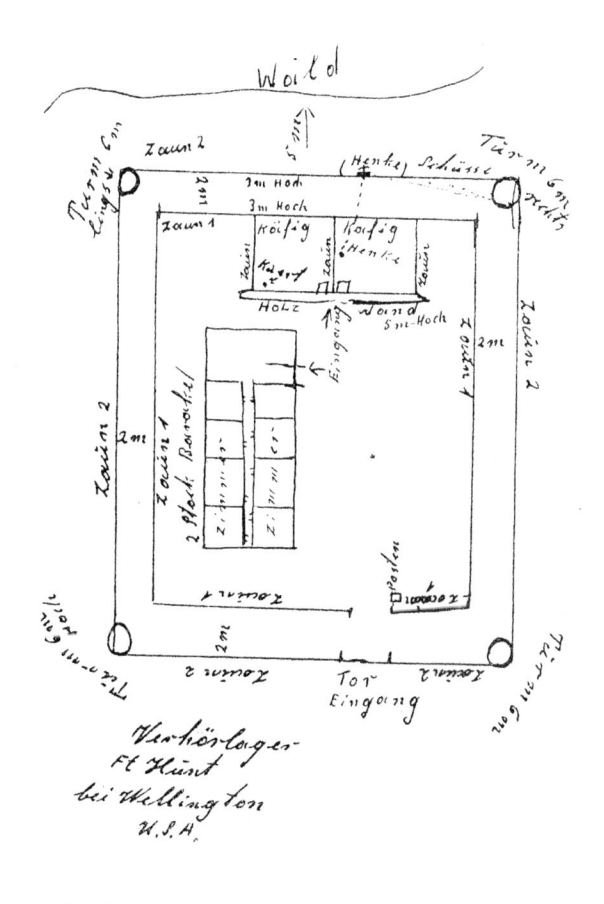

http://www.netherlandsnavy.nl/Speybank.htm

***

They shall grow not old,
As we that are left grow old;
Age shall not weary them,
Nor the years condemn.

At the going down of the sun
And in the morning,
We will remember them.

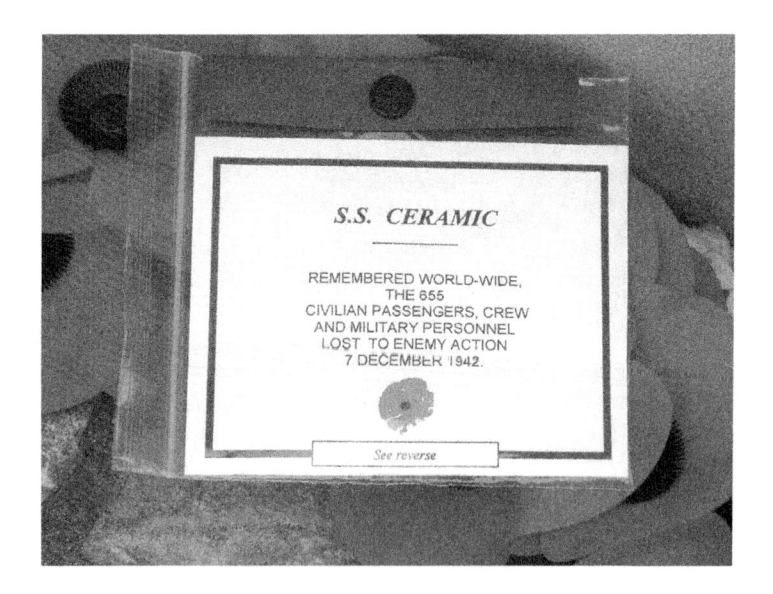

***

Wreath at newly unveiled Battle of the Atlantic memorial
laid for Eric Munday by Frank McCormick
on behalf of all *SS Ceramic* families worldwide.

Liverpool, England.
4 May 2003

S.S. CERAMIC
Sunk overnight 6th/7th December 1942

Casualty List

This list has been compiled from the following records:

Shaw, Savill & Albion: List of Passengers who embarked on the S.S. Ceramic at Liverpool on 24th November 1942.
Maritime & Coastguard Agency: Agreement and List of the Crew.
Merchant Shipping Act, 1906, and Aliens Restriction Acts, 1914 and 1919. Out-Going Passengers. Returns of Passengers leaving the United Kingdom in ships bound for places out of Europe, and not within the Mediterranean Sea.
Commonwealth War Graves Commission: List and website www.cwgc.org

Errors may be due to discrepancies in these records, or to the difficulties of transcribing longhand lists, particularly in respect of names and addresses. Any errors should be made known to the author for correction in future editions.

Clare Hardy: s.s.ceramic@btconnect.com

Civilians

ABRAHALL TERENCE HENRY
Age: **29**
Date of Birth: **30th March 1913**
Place of Birth: **Upper Holloway, London**
Occupation or Calling: **Telegraph Clerk**
Ticket No. **370**
Destination: **Cape Town**
Address in UK: 101 Halstead Road, Winchmore Hill, Middlesex.
Son of the late J. and Annette Emily Abrahall, 100 Junction Road, Upper Holloway, London.
*Recorded on Passenger List as ABRAHAM Mrs J. 101 Halstead Rd. London N21.

ALLAN THOMAS OSBORNE
Age: **51**
Occupation or Calling: **Est. Engine Fitter**
Ticket No. **217**
Destination: **Cape Town**
Address in UK: 81 Pump Lane, Rainham, Kent.

AURET JACQUELINE ELIZABETH
Age: **28**
Date of Birth: **7th July 1914**
Place of Birth: **Johannesburg**
Occupation or Calling: **Mothercraft Nurse**
Ticket No. **232**
Destination: **Cape Town**
Address in UK: Post Natal Home, Panshanger, Herts
Daughter of L. Auret, and of the late Capt. Ben Auret, Johannesburg, South Africa.

BAILE CYRIL JAMES Chartered Structural Engineer B.Sc., M.I.Struct.F., A.M.I.Mech.E.
Age: **49**
Occupation or Calling: **Government Official**
Ticket No. **213**
Destination: **Cape Town**
Address in UK: The Plantation, Daws Hill Lane, High Wycombe, Buckinghamshire
Husband of Margaret Baile

BEER MARIAN
Age: 21
Occupation or Calling: **Housewife**
Ticket No. **371**
Destination: **Durban**
Daughter of Mr. and Mrs. S. Evans, 17 Tymaen Street. Cwmavon, Aberavon, Glamorgan. Wife of W. A. C. Beer, of 2 Middleton Street, Briton Ferry, Neath, Glamorgan.
* *Travelling with her husband, Naval Telegraphist William Arthur Charles Beer, ticket 496.*

BILLINGSLEY-HEY FLORA
Age: 58
Date of Birth: **July 1884**
Place of Birth: **Bow, Devon**
Occupation or Calling: **Widow**
Ticket No. **405**
Destination: **Durban**
Address in UK: 189 (139?) Woodham Lane, New Haw, Weybridge, Surrey

BLASCHECK GRACE MARIEN ALEXANDRA
Age: 48
Date of Birth: **15th August 1894**
Place of Birth: **Corbridge**
Occupation or Calling: **Home Duties/Housewife**
Ticket No. **182**
Destination: **Cape Town**
Address in UK: Carrycoats Hall, Wark, (Birtley, Hexham), Northumberland
Daughter of Farquhar Millie Laing and Jane Grace Laing, of Farnley Grange, Corbridge, Northumberland. Wife of Capt. Joseph Henry Blascheck.
**Accompanying Masters Raymond (9) and Vernon (6) Harding, ticket no.s 181 & 182.*

BLUSGER DR ISAK NAHUM B.A., F.R.C.S.
Age: 32
Occupation or Calling: **Surgeon**
Ticket No. **267**
Destination: **Cape Town**
Address in UK: Black Notley Emergency Hospital, Nr. Braintree, Essex
Son of Soloman and Sarah Blusger, 34 Kloof Nek, Cape Town, South Africa.

BRADLEY HARRY
Age: 46 (47)
Occupation or Calling: **Farmer**
Ticket No. **189**
Destination: **Cape Town**
Address in UK: 84 Davenport Avenue, Hessle, E. Yorks.
Address given by CWGC: Ceres, Samba, Southern Rhodesia
Son of the late William Clark Bradley and Dinah Bradley, of Woodfield, Hessle, E. Yorks. Husband of the late Helen Kate Bradley.

BRADSHAW ALICE MAUD S.R.N.
Age: 41
Occupation or Calling: **Qualified Nurse**
Ticket No. **186**
Destination: **Cape Town**
Address in UK: 'Heathfield', Smedleys Street, West Matlock, Derby
Daughter of G. H. and Lizzie Bradshaw, Heathfield, Smedley Street, Matlock, Derbyshire.

BRAWN DR ROLAND DELIGNE M.R.C.S., L.R.C.P.
Age: 22 (24)
Occupation or Calling: **Doctor (Medecine)**
Ticket No. **268**
Destination: **Cape Town**
Address in UK: 20 Kensington Gardens Square, Bayswater, London
Next of Kin: Son of Essington O. and F.V. Brawn, 22 Scanlon Street, Uitenhage, South Africa.

BROUGHTON CHARLES
Age: 20
Occupation or Calling: **Labourer (Royal Navy)**
Ticket No. **499**
Destination: **Cape Town**
Address in UK: 28 Wardlebourne Road, Granton, Edinburgh
Son of Alice Rosina Broughton, 11 Evans Road, Milner Estate, East London, South Africa, and of the late William Broughton.

BUCHAN CYRIL WALTER
Age: 36
Place of Birth: **Swansea**
Occupation or Calling: **Metallurgist**

Casualty list

Ticket No. *363*
Destination: **Cape Town**
Address in UK: 11 Rhannan Road, Cathcart, Glasgow S4.
Son of D.L. Buchan, of 25 Pinewood Road, Uplands, Swansea, Glamorgan.

BUNN DR HERBERT WILFORD
M.R.C.S., L.R.C.P.
Age: *28*
Occupation or Calling: **Medical Practitioner**
Ticket No. *269*
Destination: **Cape Town**
Address in UK: Regent Palace Hotel, London W1
Son of J. H. and M. Bunn, Grosvenor Court, Summerstrand, Port Elizabeth, South Africa.

BURKE THOMAS RALPH Flt. Sgt., A.T.C.
Age: *19*
Date of Birth: *2nd November 1923*
Place of Birth: **Armthorpe, nr. Doncaster**
Occupation or Calling: **Scholar**
Ticket No. *270*
Destination: **Cape Town**
Address in UK: 31 Crescent Green, Kendal, Westmorland
Son of Mr. and Mrs. M. Burke, 14 3rd Street, Venterspost, South Africa.

CARMICHAEL VIVIENNE STELLA
Age: *22*
Place of Birth: **Glasgow**
Occupation or Calling: **Housewife**
Ticket No. *402*
Destination: **Cape Town**
Address in UK: (War Office Booking)
Husband Mr C. F. Carmichael, British Army Lieutenant
*Travelling with husband Mr C. F. Carmichael, British Army Lieutenant, ticket no. 402

CHARLES LUCY WINIFRED
Age: *60 (59)*
Place of Birth: **Peckham, London**
Occupation or Calling: **Widow**
Ticket No. *409*
Destination: **Cape Town**
Address in UK: 106 Beaufort Mansions, Chelsea, London SW3
Address given by CWGC: The Halt, Alexandra Road, Kenilworth, Cape Town. South Africa.
Wife of the late A. L. Charles.

COLES THE REVD. HORACE JOHN
Age: *55*
Date of Birth: *11th January 1887*
Place of Birth: **Bournemouth**
Occupation or Calling: **Clerk in Holy Orders**
Ticket No. *271*
Destination: **Cape Town**
Address in UK: 'Byways', Chaddesley Glen, Canford Cliffs, Bournemouth.
Son of John Samuel and Mary Louisa Coles, of Boxmore, Longfleet Road, Poole, Dorsetshire.

COLLINGBOURNE JAMES CHARLES
Age: *42*
Date of Birth: *17th June 1900*
Place of Birth: **South West Battersea, London**
Occupation or Calling: **Marine Wireless Inspector**
Ticket No. *399*
Destination: **Cape Town**
Address in UK: 38 High Brighton Street, Withernsea, E. Yorkshire.
Also: c/o. Marconi Wireless Telegraphy Co. London
Husband of Florence Collingbourne.

COOPER DOROTHY OLIVIA EMMS B.Sc.
Age: *29*
Occupation or Calling: **Housewife**
Ticket No. *184*
Destination: **Cape Town**
Address in UK: 9 Eliot Park, Lewisham, London SE13
Daughter of Arthur William Beadle, O.B.E., and Christina Beadle, of Fairlawn, Salisbury, Rhodesia, South Africa. Wife of Flying Officer Haig Allenby Cooper, of same address.

COPLANS DR CLIFFORD CROSSMAN
Age: *34*
Date of Birth: *7th January 1908*
Place of Birth: **London**
Occupation or Calling: **Medical Practitioner**
Ticket No. *283*
Destination: **Cape Town**
Address in UK: 35 Glenlion Road, Eltham, London SE9
Husband of T. Coplans.

CROAD MARY STEPHINE DOREEN
Age: 26
Date of Birth: 3rd May 1916
Place of Birth: Swaffham Prior, Cambs.
Occupation or Calling: Housewife
Ticket No. 284
Destination: Durban
Address in UK: 25 Courtfield Gardens, London SW5
Daughter of Mr. and Mrs. Woollard, of Manor House, Swaffam Prior, Cambridgeshire.
Wife of Paul Harry Cedric Croad.
*Recorded as Marie Stephanie on passenger list. Travelling with her husband, Aeronautical Engineer Paul Harry Croad, ticket no. 284

CROAD PAUL HARRY CEDRIC
Age: 25
Place of Birth: South Africa
Occupation or Calling: Aeronautical Engineer
Ticket No. 284
Destination: Durban
Address in UK: 25 Courtfield Gardens, London SW5
Son of Mr. and Mrs. Harry Croad, of 394 Ridge Road, Durban, South Africa.
Husband of Mary Stephine Doreen Croad.
*Travelling with his wife, ticket no. 284

DARROLL APOLLINE SARAH NIAY
A.R.C.M., L.R.A.M.
Age: 43
Place of Birth: South Africa
Occupation or Calling: Professor of Music
Ticket No. 272
Destination: Durban
Address in UK: Northumberland Avenue, London. N.W.1.
Also: Waldorf Hotel, Aldwych, London WC2
Daughter of George and Apolline Niay Darroll, of Cape Town, South Africa.

DAVENPORT ALFRED
Age: 53
Occupation or Calling: Engine Fitter
Ticket No. 218
Destination: Cape Town
Address in UK: 93 Talbot Road, Southsea, Portsmouth, Hants
Husband of Ethel Davenport, of 93 Talbot Road, Portsmouth.

DAVIES HENRY JOHN STANLEY
Age: 20
Date of Birth: 4th April 1922
Place of Birth: Ilford, Essex
Occupation or Calling: Civil Servant /Cotton Planter
Ticket No. 366
Destination: Cape Town
Address in UK: 110 Conway Road, Southgate, London N14
Also: c/o. Sudan Government, London
Son of H. E. and L. D. Davies, of 110 Conway Road, Southgate, Middlesex.

DIPPENAAR DR CECILIA JOHANNA
Age: 22
Date of Birth: 19th January 1920
Place of Birth: Bultfontein, South Africa
Occupation or Calling: Medical Practitioner
Ticket No. 237
Destination: Cape Town
Address in UK: Royal Liverpool Childrren's Hospital, Heswall, Cheshire
Daughter of Dr. D. Dippenaar, of Dewetsdorf, Orange Free State, South Africa.

DOLAN MARY HELEN S.R.N.
Age: 36
Place of Birth: Glasgow
Occupation or Calling: State Registered Nurse
Ticket No. 300
Destination: St. Helena
Address in UK: c/o M. McLeod, Post Office, Netherley, Nr. Stonehaven, Scotland

DU PLESSIS ADRIAAN FOSTER
Age: 37
Occupation or Calling: Civil Servant
Ticket No. 400
Destination: Cape Town
Address in UK: Sturdie House, Broomway, Weybridge, Surrey
Also: South Africa House, London WC2
Husband or H.M. Du Plessis, of Vaalbank, Colesberg, South Africa.

EWING DOREEN MARGARET
Age: 6
Occupation or Calling: Scholar
Ticket No. 358
Destination: Cape Town

Casualty list

Address in UK: (1)36 Montgomery Street, Edinburgh.
Also: 9 Northfield Avenue, Edinburgh 8, Scotland.
Daughter of A. Ewing, and of Mary Connolly Ewing, who both died on the *Ceramic*.
*Travelling with her mother Mary Connolly Ewing, ticket no. 358, and father Archibald Ewing, Naval Telegraphist, ticket no. 486.

EWING MARY CONNOLLY
Age: 32
Occupation or Calling: **Housewife**
Ticket No. 358
Destination: **Cape Town**
Address in UK: (1)36 Montgomery Street, Edinburgh.
Daughter of Mr. and Mrs. W. Topp, of the same address. Wife of A. Ewing.
*Travelling with her daughter Doreen Margaret Ewing, ticket no. 358, and husband Archibald Ewing, Naval Telegraphist, ticket no. 486.

FRASER-JONES ERNEST
Age: 50
Occupation or Calling: **Engineer**
Ticket No. 285
Destination: **Cape Town**
Address in UK: Greystones, Knowle Park, Almondsbury, Bristol.
Also: 7 Broadbent Street, Grosvenor Street, London W1.
Son of the late James and Mary Eleanor Jones, of Ravenstone, Ashby-de-la-Zouch, Leicestershire. Husband of Viola Fraser-Jones.
*Travelling with his wife, Viola Fraser-Jones and son Quentin Fraser-Jones, both ticket no. 285.

FRASER-JONES QUENTIN LAWRENCE
Age: 14
Occupation or Calling: **Scholar**
Ticket No. 285
Destination: **Cape Town**
Address in UK: Greystones, Knowle Park, Almondsbury, Bristol.
Also: 7 Broadbent Street, Grosvenor Street, London W1.
Son of Ernest and Viola Fraser-Jones, who both died on the *Ceramic*.
*Travelling with his mother, Viola Fraser-Jones and father Ernest Fraser-Jones, both ticket no. 285.

FRASER-JONES VIOLA
Age: 48
Occupation or Calling: **Housewife**
Ticket No. 285
Destination: **Cape Town**
Address in UK: Greystones, Knowle Park, Almondsbury, Bristol.
Also: 7 Broadbent Street, Grosvenor Street, London W1.
Daughter of the late Mr. P. J. Loveby-Smith.
Wife of Ernest Fraser-Jones.
*Travelling with her husband, Ernest Fraser-Jones and son Quentin Fraser-Jones, both ticket no. 285.

FREEMAN MARGARET JOYCE B.A.
Age: 31
Date of Birth: **29th September 1911**
Place of Birth: **Colwyn Bay**
Occupation or Calling: **Teacher**
Ticket No. 234
Destination: **Cape Town**
Address in UK: Colbron House, Woodville, Burton-on-Trent, Staffs.
Daughter of the Revd. and Mrs. Thomas E. Freeman, of Colbron House, Woodville, Burton-on-Trent, Staffordshire.

FRENCH LAWRENCE CUTHBERT
Age: 65
Occupation or Calling: **Mining Company Director**
Ticket No. 286
Destination: **Durban**
Address in UK: High Trees, Godalming, Surrey
Next of Kin: Husband of W. P. French, of High Trees, Godalming, Surrey.

GILES WILLIAM M.D., D.P.H., M.B., B.S.
Age: 31
Occupation or Calling: **Medical Practitioner**
Ticket No. 187
Destination: **Cape Town**
Address in UK: 103 Old Park Ridings, Grange Park, London N21
Son of Mary Giles, of Townend House, Austwick, Lancaster, and of the late John Giles.

HALSE LINDA WINIFRED
Age: 44
Occupation or Calling: **Housewife**
Ticket No. 369

Destination: **Cape Town**
Address in UK: 32 de Vere Gardens, London W8. Also: South Africa House, London WC2
Address in South Africa: The Cottage, Inanda, Johannesburg, South Africa.
Daughter of Mr. and Mrs. D. E. McConnell, of Belle Vue. Main Road. Miuzenburg, Cape Province, South Africa.
Wife of Lt. Col. S. S. Halse.
*Passenger list gives the spelling Lynda.

HARDING RAYMOND ERNEST
Age: **9**
Occupation or Calling: **Child**
Ticket No. **181**
Destination: **Cape Town**
Address in UK: 29 Malvern Avenue, South Harrow, Middlesex
Son of Horace Harding, of 29 Malvern Avenue, South Harrow, Middlesex, and of the late Ivy Gladys Harding.
*Travelling with his brother Vernon Keith Harding ticket no. 182 and accompanied by Grace Marien Alexandra Blascheck, ticket no. 182.

HARDING VERNON KEITH
Age: **6**
Occupation or Calling: **Child**
Ticket No. **182**
Destination: **Cape Town**
Address in UK: 29 Malvern Avenue, South Harrow, Middlesex
Son of Horace Harding, of 29 Malvern Avenue, South Harrow, Middlesex, and of the late Ivy Gladys Harding.
*Travelling with his brother Raymond Ernest Harding ticket no. 181 and accompanied by Grace Marien Alexandra Blascheck, ticket no. 182.

HAY WILLIAM WILFRED
Age: **52**
Occupation or Calling: **Shipwright**
Ticket No. **215**
Destination: **Cape Town**
Address in UK: 69 Dickens Road, Mile End, Portsmouth
Next of Kin: Son of Mrs. H. M. Hay. of Cartref, Leomandsley, Lichfield, Staffordshire.

HELLENBURG ARTHUR JOHN
Age: **21**
Occupation or Calling: **Civil Servant**
Ticket No. **211**
Destination: **Durban**
Address in UK: 311 Canterbury Street, Gillingham, Kent.
Son of Ernest Durrant Hellenburg and Gertrude Hellenburg, of 311 Canterbury Street, Gillingham, Kent.

HICKSON JOHN NEWTON
Age: **20**
Occupation or Calling: **Assistant Commissioner/Clerk**
Ticket No. **367**
Destination: **Cape Town**
Address in UK: Little Aston Vicarage, Sutton Coldfield, Warwickshire
Also: c/o. Sudan Government, London
Son of Dorothea Cranwell (formerly Hickson), of Little Aston Vicarage, Sutton Coldfield, Warwickshire.

HILDICK-SMITH JOAN
Age: **25**
Date of Birth: **3rd September 1917**
Place of Birth: **South Africa**
Occupation or Calling: **Nurse**
Ticket No. **287**
Destination: **Cape Town**
Address in UK: 3 Strathway House, Marylebone High St. London.
Daughter of Mr. and Mrs. G. Hildick-Smith, of Modder B. Gold Mine, East Rand, South Africa.
**Formerly of Women's Transport Service.
F.A.N.Y. (Ambulance Division).*

HOWARD ALTHENA MARGARET
Age: **2**
Occupation or Calling: **Child**
Ticket No. **273**
Destination: **Cape Town**
Address in UK: 5 Shepherds Hill, Highgate, London N6
Daughter of Joan Howard, and of the late Wing Comdr. Alex Howard, Royal Canadian Air Force.
*Travelling with her mother Joan Howard and sister Janet Mary Howard, both ticket no. 273

HOWARD JOAN
Age: **28**

Casualty list

Occupation or Calling: **Housewife**
Ticket No. 273
Destination: **Cape Town**
Address in UK: 5 Shepherds Hill, Highgate, London N6
Daughter of Edith Bagshaw, of Derwin, Sandown Road, Rondebosch, Cape Town, and of the late Thomas Ponsonby Bagshaw. Widow of Wing Comdr. Alex Howard, Royal Canadian Air Force.
*Travelling with her daughters Althena Margaret and Janet Mary Howard, both ticket no. 273

HOWARD JANET MARY
Age: **8 months**
Occupation or Calling: **Child**
Ticket No. 273
Destination: **Cape Town**
Address in UK: 5 Shepherds Hill, Highgate, London N6
Daughter of Joan Howard, and of the late Wing Comdr. Alex Howard, Royal Canadian Air Force.
*Travelling with her mother Joan Howard and sister Althena Margaret Howard, both ticket no. 273

HUME PETER JOSEPH B.A
Age: **28**
Date of Birth: **12th February 1914**
Place of Birth: **York**
Occupation or Calling: **Ambulance Unit**
Ticket No. 192
Destination: **Durban**
Address in UK: 4 Gordon Sq. London WC1.
Also: 49 Main Avenue, Heworth, Yorks.
(Deleted: Breeze Hill, Robertson House, Buxton, Derbyshire)
Son of Bertha Frances Hume, of 49 Main Avenue, Heworth, Yorkshire, and of the late Joseph Hume.

HYNE WILLIAM TAYLOR B.Sc.
Age: **29**
Occupation or Calling: **Civil Engineer**
Ticket No. 212
Destination: **Cape Town**
Address in UK: 25 Alexandra Avenue, Luton
Son of George Acland Hyne, and Emeline Taylor Hyne, of 25 Alexandra Avenue, Luton, Bedfordshire

JEFFREY AUDREY MAY
Age: **29**
Occupation or Calling: **Housewife**
Ticket No. 39
Destination: **Durban**
Address in UK: c/o. 90 Kingshall Road, Beckenham, Kent.
Also: c/o. Admiralty, London WC2
Daughter of Ernest Edward and Eva Beatrice Neil, of the same address. Wife of Lt. Alan Alexander Jeffrey, W. N. R.
*Travelling with her husband, Lieutenant Alan Alexander Jeffrey (Royal Navy), ticket no. 205.

JONES FRANK
Age: **30**
Date of Birth: **23rd August 1912**
Place of Birth: **Rochdale**
Occupation or Calling: **Engineering Turner/Civil Servant**
Ticket No. 397*
Destination: **Cape Town**
Address in UK: 3 Abbott Street, Rochdale.
Son of William and Nellie Jones, of 3 Abbott Street, Rochdale, Lancashire.

KING DENNIS GEORGE M.A.
Age: **20**
Date of Birth: **8th May 1922**
Place of Birth: **Twickenham**
Occupation or Calling: **Sudan Political Service/Civil Servant**
Ticket No. 368
Destination: **Cape Town**
Address in UK: 31 St. Winifred's Road, Teddington, Middlesex.
Also: c/o. Sudan Government, London
Son of Mr. and Mrs. George R. King, of 31 St. Winifred's Road. Teddington, Middlesex.

KING DAVID GEORGE
Age: **31 (32)**
Occupation or Calling: **Electrical Fitter**
Ticket No. 216
Destination: **Cape Town**
Address in UK: 128 Portsview Av. Fareham, Hants.
Son of Mr. and Mrs. E. H. King of Southampton Hill, Titchfield. Hampshire.
Husband of Norah Dorothy King, of Clydesdale, Portsview Avenue, Porchester, Hampshire.

LEWIN BENSON LEONARD M.P.S.
Age: 28
Date of Birth: **17th July 1916**
Place of Birth: **South Africa**
Occupation or Calling: **Pharmacist**
Ticket No. **229**
Destination: **Cape Town**
Address in UK: 39 Redpost Hill, London, SE4.
Son of Isadore Bernhardt Lewin, and Rebecca Lewin, of Church Street, Oudtshoorn, Cape Province, South Africa.
Husband of Betty May Lewin.
Travelling with his wife Betty May Lewin, ticket no. 229.

LEWIN BETTY MAY
Age: 20
Occupation or Calling: **Housewife**
Ticket No. **229**
Destination: **Cape Town**
Address in UK: 39 Redpost Hill, London, SE4.
Daughter of Mrs. A. Walters, of 35 Belle Vue Street, Swansea, Glamorgan.
Wife of Benson Leonard Lewin.
Travelling with her husband Benson Leonard Lewin, ticket no. 229.

LITTLETON CYRIL JOSEPH
Age: 36 (26)
Occupation or Calling: **Farm Manager**
Ticket No. **240**
Destination: **Cape Town**
Address in UK: The Green, Blennerhasset, Carlisle, Cumberland.
Son of Mrs. E. Littleton. of The Green, Blennerhasset, Carlisle, Cumberland.

MACLEOD ELIZABETH FRASER
Age: 27
Date of Birth: **8th April 1916**
Place of Birth: **Inchtellick, Urquhart**
Occupation or Calling: **Comptometer Operator**
Ticket No. **288**
Destination: **Cape Town**
Address in UK: 16 Marchmont Crescent, Edinburgh.
Daughter of James and Christina Macdonald, of 17 George IV Bridge, Edinburgh
Wife of the Revd. Gregor Macleod.
Travelling with her husband, Revd. Gregor McLeod, ticket no. 288.

MACLEOD THE REVD. GREGOR
Age: 32
Date of Birth: **18th May 1910**
Place of Birth: **Tain, Ross-shire**
Occupation or Calling: **Minister of Religion**
Ticket No. **288**
Destination: **Cape Town**
Address in UK: 16 Marchmont Crescent, Edinburgh.
Son of Roderick Macleod, of 2 Hartfield Street, Tain, Ross-shire.
Husband of Elizabeth Fraser Macleod.
Travelling with his wife, Elizabeth Fraser McLeod, ticket no. 288.

MADDOX THE REVD. LEONARD CECIL B.A.
Age: 26
Date of Birth: **January 1916**
Place of Birth: **Middlesex**
Occupation or Calling: **Clerk in Holy Orders**
Ticket No. **398**
Destination: **Cape Town**
Address in UK: 18 Claremont Road, Redruth, Cornwall. Also: c/o. Crown Agents for Colonies, Millbank, London.
Son of Mrs. Maddox, of 39 Tankerville Drive, Leigh-on-Sea, Essex.

MALAN FLORENCE
Age: 22
Date of Birth: **14th September 1920**
Place of Birth: **Oldfield Brow, Cheshire**
Occupation or Calling: **Planer Munitions**
Ticket No. **289**
Destination: **Durban**
Address in UK: 2 Hillcroft Road, Oldfield Brow, Altrincham
Daughter of Herbert and Lucy Darlington, of 6 Manley Road, Sale, Cheshire.
Wife of Carl Van Keerden Malan.

MARSHALL HARRY ARCHER
Age: 26
Occupation or Calling: **Civil Servant**
Ticket No. **210**
Destination: **Durban**
Address in UK: 74 Pope's Grove, Twickenham, Middlesex.
Also: R.N. Armament Depot, Dumfermline
Son of Harry and Eleanor Mabel Marshall, of 74 Pope's Grove, Twickenham, Middlesex.

Casualty list

MATHIAS PHYLLIS MILDRED
S.C.M.M.G., L.E.T., M.E.
Age: **31**
Occupation or Calling: **Masseuse**
Ticket No. **231 (Henwood)**
Destination: **Durban**
Address in UK: Lamphey Court, Lamphey, Pembrokeshire.
Also: Highclere, Haverfordwest, Pembroke
Daughter of Alice Mildred Henwood, of Entabeni, Vryheid, Natal, South Africa, and of the late Sidney Evelyn Henwood.
Wife of Wing Comdr. Lewis Mathias, R.A.F.
*Travelling with Mabel Burgess Nicholas, ticket no. 230.
Shipping Co. note: After this vessel sailed we were informed by the High Comm. for S. Africa that this passenger booked in her maiden name (Henwood - see No.142) but married Wing Comdr Mathias at Caxton Hall on the 9th Oct. 1942.

McDONALD SIR JAMES GORDON
K.B.E., Lt., Home Guard
Age: **75 (74)**
Occupation or Calling: **Retired/Government Official**
Ticket No. **183**
Destination: **Cape Town**
Address in UK: Bath Club, St. James's Street, London SW1.
Address in South Africa: Bulawayo, Rhodesia, South Africa.
Son of Hugh and Johanna McDonald, of Ellon, Aberdeenshire.

MOLLETT AUSTIN GODFREY
Age: **68**
Date of Birth: **22nd October 1874**
Place of Birth: **Port Elizabeth**
Occupation or Calling: **Mining Engineer/Business Man**
Ticket No. **299**
Destination: **Cape Town**
Address in UK: Springfield Road, Bangor, Co. Down.
Also: c/o. High Commissioner for South Africa
Address in South Africa: Crig, Port Elizabeth, South Africa.
Son of the late Revd. P. R. Mollett, of Port Elizabeth.
Husband of Catherine Adelaide Mollett.
*Travelling with his wife Catherine Adelaide Mollett and his daughter Joan Leonore Mollett, both ticket no. 299.

MOLLETT CATHERINE ADELAIDE
Age: **60**
Date of Birth: **12th October 1882**
Place of Birth: **Knoch, Ulster, N. Ireland.**
Occupation or Calling: **Housewife**
Ticket No. **299**
Destination: **Cape Town**
Address in UK: Springfield Road, Bangor, Co. Down.
Also: c/o. High Commissioner for South Africa
Address in South Africa: Crig, Port Elizabeth, South Africa.
Daughter of Mr. Todd. Wife of Austin Godfrey Mollett.
*Travelling with her husband Austin Godfrey Mollett and her daughter Joan Leonore Mollett, both ticket no. 299.

MOLLETT JOAN LEONORE
Age: **28**
Date of Birth: **2nd March 1914**
Place of Birth: **Bulawayo, South Africa.**
Occupation or Calling: **Clerk**
Ticket No. **299**
Destination: **Cape Town**
Address in UK: Springfield Road, Bangor, Co. Down.
Also: c/o. High Commissioner for South Africa
Address in South Africa: Crig, Port Elizabeth, South Africa.
Daughter of Austin Godfrey Mollett and Catherine Adelaide Mollett.
*Travelling with her father Austin Godfrey Mollett and her mother Catherine Adelaide Mollett, both ticket no. 299.

MORLAND MAVIS
Age: **27 (26)**
Occupation or Calling: **Shorthand Typist**
Ticket No. **233**
Destination: **Cape Town**
Address in UK: 381 Selby Road, Whitkirk, Leeds, Yorkshire.
Daughter of the late Harry and Edith Morland.

MORTIMER PHILIP ARTHUR JOSEPH
Age: 18
Occupation or Calling: **Student**
Ticket No. **403**
Destination: ***Cape Town***
Address in UK: 15 Upper Mall, Hammersmith, London W6.
Also: Crown Agents, Millbank SW1
Son of the Hon. Charles Edward Mortimer, C.B.E., and Winifred Mortimer of Nairobi, Kenya.

MOSCROP HENRY ABERCROMBIE
Age: 51
Occupation or Calling: **Company Secretary**
Ticket No. **274**
Destination: ***Cape Town***
Address in UK: 6 Winchfield Close, Kenton, Harrow, Middlesex.
Husband of Mary Moscrop, of 6 Winchfield Close, Kenton, Harrow, Middlesex.

NEWBY CHARLES HENRY
Age: 45
Date of Birth: **7th June 1897**
Place of Birth: **Hoyland Nether, Yorkshire**
Occupation or Calling: **Chemical Engineer**
Ticket No. **290**
Destination: ***Cape Town***
Address in UK: 88 Halifax Road, Grenoside, Sheffield.
Husband of L. Newby, of 88 Halifax Road, Grenoside, Sheffield.

NICHOLAS MABEL BURGESS C.S.M.M.G. (T.M.M.G., T.M.E.)
Age: 35
Date of Birth: **8th April 1907**
Place of Birth: **Birches Head, Hanley**
Occupation or Calling: **Masseuse**
Ticket No. **230**
Destination: ***Durban***
Address in UK: Highclere, Haverfordwest, Pembrokeshire.
Daughter of Mr. and Mrs. John Nicholas, of Highclere, Haverfordwest, Pembrokeshire.
Travelling with Phyllis Mildred Mathias (Henwood), ticket no. 231.

NICHOLLS JOHN JAMES ALFRED CHARLES
Age: 43
Occupation or Calling: **Maintenance Fitter**
Ticket No. **396**
Destination: ***Cape Town***
Address in UK: 2 Lynwood Close, North Romford, Essex.

PAINE ELSIE CECILIA
Age: 44
Date of Birth: **27th September 1898**
Place of Birth: **Knutsford, Cheshire**
Occupation or Calling: **Teacher**
Ticket No. **236**
Destination: ***Cape Town***
Address in UK: 112 Burton Road, Withington, Manchester 20.
Daughter of Mr. and Mrs. A. O. Paine, of Cragg Cottage. Grange-over-Sands, Lancashire.

PERY-KNOX-GORE BARBARA (née STUART)
Age: 27 (26)
Occupation or Calling: **Art Mistress**
Ticket No. **238**
Destination: ***Cape Town***
Address in UK: 22 St Michaels Avenue, Bramhall, nr. Stockport.
Next of Kin: Wife of Cullen Pery-Knox-Gore, of St. Michael's on Sea, S. Coast, Natal, South Africa.

PETERKEN DOROTHY BEATRICE
Age: 30
Occupation or Calling: **Housewife**
Ticket No. **298**
Destination: ***Cape Town***
Address in UK: 83 Templedene Avenue, Staines, Middlesex.
Also: 34 Colville Road, Leytonstone, London
Daughter of the late Edward Hugh and Alice Maud Johnson, of 4 The Pavement, Hainault Road, Leytonstone, Essex.
Wife of Telegraphist Walter Ernest Peterken, R.N.
Travelling with her husband Walter Ernest Peterken, ticket no. 480, and daughters Wenda Peterken and Jill Christine Peterken, ticket no. 298.

Casualty list

PETERKEN JILL CHRISTINE
Age: **3**
Occupation or Calling: **Child**
Ticket No. **298**
Destination: **Cape Town**
Address in UK: 83 Templedene Avenue, Staines, Middlesex.
Also: 34 Colville Road, Leytonstone, London.
Daughter of Telegraphist Walter Ernest Peterken, R.N., and Dorothy Beatrice Peterken.
*Travelling with her father Walter Ernest Peterken, ticket no. 480, mother Dorothy Beatrice Peterken and sister Wenda Peterken, ticket no. 298.

PETERKEN WENDA
Age: **6**
Occupation or Calling: **Child**
Ticket No. **298**
Destination: **Cape Town**
Address in UK: 83 Templedene Avenue, Staines, Middlesex.
Also: 34 Colville Road, Leytonstone, London.
Daughter of Telegraphist Walter Ernest Peterken, R.N., and Dorothy Beatrice Peterken.
*Travelling with her father Walter Ernest Peterken, ticket no. 480, mother Dorothy Beatrice Peterken and sister Jill Christine Peterken, ticket no. 298.

PICKERING ELIZABETH ELSIE
Age: **22**
Occupation or Calling: **Housewife**
Ticket No. **360**
Destination: **Cape Town**
Address in UK: c/o. Bryn Awel, Kingsway, Shotton, Chester.
Wife of John Harold Pickering, c/o. Bryn Awel, Kingsway, Shotton, Chester.
*Travelling with her husband John Harold Pickering, ticket no. 360.

PICKERING JOHN HAROLD
Age: **28**
Occupation or Calling: **Metallurgist**
Ticket No. **360**
Destination: **Cape Town**
Address in UK: c/o. Bryn Awel, Kingsway, Shotton, Chester.
Son of Mrs. M. Pickering, Highfield, Hawarden, Cheshire. Husband of Elizabeth Elsie Pickering,
c/o. Bryn Awel, Kingsway, Shotton, Chester.
*Travelling with his wife Elizabeth Elsie Pickering, ticket no. 360.

POPHAM REGINALD DAVID
Age: **41**
Occupation or Calling: **Chargeman, Engine Fitters**
Ticket No. **219**
Destination: **Cape Town**
Country of Intended Future Permanent Residence: **South Africa**
Address in UK: 17 St. Margaret's Road, Marsh Mills, Plymouth.
Husband of F. M. Popham of 17 St. Margaret's Road, Woodford Estate, Marsh Mills, Plympton, Plymouth.

POWELL MARGARET MAY
Age: **23**
Date of Birth: **8th May 1919**
Place of Birth: **Skelmorlie**
Occupation or Calling: **Housewife**
Ticket No. **275**
Destination: **Cape Town**
Address in UK: 'Dunedin', Skelmorlie, Ayrshire.

PRYOR EDIS ELAINE
Age: **27**
Date of Birth: **15th October 1915**
Place of Birth: **Felin Foel, nr. Llanelli**
Occupation or Calling: **Housewife**
Ticket No. **291**
Destination: **Cape Town**
Address in UK: Everton Villa, Bryn Avenue, Burry Port, Camarthenshire, Wales.
Daughter of Gethin Bassett, of Birdin Terrace, Felinfoel, Llanelly, Carmarthenshire.
Wife of Vincent Lorraine Pryor.
*Travelling with her husband Vincent Lorraine Pryor, ticket no. 291.

PRYOR VINCENT LORRAINE
Age: **27**
Date of Birth: **27th December 1914**
Place of Birth: **Burry, Carmarthenshire**
Occupation or Calling: **Company Director**
Ticket No. **291**
Destination: **Cape Town**
Address in UK: Everton Villa, Bryn Avenue, Burry Port, Camarthenshire, Wales.

SS CERAMIC The Untold Story

Son of Mr. W. D. Pryor, of Everton Villa, Bryn Avenue, Burry Port, Carmarthenshire.
Husband of Edis Elaine Pryor.
*Travelling with his wife Edis Elaine Pryor, ticket no. 291.

PRYTHERCH JACK DONALD
Age: *52*
Date of Birth: **5th April 1891**
Place of Birth: **Llanelli**
Occupation or Calling: **Store Manager**
Ticket No. **276**
Destination: **Cape Town**
Address in UK: Devonshire Club, St James, London SW1.

RAINE DAISY MILLICENT
Age: *49*
Date of Birth: **3rd November 1893**
Place of Birth: **Gravesend**
Occupation or Calling: **Housewife**
Ticket No. **191**
Destination: **St Helena**
Address in UK: 'Pitfield', Meopham, Kent.
Also: Electro House, Victoria Embankment WC2.
Wife of Thomas Reginald Raine.
* *Travelling with her husband Thomas Reginald Raine, ticket no. 191.*

RAINE THOMAS REGINALD
Age: *47*
Date of Birth: **26th January 1895**
Place of Birth: **Gravesend**
Occupation or Calling: **Cable Manager**
Ticket No. **191**
Destination: **St Helena**
Address in UK: 'Pitfield', Meopham, Kent.
Also: c/o. Mrs C. Speyer.
Husband of Daisy Millicent Raine.
* *Travelling with his wife Daisy Millicent Raine, ticket no. 191.*

RAWSON JESSIE MIRIAM
Age: *24*
Occupation or Calling: **Housewife**
Ticket No. **292**
Destination: **Cape Town**
Address in UK: 120 Ince Green Lane, Ince, Wigan, Lancs.
Daughter of John Gillespie, of 18 Milner Road, Woodstock, Cape Town, South Africa.

* *Travelling with her daughter Moira Alice Rawson, ticket no. 292.*

RAWSON MOIRA ALICE
Age: *1*
Occupation or Calling: **Child**
Ticket No. **292**
Destination: **Cape Town**
Address in UK: 120 Ince Green Lane, Ince, Wigan, Lancs.
Daughter of Jessie Miriam Lawson.
* *Travelling with her mother Moira Alice Rawson, ticket no. 292.*

RAY DR DAVID BRUCE
Age: *24*
Occupation or Calling: **Medical Practitioner**
Ticket No. **277**
Destination: **Cape Town**
Address in UK: 7 Glamannan Rd. Avonbridge, Stirlingshire.
Son of Dr. Robert Ray and Jeannie Bothia Ray, of 8 Jubilee Road, Parktown, South Africa.
Husband of Margaret McMillan Ray.
* *Travelling with his wife, Margaret McMillan Ray.*

RAY MARGARET MCMILLAN
Age: *26 (25)*
Occupation or Calling: **Housewife (Trained Nurse)**
Ticket No. **277**
Destination: **Cape Town**
Address in UK: 7 Glamannan Rd. Avonbridge, Stirlingshire.
Daughter of Mr. J. Muir, of 7 Slawanbar Road, Avonbridge, Falkirk, Stirlingshire.
Wife of Dr. David Bruce Ray.
* *Travelling with her husband, Dr. David Bruce Ray.*

RHODES CARL THURMAN
Age: *50*
Date of Birth: **12th June 1892**
Place of Birth: **Bedford**
Occupation or Calling: **Engineer**
Ticket No. **293**
Destination: **Cape Town**
Address in UK: c/o. Mrs A. Rhodes, 9 Halvis Grove, Firswood, Old Trafford, Manchester.
Husband of Nellie Rhodes, of Spier, Lynedoch, Cape Province, South Africa.

ROBERTSON ANGELA
Age: 12
Occupation or Calling: **Scholar**
Ticket No. **242**
Destination: **Cape Town**
Address in UK: 10 Kineton Green Road, Olton, Birmingham.
Also: c/o. Broom & Wade Ltd. High Wycombe, Bucks
Daughter of Melsom Walter and Rita Rachael Robertson.
* *Travelling with her father Melsom Walter Robertson, mother Rita Rachael Robertson and brother Richard Phillip Robertson, ticket no. 242.*

ROBERTSON MELSOM WALTER
Age: 41
Occupation or Calling: **Engineer**
Ticket No. **242**
Destination: **Cape Town**
Address in UK: 10 Kineton Green Road, Olton, Birmingham.
Also: c/o. Broom & Wade Ltd. High Wycombe, Bucks
Son of Mrs. Robertson, of 61 Eagle Road, Wembley, Middlesex, and of the late R. F. Robertson. Husband of Rita Rachael Robertson.
* *Travelling with his wife Rita Rachael Robertson, daughter Angela Robertson and son Richard Phillip Robertson, ticket no. 242.*

ROBERTSON RICHARD PHILLIP
Age: 6
Occupation or Calling: **Scholar**
Ticket No. **242**
Destination: **Cape Town**
Address in UK: 10 Kineton Green Road, Olton, Birmingham.
Also: c/o. Broom & Wade Ltd. High Wycombe, Bucks
Son of Melsom Walter and Rita Rachael Robertson.
* *Travelling with his father Melsom Walter Robertson, mother Rita Rachael Robertson and sister Angela Robertson, ticket no. 242.*

ROBERTSON RITA RACHAEL
Age: 40
Occupation or Calling: **Housewife**
Ticket No. **242**
Destination: **Cape Town**
Address in UK: 10 Kineton Green Road, Olton, Birmingham.
Also: c/o. Broom & Wade Ltd. High Wycombe, Bucks
Daughter of Mr. and Mrs. Van Geuns. of 5 Pleydell Avenue, Hammersmith.
Wife of Melsom Walter Robertson.
* *Travelling with her husband Melsom Walter Robertson, daughter Angela Robertson and son Richard Phillip Robertson, ticket no. 242.*

ROWE DANIEL DONALD
Age: 39
Occupation or Calling: **Chargeman Fitter**
Ticket No. **214**
Destination: **Cape Town**
Country of Intended Future Permanent Residence: **South Africa**
Address in UK: 53 Durham Avenue, Lipson, Plymouth.

RUSSELL CAROL MARGARET
Age: 23
Occupation or Calling: **Housewife**
Ticket No. **235**
Destination: **Cape Town**
Address in UK: Orthopaedic Dept., The Infirmary, Warrington
Address in South Africa: 79 Leinster Road, Pietermaritzburg, Natal, South Africa.
Daughter of the late William Allen Douglass Russell.

SALMON ALICE
Age: 34
Occupation or Calling: **Housewife**
Ticket No. **241**
Destination: **Durban**
Address in UK: c/o. Mr Richardson, 84 Reed Street, Burnley, Lancashire.
Wife of Peter Salmon.
* *Travelling with her daughter Jean Salmon and son Keith Salmon, ticket no. 241.*

SALMON JEAN
Age: 10
Occupation or Calling: **Scholar**
Ticket No. **241**
Destination: **Durban**
Address in UK: c/o. Mr Richardson, 84 Reed Street, Burnley, Lancashire.

SS CERAMIC The Untold Story

Daughter of Peter Salmon and of Alice Salmon.
* *Travelling with her mother Alice Salmon and brother Keith Salmon, ticket no. 241.*

SALMON KEITH
Age: 5
Occupation or Calling: **Scholar**
Ticket No. **241**
Destination: **Durban**
Address in UK: c/o. Mr Richardson, 84 Reed Street, Burnley, Lancashire.
Son of Peter Salmon and of Alice Salmon.
* *Travelling with his mother Alice Salmon and sister Jean Salmon, ticket no. 241.*

SCHNETLER PETRUS JOHANNES B.Com.
Age: 32
Occupation or Calling: **Civil Servant**
Ticket No. **296**
Destination: **Cape Town**
Address in UK: c/o. Mr Richardson, 84 Reed Street, Burnley, Lancashire.
Also: South Africa House, London WC2
Son of Daniel Schnetler and Anna Sophia Schnetler, of 130 Lunnon Road, Hillcrest, Pretoria, South Africa.

SCOTT RICHARD D. J.
Age: 41
Date of Birth: **12th July 1901**
Place of Birth: **Skirlaugh, Yorkshire**
Occupation or Calling: **Civil Engineer**
Ticket No. **359**
Destination: **Cape Town**
Address in UK: 25 Woodlands, Beverley, Yorks.

SEABROOK ETHEL CAROLINE
Age: 37
Occupation or Calling: **Housewife**
Ticket No. **239**
Destination: **Cape Town**
Address in UK: 20 Brisbane Street, Greenock, Scotland.
* *Travelling with her son Ronald John Arthur Seabrook, ticket no. 239.*

SEABROOK RONALD JOHN ARTHUR
Age: 13
Occupation or Calling: **Housewife**
Ticket No. **239**
Destination: **Cape Town**

Address in UK: 20 Brisbane Street, Greenock, Scotland.
Son of Ethel Caroline Seabrook.
* *Travelling with his mother Ethel Caroline Seabrook, ticket no. 239.*

SIBTHORPE GEORGE WILLIAM
Age: 67
Occupation or Calling: **Gatekeeper**
Ticket No. **228**
Destination: **Sydney**
Address in UK: 12 Walmer Terrace, Plumstead.

SILK HENRY
Age: 49
Date of Birth: **4th November 1893**
Place of Birth: **Kings Norton, Worcester**
Occupation or Calling: **Pattern Maker**
Ticket No. **361**
Destination: **Cape Town**
Address in UK: 260 Alcester Rd. Kings Heath, Birmingham.

SMITH MURIEL ELIZABETH AGNES
Age: 27
Occupation or Calling: **Housewife**
Ticket No. **263**
Destination: **Cape Town**
Address in UK: 126 Boulevard, Hull.
Daughter of Alfred and Emma Dorothy Goacher of the same address.
Wife of George Albert Smith.

STOYEL GLADYS EMMALINE
Age: 28
Occupation or Calling: **Housewife**
Ticket No. **297**
Destination: **Cape Town**
Address in UK: 5 Bedford Park, Plymouth.
Daughter of Thomas H. and E. T. McIntosh, of Bedford Park, Plymouth.
Wife of P.O. Reginald F. Stoyel, R.N.

TANNER THOMAS LESLEY
B.A., Ambulance Service.
Age: 32
Date of Birth: **27th May 1910**
Place of Birth: **Pollokshaws, Renfrewshire**
Occupation or Calling: **Ambulance Service**
Ticket No. **190**
Destination: **Cape Town**

Address in UK: 4 Gordon Sq. London WC1
Also: c/o. H. Tanner, Failand House, Failand, Bristol
Son of Herbert George and Agatha Mary Tanner, of Failand House, Failand, Bristol.
Husband of Dora J. Tanner, of the same address.

TAYLER NEVIL HAIG
Age: **26**
Occupation or Calling: **Engineer**
Ticket No. **280**
Destination: **Cape Town**
Address in UK: c/o. South Africa House, London WC2
Son of C. T. and Mary Tayler of 8 Barnato Street, Berea, Johannesburg, South Africa.

TETLEY MOIRA CATHERINE
Age: **22 (21)**
Occupation or Calling: **Clerk**
Ticket No. **188**
Destination: **Cape Town**
Address in UK: The Elms, Carlby, Stamford, Lincs
Daughter of Mr. and Mrs. L. Webb, of Guildford's Farm, Salisbury, S. Rhodesia.
Widow of Norman Tetley.

TURNER ETHEL LILLIAN
Age: **61**
Occupation or Calling: **Widow**
Ticket No. **408**
Destination: **Cape Town**
Address in UK: 30 Manchester Street, London, W.1.
Also: South Africa House, London WC2
Daughter of the late Sir William and Lady Burkett. Wife of Major C. Hampden Turner.

UNDERHILL GEORGE EDWARD
Age: **46**
Date of Birth: **19th September 1896**
Place of Birth: **Aston Manor, Warwickshire**
Occupation or Calling: **Engineer**
Ticket No. **278**
Destination: **Cape Town**
Address in UK: 36 Cherry Orchard Road, Handsworth Wood, Birmingham 20.
Husband of Florence Lydia Underhill, of 36 Cherry Orchard Road, Handsworth Wood, Birmingham 20.

VAN BREDA VERA ELLIN
Age: **50**
Date of Birth: **1st May 1892**
Place of Birth: **Westbury on Trym, Gloucestershire**
Occupation or Calling: **Housewife**
Ticket No. **281**
Destination: **Cape Town**
Address in UK: Pen Park House, Charlton Common, Westbury-on-Trym, Gloucestershire.
Daughter of Mrs. L. L. Waller, of Pen Park House, Charlton Common, Westbury-on-Trym, Gloucestershire.
Wife of H. J. Van Breda, of Pumula, Umkomaas, Natal, South Africa.

WATSON ELIZABETH
Age: **62**
Date of Birth: **31st May 1880**
Place of Birth: **Nottingham**
Occupation or Calling: **Housewife**
Ticket No. **185**
Destination: **Cape Town**
Address in UK: c/o. Miss Milner, Bourne Hall Cottage, Bushey, Herts.
Daughter of the late William Cooke, Castle Boulevard, Nottingham. Wife of Richard T. Watson, Theydon, S. Rhodesia.

WELCH JOSEPH PATRICK
Age: **37**
Date of Birth: **26th October 1905**
Place of Birth: **Duddeston, Warwick**
Occupation or Calling: **Toolmaker**
Ticket No. **362**
Destination: **Cape Town**
Address in UK: 66 Tintern Road, Handsworth. Birmingham.
Son of Joseph and Catherine Welch, 22 Billbrook Grove, Wesley Castle, Birmingham.
Husband of Nellie Welch, 66 Tintern Road, Handsworth. Birmingham.

WETHERED FRANCIS JOHN
B.A.; Deputy Post Warden, Westminster, London
Age: **24**
Date of Birth: **27th April 1918**
Place of Birth: **Marlow, Buckinghamshire**
Occupation or Calling: **Civil Servant**
Ticket No. **401**
Destination: **Cape Town**

Address in UK: Castle Orchard, Zeals, Wilts.
Also: 3 Hanover St. London W1.
Son of the late Lt. Col. Francis Owen Wethered.
C.M.G., T.D., D.L., J.P., and Margaret Wethered,
Remnantz, Great Marlow, Buckinghamshire.

WHITBY BARBARA ETHEL
Age: 3 (2)
Occupation or Calling: Child
Ticket No. 294
Destination: Cape Town
Address in UK: 82 Green Hill, Hampstead, London.
Also: 203 Kingsway, Widnes, Lancs.
Daughter of William Henry and Maisie Caroline Helena Whitby.
* *Travelling with her father William Henry Whitby and mother Maisie Caroline Helena Whitby, ticket no. 294.*

WHITBY MAISIE CAROLINE HELENA
Age: 38
Occupation or Calling: Housewife
Ticket No. 294
Destination: Cape Town
Address in UK: 82 Green Hill, Hampstead, London.
Also: 203 Kingsway, Widnes, Lancs.
Wife of William Henry Whitby (Engineer Officer, Merchant Navy).
* *Travelling with her husband William Henry Whitby and daughter Barbara Ethel Whitby, ticket no. 294.*

WHITE GENEVIEVE E. CLOTHILDE
Age: 24
Date of Birth: 15th December 1917
Place of Birth: Bromley, Kent
Occupation or Calling: Housewife
Ticket No. 410
Destination: Cape Town
Address in UK: 72 West Kensington Court, London W14.
Wife of Lt. Eric White, R.B., Air Service, of Wingfield, Cape Town, South Africa.

WICKERT KURT L.D.S., R.C.S., H.D.D.
Age: 26
Occupation or Calling: Dental Surgeon
Ticket No. 279
Destination: Cape Town
Address in UK: c/o. Thomson, 14 Arden Street, Edinburgh, Scotland.
Son of W. and M. Wickert, of 8 Milner Road, Bloemfontein, South Africa.

WILLIAMS DAVID GEORGE
Age: 31
Occupation or Calling: Production Foreman
Ticket No. 295
Destination: Cape Town
Address in UK: c/o. Police Station, Connah's Quay, Chester.
Husband of Joyce May Williams.
* *Travelling with his wife Joyce May Williams, ticket no. 295.*

WILLIAMS JOYCE MAY
Age: 24
Occupation or Calling: Housewife
Ticket No. 295
Destination: Cape Town
Address in UK: c/o. Police Station, Connah's Quay, Chester.
Daughter of W. Hall. of Police Station, Connah's Quay, Chester. Wife of David George Williams.
* *Travelling with her husband David George Williams, ticket no. 295.*
Listed on passenger list as Joyce Lucy Williams.

WYLLIE ALEXANDER VEITCH B.L.
Age: 43
Date of Birth: 23rd November 1899
Place of Birth: Glasgow
Occupation or Calling: Civil Servant
Ticket No. 221
Destination: Cape Town
Address in UK: 41 Furham Field, Hatch End, Pinner, Middlesex.
Also: 39 Croftburn Drive, Croftfoot, Glasgow.
Son of R. Wyllie, and of the late John Pratt Wyllie. Husband of Elizabeth Wyllie.

Alamein Memorial Egypt

BARTON VICTOR ALFRED
Age: 22
Date of Birth: **12th February 1920**
Place of Birth: **Southampton**
Engineer/Fitter/Airman
British Overseas Airways Corporation
Ticket No. **383**
Destination: **Durban**
Son of Mr. and Mrs. P. S. Barton, of Woking, Surrey.
Column 267.

CLARK ANGUS WILLIAM
Age: 24
Date of Birth: **4th December 1918**
Place of Birth: **Bril**
Engineer/Fitter/Airman
British Overseas Airways Corporation
Nationality: **British**
Ticket No. **389**
Destination: **Durban**
Son of James and Mary Annie Equenie Clark, of Knowle, Bristol.
Column 267.

GIBB ADAM
Age: 29
Civilian/Airman
British Overseas Airways Corporation
Ticket No. **392**
Destination: **Durban**
Son of George and Margaret Gibb. Husband of Nellie Emma Gibb, of Fulham, London.
Column 267.

MORGAN THOMAS RALSTON
Age: 22
Date of Birth: **13th May 1908**
Place of Birth: **Glasgow**
Engineer/Fitter/Airman
British Overseas Airways Corporation
Ticket No. **385**
Destination: **Durban**
Column 267.

MUSTOE FRANK KENNETH
Age: 21
Date of Birth: **16th July 1921**
Place of Birth: **Northleach, Glos.**
Engineer/Fitter/Airman
British Overseas Airways Corporation
Ticket No. **390**
Destination: **Durban**
Son of William Wallace Mustoe and Julia Mustoe.
Column 267.

PRATT LEONARD
Age: 26
Date of Birth: **18th April 1916**
Place of Birth: **Connah's Quay, Flintshire**
Engineer/Fitter/Airman
British Overseas Airways Corporation
Ticket No. **391**
Destination: **Durban**
Column 268.

SKINNER LAURENCE
Age: 22
Date of Birth: **30th July 1920**
Place of Birth: **Darlington**
Engineer/Fitter/Airman
British Overseas Airways Corporation
Ticket No. **384**
Destination: **Durban**
Column 268.

STOREY AMOS
Age: 22
Engineer/Fitter/Airman
British Overseas Airways Corporation
Ticket No. **387**
Destination: **Durban**
Column 268.

STROUD HENRY ARTHUR
Age: 27
Date of Birth: **13th May 1905**
Place of Birth: **Chetnole, Dorset**
Engineer/Fitter/Airman
British Overseas Airways Corporation
Ticket No. **386**
Destination: **Durban**
Husband of E. K. Stroud, of Sidmouth, Devon.
Column 268.

TEDFORD HENRY STEWART
Age: **36**
Date of Birth: **28th September 1906**
Place of Birth: **Belfast**
Engineer/Fitter/Airman
British Overseas Airways Corporation
Ticket No. **389**
Destination: **Durban**
Son of Robert Henry and Sarah Tedford.
Husband of Mary Tedford of Belfast, Northern Ireland.
Column 268

TUTT LEWIS ERNEST
Age: **45**
Storekeeper
British Overseas Airways Corporation
Ticket No. **393**
Destination: **Durban**
Son of George Hawkesley Tutt and Annie Tutt. Husband of Violet Tutt, of Morden, Surrey.
* *Previously served as 2/Lt., Royal Flying Corps, 1914-18.*
Column 267

Brookwood Memorial *Surrey*

ALLISON GEORGE THOMSON
Age: **23**
Sapper; 946229
Royal Engineers
War Office Booking
Destination: **Cape Town**
Son of George and Elsie Allison, of Brechin, Angus.
Panel 5. Column 2

ALFORD JOHN ERNEST
Age: **28**
Corporal; S/232140
Royal Army Service Corps
War Office Booking
Destination: **Cape Town**
Son of John W. H. Alford and Winifred Alford; husband of Margaret I. Alford, of Stoke, Plymouth.
Panel 15. Column 3

ANDREW CHARLES PERCIVAL KITCHENER
Age: **27**
Army; Lance Corporal; 107059
Royal Engineers
War Office Booking
Destination: **Cape Town**
Son of George and Mary Ann Andrew.
Panel 5. Column 1

ARDEN MORRIS VICTOR
Age: **23**

Army; Driver; T/112579
Royal Army Service Corps
War Office Booking
Destination: **Cape Town**
Panel 16. Column 1.

ARNOLD WILLIAM HENRY
Age: **21**
Army; Gunner; 3857066
107 Bty., 522 Coast Regt. Royal Artillery
War Office Booking
Destination: **St Helena**
Son of John Arnold, and of Mary Jane Arnold, of Timperley, Cheshire.
Panel 3. Column 1.

BAKER A. MARGARET
Army; Sister; 209761
Territorial Army Nursing Service
Ticket No. **319**
Destination: **Cape Town**
Panel 22. Column 3.

BALLARD HAROLD LAWRENCE PURVIS
Age: **30**
Army; Lieutenant; 153248
10th Bn. Duke of Wellington's (West Riding Regt.)
Ticket No. **249**
Destination: **St Helena**
Son of Jesse Purvis Ballard and Dorothea Maude Ballard.
Panel 11. Column 3.

BELL JOHN WILLIAM
Age: **32**
Serjeant; S/4341716
Royal Army Service Corps
War Office Booking
Destination: **Cape Town**
Panel 15. Column 3.

BERRY GEORGE
Age: **21**
Gunner; 1790947
Royal Artillery
War Office Booking
Destination: **St Helena**
Son of George and Kate Berry, of Hey, Lancashire.
Panel 3. Column 1.

BEVIS EVA EMILY
Age: **34**
Sister; 241733
Queen Alexandra's Imperial Military Nursing Service
Ticket No. **322**
Destination: **Cape Town**
Daughter of Lily Emily Randall Bevis, of Hamble, Hampshire.
Panel 22. Column 2.

BISS GERALD FRANCIS
Age: **20**
Gunner; 875180
531 Coast Regt. Royal Artillery
War Office Booking
Destination: **St Helena**
Son of Gilbert and Elizabeth Biss of Ely, Cardiff.
Panel 3. Column 1.

BLACKSHAW STANLEY
Age: **25**
Serjeant; 4750184
Royal Corps of Signals
War Office Booking
Destination: **St Helena**
Panel 8. Column 1.

BOOTES JAMES ELSON
Age: **27**
Sapper; 3860655
Royal Engineers
War Office Booking
Destination: **Cape Town**
Panel 5. Column 2.

BOREHAM ALFRED CLEMENT
Age: **41**
Serjeant; 7249226
Royal Army Medical Corps
War Office Booking
Destination: **Cape Town**
Son of Charles and Mary Boreham. Husband of D. L. M. Boreham, of Rettendon, Essex.
Panel 18. Column 1.

BRETHERTON FRANCIS
Age: **55**
Captain; 133078
Royal Engineers
Ticket No. **303**
Destination: **Cape Town**
Son of John and Marie Bretherton.
Panel 4. Column 3.

BROOKES GEORGE HENRY
Age: **40**
Lieutenant (Quartermaster); 168866
Royal Army Medical Corps
Ticket No. **311**
Destination: **Cape Town**
Son of William John and Elizabeth Brookes. Husband of Margaret Emma Brookes, of Abertillery, Monmouthshire.
Panel 18. Column 1.

BROWN REGINALD FRANK
Age: **37**
Private; T/10693598
Royal Army Service Corps
War Office Booking
Destination: **Cape Town**
Son of Edward Herbert and Louisa Eleanor Brown. Husband of Louisa Elizabeth Brown, Cricklewood, Middlesex.
Panel 17. Column 3.

CAREY PETER VIVIAN
Age: **22**
Lieutenant; 112899
1/7th Bn. Duke of Wellington's (West Riding Regt.)
Ticket No. **246**

Destination: **St. Helena**
Son of Maj. Peter Carey, and of Dorothy Madeline Carey, of St. Peter Port, Guernsey, Channel Islands.
Panel 11. Column 3.

CLARK HENRY
Age: *22*
Sapper; *3245975*
Royal Engineers
Ticket No. *309*
Destination: **Cape Town**
Son of H. Clark and Jean Clark, of Glasgow.
Panel 5. Column 3.

CLARKE ROY M.B., M.R.C.P.
Major; *230706*
Royal Army Medical Corps
War Office Booking
Destination: **Cape Town**
Panel 18. Column 1.

CLEAVER ERIC
Age: *21*
Gunner; *11000944*
Royal Artillery
War Office Booking
Destination: **St Helena**
Panel 3. Column 1.

CLEMENT NADIA MATHILDA
Sister; *2336422*
Queen Alexandra's Imperial Military Nursing Service
Ticket No. *323*
Destination: **Cape Town**
Panel 22. Column 2.

COOMBES ARTHUR EDWIN DENNIS
Age: *22*
Signalman; *1428625*
Royal Corps of Signals
War Office Booking
Destination: **St Helena**
Son of Ernest Michael and Amy Coombes of Fareham, Hampshire.
Panel 8. Column 1.

COULTER JOAN
Sister; *231746*
Queen Alexandra's Imperial Military Nursing Service
Ticket No. *324*
Destination: **Cape Town**
Panel 22. Column 2.

CRABTREE FRANK
Age: *28*
Warrant Officer Class I (S.S.M.) *S/2754221*
Royal Army Service Corps
formerly Black Watch (Royal Highlanders)
Ticket No. *357*
Destination: **Sydney**
Son of Walter and Annie Crabtree.
Husband of Laura Crabtree, of Hedon, Yorkshire.
Panel 15. Column 2.

CRIBB CECILIA MAUD
Age: *30*
Sister; *206920*
Queen Alexandra's Imperial Military Nursing Service
Ticket No. *346*
Destination: **Cape Town**
Daughter of Walter Henry and Maud Cecilia Cribb.
Panel 22. Column 2.

CURA LOUIS
Age: *33*
Lance Bombardier; *1712346*
Royal Artillery
War Office Booking
Destination: **St Helena**
Son of Joseph and Emily Cura.
Panel 2. Column 3.

DAVIES WILLIAM THOMAS
Age: *30*
Private; *7385575*
Royal Army Medical Corps
War Office Booking
Destination: **Cape Town**
Panel 18. Column 2.

DEER JAMES REGINALD
Age: *24*
Corporal; *T/104213*
Royal Army Service Corps
War Office Booking
Destination: **Cape Town**
Son of Claude Edgar and Beatrice Maude Deer,

of Newport, Monmouthshire.
Panel 15. Column 3.

DIVINE TOM LENNON JOHNSTONE
Age: 26
Sapper; 1916962
Royal Engineers
War Office Booking
Destination: Cape Town
Son of William and Margaret Divine.
Husband of Margaret Stuart Adam Divine, of Pinner, Middlesex.
Panel 5. Column 3.

DOLMETSCH RUDOLPH
Age: 36
Gunner; 1695369
Royal Artillery *138 Lt. A.A. Regt.*
War Office Booking
Destination: St Helena
Son of Arnold Dolmetsch and of Mabel Dolmetsch (nee Johnston).
Husband of Millicent Dolmetsch (nee Wheaton), of Godalming, Surrey.
Panel 3. Column 1.

DOLPHIN HARRY
Age: 33
Sapper; 2151815
Royal Engineers
War Office Booking
Destination: Cape Town
Panel 5. Column 33.

DRYSDALE ANDREW DOUGLAS
M.B., Ch.B. (Edin.).
Age: 23
Lieutenant 225941
Royal Army Medical Corps
Ticket No. 312
Destination: Cape Town
Son of Peter Finnie Drysdale and Annie Bonar Drysdale, of Edinburgh.
Panel 18. Column 1.

DUNN PETER
Age: 20
Private; 7405869
Royal Army Medical Corps
War Office Booking
Destination: Cape Town

Next of Kin: Son of John and Annie Dunn, of Blantyre, Lanarkshire.
Panel 18. Column 2.

ESSEX ROSEMARY NANCY
Sister; 239717
Queen Alexandra's Imperial Military Nursing Service
Ticket No. 325
Destination: Cape Town
Panel 22. Column 2.

EVANS JOHN HOWARD
Age: 28
Private; 7386933
Royal Army Medical Corps
War Office Booking
Destination: Cape Town
Son of Thomas and Margaret Evans.
Husband of Winifred Evans, of Marshfield, Bradford, Yorkshire.
Panel 18. Column 2.

EVANS MAIR ELUNED
Age: 27
Sister; 234957
Queen Alexandra's Imperial Military Nursing Service
Ticket No. 326
Destination: Cape Town
Daughter of Mr. and Mrs. B. Evans, of Nantycaws, Carmarthenshire.
Panel 22. Column 2.

FELLOWES RONALD JAMES
Age: 21
Private; 3390887
Army Dental Corps
War Office Booking
Destination: Cape Town
Panel 20. Column 2.

FINNEGAN EDWARD CHRISTOPHER
Age: 32
Corporal; 1867146
Royal Engineers
War Office Booking
Destination: Cape Town
Son of Thomas Finnegan, and of Bridget Finnegan, of Craughwell, Co. Galway, Irish Republic.
Panel 5. Column 1.

FOGWILL GEOFFREY ARTHUR
Age: 25
Serjeant; S150554
Royal Army Service Corps
War Office Booking
Destination: **Cape Town**
Son of C.P.O. F. G. Fogwill, R.N., and Mrs. F. Fogwill.
Husband of Lola Eileen Fogwill, of Gidea Park, Romford, Essex.
Panel 15. Column 3.

FORREST DAVID
Age: 30
Staff Serjeant 7645955
Royal Army Ordnance Corps
Ticket No. **406**
Destination: **Melbourne**
Next of Kin: Son of John and Agnes Forrest, of Carluke, Lanarkshire. B.LL.
Panel 18. Column 3.

FOSTER DOUGLAS CHARLES
Lieutenant; 174905
15th Bn. The Queen's Royal Regt (West Surrey)
Ticket No. **250**
Destination: **St. Helena**
Panel 8. Column 3.

FALK MORRIS
Age: 30
Serjeant 7644952
Royal Army Ordnance Corps
War Office Booking
Destination: **Cape Town**
Panel 18. Column 3.

FOX JOHN
Age: 28
Private; 7666958
Royal Army Pay Corps
War Office Booking
Destination: **Cape Town**
Son of Owen and Eunice Fox, of Tredegar, Monmouthshire.
Panel 20. Column 1.

FRASER HAMISH
Age: 20
Private; 10544535
Royal Army Ordnance Corps.

War Office Booking
Destination: **Cape Town**
Son of James and Annie Fraser, of Bonnybridge, Stirlingshire.
Panel 19. Column 2.

FRENCH HENRY RICHARD
Age: 22
Private; 7665859
Royal Army Pay Corps
War Office Booking
Destination: **Cape Town**
Panel 20. Column 1.

GANNON RICHARD WILLIAM
Age: 21
Corporal; S/57581
Royal Army Service Corps
Nationality: **British**
War Office Booking
Destination: **Cape Town**
Panel 15. Column 3.

GARDNER ANNIE MARY
Age: 26
Sister; 218360
Queen Alexandra's Imperial Military Nursing Service
Ticket No. **327**
Destination: **Cape Town**
Daughter of W. J. and Elizabeth Gardner, of Stranocum, Co. Antrim, Northern Ireland.
Panel 22. Column 2.

GIBSON COLIN JOHN RANKIN
Captain; 114311
Queen's Own Cameron Highlanders
Ticket No. **252**
Destination: **St Helena**
Panel 14. Column 2.

GILBEY HORACE PERCY
Age: 26
Private; 7378963
Royal Army Medical Corps
War Office Booking
Destination: **Cape Town**
Son of Percy Harold and Gertrude Gilbey, of Walthamstow, Essex.
Panel 18. Column 2.

Casualty list

GILL WILFRED SUTCLIFFE
Age: *25*
Private; *7368010*
Royal Army Medical Corps
War Office Booking
Destination: **Cape Town**
Son of Harry Sutcliffe Gill and Cecelia Gill.
Husband of Mary Gill, of West Town, Dewsbury, Yorkshire.
Panel 18. Column 2.

GIMPELSON HARRY L.R.C.P., M.R.C.S
Age: *30*
Lieutenant; *236042*
Royal Army Medical Corps
Ticket No. *313*
Destination: **Cape Town**
Son of Simon and Annie Gimpelson. Husband of Lucie Gimpelson of Saltdean.
Panel 18. Column 1.

GODFREY WILLIAM GERALD
Age: *23*
Private; *7537011*
Army Dental Corps
War Office Booking
Destination: **Cape Town**
Son of Bertram and Alice Godfrey.
Husband of Mary Lilian Godfrey, of Witney, Oxfordshire.
Panel 20. Column 2.

GRIFFITHS GEORGE HENRY
Age: *30*
Private; *7403309*
Royal Army Medical Corps
War Office Booking
Destination: **Cape Town**
Panel 18. Column 2.

HALL JOHN LEONARD
Age: *32*
Second Lieutenant; *219367*
Royal Army Service Corps
Ticket No. *253*
Destination: **St. Helena**
Son of John and Alice Hall.
Husband of Zena Florence Hall, of Shirley, Warwickshire.
Panel 15. Column 2.

HAROLD EDWARD
Age: *25*
Private; *4451896*
Royal Army Medical Corps
War Office Booking
Destination: **Cape Town**
Son of Edward and Emmaline Harold, of Deckham, Gateshead, Co. Durham.
Panel 18. Column 2.

HARRIS FRANK EDWARD
Age: *33*
Serjeant; *2691538*
Royal Army Medical Corps
War Office Booking
Destination: **Cape Town**
Husband of K. F. M. Harris, of South Croydon, Surrey.
Panel 18. Column 1.

HARRIS KAMON
Captain; *199790*
Royal Army Medical Corps
Ticket No. *314*
Destination: **Cape Town**
Panel 18. Column 1.

HIGHET WILLIAM BREMNER
M.B., Ch.B., F.R.C.S.
Age: *31*
Lieutenant; *246197*
Royal Army Medical Corps
War Office Booking)
Destination: **Cape Town**
Son of David Highet, and of Elsie Highet (née Bremner).
Husband of Joan Highet (née Richards), of Norwich.
Panel 18. Column 1.

HIND WILLIAM CHARLES HENRY
Age: *29*
Lieutenant; *233266*
12th Bn. Hampshire Regiment
Ticket No. *248*
Destination: **St Helena**
Son of William and Sarah Elisa Hind.
Husband of Mabel Elsie Hind, of Blackdown, Haslemere, Surrey.
Panel 11. Column 3.

HINDLE JACK VERNON
Age: 25
Private; 7671067
Royal Army Pay Corps
War Office Booking
Destination: Cape Town
Son of Viner Moorhouse Hindle and Lilly Hindle, of Boston, Lincolnshire.
Panel 20. Column 1.

HITCHENS FREDERICK
Age: 38
Lieutenant (Quartermaster); 147748
Royal Army Medical Corps
Ticket No. 315
Destination: Cape Town
Son of Joseph Edgar and Martha Hitchens. Husband of Fanny Elizabeth Hitchens, of Fleet, Hampshire.
Panel 18. Column 1.

HODKINSON BERNARD
Age: 29
Captain 96126
Royal Artillery 61 (The Denbighshire Yeomanry) Medium Regt.
Ticket No. 355
Destination: Sydney
Son of Frederick William and Emma Gertrude Hodkinson, of Bolton-le-Sands, Lancashire.
Panel 4. Column 2.

HOLLIS ENID KATHLEEN
Sister, 219022
Queen Alexandra's Imperial Military Nursing Service
Ticket No. 328
Destination: Cape Town
Panel 22. Column 2.

HOSKINS WILLIAM JAMES EDWARD
Age: 39
Warrant Officer Class II (Armt. Q.M.S.) 2215772
Royal Electrical and Mechanical Engineers
Ticket No. 253
Destination: St Helena
Panel 19. Column 3.

HOOD MARGARET ANN S.R.N., S.C.M.
Age: 35
Sister; 227175
Queen Alexandra's Imperial Military Nursing Service
Ticket No. 329
Destination: Cape Town
Daughter of John Charles and Elizabeth Lowes Hood, of Sunderland, Co. Durham.
Panel 22. Column 2.

HOWELLS DOUGLAS CHATHAM
Lieutenant; 225025
Royal Engineers
Ticket No. 304
Destination: Cape Town
Panel 4. Column 3.

HURST THOMAS HERBERT
Age: 34
Serjeant; 7344764
Royal Army Medical Corps
Ticket No. 305
Destination: Cape Town
Panel 18. Column 1.

JAQUES CLAUDE
Age: 38
Second Lieutenant 199720
Royal Engineers
Ticket No. 329
Destination: Cape Town
Husband of Elizabeth Jaques, of Harrogate, Yorkshire.
Panel 4. Column 3.

JENKINS ARTHUR RONALD
Age: 30
Sapper; 323339
Royal Engineers
War Office Booking
Destination: Cape Town
Son of Arthur and Eunice Jenkins. Husband of Phyllis Margaret Jenkins, of Hale Barns, Cheshire.
Panel 6. Column 2.

JOHNSON EDWARD ELLIS
Age: 25
Lieutenant 226244
Royal Artillery 546 Coast Regt.
Ticket No. 244
Destination: St. Helena
Son of William and Ethel Johnson, of

Peterborough, Northamptonshire.
Panel 2. Column 2.

JOLLY NORMAN
Lieutenant; 227637
Royal Army Medical Corps
Ticket No. *316*
Destination: **Cape Town**
Panel 18. Column 1

JONES THOMAS GWYN
Age: *23*
Private; 7403891
Royal Army Medical Corps
War Office Booking
Destination: **Cape Town**
Son of David and Mary Jones, of Abernant. Camarthenshire.
Panel 18. Column 2.

KAYE HUBERT
Age: *49*
Lieutenant 59529
Royal Engineers
War Office Booking
Destination: **Cape Town**
Husband of Muriel Kaye, of Horsforth, Yorkshire.
Panel 4. Column 3.

KELLY THOMAS ANTHONY
Age: *35*
Captain; 157851
Royal Army Medical Corps
War Office Booking
Destination: **Cape Town**
Son of Jack and Anne Kelly. Husband of Pauline M. Kelly, of Cork, Irish Republic. M.B., B.Ch., B.A.O.
Panel 18. Column 1.

KENNEDY DOUGLAS NORTHCOTE
Age: *22*
Bombardier; 1578016
Royal Artillery
War Office Booking
Destination: **St Helena**
Son of George Henry and Annie Jane Kennedy, of West Ealing, Middlesex.
Panel 2. Column 3.

KNIGHT GRACE LOUISE
Age: *44*
Sister; 238115
Queen Alexandra's Imperial Military Nursing Service
Ticket No. *347*
Destination: **Cape Town**
Panel 22. Column 2.

LASLETT GEORGE NEWMAN
Lieutenant; 139460
Royal Army Pay Corps
Ticket No. *349*
Destination: **Cape Town**
Panel 20. Column 1.

LEA JAMES
Age: *22*
Private; 7402425
Royal Army Medical Corps
War Office Booking
Destination: **Cape Town**
Son of George and Emma Lea. Husband of Mary Lea, of Cheadle Heath, Stockport, Cheshire.
Panel 18. Column 2.

LEADER CHARLES FREDERICK WILLIAM
Age: *37*
Captain 139433
Royal Engineers
Ticket No. *301*
Destination: **Cape Town**
Son of Fred and Rose Ellen Chetwynd Leader, of Barrow-in-Furness, Lancashire.
Panel 4. Column 3.

LEWIS KENNETH GORDON
Age: *23*
Sapper; 142861
Royal Engineers
War Office Booking
Destination: **Cape Town**
Son of William John and Beatrice Margaret Lewis, of Briton Ferry, Neath.
Panel 6. Column 2.

MASLEN ERIC JAMES
Age: *22*
Private; S/5443398
Royal Army Service Corps

War Office Booking
Destination: ***Cape Town***
Son of Arthur and Annie Maslen.
Husband of Joan Maslen, of Tickenham,
Somerset.
Panel 17. Column 3.

MATHESON DAVID BLACK
Age: ***19***
Private; T/10686619
Royal Army Service Corps
War Office Booking
Destination: ***Cape Town***
Panel 17. Column 3.

MAXWELL MARGARET
Sister; 239734
Queen Alexandra's Imperial Military Nursing Service
Ticket No. ***330***
Destination: ***Cape Town***
Panel 22. Column 2.

McBRYDE KATHERINE DAISY
Age: ***30***
Sister; 236022
Queen Alexandra's Imperial Military Nursing Service
Ticket No. ***332***
Destination: ***Cape Town***
Daughter of George Hamilton Richards and Katherine Winifred Richards, of Shortlands, Kent. *Panel 22. Column 2.*

McFADYEAN ARCHIBALD
Age: ***24***
Private; 7373405
Royal Army Medical Corps
War Office Booking
Destination: ***Cape Town***
Panel 18. Column 2.

McGREGOR MABEL DOUGLAS
Age: ***30***
Sister; 239998
Queen Alexandra's Imperial Military Nursing Service
Ticket No. ***333***
Destination: ***Cape Town***
Daughter of William and Elizabeth McGregor.
Panel 22. Column 2.

MILLER LESLIE THOMAS
Age: ***22***
Signalman; 2338081
5th Command Sigs. Royal Corps of Signals.
War Office Booking
Destination: ***St Helena***
Panel 8. Column 1.

MILNES HERBERT
Age: ***22***
Private; 7380134
Royal Army Medical Corps
War Office Booking
Destination: ***Cape Town***
Son of Charles Henry and Amy Milnes, of Leeds, Yorkshire.
Panel 18. Column 2.

MORGAN JOHN HENRY
Age: ***29***
Gunner; 1607083
Royal Artillery
War Office Booking
Destination: ***St Helena***
Son of Albert Morgan, and of Lily Morgan, of Manchester.
Panel 1. Column 3.

MORRIS DORA MARY
Age: ***27***
Sister; 239730
Queen Alexandra's Imperial Military Nursing Service
Ticket No. 331
Destination: ***Cape Town***
Daughter of David John and Dora Morris, of Blackpill, Swansea.
Panel 22. Column 2.

MURBY HARRY STOCKTON
Age: ***24***
Serjeant; S/13049465
Royal Army Service Corps
War Office Booking
Destination: ***Cape Town***
Panel 15. Column 3.

NEEDHAM EDWARD JOHN ALLPORT
Captain; 136046
Royal Army Medical Corps
Medical Officer St. Helena.

Casualty list

Ticket No. 254
Destination: **St Helena**
Panel 18. Column 1.

NEEDHAM ERIC RANDOLPH
Age: 32
Serjeant; S/267837
Royal Army Service Corps
War Office Booking
Destination: **Cape Town**
Panel 15. Column 3.

NEIL ALLAN MACDOUGALL
Age: 23
Signalman; 2330587
Royal Corps of Signals
War Office Booking
Destination: **St Helena**
Son of William and Agnes MacDougall Neil.
Husband of Mabel Neil, of Darlington, Co. Durham.
Panel 8. Column 1.

NICHOLL DAVID ILTID
Major; 942242
97 A.A. Regt. Royal Artillery
Ticket No. 354
Destination: **Sydney**
Panel 2. Column 1.

NICOLSON CHRISTINA MARGARET S.R.N.
Age: 22
Sister; 238106
Queen Alexandra's Imperial Military Nursing Service
Ticket No. 334
Destination: **Cape Town**
Daughter of Capt. James Henry Nicolson and Janet Elizabeth Nicolson.
Panel 22. Column 2.

NOLAN MARGARET
Age: 29
Sister; 238701
Queen Alexandra's Imperial Military Nursing Service
Ticket No. 335
Destination: **Cape Town**
Daughter of Patrick and Ellen Nolan, of Castlerea, Co. Roscommon. Irish Republic.
Panel 22. Column 22.

NORRIE ERNEST MURRAY
B.Sc., Econ. (Lond.)
Age: 23
Sapper; 13066548 **Royal Engineers**
War Office Booking
Destination: **Cape Town**
Son of E. S. Norrie, and of Mary E. Norrie, of Wimbledon Park, Surrey.
Panel 6. Column 3.

O'SULLIVAN MARGARET MARY
Sister; 234989
Queen Alexandra's Imperial Military Nursing Service
Ticket No. 338
Destination: **Cape Town**
Panel 22. Column 2.

PARRISH HARRY GILES
Age: 46
Major; 127709
Royal Army Ordnance Corps.
Ticket No. 356
Destination: **Cape Town**
Son of John and Emma Parrish.
Husband of Margherita Parrish of Toronto, Ontario, Canada.
Panel 18. Column 3.

PARRY KENNETH GEORGE
Age: 26
Private; 7679210
Royal Army Pay Corps
War Office Booking
Destination: **Cape Town**
Panel 20. Column 1.

PASK JAMES RONALD
Age: 26
Lieutenant; 240275
2nd Bn. West Yorkshire Regt. (Prince of Wales's Own)
Ticket No. 247
Destination: **St Helena**
Son of John and Harriet Pask.
Husband of Rita Pask, of Leeds, Yorkshire.
Panel 10. Column 1.

PERKINS JAMES ARTHUR
Captain; 152443
Royal Army Medical Corps

Ticket No. **310**
Destination: **Cape Town**
Panel 18. Column 1.

PETTIGREW JAMES STARK
Age: **26**
Serjeant; 910684
Royal Engineers
Chartered Accountant
War Office Booking
Destination: **Cape Town**
Son of James Gilchrist Pettigrew and Agnes Thomson Stark Pettigrew.
Panel 5. Column 1.

PITT JOAN
Sister; 241708
Queen Alexandra's Imperial Military Nursing Service
Ticket No. **336**
Destination: **Cape Town**
Daughter of Ernest E. Pitt and Maggie Pitt, of Banff.
Panel 22. Column 2.

POLLI SIMON
Age: **34**
Private; 7680226
Royal Army Pay Corps
War Office Booking
Destination: **Cape Town**
Son of Jacob and Sarah Polli.
Husband of Peggy Polli, of West Kensington, London.
Panel 20. Column 1.

PORTINGALE JANET SCOTT
Age: **32**
Sister; 215393
Queen Alexandra's Imperial Military Nursing Service
Ticket No. **337**
Destination: **Cape Town**
Daughter of William Robert and Helen Scott Portingale, of Victoria, British Columbia, Canada.
Panel 22. Column 2.

POTTER CLIFFORD V.
Age: **32**
Gunner; 858027
Royal Artillery *370 Coast Bty.*

War Office Booking
Destination: **St Helena**
Son of William and Ethel Johnson, of Peterborough, Northamptonshire.
Panel 3. Column 3.

PRENTIS JAMES ALAN
Age: **31**
Lieutenant; 50219
Royal Artillery
Ticket No. **243**
Destination: **St Helena**
Son of John Edward and Evelyn May Prentis.
Panel 2. Column 2.

PROUD ROBERT DAVIDSON
Age: **27**
Company Quartermaster Serjeant; 2338802
Royal Corps of Signals
War Office Booking
Destination: **St Helena**
Husband of Pauline Cecilia Proud, of Hull.
Panel 7. Column 3.

RICHMOND HUGH TAIT M.B., F.R.C.S.
Captain; 171214
Royal Army Medical Corps
Ticket No. **352**
Destination: **Cape Town**
Panel 18. Column 1.

RIDOUT FRANK EDWARD
Age: **24**
Staff Serjeant; 1431309
Royal Artillery
Ticket No. **407**
Destination: **Melbourne**
Son of Edward Charles and Mabel Annie Ridout, of Wandsworth, London.
Panel 2. Column 2.

ROBSON-CROSS WALTER M.C.
Captain 136905
Royal Engineers
Ticket No. **302**
Destination: **Cape Town**
Panel 4. Column 3.

ROWBOTHAM HARRY
Age: **24**
Sapper; 4197348

Royal Engineers
War Office Booking
Destination: **Cape Town**
Son of Henry and Ellen Rowbotham. Husband of Violet Rowbotham, of Droylsden, Lancashire.
Panel 7. Column 1.

RUSE ORVILLE THOMAS
Age: 25
Warrant Officer Class II (B.S.M.) 815196
Royal Artillery 347 Bty., 16 Coast Regt.
Ticket No. **245**
Destination: **St. Helena**
Son of Thomas and Mabel Ruse.
Panel 2. Column 2.

SIRCOM FRANCIS ALAN
Age: 37
Private; 6854573
Royal Army Ordnance Corps
War Office Booking
Destination: **Cape Town**
Panel 9. Column 12.

SLATER JOHN L.D.S.
Age: 29
Captain; 188346 **Army Dental Corps**
Ticket No. **351**
Destination: **Cape Town**
Son of George Currie Slater and Isobella Slater. Husband of Mary Slater, of Glasgow.
Panel 20. Column 2.

SMITH GORDON
Age: 22
Gunner; 1578289
Royal Artillery
War Office Booking
Destination: **St Helena**
Panel 3. Column 3.

SMITH WILLIAM
Age: 22
Signalman; 2327806
Royal Corps of Signals
War Office Booking
Destination: **St Helena**
Panel 8. Column 1.

STOKES CYRIL GEORGE
Age: 23
Gunner; 864877
Royal Artillery
War Office Booking
Destination: **St Helena**
Son of George and Blanche Grace Stokes, of Hamworthy, Poole, Dorsetshire.
Panel 3. Column 3.

STRATFORD DOROTHY MURIEL
Age: 32
Sister; 215966
Territorial Army Nursing Service
Ticket No. **318**
Destination: **Cape Town**
Daughter of Hubert and Muriel Stratford, of Worthing, Sussex. Her brother, Laurence Dacre Stratford also died on service.
Panel 22. Column 3.

SUTHERLAND BARBARA MUNRO
Age: 31
Sister; 238713
Queen Alexandra's Imperial Military Nursing Service
Ticket No. **339**
Destination: **Cape Town**
Daughter of Mr. and Mrs. George Sutherland, of Bettyhill, Sutherlandshire.
Panel 22. Column 3.

THOMPSON CHARLES FRANCIS
Age: 27
Private; 7262539
Royal Army Medical Corps
War Office Booking
Destination: **Cape Town**
Son of Mr. and Mrs. C. Thompson, of Leeds, Yorkshire.
Husband of Kathleen Thompson, of Lords Wood, Hampshire.
Panel 18. Column 3.

TOOHEY KATHLEEN
Sister; 241732
Queen Alexandra's Imperial Military Nursing Service
Ticket No. **340**
Destination: **Cape Town**
Daughter of Cornelius and Margaret Toohey, of Nenagh, Co. Tipperary, Irish Republic.
Panel 22. Column 3.

TUDOR HETTIE ANNIE
Sister; 236473
Queen Alexandra's Imperial Military Nursing Service
Ticket No. **348**
Destination: **Cape Town**
Daughter of Charles Richard and Sarah Ann Tudor of Cardigan.
Panel 22, Column 3.

WARREN JOHN GUNN
M.A. (Cantab.), M.B., B.Ch., L.R.C.P. (Lond.), M.R.C.S.
Age: 37
Lieutenant 236037
Royal Army Medical Corps
Ticket No. **312**
Destination: **Cape Town**
Son of Capt. Frank Warren, formerly of the R.A., and Bessie Warren. Husband of Nora Myfanwy Warren, of Pinhoe, Devon.
Panel 18. Column 1.

WATERS GLADYS
Age: 31
Sister; 241027
Queen Alexandra's Imperial Military Nursing Service
Ticket No. **341**
Destination: **Cape Town**
Daughter of John Waters, and of Mary Waters, of Harrington, Cumberland.
Panel 22. Column 33.

WHEELOCK LILIAN MARIA ETHEL
Age: 28
Sister; 238719
Queen Alexandra's Imperial Military Nursing Service
Ticket No. **344**
Destination: **Cape Town**
Daughter of Isaac and Ellen Jane Wheelock.
Panel 22. Column 3.

WHITE KATHERINE FRANCES MARY
Sister; 223223
Queen Alexandra's Imperial Military Nursing Service
Ticket No. **343**
Destination: **Cape Town**
Daughter of Matthew O. Byrne White and May White, of Stillorgan, Co. Dublin, Irish Republic.
Panel 22. Column 1.

WILMOT WILLIAM JAMES
Age: 32
Corporal; 3959108
158 Field Amb. Royal Army Medical Corps
War Office Booking
Destination: **Cape Town**
Son of David J. Wilmot and Gweneth Wilmot. Husband of Mary Ann Wilmot of Worplesdon, Surrey.
Panel 18. Column 2.

WINGATE ADELINE RITA
Sister; 241726
Queen Alexandra's Imperial Military Nursing Service
Ticket No. **342**
Destination: **Cape Town**
Daughter of Churchill James Wingate and Mari Wingate, of Hereford.
Panel 22. Colunin 3.

WINSER* TREVOR ERNEST
Age: 26
Date of Birth: **9th January 1916**
Place of Birth: **Hawkhurst, Kent**
Corporal; S/154859
Royal Army Service Corps
War Office Booking
Destination: **Cape Town**
Son of Ernest and Louie Winser. Husband of Joyce Winser, Hildenborough, Kent
Panel 16. Column 1.
* *Recorded on Passenger List as T. Winson*

WOOD HORACE
Age: 37
Private; 4399756
Royal Army Ordnance Corps
War Office Booking
Destination: **Cape Town**
Panel 19. Column 3.

WOOD WINIFRED MARY FRY
Age: 25
Sister; 241728
Queen Alexandra's Imperial Military Nursing Service
Ticket No. **345**

Destination: **Cape Town**
Daughter of Charles William and Winifred Fry; Adopted daughter and niece of Cyril R. J. Wood and Florence Elsie Wood, of St. Lawrence, Isle of Wight.
Panel 22. Column 3.

WOODHOUSE MARY
Age: 37
Sister; 215866
Territorial Army Nursing Service
Ticket No. 321
Destination: **Cape Town**
Daughter of George Burton Woodhouse and Mary Woodhouse.
Panel 22. Column 3.

WOOLLEY WILFRED MORTON
Age: 29
Private; 7678058
Royal Army Pay Corps
War Office Booking
Destination: **Cape Town**
Panel 20. Column 2.

Chatham Naval Memorial Kent

BEER WILLIAM ARTHUR CHARLES
Age: 28
Telegraphist; C/JX 271067
Royal Navy
Ticket No. 496
Destination: **Cape Town**
Address in UK: 2 Middleton, Briton Ferry
Son of Mr. and Mrs. W. J. Beer, of Briton Ferry, Glamorgan.
59, 2.

COOK JOHN HOLLINGWORTH ROBERTS
Age: 36
Lieutenant
Royal Naval Volunteer Reserve H.M.S. Euphrates.
Ticket No. 380
Destination: **Cape Town**
Son of Ralph Montagu Cook and Millicent Anne Cook of Paddock Wood, Kent.
66, 1.

***DYSON** JOSEPH
Age: 22
Gunner; 3392273
Royal Artillery 5 Maritime Regt.
Son of Margaret Dyson, of Chadderton, Lancashire.
67, 2.

EGAN HENRY MICHAEL
Age: 27
Petty Officer; C/JX 134609
Royal Navy
Admiralty Booking
Destination: **Cape Town**
Husband of Florence Evelyn Egan, of Rainham, Kent.
51, 3.

EWING ARCHIBALD
Age: 32
Telegraphist; C/JX 269663
Royal Navy
Ticket No. 486
Destination: **Cape Town**
Address in UK: 9 Northfield Avenue, Edinburgh
Son of Archibald and Margaret B. Ewing, of Edinburgh
59, 2.

FREESTONE EDWARD JAMES
Marine; CH/X 1265
Royal Marines H.M.S. Kongoni.
Ticket No. 491
Destination: **Cape Town**
65, 2.

*HENRICK DOUGLAS HAIG NIVELLE
Age: 25
Gunner; 5950081
Royal Artillery 5 Maritime Regt.
Son of Charles Albert and Jane Henrick, of Bedford.
67, 2.

HEWITT SIDNEY ROBERT
Age: 23
Yeoman of Signals; C/JX 140988
Royal Navy
Admiralty Booking
Destination: **Cape Town**
Son of Sidney Herbert and Alice Hewitt, of Winterton, Norfolk.
58, 2.

*HILLS FREDERICK WILLIAM
Age: 23
Gunner; 5504605
Royal Artillery 5 Maritime Regt.
Son of William and Edith May Hills, of Swanley, Kent.
67, 2.

PETERKEN WALTER ERNEST
Age: 31
Leading Telegraphist; C/JX 309423
Royal Navy
Ticket No. **480**
Destination: **Cape Town**
Address in UK: 66 Comptroller Dept., Egham
Son of Walter Bentley Peterken and Susan Peterken, of Leyton, Essex.
59, 2.

SMITH GEORGE ALBERT
Age: 33
Telegraphist; C/JX 269573
Royal Navy H.M.S. Pembroke II
Ticket No. **482**
Destination: **Cape Town**
Address in UK: 126 Boulevard, Hull
59, 3.

SMITH RAYMOND VERDUN ALBERT
Age: 26
Place of Birth: **Hereford**
Able Seaman; C/JX 236439
Royal Navy H.M.S. President III *(Crew)*
Son of Frederick and Isabella Smith; husband of Beatrice Mary Smith, of Clifford, Herefordshire. Halfway House, Brierton, Hereford.
52, 2.

WOOD HARRY
Age: 33
Lieutenant
Royal Naval Volunteer Reserve H.M.S. Assegai
Ticket No. **208**
Destination: **Durban**
Address in the UK: 206 Chessington Rd. West Ewell, Surrey
Son of John and Margaret Ann Wood, of Winton, Lancashire.
66, 1.

* *Not on the post-sinking passenger summary but believed to have been on board.*

Lee-on-Solent Fleet Air Arm War Memorial Hampshire

FORMSTONE STANLEY CLIFFORD
Age: 22
Air Mechanic 1st Class; FAA/FX. 81609
Royal Navy H.M.S. Lanka
Admiralty Booking
Destination: **Cape Town**
Son of Harold and Clara Formstone, of 9 Delvine Drive, Upton by Chester, Cheshire.
Bay 3, Panel 5.

HANDEL DONALD JOHN
Age: 22
Leading Radio Mechanic; FAA/FX. 607149
Royal Navy H.M.S. Birmingham
Admiralty Booking
Destination: **Cape Town**
Son of Mr. and Mrs. John Carl Handel.
Bay 3, Panel 6.

Casualty list

Plymouth Naval Memorial *Devon*

AITKEN HARRY AUGUSTINE
Age: 23
Able Seaman; S4401
Royal Australian Naval Reserve
Ticket No. **466**
Destination: **Sydney**
Son of Frank Rezea Aitkin and Edith May Aitkin, of Balmain, New South Wales, Australia
Panel 75, Column 2.

ARGENT THOMAS HENRY
Age: 18
Place of Birth: **Widnes**
Able Seaman; D/JX 339068
Royal Navy H.M.S. President III
(Crew)
10 Mayfair Road, Barton, Ditton, Widnes.
Panel 64. Column 1.

BRUCE CHARLES HENRY
Age: 28
Place of Birth: **New South Wales**
Leading Seaman; S1701
Royal Australian Naval Reserve
(Crew)
Son of Charles Henry and Charlot Herminea Bruce; husband of Lola Beatrice Bruce, of Campsie, New South Wales, Australia.
9A South Parade, Campsie, N.S.W.
Panel 75, Column 2.

COCHRANE JAMES
Age: 29
Serjeant; PLY/X 866
Royal Marines H.M.S. Assegai
Admiralty Booking
Destination: **Cape Town**
Son of James and C. Cochrane.
Husband of Dora M. Cochrane, of Chislehurst, Kent.
Panel 74, Column 3.

COLLIS WILLIAM CHARLES
Stoker 1st Class; D/KX 103030
Royal Navy H.M.S. Drake IV
Admiralty Booking
Destination: **Cape Town**
Panel 70. Column 1.

COUTMAN HAROLD CLIVE
Age: 20
Able Seaman S5179
Royal Australian Naval Reserve
Ticket No. **463**
Destination: **Sydney**
Son of Harold George and Elsie Eileen Coutman, of Kogarah, New South Wales, Australia.
Panel 75. Column 2.

CUTTS AUBREY RAY
Age: 24
Lieutenant
Royal Australian Naval Volunteer Reserve
Ticket No. **226**
Destination: **Sydney**
Son of Joseph Charles and Constance Cutts, of Bellevue Hill, New South Wales, Australia. Husband of Flora Cutts.
Panel 77. Column 1.

FARRELL WILFRED FRANCES
Age: 18
Marine; PLY/X 106428
Royal Marines H.M.S. Tana II
Admiralty Booking
Destination: **Cape Town**
Son of Robert Farrell, and of E. A. O. Farrell, of Droylsden, Lancashire.
Panel 74, Column 3.

GLASZIOU JOHN VICTOR
Age: 21
Leading Seaman; S4137
Royal Australian Naval Reserve
Ticket No. **461**
Destination: **Sydney**
Son of Victor and Elsie Enid Glasziou, of Belmore, New South Wales, Australia.
Panel 75, Column 2.

HALLAM WILLIAM THEODORE
Age: 44
Place of Birth: **USA**
Able Seaman; D/JX 339444
Royal Navy H.M.S. President III
(Crew)

531

Son of William and Annie Hallam.
Husband of Florence Hallam, of Bolton,
Lancashire.
25 St Helens Street, Bolton.
Panel 65, Column 1.

HEATON ROBERT
Age: **19**
Place of Birth: **Liverpool**
Able Seaman; D/JX 339442
Royal Navy H.M.S. President III
(Crew)
Son of Robert Leonard and Mary Heaton, of Liverpool.
26 Compton Street, Liverpool.
Panel 65, Column 2.

HILTON JAMES HENRY
Marine; PLY/X 106429
Royal Marines H.M.S. Tana II
Admiralty Booking
Destination: **Cape Town**
Panel 74, Column 3.

JEFFREY ALAN ALEXANDER
Age: **31**
Lieutenant
Royal Naval Reserve H.M.S. Afrikander IV
Ticket No. **205**
Destination: **Durban**
Son of Mr. and Mrs. Alexander Jeffrey.
Husband of Audrey May Jeffrey, who perished with him.
Panel 75, Column 1.

JILLARD ALFRED JOHN
Age: **29**
Place of Birth: **Spotswood**
Able Seaman; W460
Royal Australian Naval Reserve
(Crew)
Son of Alfred John and Jane Jillard; husband of Rita Doris Jillard, of Flemington, Victiora, Australia.
20 Stuart Street, Wellington.
Panel 75, Column 2.

KEENE FREDERICK EDWIN BERTRAM
Age: **32**
Corporal; PLY/X 351
Royal Marines H.M.S. Assegai
Admiralty Booking
Destination: **Cape Town**
Son of Edwin and Ellen Keene.
Husband of Heather Keene, of Warminster, Wiltshire.
Panel 74, Column 3.

LEVITZKE GUS WILLIAM
Age: **32**
Place of Birth: **Perth, Western Australia**
Able Seaman; F2481
Royal Australian Naval Reserve
(Crew)
Son of Ernest Thomas Levitzke and of Mary Jane Levitzke, of East Perth, Western Australia.
292 High Street East, Perth, Western Australia.
Panel 75, Column 2.

LLOYD GEORGE HERBERT
Age: **19**
Able Seaman S5171
Royal Australian Naval Reserve
Ticket No. **464**
Destination: **Sydney**
Son of Francis Bede Lloyd, and of Mary Lloyd, of Kingsford, New South Wales, Australia.
Panel 75. Column 2.

MAY HOWARD
Age: **35**
Marine; PLY/X 147
Royal Marines H.M.S. Assegai
Admiralty Booking
Destination: **Cape Town**
Husband of Gladys Gertrude May, of Cosham, Hampshire.
Panel 74, Column 3.

MOSCOS JOHN GEORGE
Leading Writer; 66786
South African Naval Forces
Admiralty Booking
Destination: **Cape Town**
Son of Mr. and Mrs. G. J. Moscos, of East London, Cape Province, South Africa.
Panel 74, Column 2.

NEL LOUIS
Stoker 1st Class; D/KX 96183
Royal Navy H.M.S. Drake IV
Admiralty Booking

Destination: **Cape Town**
Panel 70. Column 2.

O'DONOGHUE BASIL DAVID
Age: **28**
Lieutenant
Royal Australian Naval Volunteer Reserve
Ticket No. **225**
Destination: **Sydney**
Son of David Flynn O'Donoghue and Florence Mary O'Donoghue, of Malvern, Victoria, Australia.
Panel 77. Column 1.

*****OSBORN** LEONARD ARTHUR
Bombardier; 1549991
Royal Artillery *7/4 Maritime Regt.*
Panel 77. Column 2.

PEARSON ERNEST COURTENAY
Age: **38**
Marine; PLY/X 2646
Royal Marines H.M.S. Assegai
Admiralty Booking
Destination: **Cape Town**
Son of Courtenay and Helen Mary Pearson, of St. Budeaux, Devon.
Panel 74. Column 3.

PEEL ARTHUR HENRY FREDERICK
Age: **24**
Stoker 1st Class; D/KX 99128
Royal Navy H.M.S. Drake IV
Admiralty Booking
Destination: **Cape Town**
Son of William and Catherine Victoria Peel, of Plymouth.
Panel 70. Column 2.

PRESTON HAROLD GRESWOLDE
Age: **18**
Marine; PLY/X 106430
Royal Marines H.M.S. Tana II
Admiralty Booking
Destination: **Cape Town**
Son of Francis and Margaret Preston, of Lower Broughton, Lancashire.
Panel 74, Column 3.

ROYLE KEITH
Age: **18**
Marine; PLY/X 106431
Royal Marines H.M.S. Tana II
Admiralty Booking
Destination: **Cape Town**
Son of John W. and Alice Royle, of South Reddish, Cheshire.
Panel 74. Column 3.

SAUNDERS HERBERT HENRY
Age: **30**
Chief Petty Officer Writer 19777
Royal Australian Navy
Ticket No. **227**
Destination: **Sydney**
Son of Charles Edward and Margaret M. Saunders, of Rockdale, New South Wales, Australia.
Panel 73. Column 3.

SCRUTTON HAROLD FRANCIS
Age: **42**
Lieutenant
Royal Navy H.M.S. Assegai
Ticket No. **204**
Destination: **Cape Town**
Address in the UK: 6 Little Ash Gardens, Saltash, Plymouth.
Panel 62. Column 3.

SELBY SYDNEY JAMES
Age: **20**
Able Seaman S4769
Royal Australian Naval Reserve
Ticket No. **465**
Destination: **Sydney**
Son of Sydney George and Alice Dorothy Selby, of Wollongong, New South Wales, Australia.
Panel 75. Column 3.

SIMES FREDERICK GEORGE
Age: **24**
Stoker 1st Class; D/KX 93896
Royal Navy H.M.S. Drake IV
Admiralty Booking
Destination: **Cape Town**
Son of Charles Edward and Annie Elizabeth Simes. Native of South Africa.
Panel 70. Column 3.

SS CERAMIC The Untold Story

SIMPSON HARRY
Age: 25
Stoker 18561
Royal Australian Navy
Ticket No. 460
Destination: Sydney
Son of Walter Jessop Morton Sorrensen and Hilda Doreen Sorrensen.
Husband of Estelle Florence Sorrensen, of Windsor, Queensland, Australia.
Panel 73. Column 3.

SORRENSEN JACK MORTON
Age: 25
Able Seaman B2034
Royal Australian Naval Reserve
Ticket No. 497
Destination: Sydney
Son of Sydney George and Alice Dorothy Selby, of Wollongong, New South Wales, Australia.
Panel 75. Column 3.

STEPHEN ALFRED JOHN CARLE
Sergeant; PLY/22233
Royal Marines H.M.S. Assegai
Admiralty Booking
Destination: Cape Town
Panel 74. Column 3.

STEVENSON WILLIAM ALLISON
Age: 24
Able Seaman S2978
Royal Australian Naval Reserve
Ticket No. 460
Destination: Sydney
Son of William Allison Stevenson, and of Eileen Isabel Stevenson, of Lakemba, New South Wales, Australia.
Panel 75. Column 3.

TURNBULL JOHN CLARE
Stoker 1st Class; D/KX 96184
Royal Navy H.M.S. Drake IV
Admiralty Booking
Destination: Cape Town
Panel 70. Column 3.

UTTING RICHARD HAYNES
Age: 33
Lieutenant
Royal Australian Naval Volunteer Reserve
Ticket No. 223
Destination: Sydney
Son of James Horatio and Elna Utting, of Cottesloe, Western Australia.
Husband of Beryl Amy May Utting, of Cottesloe.
Panel 77. Column 1.

VAUGHAN KELVIN JAMES
Age: 35
Lieutenant
Royal Australian Naval Volunteer Reserve
Ticket No. 224
Destination: Sydney
Son of George Atherden Vaughan and Ethel Marion Vaughan, of Mosman, New South Wales, Australia.
Panel 77. Column 1.

WAKEFIELD SYDNEY
Marine; PLY/X 106425
Royal Marines H.M.S. Tana II
Ticket No. 353
Destination: Cape Town
Panel 75. Column 1.

WALDRON SAMUEL FREDERICK
Age: 37
Marine; PLY/21988
Royal Marines H.M.S. Assegai
Admiralty Booking
Destination: Cape Town
Son of Samuel and Elizabeth Ann Waldron.
Husband of Dorothy Beatrice Waldron, of St. Budeaux, Devon.
Panel 75. Column 1.

WALKER RICHARD
Age: 18
Marine; PLY/X 106432
Royal Marines H.M.S. Tana II
Ticket No. 353
Destination: Cape Town
Son of John W. and Annie E. Walker, of Chester.
Panel 75. Column 1.

* *Not on the post-sinking passenger summary but believed to have been on board.*

534

Portsmouth Naval Memorial Hampshire

BEDFORD THOMAS ERIC ERNEST
Age: 32
Place of Birth: **London**
Gunner; 6284164
Royal Artillery 4/2 Maritime Regt. (Crew)
Son of Thomas Ernest and Alice Bedford, of Camden Town, London.
1 Jeffrey's Place, Camden Town, London N.W.1.
Panel 72. Column 2.

BESWICK ROBERT
Age: 24
Ordnance Artificer 3rd Class; P/MX 58292.
Royal Navy H.M.S. Victory III
Ticket No. **266**
Destination: **Cape Town**
Son of Eliza Ellen Beswick.
Panel 69. Column 2.
Ordnance Artificers WW2 Memorial, Senior Rates Mess, HMS Excellent. Column 2

CHEETHAM FRANK
Age: 39
Marine; PO/X 113884
Royal Marines
Ticket No. **489**
Destination: **Cape Town**
Son of James Medwin Cheetham and Catherine Cheetham; husband of Doris Edna Cheetham, of Heaton Park, Lancashire.
Panel 70, Column 2.

DONNELL WILLIAM ORLANDO
Age: 25
Lance Bombardier; 7016831
Royal Artillery 4/2 Maritime Regt.
Son of John Joseph Donnell, and of Blanche Ellen Donnell, of Willesden Green, Middlesex.
Panel 72. Column 1.

EDWARDS ARTHUR SYDNEY
Age: 31
Able Seaman; P/JX 129891
Royal Navy H.M.S. President III
Ticket No. **493**
Destination: **Cape Town**
Son of Sydney Robert and Helen Gertrude Edwards.

Husband of Doris Mary Edwards, of Upper Tooting, Surrey.
Royal Victorian Medal.
Panel 63. Column 3.

GIBBS STANLEY VERNON
Age: 36
Chief Petty Officer, Mentioned in Despatches; P/J 105754
Royal Navy H.M.S. Victory III
Ticket No. **264**
Destination: **Cape Town**
Husband of Newell Eliza Gibbs, of Horsted Keynes, Sussex.
Panel 62. Column 2.

GOACHER PERCY WILFRED
Age: **45**
Chief Yeoman of Signals; P/J 28935
Royal Navy H.M.S. Victory III
Ticket No. **265**
Destination: **Cape Town**
Son of Alfred and Emma Goacher.
Husband of Laura Violet Goacher, of North End, Portsmouth.
Panel 66. Column 2.

HORNBROOK FRANCIS BAILEY
Age: 36
Lieutenant
Royal Naval Volunteer Reserve H.M.S. Sheba
Ticket No. **207**
Destination: **Arabia via Cape Town**
27 Station Road, Church End, London.
Panel 71. Column 1.

HOUGHTON JACK FOSTER
Age: **45**
Marine PO/216148
Royal Marines
Ticket No. **490**
Destination: **Cape Town**
Panel 70. Column 2.

JONES HARRY LIONEL
Age: **53**
Gunner
Royal Navy H.M.S. Assegai

Ticket No. 206
*Destination: **Durban***
Husband of Nellie Elizabeth Jones, of 12 Pangbourne Avenue, Cosham, Hampshire.
Panel 62. Column 1.

KING GEORGE EDGAR
Age: 32
*Place of Birth: **Nottingham***
Able Seaman; P/JX 339443
Royal Navy H.M.S. Victory III
(Crew)
Son of Edward Harvey King and Eliza Jane King.
Husband of Eva Allenby King, of Wollaton, Nottingham.
32 Ewell Road, Nottingham.
Panel 64. Column 1.

LINES CYRIL GRAHAM
Age: 31
*Place of Birth: **Birmingham***
Gunner; 7045853
Royal Artillery *4/2 Maritime Regt.*
(Crew)
Son of John Prentice Lines and Martha Helen Lines; husband of Caroline May Lines, of Warley, Worcestershire.
51 Clent Road, Warley, Oldbury, Nr. Birmingham.
Panel 72. Column 2.

LITTLE JOHN JAMES
Age: 28
*Place of Birth: **Monaghan***
Gunner; 13100704
Royal Artillery *4/2 Maritime Regt.*
(Crew)
Son of Francis and Sarah Little, of Falkirk, Stirlingshire.
36 Thornbridge Road, Falkirk.
Panel 72. Column 2.

McKENNA PATRICK JOSEPH
Age: 29
*Place of Birth: **Glasgow***
Gunner; 13055086
Royal Artillery *4/2 Maritime Regt.*
(Crew)
241 Florence Street, Glasgow C5.
Panel 72. Column 2.

RIDDELL WILLIAM FORSTER B.A. (Cantab.)
Age: 25
Lieutenant
Royal Naval Volunteer Reserve H.M.S. Tana
Ticket No. 209
*Destination: **Cape Town***
Son of William Edmiston Riddell and Emily Edmiston Riddell.
Husband of Olga Geldard Forster Riddell, of 276 Heaton Rd, Newcastle-on-Tyne.
Fellow of Gonville and Caius College, A.M.I.E.E., Freeman of the Borough of Berwick-on-Tweed.
Panel 71. Column 1.

STAPLETON RALPH ELLIS
Age: 27
*Place of Birth: **Nottingham***
Serjeant; 904443
Royal Artillery *4/2 Maritime Regt.*
(Crew)
Son of Ernest and Annie Stapleton; husband of Lorna Stapleton, of Loughton, Essex.
17 Robinson Road, Mapperley, Notts.
Panel 72. Column 1.

TIMMINS WILLIAM
Age: 27
*Place of Birth: **Blackburn***
Gunner; 3659262
Royal Artillery *4/2 Maritime Regt.*
(Crew)
Son of Bernard and Sarah Timmins; husband of Mary Timmins, of Accrington, Lancashire.
10 Charter Street, Accrington.
Panel 72. Column 3.

WELLS EDWARD ALBERT FREDERICK
Stoker 1st Class; P/K 76622
Royal Navy H.M.S. Victory
Admiralty Booking
*Destination: **Cape Town***
Panel 68. Column 3.

Casualty list

Portsmouth Naval Memorial *Hampshire*

*Not on the post-sinking passenger summary but believed to have been on board.**

BULLOCK FRANK
Age: *29*
Gunner; *4203481*
Royal Artillery *4/2 Maritime Regt.*
Son of Sydney and Jane Bullock; husband of Ethel Bullock, of Salford, Lancashire.
Panel 72, Column 2.

CARLILE JOHN HENRY
Age: *21*
Gunner; *1797607*
Royal Artillery *3/2 Maritime Regt.*
Son of John Henry and Margarett Cathrine Carlile, of Stratford, Essex.
Panel 72, Column 2.

GIBBONS ALFRED YARWOOD
Age: *27*
Gunner; *3658765*
Royal Artillery *4/2 Maritime Regt.*
Son of Thomas Bradley Gibbons and Betsy Gibbons, of Lymm, Cheshire.
Panel 72, Column 2.

NICKS WILLIAM
Age: *37*
Gunner; *1773703*
Royal Artillery *4/2 Maritime Regt.*
Panel 72, Column 2.

SULLIVAN CHARLES
Age: *27*
Gunner; *1795138*
Royal Artillery *3/2 Maritime Regt.*
Panel 72, Column 2.

VOKES EDWARD L
Age: *24*
Lance Bombardier; *1774114*
Royal Artillery *4/2 Maritime Regt.*
Son of William H. Vokes, and of Kate Vokes, of Peasedown St. John, Somerset.
Panel 72, Column 1.

A number of Royal Artillery Maritime Regiment officers are commemorated on the Chatham, Plymouth and Portsmouth Memorials, and are believed to be casualties of the SS Ceramic.

However, they are not recorded by name on the post-sinking passenger summary, and the original passenger lists only record block bookings by the War Office and Royal Navy.

It has not been possible to verify that these individuals perished on the SS Ceramic, or on one of the other sinkings on 7th December 1942, therefore these names have been recorded separately on this casualty list.

I would be pleased to update this list in any future edition of this book and welcome any further information.

ssceramic@btconnect.com

Tower Hill Memorial London

The following Merchant Seamen were not part of the SS Ceramic's crew but were travelling as passengers to their place of duty.

BALDIE EDWARD HARVEY
Age: *27*
Engineer *(Andrew Weir)*
Merchant Navy
Ticket No. *395*
Destination: **Cape Town**
Son of William and Catherine Baldie.
Husband of Margaret Baldie, of Glasgow.
281 Dumbarton Road, Glasgow.
Panel 25.

BALDWIN JAMES
Age: *29*
Date of Birth: **20th March 1913**
Place of Birth: **West Malling, Kent**
Greaser
Merchant Navy
Ticket No. *467*
Destination: **Sydney**
Panel 25.

BULBROOK BASIL JOHN
Age: *31*
Engineer Officer
Merchant Navy *(Anglo Saxon Oil Co.)*
Ticket No. *378*
Destination: **Cape Town**
Son of Percy Owen Bulbrook, and Jessie Bulbrook.
Panel 25.

BULL ALFRED VICTOR
Age: *22*
Engineer Officer
Merchant Navy *(Anglo Saxon Oil Co.)*
Ticket No. *377*
Destination: **Cape Town**
Panel 25.

CLARK WILLIAM EVAN
Age: *32*
Date of Birth: **30th November 1910**
Place of Birth: **Durban, South Africa**
Second Officer
Merchant Navy Master Mariner

Ticket No. *364*
Destination: **Cape Town**
Son of William and Eleanor Evelyn Clark.
Husband of Norah Evelyn Clark, of Durban, Natal, South Africa.
Panel 25.

DOWN ARTHUR*
Age: *21*
Electrician
Merchant Navy
Ticket No. *256*
Destination: **Sydney**
Son of Percival and Martha Down, of Punchbowl, New South Wales, Australia.
Panel 26.

EMBLETON JOHN JOSEPH
Age: *29*
Date of Birth: **19th March 1923**
Place of Birth: **Chester-le-Street, Co. Durham**
Apprentice
Merchant Navy *(Anglo Saxon Oil Co.)*
Ticket No. *374*
Destination: **Cape Town**
Panel 26.

EVANS BRIAN GEORGE*
Age: *22*
Sailor/Engineer
Merchant Navy
Ticket No. *258*
Destination: **Sydney**
Panel 26.

FLATTERY JAMES JOSEPH*
Age: *23*
Fireman
Merchant Navy
Ticket No. *468*
Destination: **Sydney**
Son of Veronica Flattery, of Stanmore, Sydney, New South Wales, Australia.
Panel 26.

FOSTER WILLIAM LOGAN
Age: 58
Master (Bibby Line)
Merchant Navy
Ticket No. 382
Destination: **Cape Town**
Panel 26.

GRAY JOHN ROBERTSON
Age: 48
Engineer Officer
Merchant Navy *(Anglo Saxon Oil Co.)*
Ticket No. 375
Destination: **Cape Town**
Son of Alexander and Isabella Gray.
Husband of Dorothy Rankin Gray, of
Cambuslang, Lanarkshire.
Panel 26.

GREEN ALBERT STANLEY*
Age: 51
Boatwain's Mate
Merchant Navy
Ticket No. 469
Destination: **Sydney**
Son of Albert and Elizabeth Alice Green.
Husband of Ada Green, of Sydney, New South
Wales, Australia.
Panel 26.

GRIFFITHS ARTHUR POTTER*
Age: 30
Date of Birth: **21st September 1912**
Place of Birth: **Sydney**
Greaser
Merchant Navy
Ticket No. 495
Destination: **Sydney**
Panel 26.

HARLOW STANLEY CHARLES*
Age: 28
Date of Birth: **9th February 1914**
Place of Birth: **Sydney**
Electrician
Merchant Navy
Ticket No. 259
Destination: **Sydney**
Son of Charles Wentworth Harlow and Ezil Harlow.
Husband of Noreen Harlow.
Panel 26.

HAWKE KENNETH MALCOLM*
Age: 18
Ordinary Seaman
Merchant Navy
Ticket No. 472
Destination: **Sydney**
Panel 26.

JOHNSON PETER WILLIAM*
Age: 21
Fireman
Merchant Navy
Ticket No. 470
Destination: **Sydney**
Son of Charles George and Eva Emma Johnson,
of Pyrmont, Sydney, New South Wales,
Australia. *Panel 26.*

KERR CHARLES REGINALD*
Age: 26
Date of Birth: **29th December 1915**
Place of Birth: **Manchester**
Engineer Officer
Merchant Navy
Ticket No. 257
Destination: **Sydney**
Panel 26.

KNOCK ALBERT JOSEPH*
Age: 52
Greaser
Merchant Navy
Ticket No. 471
Destination: **Sydney**
Son of John and Elizabeth Knock.
Panel 26.

LUTTON LAURENCE GREGORY*
Age: 17
Trimmer
Merchant Navy
Ticket No. 473
Destination: **Sydney**
Panel 26.

LODGE ARTHUR
Age: 47
Master
Merchant Navy *(Anglo Saxon Oil Co.)*
Ticket No. 372
Destination: **Cape Town**

Son of Walter and Hepzebah Lodge.
Husband of Winifred Rose Lodge, of Newcastle-on-Tyne.
Panel 26.

MARKEY EDWARD*
Age: *36*
Waiter
Merchant Navy
Ticket No. *494*
Destination: *Sydney*
Panel 26.

McGOVERN DANIEL JOHN*
Age: *40*
Cook Merchant Navy
Ticket No. *475*
Destination: *Sydney*
Panel 26.

MITCHELL FREDERICK MARRACK
Age: *24*
Engineer Officer
Merchant Navy *(Anglo Saxon Oil Co.)*
Ticket No. *379*
Destination: *Cape Town*
Son of Mr. and Mrs. W. F. Mitchell.
Stepson of Mrs. A. L. Mitchell, of Penzance, Cornwall.
Panel 26.

McMASTER KEITH ALEXANDER*
Age: *22*
Engineer Officer
Merchant Navy
Ticket No. *260*
Destination: *Sydney*
Son of Charles and Ruby May McMaster, of Sydney, New South Wales, Australia.
Panel 26.

MORRISON DOUGLAS HADLEY*
Age: *22*
Fireman
Merchant Navy
Ticket No. *474*
Destination: *Sydney*
Son of Edward and Ethel Matilda Morrison, of King's Cross, Sydney, Australia.
Panel 26.

NIVEN ALLAN ROBERT*
Junior Engineer, S.S. *"Queen Elizabeth"*
(Southampton)
Australian Merchant Navy
Ticket No. *461*
Destination: *Sydney*
Son of Robert Niven, of Rockdale, Cumberland, New South Wales. Australia.
Panel 130.

PAGE PETER*
Age: *19*
Date of Birth: **25th February 1923**
Place of Birth: **New South Wales**
Steward
Merchant Navy
Ticket No. *476*
Destination: *Sydney*
Son of William Page, and of Ina Frances Page, of Clovelly, New South Wales, Australia.
Panel 26.

RYAN JOHN JOSEPH*
Age: *24*
Trimmer
Merchant Navy
Ticket No. *477*
Destination: *Sydney*
Panel 26.

STEEDMAN WILLIAM ALFRED*
Age: *24*
Steward
Merchant Navy
Ticket No. *478*
Destination: *Sydney*
Son of Alfred and Eva Steedman, of Cabramatta, New South Wales, Australia.
Panel 27.

STEWART JOHN FORREST
Age: *43*
Engineer *(Andrew Weir)*
Merchant Navy
Ticket No. *394*
Destination: *Cape Town*
Son of John and Sophia Stewart; husband of C. C. Stewart, of Aberdeen.
Panel 27.

Casualty list

WASE JOHN ROBERTSON
Age: 37
Engineer Officer
Merchant Navy (Anglo Saxon Oil Co.)
Ticket No. 376
Destination: **Cape Town**
Son of Robert and Jane Wase.
Husband of Catherine Smith Wase, of South Shields, Co. Durham.
Panel 26.

WEST CECIL GLADSTONE SAMUEL*
Age: 26
Date of Birth: **21st August 1916**
Place of Birth: **North Sydney**
Engineer Officer
Merchant Navy
Ticket No. 262
Destination: **Sydney**
Panel 27.

WHITBY WILLIAM HENRY
Age: 47
Date of Birth: **1st July 1925**
Engineer Officer
Merchant Navy
Panel 27.

WILLIAMS OWEN GRIFFITH
Age: 31
Second Officer
Merchant Navy (Anglo Saxon Oil Co.)
Ticket No. 373
Destination: **Cape Town**
Son of Captain G.O. Williams, and of Mary Williams, of Caernarvonshire.
Panel 27.

Tower Hill Memorial London

Merchant Navy Crew

ARMSTRONG ANDREW JOHN*
Age: 24
Place of Birth: **Sydney**
Fifth Engineer Officer; R186695
Merchant Navy
Son of George and Alice Sarah Armstrong, of Waverley, New South Wales, Australia.
31 Langlee Avenue, Waverley, Sydney.
Panel 25.

ARMSTRONG GORDON*
Age: 52
Place of Birth: **Sydney, New South Wales**
Able Seaman
Merchant Navy
Villiers Street, Merrylands, Sydney, NSW.
Panel 25.

ASHCROFT JOSEPH
Age: 19
Place of Birth: **Liverpool**
Assistant Steward; R180943
Merchant Navy
Son of Ellen Teasdale, of Liverpool.
12 Chantrey Street, Liverpool.
Panel 25.

ATHERTON SAMUEL GOODEARL
Age: 47
Place of Birth: **Bolton**
First Electrician; 928311
Merchant Navy
Son of James and Mary Atherton.
Husband of Catherine Booth Atherton, of Wetherby, Yorkshire.
363 Dersley Street, Swindon
Panel 25.

ATHERTON JOSEPH
Age: 33
Place of Birth: **Liverpool**
Fireman; R234807
Merchant Navy
36 Fernhill Street, Liverpool 8.
Panel 25.

SS CERAMIC The Untold Story

ATKINSON JAMES
Age: *35*
Place of Birth: **Bootle**
Steward; *1128010*
Merchant Navy
Son of James and Elizabeth Atkinson, of Bootle, Lancashire.
11 Hornby Road, Liverpool 20.
Panel 25.

BACHEGALUP JAMES
Age: *42*
Place of Birth: **Leigh**
Greaser; *962021*
Merchant Navy
Son of Frederick and Teresa Bachegalup.
30 Kirby Street, Liverpool 3.
Panel 15.

BAKER WILLIAM ARNOLD
Age: *29*
Place of Birth: **Liverpool**
Assistant Storekeeper
Merchant Navy
11a Rainford Road, St Helens.
Panel 25.

BANKS WALTER WILLIAM
Age: *48*
Place of Birth: **Liverpool**
Third Engineer Officer; *58905; 863997*
Merchant Navy
Son of Joseph James Banks and Ellen Banks.
93 Eaton Gardens, Liverpool.
Panel 25.

BANNER JAMES ROBERT
Age: *35*
Place of Birth: **London**
Able Seaman; *1059637*
Merchant Navy
22 Redbridge Street, London E.11
Panel 25.

BANNING RONALD
Age: *16*
Date of Birth: **3rd July 1926**
Place of Birth: **New Brighton**
Deck Boy
Merchant Navy
Son of James Banning, and of Beatrice Banning, of Wallasey, Cheshire.
1 Seymour Street, New Brighton.
Panel 25.

BARTON ARTHUR REGINALD
Age: *35*
Place of Birth: **Holyhead**
Junior Engineer Officer; *R89360*
Merchant Navy
Son of Edgar and Elizabeth Barton
Husband of Annette Victoria Barton, of Holyhead, Anglesey.
9 High Terrace, Holyhead.
Panel 25.

BENEDICT LOUIS VINCENT
Age: *25*
Place of Birth: **Liverpool**
Fireman; *R261432*
Merchant Navy
19 Rivington Street, Liverpool 5.
Panel 25.

BENNION RONALD
Age: *20*
Place of Birth: **Liverpool**
Assistant Pantryman
Merchant Navy
Son of Frank and Louisa Bennion.
Husband of Evelyn C. Bennion, of Bebingdon.
14 Bromborough Road, Bebingdon.
Panel 25.

BEST NORMAN CORNTHWAITE
Age: *16*
Date of Birth: **26th January 1926**
Place of Birth: **Halifax**
Steward's Boy; *2680729*
Merchant Navy
23 Abbey Street, Newbank, Halifax.
Panel 25.

BILLINGSLEY JOHN WILLIAM
Age: *20*
Place of Birth: **Liverpool**
Steward; *R211138*
Merchant Navy
Son of Mr. and Mrs. John William Billingsley, of Liverpool.
24 Addleigh Crescent, Liverpool 13.
Panel 25.

BIRCH WALTER
Age: *29*
Place of Birth: **Liverpool**
Steward; R31360
Merchant Navy
Husband of Annie Birch, of West Derby, Liverpool.
53 Eaton Road North, Liverpool 12.
Panel 25.

BORAMAN EDWARD ALBERT
Age: *29*
Place of Birth: **Dunedin**
Fireman; R161623
Merchant Navy
Son of Edward Boraman and of Sarah Boraman (née Hudson), of Dunedin, Otago, New Zealand. Belmont, Wellington, New Zealand.
Panel 25.

BOYD WILLIAM EDWARD
Age: *50*
Place of Birth: **Belfast**
Trimmer; R259159
Merchant Navy
Son of Frederick and Clara Boyd. County Louth.
Panel 25.

BROBIN DOUGLAS GEORGE
Age: *18*
Place of Birth: **Cardiff**
Trimmer; R221127
Merchant Navy
93 Arran Street, Roath, Cardiff
Panel 25.

BRODIE GILBERT
Age: *55*
Place of Birth: **Bootle**
Steward; 833833
Merchant Navy
Son of Andrew and Isabella Brodie.
223 Strand Road, Liverpool 20.
Panel 25.

BRODIE-HALL FRANCIS JOHN
Age: *35*
Place of Birth: **London**
Assistant Steward
Merchant Navy
Son of Charles John Edward and Emily Brodie-Hall, of Pinner, Middlesex.
48 Dorners Avenue, Pinner.
Panel 25.

BROUGHTON JAMES
Age: *29*
Place of Birth: **Bury**
Steward; R132119
Merchant Navy
Son of Manley and Mary Ann Broughton.
35 Fern Street, Bury.
Panel 25.

BROWN BENJAMIN*
Age: *44*
Place of Birth: **Sydney**
Trimmer
Merchant Navy
29 Mountfield, Liverpool 19.
Panel 25.

BUCHAN ARTHUR
Age: *21*
Place of Birth: **Peterhead**
Able Seaman; R242989
Merchant Navy
48 Dingwall Drive, Peterhead.
Panel 25.

BUCHAN JOHN
Age: *21*
Place of Birth: **Peterhead**
Sailor; R2011995
Merchant Navy
51 Merchant Street, Peterhead.
Panel 25.

BURKE JOSEPH
Age: *42*
Place of Birth: **Seaham Harbour**
Steward; R82230
Merchant Navy
Son of Patrick and Bridget Burke.
25 Manor Way, Uxbridge.
Panel 25.

CAFFERY JAMES
Age: *21*
Place of Birth: **Liverpool**
Fireman: R157718

SS CERAMIC The Untold Story

Merchant Navy
Son of Christopher and Esther Caffery, of Liverpool.
Husband of Mary Caffery.
99 Victoria Square, Liverpool 3.
Panel 25.

CAHILL THOMAS JOHN
Age: *18*
Place of Birth: *Liverpool*
Ordinary Seaman; R257970
Merchant Navy
34 Marmion Avenue, Liverpool.
Panel 25.

CAINE DAVID ORRY
Age: *31*
Place of Birth: *Hale*
Chief Boots; 26994
Merchant Navy
Son of Hugh Stanley and Isabel Caine.
Husband of H. Caine, of Hale, Cheshire.
9 Oak Road, Hale.
Panel 25.

CAINE FRANK HENRY
Age: *22*
Place of Birth: *Liverpool*
Baker; R16679
Merchant Navy
Son of James and Edith Caine of Walton, Liverpool.
52 Lambourne Road, Liverpool 4.
Panel 25.

CARDWELL GEORGE
Age: *63*
Place of Birth: *Liverpool*
Greaser; 922938
Merchant Navy
Husband of Rose Cardwell, of Bootle, Lancashire.
4 Ainsdale Road, Liverpool 20.
Panel 25.

CARR FRANK
Age: *55*
Place of Birth: *Dublin*
Greaser; 620741
Merchant Navy
Husband of Mary Carr, of Waterloo, Liverpool.

16 Oxford Drive, Liverpool 22.
Panel 25.

CARTER TERENCE
Age: *18*
Place of Birth: *Liverpool*
Kitchen Porter
Merchant Navy
Son of Sarah Carter, and stepson of Ernest Price, of North Walton, Liverpool.
71 Stanley Park Avenue North, Liverpool 4.
Panel 25.

CASSINGHAM ALBERT JOHN
Age: *24*
Place of Birth: *Gravesend*
9th Engineer Officer; R211850
Merchant Navy
Ninth Son of Albert John and Emily Cassingham.
68 Kent Road, Gravesend.
Panel 25.

CHALMERS JAMES ARTHUR
Age: *20*
Place of Birth: *Dunfirmline*
Sailor; R190177
Merchant Navy
Son of Alex J. and Davina Chalmers, of Peterhead, Aberdeenshire.
22 Ugie Road, Peterhead
Panel 25.

CHESTELM THOMAS WILLIAM
Age: *47*
Place of Birth: *Liverpool*
Fireman; 1019688
Merchant Navy
32 Rendal Street, Liverpool 5
Panel 25.

CHESHIRE ARTHUR
Age: *34*
Place of Birth: *London*
Purser's Clerk
Merchant Navy
Son of Thomas and Olive Cheshire.
Husband of Maud Mary Cheshire, of Harlesden, Middlesex.
Hill Cottage, Farnhurst, Surrey.
Panel 25.

Casualty list

CHIDGEY HARRY
Age: 26
Place of Birth: Wadebridge
Carpenter's Mate; R177602
Merchant Navy
Son of Harry Chidgey, and of Kate Chidgey, of Wadebridge, Cornwall.
11 Glen Road, Wadebridge.
Panel 25.

CLARE LESLIE
Age: 17
Date of Birth: 15th February 1925
Place of Birth: Liverpool
Ordinary Seaman; R221846
Merchant Navy
Son of Thomas and Anne Clare, of Liverpool.
54 Kingsheath Avenue, Knotty Ash.
Panel 25.

CLEARY MICHAEL JOSEPH
Age: 33
Place of Birth: Wallasey
Fireman
Merchant Navy
35 Woodstock Road, Wallasey.
Panel 25.

CLEARY SYDNEY HERBERT
Age: 23
Place of Birth: Liverpool
Cook
Merchant Navy
Son of George E. and Maria Rogers.
440 Longmore Lane, Liverpool.
Panel 25.

CLUCAS GEORGE PATRICK
Age: 34
Place of Birth: Liverpool
Trimmer
Merchant Navy
Son of Pte. Thomas William Clucas, The Border Regt. *(killed in action in France, 3rd Feb., 1917)*, and of Mary Kathleen Clucas, of Bootle, Lancashire.
66 Ardley Street, Liverpool 20.
Panel 25.

COOK JOHN WILLIAM
Age: 31
Place of Birth: Wallasey
Assistant Butcher R214296
Merchant Navy
Son of Charles and Florence Cook.
Husband of Lilian E. Cook, of Wallasey, Cheshire.
66 Birkenhead Road, Wallasey.
Panel 25.

COOPER FREDERICK
Age: 19
Place of Birth: Birkenhead
Assistant Baker; R210097
Merchant Navy
Son of William Cooper, and of Alice Cooper, of Birkenhead.
99 Livingstone Street, Birkenhead.
Panel 25.

CORMACK SYDNEY JAMES
Age: 21
Place of Birth: Aberdeen
Able Seaman; R217105
Merchant Navy
Son of George and Margaret of Woodside, Aberdeen.
8 Tanfield Avenue, Aberdeen.
Panel 25.

CORRIGAN JAMES CHRISTOPHER
Age: 62
Place of Birth: Liverpool
Chief Engineer Officer; 41117
Merchant Navy
Husband of Daphne Corrigan, of Liverpool.
Casa Mia, Park Avenue, Crosby.
Panel 25.

COWIE PETER
Age: 25
Place of Birth: Buckie
Sailor; R176277
Merchant Navy
Son of Mr. and Mrs. Alexander Cowie, of Buckie. Banffshire.
9 Titness Street, Buckie.
Panel 25.

CRIDLAND DENNIS COLSTON*
Age: 31
Place of Birth: Bristol

SS CERAMIC The Untold Story

Able Seaman; R178065
Merchant Navy
Son of Joseph Henry and Kate Cridland.
53 Rose Terrace, Wayville, Adelaide, Australia.
Panel 25.

CROWE ALBERT EDWARD
Place of Birth: **Liverpool**
Age: **42**
Cook; 1046950
Merchant Navy
118 Sarcony Road, Liverpool
Panel 25.

CURRIE DUGALD
Age: **37**
Place of Birth: **Kiaries, Scotland**
Steward; R209715
Merchant Navy
41 Annette Street, Glasgow S2.
Panel 25.

CURRY ARTHUR FREDERICK
Age: **31**
Place of Birth: **Wallasey**
Assistant Steward; R90538
Merchant Navy
Son of Robert Frederick and Mary Eleanor Curry, of Wallasey, Cheshire.
56 Willoughby Road, Wallasey, Cheshire.
Panel 25.

DALE WALTER JAMES*
Age: **04**
Place of Birth: **Sydney**
Assistant Cook; 334992
Merchant Navy
The Esplanade, Mozman, Sydney NSW
Panel 25.

DAMIANO JOSEPH
Age: **41**
Place of Birth: **Springburn**
Assistant Steward; 1009276
Merchant Navy
Son of Ionta Damiano, and of Elizabeth Damiano, of Heswall, Cheshire.
The Hoven, Downham Road, Heswell.
Panel 25.

DANIELS JOHN
Age: **19**
Place of Birth: **Liverpool**
Assistant Pantryman; R252547
Merchant Navy
8 Marsh Avenue, Liverpool.
Panel 25.

DAY ALAN CHARLES
Age: **20**
Place of Birth: **Thornton Heath**
Third Refrigerator Engineer
Merchant Navy
Son of Charles Henry Day, A.M.I. Mech. E., and Maud Eugenie Day, of Thornton Heath, Surrey.
38 Malvern Road, Thornton Heath.
Panel 25.

DEASE THOMAS JAMES
Age: **22**
Place of Birth: **Liverpool**
Assistant Steward; R22040
Merchant Navy
Husband of Hannah Helen Harrington.
36 Goring Street, Liverpool 8.
Panel 25.

DEELEY RAYMOND VICTOR
Age: **20**
Place of Birth: **Birmingham**
Assistant Steward; 220913
Merchant Navy
Son of Jesse and Clara Deeley, of Northfield, Birmingham.
97 Triscott Road, Birmingham
Panel 25.

DERBYSHIRE PETER
Age: **27**
Place of Birth: **Wigan**
Assistant Steward; R160151
Merchant Navy
Husband of Helen Derbyshire, of Wigan, Lancashire.
163 Wigan Lane, Wigan,
Panel 25.

DEVINE THOMAS
Age: **33**
Place of Birth: **Liverpool**
Greaser; R1126543

Merchant Navy
Son of Thomas and Emma Devine.
Husband of Elizabeth Devine, of Bootle, Lancashire.
48 Kirk Street, Liverpool 2.
Panel 26.

DODD JOHN WILLIAM
Age: 55
Place of Birth: **Liverpool**
Steward; 629833
Merchant Navy
Husband of Gwendoline Dodd, of Llandudno Junction, Caernarvonshire.
8 Penrhoss Avenue, Llandudno Junction.
Panel 26.

DODSON SIDNEY ARTHUR FRANK
Age: 22
Place of Birth: **Yarmouth**
Steward
Merchant Navy
Son of Joseph G. and Violet L. Dodson, of Great Yarmouth, Norfolk.
3 Louise Road, Yarmouth.
Panel 26.

DONOVAN JOSEPH HENRY
Age: 26
Place of Birth: **London**
Trimmer; R268017
Merchant Navy
Son of Joseph and Anna Donovan.
Husband of Elizabeth Donovan, of Bow, London.
67 Watton Road, London E.13
Panel 26.

DORIAN DOUGLAS*
Age: 21
Place of Birth: **Sydney**
Trimmer
Merchant Navy
Son of William and Elizabeth Dorian.
16 Parry, Ryde, Sydney.
Panel 26.

DOWNES WILLIAM
Age: 25
Place of Birth: **Liverpool**
Leading Seaman; R103093
Merchant Navy
Son of James and Ellen Downes, of Seaforth, Liverpool.
14 Scotland Place, Liverpool.
Panel 26.

DRAKE WILLIAM ARTHUR
Age: 22
Place of Birth: **Southall**
Assistant Cook; R266135
Merchant Navy
5 Somerset Gardens, Bognor Regis
Panel 26.

DRINKWATER SAMUEL ARTHUR
Age: 18
Place of Birth: **Liverpool**
Assistant Steward
Merchant Navy
129 Abbotshay Avenue, Liverpool 18
Panel 26.

DUCKWORTH BADEN
Age: 42
Place of Birth: **Liverpool**
Steward; 863033
Merchant Navy
Son of James and Elizabeth Duckworth.
Husband of Bertha Duckworth of Anfield, Liverpool.
20 Sunbury Road, Liverpool 4.
Panel 26.

DUNBAR WALTER
Age: 32
Place of Birth: **Liverpool**
Steward; R76577
Merchant Navy
10 School Close, Moreton, Wallasey
Panel 26.

DUNN JAMES
Age: 43
Place of Birth: **Liverpool**
Trimmer; 903566
Merchant Navy
Husband of Elizabeth Margaret Dunn, of Liverpool.
44 Gordon Street, Liverpool.
Panel 26.

EASTWOOD EDGAR
Age: 38

Place of Birth: **Morley**
Assistant Steward
Merchant Navy
Son of Martha Ann Eastwood, of Mirfield, Yorks.
48 Greenside Estate, Hinfield, Yorkshire.
Panel 26.

EDWARDS HAROLD
Age: **35**
Place of Birth: **West Hartlepool**
Second Refrigerator Engineer; R77718
Merchant Navy
Son of Henry Wilson Edwards and Agnes Edwards.
Husband of E. Edwards, of Doncaster, Yorkshire.
33 Oakville Avenue, Scarborough.
Panel 26.

ELFORD HERBERT CHARLES
Age: **67**
Place of Birth: **Portsmouth**
Master; 031333
Merchant Navy
Son of William and Elizabeth Caroline Elford.
Husband of Elizabeth Elford, of Norwich.
Montrose Court, Finchley Road, London N.W.
Panel 25.

ELLIS AMY LOUISA
Age: **66**
Place of Birth: **London**
Stewardess; 1108788
Merchant Navy
Daughter of Alfred and Catherine Taylor.
Wife of Frank Ellis, of Shadwell, London.
285 Lodge Lane, Grays.
Panel 26.

ENNIS GEORGE
Age: **37**
Place of Birth: **Burnley**
Fireman
Merchant Navy
27 Frederick Street, Blackpool.
Panel 26.

EVANS JACK*
Age: **37**
Place of Birth: **Crewe**
Fourth Engineer Officer; R58832
Merchant Navy
East Hills, Sydney, New South Wales.
Panel 26.

EVANS WILLIAM
Age: **26**
Place of Birth: **Liverpool**
Trimmer
Merchant Navy
24 Laycester Street, Liverpool 5
Panel 26.

FALLOWS WILLIAM JAMES
Age: **35**
Place of Birth: **Liverpool**
Lounge Steward; R37407
Merchant Navy
Son of Cornelius and Susannah Fallows, of Liverpool.
83 Lewisham Road, Liverpool 5.
Panel 26.

FEELEY GEORGE HENRY
Age: **31**
Place of Birth: **Liverpool**
Ordinary Seaman; R50483
Merchant Navy
Son of George Owen Feeley, and of Amy Feeley, of Walton, Liverpool.
45 Sunmore Road, Liverpool.
Panel 26.

FELTON FREDERICK CHARLES
Age: **36**
Place of Birth: **Liverpool**
Steward; 1131196
Merchant Navy
Son of George and Mary Felton.
Husband of Annie Felton, of Waterloo, Liverpool.
20 Eastbourne Road, Liverpool 22.
Panel 26.

FITCH HENRY JAMES*
Age: **34**
Place of Birth: **Sydney**
8th Engineer Officer; R179974
Merchant Navy
Son of Henry Crathorne Fitch and Beatrice May Fitch, of Kensington.
31 Balfour Road, Kensington, Sydney.
Panel 26.

Casualty list

FLANAGAN DANIEL
Age: 31
Place of Birth: **Eire**
Fireman
Merchant Navy
Son of William and Hellen Flanagan.
Husband of Alice Flanagan.
26 Marmaduke Street, Liverpool 7.
Panel 26.

FLEMING DONALD STANLEY
Age: 35
Place of Birth: **London**
Assistant Steward; 1084959
Merchant Navy
42 North Hill, Colchester.
Panel 26.

FLEWITT DAVID CHARLES
Age: 30
Place of Birth: **Liverpool**
Assistant Steward; R43821
Merchant Navy
Son of Charles and Mary Anne Flewitt.
Husband of Christine Flewitt, of Liverpool.
Moss View Camp, Seagers Lane, Ainsdale.
Panel 26.

FOTHERGILL HERBERT
Age: 33
Place of Birth: **Foulbridge**
Third Radio Officer; C5108
Merchant Navy
Son of John and Florence Fothergill.
Husband of Norah Fothergill, of Nelson, Lancashire.
3 Station Road, Foulbridge.
Panel 26.

FOYLE ELIZABETH
Age: 49
Place of Birth: **Queens Co.**
Stewardess; R2804
Merchant Navy
Daughter of John and Mary Foyle, of Castletown. Co. Leix, Irish Republic.
3 Downs Road, Bexhill on Sea.
Panel 26.

FRASER DONALD JACK
Age: 18
Place of Birth: **Christchurch, New Zealand**
Boy
Merchant Navy
18 Parkfield Road, Liverpool 17.
Panel 26.

FRODSHAM WILLIAM CLIFFORD
Age: 44
Place of Birth: **Seacombe, Cheshire**
Engineer Officer; 1088162
Merchant Navy
Husband of Florence Frodsham, of Wallasey, Cheshire.
11 Meadowside, Leasowe Road, Wallasey.
Panel 26.

GASGUILI JOSEPH
Age: 39
Place of Birth: **Malta**
Fireman; R150775
Merchant Navy
4 Fashion Street, London E.1
Panel 26.

GIBBONS JOSEPH PATRICK
Age: 19
Place of Birth: **Ormskirk**
Fireman
Merchant Navy
Son of Joseph and Margeret Gibbons, of Ormskirk, Lancashire.
5 Ravenscroft Avenue, Ormskirk.
Panel 26.

GOODRIDGE ARTHUR HENRY
Age: 27
Place of Birth: **Tenby**
Steward; 1090899
Merchant Navy
Son of Arthur and Doris Goodridge, of Garston, Liverpool.
72 Lumley Street, Liverpool 19.
Panel 26.

GREEFF FREDERICK HAROLD
Age: 18
Place of Birth: **Cape Town**
Trimmer
Merchant Navy
5 Campbell Street, Observatory, Cape Town
Panel 26.

GRIFFITH ROBERT EVANS
Age: 27
Place of Birth: Port Madoc
Fireman
Merchant Navy
Son of Hugh and Margaret Griffith, of Port Madoc Caernarvonshire.
7 Saw Mill, Port Madoc.
Panel 26.

GRIFFITHS JAMES GEORGE
Age: 36
Place of Birth: Birkenhead
Steward; R886(6)98
Merchant Navy
Son of Robert Langford Griffiths and Caroline Griffiths.
Husband of Frances Griffiths.
54 Ariel Road, Tranmere.
Panel 26.

HAIG ERIC GERALD
Age: 27
Place of Birth: Folkestone
Assistant Steward; R179843
Merchant Navy
96 Westbourne Avenue, Bolton.
Panel 26.

HAINES JOSEPH FRANCIS
Age: 33
Place of Birth: Liverpool
Lamp Trimmer; 1139340
Merchant Navy
Husband of Sarah Haines, of Liverpool.
68 Everton Brow, Liverpool.
Panel 26.

HALEWOOD HAROLD THOMAS
Age: 20
Place of Birth: Liverpool
Assistant Steward; R177029
Merchant Navy
Son of Thomas and Winifred Halewood, of Kirkby, Lancashire.
18 Park Road, Kirby.
Panel 26.

HALSALL JAMES
Age: 40
Place of Birth: Liverpool
Steward; 1063638
Merchant Navy
15 Duncan Drive, Greasby, Cheshire.
Panel 26.

HALSALL THOMAS WALTER
Age: 53
Place of Birth: Douglas
Steward; 947396
Merchant Navy
Husband of Eliza Halsall.
8 Agate Street, Liverpool 5
Panel 26.

HAMPTON ROBERT JAMES
Age: 40
Place of Birth: Liverpool
Assistant Steward; 943772
Merchant Navy
Son of Robert Charles and Florence Hampton.
Husband of Jessie Hampton, of Liverpool.
17 Incemore Road, Liverpool.
Panel 26.

HARPER DAVID
Age: 31
Place of Birth: Glasgow
Third Officer; R65543; 43810
Merchant Navy
Son of David and Jessie Harper, of Langside, Glasgow.
38 Millbrae Crescent, Longside, Glasgow.
Panel 26,

HART TIMOTHY
Age: 38
Place of Birth: Liverpool
Fireman and Trimmer; 1089537
Merchant Navy
12 Herriott Street, Liverpool 5.
Panel 26.

HASLETT CHARLES EDWARD
Age: 47
Place of Birth: Brighton
Cook; 622301
Merchant Navy
Son of Jesse and Harriet Haslett.
Husband of Mary Ann Haslett, of Burton-on-Trent.
86 Hill Street, Station Hill, Burton-on-Trent.
Panel 26.

HAWKEN ERNEST WILLIAM*
Age: **43**
Place of Birth: **Somerville, Australia**
Purser; R53373
Merchant Navy
26 Thanet Lodge, Mapesbury Road, London W.2
Panel 26.

HAZELL LESLIE HARRY FERDINAND
Age: **37**
Place of Birth: **Liverpool**
Assistant Steward; R37562
Merchant Navy
Son of Harry and Delia Hazell.
7 Tatton Road, Liverpool 9.
Panel 26.

HEATH HENRY
Age: **51**
Place of Birth: **Kent**
Second Engineer; 928702
Merchant Navy
Husband of Irene Heath, of Crosby, Lancashire.
45 Myers Road West, Liverpool.
Panel 26.

HENDRICK PATRICK JOSEPH
Age: **29**
Place of Birth: **Liverpool**
Fireman; 163677
Merchant Navy
Husband of Honora Hendrick, of Liverpool.
60 Easby Road, Liverpool 5.
Panel 26.

HICKLING ERIC ARNOLD OBE
Age: **39**
Place of Birth: **Nottingham**
Chief Officer; 1108571; 27612
Merchant Navy
Lloyd's medal for Gallantry at sea.
Son of Edward and Mary Ellen Hickling.
Husband of Norah Winifred Hickling, of Worstead, Norfolk.
11A Hawton Crescent, Nottingham.
Panel 26.

HIGGINS JOHN
Age: **55**
Place of Birth: **Liverpool**
Greaser; R50288
Merchant Navy
5 Doncaster Street, Liverpool 5.
Panel 26.

HILL REGINALD CHARLES
Age: **29**
Place of Birth: **New Brighton**
Steward; R25623
Merchant Navy
Son of Stanley Herbert and Lucy Henrietta Hill.
Husband of Beatrice Hill, of Wallasey, Cheshire.
16 Cagmond Street, Seacombe.
Panel 26.

HITCHMAN ALBERT EDWARD
Age: **40**
Place of Birth: **Oxford**
Able Seaman; 896307
Merchant Navy
Son of Thomas and Gertude Hitchman, of Shipston-on-Stour, Warwickshire.
Shipston House, Shipston-on-Stour.
Panel 26.

HOLLIDAY ALBERT JAMES
Age: **19**
Place of Birth: **Liverpool**
Assistant Steward; R192831
Merchant Navy
122 Gladstone Road, Liverpool
Panel 26.

HOLMES CHARLES EDWARD
Age: **54**
Place of Birth: **Liverpool**
Assistant Storekeeper; 819471
Merchant Navy
Son of Charles Edward Holmes and of Emma Holmes (née Hanniford), of Waterloo, Liverpool.
Husband of Ada Thirza Holmes, of Miramar, Wellington, New Zealand.
2 Marine Crescent, Waterloo, Liverpool 22.
Panel 26.

HOPTON GRAHAM
Age: **35**
Place of Birth: **Swansea**
Assistant Purser; R81807
Merchant Navy
Son of Frank and Edith Hopton.
Husband of Edith Beryl Hopton, of Haslemere,

Surrey.
Lynwood Heath Road, nr. Haslemere, Surrey.
Panel 26.

HUGHES GEORGE
Age: *25*
Place of Birth: **Bootle**
Carpenter; R179433
Merchant Navy
20 Hornby Boulevard, Liverpool.
Panel 26.

HUGHES ROBERT JOHN
Age: *23*
Place of Birth: **Liverpool**
Trimmer
Merchant Navy
Son of Robert and Ethel R. Hughes, of Liverpool.
77 Stonefield Road, Liverpool 14.
Panel 26.

HUMPHREY REGINALD CLAUDE
Age: *29*
Place of Birth: **London**
Able Seaman; R104480
Merchant Navy
Husband of Evelyn Prince Humphrey, of Runcorn, Cheshire.
1 Seymour Street, New Brighton.
Panel 26.

HUNG PETER COLIN
Age: *21*
Place of Birth: **Liverpool**
Able Seaman; R220401
Merchant Navy
65 Curate Road, Liverpool 6.
Panel 26.

HUSTWICK PHILIP HEAP
Age: *17*
Date of Birth: **4th March 1925**
Place of Birth: **Bradford**
Apprentice
Merchant Navy
Son of Wade and Lavinia Hustwick.
Panel 26.

HUTTON IRVINE
Age: *21*
Place of Birth: **Paisley**

Electrician; R237475
Merchant Navy
10 Clarington Street, Paisley.
Panel 26.

IBBETSON FREDERICK
Age: *20*
Place of Birth: **Dewsbury**
Assistant Steward; R253230
Merchant Navy
Son of Albert and Alice Ibbetson.
15 Chapel Street, Batby, Yorkshire.
Panel 26

JACKSON KENNETH DOUGLAS (BILL)
Age: *21*
Place of Birth: **London**
7th Engineer Officer; R257758
Merchant Navy
Second son of William Harold and Elizabeth Jackson, of Harold Wood, Essex.
Woodlands, Church Road, Harold Wood.
Panel 26.

JEFFRAY ROBERT BRUCE
Age: *52*
Place of Birth: **Glasgow**
1st Refrigeration Engineer; 661484
Merchant Navy
Son of Robert and Isabella Jeffray.
Husband of Eva Alice Jeffray of Great Crosby, Lancashire.
28 Newborough Avenue, Great Crosby.
Panel 26.

JONES ROBERT LESLIE
Age: *21*
Place of Birth: **Holyhead**
Assistant Steward; R229189
Merchant Navy
Son of William Richard Jones and of Dorothy Jones, of Holyhead, Anglesey.
4 Kingsland, Holyhead.
Panel 26.

JONES WALTER
Age: *39*
Place of Birth: **Bootle**
Steward; 961499
Merchant Navy
Son of Hugh and Cathrine Jones.

Husband of Ruby Jones, of Kirkdale, Liverpool.
48 Rockby (?) Street, Liverpool 4.
Panel 26.

JONES WILLIAM TREVOR
Age: 18
Place of Birth: **Penygraig**
Trimmer; 268780
Merchant Navy
Son of Daniel and Annie Maud Jones, of Tonypandy, Glamorgan.
59 Tylacelyn Road, Penygraig, Glamorgan.
Panel 26.

KEEFE JAMES MATHEW
Age: 21
Place of Birth: **Liverpool**
Trimmer
Merchant Navy
28 Hatherley, Liverpool 8.
Panel 26.

KEENAN ALBERT
Age: 22
Place of Birth: **Liverpool**
Fireman
Merchant Navy
Son of Joseph and Catherine Keenan, of Liverpool.
36 Felton Road, Liverpool.
Panel 26.

KELLY CHARLES
Age: 31
Place of Birth: **Castletown, Isle of Man**
Fireman
Merchant Navy
8 Marsh Road, Thornton, Blackpool.
Panel 26.

KENAH JOSEPH STANLEY
Age: 27
Place of Birth: **Liverpool**
Porter; R178270
Merchant Navy
56 Louisa Street, Liverpool 5
Panel 26.

KERR ANNIE PARK
Age: 51
Place of Birth: **Lockinver**
Nursing Sister; R202669
Merchant Navy
Daughter of Andrew and Isabella Kerr.
Rowan Cottage, Coul Hill, Alross.
Panel 26.

KERSHAW WILLIAM HENRY
Age: 18
Place of Birth: **Liverpool**
Kitchen Porter
Merchant Navy
43 Danmark Street, Liverpool 22.
Panel 26.

KINEALY ROBERT JOSEPH
Age: 27
Place of Birth: **Wallasey**
Butcher R222729
Merchant Navy
Awarded the Liverpool Humane and Shipwreck Society's Silver Medal.
Son of Micheal and Mary Elizabeth Kinealy.
19 Percy Road, Wallasey.
Panel 26.

KINVIG FRANCIS JAMES
Age: 25
Place of Birth: **Liverpool**
Assistant Steward; R197059
Merchant Navy
Husband of Vera A. Kinvig, of Liverpool.
94 Spotforth Road, Liverpool 7.
Panel 26.

LARTHE HENRI ALEXANDRE
Age: 29
Place of Birth: **Anerley**
Third Officer; R158410; 49226
Merchant Navy
13 Harold Rad, London S.E.19
Panel 26.

LAWLER THOMAS
Age: 37
Place of Birth: **Liverpool**
Fireman; 1078764
Merchant Navy
7 Hillcrest Road, Liverpool 4.
Panel 26.

LAWSON JOHN FRANCIS
Age: 47
Place of Birth: **Liverpool**

Steward; 692702
Merchant Navy
Husband of Elizabeth Jane Lawson, of Bootle, Lancashire.
72 Moore Street, Liverpool 20.
Panel 26.

LEACY PATRICK JOSEPH
Age: 19
Place of Birth: Liverpool
Trimmer
Merchant Navy
Son of Patrick Joseph and Anne Leacy, of Liverpool.
11A Burnett Street, Liverpool 5.
Panel 26.

LEEMING WILLIAM ANTHONY
Age: 27
Place of Birth: Birkenhead
Leading Seaman; R156392; 5933
Merchant Navy
Son of Mr. and Mrs. W. P. Leeming.
Husband of E. R. Leeming, of Egremont, Wallasey, Cheshire.
16 Wright Street, Wallasey.
Panel 26.

LEWIS FREDERICK JAMES
Age: 30
Place of Birth: Rain Hill
Sailor
Merchant Navy
Son of Frederick Charles and Ada Lewis.
Husband of Doris Lewis, of Canvey Island, Essex.
18 Ellaby Road, Rain Hill.
Panel 26.

LIVERSIDGE KENNETH
Age: 30
Place of Birth: Leeds
Assistant Butcher
Merchant Navy
Son of Albert and Lucy Liversidge.
Husband of Elizabeth Anne Liversidge, of Mapperley, Nottingham.
73 Sefton Road, Morecambe.
Panel 26.

LLEWELLIN WILLIAM NORMAN
Age: 39

Place of Birth: Liverpool
Printer
Merchant Navy
22 Ullswater Street, Liverpool 5.
Panel 26.

LLOYD EDWARD VERNON
Age: 54
Place of Birth: Liverpool
Barman & Storekeeper; 866658
Merchant Navy
2 Marlborough Road, Southport.
Panel 26.

LOCKE JOHN JOSEPH
Age: 18
Place of Birth: Birkenhead
Trimmer
Merchant Navy
37 Carrington Street, Birkenhead.
Panel 26.

LORD JOHN FREDERICK
Age: 15
Date of Birth: 10th April 1927
Place of Birth: London
Deck Boy
Merchant Navy
Son of Harry and Edith May Lord, of Stockwell, London.
77 Hargwyne Street, Stockwell, London S.W.9
Panel 26.

LOUGHRAN FREDERICK THOMAS
Age: 35
Place of Birth: Liverpool
Assistant Steward; R26736
Merchant Navy
Son of Philip and Ann Loughran.
20 Woodville Avenue, Liverpool 23.
Panel 26.

LUTTMAN CHARLES HENRY
Age: 18
Place of Birth: Manchester
Porter; R193391
Merchant Navy
Son of Charles Henry and Beatrice Luttman, of Knowsley, Lancashire.
47 Knowsley Drive, Knowsley.
Panel 26.

Casualty list

MACKENZIE ALAN GORDON
Age: 37
Place of Birth: **Liverpool**
Second Officer; 1063295; 39662
Merchant Navy
Son of David Eason Mackenzie and Gertrude Mary Mackenzie.
Husband of Jean Prytherch Mackenzie, of Wallasey, Cheshire.
14 Barnhey Crescent, Meols.
Panel 26.

MADDISON LESLIE
Age: 38
Place of Birth: **Nottingham**
Date of Birth: **28th January 1905**
Steward; R29804
Merchant Navy
Son of Harry and Amelia Maddison.
Husband of Evelyn May Maddison, of Hill Park, Fareham, Hampshire.
277 Colmanhey Road, Ilkeston, Derby.
Panel 26.

MAGEE CHARLES PETER
Age: 28
Place of Birth: **London**
Steward; R111547
Merchant Navy
Son of Mr. and Mrs. W. N. Magee, of Clerkenwell, London.
96 Streatfield Road, Kenton.
Panel 26.

MALONEY WILLIAM
Age: 21
Place of Birth: **Liverpool**
Fireman; R218018
Merchant Navy
98 Upper Warwick Street, Liverpool 8.
Panel 26.
*Recorded on Tower Hill Memorial and in CWGC Register as William Mahoney

MALONE JOHN EDWARD
Age: 24
Place of Birth: **Liverpool**
Fireman; R167440
Merchant Navy
16B Brunswick Gardens, Liverpool 8.
Panel 26.

MANKERTS GORDON EDWARD
Age: 23
Place of Birth: **London**
Captain's Steward; R194161
Merchant Navy
Son of Henry Edward and Mary Edith Mankerts, of Edmonton, Middlesex.
Flat 1, 42 Fore Street, Edmonton N.18
Panel 26.

MANSELL ELLEN
Age: 62
Place of Birth: **London**
Stewardess; R71965
Merchant Navy
Daughter of George and Susannah Caroline Thompson.
Wife of Horace Arthur Mansell.
58 Inglehurst Garden, Ilford.
Panel 26.

MARNEY JOHN
Age: 60
Place of Birth: **Liverpool**
Greaser; 784761
Merchant Navy
Husband of Mary Ann Marney, of Liverpool.
86 Arlington Street, Liverpool 17.
Panel 26.

MARSHALL DAVID
Age: 27
Place of Birth: **Liverpool**
Able Seaman; R139829
Merchant Navy
Son of Edmund and Margaret Marshall.
Husband of Elizabeth Marshall, of Everton, Lancashire.
68 Spencer Street, Liverpool.
Panel 26.

MARSHALL FRANCIS NICHOLAS
Age: 36
Place of Birth: **Liverpool**
Steward; R31161
Merchant Navy
6 Beech Grove, Liverpool 21.
Panel 26.

MATHER JAMES
Age: 28

Place of Birth: **Liverpool**
Fireman; R265515
Merchant Navy
Son of James and Caroline Mather.
Husband of C. Mather, of Liverpool.
144 Dryden Street, Liverpool 5.
Panel 26.

McALLISTER NEIL
Age: **36**
Place of Birth: **Liverpool**
Assistant Steward; 1096367
Merchant Navy
Son of Neil and Maggie McAllister, of Buckley, Flintshire.
Glenick, 11 Mold Road, Buckley, N. Wales.
Panel 26.

McARDLE JOHN STEPHEN CROIX DE
Age: **47**
Place of Birth: **Liverpool**
Veranda Café Steward
Merchant Navy
Previously served in The London Scottish.
Son of Patrick and Ellen McArdle.
88 Aspen Grove, Lodge Street, Liverpool 8.
Panel 26.

McBRIDE WILLIAM
Age: **38**
Place of Birth: **Liverpool**
Greaser; 1090096
Merchant Navy
Son of Thomas and Martha McBride.
Husband of Bridget McBride, of Liverpool.
4B Sorthill House, Liverpool 4.
Panel 26.

McDONNELL PHILLIP
Age: **19**
Place of Birth: **Liverpool**
Assistant Cook
Merchant Navy
Son of Catherine McDonnell, of Liverpool
24 Hornby Street, Liverpool 5
Panel 26.

McFADDEN JOHN
Age: **20**
Place of Birth: **Liverpool**
Assistant Pantryman; R223182

Merchant Navy
Son of John McFadden and of Emily McFadden (née Foley), of Liverpool.
5 Nully Street, Liverpool 7.
Panel 26.

McGINN JAMES HENRY
Age: **51**
Place of Birth: **Leigh**
Assistant Steward; 1002131
Merchant Navy
Son of Michael and Helen McGinn.
73 Windsor Road, Liverpool 13.
Panel 26.

McGUINNESS WILLIAM
Age: **45**
Place of Birth: **Liverpool**
Trimmer; 944037
Merchant Navy
22 Kew Street, Liverpool 5.
Panel 26.

McKEVITT GEORGE
Age: **18**
Place of Birth: **Liverpool**
Trimmer
Merchant Navy
Son of John and Anne McKevitt.
50 Caryl Gardens, Liverpool 8.
Panel 26.

McNABB JOHN
Age: **19**
Place of Birth: **Liverpool**
Trimmer; R259174
Merchant Navy
Son of Mr. and Mrs. John McNabb, of Liverpool.
53 Tweed Street, Liverpool 6.
Panel 26.

McNALLY JAMES
Age: **28**
Place of Birth: **Liverpool**
Leading Fireman; R161944
Merchant Navy
Son of James and Mary McNally.
Husband of Grace McNally, of Liverpool.
13A Raymond Street, Liverpool 5.
Panel 26.

Casualty list

McWATERS ALFRED ERNEST
Age: **59**
Place of Birth: **Liverpool**
Laundry & Assistant Steward; 735503
Merchant Navy
Husband of Hannah McWaters, of Walton, Liverpool.
26 Sergrin Road, Roby.
Panel 26.

MELIA ANTHONY
Age: **28**
Place of Birth: **Liverpool**
Fireman; R167250
Merchant Navy
14 Mill Lane, Apply Bridge, Wigan.
Panel 26.

MERRICK JAMES
Age: **50**
Place of Birth: **Oldham**
Assistant Steward; R222668
Merchant Navy
Son of John and Martha Ann Merrick.
16 Emily Street, Oldham.
Panel 26.

MICHAELS JOHN MYER*
Age: **44**
Place of Birth: **London**
Steward; 214429
Merchant Navy
32 Belmore Street, Sydney, NSW
Panel 26.

MITCHELL HAYDN HOPKIN
Age: **19**
Place of Birth: **Aberkenfig**
Trimmer; R268783
Merchant Navy
Son of Theodore and Margaret Mitchell, of Sorn, Bridgend.
7 Heol Ganal, Sorn, Bridgend, Aberkenfig.
Panel 26.

MIZZI GERALD
Age: **32**
Place of Birth: **Malta**
Fireman; R190978
Merchant Navy
Son of Angelo Mizzi, and of Carmela Mizzi (née Schembri), of Valletta, Malta, G. C.
Husband of Salvina Mizzi, of Valletta.
128 Strada San Guiseppi, Valletta, Malta.
Panel 26.

MONKS ROBERT WILLIAM
Age: **18**
Date of Birth: **7th January 1924**
Place of Birth: **Warrington**
Apprentice
Merchant Navy
Awarded the Hobson Cup and Silver Medal of the Mercantile Marine Service Association for Great Proficiency on H.M.S. Conway in 1941.
Son of William and Annie Monks, of Harrow, Middlesex.
Panel 26.

MOON ARTHUR WILLIAM
Age: **44**
Place of Birth: **Liverpool**
Chief Butcher 997395
Merchant Navy
Son of Arthur William and Ann Jane Moon.
Husband of Elizabeth Moon of Kensington, Liverpool.
25 Cotswold Street, Liverpool 7.
Panel 26.

MORGAN ALBERT VICTOR
Age: **37**
Place of Birth: **Liverpool**
Library Steward; 1090110
Merchant Navy
Son of John and Amelia T. Morgan, of Wallasey, Cheshire.
16 Rolleston Drive, Wallasey.
Panel 26.

MORRIS COLIN*
Age: **27**
Place of Birth: **Melbourne**
Greaser; R257897
Merchant Navy
Son of Melville Arthur and Marjorie Morris, of Melbourne, Victoria, Australia.
33 Orronge Rd, Elsternwick, Melbourne.
Panel 26.

SS CERAMIC The Untold Story

MULCAHEY JEREMIAH
Age: 32
Place of Birth: **Liverpool**
Steward; R22872
Merchant Navy
Husband of Mary Mulcahey, of Liverpool.
59 Canyl Gardens, Liverpool 8.
Panel 26.

MUNRO ARCHIBALD
Age: 65
Place of Birth: **Liverpool**
Greaser; 599371
Merchant Navy
Husband of Agnes Munro, of Liverpool.
118 St Mersey Street, Liverpool 5.
Panel 26.

NEILL JOHN SAYERS
Age: 37
Place of Birth: **Belfast**
Steward
Merchant Navy
Son of William John and Mary Neill.
Husband of Catherine A. Neill, of Litherland, Liverpool.
25 Sefton Road, Liverpool.
Panel 26.

NEWNHAM HAROLD PERCY*
Age: 39
Place of Birth: **Lindfield**
Steward; R91007
Merchant Navy
20 Peel Street, South Brisbane.
Panel 26.

NEWTH TERENCE ERNEST
Age: 15
Date of Birth: **4th April 1927**
Place of Birth: **London**
Deck Boy
Merchant Navy
30 Crown Road, Billericay.
Panel 26.

O'CONNOR THOMAS
Age: 23
Place of Birth: **Liverpool**
Able Seaman; R150516
Merchant Navy

Son of Patrick and Eliza O'Connor.
Husband of K. O'Connor, of Liverpool.
18 Kirby Street, Liverpool.
Panel 26.

O'HARE HENRY
Age: 23
Place of Birth: **Liverpool**
Steward; R152577
Merchant Navy
Son of James and Ann Jane O'Hare, of Tue Brook, Liverpool.
50 Chester Road, Liverpool 6.
Panel 26.

PAGE WILLIAM HENRY
Age: 36
Place of Birth: **Shoreham**
Leading Seaman; 1079746
Merchant Navy
Son of James and Mary Jane Page, of Shoreham-by-Sea, Sussex.
43 West Street, Shoreham.
Panel 26.

PALMER LEONARD JOHN
Age: 18
Place of Birth: **Liverpool**
Assistant Steward
Merchant Navy
Son of George William and Louisa Palmer.
35 Burleigh Road North, Liverpool.
Panel 26.

PANTHER CYRIL
Age: 20
Place of Birth: **New Zealand**
Ordinary Seaman; R223249
Merchant Navy
Son of Albert and Alice May Panther, of Greymouth, Auckland, New Zealand.
99 Preston Road, Greymouth, New Zealand.
Panel 26.

PEACOCK ARTHUR CYRIL
Age: 37
Place of Birth: **Birkenhead**
Fireman
Merchant Navy
100 Corporation Road, Birkenhead.
Panel 26.

PIERCE ROBERT CHARLES
Age: 31
Place of Birth: Liverpool
Assistant Steward
Merchant Navy
12 Maple Road, Wallasey.
Panel 26.

PITT HARRY
Age: 36
Place of Birth: Manchester
Assistant Steward; R2672
Merchant Navy
48 Lordheys Avenue, Liverpool 22.
Panel 26.

PLAGE PHILIP
Age: 21
Place of Birth: Wallasey
Seaman; R172405
Merchant Navy
Son of Charles and Edith Plage.
11 Albemarle Road, Wallasey.
Panel 26.

PRESTON JOHN
Age: 28
Place of Birth: Liverpool
Fireman; R197706
Merchant Navy
Son of John and Annie Preston.
Husband of Ethel Preston, of Liverpool.
55 Ocean lane, Liverpool 5.
Panel 26.

PRICE ROBERT
Age: 27
Place of Birth: Liverpool
Fireman; R200374
Merchant Navy
Son of Elizabeth Price.
48 Woodside Road, Liverpool 7.
Panel 26.

PUDDIFER EDWARD
Age: 23
Place of Birth: Liverpool
Able Seaman; R149436
Merchant Navy
64 Scarsbick Drive, Liverpool.
Panel 26.

QUILLAN JOSEPH
Age: 19
Place of Birth: Liverpool
Trimmer; R197184
Merchant Navy
Son of James and Mary Ann Quillan, of Bootle, Lancashire.
51 Kirk, Liverpool 20.
Panel 26.

RADFORD FREDERICK
Age: 49
Place of Birth: Derby
Assistant Steward; 846221
Merchant Navy
262 Knowsley Road, Liverpool 20
Panel 26.

RAMSAY DIGBY FORSYTHE
Age: 56
Place of Birth: Westport
Greaser; 800145
Merchant Navy
Husband of Florence Elizabeth Ramsay, of Litherland, Liverpool.
30A Bridge Road, Liverpool 21.
Panel 26.

REES GEORGE
Age: 62
Place of Birth: Liverpool
Steward; 191780
Merchant Navy
Bar Temple Farm, Mellor.
Panel 26.

RICE GEORGE
Age: 31
Place of Birth: Liverpool
Greaser; R172801
Merchant Navy
Son of George Rice, and of Elizabeth Rice, of Liverpool.
44B Caryl Gardens, Liverpool 8.
Panel 26.

RICHARDSON RICHARD*
Age: 22
Place of Birth: Liverpool
Trimmer
Merchant Navy

SS CERAMIC The Untold Story

Son of Thomas and Margaret A. Richardson, of Liverpool.
102 Boundary Street, Liverpool 5.
Panel 26.
* Signed on as Andrew Michaels R226447

RIDYARD WILLIAM VALENTINE
Age: 28
Place of Birth: **Liverpool**
Assistant Steward
Merchant Navy
11 Park Street, Edgeworth, Bolton
Panel 26.

ROBERTS HARRY
Age: 18
Place of Birth: **Liverpool**
Trimmer; R253259
Merchant Navy
64c Belcest, Liverpool 8.
Panel 26.

ROGERS ANTHONY
Age: 25
Place of birth: **Cape Town, South Africa**
Fireman
Merchant Navy
137A Lower Main Road, Observatory, Cape Town, South Africa.
Panel 26.

ROSS WALTER MATHESON
Age: 47
Place of Birth: **Rosshire**
First Radio Officer; 862231
Merchant Navy
Son of Hugh and Barbara Ross, of Ardgay, Ross and Cromarty.
Gledfields Gardens, Ardgay.
Panel 26.

ROTH FRANCIS JAMES
Age: 21
Place of Birth: **Cheadle**
Pantryman; R127973
Merchant Navy
Son of Mr. and Mrs. Francis Roth, of Wallasey, Cheshire.
Stepson of May Roth, of Wallasey.
4 Geneva Road, Wallasey.
Panel 26.

RUDDOCK SAMPSON
Age: 41
Place of Birth: **Liverpool**
Fireman; 1980986
Merchant Navy
Son of P. Ruddock, and of Catherine Jane Ruddock, of Liverpool.
16 Louisa Street, Liverpool 5.
Panel 26.

SAGE JOSEPH
Age: 63
Place of Birth: **Liverpool**
Cook; 727078
Merchant Navy
Husband of Susan Sage, of Anfield, Liverpool.
1 Yelverton Road, Liverpool 4.
Panel 26.

SALTER THOMAS
Age: 40
Place of Birth: **Greenock**
Fireman; R21177
Merchant Navy
89 Wallace Street, Greenock.
Panel 26.

SAUNDERS LEONARD GILBERT
Age: 45
Place of Birth: **London**
Assistant Steward; R222667
Merchant Navy
Son of Joseph and Wihelmina Saunders.
99 Elm Drive, Hove.
Panel 26.

SCOGINGS MICHAEL
Age: 31
Place of Birth: **Liverpool**
Fireman; R265277
Merchant Navy
13 Townsend Street, Liverpool 6.
Panel 26.

SCOTT RONALD
Age: 20
Place of Birth: **Liverpool**
Assistant Steward
Merchant Navy
Son of Alexander Wood Scott and Hilda Mary Scott, of New Mills, Derbyshire.

Casualty list

4 Whittle Bank, New Mills, Derby.
Panel 26.

SCOTT ROBERT GIBB ALLAN
Age: 18
Place of Birth: Clydebank
Fireman
Merchant Navy
Son of James T. and Elizabeth Allan Scott, of Glasgow.
45 Househillwood Road, Glasgow S3.
Panel 26.

SCOTT WILLIAM EDWARD
Age: 44
Place of Birth: Glasgow
Assistant Steward; 720749
Merchant Navy
193 Ardgay Street, Glasgow C2.
Panel 26.

SCULLY JEREMIAH
Age: 52
Place of Birth: Liverpool
Greaser; 535585
Merchant Navy
78 Easby Road, Liverpool 4.
Panel 26.

SHANNON GERALD (GERARD?) JOSEPH
Age: 23
Place of Birth: Liverpool
Fireman
Merchant Navy
Son of Edward Shannon, and of Catharine Shannon, of Liverpool.
Husband of Julia Shannon, of Norris Green, Liverpool.
444 Court Ashfield Street, Liverpool.
Panel 26.

SHANNON JAMES JOHN
Age: 36
Place of Birth: Liverpool
Greaser; 1102612
Merchant Navy
Son of Edward Shannon, and of Catharine Shannon, of Liverpool.
Husband of Catherine Shannon of Liverpool.
102 Wimbourne Road, Liverpool 14.
Panel 26.

SHARKEY CHARLES JOSEPH
Age: 19
Place of Birth: Liverpool
Assistant Steward; R229779
Merchant Navy
Son of John and Ethel Sharkey, of Huyton, Lancs.
115 Wallgate Road, Wigan.
Panel 26.

SHONE ALBERT ROBERT
Age: 20
Place of Birth: Birkenhead
Vegetable Cook
Merchant Navy
16 Heygarth Drive, Greasby
Panel 26.

SHORT FRANCIS THOMAS
Age: 40
Place of Birth: Liverpool
Assistant Steward; 898529
Merchant Navy
Husband of Mary Evelyn Short, of Bootle, Lancs.
117 Linacre Road, Liverpool 21.
Panel 27.

SKINNER HERBERT HENRY
Age: 27
Place of Birth: London
Steward; R133866
Merchant Navy
31 Dudley Road, Liverpool 15
Panel 27.

SMITH ARCHIE BEAUMONT
Age: 52
Place of Birth: Ellesmere
Steward; 666306
Merchant Navy
Son of Mr. and Mrs. Charles Smith.
Husband of E.M.C. Smith, of Roby, Lancashire.
12 Valley Road, Chedderden, Derby.
Panel 27.

SMITH GEORGE
Age: 20
Place of Birth: Newcastle
Assistant Steward; R232816
Merchant Navy
Son of Ernest Smith, and of Violet Smith, of Newcastle, Staffordshire.

24 Poolfield Avenue, North Poolfield, Newcastle
Panel 27.

SMITH GEORGE HECTOR
Age: *23*
Place of Birth: **Bombay**
Assistant Steward; R158434
Merchant Navy
Son of James Edward and Annie Louisa Smith, of Walker, Newcastle-on-Tyne.
38 St Mary's Road, London N.W.10.
Panel 27.

STANTON EDWARD PATRICK
Age: *22*
Place of Birth: **Liverpool**
Trimmer
Merchant Navy
Son of Patrick and A.J. Stanton, of Liverpool.
74 Cortnell Road, Liverpool 14.
Panel 27.

STEVENS FREDERICK JOHN
Age: *19*
Place of Birth: **Hounslow**
Trimmer R268093
Merchant Navy
Son of Harry and Daisy Stevens.
56 Holloway Street, Hounslow.
Panel 27.

STRINGER JOSEPH
Age: *40*
Place of Birth: **Blackpool**
Ordinary Seaman; R262936
Merchant Navy
Husband of Mary Stringer, of Staining, Lancs.
23 Foxdale Avenue, Blackpool.
Panel 27.

TAYLOR ROBERT LOGAN
Age: *35*
Place of Birth: **Liverpool**
Assistant Steward; 1125056
Merchant Navy
Son of Mary G. Taylor, of Saughall, Cheshire.
33 Longhill Road, Moreton, Wirral.
Panel 27.

THOMPSON ARTHUR FREDERICK
Age: *28*

Place of Birth: **Liverpool**
Assistant Boots; R125080
Merchant Navy
Son of Arthur and Margaret L. Thompson, of Seaforth, Liverpool.
32 Bramble Road, Liverpool.
Panel 27.

TILSTON LIONEL FREDERICK ROBERT
Age: *42*
Place of Birth: **Chester**
Linen Keeper; 725848
Merchant Navy
Son of Frederick and Jane Tilston.
Nephew of Mrs. M. A. Griffith, of Ainsdale, Southport, Lancashire.
623 Liverpool Road, Ainsdale.
Panel 27.

TONGE JAMES
Age: *32*
Place of Birth: **Lancs**
Assistant Steward; R159656
Merchant Navy
Son of John and Mary Jane Tonge, of Farnworth, Lancashire.
62 George Street, Farnworth, Lancashire.
Panel 27.

TOWEY MICHAEL
Age: *38*
Place of Birth: **Liverpool**
Greaser; R3001
Merchant Navy
Son of Thomas and Catherine Towey.
Husband of Annie Towey, of Liverpool.
49A Kew Street, Liverpool 5.
Panel 27.

TOWNSON THOMAS HOLMES
Age: *18*
Place of Birth: **Blackburn**
Trimmer
Merchant Navy
52 Mary Street, Blackburn.
Panel 27.

TRIPP JOHN HOLLOWAY
Age: *38*
Place of Birth: **London**
Chief Steward; 1098100

Merchant Navy
Husband of Elsie Elizabeth Cecilia Tripp, of Liverpool, Buckinghamshire.
61 Dartforth Crescent, London S.E.10
Panel 27.

TUCK CLARENCE WILLIE
Age: 34
Place of Birth: Norfolk
Assistant Steward; R151164
Merchant Navy
Son of Willie and Sarah Tuck, of Rochdale, Lancs.
22 Bulmer Street, Rochdale.
Panel 27.

UNGI ERNEST
Age: 23
Place of Birth: Liverpool
Sailor; R156219
Merchant Navy
Son of John and Ethel Ungi.
Husband of Frances Ungi, of Liverpool.
3 Wharton Terrace, Liverpool.
Panel 27.

VAUGHAN ERNEST
Age: 30
Place of Birth: Bootle
Boatswain's Mate; R15907
Merchant Navy
6 Gerneth Close, Liverpool
Panel 27.

VAUGHAN EDWARD
Age: 37
Place of Birth: Bootle
Boatswain (Bosun); 1008747
Merchant Navy
6 Gerneth Close, Liverpool
Panel 27.

VERNON DONALD
Age: 17
Date of Birth: 26th May 1925
Place of Birth: Wallasey
Deck Boy
Merchant Navy
Son of Mr. and Mrs. Frank Vernon, of New Brighton, Wallasey, Cheshire.
9 The Avenue, New Brighton.
Panel 27.

WARD PETER
Age: 40
Place of Birth: Kingstown
Assistant Steward; R265634
Merchant Navy
Son of Mary Ward, of Dun Laoghaire, Co. Dublin, Irish Republic.
25 Caldwell Street, Kingstown.
Panel 27.

WATSON RICHARD
Age: 28
Place of Birth: Motherwell
Baker; R257825
Merchant Navy
Son of Mrs. W. E. A. Greatorex, of Pendleton, Manchester.
3 Gordon Street, Salford.
Panel 27.

WATTS GEORGE
Age: 42
Place of Birth: Elridge
Assistant Steward; 10154606
Merchant Navy
1 Princes Terrace, Balls Road, Birkenhead
Panel 27.

WEAVER EDWARD JAMES
Age: 40
Place of Birth: Liverpool
Chief Cook; 972560
Merchant Navy
Son of Edward and Anne Weaver.
Husband of Elizabeth Anne Weaver, of Walton, Liverpool.
24 Emery Street, Liverpool 4.
Panel 27.

WELCH JOHN HENRY
Age: 42
Place of Birth: Liverpool
Pantryman; 902719
Merchant Navy
Son of William Henry and Margret Welch.
Husband of Dorothy Mary Welch, of Speke, Liverpool.
61 Beaumont Street, Liverpool.
Panel 27.

WHARTON RICHARD HORATIO
Age: 39
Place of Birth: Carnforth
Assistant Steward; 1111262
Merchant Navy
Son of Oliver Horatio and Mary Hannah Wharton, of Warton, Carnforth, Lancashire.
Trentham, Yealand Road, Warton, Lancs.
Panel 27.

WHELAN VINCENT PAUL
Age: 20
Place of Birth: Wallasey
Assistant Cook
Merchant Navy
Son of George and Maud Mary Whelan, of Wallasey, Cheshire.
27 Albermarle Road, Wallasey
Panel 27.

WHITE CHARLES
Age: 21
Place of Birth: Liverpool
Fireman; R248869
Merchant Navy
Son of Edward White, and of Anne White, of Liverpool.
Barlow Street, Liverpool.
Panel 27.

WIGNALL RICHARD HENRY
Age: 56
Place of Birth: Liverpool
Baker; 675700
Merchant Navy
Husband of Jessie Wignall, of Wallasey, Cheshire.
11 Hill Crest, Liverpool 20.
Panel 27.

WILLIAMS RICHARD STANLEY
Age: 28
Place of Birth: Auckland
Engineer Officer; R189349
Merchant Navy
Sixth Son of James Arthur and Marion Williams, of Auckland City, New Zealand.
45 Maunsakickie Avenue, Auckland, New Zealand.
Panel 27.

WILLIAMS WILLIAM FENWICK ROBERTSON
Age: 35
Place of Birth: Liverpool
Assistant Steward
Merchant Navy
Son of Albert Edward and Esther Hay Williams.
7 Moorside Drive, Liverpool 23.
Panel 27.

WILLIAMSON FRANCIS
Age: 30
Place of Birth: Huddersfield
Assistant Baker
Merchant Navy
Husband of Mary Anne Williamson, of Almondbury, Huddersfield.
16 Green Street, Huddersfield.
Panel 27.

WILLOUGHBY JOSEPH RONALD
Age: 18
Place of Birth: Worksop
Assistant Steward; R233299
Merchant Navy
Son of William Willoughby, and of Sarah Jane Willoughby, of Worksop, Nottinghamshire.
13 Vessey Road, Worksop.
Panel 27.

WILSON THOMAS
Age: 39
Place of Birth: Liverpool
Assistant Steward; 106111
Merchant Navy
Son of Thomas James Wilson and Elizabeth Wilson.
Husband of Lily Wilson, of Liverpool.
3 Doon Street, Liverpool.
Panel 27.

WILSON SMITH NORMAN JAMES
L.R.C.P. (Edin.), L.R.C.S. (Edin.), L.R.F.P.S. (Glas.), L.D.S.R.C.S. (Edin.)
Age: 36
Place of Birth: Stirling
Surgeon; 27398
Merchant Navy
Son of Ritchie and Christina Wilson Smith.
Husband of Marie L. Wilson Smith, of Grimsby, Lincolnshire.
40 Grimsby Road, Cleethorpes.
Panel 27.

Casualty list

WINSLETT HENRY FRANCIS
Age: **41**
Place of Birth: **London**
Steward; 865188
Merchant Navy
Son of George and Annie Mary Winslett.
Husband of Charlotte Owen Winslett, of Anfield, Liverpool.
74 St Domingo Grove, Liverpool 5.
Panel 27.

WOBY BRUCE
Age: **18**
Place of Birth: **Barnetby**
Second Radio Officer; R224856
Merchant Navy
200 Legsby Avenue, Grimsby.
Panel 27.

WOLFFE JACK
Age: **29**
Place of Birth: **Derby**
Dairy Steward /Hairdresser; R87474
Merchant Navy
6 Shelthorpe, Loughborough.
Panel 27.

WOOD CHARLES
Age: **52**
Place of Birth: **Hull**
Second Engineer; 909015; 53373
Merchant Navy
Son of William Cromwell Wood and Sarah Wood.
Husband of E. Maude Wood, of Great Crosby, Lancashire.
18 Kaigh Avenue, Liverpool.
Panel 27.

WOOD THOMAS
Age: **43**
Place of Birth: **Hebburn, Tyne**
Storekeeper; R204299
Merchant Navy
Husband of Elsie Taylor Wood, of North Ormesby, Middlesbrough, Yorkshire.
2 Millfield Road, North Ormesby.
Panel 27.

WOOLFALL THOMAS ROBERT
Age: **58**
Place of Birth: **Liverpool**
Steward; 661420
Merchant Navy
Son of Thomas and Ann Woolfall.
Husband of Barbara Ann Woolfall, of Liverpool.
11 Westbrook, Saughall Massie.
Panel 27.

WORTLEY CHARLES
Age: **19**
Place of Birth: **Belfast**
Fireman; R234064
Merchant Navy
83 Imperial Street, Belfast.
Panel 27.

WRIGHT JAMES FREDERICK
Age: **40**
Place of Birth: **Bootle**
Steward; R55378
Merchant Navy
12 Queens Road, Formby.
Panel 27.

* Also commemorated on the Australian Merchant Seamen's Memorial at Canberra

Halifax Memorial Nova Scotia, Canada

DOUGHTY FREDERICK*
Age: **22**
Date of Birth: **6th May 1920**
Trimmer
Canadian Merchant Navy
23 Acton Road, London N.W. 10
Panel 21.
* Signed in as Henry George Murray, age 20, R263698, Canadian. Footnote on Crew List.

HAZEL JOSEPH
Age: **20**
Place of Birth: **Halifax, Nova Scotia**
Assistant Steward
Canadian Merchant Navy
86 Wellington Road, Liverpool
Panel 21.

Other Casualties

Non-Commonwealth and unrecorded

On the post-sinking passenger summary but unrecorded by CWGC.

CARMICHAEL C. F.*
Lieutenant **Army**
Ticket No. **402**
Destination: **Cape Town**
Next of Kin: *Travelling with wife Mrs Vivienne Stella Carmichael.
* On the post-sinking passenger summary but unrecorded by CWGC.

FORD ALFRED JAMES
Age: **31**
Occupation or Calling: **Electrical Fitter**
Ticket No. **220**
Destination: **Arabia via Cape Town**
Address in the UK: 137 Stoke Road, Gosport, Hants.
* On the post-sinking passenger summary but unrecorded by CWGC.

HARROD J.
Lieutenant
Ticket No. **307**
Destination: **Cape Town**
* On the post-sinking passenger summary but unrecorded by CWGC.

JONES FREDERICK JAMES
Age: **30/39**
Fire Officer/Admiralty Civil Servant
Royal Navy
Ticket No. **381**
Destination: **Durban**
c/o. South Africa Red Cross, South Africa House, Trafalgar Square, London.
* On the post-sinking passenger summary but unrecorded by CWGC.

Non-Commonwealth on the post-sinking passenger summary

BERNOL/DEMOL ARMAND
Age: **34**
Agent (Belgian)
Ticket No. **195**
Destination: **Cape Town**
Romilly Street, London W.1

BROKES FRANCIS
(**BROHEE** FRANCOIS JOSEPH HENRI)
Age: **43**
Belgian Forces
Ticket No. **197**
Destination: **Cape Town**
154B Willesden Lane, London N.W.6.

CHARLES JUSTINIAN (JUSTINIEN)
Age: **41**
Belgian Forces

Ticket No. **190**
Destination: **Cape Town**

GERUZET PIERRE JULES PAUL RAYMOND
Age: **34**
Belgian Forces
Ticket No. **193**
Destination: **Cape Town**

GUCHT GUSTAF PETRUS VAN
Age: **43**
Agent (Belgian)
Ticket No. **196**
Destination: **Cape Town**
65 Chelsham Road, Clapham, London S.W.4

HAAN de SAPE
Ship's Fitter (Netherland Govt.)

Casualty list

Ticket No. *404*
Destination: **Durban**

KAGEN
Petty Officer
Royal Navy

KUIPERS CARL FRIEDRICH
Age: 28
2nd Electrician
Royal Navy
Ticket No. *487*
Destination: **Cape Town**

MILO GUSTAVE
Age: 43
Agent (Belgian)
Ticket No. *194*
Destination: **Cape Town**
3 Anselm Road, London S.W.6

NAUS HUGEUS
Age: 40
Company Manager/Belgian Forces
Ticket No. *198*
Destination: **Cape Town**
c/o Wigton Hall, Wigton, Cumberland

PIRON HU(R)BERT JOSEF
Age: 20
Engineer/Belgian Forces
Ticket No. *201*
Destination: **Cape Town**
8 Old Compton Street, London W.1

PEELMANS ABEL LOUIS FERNAND HURBERT
Age: 22
Student (Belgian)
Ticket No. *202*
Destination: **Cape Town**
8 Old Compton Street, London W.1

WATTIEZ JULES MAURICE RENE AUGUSTE
Age: 32
Officer (Belgian)
Ticket No. *203*
Destination: **Cape Town**
729 Chelsea Cloisters, Sloan Avenue, London S.W.3

Failed to Embark

On the original passenger list but not the post-sinking passenger summary.

BANKS
Superintendent
Naval Surgeon
Ticket No. *222*
Destination: **Sydney**

KEW A. F.
Gunner
Ticket No. *350*
Destination: **Cape Town**

MOORE C.S.M. A.
Soldier
Ticket No. *251*
Destination: **St. Helena**

CONCANNON I
Age: 32
Surgeon
Ticket No. *282*
Destination: **Durban**
22 High Street, Eton
* Failed to embark.

CONCANNON J
Age: 27
Housewife
Ticket No. *282*
Destination: **Durban**
22 High Street, Eton
* Failed to embark.

Failed to Join

Crew

BASSETT CHARLES
Age: 24
Place of Birth: **Liverpool**
Trimmer
Merchant Navy
* Failed to join

BASSETT A.
Age: 28
Place of Birth: **Liverpool**
Fireman; R107285
Merchant Navy
11 Langley Street, Liverpool 8.
* Failed to join

BROWN COLIN
Age: 22
Place of Birth: **Liverpool**
Fireman; R172496
Merchant Navy
* Failed to join

CAMPION WILLIAM
Age: 41
Date of Birth: **29th July 1901**
Place of Birth: **Liverpool**
Fireman; R253427
Merchant Navy
149 Fernclough Road, Liverpool 14
* Failed to join (medical unfitness)

CLARO J. O.
Age: 29
Place of Birth: **Liverpool**
Able Seaman; R77099
Merchant Navy
* Failed to join

FIELD G. P.
Age: 20
Place of Birth: **Castleford**
Trimmer; R257271
Merchant Navy
* Failed to join

JAMES SIDNEY
Age: 19
Place of Birth: **Liverpool**
Trimmer; R225542 (903566)
Merchant Navy
188 Victoria Square, Liverpool.
* Failed to join
(Marginal note: S. James prosecuted fined £5 at Liverpool 21/10/43.)

MELLING RICHARD
Age: 47
Place of Birth: **Wigan**
Fireman
Merchant Navy
38 Pridley Green, Leigh, Lancs.
* Failed to join (medical unfitness)

MORAN ANDREW JOSEPH
Age: 32
Place of Birth: **Ochill, Co. Mayo**
Fireman; R253427
Merchant Navy
* Failed to join (medical unfitness)

PHARAND UBALD
Age: 29
Place of Birth: **Canada**
Fireman
Merchant Navy
77 Main Street, Sault, Quebec.
* Discharged (medical unfitness)

STEWART GORDON McD.
Age: 18
Trimmer
Merchant Navy
* Failed to join

STEWART JOHN McLEAN
Age: 20
Place of Birth: **Liverpool**
Fireman; R209426
Merchant Navy
* Failed to join

Wartime Disasters at Sea
by David Williams
Patrick Stephens Limited (Haynes Group) ISBN: 1852605650

WORST 25 WARTIME DISASTERS BY CASUALTIES

	Name	*Nationality*	*Date*	*Casualties*
1.	Wilhelm Gustloff	German	30 January 1945	c.7,800
2.	Goya	German	16 April 1945	c.6,800
3.	Cap Arcona	German	3 May 1945	c.5,000
4.	Lancastria	British	17 June 1940	c.3,050*
5.	Steuben	German	9 February 1945	c.3,000
6.	Laconia	British	12 September 1942	2,279
7.	Awa Maru	Japanese	1 April 1945	c.2,000
8.	Bahia Laura/Donau	German	30 August 1941	c. 1,700
9.	Gallia	French	4 October 1916	1,350
10.	Rakuyo Maru	Japanese	12 September 1944	c.1,350
11.	Lusitania	British	7 May 1915	1,198
12.	Rohna	British	26 November 1943	1,149
13.	Royal Edward	British	13 August 1915	935
14.	La Provence (as Provence II)	French	26 February 1916	930
15.	Amiral Magon	French	25 January 1917	c.900
16.	Nova Scotia	British	28 November 1942	863
17.	Slamat	Dutch	27 April 1941	843
18.	Leopoldville	Belgian	24 December 1944	808
19.	Arandora Star	British	2 July 1940	805
20.	Conte Rosso	Italian	24 May 1941	c.800
21.	Francesco Crispi	Italian	19 April 1943	c.800
22.	Taiyo Maru	Japanese	8 May 1942	780
23.	**Ceramic**	**British**	**6 December 1942**	**655**
24.	Mendi	British	21 February 1917	636
25.	Aragon	British	30 December 1917	610

*Lancastria possibly as high as 5000

The following ship has been omitted from David Williams' list:

| Khedive Ismail | British | 12 February 1944 | 1,297 |

The Khedive Ismail was owned by an Egyptian company (in which British shipping circles had a large interest), but had been requisitioned as a troopship by the Ministry of War Transport in October 1940, hence was under the British flag when she was sunk.

SS CERAMIC The Untold Story

This book is the result of a meeting I had with Eric Munday in 1999.

A faded newspaper clipping gave the name of the sole survivor of the Ceramic, a disaster that had claimed the life of my grandfather, and a wild stab in the phone book found the right Eric Munday, still living in the same area after 60 years.

And for those 60 years, Eric had been responding to queries just like mine, helping relatives and friends of those who had been less fortunate than he, to find out what had happened on the night of 6/7 December 1942.

With very little in print about the sinking of the Ceramic, and with much of it inaccurate or fanciful, only Eric could give a true account of what really took place. He had written diaries from that period that he lent me to read, and I realised these documents were of historical importance and the only tangible link to a forgotten wartime tragedy.

Only Eric had been there when the Ceramic had been sunk – or had he? I realised that in fact the U-boat crew would also have a first hand account of the event, and with the help of Jak Showell, who set up an introduction, Eric and I, together with Eric's wife Joan and my sister in law Helen (our interpreter) went to meet the surviving crew of U-515 at their annual reunion in 2001.

It was important for me to record first hand accounts, and these set the pattern for the rest of the book, which tells the story of the Ceramic by those who were there. I have not written this book, because I was not there. By listening to the voices of those who were, I hope you have been taken on a journey through time and feel a part of this ship's history.

Clare Hardy.

INDEX

A40, Troopship, 64
D'Aguiar, Cecil, 289
Alamein Memorial, 515
Alpen, Nurse Simone, 163
Altenburger, Gunther, 462-481
Afric, 16, 17
Arundel Castle, 136
Autograph Book, 128
Autographed Fan, 133
Azores, 322, 327, 345

Ball, Ceramic, 124
Bannister, Les, 385, 389, 406
Bastian, Harry, 184
Battalion, 5th, 72-73
Battalion, 16th, 70-71
Battalion, 18th, 75
Battalions, AIF, departures, 76
Battersby, Ian, 218-239, 242
Battle of the Atlantic Memorial, 498
Bayano, S.S., 304
Bibby Line, 294
BOAC, 329
Boiler Room, 38-40
Bombay, 96, 101
Bootle, 17, 285, 289
Bostock, Tony, 239-241
Bothnia, 305, 311
Brandt, Hermann, 463-481
Bredow, Horst, 470
Bremerhaven, 471
Bridge, 143, 156
British Governor, 307, 309
Broadway, HMS, 304-316, 318
Brochure, 146
Brookwood Memorial, 516
Bulbrook, Basil, 299

Cabin, 147, 148, 294
Caffery, J., 297
Cape Breton, 305
Cape Oreton, 311
Capetown, 127, 136-137, 166, 170-179, 241, 345
Cardiff Docks, 358
Casualty List, 499
Catrine, 305, 311
Ceramic II, 460
Ceramican, The, 82

Channings, Bill, 366, 372, 389
Chatelain, USS, 481, 483
Chatham Naval Memorial, 529
Chavasse, Lt. Cmdr. E.H., 305-316
Christmas 1942, 352
Churchill, Winston, 324, 400
Civilian Register, 499
Clifton Gardens, 63
Clyde, 152-154
Coaling, 101, 203, 235, 239, 254, 259, 269
Conroy, Dan, 288
Convoy ON149, 295, 298, 305
Coppack, Elsie, 289-290
Crossing the Line, 102
Cumberland, HMS, 161, 163

Dao, 321-323
Davenport, Phil, 180
Dewald, Herbert, 463-481
Dining Saloon, 25, 147
Disasters, 569
Doggerbank, 496-497
Dönitz, Admiral Karl, 355
Durban, 345

Electric Generators, 30
Elford, Captain H., 156, 299, 346, 407
Empire Grace, 345
Empire Heath, 308, 312
Empire Highway, 305
Empire Nugget, 307, 309
Empire Reynolds, S.S., 304
Empire Tide, 307
Engine Room, 34-39
Enterprise, H.M.S., 323, 325
Estrella, 174

Facts and Figures, 19
Fancy Dress, 141
Fans, 30-32
Flaherty, 483
Foster, Captain W. Logan, 294
Football, 134, 372, 376, 378, 383-386, 395, 398
Fort Hunt, 496
Francis, Walter, 182
Fremantle, 156, 180
Fresno Star, 305, 311

Galatea, 58-61
Gallery, Rear Admiral Daniel V., 483-490, 494-495
General Room, 27
Geneva Convention, 485-489
Giles, Dr. William, 293
Gjenvick, Corporal Ludvig K. J., 81
Gladstone Dock, 59, 127, 219, 238, 285, 287
Guadalcanal, 464, 481
Guns, 47-51, 180, 227, 262, 279, 283
Gymnasium, 28, 146

Hahn, Hans, 463-481
Halifax, 186, 205, 223, 261, 277, 283
Halifax Memorial, 565
Hanisch, Kurt, 474-481
Harland & Wolff, 14-40
Harmonic, 171
Hashagen, 466
Harrison, Ken, 363, 370, 406
Haw Haw, Lord, 300
Helgoland, 473
Henke, Werner, 319, 326, 333-336, 341, 405, 407, 469, 479, 482-496
Henry Stanley, 305, 309, 311
Herlin, Hans, 496
Hignett, Harry, 285-286, 298
Hipwell, Betty, 138-145
Hobart, 135
Honk Magazine, 77
Hood, HMS, 178
Hororata, 351
Horta, 321
Hospital Ship, 297-299

Ibbetson, Jeffery, 179
Irish Beech Hound, 313-316
Irish Plane, 312

John X. Merriman (tug), 170
Jubilee Class, 16, 17
J.W. Sauer (tug), 174

Kaspers, Hermann, 465-481
Kilpatrick, Dr. Emmett, 123
Klein, Wilhelm, 347, 464-481
Kürt, Fritz, 496-497
Kysperk, 400-402

Laing, Grace M. A., 291
Lamprecht, 466
Lamsdorf, 363
Launch, 43-45
Leacy, Peter, 289
Letters, 408
Lifeboats, 141, 327
Liley, F/Lt. Jack, 278-284
Liverpool Echo, 328
Lloyds List, 327
Lorient, 340, 345, 354, 405, 465, 468
Lounge, 147
Lyttleton, 234, 235, 240, 245, 269, 278

Maiden Voyage, 62
Man, Frank, 264-277
Marsden, T., 285-286
Mauretania, 61
McCormick, Frank, 297, 498
Medic, 16, 17
Melbourne, 63, 65, 156, 178, 180, 265
Meliskerk, 305, 306, 311
Menus, 144, 294
Mersey Pageant, 52-61
Mucker, 372, 378
Mulligan, Timothy (Lone Wolf), 341, 480
Munday, Eric, 5, 298, 327, 334-336, 338-340, 343, 348-498, 570
Munday, Ernest, 338
MOD Report, 404
Moeller, Carl, 473, 479
Molde, 304
Morden, 304
Morris, Capt. Horace C. M., 75

Newcastle Harbour, 18, 155
New York, 260, 274, 283
New Zealand Butter, 350
Norden, Robert Lee, 341

Orillia, 304

Panama Canal, 80, 182, 200, 236, 253, 270, 281
Passenger Analysis, 330-333
Paull, Capt. P. R., 66-69
Peake, Leonard G., 242-263
Peasgood, Marmaduke, 151-152

Persic, 16, 17
Peter Maersk, 305, 311, 319, 321
Plymouth Naval Memorial, 531
Pictou, 304
Piening, KK Adolf, 319-320
Pillsbury, USS, 481, 483
Polyanthus, 304, 309
Pope, 483
Port Said, 73, 100
Portsmouth Naval Memorial, 535
Prague, 402, 465
Primrose, 304
Promenade Deck, 82, 148

Radio Berlin, 333
Raksch, Walter & Waltraud, 462
Reading and Writing Room, 27
Refrigeration, 125-126, 241
Reuters, 343
Rio de Janeiro, 235, 239, 241
Roberts, Captain John, 128
Royall, Dr. Bruce, 286
Runic, 16, 17
Russians, 399, 402, 465

Saldanha Bay, 312, 317, 345
Sarpedon, S.S., 304
Schnehen, Baron & Baroness von, 401
Schwandke, 496-497
Sea Trials, 44
Seroostock, 305, 311
Sherwood, 304, 308-316, 318
Shipbuilder, The, 20
Shipping Agents, 149
Showell, Jak Mallmann, 469
Simmons, George C., 157
Singapore, 164, 264
Smoking Room, 28, 147
Souvenirs, 150
Sports, 120-122, 140
St. Helena, 296, 317, 345
Stalag 344, 380
Stalag VIIIB, 363, 405
Stapledon, Mrs K., 164
Sternberg, 366
Stewart, John McLean, 287
Stuart, Donald, 131
Stivey, Captain J., 78
Sudetanland, 365
Suevic, 16,17

Summers, Captain A. H., 124
Sydney Harbour, 16, 189, 233, 235, 265, 278

Takeover, 145
Tarantia, 305
Taylor, Charles R. J., 295, 298, 345
Telegraphy, 33
Testbank, 161-179
Ticket, 124
Tower Hill Memorial, 538
Towey, Michael, 158
Trophy Cup, 120
Turner, Nathan Redvers, 178-179

U-43, 496-497
U-155, 319
U-515, 319, 349, 461-497
U-Boat Archive, 470

Vaughan, Bosun, 227, 228, 328
Verandah Cafe, 146
Viceroy of India, 161, 163, 166, 168

Walvis Bay, 162, 169, 175
War Cabinet, 310, 322, 324
Wellington, 182, 184
Whale, Derek, 288
Wilhelmshaven, 356, 360
Willis, George Samuel, 74
Wigglesworth, Charles, 159
Wilson, Sgt/Pilot Ralph A., 187-217
Winser, Trevor, 4-11, 294
Working Party, 389
Wragg, Clarry, 364, 371
WW1, 64-81
WW2, 158-569

Printed in Great Britain
by Amazon